ADVANCE PRAISE FOR
PATHOLOGICAL ALTRUISM

"While other-regarding actions are rightly deemed the moral alternative to self-ishness, and while a new biological science of generosity shows that such prosocial actions are in general associated with flourishing and health in the agent, there is always the problem of a good thing going bad. Barbara Oakley and her colleagues have addressed the dark side of altruism, for the altruistic personality can be manipulated by nefarious ideologies and overwhelmed by excessive expectations, can ignore the due care of the self and be unwise in its application. *Pathological Altruism* surveys the dark side of a human capacity that is otherwise one of our saving graces. In this regard, altruism, hope, forgiveness, creativity, purpose, and so many positive human assets can easily be distorted. It is good to have such discussions available."

—Stephen G. Post
Director, Center for Medical Humanities, Compassionate Care, and Bioethics
Department of Preventive Medicine, Stony Brook University
Editor, *Altruism and Health: Perspectives from Empirical Science*

"Pathological altruism? Sounds like an oxymoron, but this fascinating book quickly convinces you that altruism can go seriously mad and bad. The great breadth and quality of contributors to this book from psychiatry, psychology, and philosophy—and that's just the 'P's'—shed light on the dark side of our evolutionary propensity towards altruism, which can be subverted to a wide range of pathologies such as survivor guilt, drug co-dependency, personality disorders, and eating disorders. When within-group altruism is exploited to between-group hostility, it can lead to suicide martyrdom and genocide."

—Robert Plomin
MRC Research Professor and Deputy Director
Social, Genetic and Developmental Psychiatry Centre
Institute of Psychiatry, King's College London
Past-President of the Behavior Genetics Association
Author of *Behavioral Genetics* (now in its 5th edition)

PATHOLOGICAL ALTRUISM

A new perspective regarding altruistic actions and their consequences.
Image © Kevin Mendez-Aracena and Barbara Oakley

PATHOLOGICAL
ALTRUISM

EDITED BY

Barbara Oakley

Ariel Knafo

Guruprasad Madhavan

David Sloan Wilson

FOREWORD BY

Francisco J. Ayala

OXFORD
UNIVERSITY PRESS

Oxford University Press, Inc., publishes works that further
Oxford University's objective of excellence
in research, scholarship, and education.

Oxford   New York
Auckland   Cape Town   Dar es Salaam   Hong Kong   Karachi   Kuala Lumpur
Madrid   Melbourne   Mexico City   Nairobi   New Delhi   Shanghai   Taipei   Toronto

With offices in
Argentina   Austria   Brazil   Chile   Czech Republic   France   Greece   Guatemala   Hungary   Italy
Japan   Poland   Portugal   Singapore   South Korea   Switzerland   Thailand   Turkey   Ukraine   Vietnam

Published by Oxford University Press, Inc.
198 Madison Avenue, New York, New York 10016

Library of Congress Cataloging-in-Publication Data
    Pathological altruism/Barbara Oakley . . . [et al.].
      p. cm.
    Includes bibliographical references and index.
ISBN 978-0-19-973857-1 (hbk.)
1. Altruism. I. Oakley, Barbara A., 1955–
BF637.H4P38   2011
155.2'32—dc22   2010041920

To the late Fred Preston
Whose contributions to this volume are sorely missed

FAUST: All right—who are you, then?

MEPHISTOPHELES: Part of that force which would do ever evil, and does ever good.

—Johann Wolfgang von Goethe

CONTENTS

PART I   THE PSYCHOLOGY OF PATHOLOGICAL ALTRUISM. . . . 1

CHAPTER 1   PATHOLOGICAL ALTRUISM—AN INTRODUCTION 3
Barbara Oakley, Ariel Knafo, and Michael McGrath

- *Pathological altruism* might be thought of as any behavior or personal tendency in which either the stated aim or the implied motivation is to promote the welfare of another. But, instead of overall beneficial outcomes, the "altruism" instead has irrational (from the point of view of an outside observer) and substantial negative consequences to the other or even to the self.
- Many harmful deeds—from codependency to suicide martyrdom to genocide—are committed with the altruistic intention to help companions or one's own in-group. Thus, it is worthwhile to study how well-meaning altruism can shade into pathology.
- Studies of pathological altruism provide for a more nuanced and sophisticated understanding of altruism.

CHAPTER 2   EMPATHY-BASED PATHOGENIC GUILT, PATHOLOGICAL ALTRUISM, AND PSYCHOPATHOLOGY. 10
Lynn E. O' Connor, Jack W. Berry, Thomas B. Lewis, and David J. Stiver

- Empathic reactions to pain or distress in others are instantaneous and begin the path to both normal and pathological altruism. These reactions move quickly to implicit empathy-based guilt, linked to a belief that one should try to relieve the suffering of others.
- Empathic guilt is further linked to evaluations of fairness, equality, and the equitable distributions of resources.
- Survivor guilt (inequity guilt) is a specific form of empathic guilt that tends to become pathogenic when based on a false belief that one's own success, happiness, or well-being is a source of unhappiness for others, simply by comparison. People with high survivor guilt may falsely believe they are "cheaters."
- *Pathogenic guilt leads to pathological altruism.* In pathological altruism, the altruistic behavior helps no one and potentially harms the altruist, the recipient of the altruism, or both.
- Empathic concern and empathic guilt are evolved psychological mechanisms sustaining mammalian group cohesion. Altruism may fail to favor fitness at the level of the individual in within-group competition, while increasing fitness at the level of the group in between-group competition.

• Pathogenic guilt and pathological altruism are commonly found in mental disorders, such as depression, posttraumatic stress disorder (PTSD), and obsessive-compulsive disorder (OCD).

• In the same way that the process of natural evolution selects features of the human species, the cultural environment selects for patterns of behaviors during the lifetime of an individual or a group.
• One particular form of human behavior, language, is of great survival value. But language also amplifies the way we experience both the positive and negative aspects of the world. This can reinforce behaviors that are damaging for individuals and groups.
• Some behaviors that may play a role in pathological altruism are *experiential avoidance*, a *conceptualized self*, *perspective-taking*, and *values-based action*.
• *Acceptance and commitment therapy* and *relational frame theory* lay forth a scientific framework and provide tools to modify such behaviors, which points to their potential utility to reduce pathological altruism.

• Codependency is an inability to tolerate a perceived negative affect in others that leads to a dysfunctional empathic response.
• Codependency likely shares roots with pathological altruism.
• There are evolutionary, genetic, and neurobiological components to the expression and propagation of codependent behaviors.

• The word, "addiction" appears to limit our perception of a wider realm—*general behavioral reinforcement* within the human brain. If neurochemical processes reinforce "good" habits such as love, loyalty, joy in music or skill, then addiction should be studied in a larger context.
• If a mental state causes pleasurable reinforcement, there will be a tendency to return to it. Meditation, adoration, gambling, rage, and indignation might all, at times, be "mental addictions."
• This more general view of reinforcement suggests potential ways to reduce or eliminate drug addiction, as well as self-induced rage.
• Self-righteousness and indignation may sometimes be as much about chemical need as valid concerns about unfair actions. Among other outcomes, this may cause "pathologically altruistic" behavior.
• Moderate-progressives who seek problem-solving pragmatism may get a boost if it were proved that dogmatic self-righteousness is often an "addiction."

- The Five-Factor Model of personality can be used to describe adaptive and maladaptive variants of altruism.
- Research suggests that maladaptive altruism is a component of dependent personality disorder.
- Case studies illustrate how maladaptive altruism, combined with differing levels of neuroticism, may impact treatment.

- Individuals with eating disorders tend to sacrifice their own needs and interests and devote themselves instead to helping and serving others.
- Selflessness and concern for appropriateness, concepts linked to pathological altruism, have been shown to characterize women with eating disorders.
- Developmental, interpersonal, family, cultural, genetic, personality, and social factors no doubt combine to make pathological altruism a characteristic of people who develop eating disorders.

- In animal hoarding, animals are used to support the hoarder's own emotional needs with respect to intimacy, self-esteem, control, identity, and fear of abandonment.
- Self- versus other-centeredness in animal hoarding reflects a lack of empathy and often leaves the true needs of animals unmet.
- Precipitating factors for animal hoarding likely include failure to develop functional attachment styles during childhood as a result of caregiver unavailability, neglect, or abuse.
- A hoarder's feeling of being a savior of animals is not the same as actually saving those animals. Although believing they are animals' saviors, rescuer hoarders fail to provide for the animals' basic life requirements.

- Williams syndrome illustrates how atypical development can affect social functioning.
- Individuals with the disorder are often referred to as caring, empathetic, and hypersociable.
- The Williams syndrome style of social engagement occurs alongside high levels of anxiety and social vulnerability in adults.

- Believing that you are acting in another's best interest is not synonymous with acting in another's best interest. It is a belief, not a fact.
- Moral judgments, such as "good intentions," arise out of basic biological drives, not out of inherent goodness or evilness.
- Justifications of behavior such as "I'm just trying to help," should be used with great restraint and viewed with great skepticism.

- Individuals who disavow their own need for support may be vulnerable to distress in the context of medical illness, both as patients themselves and as caregivers to others.
- The term "pathological altruism" has heuristic appeal, but is problematic in the context of life-threatening illness in that:
  - The term "pathology" in this circumstance implies a categorical external judgment of behavior and motivation, based on an arbitrary threshold that does not necessarily account for the social or relational context or the degree of suffering of the other.
  - The concept of altruism implies a dichotomy, often false, between the interests of self and those of the other.
  - Humans are relationally organized, such that acts of caregiving, particularly toward family members or loved ones, are often intrinsically rewarding and therefore not purely altruistic.
- The multiple determinants of altruism in the cancer caregiving context challenge us to develop a new nosology of such behavior and concern, informed by biological, social, and psychodynamic theory.

- Therapeutic jurisprudence and neuroimaging are valuable tools when considering the treatment of pathological altruism in the law, in cases of organ donations to strangers and cases raising "cultural defenses."
- Therapeutic jurisprudence gives us a benchmark by which we can assess whether the pathological altruist (if, indeed, the altruist is pathological) has sacrificed her dignity to do the putatively pathologically altruistic act, an assessment process that can also illuminate whether the underlying behavior is irrational, harmful to others, or self-harming.
- Neuroimaging gives us new tools to potentially assess whether the pathological altruist is a rational moral agent in doing such acts.

- Healthy forms of altruism and pathological altruism are distinguished by the compulsion to be altruistic coupled with a maladaptive outcome.
- Pathological altruism may be found in association with criminal behavior, in which the altruist may be the victim, the victimizer, or both.
- Pathological altruism may be viewed as a manifestation of cognitive distortions resulting from genetic, chemical, environmental, or developmental factors acting alone or in concert.
- Pathologically altruistic behavior can be classified into four major types: *protective*, *defensive*, *masochistic*, and *malignant*, each having both psychotic and nonpsychotic incarnations.

- Pathological altruism can be briefly summarized as altruism that:
  - is unnecessary or uncalled for
  - has consequences that cause the actor to complain, yet the actor continues doing it anyway
  - is motivated by values or needs within the altruist that are irrational or are symptoms of psychological disturbance
  - is of no real benefit to anyone, and a reasonable person would have foreseen this
- The higher the level of altruistic behavior reported by subjects, the higher their level of criminal victimization.
- Self-reported altruism has been found to be a significant predictor of both property and personal crime victimization.
- The relationship between altruism and victimization has been found to be especially due to *risky altruism*, which in turn is correlated with the basic personality trait of Sensation Seeking.

- Suicide attacks are a combative tactic arising from a lethal, nonpathological altruism in some warfare contexts.
- Altruism is the only widely agreed upon temperamental attributes of suicide attackers.
- Strong altruistic dispositions are increasingly being found to have underlying biological mediators.
- Understanding the neurocognitive underpinnings of willingness to commit extreme altruistic acts may help us understand suicide attacks.

- Low self-control, which is a major covariate of criminal behavior, appears early in life and is relatively stable over the life course.
- Levels of self-control may vary across historical periods as people become more sensitive to socially intrusive behavior.
- The perplexing levels of obedience in major genocides do not reflect deficiencies in self-control but suggest the oversocialization of the internal executive function by external social hierarchies.

- Altruism and emotional contagion have a powerful capacity to mobilize financial and humanitarian aid to impoverished nations.
- Although external economic assistance has been helpful for many countries, a large number of altruistic, non-strategic, foreign aid programs over the past several decades have failed—worsening the very situation they were meant to help. Many other humanitarian programs have also been ineffective at enormous cost.
- Altruistic efforts for social improvements must be guided, not purely by emotion, but with a well thought-out objective strategy and endpoint.
- Neuroscience is allowing us to understand how default emotional approaches to helping others can backfire and cripple otherwise noble intentions.
- Public policies and interventions that have incorporated smart, strategic, and tempered altruism may be effective in alleviating poverty and stimulating economic development.
- There may be value in recruiting a new breed of non-traditional talent that is capable of reframing the way development assistance is carried out.

- Finding Truth was Gandhi's ultimate objective.
- Nonviolence is a key means for obtaining Truth.
- Nonviolence can, on occasion, become a pathologically altruistic enterprise, unnecessarily hurting others, and it cannot be dogmatically followed if the greater good of Truth is to be attained.

- Much of what is called "altruistic" behavior in nature can have self-serving, kinship, or game-based roots that we should not ignore simply out of aesthetic Puritanism.
- Unselfish altruism can emerge out of satiability, satiation, empathy, and sympathy, as well as cultural and individual values. Although sometimes implemented in ways that are ill-conceived or pathological, this trait is viewed as a high feature of intelligence.
- Occasionally, altruism *between species* seems to be unleashed by full bellies and sympathy, (sometimes) along with enlightened self-interest in the long-term survival of an entire world.
- Modern Western society disavows the notion that ideas are inherently dangerous or toxic, or that an elite should guide gullible masses toward correct thinking. However, virtually every other culture held the older, prevalent belief in "toxic memes." As yet, there is no decisive proof supporting one side over the other.
- Western assumptions color the "search for extra-terrestrial intelligence" (SETI), just as previous "first-contact" events were driven by cultural assumptions of past eras. Especially pervasive—and unwarranted—is the belief that all advanced civilizations will automatically be altruistic.

Bernard Berofsky

- Ethical altruism can be defined either as the view that we have obligations to others or that altruism is a virtue. Ethical egoists believe that we have obligations only to ourselves and that altruism is not a virtue.
- Psychological egoists deny that there are altruists. Since altruism is characterized by intention rather than outcome, and there are people who act with the intention to help others at their own expense, psychological egoism seems clearly false.
- Since a conscious intention to help can conceal an unconscious motivation to harm, one can redefine psychological egoism more plausibly as the view that no one is really motivated to sacrifice his or her own interests to help others.
- If the psychological egoist is right and there are no altruists, how can there be pathological altruists?
  - First answer: Pathological types have some common characteristics—compulsiveness, destructiveness, ignorance of motivation.
  - Second answer: More importantly, the pathological altruist's altruistic *intention* is an essential expression of his self-regarding *motivation*. He must intend to help in order to serve his own destructive needs.

John W. Traphagan

- Altruism and pathology are concepts that do not necessarily translate well from one culture to another; this raises questions for how biological and cultural aspects of these concepts influence behavior.
- Certain features of altruistic behavior may be relatively consistent across different cultures, but nuances of meaning vary, necessarily implying that deviation from the "norm" will vary as well.
- Pathological altruism is behavior that deviates from norms of action that shape concepts of altruism in particular cultures, but those acts themselves have no moral value and are not necessarily parallel from one culture to another.

Joan Y. Chiao, Katherine D. Blizinsky, Vani A. Mathur, and Bobby K. Cheon

- Western and East Asian cultures vary in individualism and collectivism, or cultural values that influence how people think about themselves in relation to others.
- Cultural differences in social behavior are associated with cultural differences in allelic frequency of serotonin transporter-linked polymorphic region v (*5-HTTLPR*) variants.
- Culture–gene coevolution between individualism–collectivism and the *5-HTTLPR* may influence brain regions associated with empathy and altruism.

Jorge M. Pacheco and Francisco C. Santos

- Without additional mechanisms, cooperation is not an evolutionarily viable behavior, as the *tragedy of the commons* often emerges as the final doomsday scenario.

- In a black-and-white world in which individuals' actions are limited to cooperate or to defect, pathological altruists can be seen as obstinate cooperators, who go to all lengths to maintain their behavior.
- Pathological altruists cooperate indiscriminately, being unmoved by the temptations of greed and fear that lead to defection.
- A single pathological altruist can obliterate the evolutionary advantage of defectors, letting others ignore the temptation to cheat and become, themselves, cooperators. Hence, they generate a messianic effect, which spreads through the entire community.
- Pathological altruists catalyze social cohesion, as their presence benefits the entire community even when defection remains as the single rational option and individuals act in their own selfish interest.

- Psychologically altruistic acts may not necessarily be evolutionarily altruistic.
- Battered women and their violent mates have more sons than others.
- Therefore, battered women's decision to stay with their abusers may be psychologically altruistic, but evolutionarily self-interested, as they gain the genetic benefit of producing violent sons.

- Empathy emerges early in life and often motivates caring, prosocial actions toward others. This leads to social competence and healthy emotional development.
- Children's empathy can lead to pathogenic guilt, anxiety, and a sense of personal failure when early family environments require too much of them.
- Parental depression contributes to pathogenic guilt in children which, in turn, creates conditions conducive to risk for developing depression.
- Genetic and environmental factors combine to determine why some children, especially girls, are likely to develop empathy-based pathogenic guilt and depression.

- Empathy involves two very different neural processes: affective (feeling an emotion appropriate in response to another person's thoughts and feelings), and cognitive (also called Theory of Mind—that is, being able to imagine someone else's thoughts or feelings).
- The ability to empathize forms one pole of a personality-related dimension—the opposite pole is the ability to systemize. (Put briefly, systemizing is the drive to create and understand systems, for example, the mechanical system of an old-fashioned clock).
- On average, empathizing is stronger in females, whereas systemizing is stronger in males.

- Empathizing-Systemizing theory can be used to quantify people's drive to empathize and systemize. More importantly, it makes predictions regarding the origins of conditions such as autism, which involves intact or even strong systemizing alongside difficulties in empathy.
- Empathizing-Systemizing theory also predicts that some individuals will have difficulties systemizing, but an intact or even a strong drive to empathize. These "hyper-empathizers" may escape clinical notice.

- People are social animals who go to great lengths to belong—a need that may be rooted in biology. This behavior and biology directed toward social belonging may result in heightened altruism toward some and diminished empathy toward others.
- Whether altruism is pathological depends on its context, as empathy may be selective toward particular individuals or one's own in-group, at the expense of other individuals or groups.
- Oxytocin and vasopressin systems, structurally flexible and capable of rapid changes, appear to be key in understanding social behaviors in rapidly changing human societies.
- A "seduction super-response" may be rooted in biological systems for how receptive one is to social signals, such as vocalizing. Similarly, impaired sensitivity to social signals may lead to "hyper-trust" in failing to detect social threats.
- More broadly, social signals are transmitted through groups; a seduction super-response or undue hyper-trust may be a response to social contagions involving neurosensory or chemosensory means yet to be discovered.

- Compassion fatigue is introduced as a form of pathological altruism since it is altruistically motivated and gives rise to symptoms of burnout.
- Empirical findings are discussed that dissociate different forms of vicarious responses.
- We conclude that the term *compassion fatigue* should be replaced by the term *empathic distress fatigue*.

- Pathological altruism emerges as a by-product of a runaway process of selection for in-group favoritism and self-deception.
- In-group favoritism coupled with self-deception or denial of the other, leads to pathological commitment to one group's ideology, coupled with out-group antagonism that can lead to mass genocides.
- Self-sacrifice and martyrdom represent the ultimate forms of pathological altruism, at least from the perspective of the victims. From the perspective of the pathological altruist's group (e.g., religion), however, it is divine altruism, revered, and adaptive for the martyr's faith.

• When pathological altruism runs away, it can lead to mass genocides, as obstinate cooperators disregard the humanity—and human rights—of all who interfere with the ideological cause.

Joachim I. Krueger

• Personality-based approaches to pathological altruism are either typological or dimensional, with distinct implications for the question of how pathological altruism is propagated.
• In a mixed population of individuals with different social preferences, altruists do poorly. They may not see it that way, however, which makes their behavior pathological.
• In a Volunteer's Dilemma, altruists suffer when interacting with other altruists.
• When interpersonal dilemmas are nested within intergroup dilemmas, the meaning of altruism is contingent on perspective.
• Evolution has favored parochial morality (altruism), leaving us with the intractable problem of how to satisfy the local group and the general population at the same time.

David Sloan Wilson

• The concept of a pathological adaptation might seem like a contradiction of terms, but traits that count as adaptive in the evolutionary sense can be harmful to others and even to oneself over the long term.
• When altruism is defined in terms of behavioral consequences, it is inherently vulnerable to exploitation by selfishness and evolves only when altruists manage to confine their interactions with each other. Even when altruism evolves because it is more successful than selfishness, on average, some altruists still encounter selfish individuals and are harmed by their own behavior.
• Social environments are pathological when they are structured to make altruists vulnerable to exploitation. Much can be done to create social environments that favor altruism as a successful behavioral strategy.
• Altruism at one level of a multitiered hierarchy (e.g., within groups) can be used for selfish purposes at higher levels (e.g., between-group conflict). The costs and benefits of altruism are repeated at all levels.
• When altruism is defined in psychological terms, it can be regarded as a proximate mechanism for motivating altruistic behavior. Just as there are many ways to skin a cat, there are many proximate mechanisms for motivating altruistic behavior that can be expected to vary among individuals and cultures.
• The analysis of pathological altruism in this volume should be extended to other traits associated with morality and group-level functional organization.

ACKNOWLEDGMENTS

WE WOULD LIKE TO THANK Lori Handelman for her superb insight and encouragement from the initial idea to the final arrival of the manuscript at Oxford, and Abby Gross for her masterful stepping up to the task of shepherding the book into publication. Anindita Sengupta, the project manager was top notch; Karen Kwak has been a first-rate production editor; and Joanna Ng has been a godsend at every phase. Annie Woy's copyediting was superb. Authors couldn't ask to work with a better publishing dream team. Our thanks also to our brilliant literary agent, Rita Rosenkranz, for her commitment to perfection and wise guidance. Our appreciation also to Noe Zamel for his insightful suggestions, and Patrick Finlinson for his knowledgeable encouragement. Virginia Postrel's work, particularly her seminal *The Future and Its Enemies: The Growing Conflict Over Creativity, Enterprise, and Progress*, has served as an inspiration.

Lastly, we would like to thank Jeff Miller of faceoutstudio for his cover design. According to Jeff and Oxford editor Abby Gross, "The onion in the cover page illustrates how something rooted in what we think of as purity—the white, clear-ish center—could reverberate out or develop into something dark—the brown, crinkly outer layers. Layers within layers are also symbolic of human nature, from emotions to motives to behaviors and beyond that, the impact of behaviors outside of the self." No editors could be happier with such beauty, originality, or insight, all wrapped into one seemingly simple image.

FOREWORD

MY DICTIONARY (*Merriam Webster Collegiate Dictionary*, 10th edition) defines altruism as "unselfish regard to or devotion to the welfare of others." The dictionary adds a second definition: "behavior by an animal that is not beneficial to or may be harmful to itself but that benefits others of its species." This second definition relates to "biological" altruism, which applies to all animals and makes explicit what is implied by "unselfish" in the first definition—namely, that the agent need not benefit and, indeed, may be harmed by the behavior. Biological altruism is assayed in reproductive terms. Human altruism has a broader scope, "the welfare of others," and it does not necessarily connote action, but simply "regard" or "devotion."

The target of the regard or the behavior is, in both definitions, the welfare or the benefit of others. If such is the case, it would seem that "pathological altruism" might be a contradiction in terms. It is not so, precisely because *human* altruism, which is the subject of the present book, necessarily denotes only regard or consideration of others, not necessarily action beneficial to them. A person's actions may harm others who are held in high regard by that person, because of misjudgment, or because the intended beneficiaries are some third party, not the immediate targets of the action. Think of suicide bombers. The terrorists that destroyed the New York Twin Towers surely thought that they were acting for the benefit of Islam.

All these issues and many more are extensively and profoundly explored in *Pathological Altruism*. I offer here the simple points made in the previous paragraph, because I presume many potential readers may react to the book's title as I did when I was first introduced to this book. I was puzzled. Why "pathological" altruism? Is it not the case that altruism bespeaks benefits to others and virtuous intentions by the altruist? Upon reflection, I imagined that instances of pathological altruism might sometimes occur. I read the manuscript and discovered that pathological altruism is not an aberration that might occasionally be the case, but rather a behavior that overwhelmingly occurs in human social intercourse.

Reading *Pathological Altruism* has been for me an adventure of discovery, taking place at many levels. This book skillfully explores the cognitive and emotional foundations of pathological altruism; the associated psychiatric conditions; its diverse and profound societal consequences; how cultures deal with misplaced altruism and how evolution shaped it; and the development of pathological altruism at the individual level. I am certain that *Pathological Altruism* will be also, for other readers, a stimulating, profitable, and enjoyable enterprise. All chapters are written by experts, conveying their message, even when somewhat esoteric, with clarity and, often, with verve. The concluding chapters are a suitable colophon for an exciting book, engaging overviews encompassing evolutionary, psychological, philosophical, and cultural perspectives.

Read this book. You will learn much that would be new to you, whatever your expertise or interest. And I would be surprised if you don't enjoy this voyage of discovery.

Francisco J. Ayala
Templeton Prize Laureate
University Professor
Donald Bren Professor of Biological Sciences
University of California, Irvine

CONTRIBUTORS

Francisco J. Ayala
University Professor and Donald
  Bren Professor of Biological
  Sciences
University of California, Irvine
Irvine, California

Rachel Bachner-Melman
Licensed Clinical Psychologist
Coordinator, Eating Disorders Unit
  Adult Psychiatric Ward
Hadassah University Medical
  Center
Ein Karem, Jerusalem, Israel

Simon Baron-Cohen
Professor of Developmental
  Psychopathology
Director of the Autism Research
  Centre
University of Cambridge
Cambridge, United Kingdom

Bernard Berofsky
Professor Emeritus
Department of Philosophy
Columbia University
New York, New York

Jack W. Berry
Assistant Professor
Department of Psychology
Samford University
Birmingham, Alabama; and
Codirector of the Emotion,
  Personality, and Altruism
  Research Group
Wright Institute
Berkeley, California

Katherine D. Blizinsky
Graduate Student
Interdepartmental Neuroscience
  Program
Northwestern University
Evanston, Illinois

Augustine Brannigan
Professor of Sociology and Fellow
Centre for Military and Strategic
  Studies
University of Calgary
Calgary, Canada

David Brin
Scientist and Author
Encinitas, California

Vicki Bruce
Professor and Head of the School
  of Psychology
Newcastle University
Newcastle upon Tyne, United
  Kingdom

Robert A. Burton
Former Associate Chief
Department of Neurosciences
UCSF Medical Center at
  Mount Zion
University of California,
  San Francisco
San Francisco, California

Bobby K. Cheon
Graduate Student
Department of Psychology
Northwestern University
Evanston, Illinois

Joan Y. Chiao
Assistant Professor
Department of Psychology
Northwestern University
Evanston, Illinois

Arun Gandhi
Founder/President
Gandhi Worldwide Education
  Institute
(www.gandhiforchildren.org)
University of Rochester
Rochester, New York

Marc D. Hauser
Professor
Departments of Psychology and
  Human Evolutionary Biology; and
Director, Cognitive Evolution
  Laboratory
Harvard University
Cambridge, Massachusetts

Steven C. Hayes
Nevada Foundation Professor
Department of Psychology
University of Nevada, Reno
Reno, Nevada

Robert J. Homant
Professor
Department of Criminal Justice
University of Detroit Mercy
Detroit, Michigan

Ali Jawaid
MD/PhD Student
Institute of Neuropathology
University of Zurich
Zurich, Switzerland

Satoshi Kanazawa
Reader in Management
Managerial Economics and
  Strategy Group
Department of Management
London School of Economics and
  Political Science
London, United Kingdom

Daniel B. Kennedy
Forensic Criminologist
Oakland University
Rochester, Michigan

Olga Klimecki
Doctoral Student
Department of Social
  Neuroscience
Max Planck Institute for
  Human Cognitive and
  Brain Sciences
Leipzig, Germany

Ariel Knafo
Associate Professor
Psychology Department
The Hebrew University of Jerusalem
Jerusalem, Israel

Joachim I. Krueger
Professor
Department of Cognitive, Linguistic,
  & Psychological Sciences
Brown University
Providence, Rhode Island

Thomas B. Lewis
Assistant Clinical Professor
  of Psychiatry
School of Medicine
University of California,
  San Francisco; and
Professor
Fromm Institute
University of San Francisco
San Francisco, California

Madeline Li
Assistant Professor
Department of Psychiatry
University of Toronto; and
Clinician-Scientist
Department of Psychosocial
  Oncology and Palliative Care
Division of Behavioural Sciences
  and Health Research
Princess Margaret Hospital
Toronto, Canada

Guruprasad Madhavan
Program Officer
Policy and Global Affairs
National Academy of Sciences
Washington, District of Columbia

Vani A. Mathur
Graduate Student
Department of Psychology
Northwestern University
Evanston, Illinois

Michael McGrath
Clinical Associate Professor
Department of Psychiatry
University of Rochester School of
  Medicine and Dentistry; and
Medical Director and Chair
Department of Behavioral Health
Unity Health System
Rochester, New York

Jane N. Nathanson
Social Work and Rehabilitation
  Consultant
Member,
Hoarding of Animals Research
  Consortium
Boston, Massachusetts

Barbara Oakley
Associate Professor of Engineering
School of Engineering & Computer
  Science
Oakland University
Rochester, Michigan

Lynn E. O'Connor
Professor
Director of the Emotion, Personality,
  and Altruism Research Group
Wright Institute
Berkeley, California

Jorge M. Pacheco
Professor
Department of Mathematics
University of Minho
Campus of Gualtar
Braga, Portugal

Gary J. Patronek
Vice President for Animal Welfare
  and New Program Development
Animal Rescue League of Boston
Boston, Massachusetts

Michael L. Perlin
Professor of Law
Director of the Online Mental
  Disability Law Program
Director of the International
  Mental Disability Law Reform
  Project
Justice Action Center
New York Law School
New York, New York

Karol M. Pessin
Biotechnology Intellectual Property
  Lawyer
Westlake Village, California

Jennifer Ruth Presnall
Graduate Student
Clinical Psychology Program
University of Kentucky
Lexington, Kentucky

Deborah M. Riby
Lecturer
School of Psychology
Newcastle University
Newcastle upon Tyne, United
  Kingdom

Gary Rodin
Professor of Psychiatry
University of Toronto; and
Harold and Shirley Lederman Chair
  in Psychosocial Oncology and
  Palliative Care
Princess Margaret Hospital
Toronto, Canada

Francisco C. Santos
Associate Researcher
Department of Computer
  Science
New University of Lisbon
Lisbon, Portugal

Tania Singer
Director
Department of Social Neuroscience
Max Planck Institute for Human
  Cognitive and Brain Sciences
Leipzig, Germany

David J. Stiver
Librarian–Archivist
Graduate Theological Union
Berkeley, California

Adolf Tobeña
Professor of Psychiatry and Chair
Department of Psychiatry and
  Forensic Medicine
Autonomous University of Barcelona
Barcelona, Spain

John W. Traphagan
Associate Professor of Religious
  Studies and Anthropology
University of Texas at Austin
Austin, Texas

Brent E. Turvey
Forensic Criminologist
Forensic Solutions
Sitka, Alaska
Adjunct Professor of Justice Studies
Oklahoma City University
Oklahoma City, Oklahoma

Carol Van Hulle
Assistant Scientist
Waisman Center
University of Wisconsin–Madison
Madison, Wisconsin

Roger Vilardaga
Doctoral Student
Department of Psychology
University of Nevada, Reno
Reno, Nevada

Thomas A. Widiger
T. Marshall Hahn Professor of
  Psychology
University of Kentucky
Lexington, Kentucky

David Sloan Wilson
Distinguished Professor
Departments of Biology and
  Anthropology
Binghamton University
State University of New York
Binghamton, New York

Carolyn Zahn-Waxler
Research Scientist
Departments of Psychology and
  Psychiatry
Center for Investigating Healthy
  Minds, Waisman Center
University of Wisconsin–Madison
Madison, Wisconsin

PART I

THE PSYCHOLOGY OF PATHOLOGICAL ALTRUISM

CHAPTER 1

PATHOLOGICAL ALTRUISM—AN INTRODUCTION

Barbara Oakley, Ariel Knafo, and Michael McGrath

KEY CONCEPTS

- *Pathological altruism* might be thought of as any behavior or personal tendency in which either the stated aim or the implied motivation is to promote the welfare of another. But, instead of overall beneficial outcomes, the "altruism" instead has irrational (from the point of view of an outside observer) and substantial negative consequences to the other or even to the self.
- Many harmful deeds—from codependency to suicide martyrdom to genocide—are committed with the altruistic intention to help companions or one's own in-group. Thus, it is worthwhile to study how well-meaning altruism can shade into pathology.
- Studies of pathological altruism provide for a more nuanced and sophisticated understanding of altruism.

THE PAST DECADE has seen an explosion in research and interest in altruism,[1] and for good reason—not only is altruism beneficial, but neuroscience and genetics are now providing fresh and useful insights. For researchers, it is the best of all worlds—modern breakthroughs can allow us to help others by studying the very phenomenon of altruistically helping others.

The benefits of altruism appear so obvious, and a high regard for altruism is so deeply ingrained in modern Western culture, that it seems almost heretical to suggest that altruism may have a dark side. But some of human history's most horrific episodes have risen from people's well-meaning altruistic tendencies. Consider Oliver Wendell Holmes, one of America's most admired Supreme Court justices, whose well-intentioned rhetoric supported eugenic forced sterilization: "It is better for all the world, if instead of waiting to execute degenerate offspring for crime, or to let them starve for their imbecility, society can prevent those who are manifestly unfit from continuing their kind" (*Buck v. Bell*, 1926). Or, master manipulator Adolph Hitler, who confided: "When I appeal . . . for sacrifice, the first spark is struck" (Waite, 1977, p. 396).

> Some of human history's most horrific episodes have risen from people's well-meaning altruistic tendencies.

Pathological altruism might be thought of as any behavior or personal tendency in which either the stated aim or the implied motivation is to promote the welfare of another or others. But, instead of overall beneficial outcomes, the "altruism" instead has irrational and substantial negative consequences to the other or even to the self. Marc Hauser, (Chapter 29), rightly notes that when discussing a pathological altruist, motivation becomes important. A working definition of pathological altruist (besides the obvious "a person who engages in pathological altruism"), might then be: "A person who *sincerely* engages in what he or she intends to be altruistic acts, but who harms the very person or group he or she is trying to help, often in unanticipated fashion; or harms others; or irrationally becomes a victim of his or her own altruistic actions." Thus, a con artist who solicited funds for orphan children, when his real intention was to spend money on himself, would not be a pathological altruist. But the person who gave to the con man *could* be a pathological altruist.

The many authors showcased in this volume have viewed the central idea of pathological altruism from differing perspectives. Each of their approaches points to one disturbing truth: What we value so much, the altruistic "good" side of human nature, can also have a dark side. Altruism can be the back door to hell.

This book focuses on basic psychological schemata designed to explain pathological altruism from a straightforward psychological perspective. But one of its strengths is its accompanying exploration of the underlying neuropsychological and biological processes that actually account for it. Part I deals with the cognitive and emotional foundations that are most visible as the roots of pathological altruism. At their extreme, these involve those psychiatric conditions that are considered in Part II. The diverse and profound societal implications of pathological altruism are discussed in Part III. In Part IV, we turn to the social and macrobiological basis of pathological altruism—how do cultures deal with it, and how did evolution shape it? Part V explores the development of altruism and pathological altruism at the individual level, taking into account the neural processes involved. And finally, in Part VI, three of the most provocative and sophisticated authors in the field (Marc Hauser, Joachim Krueger, and David Sloan Wilson) undertake overall integrations of the subject matter, which encompass evolutionary, psychological, philosophical, and cultural perspectives (see Chapters 29, 30, and 31).

> What we value so much, the altruistic "good" side of human nature, can also have a dark side. Altruism can be the back door to hell.

A major strength of this volume is that the contributing authors bring a combination of eclectic backgrounds and viewpoints to the study of pathological altruism, helping ground the subject in a scientific, social, and cultural matrix. For example, Augustine Brannigan's background as a sociologist helps him form his elegant hypothesis of genocide and pathological altruism based largely on social theory (Chapter 16). Adolf Tobeña, on the other hand, in Chapter 15, uses his clinical perspective as a psychiatrist, and his firm views on the importance of biological influences, to form a theory of suicide bombings that complements Brannigan's work in an intriguing fashion. Madeline Li and Gary Rodin (Chapter 11) bring their wealth of psychiatric experience from cancer wards, where those who were previously the caretakers become, in turn, the most difficult patients to care for.

Social worker Jane Nathanson and veterinarian Gary Patronek (who also has a background in humane law enforcement) discuss the pathological altruism involved in animal hoarding in Chapter 8. Roger Vilardaga and Steven Hayes (Chapter 3) use their clinical sensitivity and behavioral theory of cognition to explain how our language abilities can become a double-edged sword, allowing us to become genuinely altruistic but also keeping us stuck at times in a state of psychological suffering that can ultimately affect others. And Bernard Berofsky brings to bear his philosophical training to illuminate the logic of the key concepts in Chapter 20. In so doing, he shows how "pathological altruism" is an appropriate label, despite the fact that pathological altruists are not really altruists.

The first known reference to *pathological altruism* in the professional litera-ture is from a 1984 paper by Nancy McWilliams "The Psychology of the Altruist" (McWilliams, 1984). The subject was given a more comprehensive psychoana-lytic treatment in a 2001 paper by Beth Seelig and Lisa Rosof: "Normal and Pathological Altruism"(Seelig & Rosof, 2001). Early psychoanalysts had been encouraged to think of all altruism as arising from masochistic impulses. But Seelig and Rosof relied on a psychoanalytic framework to discriminate between forms of altruism ranging from the "protoaltruism" observed in animals and parental nurturing, to the "psychotic altruism" of bizarre caretaking behavior seen in deeply disturbed individuals. In this volume, Brent Turvey (Chapter 13) provides an updated perspective on Seelig and Rosof's work, grounded in Turvey's substantial experience as a forensic scientist and criminal profiler.

The lack of systematic research and theory in regard to pathological altruism does not mean that maladaptive variants of altruism (as, for example, excessive self-sacrifice) have completely escaped clinical notice: Thomas Widiger and Jennifer Presnall (Chapter 6) connect the concept to dependent personality dis-order in the *Diagnostic and Statistical Manual of Mental Disorders, 4th Edition, Text Revision* (DSM-IV-TR), as well as to the maladaptive form of agreeableness in the Five-Factor Model of personality.[2]

Pathologies involving altruism, however, have broader implications and pro-found importance in understanding the human condition from neuroscientific, psychological, psychiatric, and social perspectives. For example, autism involves a well-studied syndrome most often seen in males; it is characterized by strong systemizing skills coupled with little or no empathy. But, as described by Simon Baron Cohen in Chapter 26, there is evidence for a converse of autism more often experienced by females. This hyperempathetic condition would be characterized by superior empathizing skills and poor systemizing ability. Although lack of sys-temizing abilities would severely restrict career choices for the women involved, conditions of hyperempathy have drawn comparatively little research interest.

Indeed, as Michael McGrath and Barbara Oakley point out in Chapter 4, con-ditions involving hyperempathy may well underlie the mass appeal of such ill-defined concepts as codependency, so little studied from a scientific perspective. "Codependents" may, in pathologically altruistic fashion, support their par-amours' drug addiction while endlessly forgiving their emotional and physical abuse. Or, they may simply be "nice" people who are easily taken advantage of. As Karol Pessin explains in Chapter 27, variations in alleles related to vasopressin and oxytocin may well lie behind this type of behavior, and in fact, may lead to hyperresponsiveness to social signals of all sorts. In another vein of research explored by Debbie Riby and her colleagues, the overfriendliness of Williams syn-drome, which can lead to increased risk of victimization, might also shed light on the genetics underlying some forms of codependent behavior (see Chapter 9).

In fact, pathologies of altruism may be related to a variety of conditions. As Rachel Bachner-Melman explains in Chapter 7, treating the selflessness of eating-disordered patients is an important aspect of recovery that goes beyond a focus on issues of food and weight. Olga Klimecki and Tania Singer (Chapter 28) explain how empathy can inadvertently lead to what is commonly called *compassion fatigue*—their chapter shows how the term would be more aptly termed *empathic distress fatigue*. Lynn O'Connor and her colleagues describe survivor guilt, empathy, altruism, and pathological altruism from the perspective of multilevel selection theory (Chapter 2). Carolyn Zahn-Waxler and Carol Van Hulle describe a pathway whereby empathy-based pathogenic guilt in children of depressed parents may lead to costly altruism and eventually culminate in depression (Chapter 25).

Pathological altruism—in the sense of an unhealthy focus on others to the detriment of one's own needs—may have a very early start, and can be seen in developmental personality processes. (Roth, 2008). This can be quantified using data from toddler-age twins (Knafo, 2006). Children were designated as highly *altruistic* if they were in the top 20% in measured prosocial behavior (Goodman, 1997). Another category related to *self-actualizing* behavior, such as "shows pleasure when s/he succeeds," "continues trying, even when something is hard," or "wants to do things by him/herself." Children were rated as *low* in self-actualizing behaviors if they ranked in the bottom 20% of that category. Twins were thought to potentially show the beginning of a form of pathological altruism if they simultaneously ranked in the top 20% of altruistic behaviors and the bottom 20% of self-actualizing behaviors. Of 2,496 children, 73 (3%) met both criteria. That is, these children were very likely to share, care for other children, and help around the house, but were not at all likely to be characterized by "shows pleasure when s/he succeeds," "continues trying, even when something is hard," or "wants to do things by him/herself."

> Some forms of pathological altruism may exact a psychological price even at an early age.

Interestingly, these children were different from other children in their measured temperament. They were less likely to show high degrees of activity, and—unsurprisingly—were slightly more sociable (high motivation for sharing the company of others). Figure 1.1 demonstrates that pathological altruism can have some benefits for children's adjustment, as it was associated with low degrees of conduct problems (aggression, tantrums). On the other hand, it may exact a psychological price even at this early age, as shown by the high scores in emotional symptoms, including worries, unhappiness, fear, nervousness, and somatization.

Viewing altruism as a potentially negative influence provides a new and surprisingly valuable perspective for a variety of complex problems. For example, altruism by its very nature can position the altruist for various types of victimization, as well as praise. Even if groups of altruists out-compete groups of nonaltruists, how could altruism have spread within a community in the first place? Jorge Pacheco and Francisco Santos's "The Messianic Effect of Pathological Altruism" (Chapter 23) provides an elegant new approach to this crucial, evolutionary conundrum. In some sense, unrequited altruism, even when it has apparently negative aspects from every perspective, can still have positive implications.

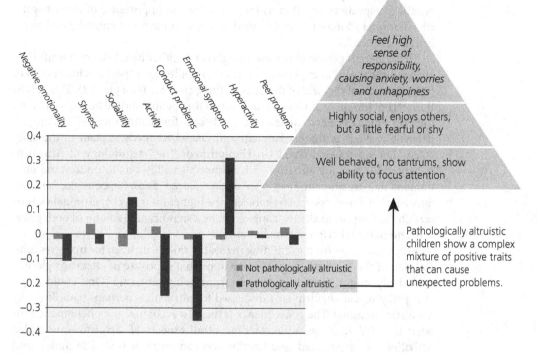

FIGURE 1.1
Mean levels of temperament and behavior problems of 3-year-old twins who display early signs of pathological altruism, as compared with other twins without the syndrome. One twin was selected per pair ($N = 1,248$ pairs). The data presented are based on mother-reported scores standardized separately for girls and boys.
* difference significant ($p < 0.05$ or lower).

One simple way of defining pathological altruism is to say that it involves well-meaning efforts that worsen the very situation they mean to help. This is explored by coeditors Guruprasad Madhavan and Barbara Oakley in their "Too Much of a Good Thing? Foreign Aid and Pathological Altruism" (Chapter 17). Such well-meaning behavior often involves self-righteousness, as explained by neurologist Robert Burton, in his personal story of one doctor's abuse of power to "help" a mortally ill patient (Chapter 10). The dangers of "altruistic" self-righteousness in political partisanship (Chapter 5) are underscored by physicist and science fiction grand master David Brin, who also explores the dangers of modern Western notions of altruism as panacea in regard to the Search for Extra-Terrestrial Intelligence (SETI) project in Chapter 19.

> Viewing altruism as a potentially negative influence provides a new and surprisingly valuable perspective for a variety of complex problems.

A more sophisticated, nuanced view of altruism allows us to understand cultural differences in the concept, which in turn offers a better understanding of altruism's core, as anthropologist John Traphagan explains in "Altruism, Pathology, and Culture" (Chapter 21). Similar sentiments are conveyed from a surprising evolutionary perspective by Satoshi Kanazawa in his "Battered Women, Happy Genes: There Is No Such Thing As Altruism, Pathological or

Otherwise" (Chapter 24). Joan Chiao and her colleagues knit both cultural and genetic perspectives together as they describe the importance of culture–gene coevolutionary forces in shaping distinct cultural norms of empathy and altruism in Chapter 22.

That different people may view a single act as either beneficial or harmful has legal ramifications, as explored by mental disability law expert Michael Perlin in his discussion of the field of therapeutic jurisprudence (Chapter 12). This cuts to the heart of life-or-death issues, such as whether people should be allowed to sell their own kidneys, or whether a cultural defense for beating one's wife is, indeed, defensible. And, as Robert Homant and Daniel Kennedy explain in the aptly titled "Does No Good Deed Go Unpunished? The Victimology of Altruism" (Chapter 14) viewing altruism with nuance also allows us to understand phenomena that are often unmentioned or unexplored. Thus, for example, the more altruistic behavior reported by subjects, the higher their level of criminal victimization: Self-reported altruism appears to be a significant predictor of both property and personal crime victimization.

Researchers shy from examining the seamy side of altruism for many reasons. But one of the most important seems to be that exposure of altruism's gloomy underbelly might discourage people from being altruistic. One could argue that pathological altruism isn't discussed for altruistic—perhaps pathologically altruistic—reasons. The consequence is that few recognize the phenomenon for what it is. Without an understanding of all aspects of altruism—misguided activities are perpetuated, and horrific acts can result. It is vital to understand how attempts to do good can inadvertently worsen the very situation they were meant to solve, or create other problems, either anticipated or unanticipated. This is set into sharp view in Chapter 15, where Adolf Tobeña notes the single shared characteristic of suicide bombers—their altruism. And Augustine Brannigan points out, in Chapter 16, that genocide is committed by those seeking to *help* their fellow man.

> Without an understanding of all aspects of altruism, misguided activities are perpetuated, and horrific acts can result. It is vital to understand how attempts to do good can inadvertently worsen the very situation they were meant to solve, or create other problems, either anticipated or unanticipated.

Pathologies of altruism, it seems, form a great, dark, unexplored frontier. *Pathological Altruism* is the first work to explore this phenomenon from multiple perspectives, rather than relying on a merely (and from some perspectives, outmoded) psychoanalytic approach. The volume synthesizes work from multiple fields, offering many viewpoints on aspects of pathological altruism. Each author brings a unique background to the work. The sum of their contributions will, it is hoped, serve as a scientifically grounded focal point for a new field—pathological altruism—providing a nuanced counterbalance to the study of altruism.

Let us introduce this volume's contributions by following Goethe's lead, as Faust asks:

"All right—who are you, then?"

and Mephistopheles answers:

"Part of that force which would do ever evil, and does ever good."

Acknowledgment

The Longitudinal Israeli Study of Twins (LIST) is supported by grant No. 31/06 from the Israel Science Foundation to Ariel Knafo.

Notes

1. A succinct parsing of altruism is provided by Jacob Neusner and Bruce Chilton in their *Altruism in World Religions* (p. xi):

A standard dictionary definition describes altruism as "unselfish concern for the welfare of others: opposed to egoism." The four components of this definition distinguish altruism from other kinds of care for others. "Unselfish" carries with it the notion that the altruist acts for the sake of the other rather than himself or herself. "Concern" suggests that altruism entails a motivation as well as an action. "Welfare" means that the goal is to benefit, rather than harm, the other. And "others" implies that the altruist is capable of seeing the object of concern as someone distinct from himself or herself. (Neusner & Chilton, 2005)

2. The domains of the Five-Factor Model are neuroticism, extraversion (versus introversion), openness to experience, agreeableness (versus antagonism), and conscientiousness.

References

Buck v. Bell, 274 U.S. 207 (1926).

Goodman, R. (1997) The strengths and difficulties questionnaire: A research note. *Journal of Child Psychology and Psychiatry*, **38**, 581–586.

Knafo, A. (2006). The Longitudinal Israeli Study of Twins (LIST): Children's social development as influenced by genetics, abilities, and socialization. *Twin Research and Human Genetics*, 9(6), 791–798.

McWilliams, N. (1984). The psychology of the altruist. *Psychoanalytic Psychology*, 1, 193–213.

Neusner, J., & Chilton, B. (2005). *Altruism in world religions*. Washington DC: Georgetown University Press.

Roth, G. (2008). Perceived parental conditional regard and autonomy support as predictors of young adults' self-versus other-oriented prosocial tendencies. *Journal of Personality*, 76(3), 513.

Seelig, B. J., & Rosof, L. (2001). Normal and pathological altruism. *Journal of the American Psychoanalytic Association*, 49(3), 933–959.

Waite, R. G. L. (1977). *The psychopathic god: Adolf Hitler*. New York: Basic Books, Inc.

CHAPTER 2

EMPATHY-BASED PATHOGENIC GUILT, PATHOLOGICAL ALTRUISM, AND PSYCHOPATHOLOGY

Lynn E. O'Connor, Jack W. Berry, Thomas B. Lewis, and David J. Stiver

> But to help others, it is not sufficient merely to wish to do so (that is to free others from sorrow and bring about their happiness). Indeed, altruistic thoughts can become an obsession and increase our anxiety . . . . When such good and positive thoughts are combined with wisdom, we know how to help beings effectively and can actually do so. (p. 26)
>
> —H. H. The Dalai Lama, *For the Benefit of All Beings: A Commentary on the Way of the Bodhisattva (2009)*

KEY CONCEPTS

- Empathic reactions to pain or distress in others are instantaneous and begin the path to both normal and pathological altruism. These reactions move quickly to implicit empathy-based guilt, linked to a belief that one should try to relieve the suffering of others.
- Empathy-based guilt is further linked to evaluations of fairness, equality, and the equitable distribution of resources.
- Survivor guilt (inequity guilt) is a specific form of empathy-based guilt that tends to become pathogenic when based on a false belief that one's own success, happiness, or well-being is a source of unhappiness for others, simply by comparison. People with high survivor guilt may falsely believe they are "cheaters."
- *Pathogenic guilt leads to pathological altruism.* In pathological altruism, the altruistic behavior helps no one and potentially harms the altruist, the recipient of the altruism, or both.

- Empathic concern and empathic-based guilt are evolved psychological mechanisms sustaining mammalian group cohesion. Altruism may fail to favor fitness at the level of the individual in within-group competition, while increasing fitness at the level of the group in between-group competition.
- Pathogenic guilt and pathological altruism are commonly found in mental disorders, such as depression, posttraumatic stress disorder (PTSD), and obsessive-compulsive disorder (OCD).

IN THIS CHAPTER, we discuss empathy-based guilt, an evolved psychological mechanism that, when misdirected or excessive, can become pathogenic and lead to pathological altruism. Empathy-based guilt often hovers behind pathological acts of altruism, generating the considerable energy spent in sometimes futile and often self- and other-destructive efforts to help. A theme of this chapter is that empathy-based guilt becomes pathogenic when it provokes cognitive errors in understanding causality. When people who feel empathy at witnessing another's misfortunes falsely believe that they caused the other's problems, or falsely believe that they have the means to relieve the person of suffering, they have erred in their analysis of the situation. In the following discussion of guilt and pathological altruism, we are primarily speaking from the perspective of individual fitness pertaining to within-group competition. However, a trait that is detrimental on the level of individual fitness may be adaptive for fitness at the level of the group in between-group competition (i.e., group selection).

As is evidenced throughout this volume, we are seeing a rapid rise of interest in empathy, prosociality, and altruism (Bekoff & Pierce, 2009; Decety & Ickes, 2009; Frith, 2007; Haidt, 2006; Hauser, 2006; Keltner, 2009; Singer, et al, 2006; Tomasello, 2009). For decades, both science and popular culture viewed psychological, social, and economic phenomena from the perspective of an individualistic, competitive worldview (Dawkins, 1976; Williams 1966). Altruism was interpreted as ultimately self-serving, either psychologically or biologically, through the mechanism of inclusive fitness (kin selection), reciprocal altruism, or "costly display." Today, there are numerous reports of empathy and altruism—with authentic focus on "the other"—expressed throughout the human and non-human animal kingdom (de Waal, 2006; de Waal, 2008; Hauser, 2006; Preston & de Waal, 2002). Many now consider altruistic motivation as fundamental and truly other-directed.

As empathy and altruism emerged to take center stage, multilevel selection theory became an obvious solution to the longstanding puzzle over altruism. Furthermore, inspired in part by complexity science illustrating the tendency of agents to "self-organize" with increasing complexity (Barabasi, 2002; Byrne, 2002), the role of cooperation in biology is recognized; cooperation is found at every level of biological organization. Mammals regularly engage in acts of altruism toward conspecifics. At remarkably young ages, human infants and toddlers exhibit empathy, followed by efforts to help (See Eisenberg, 2000 for review; Warneken & Tomasello, 2006; Zahn-Waxler, Radke-Yarrow, & King, 1979; Zahn-Waxler, Radke-Yarrow, Wagner, & Chapman, 1992). In sync with this shifting worldview, a kinder, more adaptive unconscious mind has been uncovered through studies in psychology, social neuroscience, and economic behaviors

(Gintis, Bowles, Boyd, & Fehr, 2006; Hassin, Uleman, & Bargh, 2005; Kihlstrom, 1987).

Accompanying this changing scientific landscape, the theory of group selection has been resurrected and recognized as a viable evolutionary force (Wilson & Sober, 1994; Wilson & Wilson, 2007). Multilevel selection theory (the simultaneous operation of natural selection at the group and the individual levels) provides an explanation for the evolution of empathy-based guilt and altruism, enhancing fitness in between-group competition, but not infrequently causing trouble for the individual in within-group competition. Groups with more altruists do better in competition with groups with fewer altruists. From the point of view of group selection, the evolution of altruism is advantageous for mammals (and other group animals) living together in interdependent social groups. Boehm (2008) notes that, in our species, there has been a preference for generous mates over a period of 45,000 years, in a process of "runaway selection" suggesting that altruistic traits are preferred from multiple levels of selection.

The Positive Role of Empathy-based Guilt

Empathy-based guilt, and survivor guilt broadly defined (inequity guilt), illustrates the contradiction between individual and group fitness. Survivor guilt sometimes refers to the guilt people feel when someone else dies. More broadly, survivor guilt refers to the emotion people may experience when they are surpassing others and believe they are therefore hurting those who are less successful, simply by comparison. In a pilot study carried out by David Sloan Wilson and colleagues, undergraduates who had been assessed on the Interpersonal Guilt Questionnaire (IGQ: O'Connor, Berry, Weiss, Bush, & Sampson, 1997) participated in an economic game. Results demonstrated the positive role of survivor guilt at the level of the group. Individually, students who were high in survivor guilt were also high in other measures indicating psychological difficulties. However, at the level of the group, those who were higher in survivor guilt were significantly more likely to be cooperators (O'Connor, Berry, Lewis, Mulherin, & Crisostomo, 2007; Wilson, personal communication, 2006).

Historically, empathy-based guilt made it possible in our highly social species to live relatively peacefully in large, stable, interdependent groups, despite wide variations in access to food and shelter. Likewise, our altruistic motivation, the way we identify with one another (often outside of awareness) and react to others' pain as if we are feeling it ourselves, is often followed by an impulsive, hardwired, effort to help. This process makes our highly social lifestyle reliable (Singer, 2006). The ability to cooperate, share, and empathize with another's pain contributes to our feeling of belonging, and this in turn helps to regulate our emotions through our ordinary daily interactions (Baumeister & Leary, 1995; Lewis, Amini, & Lannon, 2002; O'Connor, 2001).

Survivor guilt is a common emotion. Antecedents to survivor guilt—discomfort at inequity eliciting begging and sharing—may first be seen in mammals whose infants remain dependent on parents for food and protection, often for years. In humans, children and adolescents are not fully developed and capable of being self-sustaining until around the age of 20. Furthermore, reports of nonhuman animals sharing in nonfamilial relationships are emerging. Bonobos, perhaps our closest relatives, instead of fighting over resources, use sexual encounters to reduce aggression in the group, allowing them to share whatever food becomes available. In experimental conditions, bonobos, given a favorite food, will open an adjacent cage door housing another bonobo, preferring to share and eat with a conspecific rather than eating the treat alone (Hare & Kwetuenda, 2010). Chimpanzees in the wild share food and demonstrate altruism even to non-related conspecifics. Boesch, Bolé, Eckhardt, and Boesch (2010) report that male and female chimpanzees in the wild will adopt nonrelated orphans and "mother" them through adulthood.

Begging behavior in a species suggests the complementary existence of empathic concern or distress, relieved by sharing. This reaction to begging may be a predecessor to the capacity to feel survivor guilt. Although sharing and cooperation may point to an ultimate biological purpose to altruistic behavior (success in between-group competition), the relief of empathy-based guilt, reflecting an authentic concern for others, may be a proximate purpose of the same behaviors.

Development of Empathy, Guilt, and Altruism

Between our empathy system and altruistic behavior lies a complex network of emotions and impulses to help someone in trouble. These emotions and motivations are involved in our inclination to take responsibility for the well-being of others. From birth, infants feel distress at the distress of others (Sagi & Hoffman, 1976). When newborns listen to an audio recording of other babies crying, they begin to cry, more so than when they hear a recording of their own crying. By a year of age, if someone is upset or unhappy in their environment, infants make an effort to engage their mother as a helper. By 16 months, toddlers respond to other's distress by trying to do something to relieve it. Toddlers and young children are already demonstrating individual differences in reactions to other's suffering. Some toddlers are precocious in their altruistic efforts, and some who have been neglected, abused, or otherwise living in a contentious atmosphere may react to other children's distress with aggression. When highly empathic toddlers and children are unable to help another child or parent in distress, they may experience the antecedants of empathy-based guilt, or survivor guilt. As children develop into adolescents, empathy-based guilt continues to dominate the complex road from empathy to altruistic behavior. (See Chapter 25, Zahn-Waxler and Carol Van Hulle, pp. 243–259 for a more complete discussion.)

Both genetics and environment—shared and nonshared—may account for individual differences in the path from empathy, to guilt, to action in response to the suffering of another (Knafo, Zahn-Waxler, Van Hulle, Robinson, & Rhee, 2008; Zahn-Waxler, 2000). Francis (2009) found that epigenetics accounts for individual differences in maternal behavior in rats. This has implications for individual differences in empathic responses and altruism, both pathological and authentically helpful. The epigenome is sensitive to environmental influences and may account for how and when genes related to altruism are turned on or off. Individual differences that appear nongenetic may be influenced by the environment through epigenetic processes.

> Empathy-based guilt with associated pathogenic beliefs often underlies pathological altruism.

Cognitive evaluations, often unconscious, mediate the relationship between empathy and altruism, by way of explanations that may elicit guilt. These cognitions are related to attributions of causality, whereby a person feels responsible for another's suffering. Depending on the nature of this unconscious mental

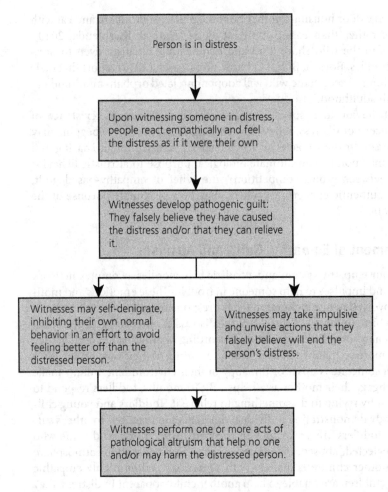

FIGURE 2.1
Upon witnessing someone in distress, people tend to react empathically and feel the distress as if it were their own. In some cases, people almost instantly and implicitly feel pathogenic guilt; that is, they erroneously believe they caused the distress, and/or that they have the power to relieve it. Based on this false belief related to causality, they then may engage in pathological acts of altruism, failing to help, or even harming, the person in distress as well as themselves.

processing, empathic perceptions of distress in others can trigger either helpful or pathological forms of altruistic response. In short, empathy-based guilt when associated with pathogenic beliefs, often underlies pathological altruism.

Pathogenic beliefs related to causality produce the implicit experience of guilt. When people falsely believe their own well-being is directly linked to others' misfortunes (the beliefs underlying survivor guilt), attempts to be altruistic are likely to be pathological (Figure 2.1). An act of altruism may harm the altruist and still not be pathological (by our definition), but when harm occurs without any benefit to the object of altruism, we are looking at pathological altruism, which is associated with several types of psychopathology.

Empathy-based guilt, often nonpathogenic, is a necessary ingredient in many social situations; for example, guilt is the driver in forgiveness. If someone causes harm to another, the victim is more able to forgive the perpetrator if the perpetrator feels regretful and guilty, and signals this to the victim (Acker, 2011; Worthington et al., 2005).

Our ability to respond to one another with empathy, to experience guilt when we believe we have harmed another, allows us to overcome many common social conflicts that might, without empathy-based guilt, destroy our relationships and render us isolated. Altruistic behavior has been demonstrated to have numerous benefits for the altruist, including better physical and mental health, and increased fitness. Altruism, then, may be beneficial in both within- and between-group competition.

From a clinical and research perspective, we find that empathy-based guilt may become excessive, unrealistic in scope and perspective, and lead to altruistic behaviors that tend to be pathological. Pathogenic guilt, by definition, is associated with incorrect explanations of causality that result in psychopathology and pathological altruism. Self-blaming narratives are often under the surface of conscious awareness and cover a wide territory. Examples of empathy-based guilt that becomes pathogenic and leads to pathological altruism abound:

- The battered wife falsely believes that she has made her partner become violent and that if she were to leave him, he might commit suicide. In an effort to save his life, she stays in the abusive relationship.
- The man who is happily married and also loves his job errs when he believes that his happiness is making his less fortunate brother feel inadequate by comparison. In an effort to make things more equal, he begins fighting with his wife for no apparent reason.
- The woman with recurring depression and relapses in alcoholism falsely believes that if she kills herself, she will cease being a burden to her family members. As a result she commits suicide.
- The bullied husband errs when he believes his histrionic wife will destroy herself if he doesn't respond to her every demand. Increasingly, he finds himself tiptoeing around, afraid of her outbursts and inhibiting the expression of his own personality to keep her placated.

In each situation, neither empathy nor altruistic motivation is inherently problematic; pathology begins when people believe, erroneously, that they are the source of someone else's problems and/or that they have the ability to relieve the other of his or her difficulties. In each example, the link between empathy and pathological altruism is guilt. The self-destructive actions that follow are all acts of pathological altruism, driven by pathogenic guilt.

Survivor Guilt, Fairness, and Inequity

Recent studies in primates and other mammals suggest that some (perhaps many) species have fairly well-developed capacities for assessing fairness (Brosnan, 2006; Brosnan & de Waal, 2003; de Waal & Berger, 2000; Hauser, Teixidor, Fields, & Flaherty, 1993). Our propensity to assess fairness may be a positive force in one set of circumstances, encouraging our giving nature, while in other conditions it may leave us depressed and self-defeating. Discomfort at inequity is not limited to feelings about close friends, family, or what we consider our "in-group." We feel survivor guilt when we see a homeless older woman, despondent and dirty, on the street in front of the Walgreens, her hand out begging for money. How many of us avert our eyes, avoiding that moment of intimate contact, because we feel guilty about our comparative good fortune?

Survivor guilt is often functioning when we compare ourselves to others and may be the downside of winning in a social comparison. The tendency to respond to misfortune in others with a feeling of guilt was shaped by our species' adaptations to the environment in which we evolved. In the Pleistocene, in our hunter and gatherer origins, we lived in environments where access to food was variable. A variety of ecological reasons—the lack of refrigeration, the sheer size of the prey of a successful hunting party—all contributed to a social system based on equality. Survivor guilt serves to promote equality and sharing; it provides a leveling mechanism required by a culture that, by necessity, must maintain an equitable distribution of resources. Thus, the equitable social system of our early relatives served an ultimate evolutionary purpose.

The development of cooperation and equity in our species is further supported by altruistic punishment (Fehr & Fischbacher, 2003). People are armed with a fine capacity to detect cheaters, or nonaltruistic people. Although there is at present some debate as to whether or not a specific "cheater-detection" module exists in our neurocircuitry (Carlisle & Shafir, 2005), it is remarkable just how early and how well we are able to detect cheaters. Cosmides and Tooby (1992) found that, when they posed a logical problem to a group of subjects and asked them to assess how to solve it, almost all failed to do so. When, however, they changed the problem to reflect one that focused upon detecting cheaters, the subjects were remarkably successful.

Survivor guilt, then, depends on the capacity to make social comparisons and to evaluate the distribution of resources in order to ensure it is equitable. Although the ability to detect cheaters has been described as something we use to judge others, in survivor guilt, cheater detection is turned upon the self. When experiencing survivor guilt, a person believes that he or she is getting more of the "goods" than is deserved, while another member of the group is suffering because of this unfair distribution. Studies of moral self-regulation have revealed that we are in a continuous process of judging our own morality (Sachdeva, Iliev, & Medin, 2009). When the moral system is on overdrive and based on an unrealistic judgment of ourselves as responsible for the suffering of others, we begin to find empathy-based pathogenic guilt, resulting in psychopathology and pathological altruism.

Survivor guilt, when experienced internally but acted upon only after realistic consideration, is not likely to be pathogenic. But when it is followed rapidly by impulsive and ineffective efforts to equalize or level the playing field, the guilt has become pathogenic.

Survivor Guilt in the Clinic

Survivor guilt was first conceptualized as a painful emotion that often emerges when someone survives the death of a loved one. Darwin (1872/1965) described a woman, in the wake of her father's death, walking around wringing her hands, thinking "I should have done more to help him." Freud (1897/1960) also touched upon survivor guilt in relation to his own brother's death, writing of "the great remorse that follows . . . ." Almost 60 years later, Neiderland (1961) described his work with survivors of the prison camps of World War II, noting their intense suffering, insomnia, nightmares, anxiety and depression, and haunting words: "What right do I have to be alive when everyone else in my family is dead?" Two psychoanalysts, Modell (1965; 1971) and Weiss (1986), began to write about survivor guilt, more broadly defined. Their conceptualization included the

emotional suffering of patients who believed that their being successful or satisfied with their lives, their work, or relationships was harming others, especially
less successful family members, close friends, and associates. These patients
believed their loved ones were suffering simply by comparison with their own
successful lives. Burdened with survivor guilt, people tend to inhibit their own
healthy goal-seeking behaviors, so as not to be better off than others. In the case
of World War II concentration camp survivors, some nearly ceased living, holding themselves in a paralyzed condition, unable to experience joy.

There are situations in which people compete for a reward that only one
person can win, and although winning is the goal, it is often marred by survivor
guilt. Here, survivor guilt is entirely conscious, based on the realistic situation,
and rarely leads to pathological acts of altruism. Furthermore, people with well-
developed skills in affect regulation are able to experience survivor guilt without
it resulting in a compulsion to level the playing field. They are able to recognize
their empathic response to someone else's suffering, but may successfully regulate the intensity and cognitive assessment of the feeling. Some people—perhaps
those with an extraverted and even narcissistic personality—claim to never feel
survivor guilt. However, it often comes to light that they defend themselves
against it by externalizing, blaming others, and getting angry.

The *Diagnostic and Statistical Manual of Mental Disorders, 4th Edition, Text
Revision (DSM-IV-TR)* notes that people who are depressed also tend to feel
excessively guilty and engage in ruminative self-blaming cognitions. Anecdotal
case observations reveal that empathy-based guilt also looms irrationally in anxiety disorders. In obsessive-compulsive disorder (OCD), the fearful situations
expected are often found to be something patients fear will happen to a loved
one, not to themselves. For example, a woman who washes her hands so much
each day that they are red and peeling, when questioned about the reasons for
her compulsion, will often say something like: "If I don't wash my hands I might
contaminate the food I cook for my husband and daughter; I might be responsible for killing them with some infectious disease." Another form of OCD,
regarded as "hyperscrupulosity," is defined by patients' obsession with morality
in themselves and others. Catholic priests in the 16th century came to recognize
the condition and developed a treatment for parishioners who came to confes-
sion daily, or multiple times a day, to confess "sins" that the priests considered to
be imaginary crimes. The clergy discovered what is now standard behavioral
treatment for OCD—that is, exposure and response prevention. They told their
hyperscrupulous parishioners that they were forbidden to look at the Bible, or
any form of scriptures. This, of course, filled the afflicted with anxiety, but as
with modern-day treatment, their anxiety would peak and often the obsessions
then subsided.

A sufferer from an OCD spectrum disorder, hoarding, tells her OCD peer
support group that she can't stop picking up papers from the floor of the super-
market. Her reason: She is convinced that if the papers are left on the floor, some
old woman with poor coordination might slip on one of them, fall down, and be
lethally injured—all because she failed to pick up the pieces of paper.

People suffering from posttraumatic stress disorder (PTSD), so common now
in our military personnel returning from tours in Iraq or Afghanistan, are tor-
mented by their memories of a trauma. In many cases, the trauma was seeing their
comrade(s) maimed or killed from a sudden bomb blast or unexpected sniper fire.
What turns these sad stories into PTSD is, again, erroneous causal attribution. In
each case, we hear some reason, an often convoluted and unrealistic explanation,

of how the surviving soldier is at fault in his buddy's death. "If only I had taken my turn being the first in line watch person" or "If only I had been more alert to what was going on around us." In a recent empirical study of 79 American soldiers who served in Afghanistan and/or Iraq, Morgan (2010) found the trauma of witnessing harm to others more significant in PTSD-related obsessions than was the trauma of harm to oneself.

Children who witness the abuse of their mother or siblings while escaping themselves seem to develop a tendency for guilt and faulty reasoning about causality that leads to chronic, pathogenic guilt and self-blame. Witnessing domestic violence may be a more pathogenic experience than being beaten oneself. Children who grow up in dysfunctional families, in which violence is the norm, necessarily begin to confuse causal information, taking on guilt themselves instead of blaming their parents. This is yet another act of pathological altruism.

The Neuroscience of Guilt and Pathological Altruism

The past decade has seen a dramatic leap in understanding the neural substrates underlying healthy altruism. This also suggests possible origins for dysfunction in pathological altruism. A detailed review of this fascinating material is, regrettably, beyond the scope of this chapter. Instead, we present a simplified neurobiological model in which we explore two networks, each comprised of multiple linked areas: the network underlying empathic distress, and the network underlying prosocial emotions such as guilt, compassion, and inequity aversion.

Normal people typically create internal simulations of much of the behavior they witness, including actions, sensations, and emotions of the people around them (Iacoboni & Dapretto, 2006). This ubiquitous "covert modeling" of other's behavior constitutes one of the principal mechanisms of empathy (Decety & Chaminade, 2003). Covert simulation occurs in response to observed facial expressions, postures, body movements, tone of voice, sensations, pain, and even moral attitudes. Through the internal simulation of observed sensations and actions, we are able to experience some portion of what others are themselves feeling and doing.

Empathic modeling gives rise to one of the mechanisms that promotes altruism: because other people's sensations are simulated inside an observer's brain, normal observers experience distress at witnessing the distress of others; they experience pain at witnessing the pain of others. Thus, normal observers are motivated to reduce pain and distress in others to minimize discomfort generated by simulations of that pain in their own brains.

Several brain areas are crucial in representing emotional distress and thus critical to the normal functioning of altruism. The amygdala (Figures 2.2 and 2.3) has been implicated in representing negative emotion in response to experiencing or witnessing aversive stimuli, whereas the anterior temporal pole has been implicated in processing the social meaning of events (Moll, Zahn, de Oliveira-Souza, Krueger, & Grafman, 2005). The insula (Figure 2.4), which can be conceptualized as the sensory cortex of the limbic system, is activated by a wide variety of emotional stimuli, including experiencing or witnessing emotional distress or pain (Jackson, Meltzoff, & Decety, 2005).

Interruption in the function of any of these areas can produce profound disturbances in empathy and altruistic behavior. In frontotemporal dementia (FTD), for instance, the anterior temporal pole undergoes gradual deterioration. Patients with FTD commonly develop an empathic deficit and insensitivity to the pain of others that is surprising and disturbing to family members (Rankin et al., 2006). In addition, psychopathic individuals have been found to exhibit not only reduced activity (Birbaumer et al., 2005) but also volume loss in the anterior temporal cortex and the insula (de Oliveira-Souza et al., 2008); this may be related to their callousness and inability to "feel" other people's pain, as well as their indifference to the social dimensions of their actions.

Psychopathy and FTD may represent syndromes of decreased function in one or more areas related to internal models of others' distress. It is possible that analogous syndromes of hypersensitivity also exist. If the brain areas most important in modeling emotional distress—amygdala, anterior temporal cortex, and insula—are abnormally sensitive in some individuals, they could experience supra-normal levels of empathic distress, and, consequently, would experience a powerful motivation to alleviate or reduce that distress, even in situations in which such behaviors may not be appropriate. It is possible, for instance, that some observers in this supra-normal group experience more distress and pain from the empathic simulation generated in their own brains than does the person suffering the actual injury being witnessed.

The second circuit we will consider is that underlying prosocial moral emotions, including guilt, compassion, and inequity aversion. Moral emotions, which arose late in the evolution of emotion systems, guide and motivate behaviors to facilitate interactions within the large social group that constitutes the environment in which *Homo sapiens* resides (Haidt, 2003). The moral emotions include a prosocial or cohesiveness-promoting group of emotions such as guilt, embarrassment, compassion, and gratitude, which serve to maximize helping behaviors and maintain the social order.

The location of the brain areas involved in producing the prosocial moral emotions has been the subject of recent research. Several areas are consistently implicated across studies.

First, the subgenual cingulate cortex (Figure 2.4) has been observed to be activated under conditions of guilt (Zahn et al., 2009). This is of particular interest, since abnormally increased activity in the subgenual cingulate cortex has been linked to the disease state of major depression (Greicius et al., 2007), in which guilt-ridden ruminations are often a prominent symptom. The subgenual cingulate has also been linked to the presence of charitable donation behavior (Moll et al., 2006). Second, the anterior portions of the medial prefrontal cortex (Figure 2.4) have been implicated in the production of prosocial feelings, such as compassion and the urge to donate to charity at a cost to oneself. Finally, some investigators have reported activation of the mesolimbic reward system (Figure 2.4) during the elicitation of prosocial emotions (Moll et al., 2007), indicating the likelihood that evolution has linked altruistic behaviors to intrinsic reward as a mechanism for promoting the acting and repetition of such behaviors.

The areas most relevant to the production of prosocial emotions—the subgenual cingulate, anterior medial prefrontal cortex, and mesolimbic reward system—suggest mechanisms relevant to the production of pathological altruism.

Major depression, a syndrome that includes overactivation of the subgenual cingulate, is not infrequently accompanied by acts of attempted but pathological altruism, as when severely depressed patients evidence a sincere belief that by committing suicide they could substantially improve the lives of those around them. Increased activity in anteromedial prefrontal cortical areas may produce unusually strong motivations toward compassionate or self-sacrificing altruism. Finally, increased mesolimbic reward activity with respect to prosocial motivations could

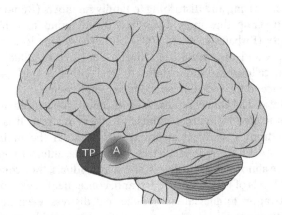

FIGURE 2.2
Lateral view of the human brain, illustrating the anterior temporal pole (TP) and the amygdala (A). The amygdala, located deep within the temporal lobe, represents negative emotions, whereas the temporal pole has been linked to processing the social meaning of behavior. Together, they constitute crucial components of a person's ability to feel empathic concern, and, if too sensitive, could motivate pathological altruism.

Adapted from an illustration by Patrick J. Lynch, medical illustrator. Creative Commons Attribution 2.5 License 2006.

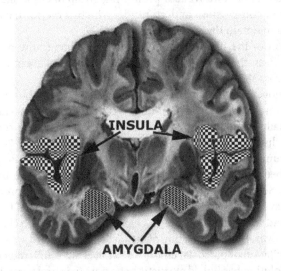

FIGURE 2.3
Coronal section of the human brain, illustrating the bilateral insula (checkerboard pattern) and amygdala (tread pattern). The insular cortex, sometimes called "the sensory cortex of the limbic system," represents the visceral sensations pertaining to emotional experiences—e.g., chest tightening, butterflies in the stomach, chills up and down the spine. Witnessing pain in others produces intense insular activation, whereas some forms of empathy deficiency (sociopathy) involve restricted insular function and reduced insula volume.

Adapted from Mobbs, D., Lau, H. C., Jones, O. D., & Frith, C. D. (2007). Law, responsibility, and the brain. PLoS Biol 5(4): e103. doi:10.1371/journal.pbio.0050103; available through the Creative Commons Attribution License.

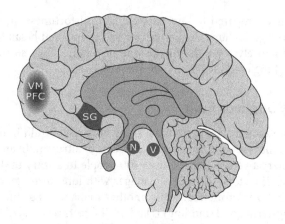

FIGURE 2.4

Sagittal view of the human brain, illustrating the ventromedial prefrontal cortex (VMPFC), the subgenual cingulate (SG), and the two major components of the mesolimbic reward system, the ventral tegmental area (V) and the nucleus accumbens (N). The VMPFC has been associated with altruistic behaviors, like charitable donations that occur at a cost to oneself. Activity in the SG has been linked to feelings of guilt, and, interestingly, is frequently hyperactive in the state of major depression. The mesolimbic reward system N and V is activated by behaviors that directly advance reproductive fitness (e.g., sex and food) and serves to ensure the repetition of such behaviors. The activation of N and V in altruistic states suggests that these states enjoy a primary reward valence, which in some persons could become overly activated and result in maladaptive altruistic acts.

Adapted from an illustration by Patrick J. Lynch, medical illustrator. Creative Commons Attribution 2.5 License 2006.

make self-sacrificing acts profoundly reinforcing in certain individuals, perhaps providing the enthusiasm with which some missionaries and saints have thrown themselves into situations in which their martyrdom was virtually assured.

Empirical Studies of Empathy, Guilt, Pathological Altruism, and Psychopathology

Moving from anecdotal and clinical examples, we set out to examine empirically the connection between empathy-based guilt, altruism, and psychopathology. We first developed a reliable and valid measure, the Interpersonal Guilt Questionnaire (IGQ-67), designed to quantify survivor guilt and closely related constructs. We consistently found high levels of survivor guilt significantly correlated with depression, anxiety, obsessive thinking and the OCD spectrum disorders along with most of the Axis II personality disorders (O'Connor, Berry, & Weiss, 1999; O'Connor, Berry, Weiss, Schweitzer, & Sevier, 2000; O'Connor, Berry, Weiss, & Gilbert, 2002). In several studies, we have found survivor guilt also present in PTSD (O'Connor et al, 2002; Pole, D'Andrea, O'Connor, & Santarlasci, unpublished manuscript).

Research on attributional style (Seligman, Abramson, Semmel, & von Baeyer, 1979), or how people explain both bad and good events, demonstrates that pessimists—those who blame themselves for bad outcomes and who attribute good outcomes to something outside themselves (like luck for example)—are highly prone to depression when facing adversity. We found that survivor guilt is significantly correlated with a pessimistic explanatory style (Menaker, 1995). Most noteworthy, the association was greater in terms of how people explain fortunate events compared to how they explain misfortunes. Although people high in survivor guilt blame themselves for bad events that befall them (as they often blame themselves for the misfortune of others), they seem particularly incapable of taking credit for their own successes.

Everyday Survivor Guilt

We next conducted an experimental study of survivor guilt in daily life, outside the clinic, that precipitated pathological acts of altruism. In an online study, we collected narrative reactions of over 400 people to a story of downsizing in the workplace. The story is about a manager with long-term good standing in the company who is promoted, while another manager in a different division (also with long-term good standing) is laid off. Subjects responded to one of four conditions, determined randomly, that varied only in the closeness of the relationship between the two managers. In one condition, the employee who was terminated was a sibling; in another, it was a friend; in a third, it was a distant acquaintance, unlikely to cross paths in the future; and in the fourth, it was someone who had been a long-time rival who often behaved unethically. Subjects wrote narratives about the thoughts, feelings, and behaviors they expected from the manager who was promoted. We found that the closer the relationship between the managers, the greater the likelihood that the promoted worker was expected to feel guilty, to experience a decrease in productivity, and to exhibit inhibitions on activities that are normally enjoyable, which we interpret as pathological altruism (O'Connor, Berry, Crisostomo, et al., 2007).

A Structural Model of Empathy, Guilt, Inhibition, and Altruism

Using a structural model, we illustrate our hypotheses about the relationships between empathy, guilt and pathological altruism using data from an online survey. Participants were 450 community adults with varied ethnicity who completed a brief Big Five Inventory, the Interpersonal Reactivity Index (IRI; with scales for Empathic Concern, Perspective-Taking, and Empathic Distress; Davis, 1983), and the IGQ-67 subscales for Survivor Guilt and Omnipotent Responsibility Guilt (exaggerated responsibility for the well-being of others). In addition, participants completed the Dispositional Altruism Scale (DAS; Berry, et al, 2005), an instrument adapted from the Social Support Behaviors Scale (Vaux, Riedel, & Stewart, 1987), assessing social support received from family and friends. We reversed the direction of empathic behavior—instead of a person receiving social support, the person is now extending social support to others. We changed the wording to express the frequency with which the test-taker provides support to others and added a subscale for altruism toward strangers. We used the sum of scores across family, friends, and strangers as a global measure of the disposition to engage in altruistic acts. Psychometric evaluation of the DAS, based on item-response theory (IRT), along with correlations with theoretically relevant constructs, supported reliability and validity.

We tested our hypotheses about the origins of pathological altruism in empathy-based guilt, using structural equation modeling (see Figure 2.5 for model). We hypothesized that empathic concern and perspective-taking would form a latent construct of empathy, and that survivor guilt and omnipotent responsibility would form a latent guilt factor. Finally, we hypothesized that

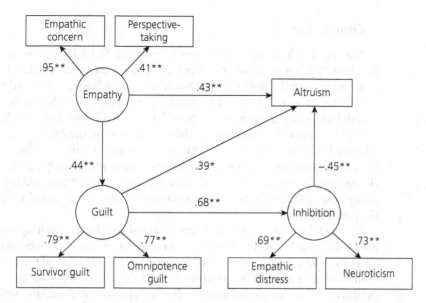

FIGURE 2.5
Structural model of the relationships among empathy, guilt, psychological inhibitions, and dispositional altruism.
This model illustrates the complex relationships between empathy, guilt and altruism. In this model, empathy gives
rise to guilt, and both empathy and guilt have a direct positive influence on altruistic actions. However, empathy-
based guilt, by way of significant associations with neuroticism and empathic distress, is also positively associated
with psychological inhibitions. This may interfere with altruistic behaviors and constitute the potential downside of
empathy-based guilt.

Note. Standardized coefficients. Model Fit Statistics: x^2 (10) = 89.8, $p < 0.01$; Cumulative Fit Index (CFI) = 0.93; Root Mean
Square Error of Approximation (RMSEA) = 0.08; Standardized Root Mean Square Residual (SRMR) = 0.05.
*$p < 0.05$, ** $p < 0.01$

empathic distress (the tendency to become upset and anxious when witnessing
the distress of others) and neuroticism (a broad trait reflecting proneness to
experience negative affect) would form a factor of guilt-based psychological
inhibitions.

We proposed that when empathy gives rise to pathogenic guilt, a person's
altruistic impulses may take pathological forms, such as the development of
psychological inhibitions and symptoms—in other words, putting the lid on
one's achievements. These inhibitions—behavioral reflections of empathy-based
guilt—may limit ones' own developmentally adaptive actions, in addition to
interfering with truly helpful and effective acts of altruism toward others. Our
statistical model of the path from empathy through guilt and inhibitions to
altruism is shown in Figure 2.5. The latent empathy, guilt, and inhibition factors
that we hypothesized were supported by the data. According to the model,
empathy has a positive direct effect on altruistic actions. However, in the model,
empathy is also positively related to the guilt associated with psychological inhibitions that interfere with effective altruistic efforts. Guilt also had a direct positive effect on altruism. This suggests that some element of empathy-based guilt,
instead of being pathogenic, contributes positively to altruistic actions.
(Theoretically, effective altruistic behaviors may serve to relieve the intense discomfort of empathy-based guilt, suggesting a proximate purpose of altruism.)
These data are consistent with our understanding of pathological altruism and
its association with guilt and altruistically motivated inhibitions.

Conclusion

We began this chapter with a quote from the Dalai Lama, former head of the state of Tibet in Exile and ongoing religious leader of Tibetan Buddhists scattered around the world. Many Buddhist lamas, scholars, yogis, and practitioners have, as a recognized life purpose, the goal of attaining the state of a Bodhisattva, a person who has been "enlightened" and dedicates his or her life to the "liberation of all sentient beings." Following the Mahayana tradition, Tibetan Buddhists believe the path to happiness is helping others and that the goal of practice is to be reborn in order to continue helping others, until all sentient beings are liberated (Dalai Lama, 1994; Rinchen/Atisha, 1997; Shantideva, 2003); only then is a true state of Nirvana or the end of suffering (for all) possible.

For over 50 years, Tibet has been occupied by China, enduring what some have called the "Tibetan Holocaust." Since 1959, millions of Buddhists within Tibet have been killed, imprisoned, and tortured. A majority of their numerous monasteries, traditionally the centers of religion, learning, and culture, were destroyed. The full expression of Tibetan religion and culture was greatly restricted, stripping away from this very spiritual country what had been the center of life. In Tibet, almost every family had at least one son and/or daughter in a monastery. Thus, the attacks on religion extended beyond what may be perceived as a privileged class of monastics. Although there remained class divisions within monasteries and modernization was called for, the changes brought in with the Chinese takeover were accompanied by a violent and massive assault on the Tibetan people. Many Tibetans who were able undertook the dangerous escape by foot, over the Himalayas, to the safety of Nepal and India. Keller et al. (2006), in studies comparing people from different regions of origin who have undergone political torture, found significant variation in PTSD symptoms in Tibetan exiles. In contrast to the experience of many who have fled from their countries and cultures of origin because of political or religious oppression (including refugees living on the Thai-Burmese border, Somali and Oromo refugees, and the often-mentioned example of European Jews who survived the Nazi concentration camps), many Tibetan Buddhists in exile seem to be somewhat psychologically protected from assuming unrealistic responsibility for loved ones still suffering in Tibet. Unlike concentration camp and other political torture survivors, and differing from the present-day U.S. military returning from Iraq or Afghanistan, many of whom suffer from suicidal intentions, or even, on a smaller scale, survivors of traumatic family situations, Tibetans in exile appear relatively resilient and optimistic. Sachs et al. (2008) and Keller et al. (2006) hypothesized that something in the Tibetan Buddhist religion serves as a buffer.

Several studies have described an increase in anxiety, but not depression in Tibetan exiles. In a recent study, 769 Tibetan exiles arriving over a 2-week period in Dharamsala, India, were assessed for degree of trauma, psychological distress, and coping. Although data demonstrated a correlation between degree of torture endured and psychological problems, as a whole, the new exiles were remarkably free of serious pathology. Out of the whole sample, only one case of PTSD was diagnosed. Furthermore, relatively low levels of other mental disorders associated with trauma (depression and anxiety for example) were noted (Sachs, Rosenfeld, Lhewa, Rasmussen, & Keller, 2008). Another, earlier study examining responses to trauma from a cross-cultural perspective found a significantly lower rate of PTSD symptoms among Buddhist refugees, almost all of whom were Tibetans in exile (Keller et al., 2006). These results were supported by other studies (Crescenzi et al., 2002).

The authors suggest that coping activities, most often religious, and subjective appraisal of trauma severity, may account for these unexpected findings. Subjects consistently seemed to believe that the degree of trauma they experienced was of lesser intensity than that endured by others. Sachs et al. suggest that the belief system embodied in the religion and religious coping strategies may provide some explanation. It may be inferred that particular beliefs and practices cut into the sources of pathogenic beliefs, pathological altruism, and associated psychopathology, indicating new avenues of treatment and prevention. The meditative practices of Tibetan monks have now been studied by Western neuroscientists, and have demonstrated the positive effects these practices have on emotion regulation (Lutz, Brefczynski-Lewis, Johnstone, & Davidston, 2008; Lutz, Slagter, Dunne, & Davidson, 2008). Negative emotions, such as excessive or pathogenic guilt, may be modified, along with anger and fear. Furthermore, when the Dalai Lama notes that altruistic thoughts and wishes, without wisdom, increase obsessional thinking and anxiety, it is likely he is speaking from experience and is addressing the distortions in causal thinking or attributions that we have emphasized in this chapter. In support of these hypotheses, a recent study of 98 Tibetan Buddhists, 85% of whom were from the United States or Europe, found the sample to be significantly lower in Separation and Omnipotent Responsibility Guilt, Empathy-Distress, and Depression and significantly higher in Altruism toward Strangers, when compared to a sample of 444 non-Buddhists, also from the United States or Europe. In addition, Buddhists were significantly higher on the Big-5 personality factors of Agreeableness and Conscientiousness and significantly lower in Neuroticism. Within the sample of Tibetan Buddhists we found intensity of meditation (frequency and duration) to be significantly associated with lower depression, Neuroticism, Omnipotent Responsibility Guilt, and Empathy-Distress and with higher Conscientiousness, Empathy-Perspective-taking, and Altruism towards strangers (O'Connor, Berry & Stiver, (2011).

When Tibetan Buddhists speak of "wisdom," they are addressing a philosophical concept central to their worldview: *shunyata*, usually translated as "emptiness," "voidness," "nothingness," or even "relativity." Accepting the idea of emptiness as a descriptor may pave the way to holding a more realistic perspective on oneself and one's capacities. In this Buddhist worldview, we are all impermanent and interdependent; we are "empty" of independent, intrinsic existence, excluding the possibility of omnipotent, permanent responsibility for things we can't control or even necessarily influence. If we believe that no one is entirely independent or permanent, and that everyone is interdependent, it follows that no one can be liberated until everyone is liberated. Believing that we are all closely connected and impermanent results in the strong motivation to liberate all "sentient beings" from suffering, without taking on unrealistic and irrationally grandiose beliefs associated with the errors in causal attributions we have seen so associated with empathy-based guilt and pathological altruism. Thus, this construct we have translated as "emptiness" describes a perspective that may provide a protective factor, mediating exaggerated pathogenic guilt that leads to pathological altruism, despite a history of trauma.

Other religious and philosophical worldviews that emphasize realistic limitations on human proneness to omnipotent thinking may also offer protection from pathogenic guilt and pathological altruism. In fact, some research demonstrated that people with different ethnic backgrounds and religious affiliations may have different levels of pathogenic guilt and pathological altruism (Albertsen, O'Connor, & Berry, 2006). Specific practices, such as meditation, rituals, and prayers found in many religions, may contribute to the relief they offer to practitioners. The rise of interest in contemplative science in psychology and education points in that direction. Relief from the burden of cognitive distortions may serve to make it possible for people to nurture their natural compassion and engage in healthy altruism, more effectively helping others, in line with our wired-in propensity for kindness, while avoiding self- and other destructive actions that are described in this book as pathological altruism.

Acknowledgments

The authors wish to thank the Meehan Foundation for funding this project and the research conducted by the Emotion, Personality & Altruism Research Group that is reported in this manuscript. We thank Carolyn Zahn-Waxler for her careful reading of the manuscript, Roland Zahn for his review and commentary on the neuroscience in pathological altruism, Emiliana Simon-Thomas for her detailed review of the manuscript and helpful suggestions, and Alexandria Leedy and Deborah Chase for their thoughtful comments. We also thank Ven Losang Monlam and David Bullard for their insightful commentaries on Tibetan Buddhism, and Stephen Hinshaw for reading and commenting on the manuscript, with a uniquely broad knowledge and perspective on clinical psychology. We thank Charles Smith and members at Tse Chen Ling, San Francisco, Losang Monlam, the Mongolian Buddhist Cultural Center, Bloomington, Indiana, for their help gathering data, and Sze Gee Toh for her work as a translator. We thank Suluck Chaturabul, Project Manager of EPARG, whose help has been invaluable as we were working on this manuscript, and our UC Berkeley Research Assistant Mina Yadegar, who managed to find difficult-to-locate literature. Finally, we wish to thank Kathy Mulherin, who is our ongoing, very patient and encouraging reader.

References

Acker, K. (2011). When do we forgive? An examination of the role of apology and empathy-based guilt in promoting forgiveness. Doctoral Dissertation. Wright Institute Berkeley, CA.

Albertsen, E. J., O'Connor, L. E., & Berry, J. W. (2006). Religion and interpersonal guilt: Variations across ethnicity and spirituality. *Mental Health, Religion & Culture, 9*(1), 67–84.

Barabasi, A. L. (2002). *Linked: The new science of social networks.* New York: Basic Books.

Baumeister, R. F., & Leary, M. R. (1995). The need to belong: Desire for interpersonal attachments as a fundamental human motivation. *Psychological Bulletin, 117*(3), 497.

Bekoff, M., & Pierce, J. (2009). *Wild justice: The moral lives of animals.* Chicago, IL: University of Chicago Press.

Berry, J.W., O'Connor, L.E., Crisostomo, P., & Yi, E. (February, 2005). Altruism and empathy based guilt across five cultures. In G. Fricchione (Chair), Identifying altruism. Symposium conducted at the 34th Annual Conference of the Society for Cross-Cultural Research, Santa Fe, New Mexico.

Birbaumer, N., Veit, R., Lotze, M., Erb, M., Hermann, C., Grodd, W., & Flor, H. (2005). Deficient fear conditioning in psychopathy: A functional magnetic resonance imaging study. *Archives of General Psychiatry, 62*(7), 799.

Boesch, C., Bolé, C., Eckhardt, N., & Boesch, H. (2010). Altruism in forest chimpanzees: A case for adoption. *PLoS ONE, 5*(1), 1–6. doi:10.1371/journal.pone.0008901.

Boehm, C. (2008). Purposive social selection and the evolution of human altruism. *Cross-Cultural Research, 42* (4), 319–352.

Brosnan, S. F. (2006). Nonhuman species' reactions to inequity and their implications for fairness. *Social Justice Research, 9*(2), 153–185.

Brosnan, S. F., & de Waal, F. B. M. Letters to nature - Monkeys reject unequal pay. *Nature, 425*(6955), 297–299. doi:10.1038/nature01963.

Brosnan, S. F. (2006). Nonhuman species' reactions to inequity and their implications for fairness. *Social Justice Research, 9.*

Dalai Lama XIV, (1994). *A flash of lightning in the dark of night: A guide to the Bodhisattva's way of life* (Padmakara Translation Group, Trans.). Boston: Shambhala.

Byrne, D. (2002). *Complexity Theory and the Social Sciences.* New York: Taylor & Francis.

Carlisle, E. & Shafir, E. (2005). Questioning the cheater-detection hypothesis: New studies with the selection task. *Thinking and Reasoning, 11*(2), 97–122.

Cosmides, L., & Tooby, J. (1992). Cognitive adaptations for social exchange. In J.H. Barlow, L. Cosmides, & J. Tooby (Eds.), *The adapted mind: Evolutionary psychology and the generation of culture* (pp. 163–228). Oxford: Oxford University Press.

Crescenzi, A., Ketzer, E., Van Ommeren, M., Phunsok, K., Komproe, I., & de Jong, J. T. V. N. (2002). Effect of political imprisonment and trauma history on recent Tibetan refugees in India. *Journal of Traumatic Stress, 15,* 369–375.

Dalai Lama, H. H. (2009). *For the benefit of all beings: A commentary on the way of the bodhisattva.* Boulder, CO: Shambala Press.

Darwin, C. (1872/1965). *The expression of the emotions in man and animals.* Chicago: University of Chicago Press.

Davis, M. H. (1983). Measuring individual differences in empathy: Evidence for a multidimensional approach. *Journal of Personality and Social Psychology, 44,* 113–126.

Dawkins, R. (1976). *The selfish gene.* Oxford, UK: Oxford University Press.

Decety, J. & Ickes, W. (Eds). (2009). *The social neuroscience of empathy.* Cambridge, MA: MIT Press.

Decety, J., & Chaminade T. (2003). Neural correlates of feeling sympathy. *Neuropsychologia, 41*(2), 127–138.

de Oliveira-Souza, R., Hare, R. D., Bramati, I. E., Garrido, G. J., Azevedo Ignácio, F., Tovar-Moll, F., & Moll, J. (20April 08, 15). Psychopathy as a disorder of the moral brain: Fronto-temporo-limbic grey matter reductions demonstrated by voxel-based morphometry. *Neuroimage, 40*(3), 1202–1213.

de Waal, F. B. M. (2008). Putting the altruism back into altruism: The evolution of empathy. *Annual Review of Psychology, 59,* 279–300.

de Waal, F. B. M. (2006). *Our inner ape: A leading primatologist explains why we are who we are.* New York: Riverhead Books.

de Waal, F. B. M., & Berger, M. L. (2000). Payment for labor in monkeys. *Nature, 404,* 563.

Eisenberg, N. (2000). Empathy and sympathy. In M. Lewis, & J. M. Haviland-Jones (Eds.), *Handbook of emotions* (2nd ed., pp. 677–691). New York: Guilford.

Fehr, E., & Fischbacher, U. (2003). The nature of human altruism. *Nature, 425*(6960), 785–791.

Francis, D. D. (2009). Conceptualizing child health disparities: A role for developmental neurogenomics. *Pediatrics, 124*(Sup3), S196–S202. doi:10.1542/peds.2009–1100G.

Frith, C. (Ed.) (2007). *Empathy and fairness.* Novartis Foundation Symposium, No. 278. London: John Wiley & Sons Ltd.

Gintis, H., Bowles, S., Boyd, R. T., & Fehr, E. (2006). *Moral sentiments and material interests: The foundations of cooperation in economic life.* Cambridge: MIT Press.

Greicius, M. D., Flores, B. H., Menon, V., Glover, G. H., Solvason, H. B., Kenna, H., et al. (2007). Resting-state functional connectivity in major depression: Abnormally increased contributions from subgenual cingulate cortex and thalamus. *Biological Psychiatry, 62*(5), 429.

Haidt, J. (2006). *The happiness hypothesis.* Cambridge MA: Basic Books.

Haidt, J. (2003). The moral emotions. In R. J. Davidson, K. R. Scherer, & H. H. Goldsmith (Eds.), *Handbook of affective sciences* (pp. 852–870). Oxford, UK: Oxford University Press.

Hare, B., & Kwetuenda, S. (February 2010). Buddy, can you spare a banana? Study finds that bonobos share like humans. *ScienceDaily.* Retrieved February 18, 2010, from http://www.sciencedaily.com/releases/2010/02/100212125708.htm.

Hassin, R. R., Uleman, S., & Bargh, J. A. (Eds.). (2005). *The new unconscious.* New York: Oxford University Press.

Hauser, M. D. (2006). *Moral Minds.* New York: Harper Collins Publishers.

Hauser, M. D., Teixidor, R., Fields, L., & Flaherty, R. (1993). Food elicited calls in chimpanzees: Effects of food quantity and divisibility. *Animal Behaviour, 45*(4), 817–819.

Iacoboni, M., & Dapretto, M. (2006). The mirror neuron system and the consequences of its dysfunction. *Nature Reviews. Neuroscience. 7*(12), 942. doi:10.1038/nrn2024.

Jackson, P. L., Meltzoff, A.N., & Decety, J. (2005). How do we perceive the pain of others? A window into the neural processes involved in empathy. *Neuroimage, 24*(3), 771–779.

Jones, E. (Ed.). (1960). *The letters of Sigmund Freud* (1897). New York: Basic Books.

Keller, A., Lhewa, D., Rosenfeld, B., Sachs, E., Asher, A., Cohen, I., et al. (2006). Traumatic experiences and psychological distress in an urban refugee population. *Journal of Nervous and Mental Disease, 194,* 188–194.

Keltner, D. (2009). *Born to be good: The science of a meaningful life.* New York: WW Norton & Company.

Kihlstrom, J. F. (1987). The cognitive unconscious. *Science, 237,* 1445–1452.

Knafo, A., Zahn-Waxler, C., Van Hulle, C., Robinson, J. L., & Rhee, S. H. (2008). The developmental origins of a disposition toward empathy: Genetic and environmental contributions. *Emotion, 8,* 737–752.

Lewis, T., Amini, F., & Lannon, R. (2002). *A general theory of love.* New York: Random House.

Lutz, A., Brefczynski-Lewis, J., Johnstone, T., & Davidson, R. J. (2008). Regulation of the neural circuitry of emotion by compassion meditation: Effects of meditative expertise. *PLoS ONE, 3*(3), e2897.

Lutz, A., Slagter, H. A., Dunne, J. D., & Davidson, R. J. (2008). Attention regulation and monitoring in meditation. *Trends in Cognitive Science, 12*(4), 163–169.

Lutz, A., Brefczynski-Lewis, J., Johnstone, T., & Davidson, R. J. (2008). Regulation of the neural circuitry of emotion by compassion meditation: Effects of meditative expertise. *PLoS ONE, 3,*

Menaker, A. (1995). *The relationship between attributional style and interpersonal guilt.* Doctoral Dissertation, California School of Professional Psychology, Alameda, CA.

Mobbs, D., Lau, H.C., Jones, O.D., Frith, C.D. (2007). Law, responsibility, and the brain. *PLoS Biology, 5*(4), e103. doi:10.1371/journal.pbio.0050103.

Modell, A. H. (1971). The origin of certain forms of pre-oedipal guilt and the implications for a psychoanalytic theory of affects. *International Journal of Psychoanalysis, 52,* 337–346.

Modell, A.H. (1965). On having the right to a life: An aspect of the superego's development. *International Journal of Psycho-Analysis, 46,* 323–331.

Moll, J., de Oliveira-Souza, R., Garrido, G. J., Bramati, I. E., Caparelli-Daquer, E. M., Paiva, M. L., & Grafman, J. (2007). The self as a moral agent: Linking the neural bases of social agency and moral sensitivity. *Social Neuroscience, 2*(3–4), 336–352. doi: 10.1080/17470910701392024.

Moll, J., Krueger, F., Zahn, R., Pardini, M., de Oliveira-Souza, R., & Grafman, J. (2006). Human fronto-mesolimbic networks guide decisions about charitable donation. *Proceedings of the National Academy of Sciences USA, 103*(42), 15623–15628.

Moll, J., Zahn, R., de Oliveira-Souza, R., Krueger, F., & Grafman, J. (2005). Opinion: the neural basis of human moral cognition. *Nature Reviews Neuroscience, 6*(10), 799–809.

Morgan, J. (2010). Study of the Military and Facebook. Doctoral Dissertation, Wright Institute, Berkeley, CA.

Neiderland, W. G. (1961). The problem of the survivor. *Journal of Hillside Hospital, 10,* 233–247.

O'Connor, L. E., Berry, J. W., Weiss, J., Bush, M., & Samspson, H. (1997). Interpersonal guilt: Development of a new measure. *Journal of Clinical Psychology, 53*(1), 73–89.

O'Connor, L. E., Berry, J. W., & Weiss, J. (1999). Interpersonal guilt, shame, and psychological problems. *Journal of Social and Clinical Psychology, 18*(2), 181–203.

O'Connor, L. E., Berry, J. W., Lewis, T., Mulherin, K., & Crisostomo, P. (2007). Empathy and depression: The moral system on overdrive. In T. Farrow, & P. Woodruff (Eds.), *Empathy and mental illness*. London: Cambridge U. Press.

O'Connor, L. E., Berry, J. W., Weiss, J., Schweitzer, D., & Sevier, M. (2000). Survivor guilt, submissive behaviour and evolutionary theory: The down-side of winning in social comparison. *British Journal of Medical Psychology, 73*(4), 519–530.

O'Connor, L. E., Berry, J. W., Weiss, J., & Gilbert, P. (2002). Guilt, fear, submission, and empathy in depression. *Journal of Affective Disorders, 71,* 19–27.

O'Connor, L.E., Berry, J.W.,Stiver, D.J.,Monlam, J., & Chaturabul, S.,(April 2011). Empathy, guilt and altruism: Tibetan Buddhist meditation practices. Presentation, Annual Meeting of the Western Psychological Association, Los Angeles CA.

O'Connor, L. E., Berry, J. W., Crisostomo, P. S. Chaturabul, S., Hume, A., & Imp, S. (2007). *Survivor guilt and altruism: Responses to inequality in the work place*. Presentation, Human Behavior and Evolution Society, Williamsburg, VA.

O'Connor, L.E. (2001). Pathogenic beliefs and guilt in human evolution: Implications for psychotherapy. In P. Gilbert & K. Bailey (Eds.), *Genes on the couch: Explorations in evolutionary psychology* (pp.276–303). London: Brunner-Routledge.

Pole, N., D'Andrea, W., O'Connor, L. E., Santarlasci, A. *The role of empathy-based guilt in predicting PTSD symptoms in retired police officers*. Unpublished manuscript.

Preston, S. D., & de Waal, F. B. M. (2002). Empathy: Its ultimate and proximate bases. *Behavioral and Brain Sciences, 25*(1), 1–72.

Rankin, K. P., Gorno-Tempini, M. L., Allison, S. C., Stanley, C. M., Glenn, S., Weiner, M. W., & Miller, B. L. (2006). Structural anatomy of empathy in neurodegenerative disease. *Brain, 129*(11), 2945–2956. doi:10.1093/brain/awl254.

Rinchen, S. (1997). *Atisha's lamp for the path to enlightenment*. (R. Sonam, Trans.). Ithaca, NY: Snow Lion Publications.

Sachdeva, S., Iliev, R., & Medin, D. L. (2009). Sinning saints and saintly sinners: The paradox of moral self-regulation. *Psychological Science, 20*(4), 523–528.

Sachs, E., Rosenfeld, B., Lhewa, D., Rasmussen, A., & Keller, A. (2008). Entering exile: Trauma, mental health, and coping among Tibetan refugees arriving in Dharamsala, India. *Journal of Traumatic Stress, 21*(2), 199–208.

Sagi, A., & Hoffman, M. L. (1976). Empathic distress in the newborn. *Developmental Psychology, 12,* 175–176.

Shantideva. (2003). Guide to the Bodhisattva's way of life: A Buddhist poem for today. (K. Gyatso & N. Elliott, Trans.). Ulverston, Cumbria: Tharpa Publications.

Seligman, M. E., Abramson, L. Y., Semmel, A., & von Baeyer, C. (1979). Depressive attributional style. *Journal of Abnormal Psychology, 88*(3), 242–247.

Singer, T. (2006). The neuronal basis and ontogeny of empathy and mind reading: Review of literature and implications for future research. *Neuroscience and Biobehavioral Reviews, 30*(6), 855–863.

Singer, T., Seymour, B., O'Doherty, J. P., Stephan, K. E., Dolan, R. J., & Frith, C. D. (2006). Empathic neural responses are modulated by the perceived fairness of others. *Nature, 439*(7075), 466–469.

Tomasello, M. (2009). *Why we cooperate.* Cambridge, MA: MIT Press.

Vaux, A., Riedel, S., & Stewart, D. (1987). Modes of social support: The Social Support Behavior (SS-B) scale. *American Journal of Community Psychology, 15*(2), 209–237.

Warneken, F., & Tomasello, M. (2006). Altruistic helping in human infants and young chimpanzees. *Science, 311*(5765), 1301.

Weiss, J. (1986). Unconscious guilt. In J. Weiss, & H. Sampson (Eds.), *The psychoanalytic process: Theory, clinical observation and empirical research* (pp. 43–67). New York: Guilford.

Williams, G. (1966). *Adaptation and natural selection: A critique of some current evolutionary thought.* Princeton, NJ: Princeton University Press.

Wilson, D. S., & Sober, E. (1994). Reintroducing group selection to the human behavioral sciences. *Behavioral and Brain Sciences, 17*(4), 585–654.

Wilson, D. S. & Wilson, E. O (2007). Rethinking the theoretical foundation of sociobiology. *Quarterly Review of Biology, 82*(4), 328–348.

Worthington, E. L., Jr., O'Connor, L. E., Berry, J. W., Sharp, C., Murray, R., & Yi, E. (2005). Compassion and forgiveness: Implications for psychotherapy. In P. Gilbert (Ed.), *Compassion: Conceptualisations, research and use in psychotherapy* (pp.168–192). London: Brunner-Routledge.

Zahn, R., Moll, J., Paiva, M., Garrido, G., Krueger, F., Huey, E. D., & Grafman, J. (2009). The neural basis of human social values: Evidence from Functional MRI. *Cerebral Cortex, 19*(2), 276–283. doi:10.1093/cercor/bhn080.

Zahn-Waxler, C. (2000). The development of empathy, guilt, and internalization of distress: Implications for gender differences in internalizing and externalizing problems. In R. J. Davidson (Ed.), *Anxiety, depression, and emotion: Wisconsin symposium on emotion,* Vol. 1 (pp. 222–226). New York: Oxford University Press.

Zahn-Waxler, C., Radke-Yarrow, M., & King, R. A. (1979). Child rearing and children's prosocial initiations towards victims of distress. *Child Development, 50*(2), 319–330.

Zahn-Waxler, C., Radke-Yarrow, M., Wagner, E., & Chapman, M. (1992). Development of concern for others. *Developmental Psychology, 28*(1), 126–136.

CHAPTER 3

A CONTEXTUAL BEHAVIORAL APPROACH TO PATHOLOGICAL ALTRUISM

Roger Vilardaga and Steven C. Hayes

KEY CONCEPTS

- In the same way that the process of natural evolution selects features of the human species, the cultural environment selects for patterns of behaviors during the lifetime of an individual or a group.
- One particular form of human behavior, language, is of great survival value. But language also amplifies the way we experience both the positive and negative aspects of the world. Verbal processes can reinforce behaviors that are damaging for individuals and groups.
- Some verbal behaviors that may play a role in pathological altruism are *experiential avoidance*, a *conceptualized self*, *perspective-taking*, and *values-based action*.
- *Acceptance and commitment therapy* and *Relational Frame Theory* lay forth a scientific framework and provide tools to modify such behaviors, which points to their potential utility to reduce pathological altruism.

THE CONCEPT OF altruism has intrigued researchers and philosophers over the centuries (Batson, 1991a); it seems central for the understanding of human relationships and the organization of societies. The degree of cooperation and altruism among humans, as shown by their varied organizations and other social units (e.g., universities, governments, religious groups, business corporations, etc.), far exceeds other social animals. The survival of the human species in an astonishing array of ecosystems on Earth is arguably due in part to these varied forms of behavior[1] (Fehr & Fischbacher, 2003).

Altruism has been described as a voluntary act that is an end in itself—it does some good to the other, is not directed toward self-gain (Leeds, 1963), and generally implies some sense of self-sacrifice (Krebs, 1970). In a more fundamental way, altruism has also been described as "costly acts that confer economic benefits on other individuals" (Fehr & Fischbacher, 2003, p. 785).

Pathological altruism, as a special case of altruistic behavior, is the subject of consideration in this volume. As the chapters themselves show, the concept has a variety of interpretations. This is not surprising. Lay terms such as *altruism*, although quite frequent in scientific writing, cannot be clearly defined scientifically. Such terms are vague and hard to define for the very same reason they are widely adopted and highly accepted—that is, because they can be used in a variety of settings and with a variety of connotations.

Our understanding of the term "pathological altruism" suggests it is generally used to refer to (a) the actions of individuals with the intention of promoting the welfare of others that cause needless harm to themselves or others, (b) an excess of the "self-sacrificing" aspect of altruism implicit in most common definitions of altruism itself, and (c) a repetitive pattern of this feature that makes the pattern of action more pervasive and more problematic.

In other words, we take as the domain of our analysis socially well meaning but harmful and excessive forms of self-sacrifice that become more pervasive and problematic over time. Examples of pathological altruism might include workaholism (e.g., Scott, Moore, & Miceli, 1997), excessive ascetics or helping behavior (e.g., Fallon & Horwath, 1993), or the damage of maintaining a relationship with a physical or sexual abuser (e.g., Campbell, 2002).

In this chapter, we will develop a more precise account of these three aspects of pathological altruism on the basis of a contextual behavioral science (CBS) approach (Hayes, Levin, Plumb, Boulanger, & Pistorello, in press; Vilardaga, Hayes, Levin, & Muto, 2009). CBS refers to a set of analytic assumptions and strategic choices regarding scientific development that have emerged from behavior analysis that have been applied in the creation of an approach to human language and cognition called Relational Frame Theory (RFT; Hayes, Barnes-Holmes, & Roche, 2001). In addition, an applied model of intervention emerged based on RFT called *acceptance and commitment therapy* (ACT; Hayes, Strosahl, & Wilson, 1999). We will provide an interpretation of pathological altruism from within that perspective.

Contextual Behavioral Science and Pathological Altruism

The cultural/verbal environment can select human behaviors in very specific ways, but it would be unscientific to simply refer to the "influence" of cultural factors without further analysis. For this reason, in this section we will introduce RFT (Hayes et al., 2001), a theory that explains the interactions between the cultural/verbal environment and human behavior. We will also introduce key concepts of this approach that are relevant to the organization of human beings into groups and to the topic of pathological altruism. This will require explaining some of the technical terms in RFT.

Relational Frame Theory and the Importance of Language Contexts

Relational Frame Theory is a contextual behavioral account of language and cognition that argues verbal stimuli have their impact on human behavior because of their participation in what we call *relational frames*. All complex organisms learn to respond relationally to the environment. For example, a primate learning to choose the larger of two small piles of food will abandon the large pile if the choice of an even larger pile is now available.

But human beings with the right kind of learning histories seem to be able to bring such *relational responding* under the control of arbitrary cues and then to respond relationally to events as specified by these cues. For example, a 3-year-old may prefer a nickel over a dime because it is larger (based upon the formal property, its size); but a 6-year-old will prefer a dime over a nickel because *it is larger* (based upon its arbitrary property, its value). Specific forms of this kind of arbitrary applicable responding[2] are termed relational frames.

Relational frames have three distinct features: *mutual entailment, combinatorial entailment*, and *transformation of stimulus functions*. Mutual entailment occurs when a human organism learns a relation between event "A" and "B" and then derives the relation between "B" and "A." For example, a person who learns that the French word *secours* is the same as the word *help*, may derive that *help* is the same as *secours*. The same individual, told that the word *help* is the same as the word Spanish word *ayuda*, may derive that the word *ayuda* is the same as the word *secours*. This quality of relational frames is referred to as combinatorial entailment. If this person is walking on the street in France and hears "Ayuda! Ayuda!" new behavioral functions may emerge, such as feelings of fear in the presence of those words, or seeking help by shouting "Secours! Secours!" This is an example of transformation of stimulus functions (the word "Ayuda!" acquires the functions of the word "Help!"), which is a change in the functions of related events based on specific functional cues and the mutual and combinatorial relations among them. In this case, calling "Help!" and feeling fear in response to that call from others is now available in other functional contexts with regard to *secours* and *ayuda*. What is learned is not necessarily the relations among a series of events, but rather a response frame.

Relational framing is readily demonstrable in human infants (Lipkens, Hayes, & Hayes, 1993), and a variety of studies have shown that a history of multiple exemplars seems to be needed to learn relational frames (e.g., Berens & Hayes, 2007; Luciano, Becerra, & Valverde, 2007). The advantage of relational responding occurred even before elaborate forms of language evolved culturally (e.g., metaphor, logic, storytelling). A human ancestor, unlike other organisms, would be able to communicate with others by pronouncing "food" upon seeing food and to search for food upon being told the word "food." From an RFT point of view, the small step forward, evolutionarily speaking, of regulating relational responses by arbitrary contextual cues, provides a profound way to analyze language and cognition.

If human beings are advantaged in their ability to walk on two feet, that evolutionary step was not intentional. It was merely selected. The same is true within the lifetime of individuals. The core unit in language responding, relational framing, develops ontogenetically[3] due to the selective process performed by the social and cultural environment. The same applies to the elaboration of language functions that are built on the foundation of relational framing.

> The core unit of language, *relational framing*, develops across the life of an individual due to the specific selective processes performed by the social and cultural environment.

Language contexts provide many advantages to the human species. They further the organism's ability to manipulate long-term events and have more effective control over the environment. Relational responding transforms the way learning normally occurs. It both produces and constrains behavioral variability, which ultimately leads to an accelerated process of adaptive behavior. If a person is told, "You will have food next winter if you plant seeds now," this person can learn the value of the specified action based on consequences experienced months later. This restricts variability in one sense (e.g., to effective forms of food production) but in another sense expands it (e.g., to include forms of behavior that would be difficult to be arrived at by trial and error). As will be seen later, an organisms' ability to predict and control is a key feature that helps explain some of the advantages and disadvantages of relational responding.

Relational responding also increases the ability of humans to interact with one another in specific ways at the group level, increasingly overcoming the limits of physical and temporal proximity. This has been expanded enormously by human inventions (i.e., written language, printing presses, Morse code, radio, television, cellular phones, satellite transmission, the Internet, text messaging), themselves based in part on these same relational abilities. The ability of these inventions to organize group behavior is obvious, as when during the 2009 elections in Iran, Twitter allowed protesters to organize themselves and to coordinate their behavior to avoid being caught by government officials (Morozov, 2009).

> Language contexts seem to function virtually as a kind of behavioral "organ" at the level of the group. This "organ" is transmitted from generation to generation regardless of the survival of specific individuals.

Furthermore, because derived relations are arbitrarily applicable, the group can regulate behavior in increasingly fine-grained ways. Highly precise and arbitrary cultural practices, rituals, and distinctions can be readily made via human language. Language contexts seem to function virtually as a kind of behavioral "organ" at the level of the group. This "organ" is transmitted from generation to generation regardless of the survival of specific individuals.

The evolutionary and social/cultural contingencies that have selected the ability to acquire relational responding do not ensure that life is "better" for those with these responses. Language contexts can be both harmful and helpful.

The Dark and Light Sides of Human Language

Experiential Avoidance

Verbal stimuli are regulated by context, but in the social world these contexts become so overextended that language begins to harm human functioning in certain domains. For example, human language can increase the pervasiveness of aversive events. If an individual's relational ability leads to establishing a relation between the name of certain flower and the loss of a previous romantic relationship, this in turn can lead to experiencing the sadness associated with this original event upon hearing the name of the flower. This process of aversive conditioning may generalize via relational framing, perhaps leading the person to avoid any verbal reference to such flowers. Because framing is not mere association, even wildly different contexts can have the same effect if they are related to flowers in ways such as opposition, distinction, or hierarchy: Even a desert landscape could evoke the idea "no flowers could grow there" and sadness might now show up in the context of barren landscapes.

A natural result is experiential avoidance: the attempt to suppress, change, and alter the form, frequency, or intensity of uncomfortable thoughts, feelings, and memories (Hayes, Wilson, Gifford, & Follette, 1996). Experiential avoidance has a paradoxical and pervasive negative effect in human's functioning, often narrowing an individual's options or choices. Numerous studies showed that this process is related to depression, anxiety, trauma, and low quality of life (Hayes et al., 2004b; Hayes, Luoma, Bond, Masuda, & Lillis, 2006) among others.

> Experiential avoidance is the individual's attempt to suppress, change, and alter the form, frequency, or intensity of uncomfortable thoughts, feelings, and memories.

The Conceptualized Self

"Self," from a behavioral perspective (e.g., Skinner, 1974), refers to an organism's ability to discriminate its own behavior and respond to a current situation on that basis. Among humans, this process is in part verbal (Dymond & Barnes, 1995, 1997; Hayes & Wilson, 1993). When people describe themselves or hear others describe them, they form a self-concept. In a sense "who they are" can become a coordinated list of central evaluative and descriptive relations.

This natural process can also become repertoire narrowing. The terms used to characterize people are easily overextended, both positively and negatively. A person may be "stupid" because she does not have skills in just a few areas, or "kind" despite the fact that in some contexts he is not. Further, people can easily become excessively dependent on the views (or perspectives) of others. Children who receive too strong, aversive, or inconsistent training linked to self-conceptualizations from others may become hypersensitive to cues of this kind.[4] Experiential avoidance and entanglement with a conceptualized self are examples of the repertoire narrowing effects of language. Other language processes are more helpful as they apply to the topic of this chapter.

Deictic Framing

From an RFT point of view, *deictic framing* is a form of relational responding that establishes a specific relation based on the perspective of a speaker such as I–you, here–there, and now–then. What is unique about deictic frames is that they can only be taught via demonstration since there are no parallel relations defined by the formal properties of the objects that are related. For other relational frames (i.e., comparison), a nonarbitrary relationship (i.e., "This object is bigger than that one") exists, which later can be abstracted and be verbally applied (i.e., "A nickel is smaller than a dime"). Deictic frames are not like that. For example, "here" versus "there" is defined only with regard to a perspective or point of view.

What training in deictic framing skills establishes is what is commonly known as "perspective-taking." As children learn deictic relational responses, they learn to adopt different perspectives in order to disambiguate these relations. They learn there is a perspective of "I/here/now" but that it is different from the perspective of others, or of themselves at another time and place.

> Deictic frames are a set of relations based on the perspective of a speaker (ie, I–you, here–there, and now–then).

Despite their complexity, these skills are fundamental to the use of language in several areas. Storytelling, for example, requires that a listener possess perspective-taking skills (the ability to imagine how the story unfolds from the perspective of various characters) or a great deal of the story will be missed.

Relational Frame Theory researchers have found that deictic framing emerges developmentally over time (McHugh, Barnes-Holmes, & Barnes-Holmes, 2004a) and can be trained (Weil, 2007). Further, lack of deictic framing is associated with such key social phenomena as social anhedonia (Villatte, Monestes, McHugh, Freixa i Baqué, & Loas, 2008), empathy and stigma (Vilardaga et al., 2008), schizophrenia (Villatte, Monestes, McHugh, Freixa i Baqué, & Loas, 2010), theory of mind (Weil, in press), sense of self (Rehfeldt, Dillen, Ziomek, & Kowalchuk, 2007b), and false belief and deception (McHugh, Barnes-Holmes, & Barnes-Holmes, 2004b).

Values-based Actions

Values have been defined within a CBS approach as "freely chosen, verbally constructed consequences of ongoing, dynamic, evolving patterns of activity, which establish predominant reinforcers for that activity that are intrinsic in engagement in the valued behavioral pattern itself" (Wilson & DuFrene, 2009, p. 66). We call these behaviors *values-based actions*, that is, behaviors selected by positive relational contingencies (see Dahl, Plumb, Stewart, & Lundgren, 2009, for a book length presentation of values).

> Values are freely chosen, verbally constructed consequences of ongoing, dynamic, evolving patterns of activity, which establish predominant reinforcers for that activity that are intrinsic in engagement in the valued behavioral pattern itself.

Relational responding can establish appetitive functions even in difficult current environments. Consider the work of a scientist. Even if the research has so far failed to yield important results, and extrinsic rewards are few, the work can be intensely meaningful. Every day can be a joyful exploration, because it is about something relationally construed as valuable (i.e., contributing to a "better world"). Values-based actions are more likely to promote and sustain constructive patterns of behavior over time than experientially avoidant actions, and have been linked to a variety of positive outcomes (e.g., Elliot, Sheldon, & Church, 1997; Sheldon & Elliot, 1999; Sheldon, Kasser, Smith, & Share, 2002).

Redefining Pathological Altruism from a Contextual Behavioral Approach

The verbal processes just described can go a long way toward explaining the three aspects of pathological altruism described earlier. Pathological altruism, we argue, may be a form of experiential avoidance, made more likely by weaknesses in a deictic framing repertoire and entanglement with a conceptualized self, in combination with a specific set of ongoing values. Generally healthy prosocial processes, such as empathy and values-based action, are harnessed by this avoidant process, which self-amplifies due to its rule-governed and avoidant nature. In the sections below, we briefly walk through each of these claims following the model presented in Figure 3.1. We will use clinical examples to facilitate our presentation of the model throughout.

In this model, deictic framing has a central role, since it has a theoretical link to both the dysfunctional side of language (e.g., the formation of experiential avoidance and a conceptualized self) and the mediation of our social interactions,

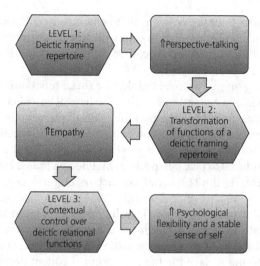

FIGURE 3.1
A three-level perspective-taking model to account for psychological flexibility and a stable sense of self.

as well as in the undermining of such effects through the development of a more stable sense of self (see Vilardaga & Hayes, in press, for a presentation of this model in the context of the therapeutic relationship). The ultimate utility of such a model is not to represent the "reality" of the phenomena, but to aid the researcher in thinking about the subject matter in a more effective way.

A Deictic Framing Repertoire

According to this model, deictic framing allows the individual take multiple perspectives. This basic ability could account for an individual's tendency to acknowledge other individual's needs. The ability to take multiple perspectives can have both a positive and negative impact at the level of the group as we will later see (Figure 3.2).

Deictic framing may be essential for an optimal psychological functioning and for establishing healthy human interactions. Research has shown that per-spective-taking is related to prosociality (Underwood & Moore, 1982), reduced delinquency (Chandler, 1973), and increased social competence and knowledge

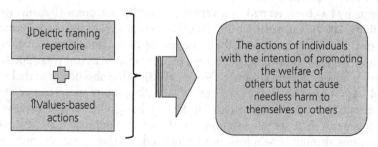

FIGURE 3.2
First level: Pathological altruism and deictic framing.

(Silvern, Waterman, Sobesky, & Ryan, 1979) among others.[5] In addition, lack of perspective-taking has been noted in eating disorders, schizophrenia and social phobia (Imura, 2002; Rupp & Jurkovic, 1996; Schiffman et al., 2004; Wells, Clark, & Ahmad, 1998).

Deictic framing may be an essential skill for social functioning, but its effects are not always positive. Sometimes adults who have acquired complex perspective-taking abilities do not use them in their social interactions (Keysar, Lin, & Barr, 2003). There are also circumstances under which perspective-taking does not lead to prosocial outcomes, such as when people dislike the individuals for whom they are induced to take perspective (McPherson Frantz & Janoff-Bulman, 2000), when there is limited social contact or cultural exposure to others (Aberson & Haag, 2007; Lee & Quintana, 2005), or in competitive situations (Epley, Caruso, & Bazerman, 2006; Tjosvold, Johnson, & Johnson, 1984).

Pathological altruism may occur due to a lack of a deictic framing repertoire or its failure to be evoked in a given situation. For example, consider a doctor who insists on trying to save the life of a terminal patient despite the patient's requests. Help may be designed to accomplish a verbally framed outcome of helping others (it is a values-based action), but if the doctor fails to view the helping behavior from the point of view of the person being "helped" it can cause more harm than good. This exemplifies the first aspect of our definition of pathological altruism; that is to say, the actions of individuals with the intention of promoting the welfare of others but that cause needless harm to themselves or others.

However, strong deictic framing repertoires can also be used to exploit others from within another set of values that is less prosocial. "Opportunists" in a social environment may appreciate the perspective of others and use that knowledge against them—as with the psychopath who uses knowledge of how his actions induce terror to increase his victim's terror even further. Thus, a deictic framing repertoire is a necessary but not sufficient step toward healthy altruism.

The Transformation of Functions of a Deictic Framing Repertoire

Some verbal contexts cue a relational response; others cue specific functions that are transformed by those same relational repertoires. A person may know that a hurricane is more dangerous than a mosquito; it is another matter to feel that difference emotionally. In the same way, once the individual has taken another individual's perspective, it is another matter to respond to the aversive (interpersonal distress) or appetitive (empathic concern or sympathy) states of others. This is the issue of *empathy* (Figure 3.3).

Empathy has been related to a variety of healthy outcomes (Batson, 1991b; Eisenberg, 2000). It is worth noting that this second level of the model implies a relational repertoire and is not the same process, functionally speaking, as the empathic responses commonly observed in other mammals (de Waal, 2008) and in very young children (Decety & Meyer, 2008) in the absence of verbal (relational) repertoires. More primal forms of empathy require the presence of specific stimuli (i.e., witnessing an actual individual being attacked), whereas verbal repertoires can elicit the same response in almost any circumstance (i.e., looking at the snow through a window and feeling sad for those who do not have a home). Others have noted that these more primal forms of empathy can later be integrated with higher cognition, in what psychologists have referred to as

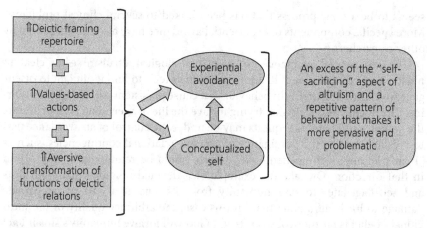

FIGURE 3.3
Second level: Pathological altruism, experiential avoidance, and the conceptualized self.

"empathic concern" (e.g., Decety, Michalska, & Akitsuki, 2008; de Waal, 2008; Moriguchi et al., 2007). This second aspect of the model characterizes individuals who not only perceive the point of view of others as in the first level of the model, they also tend to be *affected* by it.

Arousal of this kind has been discussed as a motivator for prosocial behavior (e.g., Hornstein, 1991; Krebs, 1970; Preston & de Waal, 2002), but negative arousal can be difficult to cope with effectively for some individuals, and may lead to attempts to suppress, reject, or undermine the impact of such functions by engaging in a process of experiential avoidance. Excessive altruistic acts hold out hope of removing some forms of discomfort, such as acknowledgment of the finite nature or inherent pain of life. Threats to a conceptualized self are especially likely to give rise to negative arousal; individuals will fight to retain their self-image, even at the cost to others or themselves, in order to avoid this kind of discomfort (i.e., "If I don't help, I'm a bad person, so I will help even if it is unwelcome or harmful"). These two processes, experiential avoidance and a conceptualized self, are repertoire narrowing, and can inhibit the individual's ability to successfully engage in values-based actions. They seemingly can account for the remaining two aspects of our definition of pathological altruism (1) a pattern of behavior that is based in part on an excess of the "self-sacrificing" aspect of altruism implicit in most common definitions of altruism itself, and (2) a repetitive pattern of this feature that makes the pattern of action more pervasive and more problematic.

By conceptualizing pathological altruism as a form of experiential avoidance, we can make sense of the repetitive pattern of behavior implied by the word "pathological." Experiential avoidance is negatively reinforced, meaning that once an individual successfully reduces contact with the relationally framed interpersonal suffering or distress, this action will be evoked when future signals of personal distress from others arise. These signals in combination with other biological predispositions can promptly elicit the same pattern, again and again, even if it is unhelpful or even harmful.

Although we do not yet possess specific data that link pathological altruism to experiential avoidance, an increasing body of literature indicates the negative impact of experiential avoidance in a variety of areas. Experiential avoidance seems to be a toxic process that has been linked to several clinical problems.[6] More specific components of experiential avoidance have also been explored by other researchers.[7]

The experiential avoidance aspect of pathological altruism seems clear in most extended examples of it. Some individuals tend to find it difficult to disengage from certain patterns of behavior that cause persistent psychological suffering. The doctor who insists on trying to save the life of a terminal patient despite the patient's and family's requests may be under the control of an avoidance pattern established by the dominance of aversive relational contingencies, such as "I can't let any of my patients die," which would be reinforced by any action in that direction. Or, take the example of a devoted religious man who fasts and self-flagellates to save humanity from its sins at a cost of irreparable damage to his health. Note that, in this case, the arbitrary quality of the individuals' belief is far more obvious (e.g., "God will forgive humanity's sins if I act this way").

In the previous two levels of the model, we have seen how perspective taking can be a process that fosters both positive and negative outcomes. In the next section, we will address some of the contextual factors that can help reduce the impact of experiential avoidance.

Extended Contextual Control over the Transformation of Functions of a Deictic Framing Repertoire

A third level of perspective taking, the emergence of a stable sense of self, is important to further adaptability with respect to the individual and the group (Figure 3.4). A stable sense of self is more likely when an individual has been exposed to enough variations of verbal contexts. Most psychotherapy situations can be characterized by a continuum exposure to verbal contexts such as "what are YOU feeling

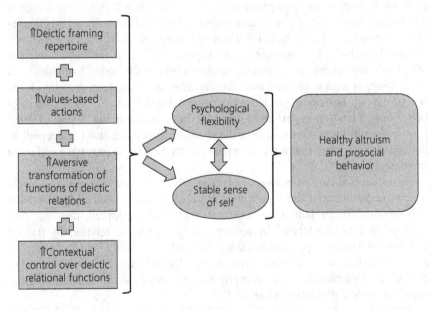

FIGURE 3.4
Third level: Healthy altruism, psychological flexibility, and a stable sense of self.

NOW?," "what were YOU feeling THEN?," "what are YOU thinking HERE?," "what were YOU thinking THERE?," etc. This iterative process does not suggest that simple exposure to enough variations of verbal contexts can make for an integrated sense of self; it simply suggests that it is more *likely* to occur. Experiencing self as the only invariant across a myriad of cognitive and emotional experiences has been conceptualized as the core of "spirituality," mindfulness, and a sense of transcendence (Hayes, 1984), which we argue allows healthy self-control and provides well-being.

Additionally, a more integrated sense of self ameliorates the aversive functions of some deictic frames, since it contextualizes them and therefore it allows for more effective behaviors to arise. Contextual control is crucial, and it relates to the notion of *psychological flexibility* or the ability to *engage* or *disengage* in behavior in the service of chosen values, and to contact the present moment as a fully conscious being (Hayes, Levin, & Vilardaga, in press).

This integrated sense of self increases individuals' self-awareness and enables them to respond to the current environment in a more effective manner, given their set of core values. It does not really imply a disconnection from their perspective-taking ability; on the contrary, it implies that the individuals' behavior is under the control of a broader sense of perspective.

This process of awareness has been defined as *self-as-context* by ACT proponents (Hayes et al., 1999). It contributes to a reduction of the individuals' psychological inflexibility and allows more healthy and fluid interactions with the group. This kind of sense of self allows a given individual to not only take perspective regarding the other person, but also to take perspective regarding his own private experiences and therefore make room for more effective values-based actions.

Final Remarks

Although no specific data support the interpretative account of pathological altruism laid out here, there are data in support of the three levels of the model just described in the context of social anhedonia, which is a subclinical behavioral pattern predictive of schizophrenia (Chapman, Chapman, Kwapil, Eckblad, & Zinser, 1994). Because social anhedonia and pathological altruism are within a sociality proneness continuum, and this model provides a framework for considering healthy and pathological forms of social functioning, a brief description seems warranted. In a recent study (Vilardaga, Estévez, Levin, & Hayes, in press), 110 colleges students completed a battery of questions that evaluated their deictic framing ability (Deictic Relational Task; Vilardaga et al., 2009), empathic concern (Interpersonal Reactivity Index; Davis, 1980), experiential avoidance (Acceptance and Action Questionnaire; Hayes et al., 2004a), and social anhedonia (revised Social Anhedonia Scale; Eckblad, Chapman, Chapman, & Mishlove, 1982). Analyses revealed that deictic framing, empathy, and experiential avoidance had a large-sized effect on social anhedonia after taking into consideration age and gender. This preliminary data is promising, particularly in light of a growing body of evidence that interventions such as ACT can target the processes of experiential avoidance, conceptualized self and, effective values-actions across multiple problems (Hayes et al., 2006). The evidence also shows that changes in these processes mediate outcomes (Hayes et al., 2006). In other words, these processes can be manipulated; when they are changed, changes in outcome follow. This fact suggests that this model could be a promising line of investigation with regard to pathological altruism at a behavioral level.

Conclusion

Behavior analysis, at least the variant from which the CBS approach has emerged, is poorly understood. Although Skinner's behaviorism deviated from the black box paradigm of stimulus–response psychology and opened the door to the behavioral analysis of emotion and cognition and the world within (Skinner, 1945), errors in the analysis of language and cognition led behavior analysts to conclude that an analysis of cognition and emotion was not essential to the understanding of overt behavior (Hayes, 1989).[8] Unfortunately, many forms of complex human phenomena would not yield to a direct contingency account alone. Furthermore, behaviorists applied a narrow range of methodologies, which made it difficult to analyze more complex forms of behavior and to an excessive reliance on interpretation when dealing with behaviors beyond the reach of a direct contingency analysis (Hayes, 1987). An additional problem might be that the technical terms developed by behavior analysts did not refer to "internal causes," such as the structural aspects of the brain, but instead to ecological and systemic aspects of the environment in interaction with the organisms' behavior (which are entirely physical as well, although less intuitive and acceptable in traditional views of science, such as in the medical model).

By defining what "cognition" is via derived relational responding, a contextual behavioral approach can proceed in a more effective way. From an RFT point of view, two ontogenetic contingency streams exist at the psychological level of analysis. One is composed of the direct contingencies that impact behavior in the organism–environment interaction. The other is composed of events, actions, and consequences involved in derived relational responses. These two streams interact, and are in turn embedded in contingency streams at the cultural and biological level. The metatheory involved in this approach is evolutionary science, with variation and selection operating simultaneously at all of these levels.

The CBS approach to pathological altruism does not put emphasis on the individual's "intent" to help or to be selfish. The focus instead is on the verbal contexts that select deictic framing repertoires, making experiential avoidance possible, and also putting it under more appropriate contextual control. Pathological altruism can be conceptualized at the psychological level of analysis as a form of behavior that is influenced and maintained by the verbal context of a certain cultural environment (e.g., the context of an individual's history and current circumstances). This verbal context can select certain forms of behavior, such as experiential avoidance and entanglement with a conceptualized self, that can lead to pathological altruism given the proper conditions. Instead, healthy forms of altruism tend to be the result of verbal contexts that select values-based action and a strong deictic framing repertoire that involves not only being aware of one's own suffering and that of others, but also of developing a stable sense of self with high psychological flexibility.

Since there has been little direct research on pathological altruism from a CBS perspective, the present analysis is designed more to guide subsequent investigation than to prove the adequacy or applicability of the present account. We hope the current chapter provides preliminary guidance and encourages other researchers to consider the value of a contextual behavioral strategy.

Notes

1. In this chapter, we use the term *behavior* to refer to the activity of an organism, which includes external actions but also private events, such as thoughts, emotions, or physical perceptions.

2. Arbitrary applicable relational responding (AARR) is a technical term in RFT that refers to the abstraction of patterns of responding among set of stimuli that are brought under the control of an arbitrary contextual cue. A more detailed description of this process, along with the experimental preparations that lead to the development of this concept, can be found in Hayes, Barnes-Holmes, and Roche (2001, p. 25, Section 2.1.3).

3. Ontogeny refers to the development or course of development of an individual organism. This is as opposed to phylogeny—the development of species as they slowly emerge over time.

4. See Chapter 26, by Carolyn Zahn-Waxler and Carol Van Hulle, for a more extended description of this clinical presentation.

5. See also the benefits of perspective-taking in the development of children (e.g., Baron-Cohen, Leslie, & Frith, 1985; Blacher-Dixon & Simeonsson, 1981; Charlop-Christy & Daneshvar, 2003; LeBlanc et al., 2003; Rehfeldt, Dillen, Ziomek, & Kowalchuk, 2007a), conflict resolution (Corcoran & Mallinckrodt, 2000; Drolet, Larrick, & Morris, 1998), stigma (Galinsky & Ku, 2004; Vescio, Sechrist, & Paolucci, 2003), and marital adjustment (Long, 1993).

6. These problems include sexual victimization (Polusny, Rosenthal, Aban, & Follette, 2004), posttraumatic stress disorder (Marx & Sloan, 2005; Plumb, Orsillo, & Luterek, 2004), self-harm behaviors (Chapman, Gratz, & Brown, 2006), and parental distress (Greco et al., 2005).

7. For example, emotional suppression has been related to depression (Degenova, Patton, Jurich, & Macdermid, 1994), substance abuse (Malow et al., 1994), and difficulties in recovery from distress (Cioffi & Holloway, 1993; Masedo & Esteve, 2007).

8. An extended presentation of the conceptual problems of traditional behavioral accounts of language can be found in Hayes and Hayes (1992).

References

Aberson, C. L. & Haag, S. C. (2007). Contact, perspective taking, anxiety as predictors of stereotype endorsement, explicit attitudes, implicit attitudes. *Group Processes & Intergroup Relations, 10*, 179–201.

Baron-Cohen, S., Leslie, A. M., & Frith, U. (1985). Does the autistic child have a "theory of mind"? *Cognition, 21*, 37–46.

Batson, C. D. (1991a). *The altruism question: Toward a social psychological answer.* Hillsdale, NJ: Lawrence Erlbaum.

Batson, C. D. (1991b). *The altruism question: Toward a social-psychological answer.* Hillsdale, NJ, England: Lawrence Erlbaum Associates, Inc.

Berens, N. M., & Hayes, S. C. (2007). Arbitrarily applicable comparative relations: Experimental evidence for a relational operant. *Journal of Applied Behavior Analysis, 40*, 45–71.

Blacher-Dixon, J., & Simeonsson, R. J. (1981). Perspective-taking by mentally retarded children: A one-year follow-up. *American Journal of Mental Deficiency, 85*, 648–651.

Campbell, J. C. (2002). Health consequences of intimate partner violence. *Lancet, 359*, 1331–1336.

Chandler, M. J. (1973). Egocentrism and antisocial behavior: The assessment and training of social perspective-taking skills. *Developmental Psychology, 9*, 326–332.

Chapman, A. L., Gratz, K. L., & Brown, M. Z. (2006). Solving the puzzle of deliberate self-harm: The experiential avoidance model. *Behaviour Research and Therapy, 44*, 371–394.

Chapman, L. J., Chapman, J. P., Kwapil, T. R., Eckblad, M., & Zinser, M. C. (1994). Putatively psychosis-prone subjects 10 years later. *Journal of Abnormal Psychology, 103*, 171–183.

Charlop-Christy, M. H., & Daneshvar, S. (2003). Using video modeling to teach perspective taking to children with autism. *Journal of Positive Behavior Interventions, 5*, 12–21.

Cioffi, D., & Holloway, J. (1993). Delayed costs of suppressed pain. *Journal of Personality and Social Psychology, 64*, 274–282.

Corcoran, K. O., & Mallinckrodt, B. (2000). Adult attachment, self-efficacy, perspective taking, and conflict resolution. *Journal of Counseling & Development, 78*, 473–483.

Dahl, J., Plumb, J. C., Stewart, I., & Lundgren, T. (2009). *The art and science of valuing in psychotherapy.* Oakland, CA: New Harbinger.

Davis, M. H. (1980). A multidimensional approach to individual differences in empathy. *Catalog of Selected Documents in Psychology, 10*, 1–17.

de Waal, F. B. M. (2008). Putting the altruism back into altruism: The evolution of empathy. *Annual Review of Psychology, 59*, 279–300.

Decety, J., & Meyer, M. (2008). From emotion resonance to empathic understanding: A social developmental neuroscience account. *Development and Psychopathology, 20*, 1053–1080.

Decety, J., Michalska, K. J., & Akitsuki, Y. (2008). Who caused the pain? An fMRI investigation of empathy and intentionality in children. *Neuropsychologia, 46*, 2607–2614.

Degenova, M. K., Patton, D. M., Jurich, J. A., & Macdermid, S. M. (1994). Ways of coping among HIV-infected individuals. *Journal of Social Psychology, 134*, 655–663.

Drolet, A., Larrick, R., & Morris, M. W. (1998). Thinking of others: How perspective taking changes negotiators' aspirations and fairness perceptions as a function of negotiator relationships. *Basic and Applied Social Psychology, 20*, 23–31.

Dymond, S., & Barnes, D. (1995). A transformation of self-discrimination response functions in accordance with the arbitrarily applicable relations of sameness, more than, and less than. *Journal of the Experimental Analysis of Behavior, 64*, 163–184.

Dymond, S., & Barnes, D. (1997). Behavior-analytic approaches to self-awareness. *Psychological Record, 47*, 181–200.

Eckblad, M. L., Chapman, L. J., Chapman, J. P., & Mishlove, M. (1982). *The revised social anhedonia scales.* (Available from T. Kwapil at t_kwapil@uncg.edu or write him at Department of Psychology, University of North Carolina at Greensboro, 281 Bruce M. Eberhart Bldg., Greensboro, NC 27410).

Eisenberg, N. (2000). Emotion, regulation, and moral development. *Annual Review of Psychology, 51*, 665–697.

Elliot, A. J., Sheldon, K. M., & Church, M. A. (1997). Avoidance personal goals and subjective well-being. *Personality and Social Psychology Bulletin, 23*, 915–927.

Epley, N., Caruso, E., & Bazerman, M. H. (2006). When perspective taking increases taking: Reactive egoism in social interaction. *Journal of Personality and Social Psychology, 91*, 872–889.

Vilardaga, R., Estévez, A., Levin, M. E., Hayes, S. C. (in press). Deictic Relational Responding, Empathy and Experiential Avoidance as Predictors of Social Anhedonia in College Students, *The Psychological Record.*

Fallon, B. A., & Horwath, E. (1993). Asceticism - Creative spiritual practice or pathological pursuit. *The Psychological Record, 56,* 310–316.

Fehr, E., & Fischbacher, U. (2003). The nature of human altruism. *Nature, 425,* 785–791.

Galinsky, A. D., & Ku, G. (2004). The effects of perspective-taking on prejudice: The moderating role of self-evaluation. *Personality and Social Psychology Bulletin, 30,* 594–604.

Greco, L. A., Heffner, M., Poe, S., Ritchie, S., Polak, M., & Lynch, S. K. (2005). Maternal adjustment following preterm birth: Contributions of experiential avoidance. *Behavior Therapy, 36,* 177–184.

Hayes, S. C. (1984). Making sense of spirituality. *Behaviorism, 12,* 99–110.

Hayes, S. C. (1987). Language and the incompatibility of evolutionary and psychological continuity. *Behavior Analysis, 22,* 49–54.

Hayes, S. C. (1989). *Rule-governed behavior: Cognition, contingencies, and instructional control.* New York: Plenum Press.

Hayes, S. C., Barnes-Holmes, D., & Roche, B. (2001). *Relational frame theory. A post-Skinnerian account of human language and cognition.* New York: Kluwer Academic.

Hayes, S. C. & Hayes, L. J. (1992). Verbal relations and the evolution of behavior analysis. *American Psychologist, 47,* 1383–1395.

Hayes, S. C., Levin, M. E., Plumb, J., Boulanger, J., & Pistorello, J. (in press). Acceptance and commitment therapy and contextual behavioral science: Examining the progress of a distinctive model of behavioral and cognitive therapy. *Behavior Therapy.*

Hayes, S. C., Levin, M. E., & Vilardaga, R. (in press). Acceptance and commitment therapy: Applying an iterative translational research strategy in behavior analysis. In *APA Handbook of Behavior Analysis.*

Hayes, S. C., Luoma, J. B., Bond, F. W., Masuda, A., & Lillis, J. (2006). Acceptance and commitment therapy: Model, processes and outcomes. *Behaviour Research and Therapy, 44,* 1–25.

Hayes, S. C., Strosahl, K., Wilson, K. G., Bissett, R. T., Pistorello, J., Toarmino, D., et al. (2004a). Measuring experiential avoidance: A preliminary test of a working model. *Psychological Record, 54,* 553–578.

Hayes, S. C., Strosahl, K., Wilson, K. G., Bissett, R. T., Pistorello, J., Toarmino, D., et al. (2004b). Measuring experiential avoidance: A preliminary test of a working model. *Psychological Record, 54,* 553–578.

Hayes, S. C., Strosahl, K. D., & Wilson, K. G. (1999). *Acceptance and commitment therapy: An experiential approach to behavior change.* New York: Guilford Press.

Hayes, S. C., & Wilson, K. G. (1993). Some applied implications of a contemporary behavior-analytic account of verbal events. *Behavior Analyst, 16,* 283–301.

Hayes, S. C., Wilson, K. G., Gifford, E. V., & Follette, V. M. (1996). Experiential avoidance and behavioral disorders: A functional dimensional approach to diagnosis and treatment. *Journal of Consulting and Clinical Psychology, 64,* 1152–1168.

Hornstein, H. A. (1991). Empathic distress and altruism: Still inseparable. *Psychological Inquiry, 2,* 133–135.

Imura, O. (2002). Schizophrenia and perspective taking: A comparison of schizophrenic and transient psychotic disorder patients. *Japanese Journal of Psychology, 73,* 383–390.

Keysar, B., Lin, S., & Barr, D. J. (2003). Limits on theory of mind use in adults. *Cognition, 89,* 25–41.

Krebs, D. L. (1970). Altruism - Examination of concept and a review of literature. *Psychological Bulletin, 73,* 258–302.

LeBlanc, L. A., Coates, A. M., Daneshvar, S., Charlop-Christy, M. H., Morris, C., & Lancaster, B. M. (2003). Using video modeling and reinforcement to teach perspective-taking skills to children with autism. *Journal of Applied Behavior Analysis, 36,* 253–257.

Lee, D. C., & Quintana, S. M. (2005). Benefits of cultural exposure and development of Korean perspective-taking ability for transracially adopted Korean children. *Cultural Diversity & Ethnic Minority Psychology, 11*, 130–143.

Leeds, R. (1963). Altruism and the norm of giving. *Merrill-Palmer Quarterly, 9*, 229–232.

Lipkens, R., Hayes, S. C., & Hayes, L. J. (1993). Longitudinal study of the development of derived relations in an infant. *Journal of Experimental Child Psychology, 56*, 201–239.

Long, E. C. J. (1993). Maintaining a stable marriage: Perspective taking as a predictor of a propensity to divorce. *Journal of Divorce & Remarriage, 21*, 121–138.

Luciano, C., Becerra, I. G., & Valverde, M. R. (2007). The role of multiple-exemplar training and naming in establishing derived equivalence in an infant. *Journal of the Experimental Analysis of Behavior, 87*, 349–365.

Malow, R. M., Ireland, S. J., Halpert, E. S., Szapocznik, J., Mcmahon, R. C., & Haber, L. (1994). A description of the maternal addiction program of the University of Miami, Jackson Memorial Medical Center. *Journal of Substance Abuse Treatment, 11*, 55–60.

Marx, B. P., & Sloan, D. M. (2005). Peritraumatic dissociation and experiential avoidance as predictors of posttraumatic stress symptomatology. *Behaviour Research and Therapy, 43*, 569–583.

Masedo, A. I., & Esteve, M. R. (2007). Effects of suppression, acceptance and spontaneous coping on pain tolerance, pain intensity and distress. *Behaviour Research and Therapy, 45*, 199–209.

McHugh, L., Barnes-Holmes, Y., & Barnes-Holmes, D. (2004a). Perspective-taking as relational responding: A developmental profile. *Psychological Record, 54*, 115–144.

McHugh, L., Barnes-Holmes, Y., & Barnes-Holmes, D. (2004b). Relational frame account of the development of complex cognitive phenomena: Perspective-taking, false belief understanding, and deception. *International Journal of Psychology & Psychological Therapy, 4*, 303–324.

McPherson Frantz, C., & Janoff-Bulman, R. (2000). Considering both sides: The limits of perspective taking. *Basic and Applied Social Psychology, 22*, 31–42.

Moriguchi, Y., Decety, J., Ohnishi, T., Maeda, M., Mori, T., Nemoto, K., et al. (2007). Empathy and judging other's pain: An fMRI study of alexithymia. *Cerebral Cortex, 17*, 2223–2234.

Morozov, E.(2009, June 17). Iran elections: A twitter revolution? *The Washington Post.*

Plumb, J. C., Orsillo, S. M., & Luterek, J. A. (2004). A preliminary test of the role of experiential avoidance in post-event functioning. *Journal of Behavior Therapy and Experimental Psychiatry, 35*, 245–257.

Polusny, M. A., Rosenthal, M. Z., Aban, I., & Follette, V. M. (2004). Experiential avoidance as a mediator of the effects of adolescent sexual victimization on negative adult outcomes. *Violence and Victims, 19*, 109–120.

Preston, S. D., & de Waal, F. B. M. (2002). Empathy: Its ultimate and proximate bases. *Behavioral and Brain Sciences, 25*, 1–2.

Rehfeldt, R. A., Dillen, J. E., Ziomek, M. M., & Kowalchuk, R. K. (2007a). Assessing relational learning deficits in perspective-taking in children with high-functioning autism spectrum disorder. *Psychological Record, 57*, 23–47.

Rehfeldt, R. A., Dillen, J. E., Ziomek, M. M., & Kowalchuk, R. K. (2007b). Assessing relational learning deficits in perspective-taking in children with high-functioning autism spectrum disorder. *Psychological Record, 57*, 23–47.

Rupp, G. L., & Jurkovic, G. J. (1996). Familial and individual perspective-taking processes in adolescent females with bulimic symptomatology. *American Journal of Family Therapy, 24*, 75–82.

Schiffman, J., Lam, C. W., Jiwatram, T., Ekstrom, M., Sorensen, H., & Mednick, S. (2004). Perspective-taking deficits in people with schizophrenia spectrum disorders: A prospective investigation. *Psychological Medicine, 34,* 1581–1586.

Scott, K. S., Moore, K. S., & Miceli, M. P. (1997). An exploration of the meaning and consequences of workaholism. *Human Relations, 50,* 287–314.

Sheldon, K. M., & Elliot, A. J. (1999). Goal striving, need satisfaction, and longitudinal well-being: The self-concordance model. *Journal of Personality and Social Psychology, 76,* 482–497.

Sheldon, K. M., Kasser, T., Smith, K., & Share, T. (2002). Personal goals and psychological growth: Testing an intervention to enhance goal attainment and personality integration. *Journal of Personality, 70,* 5–31.

Silvern, L. E., Waterman, J. M., Sobesky, W. E., & Ryan, V. L. (1979). Effects of a developmental model of perspective taking training. *Child Development, 50,* 243–246.

Skinner, B. F. (1945). The operational analysis of psychological terms. *Psychological Review, 52,* 270–277.

Skinner, B. F. (1974). *About Behaviorism.* New York: Knopf.

Tjosvold, D., Johnson, D. W., & Johnson, R. (1984). Influence strategy, perspective-taking, and relationships between high- and low-power individuals in cooperative and competitive contexts. *Journal of Psychology: Interdisciplinary and Applied, 116,* 187–202.

Underwood, B., & Moore, B. (1982). Perspective-taking and altruism. *Psychological Bulletin, 91,* 143–173.

Vescio, T. K., Sechrist, G. B., & Paolucci, M. P. (2003). Perspective taking and prejudice reduction: The mediational role of empathy arousal and situational attributions. *European Journal of Social Psychology, 33,* 455–472.

Vilardaga, R., & Hayes, S. C. (in press). Acceptance and Commitment Therapy and the therapeutic relationship stance. *European Psychotherapy.*

Vilardaga, R., Hayes, S. C., Levin, M. E., & Muto, T. (2009). Creating a strategy for progress: A contextual behavioral science approach. *Behavior Analyst, 32,* 133.

Vilardaga, R., Levin, M. E., Waltz, T., Hayes, S. C., Long, D., & Muto, T. (2008). Testing a new perspective-taking procedure in the context of attitudes, emotional reactions and behaviors towards different cultural groups. In R. Vilardaga (Chair), *Recent applications of relational frame theory using deictic framing procedures.* Symposium to be conducted at the 34rd Annual Convention of the Association for Behavior Analysis International, Chicago, IL.

Vilardaga, R., Waltz, T., Levin, M. E., Hayes, S. C., Stromberg, C., & Amador, K. (2009). Deictic relational framing and connectedness among college students: A small analog study. In L. McHugh (Chair), *Applications of deictic relational framing.* Symposium to be conducted at the Third World Conference on ACT, RFT, and Contextual Behavioral Science, Enschede, The Netherlands.

Villatte, M., Monestes, J. L., McHugh, L., Freixa i Baqué, E., & Loas, G. (2008). Assessing deictic relational responding in social anhedonia: A functional approach to the development of Theory of Mind impairments. *International Journal of Behavioral Consultation and Therapy, 4,* 360–373.

Villatte, M., Monestes, J. L., McHugh, L., Freixa i Baqué, E., & Loas, G. (2010). Adopting the perspective of another in belief attribution: Contribution of Relational Frame Theory to the understanding of impairments in schizophrenia. *Journal of Behavior Therapy and Experimental Psychiatry, 41,* 125–134.

Weil, T., Hayes, S.C., & Capurro, P. (in press). Establishing a Deictic Relational Repertoire in Young Children. *The Psychological Record.*

Wells, A., Clark, D. M., & Ahmad, S. (1998). How do I look with my minds eye: Perspective taking in social phobic imagery. *Behaviour Research and Therapy, 36,* 631–634.

Wilson, K. G., & DuFrene, T. (2009). *Mindfulness for two: An acceptance and commitment therapy approach to mindfulness in psychotherapy.* Oakland, CA: New Harbinger.

CHAPTER 4

CODEPENDENCY AND PATHOLOGICAL ALTRUISM

Michael McGrath and Barbara Oakley

No man is an island.
—John Donne

KEY CONCEPTS

- Codependency is an inability to tolerate a perceived negative affect in others that leads to a dysfunctional empathic response.
- Codependency likely shares roots with pathological altruism.
- There are evolutionary, genetic, and neurobiological components to the expression and propagation of codependent behaviors.

CODEPENDENCE IS BEHAVIOR on the part of a person that enables another's highly dysfunctional behavior. This generally involves a spouse or significant other, such as a lover, parent, child, or anyone with whom an important relationship is shared. The behavior of the codependent person can involve overt acts, such as lying to a spouse's employer to help cover an absence, or acts of omission, such as finding an alcoholic's hidden alcohol and not disposing of it. The concept of codependence was initially associated with substance abuse, but it is now thought to relate to any dysfunctional behavior, including spousal abuse, elder abuse, or even crime; as when help is given to procure victims. (The latter can involve a murky line as codependent shades into coconspirator.) Even a caretaker who continues to feed a morbidly obese child could be considered codependent.

Not all codependent relationships are the same. In some, a person begins a relationship that sours after initial harmony. In others, it is the dysfunctional behavior itself that attracted the codependent person. Additionally, the codependency may be the by-product of a predetermined relationship, such as a sibling, parent, child, or coworker. Generally, the closer the relationship is genetically (or culturally, as with a stepparent or stepchild), the harder it is to break the codependency bond. Although it might be difficult to end a relationship with a dysfunctional spouse or domestic partner, most (but not all) would find it more emotionally wrenching to end a codependent relationship with their child.

> Simply being connected to or involved in the care of a dysfunctional individual does not make one codependent. It is continuing the relationship in a manner that overtly or covertly supports the dysfunctional behavior that makes one codependent.

In the codependent relationship, not all actors are equal. One who helps maintain the dysfunctional behavior of another is often referred to as an *enabler*. This term is relative, as it is possible for both players to enable each other in differing ways. A relationship does not have to rise to the level of abuse for either partner to be viewed as codependent. As such, codependency is a fluid and broad concept, leading some to opine that the phenomenon is not generalizable, as different populations with different behaviors can be labeled with the same pathology. But it is clear that there is indeed a common trait: the inability or unwillingness to end a dysfunctional relationship or behavior. Simply being connected to or involved in the care of a dysfunctional individual does not make one codependent. It is continuing the relationship in a manner that overtly or covertly supports the dysfunctional behavior that makes one codependent.

Self-help and Professional Literature

Mellody, Miller, and Miller (1989, pp. 7–42) offer five core symptoms of codependence:

- Difficulty experiencing appropriate levels of self-esteem
- Difficulty setting functional boundaries
- Difficulty owning one's own reality
- Difficulty acknowledging and meeting one's own needs and wants
- Difficulty experiencing and expressing one's reality in a moderate fashion (i.e., avoiding extremes)

As will be seen with subsequent authors, the criteria suggested are vague and easily generalizable, leading to over inclusiveness. The authors (Mellody, Miller, & Miller, 1989) presumed that the disorder of codependence resulted from dysfunctional family dynamics, especially abuse. The theories put forth appear to be based on the authors' anecdotal experiences; no empirical study is offered in support.

Beattie (1992, 2009), one of the most well-known self-help codependency authors, points out that many behaviors labeled as codependent are normal (to a point), and become dysfunctional when people begin to allow themselves to be defined by others. Beattie (1992, pp. 42–54) describes the *characteristics* of codependency as:

- Caretaking
- Low self-worth
- Repression of feelings
- Obsessing over things
- Attempting to control
- Denial
- Dependency
- Poor communication
- Weak (personal) boundaries

- Lack of trust of self and others
- Anger
- Sexual problems
- Miscellaneous

Beattie presents these characteristics with qualifiers, such as "*many* codependents," "codependents *tend to*," "codependents *frequently*," and "*some* codependents" [Italics added]. The qualifiers make it easy to designate essentially anyone as codependent. The offered characteristics are vague, broad in scope, and found in a myriad of conditions, diagnosable or otherwise. Beattie (2009, p. 13) believes codependent behaviors have "mainstreamed into the culture," and many have learned to camouflage them. She suggests setting personal boundaries and other (this author would argue) intuitive strategies (Beattie, 1992, 2009). As with most self-help literature, a belief in a higher power (i.e., a god), is presumed, a trait shared with the 12-step alcohol dependency program from which the codependency movement emerged. In spite of Beattie's well-meaning approach, the advice she offers is essentially anecdotal, with no scientific basis. It seems everyone is codependent until proved otherwise (Katz & Liu, 1991).

As further proof that no one can escape the label of codependent, Subby, another codependency author who got his professional start in the chemical-dependency treatment arena (1987, p. 16) has offered the concept of "paradoxical codependency," in which the persona of self-sufficiency is a front for feelings of inadequacy and self-doubt. So, apparently, if you do not show signs of codependency this would be proof that you are (paradoxically) codependent. As with most other self-help authors on codependency, Subby identifies codependency's origin in dysfunctional family rules or styles of interaction. There is no apparent room for a more scientific approach (p.53): "These rules are passed down from one generation to the next, not by heredity or genetics, but by learning ... by watching and mimicking" [Ellipsis in original]. As to explaining how all family members exposed to the same "rules" are not uniformly codependent (p. 53): "We don't know for sure ...."

O'Gorman (1993), while describing the codependency phenomenon, reinforced the belief that it is a (family) learned behavior, incorporating learned helplessness into her description. Further, O'Gorman (1993, p. 208) advised, "The alcoholic family literally teaches that all family members are secondary to the alcoholic, which reinforces societal views of women as 'less than beings,' and ... (p. 209) 'Being a woman in our society can set the stage for codependency... As we can see three of the four themes[1] of learned helplessness are in evidence in the development of women even before the specific impact of the alcoholic or other dysfunctional family begins.' There is no mention of why not all children of alcoholics exhibit codependent behavior, nor what, if anything, is different about young males growing up in alcoholic families."

Schaef (1986, p. 25) prefers to take a "big picture" approach, suggesting that, "what we are calling codependence is, indeed, a *disease* that has many forms and expressions and that grows out of a disease process that is inherent in the system in which we live. I call this disease the *addictive process* ... an unhealthy and abnormal disease process, whose assumptions, beliefs, behaviors, and lack of spirituality lead to a process of non-living that is progressively death oriented. This basic disease, from which spring the subdiseases of codependence and alcoholism—among others—is tacitly and openly supported by the society in which we live" [Italics in original]. In case the reader might question their ability to follow Schaef's line of thinking, she clarifies (p. 25): "I also believe that trying to generate definitions from a rational, logical premise is actually a manifestation of the disease process. I want to avoid that sort of analysis."

Braiker (2001), the psychologist of *The Disease to Please*, conceptualizes codependency as the need to please others at the expense of the codependent person. She is clear that she is not talking about ". . . nice people who occasionally go too far in trying to make others happy." Braiker's "disease to please" is thought to be "a debilitating psychological problem with far-reaching, serious consequences" (p. xi). The reader takes a 24-item true–false test, and based on the number of "true" endorsements, is assigned one of four levels of "people pleasing" or codependency, ranging from "mild or none" to "deeply ingrained and serious" (p. 2–4). Next, readers check subscales to determine whether they are controlled by thoughts, behaviors, or emotions—the three corners of the "disease to please" triangle. No empirical basis is offered to support any of the inferences made or recommendations to treat the purported codependent diagnosis.

> The concept of codependency is a product, to some degree, of the culture in which it appeared.

The concept of codependency is a product, to some degree, of the culture in which it appeared. For some within this culture, recovering from codependency becomes a way of life, a way of making sense of problems, and a way of defining themselves. As Rice (1996, p. 11) notes, being a part of the codependency movement "entails holding very specific beliefs, and those beliefs provide a means of making sense of and organizing one's life." If codependency is to be studied in a more scientific manner, it is necessary to separate the concept of codependency from the codependency recovery movement/industry and restrict it to significantly dysfunctional interpersonal behaviors that can be identified and studied. As an example of the need for such a separation, estimates of codependency are clearly exaggerated by codependency advocates.[2]

The mainstream psychiatric community has paid little formal notice to codependency. For example, the subject of codependence is allotted four paragraphs in a chapter on substance-related disorders in the ninth edition of *Kaplan & Sadock's Comprehensive Textbook of Psychiatry* (Strain & Anthony, 2009). And this includes a disclaimer that mentioning *enabling* and *denial* as frequently listed aspects of codependence was not an endorsement that an actual syndrome (i.e., codependency) exists. The terms codependency and codependent are nowhere to be found in the index of *The American Psychiatric Publishing Textbook of Psychiatry*, fifth edition (Hales, Yudofsky, & Gabbard, 2008). *The American Psychiatric Publishing Textbook of Substance Abuse Treatment*, fourth edition (Galanter & Kleber, 2008), does not list *codependent, codependency*, or *codependence* in its index. Nor is the term(s) found in the *Diagnostic and Statistical Manual of Mental Disorders, 4th Edition, Text Revision* (DSM-IV-TR) (American Psychiatric Association [APA], 2000). In *Principles of Addiction Medicine*, fourth edition (Liepman, Parran, Farkas, & Lagos-Saez, 2009), codependence is mentioned briefly in the context of enabling. Codependency is simply mentioned as one item to assess when taking a history in the *Clinical Textbook of Addictive Disorders*, third edition (Stanton & Heath, 2005, p. 534). No definition of the term is provided.

Most, although not all, peer-reviewed literature on codependency appears in relation to spouses and families of substance abusers. Articles tend to be either

very critical or naively accepting of the concept. A significant amount of what has been
offered professionally borders on unsup-
ported speculation.

> Research articles on codependency tend to be either very critical or naively accepting of the concept. A significant amount of what has been offered professionally borders on unsupported speculation.

There has been (Stafford, 2001) a lack of
shared operational definition for codependency in the literature, which makes evaluat-
ing the validity of the construct difficult.
Morgan (1991) observed that codependency
suffers from diverse definitions, formulation,
and treatment approaches, all of which lack any systematic research basis. He
further notes (p. 722) that the term has at least three levels of meaning (as a
didactic tool, a psychological concept, and as a disease), with little distinction
made by those who use the term. Even worse, it is sometimes difficult to separate
scholarly professional literature from popular self-help published works. As an
example, Stafford (2001, p. 277) cites a (presumably) peer-reviewed psychiatric
nursing article (Martsoff, et al., 1999) that claimed 40 million Americans had
been accurately labeled codependent, basing the claim on an article (Goff &
Goff, 1988) published 11 years earlier in a journal that deals with personnel
issues.

Codependency is considered by some as most consistent with the DSM-III
Dependent Personality Disorder (APA, 1980; Morgan, 1991). (See also Widiger
and Lowe in this volume.) Cermak (1986) proposed including codependency as
a personality disorder in the DSM-III-R (APA, 1987), which did not occur. He
addressed, to some extent, the issue of pathologizing common (culturally
accepted female role) behaviors by noting the difference the DSM-III (and later
the DSM–IV [APA, 1994]) makes between personality traits and personality
disorders. Personality traits morph into a disorder when they become "inflexible
and maladaptive and cause either significant functional impairment or subjective distress" (APA, 1980, p. 305). Cermak (1986, p. 15) suggested a Codependent
Personality Disorder with the following criteria:

A. Continued investment of self-esteem in the ability to control both
    oneself and others in the face of serious adverse consequences.
B. Assumption of responsibility for meeting other's needs, to the
    exclusion of acknowledging one's own.
C. Anxiety and boundary distortions around intimacy and separation.
D. Enmeshment in relationships with personality disordered, chemically
    dependent, other codependent, and/or impulse disordered individuals.
E. Three or more of the following:
    - Excessive reliance on denial
    - Constriction of emotions (with or without dramatic outbursts)
    - Depression
    - Hypervigilance
    - Compulsions
    - Anxiety
    - Substance abuse
    - Has been (or is) the victim of recurrent physical or sexual abuse
    - Has remained in a primary relationship with an active substance
      abuser for at least 2 years without seeking outside help
    - Stress-related medical illnesses

Unfortunately, the diagnostic criteria offered have no empirical basis, overlap with other disorders on many levels, and offer little if any specificity in diagnosing a disorder that arguably, to date, has not been proven to actually exist. For example, some of the items listed for criterion E have no intrinsic relationship to the concept of codependency, and others involve circular reasoning, although certainly codependent individuals might exhibit some of these symptoms or parameters. Criterion A appears reasonable, as does criterion B. Criterion C is vague and a better description of a borderline personality constellation, than codependence. Criterion D reinforces the presumed connection to substance abuse. As noted above, this diagnostic category did not make it into the DSM-III-R (APA, 1987) or the DSM-IV (APA, 1994).

Regarding attempts to use a personality disorder diagnosis as a way of capturing the codependent construct, Harper and Capdevilla (1990, p. 289) opined that "[c]odependency is so conceptually complex . . . that it would require four separate *DSM* categories to contain it, combining characteristics found in Alcoholism, and the Dependent, Borderline, and Histrionic Personality Disorders, as well as an additional category made up of 'associated features.'" Stafford (2001) points out that, although a woman might meet some of Cermak's (1986) criteria for codependency, when the situation is reviewed from a societal role context, "codependent" behaviors may be more indicative of role conflict than individual psychopathology.

> It might be better to conceptualize codependency as dysfunctional behaviors to identify, rather than a disorder to diagnose.

This author would suggest it might be better to conceptualize codependency as dysfunctional behaviors to identify, rather than a disorder to diagnose. A person might exhibit codependent behaviors, rather than suffer from codependency per se. Such an individual might have a diagnosable mental disorder, but the codependency itself would be subsumed under a larger rubric. Also, any given individual might exhibit codependent behavior in one or more relationships, but not in others.

Cleary (1994) observed that although codependency is widely accepted in the substance abuse treatment field and often relied on when prescribing treatment modalities, there is little to no support for the concept. Harper and Cadevila (1990) noted that many clinicians in substance abuse treatment settings were providing codependency treatment without any formal training in family therapy. Cleary's (1994) review of literature from 1984 to 1994 found no reliance on systematic studies, with research consisting mostly of case descriptions by social workers and substance abuse counselors from their own clinical work. J. Miller (1994, p. 341) also noted that "[t]here is no clinical, experimental, or descriptive research, only impressionistic assertions. In fact, many publications on codependency are written by members of Al-Anon, who describe their own personal experiences (e.g., Beattie, 1987) . . . Consequently, even if the concept were clearly defined, its validity must be seriously questioned . . . it is not surprising that empirical research fails to find any of the descriptive features suggested by the disease model . . . indeed, many spouses react in a controlled and adaptive fashion."

Miller (1994, p. 342) noted that "[t]he disease model creates a 'codependent/noncodependent' dichotomy that does not exist in the real world." Cleary (1994) echoes Gierymski and Williams' (1986) concern that there is no convincing support that the myriad of behavioral and emotional problems presumed to be correlated with codependency (associated with substance abuse) were not shared by families dealing with and adapting to family members suffering from chronic diseases such as schizophrenia, Alzheimer disease, mental retardation, or diabetes. To date, it does not appear anyone has researched this issue.

Assuming that codependency exists (certainly the behaviors associated with it do), can it be separated out from its chemical dependency treatment milieu roots? O'Brien and Gaborit (1992) studied 115 American undergraduate students in an attempt to answer two questions: Does codependency exist apart from chemical dependency? And, are codependent people more depressed than non-codependents? The study findings found support for the belief that codependency exists outside of substance abuse, and did not find support for the supposition that codependent individuals are more depressed than others.

A lack of psychometrically sound instruments to measure the phenomenon has hampered research into codependency (Dear & Roberts, 2005). Stafford (2001) reviewed eight self-report instruments[3] used to measure codependency as a personality variable, finding that (pp. 282–283):

> A lack of psychometrically sound instruments to measure the phenomenon has hampered research into codependency.

> Although favorable reliability coefficients are reported on the codependency instruments that have been tested, they have been subjected to limited scrutiny with community and clinical samples in extant research. Most of the tools have been tested on undergraduate students (who then acquire additional course credit) and on self-identified codependent persons. Thus it would seem that there is an absence of robust normative data on these instruments. Although many individuals thought to be codependent may share similar behaviors, histories, and so forth, suggesting high validity for the construct, the diagnostic criteria are so protean and vague that clinicians have difficulty achieving consensus on who really has this disorder, suggesting questionable reliability for the concept. (Maxmen & Ward, 1995)

In spite of the recognition of enabling behaviors among significant others of substance abusers, specific data involving enabling behaviors are scarce (Rotunda, et al., 2004). It should be noted that, just as enabling can be indicative of hopelessness and avoiding conflict while maintaining a dysfunctional relationship, such behavior could be an adaptive and effective way of protecting the substance abuser and others from potentially negative consequences.

Dear and Roberts (2000) developed the Holyoake Codependency Index (HCI) at an Australian substance abuse treatment center. Thirty-nine men and 268 women with a family member in substance abuse treatment were given a 28-item pilot version. This was later pared to a 13-item form comprised of three subscales measuring *external focus*, *self-sacrifice*, and *reactivity*. This latter version was replicated with a community sample of 303 women. Although the parameters assessed encompass presumed facets of codependency, this research (as is the case with most research on codependency) was carried out in the context of the substance abuse milieu. The *external focus* subscale assesses the tendency to rely on external (other people's) feedback "for approval and a sense of identity." The *self-sacrifice* subscale items identify "a tendency to regard others' needs as more important than one's own," while the *reactivity* subscale measures the feeling of being controlled by the behavior of another (p. 995).

Dear (2002) reported on a study examining whether the results of the HCI were consistent across genders in a nontreatment-related sample, using undergraduate university students. Factorial validity was found to be consistent with prior studies and across genders. Test–retest reliability (Dear, 2004) was assessed using 59 university students who were retested (from an original test group of 96) three weeks after taking the HCI. It was reported that (p. 483) "this index is sufficiently psychometrically sound for research. The index is content valid; the subscale structure is stable across samples and sexes; the subscales are internally consistent and have good retest reliability over 3 wk.; and there is adequate initial evidence of construct validity." Dear (2004) notes that it is difficult to examine the concurrent validity due to the limitations of other published codependency scales, and that retesting would need to be assessed at intervals of greater than 3 weeks. Study replication would also be necessary.

In a later review of the HCI data, Dear and Roberts (2005, p. 294) state "the HCI is the only measure of codependency that was deliberately developed not to contain items that confound the measure with other variables, such as self-esteem or emotional distress," and possessing a subscale structure that is content valid and stable across samples. They admit it is still problematic regarding assessment of construct validity, and list five main limitations of the HCI:

- It does not assess interpersonal or emotional aspects of codependency.
- The reactivity subscale contains only three items and is related to the partner's behavior.
- The reactivity subscale will have limited, if any, relevance to samples in which the majority of participants are not in a current problematic relationship.
- The construct validity of the self-sacrifice subscale needs further examination.
- The only data so far is from the developers of the HCI.

Dear and Roberts have concluded that the psychometric properties of the HCI are superior to those of any currently published codependency measure and that the HCI can be used to reliably assess at least two core constructs of codependency, *external focus* and *self-sacrifice*. This author would suggest that by maintaining a focus on the two domains of *external focus* and *self-sacrifice*, it will be easier for various researchers to be confident that they will be studying the same thing.

Roots of Codependency

> Codependence can be viewed as a dysfunctional empathic response, a displaced mutual aid endeavor in which the main defect is an inability to tolerate negative affect in the important other.

Why would a person remain in a dysfunctional relationship with a stress-inducing other? It may be that ending the relationship would create more stress (if only transient) than remaining in the relationship. Or, perhaps the dysfunction meets the psychological needs of both actors. Maybe the prime focus of researchers in this area should be the inability of enablers to modulate their own overly empathic response to the negative affective state induced in the other when they confront the dysfunctional behavior or attempt to set limits on it. (See Figure 4.1) This author

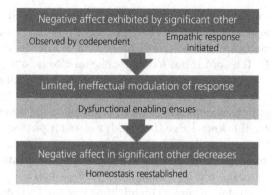

FIGURE 4.1
The codependent individual perceives negative affect in another and fails to modulate their empathic response. Enabling behavior leads to a decrease in negative affect in the dysfunctional other and the enabler.

believes codependence can be viewed as a dysfunctional empathic response, a displaced mutual aid endeavor in which the main defect is an inability to tolerate negative affect in the important other.

Humans have evolved to cohabit and interact with other humans. In a telling illustration of man's social nature, de Waal (2006) points out that, absent the death penalty, solitary confinement is probably the most extreme punishment we have. But from where does this human need to interact with others arise? Evidence is pointing to the newborn human entering the world already innately primed to engage.

There is reason to believe that prosocial skills develop early, in tandem with other capacities, such as conscience and empathy, rather than being environmentally instilled or taught (Thompson, Meyer, & McGinley, 2005). Rochat (2004) believes a rudimentary sense of self versus nonself and a drive to interact with other humans are present at birth, consistent with a genetic/evolutionary basis for social behaviors. Decety and Meyer (2008, p. 1058) concur, stating: "In sum, the developmental data suggest that the mechanism subserving emotion (as the observable expressions of feelings and affects) sharing between infant and caretaker is immediately present from birth. Newborns are innately and highly attuned to other people and motivated to socially interact with others." Since some prosocial behaviors are apparent at birth, the fetus must have become capable of them in utero.

Very likely, there are evolutionarily early neurological systems or pathways for emotional empathy and evolutionarily later systems or pathways that allow for a more advanced response to the perception of the emotional state of others—what would be called a *cognitive empathy* (de Waal, 2008; Shamay-Tsoory et al., 2009). Decety and Jackson (2004) describe empathy as consisting of the macrocomponents of shared neuronal representations, self-awareness (awareness of self as self and as different from others), mental flexibility (ability to adopt someone else's perspective), and emotion regulation. Empathy is clearly an advantageous facet of human cognition. Where the codependent individual may stray is in the modulation of the affect it generates in the observer.

The *theory of mind* (ToM)—closely related to the concept of cognitive empathy—suggests that to empathize with others, we must be able to identify a mental state in another, understand what it likely means to the other, and still know that it is not our own mental state (Flavell, 2004). Such ability would allow us to predict the behavior of others based on our prior experiences of self and others' mental states and the behaviors that did or did not follow (Premack & Woodruff, 1978). The ToM is posited to operate on a conscious and an unconscious level and implies that we understand that others have their own thoughts, feelings, and intentions. ToM includes our being aware that the beliefs of others are not necessarily based on reality, but can be based on the other person's perception of reality. This knowledge (i.e., ToM) allows for prosocial interactions, but also sets the stage for deception. Some researchers (Baron-Cohen, 1995) view ToM as a brain module, whose disruption explains autism. Buller (2006) critiques ToM, pointing out that there is no strong empirical evidence for us possessing a ToM module, as well as highlighting that autism is much more than not being able to understand the minds of others. Regardless of whether there is a module in the mammalian brain analogous to ToM, the concept is helpful in explaining empathy, if not autism.

It would seem obvious that our behaviors, even those that are seemingly detrimental on an individual basis, would need to in some way confer a broader evolutionary advantage. A potentially confounding issue is the *savannah principle* (Kanazawa, 2004), which posits that the human brain is adapted to an ancestral environment of 10,000 years ago and has had little opportunity to adapt itself to the current environment. But such claims are speculative. Currently, data from the well-known Framingham Heart Study (2009) are being analyzed from an evolutionary perspective to see if there is evidence for natural selection and genetic response to such selection in modern humans (Dolgin, 2009). Buller (2006) believes that there must have been some adaptive psychological evolution in the past 10,000 years. And Hawks et al. (2007, p. 2057) believe "the rapid cultural evolution during the Late Pleistocene created vastly more opportunities for further genetic change, not fewer, as avenues emerged for communication, social interactions, and creativity."

> Similar to codependency, can altruism take well-meaning behavior too far?

Assuming human behaviors are the product of genes, evolution, and environment, how do we explain codependent behavior that does not appear to benefit the codependent individual, and in fact seems detrimental to his or her well-being? Altruism is a behavior associated with empathy. Similar to codependency, can altruism take well-meaning behavior too far?

Pathological Altruism

Homant and Kennedy (see Chapter 14) describe pathological altruism as a type of maladaptive altruism, suggesting it could be characterized by one or more of the following: behavior that is unnecessary or uncalled for; the altruist complains about the effect of the altruistic behavior on him- or herself, in the context of performing the behavior; the underlying motivation may be irrational or a product of a psychological disturbance; and the outcome fails to benefit anyone and this was foreseeable to a reasonable person. Homant and Kennedy's characterization would offer guidance in sorting out goal-directed self-sacrifice from pathological altruism. Under their paradigm, Jesus, Gandhi, and Martin Luther King, Jr., could be seen as self-sacrificing, rather than pathologically altruistic.

The self-sacrificing individual accepts the psychological and/or physical pain he endures as a necessary part of the "helping-others" equation. For the pathological altruist, perhaps the pain and suffering is the goal.

The Root of Empathy

The evolutionary and genetic bases of altruism have received significant attention. From the moment two cells adhered, resulting in improved survival, biological cooperation was off and running. Just as different organs in an organism work cooperatively to enhance an organism's survival, different organisms working cooperatively gained an evolutionary advantage. As noted by Harris (2007, p. 168), "Mutual aid between and among members of a species may be the most potent force in evolution." That empathy will facilitate mutual cooperation would appear to require little argument.

The precursor to altruism is empathy. Human (mammalian) altruism has its roots in parental[5] caring for the infant, but the interaction is not a one-way street, as one of the most powerful reinforcements for parental attention is when the infant smiles back at the caretaker (Strathearn, Li, Fonagy, & Montague, 2008). Studies support a very early ability, including at birth, of the human neonate to recognize (prefer) the mother's face (Bushnell, Sai, & Mullin, 1989; Slater & Quinn, 2001). It would appear we come "off the shelf" ready to engage, primed for empathy with those who care for us. As we move outside of our immediate gene pool, the evolutionary rationale for supporting or helping another diminishes. When we reach the periphery (no familial ties), and we help someone without expectation of benefit to ourselves, we are being truly altruistic.

Hamilton (1964) developed the concept of inclusive fitness or *kin selection* to help explain the altruistic acts of those closely related genetically. Trivers (1971) introduced *reciprocal altruism*, whereby we act altruistically toward a nonrelated other. There would be an expectation that the benefited other would at some future point act in a manner to benefit the original actor or some close genetic relative of the original actor. In this way, the altruism of the individual benefits the whole in a cave man equivalent of "what goes around comes around." Multilevel-Selection Theory (McAndrew, 2002; Wilson, 1997) proposed that natural selection can operate at a group level, thus offering an evolutionary explanation for behaviors that would benefit a group but not an individual. This assumes competing groups, in which evolutionary group selection pressures would be expected to select for traits that increase the survival of one group over similar groups.

> It would appear we come "off the shelf" ready to engage, primed for empathy with those who care for us.

Turning back to codependent behaviors, although it may not make much sense on an individual basis for the codependent person to maintain the dysfunctional relationship, on a group level the codependent behavior must convey some benefit to maintain it. Altruism makes the most sense when people do not cheat; that is, the person benefiting from another's altruism in turn passes that altruistic behavior forward. Said another way, for altruism to work, those performing altruistic acts should be able to assume that they are not helping a cheater or one who takes advantage of others, such as a psychopath. Yet, any behavioral scientist can describe how easy it is to run from someone with a knife, but how hard to run from someone who cuts with a caress. Are humans any good at spotting cheaters? Perhaps they are good at spotting the unshaven pick-pocket, but not the charming murderer. Is codependence an issue of inability to identify the cheater, or is it the opposite, the ability to find the cheater?

Do we make altruist–cheater decisions based on underlying genetic predis-positions, rather than logical assessments of a situation? The answer might be yes. Brown and Moore (2000, p. 33) conducted a study (total $n = 60$) with find-ings consistent with such a hypothesis, noting that, "subjects are detecting altru-ists rather than giving logically correct responses." In other words, it appeared test subjects were unknowingly eschewing logic for innate "information pro-cessing capabilities designed by natural selection to detect whether a helpful act was motivated by genuine concern for others (p. 27)."

Disorders of diminished empathy are well known and include the Autistic Spectrum Disorders (for example, autism and Asperger syndrome), some per-sonality disorders, and psychopathy. On some level, these disorders are believed to reflect a decreased ability to identify the inner affective states of others, or to understand what the other is feeling and to react appropriately. The defect can be striking, as in childhood autism and psychopathy, or more subtle, as in a histri-onic personality disorder, where gaining attention is the goal and the feelings of others are secondary.

The Basis of Codependency

In the following sections, I will discuss the possible evolutionary, genetic, and neurobiological bases for codependency. This breakdown is artificial, as all human traits have developed in the simultaneous context of these three areas.

Evolutionary Basis/Pressure for Codependence

Battered women are often viewed as codependent. Is this consistent with the savannah principle (Kanazawa, 2004), a by-product of the female *Homo sapiens* relying on the hunter males of the species to feed and protect them? Possibly, but not all codependent individuals are female. Many men are involved as the enabler in codependent situations, and it is no secret that men are also battered by their female domestic partners (Straus, 1999). The evolutionary pressure for codepen-dency would seem to be more a function of group pressure to maintain the smooth functioning of the group, rather than any individual advantage.

It is possible that a multilevel selection process favors submissive partners for some dyads. After all, in every dual relationship, one member will have more of one trait than another. The question in a codependent relationship, however, is not necessarily why a person enters into the relationship, but rather why he or she maintains the relationship in spite of the failure of the partner to provide appropriate reciprocity. In the context of the savannah principle, Kanazawa (see Chapter 25) suggests that there was an evolutionary advantage for battered women in maintaining the relationship with the batterer. Batterers are violent men. Until fairly recently in the human story, women were best protected by men who would resort to violence when necessary. If a cave woman were in danger, she would probably prefer a brutal Stanley Kowalski between her and the threat, as opposed to a dweebish Barney Fife. In Kanazawa's formulation, being beaten by a violent man would be part of the cost of being protected by him. Kanazawa suggests that domestic violence can be explained on an evolu-tionary basis through the fact that battered women appear to have more sons than the general population (Kanazawa, 2008), even if the observed effect is weak. Also, analysis of British and American samples (Kanazawa, 2006) appears to demonstrate that male batterers have more sons than do nonbatterers.

It should be kept in mind that, for a trait to be selected for on an evolutionary basis, it is not required that every individual person (collection of genes) acts in a particular manner, but only that a certain threshold percentage does. This threshold percentage can be quite small. Also, although the trait might appear counterproductive on an individual level, it might be selected for on an environmental basis, as is the case with sickle cell anemia. Although sickle cell anemia would be expected to be selected against, the trait (only one sickle cell allele, instead of two) provides some protection against malaria (Allison, 1956). Another possible mechanism for the propagation of altruism, and by inference, codependence, is genetic hitchhiking. Such a model (Barton, 2000; Santos & Szathmary, 2008) could allow for propagation of a trait such as "strong altruism" without invoking kin selection. A gene or series of genes for altruism, even if the trait is selected against, could survive if linked to another gene that enhanced fitness.

Porges' (2001) polyvagal theory uses the development of the autonomic nervous system (ANS) as an organizing basis for social behavior. The theory posits three important stages in neural regulation of the ANS. The earliest is an immobilization strategy, in which stress is met with decreased metabolic activity. The second stage is a mobilizing strategy mediated through a sympathetic nervous system that increases metabolic activity—what is commonly referred to as "fight or flight." The third and latest stage, unique to mammals, is distinguished by a more developed (myelinated) vagus nerve adjusting heart rate in response to environmental stimuli. It would be interesting to see if the ANS responses of codependents differ in any meaningful way from controls. An interesting part of the polyvagal theory is that the mammalian vagus is neuroanatomically linked to other cranial nerves involved in the regulation of social behaviors through vocalization and facial expressions (Porges, 2001).

Genetic Basis for Codependence

Human personality/behavioral traits clearly have a genetic basis, even if the genetic connection is complicated (McGuffin, Riley, & Plomin, 2001). If codependency is a genuine syndrome or group of behaviors, there must be some genetic basis for it. But, as with personality syndromes in general, it will be difficult to tease out the specific characteristics that define codependency, especially since traits and behaviors ordinarily appear on a continuum, as opposed to discrete quanta. Some syndromes appear to demonstrate that empathic and trusting traits have a genetic basis.

Williams syndrome is not sex-linked and encompasses a multitude of features, including a characteristic facies, cardiovascular abnormalities, musculoskeletal problems, attention deficit disorder, mild to moderate mental retardation, and more (National Institutes of Health, 2008). It appears to be the result of a missing 21-gene segment that includes the elastin[6] gene (ELN) at the 7q11.2 chromosomal locus (Morris, 2006). In addition to the features noted above, those afflicted with Williams syndrome have an interesting deficit, tending to be hypersocial and overly trusting of strangers. They are described as overempathic. This disorder supports a genetic (hence neural) substrate for empathic and trusting behaviors. (See Chapter 9 by Riby et al.)

Disorders associated with high rates of the empathy-spectrum disorders of autism, such as fragile X syndrome, are consistent with a genetic component to social behavior disorders. Fragile X syndrome is a single gene mutation on the X chromosome and interferes with production of a protein required for proper synaptic development (Hagerman, 2006). Hard numbers are elusive, as diagnostic variability and study limitations cloud the issues, but up to 4% of those diagnosed with autism have fragile X syndrome. A striking finding, though, is that of those with fragile X syndrome, ranges of autism run reliably from 18% to 33% (Belmonte & Bourgeron, 2006). That up to a third of individuals with a specific genetic defect can be diagnosed with an empathy-related disorder speaks strongly for a genetic basis to empathy.

Anckarsater and Cloninger (2007, p. 262) note that there is a "substantial body of data showing a moderate to strong heritability for traits related to empathy." Thus, there is reason to assume that other traits, such as a tendency to codependency, would also have a similar heritability. Further, Anckarsater and Cloninger (p. 272) point out that there is "clear and consistent evidence for genetic contributions to normal and abnormal personality traits, whether they are measured as quantitative traits or as clusters of personality disorders." These data come from twin studies and suggest heritability of up to 50% for various dimensions of personality, including those related to empathy. Anckarster and Cloninger (2007) suggest that a broad spectrum of child and adolescent disorders associated with empathy deficits have a strong genetic basis and are related to personality disorders and other mental disorders found in adults.

Some (Cermack, 1986) would claim that severely codependent individuals would meet criteria for a DSM-IV-TR-like dependent personality disorder (APA, 2000). Widiger and Presnall (Chapter 6) believe pathological altruism is a key feature of a dependent personality disorder. It should be kept in mind that universal agreement is lacking on the validity of the DSM, especially when it comes to personality disorders. For example, Widiger (2007) notes issues related to diagnostic unreliability, excessive diagnostic co-occurrence, inconsistent and unstable diagnostic boundaries, and an inadequate scientific basis for most categories of personality disorder. Some psychiatric diagnoses may fit a dimensional (continuum) model, whereas others may be better suited to a categorical (discrete syndrome) model (Haslam, 2003). Also (Schmidt, Kotov, & Joiner, 2004, p. x), the categories and indicators of psychopathology that make it into the *DSM* series (which rely on categories, not dimensions), although informed by science, are "decided more by committee than by science. While it is true that the *DSM* committees pay careful attention to available psychopathology science, it is also true that the basic methodology of the *DSM* for inclusion and delineation of disorders is based on committee consensus, the pitfalls and gross errors of which can be substantial."

Bilder et al. (2009) believe a broader approach to psychiatric diagnosis needs to be adopted to take into account the study of phenotypes on a genome-wide scale, what has been labeled *neuropsychiatric phenomics*.[7] Defining syndromes (i.e., diagnoses) as discrete entities may not be appropriate when taking into account the underlying genetic basis to many behaviors—especially when this genetic inheritance is filtered through the molecular maelstrom of embryonic development, and in turn influenced by the environment and the plasticity of the central nervous system (CNS). It may make more sense to look for a genetic basis for the symptoms or behaviors people exhibit, rather than the diagnosis they currently have been given. "The phenomics strategy explicitly calls for efforts to redefine phenotypes as multilevel combinations of measures that may offer more realistic constraints on the mechanistic paths leading from genome to syndrome" (Bilder et al., 2009, p. 3). A database to explore such an approach is in progress (Sabb et al., 2008)—heredity is appearing to be more complicated than simply locating a suspect gene or collection of genes on a chromosome.

Neurobiological Correlate for Codependence

Although no specific neurobiological correlate for codependency has been identified, it is likely that future research will uncover pathways overlapping those involved in emotional and cognitive empathy. The problem is that the behaviors and/or trait of codependency are unlikely to utilize a simple neuronal pathway. Instead, as with many human behaviors requiring cognition, they will surely use multilevel pathways, both excitatory and inhibitory, with an amorphous reward system that may involve a decrease in anxiety or negative affect. Singling out critical aspects for study will be a daunting task, worsened by the fact that codependency is itself such a fluid concept. There are promising leads, though. Decety and Meyer (2008, p. 1073) argue that empathy is the end product of "bottom-up processes, which are driven by emotion expressions, and top-down processes, including self-regulation and executive control," and suggest the prefrontal cortex (PFC) would likely be the top-down regulator. Failure of the PFC to inhibit empathic responses could play a role in codependence.

One part of the neurological substrate for empathy may be analogous to the mirror neuron system (MNS), in which the observer of an action performed by another has brain activity similar to that observed, as if he or she had actually performed the action. The direct research on motor neurons was performed on macaque monkeys (Rizzolatti & Craighero, 2004) with indirect functional magnetic resonance imaging (fMRI) research in humans (Dinstein, Gardner, Jazayeri, & Heeger, 2008). Neuronal activity in an observer similar to that in a performer would suggest identification of a behavior as well as possibly the mind state of the actor. This could occur on a conscious or unconscious level. Schulte-Ruther et al. (2007) lend support to the view that the MNS is involved in empathy. Shamay-Tsoory et al. (2009, p. 618) comment on recent studies (Carr, Lacoboni, Dubeau, Mazziotta, & Lenzi, 2003; Seitz et al., 2008) in which the MNS of the inferior frontal gyrus (IFG) is activated by emotion recognition (phylogenically early) and emotional empathy (phylogenically later) (Jabbi, Swart, & Keysers, 2007; Schulte-Ruther et al., 2007). Shamay-Tsoory and her colleagues also suggest the core structure of emotional empathy is the IFG which (p. 618) "appears to be involved mainly [in] emotional contagion and emotion recognition." Functional MRI studies are usually correlational and not causal, but Jabbi and Keysers (2008, p. 779) believe they developed evidence "in support of the idea that motor simulation is causally linked to emotional simulation." (See Figure 4.2.)

> Failure of the prefrontal cortex to inhibit empathic responses could play a role in codependence.

Sex differences in empathy (and possibly codependence) are controversial, with a bias toward women being inherently more empathic and therefore more prone to codependency than men. Eisenberg and Fabes (1990) found that sex differences in empathy that were present when subjects could tell that empathy was being studied were limited or disappeared when the subject was not aware

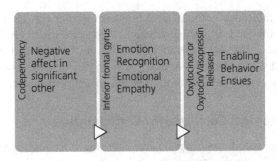

FIGURE 4.2
The significant other presents with negative affect. This affect is recognized by the codependent person. The inferior frontal gyrus fails in its modulating role, and oxytocin, vasopressin, or some combination of the two is released, leading to a prosocial empathic response, even if the result is an enabling behavior.

of the intent of the questions. Although interesting, the N was small, with 30 married men and 30 married women. Goldsmith and Dun's (1997) study of 119 college students found little difference between men and women, citing situational factors as much more controlling. A 1998 meta-analysis by Fabes and Eisenberg (1998) found that adult prosocial behavior was inconsistent across studies and varied as a function of the quality of the studies. They summarize their meta-analysis by noting that, although girls appear to be more prosocial than boys, the issue of sex differences in prosocial behaviors and their origins remained unresolved.

An even more recent study of children by Auyeung et al. (2009) seems to confirm that there *is* a sex difference, with females being more empathic than males. A confounding issue could be that since the study relied on questionnaires filled out by parents, it is possible that parental societal expectations crept into the data. Regardless, a female-greater-than-male empathic stance could be expected, especially in light of the strong male predominance in autism spectrum disorders of about 4 to 1 (Chakrabarti & Fombonne, 2005) and up to almost 11 to 1 in Asperger syndrome (Gilberg et al., 2006), and the greater role of the peptide oxytocin (see below) in females over males. Although, as Goldsmith and Dun (1997) suggested, when it comes to empathy, men and women are probably more alike than different. What remains to be seen is whether an empathy differential is an artifact of empathic thinking as opposed to empathic action. Although it appears that woman are prone to be more empathic in general than are males, the recipient of the empathy might be interested in which sex is more likely to act altruistically in a dangerous situation.

As noted earlier, empathy has both an emotional and a cognitive facet. Thus, it is possible that codependence may be characterized by impaired cognition as well as emotion. In other words, the codependent individual may have limited ability to put the emotional aspect of what she is feeling (empathy) into a broader perspective; she cannot modulate her empathy adequately due to dysfunction in a cognitive empathy pathway. This pathway would be phylogenically newer than the emotional empathy pathway, and would modulate the empathic response. Shamay-Tsoory et al. (2009) suggest that this facility may be located in the ventromedial prefrontal (VM) gyrus, and, further, identify Brodmann area 44 to be involved in emotional empathy, whereas areas 11 and 10 appear to be involved in cognitive empathy. Clearly, more research in areas such as these is needed, but the implications are clear. Neural mechanisms exist that allow us to observe others and know (or at least guess) what they are feeling. Similar mechanisms have been identified in relation to observing others in pain (Loggia, Mogil, & Bushnell, 2008), a sensation that has significant emotional connections, especially regarding empathy. As a correlate of empathy, codependence will likely involve such mechanisms.

Some studies assessing brain function using fMRI after cognitive behavioral therapy for the treatment of obsessive-compulsive and phobic disorders (Linden, 2006) have found decreases in metabolism in the right caudate nucleus, as well as in limbic and paralimbic areas. These changes parallel similar changes after antidepressant treatment with selective serotonin uptake inhibitors. Findings such as these support the position that changes in thought are reflected in brain functioning and adjustments in brain function can be reflected in changes in thought. In other words, "brain change" can be top-down or bottom-up. Findings such as this should come as no surprise, since nothing happens (i.e., no thinking) in the brain without electrochemical activity at synapses. The prior entrenched belief that the brain stopped shaping itself and no new neurons could develop after a certain (young) age has been overturned, with evidence of stunning neural plasticity being published on a regular basis (Begley, 2009; Doidge, 2007).

It is logical to postulate that codependence may share some of the neural pathways involved in maternal or romantic love. After all, negative affect in those we love likely evokes a higher level of empathy than in those we are less connected to. And codependence involves interference with judgment and assessment of others' intentions, arguably a correlate to the state of being in love. Various neurotransmitters and hormones will be implicated, with arginine vasopressin and oxytocin appearing to play important roles (Bartels & Zeki, 2004). Oxytocin is a hormone correlated with social decision-making across vertebrates. Israel et al. (2009) propose a substantial genetic basis for prosocial decision-making mediated through oxytocin receptors. Arginine vasopressin is a second hormone linked to regulation of social behavior in humans (Bachner-Melman et al., 2005) including social bonding and attachment (Bartz & Hollander, 2006) in animals. The roles of oxytocin and vasopressin in human behavior are being researched on both a behavioral, genetic, and molecular level (Israel et al., 2008).

> It is logical to postulate that codependence may share some of the neural pathways involved in maternal or romantic love.

Dopamine and serotonin have also been attributed a role in prosocial attitudes or behaviors (Meeks & Jeste, 2009). Serotonin may play a role in codependency by increasing the aversion to harm others. A recent study (Crockett, et al, 2010) claims evidence that serotonin directly alters moral judgment and behavior, by enhancing an individual's distaste to personally harming another. Enablers often (emotionally) equate setting limits on codependent dysfunctional behavior with harming the other.

Oxytocin and vasopressin are peptides[8] that have been around in some form for at least 700 million years in organisms as diverse as hydra, worms, insects, and vertebrates (Donaldson & Young, 2008). Mammalian oxytocin and vasopressin[9] are nine amino acids long and vary from each other at only two amino acid positions. The genes coding for them are located near each other on the same chromosome: 20.[10] These peptides have been evolutionarily conserved over the millennia and appear to strongly influence social behavior. It may be that diversity in the genetic regulation of the oxytocin and vasopressin receptors underlies the natural variation observed in social behaviors, both within and between species (Donaldson &Young, 2008). There are sex differences, but it is clear that both peptides play a role in modulating social behavior in males and females. Generally, it appears that, in humans, oxytocin lowers amygdala (fear, rage) activity and has an anxiolytic effect, promoting social interaction (Heinrichs, von Dawans, & Domes, 2009). Vasopressin acts not only on the nervous system, but also to constrict blood vessels (raise blood pressure) and as an antidiuretic (preserves fluid) in the kidneys. It has been implicated mostly in male-typical social behaviors, including aggression and stress-responsiveness among others, with the potential to increase anxiety (Heinrichs et al., 2009). Cortisol may well be implicated, as it helps modulate limbic activity during stress (Shirtcliff et al., 2009), and codependency is nothing if not stressful (see Chapter 28 by Karol Pessin), and vasopressin can increase cortisol levels (Ebstein et al., 2009).

A recent study by Baumgartner et al. (2008) offers support for the belief that oxytocin is one factor modulating trust in humans. Trusting behaviors were associated with decreased activation on fMRI in the brain areas modulating fear (amygdala and midbrain regions). They (Baumgartner et al., 2008) found, using a double-blind model, that subjects exposed to (intranasal) oxytocin ignored feedback regarding breaches of trust, whereas those receiving placebo took such information into account and modified their willingness to trust others. In another study (Zak, Stanton, & Ahmadi, 2007), oxytocin increased generosity to strangers. Adult animals given oxytocin exhibit enhanced sociality and parental behaviors (Harris, 2007). Generosity and trusting behaviors can be contrasted with traits seen in psychopathy, a disorder almost defined by a lack of empathy.

Conclusion

Codependence can be viewed as a dysfunctional empathic response (see Figure 4.3) The codependent individual observes a negative affect in the significant other, perhaps via a mirror-neuron type system. An emotional empathic response ensues, leading the codependent individual to attempt to alleviate the

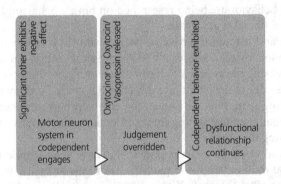

FIGURE 4.3
An empathic recognition of a negative affect in another is facilitated by the motor neuron system. Oxytocin, vasopressin, or a combination of the two is released, and prosocial behavior is enhanced, even overriding one's judgment with enabling behavior following.

negative affect. Proper boundary modulation (i.e., inhibition as mediated by a cognitive empathy system) of this response is lacking or impaired. This occurs even though the codependent actor may know that enabling the other is not really in the other's (and also their own) long-term best interest. Essentially, codependency may be the inability of the codependent person to tolerate the negative affect in the other. This leads to enabling behaviors designed to lower the negative affect of both in the short term, but which propagate the dysfunctional behaviors in the long term. This can occur even in the context of our being made aware that enabling the other is counterproductive.

On a psychodynamic level, low self-esteem and dependency traits can account for much of the codependency dyad, and interestingly, codependent behavior can be a subtle means of control. For example, the wife batterer is dependent on his dysfunctional domestic relationship, as is evidenced often by the rage that can ensue when the wife (or other) decides to end the relationship. But the psychodynamics are the explanation we place on a behavior (or collection of behaviors) that is, to a significant degree, programmed genetically, a result of our evolutionary journey to the present. And the reader is reminded that one can display codependency in one relationship and not in others.

Does this place us at the mercy of our genes? The answer is both yes and no. All behavior is observed on a continuum, and various individuals will have incremental contribution from various sectors, be it genetic or environmental. Human social skills, although apparently innate, are dependent on stimuli and environment during crucial developmental periods, both pre- and postnatal. These social skills and their resultant behaviors are mediated by neural pathways dependent upon chemical regulation, both for their development and for their ongoing mediation. Advances in neuroscience have shown that the brain is much more plastic than envisioned even just a few years ago.

Future research on codependency may be best served by focusing identification of codependency on the domains of *external focus* and *self-sacrifice* to avoid dilution of the construct. Bootstrapping onto research into empathy and altruism, codependence may be able to be ferreted out, with neurotransmitters identified and neural pathways elucidated, as is currently the case for empathy. As the field of *neuropsychiatric phenomics* matures, the genetic basis for behavioral traits, including codependency may be easier to trace.

Notes

1. As listed by O' Gorman (1993, p. 201), the four themes are: (1) no perceived control of the environment, (2) no task involvement (i.e., passivity), (3) disrupted normal routines, and (4) avoidance of social support. It is not clear to this author which of the four themes has been left out.

2. For example, Schaef (1986, p. 71) variously suggested that up to 96% of the population is codependent (by citing Sharon Wegscheider-Cruse without a specific citation) and also suggested that the total number of codependent individuals in the United States exceeded the actual population (p. 22).

3. The Friel Adult Child/Codependency Assessment inventory (Friel, 1985); The Codependency Assessment Questionnaire (Potter-Efron & Potter–Effon, 1989); The Co-Dependency Inventory, developed from the Co-Dependents Anonymous Checklist (no known studies on psychometric characteristics of this instrument have been located in the professional literature to 2001 [Stafford, 2001, p. 278]); The Spann-Fischer Codependency Scale (Fischer, Spann, & Crawford, 1991); The Beck Codependency

Assessment Scale (Beck, 1991); The Eight-Factor Codependency Scale (Kottke, Warren, Moffett, & Williams., 1993); Codependent Questionnaire (Roehling & Gaumond, 1996); The Codependency Assessment Tool (Hughes-Hammer, et al., 1998)

4. As explained by Maxmen and Ward (1995, p. 5), the validity can be considered high as (in their opinion) a "codependent personality" describing people who share basic clinical features probably exists, but clinicians have trouble agreeing on a definition.

5. The vast majority of research focuses on the mother–infant interaction.

6. Elastin is a protein important to the stretching of skin, blood vessels, and other tissues. Lack of it leads, among other problems, to dysfunction of blood vessels and joints.

7. *Neuropsychiatric phenomics* can be described as the study of the vast array of observable human traits and characteristics (the phenome). It is viewed by Bilder et al. (2009) as a *transdiscipline*, requiring input from multiple scientific fields. In essence, it is an attempt to understand the human being from the molecular level to the "observable" (phenotype).

8. Also referred to as *neuropeptides* when released at a synapse, as they function as neurotransmitters, and referred to as *neurohormones* when released outside the central nervous system. These are very versatile molecules.

9. Arginine vasopressin is the vasopressin found in mammals.

10. There is little space between the two genes in question. This could potentially be a type of genetic hitchhiking.

References

Allison, A. C. (1956). Sickle cells and evolution. *Scientific American, 195*, 87–94.

American Psychiatric Association (APA). (1980). *Diagnostic and statistical manual of mental disorders* (3rd ed.) (DSM-III). Washington, DC: Author.

American Psychiatric Association (APA). (1987). *Diagnostic and statistical manual of mental disorders* (3rd ed., revised) (DSM-III-R). Washington, DC: Author.

American Psychiatric Association (APA). (1994). *Diagnostic and statistical manual of mental disorders* (4th ed.) (DSM-IV). Washington, DC: Author.

American Psychiatric Association (APA). (2000). *Diagnostic and statistical manual of mental disorders* (4th ed., text revised) (DSM-IV-TR). Washington, DC: Author.

Anckarsater, H., & Cloninger, C. R. (2007). The genetics of empathy and its disorders. In T. Farrow, & P. Woodruff (Eds.), *Empathy in mental illness* (pp. 260–288). New York: Cambridge University Press.

Auyeung, B., Wheelwright, S., Allison, C., Atkinson, M., Samarawickrema, N., & Baron-Cohen, S. (2009). The children's empathy quotient and systemizing quotient: Sex differences in typical development and in autism spectrum conditions. *Journal of Autism and Developmental Disorders, 39*(11), 1509–1521. doi: 10.1007/s10803–009–0772-x.

Bachner-Melman, R., Zohar, A. H., Bacin-Schnoor, N., Elizur, Y., Nemanov, L., Gritsenko, I., & Ebstein, R. P. (2005). Link between vasopressin receptor AVP R1 promoter region microsatellites and measures of social behavior in humans. *Journal of Individual Differences, 26*(1), 2–10. doi: 10.1027/1614–0001.26.1.2.

Baron-Cohen, S. (1995). *Mindfulness: An essay on autism and theory of the mind.* Cambridge, MA: MIT Press.

Bartels, A., & Zeki, S. (2004). The neural correlates of maternal and romantic love. *NeuroImage, 21*, 1155–1166. doi: 10.1016/j.neuroimage.2003.11.003.

Barton, N. H. (2000). Genetic hitchhiking. *Philosophical Transactions of the Royal Society of London. Series B, Biological Sciences, 355*(1403), 1553–1562. doi: 10. 1098/rstb.2000.0716.

Bartz, J. A., & Hollander, E. (2006). The neuroscience of affiliation: Forging links between basic and clinical research on neuropeptides and social behavior. *Hormones and Behavior, 50,* 518–528. doi: 10.1016/j.yhbeh.2006.06.018.

Baumgartner, T., Heinrichs, M., Vonlanthen, A., Fischbacher, U., & Fehr, E. (2008). Oxytocin shapes the neural circuitry of trust and trust adaptation in humans. *Neuron, 58,* 639–650. doi: 10.1016/j.neuron.2008.04.009.

Beck, W. H. (1991). *William Beck assessment scale manual.* Chicago: Administrative Services.

Beattie, M. (1987). *Codependent no more.* Center City, MN: Hazelden.

Beattie, M. (1992). *Codependent no more. 2nd ed.* New York: MJF Books.

Beattie, M. (2009). *The new codependency.* New York: Simon & Shuster.

Begley, S. (2009). *The plastic mind: New science reveals our extraordinary potential to transform ourselves.* London: Constable & Robinson Ltd.

Belmonte, M. K., & Bourgeon, T. (2006). Fragile X syndrome and autism at the intersection of genetic and neural networks. *Nature Neuroscience, 9*(10), 1221–1225. doi: 10.1038/nn1765.

Blair, R. J. R. (2007). Subcortical brain systems in psychopathy: The amygdala and associated structures. In C. J. Patrick (Ed.), *Handbook of psychopathy* (pp. 296–312). New York, NY: The Guilford Press.

Bilder, R. M., Sabb, F. W., Cannon, T. D., London, E. D., Jentsch, J. D., Parker, D. S., et al. (2009). Phenomics: The systematic study of phenotypes on a genome-wide scale. *Neuroscience, 164*(1), 30–42. doi: 10.1016/j.neuroscience.2009.01.027.

Braiker, H. B. (2001). *The disease to please: Curing the people-pleasing syndrome.* New York: McGraw-Hill.

Brown, W. M., & Moore, C. (2000). Is prospective altruist-detection an evolved solution to the adaptive problem of subtle cheating in cooperative ventures? Supportive evidence using the Wason selection task. *Evolution and Human Behavior, 21,* 25–37. doi: 10.1016/S1090-5138(99)00018-5.

Buller, D. J. (2006). *Adapting minds: Evolutionary psychology and the persistent quest for human nature.* Cambridge, MA: MIT Press.

Bushnell, I. W. R., Sai, F., & Mullin, J. T. (1989). Neonatal recognition of the mother's face. *British Journal of Developmental Psychology, 7*(1), 3–15.

Carr, L., Lacoboni, M., Dubeau, M. C., Mazziotta, J. C., & Lenzi, G. L. (2003). Neural mechanisms of empathy in humans: A relay from neural systems for imitation to limbic areas. *Proceedings of the National Academy of Sciences USA, 100,* 5497–5502.

Cermak, T. L. (1986). *Diagnosing and treating co-dependence.* Minneapolis, MN: Johnston Institute Books.

Chakrabarti, S., & Fombonne, E. (2005). Pervasive developmental disorders in preschool children: Confirmation of high prevalence. *The American Journal of Psychiatry, 162,* 1133–1141.

Cleary, M. J. (1994). Reassessing the codependency movement: A response to Sorentino. *Health Care Management Review, 19*(1), 7–10.

Crockett, M.J., Clark, L., Hauser, M.D., & Robbins, T.W. (2010). Serotinin selectively influences moral judgment and behavior through effects on harm aversion. Proc Natl Acad Sci, 107(40):17433-8.

de Waal, F. (2006). Morally evolved: Primate social instincts, human morality, and the rise and fall of the "Veneer Theory." In S. Macedo, & O. Ober (Eds.), *Primates and philosophers: How morality evolved* (pp. 1–80). Princeton, NJ: Princeton University Press.

de Waal, F. (2008). Putting the altruism back in altruism: The evolution of empathy. *Annual Review of Psychology, 59,* 279–300. doi: 10.1146/annurev.psych.59.103006.093625.

Dear, G. E. (2002). The Holyoake codependency index: Further evidence of factorial validity. *Drug and Alcohol Review, 21,* 47–52. doi: 10.1080/09595230220119354.

Dear, G. E. (2004). Test-retest reliability of the Holyoake codependency index with Australian students. *Psychological reports, 94,* 482–484.

Dear, G. E., & Roberts, C. M. (2000). The Holyoake codependency index: Investigation of the factor structure and psychometric properties. *Psychological Reports, 87,* 991–1002.

Dear, G. E., & Roberts, C. M. (2005). Validation of the Holyoake codependency index. *The Journal of Psychology, 139*(4), 293–313.

Decety, J., & Jackson, P. L. (2004). The functional architecture of human empathy. *Behavioral and Cognitive Neuroscience Reviews, 3,* 71–100. doi: 10.1177/1534582304267187.

Decety, J., & Meyer, M. (2008). From emotion resonance to empathic understanding: A social developmental neuroscience account. *Development and Psychopathology, 20,* 1053–1080. doi:10.1017/S0954579408000503.

Dinstein, I., Gardner, J. L., Jazayeri, M., & Heeger, D. J. (2008). Executed and observed movements have different distributed representations in human aIPS. *Journal of Neuroscience, 28*(44), 11231–11239. doi:10.1523/JNEUROSCI.3585–08.2008.

Dolgin, E. (2009). Evolving heart. *The Scientist, 23*(8), 19. Retrieved August 25, 2009 from http://the-scientist.com/article/display/55844/

Doidge, N. (2007). *The brain that changes itself: Stories of personal triumph from the frontiers of brain science.* New York, NY: Penguin Books.

Donaldson, Z. R., & Young, L. J. (2008). Oxytocin, vasopressin, and the neurogenetics of sociality. *Science, 322*(5903), 900–904. doi: 10.1126/science.1158668.

Ebstein, R. P., Israel, S., Lerer, E., Uzefovsky, F., Shalev, I., Gritsenko, I., et al. (2009). Arginine vasopressin and oxytocin modulate human social behavior. *Annals of the New York Academy of Science, 1167,* 87–102. doi: 10.1111/j.1749–6632.2009.04541.x.

Eisenberg, N., & Fabes, R. A. (1990). Empathy: Conceptualization, measurement and relation to prosocial behavior. *Motiv Emotion, 14,* 131–149.

Fabes, R. A., & Eisenberg, N. (1998). *Meta-analyses and sex differences in children's and adolescents' prosocial behavior.* Arizona State University. Retrieved October 10, 2009 from www.public.asu.edu.~rafabes/meta.pdf.

Fischer, J., Spann, L., & Crawford, D. (1991). Measuring codependency. *Alcoholism Treatment Quarterly, 8,* 87–99. doi: 10.1300/J020V08N01_06.

Flavell, J. H. (2004). Theory-of-mind development: Retrospect and prospect. *Merrill-Palmer Quarterly, 50*(3), 274–290. doi: 10.1353/mpq.2004.0018.

Framingham Heart Study (2009). Retrieved September 15, 2009 from http://www.framinghamheartstudy.org/.

Friel, J. C. (1985). Co-dependency assessment inventory: A preliminary research tool. *Focus on Family and Chemical Dependency, 8,* 20–21.

Galanter, M., & Kleber, H. D. (2008). *The American Psychiatric Publishing Textbook of Substance Abuse Treatment* (4th ed.). Arlington, VA: American Psychiatric Publishing, Inc.

Gierymski, T., & Williams, T. (1986). Codependency. *Journal of Psychoactive Drugs, 19*(1), 7–13.

Gillberg, C., Cederlund, M., Lamberg, K., & Zeijlon, L. (2006). Brief report: "The autism epidemic" The registered prevalence of autism in a Swedish urban area. *Journal of Autism and Developmental Disorders, 36,* 429–435. doi: 10.1007/s10803–006–0081–6.

Giff, L., & Goff, P. (1998). Trapped in codependency. *Personnel Journal, 67,* 50–57.

Goldsmith, D. J., & Dun, S. A. (1997). Sex differences and similarities in the communication of social support. *Journal of Social and Personal Relationships, 14*(3): 317–337. doi: 10.1177/0265407597143003.

Hagerman, R. J. (2006). Lessons from fragile X regarding neurobiology, autism, and neurodegeneration. *Journal of Developmental and Behavioral Pediatrics, 27*(1), 63–74.

Hales, R. E., Yudofsky, S. C., & Gabbard, G. O. (Eds.). (2008). *The American Psychiatric Publishing Textbook of Psychiatry* (5th ed.). Arlington, VA: American Psychiatric Publishing, Inc.

Hamilton, W. D. (1964). The genetic evolution of social behaviour I, II. *Journal of Theoretical Biology, 7*, 1–52.

Harper, J., & Capdevila, C. (1990). Codependency: A critique. *Journal of Psychoactive Drugs, 22*(3), 285–292.

Harris, J. (2007). The evolutionary neurobiology, emergence and facilitation of empathy. In T. Farrow, & P. Woodruff (Eds.), *Empathy in mental illness* (pp. 168–186). New York: Cambridge University Press.

Haslam, N. (2003). Categorical versus dimensional models of mental disorder: The taxometric evidence. *Australian and New Zealand Journal of Psychiatry, 37*, 696–704. doi: 10.1080/j.1440–1614.2003.01258.x.

Hawks, J., Wang, E. T., Cochran, G. M., Harpending, H. C., & Moyzis, R. K. (2007). Recent acceleration of human adaptive evolution. *Proceedings of the National Academy of Sciences, 104*, 20753–20758. doi: 10.1073/pnas.0707650104.

Heinrichs, M., von Dawans, B., & Domes, G. (2009). Oxytocin, vasopressin, and human social behavior. *Frontiers in Neuroendocrinology, 30*, 548–557. doi: 10.1016/j.yfrne.2009.05.005.

Hughes-Hammer, C., Martsolf, D.S., & Zeller, R.A. (1998). Development and testing of the codependency assessment tool. *Archives of Psychiatric Nursing, 12*(5), 264–272.

Israel, S., Lerer, E., Idan, S., Uzefovsky, F., Riebold, M. E., Bachner-Melman, R., et al. (2008). Molecular genetic studies of the arginine vasopressin 1a receptor (arginine vasopressinR1a) and the oxytocin receptor (OXTR) in human behavior: From autism to altruism with some notes in between. In I. D. Newman, & R. Landgraf (Eds.), *Progress in Brain Research,* Vol. 170 (pp. 435–449). doi: 10.1016/30079–6123(08)00434–2.

Israel, S., Lerer, E., Idan, S., Uzefovsky, F., Riebold, M., Laiba, E., et al. (2009) The oxytocin receptor (OXTR) contributes to prosocial fund allocations in the dictator game and the social value orientations task. *PLoS ONE, 4*(5), e5535. doi: 10.1371/journal.pone.0005535.

Jabbi, M., Swart, M., & Keysers, C. (2007). Empathy for positive and negative emotions in the gustatory cortex. *Neuroimage, 34*, 1744–1753. doi: 10.1016/j.neuroimage.2006.10.032.

Jabbi, M., & Keysers, C. (2008). Inferior frontal gyrus activity triggers anterior insula response to emotional facial expressions. *Emotion, 8*(6), 775–780. doi: 10.1037/a0014194.

Kanazawa, S. (2004). The savanna principle. *Managerial and decision economics, 25*, 41–54. doi: 10.1002/mde.1130.

Kanazawa, S. (2006). Violent men have more sons: Further evidence for the generalized Trivers-Willard hypothesis (gTWH). *Journal of Theoretical Biology, 239*, 450–459. doi: 10.1016/j.jtbi.2005.08.010.

Kanazawa, S. (2008). Battered woman have more sons: A possible evolutionary reason why some battered women stay. *Journal of Evolutionary Psychology, 6*, 129–139. doi: 10.1556/JEP.2008.1007.

Kanazawa, S. (2008). Why human evolution pretty much stopped about 10,000 years ago. *Psychology Today.* Retrieved from http://www.psychologytoday.com/blog/the-scientific-fundamentalist/200810/why-human-evolution-pretty-much-stopped-about-10000-years-

Katz, S. J., & Liu, A. E. (1991). *Codependency conspiracy: How to break the recovery habit and take charge of your life*. New York, NY: Warner Books, Inc.

Kottke, J. L., Warren, L. W., Moffett, D., & Williams, R. (1993, April). *The meaning of codependency: Psychometric analysis of a construct.* Paper presented at the meeting of the Western Psychological Association, Phoenix, AZ.

Liepman, M. R., Parran, T. V., Farkas, K. J., & Lagos-Saez, M. (2009). Family involvement in addiction, treatment and recovery. In R. L. Ries, D. A. Fiellin, S. C. Miller, & R. Saitz (Eds.), *Principles of addiction medicine* (4th ed., pp. 857–868). Philadelphia, PA: Lippincott, Williams and Wilkins.

Linden, D. E. J. (2006). How psychotherapy changes the brain–the contribution of functional neuroimaging. *Molecular Psychiatry, 11*, 528–538. doi: 10.1038/sj.mp.4001816.

Loggia, M. L., Mogil, M. S., & Bushnell, M. C. (2008). Empathy hurts: Compassion for another increases both sensory and affective components of pain perception. *Pain, 36*(1), 168–176. doi: 10.1016/j.pain.2007.07.017.

Martsoff, D. S., Hughes-Hammer, C., Estok, P., & Zeller, R. A. (1999). Codependency in male and female helping professionals. *Archives of Psychiatric Nursing, 13*, 97–103. doi: 10.1016/S0883–9417(99)80026–0.

Maxmen, J. S., & Ward, N. G. (1995). *Essential psychopathology and its treatment.* New York: W. W. Norton.

McAndrew, F.T. (2002). New evolutionary perspectives on altruism: Multi-level selection and costly-signaling theories. Current Directions in Psychological Science, 11(2), 79–82.

McGuffin, P., Riley, B., & Plomin, R. (2001). Genomics and behavior: Toward behavioral genomics. Science, 291(5507), 1232–12–49. doi: 10.1126/science.1057264.

Meeks, T. W., & Jeste, D. V. (2009). Neurobiology of wisdom: A literature overview. *Archives of General Psychiatry, 66*(4), 355–365.

Mellody, P., Miller, A. W., & Miller, J. K. (1989) *Facing codependency: What it is, where it comes from, how it sabotages our lives.* New York: Harper Collins Publishers.

Miller, J. K. (1994). The codependency concept: Does it offer a solution for the spouses of alcoholics? *Journal of Substance Abuse Treatment, 11*(44), 339–345.

Morgan, J. P., Jr. (1991). What is codependency? *Journal of Clinical Psychology, 47*(5), 720–729.

Morris, C. A. (2006). Williams Syndrome. *GeneReviews.* Retrieved 5/31/09 from www.ncbi.nih.gov/bookshelf/br.fcgi?book=gene&part=williams.

National Institutes of Health. (2008). *Medical Encyclopedia: Williams Syndrome.* Retrieved May 31, 2009 from www.nlm.nih.gov/medlineplus/ency/article/001116.htm.

O'Brien, P. E., & Gaborit, M. (1992). Codependency: A disorder separate from chemical dependency. *Journal of Clinical Psychology, 48*, 129–136. doi:10.1002/1097–4679(199201)48:1<129::AID-JCLP2270480118>3.0.CO;2-C.

O'Gorman, P. (1993). Codependency explored: A social movement in search of definition and treatment. *Psychiatric Quarterly, 64*(2), 199–212.

Potter-Efron, R. T., & Potter-Efron, P. S. (1989). Assessment of codependency with individuals from alcoholic and chemically dependent families. *Alcoholism Treatment Quarterly, 6*, 37–57.

Premack, D., & Woodruff, G. (1978). Does the chimpanzee have a theory of mind. *Behavioral and Brain Sciences, 1*(4), 515–526.

Porges, S. W. (2001). The polyvagal theory: Phylogenetic substrates of a social nervous system. *International Journal of Psychophysiology, 42*, 123–146. doi: 10.1016/S0167–8760(01)00162–3.

Rice, J. S. (1996). *A disease of one's own: Psychotherapy, addiction and the emergence of co-Dependency*. New Brunswick, NJ: Transactions Publishers.

Rizzolatti, G., & Craighero, L. (2004). The mirror-neuron system. *Annual Review of Neuroscience, 27*, 169–192. doi: 10.1146/annurev.neuro.27.070203.144230.

Rochat, P. (2004) *The infant's world*. Cambridge, MA: Harvard University Press.

Roehling, P. V., & Gaumond, E. (1996). Reliability and validity of the Codependent Questionnaire. *Alcoholism Treatment Quarterly, 14*, 85–95.

Rotunda, R. J., West, L., & O'Farrell, T. J. (2004). Enabling behavior in a clinical sample of alcohol-dependent clients and their partners. *Journal of Substance Abuse Treatment, 26*, 269–276. doi: 10.1016/j.jsat.2004.01.007.

Sabb, F. W., Bearden, C. E., Ghan, D. C., Parker, D. S., Freimer, N., & Bilder, R. M. (2008). A collaborative knowledge base for cognitive phenomics. *Molecular Psychiatry, 13*, 350–360. doi: 10.1038/sj.mp.4002124.

Santos, M., & Szathmary, E. (2008). Genetic hitchhiking can promote the initial spread of strong altruism. *BioMed Central Evolutionary Biology, 8*, 281. doi:10.1186/1471–2148-8–281.

Schaef, A. W. (1986). *Co-dependence: Misunderstood—mistreated*. New York, NY: HarperCollins Publishers.

Schmidt, N. B., Kotov, R., & Joiner, T. E., Jr. (2004). *Taxometrics: Toward a new scheme for psychopathology*. Washington, DC: American Psychological Association.

Schulte-Rüther, M, Markowitsch, H. J., Fink, G. R., Piefke, M. (2007). Mirror neuron and theory of mind mechanisms involved n face-to-face interactions: A functional magnetic resonance imaging approach to empathy. *Journal of Cognitive Neuroscience, 19*, 1354–1372. doi: 10.1162/jocn.2007.19.8.1354.

Seitz, R. J., Schäfer, R., Scherfeld, D., Friederichs, S., Popp, K., Wittsack, H. J., et al. (2008). Valuating other people's emotional face expression: A combined functional magnetic resonance imaging and electroencephalography study. *Neuroscience, 152*(3), 713–722. doi: 10.1016/j.neuroscience.2007.10.066.

Shamay-Tsoory, S., Aharon-Peretz, J., & Perry, D. (2009). Two systems for empathy: A double dissociation between emotional and cognitive empathy in inferior frontal gyrus versus ventromedial prefrontal lesions. *Brain, 132*, 617–617. doi: 10.1093/brain/awn279.

Shirtcliff, E. A., Vitacco, M. J., Graf, A. R., Gostisha, A. J., Merz, J. L., & Zahn-Waxler, C. (2009). Neurobiology of empathy and callousness: Implications for the development of antisocial behavior. *Behavioral Sciences and the Law, 27*, 137–171. doi: 10.1002/bsl.862.

Slater, A., & Quinn, P.C. (2001). Face recognition in the newborn infant. *Infant and Child Development, 10*, 21–24. doi: 10.1002/icd.241.

Stafford, L. L. (2001). Is codependency a meaningful concept? *Issues in Mental Health Nursing, 22*, 273–286. doi: 10.1080/01612840121607.

Stanton, D., & Heath, A. W. (2005). Family-based treatment: Stages and outcomes. In R. J. Frances, S. J. Miller, & A. H. Mack (Eds.), *Clinical textbook of addictive disorders* (3rd ed., pp. 528–548). New York: The Guilford Press.

Strain, E. C., & Anthony, J. C. (2009). Substance-related disorders: Introduction and overview. In B. J. Sadock, V. A. Sadock, & P. Ruiz (Eds.), *Kaplan & Sadock's Comprehensive textbook of psychiatry*, Vol. 1 (9th ed., pp. 1237–1267). Philadelphia, PA: Lippincott, Williams and Wilkins.

Straus, M. A. (1999). The controversy over domestic violence by women: A methodological, theoretical, and sociology of science analysis. In X. B. Arriaga, & S. Oskamp (Eds.), *Violence in intimate relationships* (pp. 17–44). Thousand Oaks, CA: Sage.

Strathearn, L., Li, J., Fonagy, P., & Montague, P. R. (2008). What's in a smile? Maternal brain responses to infant facial cues. *Pediatrics, 122*(1), 40–51. doi: 10.1542/peds. 2007–1566.

Subby, R. (1987). *Lost in the shuffle: The co-dependent reality*. Deerfield Beach, FL: Health Communications.

Thompson, R. A., Meyer, S., & McGinley, M. (2005) Understanding values in relationship: The development of conscience. In M. Killen, & J. Smetana (Eds.), *Handbook of moral development* (pp. 267–297). Hove, UK: Psychology Press.

Trivers, R. L. (1971). The evolution of reciprocal altruism. *The Quarterly Review of Biology*, *46*(1), 35–57.

Wegscheider-Cruse, S., & Cruse, J. R. (1990). *Understanding codependency*. Deerfield Beach, FL: Health Communications.

Widiger, T. A. (2007). Alternatives to DSM-IV Axis II. In W. T. O'Donohue, K. A. Fowler, & S. O. Lilienfield (Eds.), *Personality disorders: Toward the DSM-V* (pp. 21–40). Thousand Oaks, CA: Sage Publications, Inc.

Wilson, D. S. (1997). Altruism and organism: Disentangling the themes of multilevel selection theory. *The American Naturalist, 150*, S122–S134. doi: 10.1086/286053.

Zahn-Waxler, C., Hollenbeck, B., & Radke-Yarrow, M. (1984). The origins of empathy and altruism. In L. W. Fox, & L. D. Mickey (Eds.), *Advances in animal welfare science* (pp. 21–39). Washington, DC: Humane Society of the United States.

Zak, P. J., Stanton, A. A., & Ahmadi, S. (2007). Oxytocin increases generosity in humans. *Plos ONE, 2*(11): e1128. doi: 10.1371/journal.pone.0001128.

PART II

PSYCHIATRIC IMPLICATIONS OF PATHOLOGICAL ALTRUISM

CHAPTER 5

SELF-ADDICTION AND SELF-RIGHTEOUSNESS[1]

David Brin

KEY CONCEPTS

- The word, "addiction" appears to limit our perception of a wider realm—*general behavioral reinforcement* within the human brain. If neurochemical processes reinforce "good" habits such as love, loyalty, joy in music or skill, then addiction should be studied in a larger context.
- If a mental state causes pleasurable reinforcement, there will be a tendency to return to it. Meditation, adoration, gambling, rage, and indignation might all, at times, be "mental addictions."
- This more general view of reinforcement suggests potential ways to reduce or eliminate drug addiction, as well as self-induced rage.
- Self-righteousness and indignation may sometimes be as much about chemical need as valid concerns about unfair actions. Among other outcomes, this may cause "pathologically altruistic" behavior.
- Moderate-progressives who seek problem-solving pragmatism may get a boost if it were proved that dogmatic self-righteousness is often an "addiction."

Generalizing the Word "Addiction"

For years I have followed—albeit as an outsider—advances that investigate *reinforcement processes in the human brain,* especially those that are active in mediating pleasure response. This falls generally into research on addiction: some of the august workers who have spared time to talk to me about this topic have included Hans Breiter, Rich Wilcox, Stanley Glick, Jonathan D. Cohen, Alan I. Leshner, Gregory Berns, Dan Ariely, Steven Grant, and Seth Boatwright-Horowitz. Alas, like the subject of global warming, research related to addiction draws so much political heat that it's a wonder anything can get done at all.

Despite some important accomplishments, I believe the field of addiction may be missing an important component area—that of *volitionally or habitually self-stimulated secretion*—or, more simply, *self-doping.* In other words, the power that individuals have to trigger the release of psychoactive chemicals simply by entering into certain types of consciousness or states of mind.

I am not talking about mysticism or New Age levels of awareness. True, some workers have measured the neurochemical effects of meditation and other Eastern arts. But this ignores a great many other pleasurable or semipleasurable mental states that require considerably less discipline to access than the meditative plateau. States that are accessible to nearly everyone, almost every day.

Of course, this overall effect has been known ever since William James wrote *Varieties of Religious Experience*. But I'd like to suggest strong reasons to study autonomous self-stimulation along new directions that are tangentially related to those already being pursued. For one thing, new research trends seem to offer potential hope for getting out of the horrible "Drug War." For another, it might offer useful insights into why some pathologically altruistic individuals pursue well-meaning behavior that ultimately harms those they mean to help.[2]

Progress in Studying "Self-addiction"

Of course, we know that individuals who are addicted to psychoactive chemicals can often wind up behaving in socially harmful ways while in pursuit of their high. But what of many *other* compulsively harmful behaviors we see practiced around us? Might some of them have similar roots? What if many irrationally harmful, self-defeating, or "codependent" actions arise from attempts to trigger a self-doped pleasure response?

Consider studies of gambling. Researchers led by Dr. Hans Breiter of Massachusetts General Hospital examined with functional magnetic resonance imaging (fMRI) which brain regions activate when volunteers won games of chance—regions that overlapped with those responding to cocaine. "Gambling produces a similar pattern of activity to cocaine in an addict," according to Breiter (*Newsweek*, 2001).

Moving along the spectrum toward activity that we consider more "normal"—neuroscientists at Harvard have found a striking similarity between the brain states of people trying to predict financial rewards (for example, via the stock market) and the brains of cocaine and morphine users.

Along parallel lines, prior to the 2004 presidential election, researchers at Emory University monitored brain activity while asking staunch Democrats and Republicans to evaluate information that threatened their preferred candidate. "We did not see any increased activation of the parts of the brain normally engaged during reasoning," said Drew Westen, Emory's director of clinical psychology. "Instead, a network of emotion circuits lit up... reaching biased conclusions by ignoring information that could not rationally be discounted. Significantly, activity spiked in circuits involved in *reward*, similar to what addicts experience when they get a fix," Westen explained (Westen, Blagov, Harenski, Kilts, & Hamann, 2006).

How far can this spectrum be extended? Perhaps all the way into those realms of behavior—and mental states—that we label as wholesome? Rich Wilcox, of the University of Texas, says: "Recovery process in addiction is based to a great extent on cognitively mediated changes in brain chemistry of the frontal/prefrontal cortex system. Furthermore... there is even a surprising amount of literature cited in PubMed suggesting that prayer also induces substantial changes in brain chemistry" (R. Wilcox, personal communication).

Clearly, this spectrum of "addiction" includes reinforcement of behaviors that are utterly beneficial and that have important value to us, such as our love for our children. I get a jolt every time I smell my kids' hair, for instance. The "Aw!" that many people give when they see a baby smile is accompanied by skin flushes and iris dilation, reflecting physiological pleasure. Similar jolts come to people from music, sex, exercise, and the application of a skill.

A great deal of recent research has danced along the edges of this area (Brooks, 2005; Dietrich & McDaniel, 2004; Elias, 2004; Graham, 2005; Lim, Murphy, & Young, 2004; Markey, 2003; Yao et al., 2005). But the core topic appears to have been neglected. I'm talking about the way that countless millions of humans either habitually or volitionally pursue drug-like reinforcement cycles—either for pleasure or through cycles of withdrawal and insatiability that mimic addiction—purely as a function of entering an addictive *frame of mind.*

For a majority, indeed, this process goes unnoticed because there is no pathology. Reiterating; it is simply "getting high on life." Happy or at least contented people, who lead decent lives, partake in these wholesome addictive cycles, which have escaped much attention from researchers simply because these cycles operate at the highest levels of human functionality. (It is easy to verify that there is something true underlying the phrase "addicted to love.")

This wholesomeness should no longer mask or exclude such powerfully effective mental states from scientific scrutiny. For example, we might learn more about the role of oxytocin in preventing the down-regulating or tolerance effects that exacerbate drug addiction. Does this moderating effect provide the more wholesome, internally generated "addictions" with their long-lasting power? Suppose that, instead of preaching to substance abusers that they should "get high on life," we could actually train them in self-triggered endorphin/dopamine-releasing methods? Methods the rest of us learn unconsciously in childhood. These would be *better* addictions that do not suffer from receptor down-regulating and other problems, such as depression or insatiability.

Even more attractive would be to shine light on patterns of volitional or habitual addictive mentation that are *not* helpful, functional, or desirable. Gambling has already been mentioned. *Rage* is obviously another of these harmful patterns, which clearly have a chemical-reinforcement component. Many angry people report deriving addictive pleasure from *fury,* and this is one reason why they return to the state, again and again. Thrill-seeking can also be like this, when it follows a pathology of down-regulating satiability. Ernst Fehr, Brian Knutson, and John Hibbing have written about the pleasure-reinforcement of *revenge,* which Hollywood films tap incessantly in plot lines that give audiences a vicarious thrill of payback against villains-who-deserve-it.

This, indeed, may be a key element behind pathologically altruistic activities— that is, well-meaning efforts that actually worsen the very situation they are meant to help. Above all, it contributes to understanding why the pathological altruist may be incapable of error-correction, refining the well-intended activity to improve its actual, rather than delusional, helpfulness: Because the superficial goal is less important than the real thing sought—an addictive state of mind.

The Most Common, but Unstudied, Form of Self-addiction

So far, we are on ground that is supported by copious (if peripheral) research. If nothing else, at least there should be an effort to step back and notice the forest for the trees, generalizing a view of this whole field as we've described it so far to form a general paradigm of self-reinforcement.

Only now, taking this into especially important new territory, we should consider something more specific. An emotional and psychological pathology that both illustrates the general point and demands attention on its own account: that of *self-righteous indignation*. (For the purposes of this chapter, we shall assume that many of the pathologically altruistic also fall into this category.)

We all know self-righteous people. (And, if we are honest, many of us will admit having wallowed occasionally in self-righteousness ourselves.) It is a familiar and rather normal human condition, supported—even promulgated— by messages in mass media. Although there are many drawbacks, self-righteousness can also be heady, seductive, and even . . . well . . . addictive. Any truly honest person will admit that the state *feels good*. The pleasure of knowing, with subjective certainty, that you are *right* and your opponents are deeply, despicably *wrong*. Or, that your method of helping others is so purely motivated and correct that all criticism can be dismissed with a shrug, along with any contradicting evidence.

> Sanctimony, or a sense of righteous outrage, can feel so intense and delicious that many people actively seek to return to it, again and again.

Sanctimony, or a sense of righteous outrage, can feel so intense and delicious that many people actively seek to return to it, again and again. Moreover, as Westin and his colleagues have found, this trait, when applied to politics, crosses all boundaries of ideology (Brin, 1998). Indeed, one could look at our present-day political landscape and argue that a relentless addiction to indignation may be one of the chief drivers of obstinate dogmatism and an inability to negotiate pragmatic solutions to a myriad modern problems. It may be the ultimate propellant behind the current "culture war."

If there is *any* underlying truth to such an assertion, then acquiring a deeper understanding of this one issue of addictive self-righteousness may help us deal with countless others, ranging from codependency to outrageously self-defeating political partisanship.

A Set of Core Questions

Let me boil this down to a key set of questions, not only for researchers in addiction and psychologically active brain chemistry, but for anyone else interested in the topic.

1. Do you perceive—as I do—a gap in addiction-related research, when it comes to studying cycles of reinforcement that take place entirely within the brain, without external stimulation?
2. Might studying the most wholesome cycles of "addictive" reinforcement—such as love, music, or skill—result in a wider perspective on a natural human process?
3. Might "addiction" be viewed as the hijacking of natural reinforcement processes by unwholesome—or socially disapproved—substitutes such as drugs or rage? Would it help to better understand environmental circumstances, as well as genetic or epigenetic biological predispositions?

4. Might this broadened knowledge of addiction and addictive behaviors allow for retraining the brain, even in those with biological predispositions, to allow people to learn healthier forms of auto-reinforcement? This could form the basis of new therapies such as acquisition of new skills, anger management, access to wholesome thrills, or diversion toward sanely satisfying altruistic activities.
5. Would such a broadened definition and broadening of research efforts have positive social effects, bringing more realistic expectations and strategies to the "Drug War?"
6. Might it be worthwhile to demonstrate that *indignation* and *self-righteousness* are clinically measurable physiological states, reinforced in some by the semivolitional or habitual release of psychologically active chemicals in the brain?
7. If we could show clearly, publicly, and decisively that indignation and self-righteousness can be addictions, might this help empower moderates in every political movement, so that negotiation and pragmatism would become more fashionable than dogmatic purity and outrage?
8. Could addictive indignation and self-righteousness underlie at least some forms of pathological altruism?

Difficulties

There are many reasons why researchers have shied away from studying internal stimulation in favor of external stimulations, like gambling and drugs. As the University of Southern California's Joseph Miller has written in our correspondence on the subject:

> There are incredible problems with any sort of research which seeks to quantify a mental state. It is orders of magnitude more difficult to study internal stimuli than external stimuli. Subjects lie, often without any real consciousness of the act. And mental states can change more rapidly than relatively slow procedures like MRI can hope to capture. And subjects are highly distractible.
>
> Having said that, there is ongoing work along the lines you suggest, although it seems to be more directed at gambling, drug addictive states, internal religious states, etc. One way to approach this is to have the subject engage in some behavior which naturally requires the mental state you are trying to study, e.g., simulated slot machines for studying the gambling response etc . . . . I can imagine having a right-winger read pronouncements of UN rep, Ambassador Bolton—(or Hillary Clinton?)—and see what brain changes are observable. I'm sure the "usual suspects" would be involved, e.g., *ventral striatum*, aka *nucleus accumbens*.

Putting aside specific politics, one could offer a dozen suggestions for how blind or double-blind experiments might be performed. Subjects might name their own emblems of outrage, for example, choosing in advance the symbols and people most likely to trigger their own indignation. Experiments could narrow down the range and subjectivity of studying self-induced mental states. After all, in the beginning, we would not be seeking to "cure" anybody—only to get a better handle on how these cycles work.

Might those who are addicted to indignation exhibit different patterns of trigger-response, latency, persistence, and recovery than people who are merely righteous on occasion? These patterns might be similar to the way that a stiff drink has measurably different effects upon a social drinker than an alcoholic.

In a related fashion, perhaps individuals who have fallen into codependent behavioral patterns might be studied to see whether the "usual suspect" neurological reward system is activated by codependent-related activities.

> Might those who are addicted to indignation exhibit different patterns of trigger-response, latency, persistence, and recovery than people who are merely righteous on occasion?

Suppose the expected, poststimulation high is blocked by chemical inhibitors. Might indignation addicts and codependents show a very different set of behaviors when the expected high is inhibited, than a merely righteous or helpful person would display, even if they agreed about the triggering dogma or image? Researchers might use knowledge gained from studying the dysfunction of drug addicts and alcoholics, where behaviors are explicit, measurable, and objective. Could not potentially vast social effects come simply from demonstrating such patterns, thereby showing that indignation and perhaps even codependence are pernicious, addictive habits?

Why the Issue Has Grown Urgent

Beyond drug addiction and codependence lie the deeply pernicious aspects of political ideology. We have entered an era of rising ideological division and a "culture war" that increasingly stymies our knack for problem-solving. Nowadays, few adversarial groups seem capable of negotiating peaceful consensus solutions to problems, especially with opponents who are perceived as even *more* unreasonably dogmatic than they are. This cycle is often driven by the irate stubbornness of a few vigorous leaders. After all, the indignant have both stamina and dedication, helping them take high positions in advocacy organizations, from Left to Right.

Might recent exaggerated levels of bilious social division be partly attributed to an all-too-human tendency to fall into addictive patterns of self-doping, by wallowing in a pleasurable mental state? A state that undermines our ability to empathize with opponents, accept criticism, or negotiate practical solutions to problems? May I boldly suggest that this insidious type of reinforcement may cause *vastly more overall social harm* than every illegal drug on the street?

> Suppose it were openly *demonstrated* that the self-righteous mental state is reinforced chemically by hijacking internal "addiction" mechanisms. Given enough publicity, *might such a finding help empower pragmatists and moderates of all kinds?*

At risk of growing repetitious, suppose it were openly *demonstrated* that the self-righteous mental state is reinforced chemically by hijacking internal "addiction" mechanisms. Given enough publicity, *might such a finding help empower pragmatists and moderates of all kinds?*

Certainly, some will oppose such research, calling it improper interference by science into political realms that are best left to individual subjectivity. Too late. Already, serious effort has been expended in studying political inclinations using fMRI. Ideologues across the spectrum are studying methods of "mind control." Obviously, this is an area that will receive ever greater attention in coming years, like it or not.

At least the aim here is to *lessen* the influence of indignant dogmatism and empower those in society who are inclined toward calm and judgment.

Conclusion

Can Science Rescue Us From Dogmatism?

I have for some years written to researchers in related fields, asking about ways to study abuse of natural reinforcement processes. It would seem the addictive properties of rage and self-righteousness could easily be either proved or disproved. (And yes, of course, I might be wrong!) A number of researchers have kindly given me time. Some offered enthusiastic encouragement. I have even given a talk on the subject, in 2009, at the National Institute on Drug Abuse.

Nevertheless, as we observe a relentless increase in irrationally indignant, self-righteous, or pathologically altruistic behavior everywhere in society and across all political spectra, I cannot help but wish for research in this area to happen with much greater urgency. That is, of course, unless this urgency arises from an addictive sense of self-importance, mediated and reinforced by the reward systems of a pathologically altruistic brain.

Late Note

Recent research supports the general thrust of this article. A major roadblock in any negotiation can often be that each side believes their opponent's position is unmovable, according to a group of researchers in Israel. Stand-offs, they say, can end if those involved think their counterparts can adopt a flexible mindset. Eran Halperin of the Interdisciplinary Center Herzliya in Israel and colleagues surveyed 500 Israeli Jews on whether they believed groups of people had fixed natures, and on their attitudes towards the Palestinians. Volunteers who believed that groups could change tended to have more positive attitudes towards a negotiated peace process. Halperin found that just priming individuals with the notion that their opponents might be flexible enhances flexibility in the test subjects. According to Halperin, this suggests that "when you make people believe that groups have malleable characteristics, they change their attitudes towards the other group and are more willing to make specific compromises for peace." (Marshall, 2011)

Notes

1. Originally published in somewhat different form online at http://www.davidbrin.com/addiction.htm as "An Open Letter to Researchers of Addiction, Brain Chemistry, and Social Psychology," Copyright © 2005. All rights reserved.

2. Pathological altruism in this chapter follows the definition of Homant and Kennedy (Chapter 14). It is characterized as "helpfulness" that has one or more of the following traits:

- It is unnecessary or uncalled for. Either the distress in the other is not sufficient to warrant the costs or risks to the actor, or there are better ways of meeting the other's needs.
- Or, it is performed by an actor who is likely to complain about the consequences of the altruism, yet continues doing it anyway.
- Or, it is motivated by irrationality or symptoms of psychological disturbance.
- Or, it is of no real benefit to anyone, and a reasonable person would have foreseen this.

References

Begley, S. (2001). Your brain on poker. *Newsweek*. Retrieved http://www.newsweek.com/id/79003

Brin, D. (1998). *The transparent society: Will technology force us to choose between privacy and freedom?* New York: Basic Books.

Brooks, M. (2005). 13 things that do not make sense: The placebo effect. Retrieved from http://www.newscientist.com/article/mg18524911.600-13-things-that-do-not-make-sense.html?full=true

Dietrich, A., & McDaniel, W. (2004). Endocannabinoids and exercise. *British Medical Journal*, 38(5), 536–541.

Elias, P. (2004). Brain scans may unlock candidates' appeal. *Live Science*. Retrieved from http://www.livescience.com/health/brain_politics_041029.html\

Graham, S. (2005). Brain scans help scientists 'read' minds. *Scientific American*. Retrieved from http://www.scientificamerican.com/article.cfm?id=brain-scans-helps-scienti

Lim, M., Murphy, A., & Young, L. (2004). Ventral striatopallidal oxytocin and vasopressin V1a receptors in the monogamous prairie vole (*Microtus ochrogaster*). *The Journal of Comparative Neurology*, 468(4), 555–570.

Markey, S. (2003). Monkeys show sense of fairness, study says. Retrieved from http://www.primates.com/monkeys/fairness.html

Marshall, M. (August 25, 2011). To resolve conflict, believe that people can change. New Scientist. Retrieved from http://www.newscientist.com/article/dn20833-to-resolve-conflict-believe

Westen, D., Blagov, P. S., Harenski, K., Kilts, C., & Hamann, S. (2006). The neural basis of motivated reasoning: An fMRI study of emotional constraints on political judgment during the U.S. Presidential election of 2004. *Journal of Cognitive Neuroscience*, 18(11), 1947–1958.

Yao, L., McFarland, K., Fan, P., Jiang, Z., Inoue, Y., & Diamond, I. (2005). Activator of G protein signaling 3 regulates opiate activation of protein kinase A signaling and relapse of heroin-seeking behavior. *Proceedings of the National Academy of Sciences*, 102(24), 8746–8751.

CHAPTER 6

PATHOLOGICAL ALTRUISM AND PERSONALITY DISORDER

Thomas A. Widiger and Jennifer Ruth Presnall

KEY CONCEPTS

- The Five-Factor Model of personality can be used to describe adaptive and maladaptive variants of altruism.
- Research suggests that maladaptive altruism is a component of dependent personality disorder.
- Case studies illustrate how maladaptive altruism, combined with differing levels of neuroticism, may impact treatment.

THE PURPOSE OF this chapter is to understand pathological altruism from the perspective of personality theory and research. We will begin with a description of the general model of personality that we will be working from, followed by a discussion of pathological altruism from the perspective of this model.

Everybody has a personality, or a characteristic manner of thinking, feeling, behaving, and/or relating to others. These personality traits are often felt to be integral to each person's sense of self, as they involve what persons value, what they do, and what they are like almost every day throughout much of their lives. Almost every personality trait can be understood in terms of the Five-Factor model (FFM). The FFM was originally derived from studies of the English dictionary, with an aim toward developing a comprehensive lexicon of personality structure (Ashton & Lee, 2001). The relative importance of a personality trait is indicated by the number of terms developed within a language to describe the different magnitudes and nuances of that trait, and the structure of the traits is evident by the empirical relationship among these trait terms. Lexical studies have been conducted on many languages (e.g., Czech, Dutch, Filipino, German, Hebrew, Hungarian, Italian, Korean, Polish, Russian, Spanish, and Turkish), and this research has confirmed the existence of the FFM domains (Ashton & Lee, 2001). These five broad domains have been identified as neuroticism, extraversion (vs. introversion), openness to experience, agreeableness (vs. antagonism), and conscientiousness (McCrae & Costa, 2003).

Considerable empirical support exists for the construct validity of the FFM, including multivariate behavior genetic support for the heritability of the personality structure, childhood antecedents, temporal stability across the lifespan, and cross-cultural validity, both through emic studies that consider the trait terms indigenous to a particular culture and etic studies that consider the validity of a particular model of personality applied to the culture (Widiger & Trull, 2007).

Each of these five broad domains has been differentiated into six facets by Costa and McCrae (1992) through their construction of and research with the NEO Personality Inventory-Revised (NEO PI-R). For example, the broad domain of agreeableness (vs. antagonism) includes such facets as trust, straight-forwardness, compliance, modesty, tender-mindedness, and, of most relevance for this text, altruism.

Persons characterized by moderately high levels of altruism "have an active concern for others' welfare as shown in generosity, consideration of others, and a willingness to assist others in need of help" (Costa & McCrae, 1992, p. 18). All persons vary in the extent to which they can be said to be characteristically high or low in altruism. Women are, on average, more altruistic than men (Costa, Terracciano, & McCrae, 2001). Canadians think they are more altruistic than they really are, whereas Americans think they are less altruistic than they really are (McCrae & Terracciano, 2006). In a comparison of levels of altruism across 36 different countries, the most altruistic persons were from Canada, the least were from Japan (McCrae, 2002). However, it should be emphasized that the overlap in the distributions of levels of altruism across both gender and country are quite substantial. In other words, a substantial proportion of the population of men and Japanese are characteristically very altruistic.

In modern Western society, it is thought to be better for the person (and for those around him or her) to be altruistic than not to be. However, Widiger, Costa, and McCrae (2002) have suggested that each of the 60 poles of the 30 facets of the FFM have both adaptive and maladaptive variants. For example, one of the facets of agreeableness is trust. It is generally adaptive and beneficial to be trusting (high in trust), but not to the point of being characteristically gullible. Similarly, it can also be adaptive and beneficial to be skeptical (low in trust), but not to the point of being consistently mistrustful and paranoid.

> It is generally adaptive and beneficial to be trusting (high in trust), but not to the point of being characteristically gullible.

The same can be said for the trait of altruism. It is generally good to be giving, helpful, and even generous (high in altruism), but not to the point of suffering numerous debilitating consequences secondary to a characteristically self-sacrificing selflessness. Always placing oneself second to the interests, desires, needs, and whims of others will clearly result in mounting losses and accumulating deprivations, and at the most extreme, perhaps even victimization and abuse.

It is "when personality traits are inflexible and maladaptive and cause significant functional impairment or subjective distress [that] they constitute Personality Disorders" (American Psychiatric Association [APA], 2000, p. 686). The *Diagnostic and Statistical Manual of Mental Disorders, 4th Edition, Text Revision* (DSM-IV-TR; APA, 2000) is the official nomenclature for the classification and diagnosis of mental disorders. Included within DSM-IV-TR are ten officially recognized personality disorders, one of which is the Dependent Personality Disorder (DPD). Well before ever considering the DSM-IV-TR personality disorders as maladaptive variants of the FFM, Costa and McCrae (1985) had suggested that "agreeableness can also assume a pathological form, in which it is usually seen as dependency" (p. 12). Pathological altruism (self-sacrifice) is indeed one of the key features of this personality disorder. As expressed in the text of DSM-IV-TR, persons with this disorder "are willing to submit to what others want, even if the demands are unreasonable" (APA, 2000, p. 722). "They may make extraordinary self-sacrifices or tolerate verbal, physical, or sexual abuse" (APA, 2000, p. 722).

> Always placing oneself second to the interests, desires, needs, and whims of others will clearly result in mounting losses and accumulating deprivations, and at the most extreme, perhaps even victimization and abuse.

Dependency and Altruism

There is compelling empirical support to consider DPD as a maladaptive variant of the domain and facets of FFM agreeableness, including the facet of altruism, as indicated in studies of clinicians' ratings of prototypic cases of DPD, researchers' descriptions of prototypic cases, and peers ratings of persons with dependent personality traits (Presnall, Edmundson, & Widiger, in press). However, most self-report inventory studies have failed to confirm the expected relationship between altruism and dependency (Bornstein & Cecero, 2000; Miller & Lynam, 2008; Samuel & Widiger, 2008), leading some to question the validity of the hypothesized association (Miller & Lynam, 2008).

The weak to inconsistent relationship within self-report measure inventory research appears to be due largely to reliance on the NEO-PI-R (Costa & McCrae, 1992) for the assessment of agreeableness. The NEO-PI-R was constructed to provide a measure of normal personality functioning. Haigler and Widiger (2001) indicated that 83% of the NEO-PI-R agreeableness items assess an adaptive rather than a maladaptive trait. They constructed an experimentally altered version of the NEO-PI-R by inserting words into the items to alter the adaptive items into maladaptive items, without otherwise altering their content. For example, the NEO-PI-R altruism items "I try to be courteous to everyone I meet," "Some people think of me as cold and calculating" (keyed false), "I think of myself as a charitable person," "Some people think I'm selfish and egotistical" (keyed false), and "I go out of my way to help others if I can" (Costa & McCrae, 1992, p. 72) all describe behavior for which it would be preferable (or adaptive) to endorse the item in the altruistic direction. The experimentally altered versions of each respective item were "I am overly courteous to everyone I meet," "I can be cold and calculating when it's necessary" (keyed negatively), "I am so charitable that I give more than I can afford," "Most people think that I take good care of my own needs" (keyed negatively), and "I have sacrificed my own needs to help others." The correlations of agreeableness with three independent measures of DPD increased from 0.04, 0.17, and 0.04 using the NEO-PI-R to 0.57, 0.66, and 0.45, respectively, using the experimentally altered version. These findings were subsequently replicated and extended to additional measures of trait dependency by Presnall et al. (in press).

Pathological Altruism and Abuse

Persons who are pathologically altruistic are so selfless that they are prone to being used, exploited, and victimized by others. They may even subject themselves to abuse, humiliation, degradation, or financial ruin. However, it can at times be quite difficult to determine whether such behaviors reflect a personality trait or a situational reaction to a punitive, controlling, dictatorial, or threatening environment (Bornstein, 2006; Widiger, 1995).

A proposal for DSM-III-R (APA, 1987) was a diagnosis titled Masochistic Personality Disorder, which included such features as "remains in relationships in which others exploit, abuse, or take advantage of him or her, despite opportunities to alter the situation," "almost always sacrifices own interests for those of others," and "rejects help, gifts, or favors so as not to be a burden on others" (Work Group to Revise DSM-III, 1985, p. 134), all of which would be seen in persons characterized by a pathological altruism. This proposed diagnosis generated considerable controversy as it could (and would likely) be applied to some women who are within physically abusive relationships. It might stigmatize unfairly many of these women, suggesting that perhaps they were seeking or desiring the abuse, perhaps even effectively blaming the women for the harm they were receiving from others (Caplan, 1984).

There are even historical examples within the scientific literature of a masochistic diagnosis being applied to victims of spouse abuse (e.g., Snell, Rosenwald, & Robey, 1964). It was largely for this reason that the masochistic diagnosis failed to receive official recognition and was placed within an appendix to DSM-III-R for proposed diagnoses needing further study (APA, 1987). The DSM-IV Personality Disorders Work Group rejected the proposal altogether, eliminating it even from the appendix (Pincus, Frances, Davis, First, & Widiger, 1992).

There are many possible motives for staying within an abusive relationship, including fear of injury or even death (e.g., it is perhaps better to be occasionally beaten than risk losing one's life), love (the abusing spouse will often beg and plead for forgiveness), unrealistic expectation that the abuse will end (the abusing spouse will often vow never to do it again), financial dependence, and absence of any viable alternative or means of escape (Bornstein, 2006; Caplan, 1984). None of these motivations for the excessive self-sacrifice suggests the presence of a personality disorder, and there is little research on the ability of clinicians (or even researchers) to effectively differentiate between these very different explanations for the self-sacrificing behavior.

Case Studies

Sofia

Sofia was a 33-year-old married woman with two children, ages 14 and 15. Sofia had emigrated to the United States from Argentina about 5 years before, with her husband, Carlos, who came to the United States seeking better employment. Sofia came to the Comprehensive Care Center after a visit by the police to their home, responding to a call from a neighbor upon seeing Sofia's condition: She had been beaten by her husband.

It was not the first time Sofia had been beaten. She had suffered at his hands a number of times, although perhaps not so severely as the episode that led to the police investigation. But Sofia did not want charges to be filed. She did not feel that her husband had done anything that terribly wrong. She recognized that he had difficulty controlling his temper, but she felt that it was a relatively small character flaw that she'd become accustomed to. She felt it was essentially her destiny, to suffer these consequences—that her husband was in general a decent

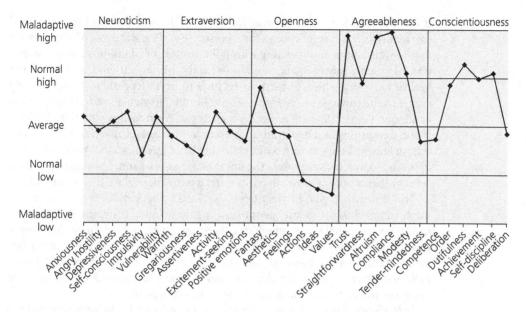

FIGURE 6.1
Sofia's Five-Factor Model profile: Note the elevation with regard to *Agreeableness.*

man and a good husband, providing support for their family. He rarely drank, did not cheat on her, and worked hard.

As part of a routine psychological evaluation at the Comprehensive Care Center, Sofia completed the NEO-PI-R (Costa & McCrae, 1992) to obtain insight into her personality as described by the Five-Factor Model. The results are shown in Figure 6.1. NEO-PI-R scores are typically interpreted relative to the norms provided within the test manual, which are separate for males and females. There are also considerable data on cross-cultural variation in NEO-PI-R scores, including data from Argentina (McCrae et al., 2005). A consideration of cultural norms was particularly important in this case, given Sofia was from a culture in which women have generally less power and authority within the marital relationship (as well as a country that has a relatively higher rate of spousal abuse). Sofia's elevations on the facets of agreeableness, conscientiousness, and closedness to experience were well above the norms for her gender and culture.

As Figure 6.1 reveals, Sofia is a trusting, compliant, straightforward, modest, and altruistic person. She is dutiful, self-disciplined, and competent, as well as somewhat low in openness to new ideas, values, and activities. Sofia's elevated scores on the NEO-PI-R were further explored through the administration of the Structured Interview for the Five-Factor Model (SIFFM; Trull & Widiger, 1997). The SIFFM assesses for maladaptive variants of elevated facet scores. For example, for the facet of altruism, if a person states that she is generous or charitable toward others, she is asked further if she has ever been exploited or used by others due to her apparent generosity. If she indicates that she often goes out of her way to help others who are in need, she is further asked if she often does this at the sacrifice of her own best interests. Sofia endorsed these maladaptive variants of altruism, and went much further to describe a history of self-sacrifice—being victimized and exploited even long before her current relationship.

Sofia was a devoted mother, at times perhaps to excess, but the sacrifices she made for her children did appear to be for the most part normative and healthy.

It was the sacrifices that she made for her marriage and husband that appeared maladaptive. It is fine, of course, for a person to embrace the role of a housewife, to find satisfaction and meaning within the context of a long-term, healthy relationship. Sofia, however, appeared to live only for her husband, and under the heel of his every whim. She expressed little to no independent thought, rarely expressed her own needs or wishes, and submitted to virtually anything her husband might desire. She did not enjoy their sexual relationship, which she at times found demeaning and denigrating. She would not contact anyone, including her own original nuclear family, without her husband's permission. When asked her opinion, Sophia would express the opinion of her husband. She was more like a servant than a wife, at times even appearing more like a slave than a servant.

The immediate goal of treatment was Sofia's physical safety, as well as the safety of her children. Subsequent to settling these initial concerns, focus shifted to Sophia's personality, for which treatment was going to be difficult. The therapist used cognitive therapy techniques to help her appreciate the irrationality and maladaptivity of her characteristic view of herself and others, along with behavioral techniques to develop the ability to act more assertively, express her opinions and rights, and to stand up and protect herself.

Sofia's high scores on conscientiousness boded well for being a responsible, hardworking, and dedicated patient, but her low scores on openness suggest a lack of willingness, perhaps even ability, to see and appreciate alternative perspectives. She lacked a strong motivation to change. She did agree that the physical beatings were excessive and harmful (as well as illegal), but she felt it was "in her nature" to be self-sacrificing, docile, and compliant. She felt that she had always been that way, and could not really imagine behaving otherwise.

Mallory

Mallory was a 26-year-old married woman with no children. Mallory was happy with her marriage (3 years earlier), as she had feared for many years it simply would not happen. Her first psychological treatment occurred when she was an undergraduate at college. She became significantly depressed after the break-up with a boyfriend of approximately 1 year in duration. At the time, she felt convinced that she would never find another man, and that she would be alone and lonely forever. For her, life had no meaning or value without a relationship.

Treatment had been successful in ameliorating her depression, but the therapist could not help noticing that the remission of Mallory's depression coincided with the beginning of a new relationship. Feelings of pessimism changed to hope; dismay and sorrow to joy and happiness. However, Mallory remained stricken with foreboding that her happiness would not last, that her boyfriend would eventually leave her like every previous boyfriend, and that she would again, someday, be alone.

Mallory was in treatment due to her husband's encouragement. She acknowledged that it was difficult for her to feel secure within her relationship. She was repeatedly perceiving and exaggerating signs of disinterest on his part, responding with dismay and emotional turmoil, and even straining the relationship by repeatedly demanding reassurance that everything was really fine.

Figure 6.2 provides Mallory's FFM personality profile. Like Sofia, Mallory is characterized in part by maladaptively high levels of altruism and compliance. Her pathological altruism was expressed in part through her unsolicited willingness to be the one who makes the sacrifices within the relationship. She was not

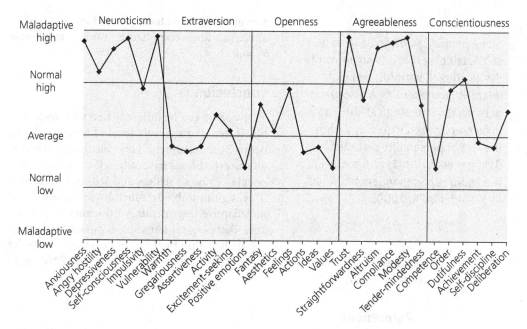

FIGURE 6.2
Mallory's Five-Factor Model profile: Note elevations within *Neuroticism* and *Agreeableness*.

about to ever do, ask, or say anything that might be perceived by her husband as being self-centered or selfish. She wanted him to be fully and entirely happy and content.

Mallory's husband would admit that initially, and still at times to this day, he found Mallory's self-sacrifices to be agreeable, if not pleasing. She was tremendously easy to get along with. None of his quirks and foibles seemed to trouble her, and it was rather nice to be "number one" within the relationship, an experience he had never felt so strongly before. However, in time, it became troublesome. It just didn't seem realistic, honest, or right. He didn't really want her to always be the one who made the sacrifice. He grew to realize that he wanted the relationship to be much more equal. Ironically, Mallory was perhaps driving her husband away precisely through her effort to keep him.

Mallory's neuroticism would be easier to treat than Sofia's maladaptive agreeableness, in part because neuroticism can lack the "ego-syntonic" experience of other personality traits. Sofia, in contrast, was largely comfortable with her personality traits. She did not consider them to be the source of her problems. However, Mallory's feelings of anxiousness, depressiveness, vulnerability, and self-consciousness are inherently troubling. Most of the facets of neuroticism are explicit and direct expressions of pain and suffering.

Mallory's elevated neuroticism, though, did complicate the therapist's understanding of the case. It was quite possible that Mallory's anxiousness, dysphoria, self-consciousness, and feelings of vulnerability drove her compliant, sacrificial behavior (Presnall et al., in press; Miller & Lynam, 2008). Much of the behavior of persons with DPD is said "to arise from a self-perception of being unable to function adequately without the help of others" (APA, 2000, p. 721). Their self-sacrificing behavior might then reflect their feelings of vulnerability and incompetence. Once the feelings of insecurity, self-confidence, and vulnerability

> Some people can be so selfless and self-sacrificing that it is significantly dysfunctional, harmful, and maladaptive, representing a disorder of personality. Pathological altruism is in fact recognized explicitly within the FFM of personality disorder (Widiger et al., 2002) and is one of the features of dependent personality disorder (APA, 2000).

are successfully treated, perhaps the self-sacrifice, altruism, and compliance would ameliorate as well.

Conclusion

Everyone can be differentiated with respect to his or her characteristic level of altruism. Some people are routinely very altruistic, whereas others are characteristically self-centered. Some people can be so selfless and self-sacrificing that it is significantly dysfunctional, harmful, and maladaptive, representing a disorder of personality. Pathological altruism is in fact recognized explicitly within the FFM of personality disorder (Widiger et al., 2002) and is one of the features of Dependent Personality Disorder (APA, 2000).

References

American Psychiatric Association. (1987). *Diagnostic and statistical manual of mental disorders.* (3rd ed., rev. ed.). Washington, DC: Author.

American Psychiatric Association. (2000). *Diagnostic and statistical manual of mental disorders. Text revision* (4th ed., rev. ed.). Washington, DC: Author.

Ashton, M. C., & Lee, K. (2001). A theoretical basis for the major dimensions of personality. *European Journal of Personality, 15,* 327–353.

Bornstein, R. F. (2006). The complex relationship between dependency and domestic violence. Converging psychological factors and social forces. *American Psychologist, 61,* 595–606.

Bornstein, R. F., & Cecero, J. J. (2000). Deconstructing dependency in a five-factor world: A meta-analytic review. *Journal of Personality Assessment, 74,* 324–343.

Caplan, P. J. (1984). The myth of women's masochism. *American Psychologist, 39,* 130–139.

Costa, P. T., & McCrae, R. R. (1985). *The NEO personality inventory manual.* Odessa, FL: Psychological Assessment Resources.

Costa, P. T., & McCrae, R. R. (1992). *Revised NEO Personality Inventory (NEO-PI-R) and NEO Five-Factor Inventory (NEO-FFI) professional manual.* Odessa, FL: Psychological Assessment Resources, Inc.

Costa, P. T., Terracciano, A., & McCrae, R. R. (2001). Gender differences in personality traits across cultures: Robust and surprising findings. *Journal of Personality and Social Psychology, 81,* 322–331.

Haigler, E. D., & Widiger, T. A. (2001). Experimental manipulation of NEO PI-R items. *Journal of Personality Assessment, 77,* 339–358.

McCrae, R. R. (2002). NEO PI-R data from 36 cultures. In R. R. McCrae, & J. Allilk (Eds.), *The five-factor model of personality across cultures* (pp. 105–125). New York: Kluwer Academic.

McCrae, R. R., & Costa, P. T. (2003). *Personality in adulthood. A five-factor theory perspective* (2nd ed.). New York: Guilford.

McCrae, R. R., & Terracciano, A. (2006). National character and personality. *Current Directions in Psychological Science, 15,* 156–161.

McCrae, R. R., Terracciano, A., & 79 members of the Personality Profiles of Cultures Project. (2005). Personality profiles of cultures: aggregate personality traits. *Journal of Personality and Social Psychology, 89*, 407–425.

Miller, J. D., & Lynam, D.R. (2008). Dependent personality disorder. Comparing an expert generated and empirically derived five-factor model personality disorder count. *Assessment, 15*, 4–15.

Pincus, H. A., Frances, A. J., Davis, W. W., First, M. B., & Widiger, T. A. (1992). DSM-IV and new diagnostic categories: holding the line on proliferation. *American Journal of Psychiatry, 149*, 112–117.

Presnall, J. R., Edmundson, M., & Widiger, T. A. (in press). Assessment of dependency, agreeableness, and their relationship. *Psychological Assessment.*

Samuel, D. B., & Widiger, T.A. (2008). A meta-analytic review of the relationships between the five-factor model and DSM-IV-TR personality disorders: A facet level analysis. *Clinical Psychology Review, 28*, 1326–1342.

Snell, J., Rosenwald, R., & Robey, A. (1964). The wifebeater's wife. A study of family interaction. *Archives of General Psychiatry, 11*, 107–112.

Trull, T. J., & Widiger, T. A. (1997). *Structured interview for the five factor model of personality.* Odessa, FL: Psychological Assessment Resources.

Widiger, T. A. (1995). Deletion of the self-defeating and sadistic personality disorder diagnoses. In W. J. Livesley (Ed.), *The DSM-IV personality disorders* (pp. 359–373). New York: Guilford.

Widiger, T. A., Costa, P. T., & McCrae, R. R. (2002). A proposal for Axis II: Diagnosing personality disorders using the five factor model. In P. T. Costa & T. A. Widiger (Eds.), *Personality disorders and the five factor model of personality* (2nd ed., pp. 431–456). Washington, DC: American Psychological Association.

Widiger, T. A., & Trull, T. J. (2007). Plate tectonics in the classification of personality disorder: Shifting to a dimensional model. *American Psychologist, 62*, 71–83.

Work Group to Revise DSM-III. (1985). *DSM-III-R in development.* Washington, DC: American Psychiatric Association.

CHAPTER 7

THE RELEVANCE OF PATHOLOGICAL ALTRUISM TO EATING DISORDERS

Rachel Bachner-Melman

KEY CONCEPTS

- Individuals with eating disorders tend to sacrifice their own needs and interests and devote themselves instead to helping and serving others.
- Selflessness and concern for appropriateness, concepts linked to pathological altruism, have been shown to characterize women with eating disorders.
- Developmental, interpersonal, family, cultural, genetic, personality, and social factors no doubt combine to make pathological altruism a characteristic of people who develop eating disorders.

IT IS NOT uncommon to observe people on self-imposed starvation diets deriving pleasure from serving food to others or cooking for them. This tendency of individuals with eating disorders (anorexia nervosa, bulimia nervosa, binge eating disorder, and eating disorder not otherwise specified) to deprive themselves while satisfying others' needs is by no means restricted to nutrition, and has been frequently observed and described in research and in clinical settings. It is common for eating-disordered patients in treatment programs to devote themselves to taking care of each other. According to self-psychologists (Bachar, 1998; Geist, 1998; Goodsitt, 1997), patients with eating disorders feel and behave like selfless souls serving others' needs. Salvador Minuchin, a family therapist, described the self-sacrifice of anorexic patients in the service of their family's needs (Minuchin, Rosman, & Baker, 1987). Women with anorexia nervosa interviewed by Wechselblatt, Gurnick, and Simon (2000) felt they had been encouraged by their families and cultural environments to substitute others' needs for their own.

A self-report Selflessness Scale measuring the tendency to relinquish one's own interests and ignore one's own needs in order to serve the interests and well-being of others has been developed by Eytan Bachar and his colleagues for use in empirical research (Bachar et al. 2002). Scores on this questionnaire have been found to distinguish between women with eating disorders and control women (Bachar et al., 2002) to be positively associated with the severity of anorexic symptomatology (Bachner-Melman, Zohar, Ebstein, & Bachar, 2007) and to predict the development of eating pathology in adolescent schoolgirls with 82% sensitivity and 63% specificity.

> Women with anorexia nervosa . . . felt they had been encouraged by their families and cultural environments to substitute others' needs for their own.

Low selflessness scores seem to offer some degree of protection from eating problems (Bachar, Gur, Canetti, Berry, & Stein, 2010).

Research conclusions may be convincing and rational, yet the most potent descriptions of pathological altruism as part and parcel of eating disorders come, perhaps, from those in recovery. "All of my life I lived for other people," writes one ex-patient, "not out of choice, but because I didn't know any other way. It wasn't until years later that I found out that I didn't actually have a self. I became what other people liked, thought, said, and did: without respect for myself, going day by day trying to please other people so that I could be good enough" (Claude-Pierre, 1997; p. 256). A 44-year-old woman recovering from anorexia after over 20 years of illness, writes: "I was a pleaser from a very young age to my father, mother, and other family members and friends, and this took away my freedom to make choices that were right for me. . . . The happiness of others was primary in my life . . . I was the super woman at our local swim club where my kids swam. I did everything from ordering suits to running meets. I volunteered for every job, every week" (D. Friedman, personal communication, September 7, 2009).

The vast majority of eating-disordered patients (approximately 90%) are women. Sociological theories suggest that women, in general, focus more than men on the needs of other people (Gilligan, Rogers, & Tolman, 1991). Moreover, even the healthiest people—women and men—derive a sense of competence, pleasure, and self-worth from being kind, helpful, and generous toward others.

> "All of my life I lived for other people," writes one ex-patient, "not out of choice, but because I didn't know any other way. It wasn't until years later that I found out that I didn't actually have a self."

How, then, can altruism be pathological? The point at which giving becomes unhealthy is difficult to define. The crucial factors differentiating "normal altruism" from "pathological altruism," as seen in the eating disorders, include the motivation for giving, the price paid, and the degree of sacrifice and associated negative affect involved.

The major motivations for giving in healthy altruism are openness to new experiences and a desire for personal growth (Stone, 2000). In contrast, the major motivation for giving in eating-disordered individuals is to please others, gain approval, and avoid criticism and rejection. Unlike healthy altruism, pathological altruism enhances a sense of self-worth via significant self-sacrifice and self-deprivation (Seelig & Rosof, 2001). Hilde Bruch, a psychoanalyst and pioneer in the treatment of eating disorders, pointed out that individuals with eating disorders give to others at great expense to the development of their own identity. They often crave connections and wish to maintain them at all costs. A frequent motivation for giving and accommodating themselves to others' tastes, opinions, and needs is the hope of receiving much-needed affection and acceptance. Giving to other people may be seen as a precondition for love or positive regard. The other side of this coin is a fear of rejection and of feeling lost should a relationship be disrupted (Bruch, 1978).

> The major motivations for giving in healthy altruism are openness to new experiences and a desire for personal growth. In contrast, the major motivation for giving in eating-disordered individuals is to please others, gain approval, and avoid criticism and rejection.

In the pathological altruism that so often accompanies eating disorders, the simple and natural joy of giving is tainted by anger and frustration, conscious or unconscious, at sacrificing so much and receiving so little in return. The tendency of women with anorexia to repress needs and feelings, especially anger, to protect interpersonal relationships has been supported from a cognitive and sociological perspective by Geller, Cockell, Goldner, and Flett (2000). Yet, even though a high emotional price is paid for constant compromise, pathological altruism has significant adaptive value for eating-disordered patients, because in the short term its rewards mask and provide relief from feelings of worthlessness and inefficacy. Since pathological altruism in the eating disorders often involves satisfaction as part of the inner conflict created by giving, it would usually be defined by Seelig and Rosof (2001) as "conflicted" as opposed to healthy or "generative" altruism. However, in cases when caretaking becomes compulsive, joyless, and martyr-like, it might fall into their category of "pseudoaltruism."

How and when do eating-disordered individuals come to prioritize others' needs above their own? Clinicians and theoreticians have described developmental processes explaining the emergence of pathological altruism long before the onset of an eating disorder (usually in adolescence or early adulthood). Since prospective research on these processes remains impractical and sparse, support for these explanations must generally be gathered retrospectively, after the onset of the disorder. For this reason, descriptions of and explanations for the development of pathological altruism in childhood as a precursor to eating disorders should currently be regarded as hypotheses supported by much anecdotal, clinical, theoretical, and retrospective narrative evidence. Whereas pathological altruism is in no way limited to individuals who go on to develop eating disorders, it seems to be particularly characteristic of this population.

The etiology of eating disorders is complex and multifactorial. Genetic, biological, temperamental, developmental, family, personality, sociocultural, interpersonal, and circumstantial factors contribute collectively to risk. The developmental and interpersonal processes described below fit into a large and intricate puzzle explaining the development of eating disorders, yet are presented here because they seem central to an understanding of pathological altruism as a contributing factor. Heinz Kohut's self-psychology (Kohut, 1971, 1977), in particular, provides us with a theoretical framework that lends itself aptly to a description of the development of pathological altruism as seen in the eating disorders.

To develop healthily, children need the feeling that they are special, appreciated, and worthy of admiration—"mirroring," in Kohut's terminology. It is age-appropriate, for example, for small children to believe that they are cute and gorgeous, their scribbles are masterpieces, what they say is worth listening to, and they are the center of their parents' world. Kohut (1971) believed this infantile or "archaic" grandiosity to be normal and necessary for the development of a cohesive sense of self, good self-esteem, and healthy goals. Children whose mirroring (and other) needs are met are able to develop a wholesome sense of identity and to be confident that their basic needs can be satisfied by those close to them. They are able to turn to others in a healthy way and use them as "selfobjects," as Kohut (1968) called people who serve the function of fulfilling others' needs.

When parents or caregivers are immersed in their own physical, psychological, interpersonal, and/or circumstantial preoccupations, they are not fully available, responsive, and empathic to the needs of their children. Possible evidence for a tendency of mothers of girls with eating disorders to be preoccupied with their own issues was found in a recent study showing low levels of selflessness in mothers of daughters with anorexia (Bachar et al., 2010). Interestingly, the daughters showed heightened selflessness when their mothers, but not their fathers, exhibited depressive tendencies. Although these results may highlight a tendency in girls with anorexia to worry about and try to protect their mothers by adopting their concerns, this study was conducted after the onset of anorexia, leaving the premorbid picture unclear.

According to Kohut's theory, when needs for external mirroring are insufficiently met in childhood, the "archaic grandiosity" (Kohut, 1971) described above is not transformed and incorporated into a cohesive, healthy self. As a result, an exaggerated and permanent need for responsiveness from others develops, to the extent that some people come to feel they exist largely in the eye of the beholder (Goodsitt, 1984). Alas, as time passes, the sense of positive self-esteem that failed to crystallize during early childhood is less and less likely to be established. Later on, receiving good things may provoke a sense of unease and guilt. Compliments, acts of caring, and admiration for genuine virtues, intelligence, talents, skills, or competencies often fall like water from a duck's back, leaving the individual tragically starved for the very reinforcement being offered.

Such circumstances are not limited to objectively deprived or abused children. Sometimes the subjective experience of unmet needs may result from an extreme sensitivity to the social environment resulting primarily from genetic, temperamental, and/or biological factors, or from a mismatch between the child's personality and parenting style (Strober, 1991). How do sensitive children cope with the unmet needs they experience to be cared for, held, understood, and admired? They cut off and ignore them. They come to regard them as excessive and unjustified. They become ashamed of their desire to be seen, helped, and served; ashamed of being dependent on others; ashamed of needs for acknowledgment and mirroring. Some children who sense their caretakers are burdened learn very early on not to add to their burden and strive to lighten it by not making demands and coping with life on their own. In extreme cases, they make it a top priority not to be a burden on anybody. Ashamed of their "true" self, they hide behind an appearance of self-sufficiency (Modell, 1965) and develop a façade molded by other's expectations—coined a "false self" by the psychoanalyst and leading object-relations theorist Donald Winnicott (Winnicott, 1965). Desperate for appreciation and longing to be listened to, they dismiss their inner values, experiences, initiatives, and needs (Goodsitt, 1984).

Clinicians and theoreticians have described this in eating disorders. Bruch (1978), for example, wrote that her anorexic patients had spent their lives learning how to adapt themselves to others in order to lessen demands on them. Selvini Palazzoli (1978), a family therapist from the Milan systems group of therapists, emphasized the guilt experienced by children who later develop eating disorders in response to their needs, and described family dynamics that lead them to feel responsible for their parents' well-being. Richard Geist (1989a) and Eytan Bacher (1998), Kohutian "self-psychologists," point out that eating-disordered patients often recall feeling responsible for their parents and taking on a comforting, organizing role in the home.

The core symptom of eating disorders involves denial of one of the most basic biological needs: the need for food. In eating disorders, food ingestion comes to be regarded as an unjustifiable self-indulgence, a selfish and illegitimate act. In anorexia, the rejection of pleasure and condemnation of anything that smacks of indulgence (Mogul, 1980) is communicated via an emaciated body shape. Eating disorders involve a denial of needs far beyond the need for food, often including denial of other biological needs, such as the need for rest, sleep, sex, and medical care, and of interpersonal needs for affection, support, and help. Eating healthily means caring for oneself, giving oneself sustenance, responding to inner needs, and allowing oneself pleasure. All these things are problematic for those suffering from eating disorders.

Eating disorders provide an effective strategy to avoid satisfying inner wishes and needs via a highly regimented and ritualized daily schedule regulated by behavioral and moral rules. Helping others usually appears very high up on a long list of obligations. Much anger and aggression is inherent in the symptoms of an eating disorder. People with these disorders invariably disown and condemn anger, aggression, and greed, and often devote themselves to listening to others, taking care of them, helping and serving them (Bruch, 1973). Feeling they have no right to exist in their own right (Goodsitt, 1997), they consistently adopt, in the language of self-psychology, the role of selfobject. Their raison d'être becomes to maintain others' well-being. They give what they themselves would like to receive but cannot. Their illness could even be seen as thinking so much of other people and so little of themselves that others are forced to step in and take over the function of self-care. In other words, they are "consummate caretakers" (Bruch, 1978) or experts in "pathological altruism."

Contemporary society overvalues independence (Fineman, 2005), causing autonomy to appear deceptively adaptive. Those who appear to cope without help tend to be admired at the personal, familial, and broader cultural level. Pathological altruism, too, can look misleadingly healthy. Altruism is socially approved; parents, teachers, religious leaders, and society at large teach us the value of giving to family members, siblings, classmates, friends, and the needy. The autonomy and altruism of children and adolescents who go on to develop eating disorders are all too often misinterpreted as signs of health and good adjustment by parents, peers, loved ones, colleagues, teachers, and society at large. It is not uncommon for the parents of adolescents with eating disorders, particularly anorexia, to overlook and deny their child's illness as long as possible and to react with incredulity and disbelief when confronted with it. How, they ask, could such an easy, sweet-natured, undemanding, and disciplined person possibly be ill?

> The autonomy and altruism of children and adolescents who go on to develop eating disorders are all too often misinterpreted as signs of health and good adjustment by parents, peers, loved ones, colleagues, teachers, and society at large.

Parents are on no account to be blamed for their children's eating disorders. Whereas the vast majority of parents are self-absorbed to varying degrees, very few children become pathological altruists, and a tiny majority eventually develop eating disorders. Gender is the most significant risk factor for an eating disorder, and the role of genetics is paramount (Bulik et al., 2008; Holland, Sicotte, & Treasure, 1988; Mazzeo et al., 2009; Strober, Freeman, Lampert, Diamond, & Kaye, 2000). Not only does heredity play a role in eating disorders, but also in altruism; conceivably, certain genetic pathways are shared. Twin studies have demonstrated that a significant proportion of the differences between people's prosocial attitudes is due to heredity (Asbury, Dunn, Pike, & Plomin, 2003), and specific genes associated with altruism as measured by the Selflessness Scale (*DRD4, IGF2,* and *DRD5*) have been preliminarily identified (Bachner-Melman et al., 2005). Interestingly, two of these genes are related to the "reward" neurotransmitter dopamine, supporting the notion that helping others may be reinforced by reward. What exactly is passed on genetically is not clear. It is possible that an inherited sensitivity factor predisposes some children to be particularly attuned to interpersonal cues, and later to take on responsibility for other's well-being, and that interaction with other genetic and environmental factors contributes to risk for an eating disorder.

A lack of clear self-definition, so intricately linked to pathological altruism, interacts with cultural, biological, personality, and genetic factors to create a risk profile for the development of eating disorders. Michael Strober, for example, sees anorexia nervosa basically as a failure to establish a clear and stable sense of self, but his conceptualization extends beyond this. He believes that a specific, genetically based personality style as measured by Cloninger's (1987) Tridimensional Personality Questionnaire (high harm-avoidance, low novelty seeking, and high reward dependence) inhibits the natural exploration necessary for normal self-development and contributes to a lack of goodness-of-fit between child and parenting style (Strober, 1991).

Pathologically altruistic behavior that stems from a lack of a sense of self involves reading, anticipating, or guessing others' needs and giving these priority over one's own. People with eating disorders appear to be very adept at this. External environment and circumstances take precedence over an internal compass of what is beneficial for self. Such an internal compass seems absent in women with eating disorders. Bruch (1973, 1978) commented that women with anorexia depend on external sources for their self-esteem and become experts at reading cues from others about how to feel and behave. Vitousek and Ewald (1993) emphasized the combined contribution of genetic and environmental factors to the failure to develop a clear sense of self, leading to an overreliance on social and environmental cues. Boskind-Lodahl (1976) emphasized cultural and social pressures in the lack of identity experienced by girls with eating disorders. In Schupak-Neuberg and Nemeroff's (1993) view, the absence of a true self underlying bulimia nervosa stems from an overemphasis on cultural factors and physical appearance.

> Pathologically altruistic behavior that stems from a lack of a sense of self involves reading, anticipating, or guessing others' needs and giving these priority over one's own.

Endorsement of the current thin beauty ideal that underlies disturbed eating attitudes and behaviors might be seen as an extended expression of pathological altruism, in the sense that the biological need to eat is sacrificed for the broader "needs" or dictates of society concerning body shape. This hypothesis was explored in research (Bachner-Melman et al., 2009) using the construct "concern for appropriateness," first introduced in the field of social psychology and measured by a self-report questionnaire called the Concern for Appropriateness Scale (Lennox & Wolfe, 1984). Concern for appropriateness involves constant efforts to read others' needs and expectations in order to evaluate appropriate behavior strategies and adopt them, out of a fear of being different or standing out. It is associated with a general tendency to understand and be influenced behaviorally by interpersonal and media messages (Bearden & Rose, 1990; Johnson, 1989).

What counts as a desirable, socially "appropriate" identity varies sharply from one cultural-historical setting to another (Schlenker, 1982). In contemporary Westernized societies, a steady diet of stereotyped thin images persists in the media and motivates many women to strive for thinness. Yet, not all women exposed to the media are similarly influenced by the messages to which they are exposed.

> It was hypothesized that people concerned with appropriateness may be more vigilant than others concerning cultural norms on physical appearance and the culturally "appropriate" body shape, motivating them to attain it at any price, even if they have to sacrifice their health to do so.

It was hypothesized that people concerned with appropriateness may be more vigilant than others concerning cultural norms on physical appearance and the culturally "appropriate" body shape, motivating them to attain it at any price, even if they have to sacrifice their health to do so. Concern for appropriateness was indeed found to characterize women with a present or past history of anorexia nervosa and to be associated with symptom severity (Bachner-Melman et al., 2009). Moreover, this association was fully mediated by sociocultural attitudes toward appearance. The most plausible interpretation of these results is that women highly concerned with social appropriateness tend to endorse, inter alia, prevailing cultural attitudes toward appearance, including the importance of being thin. The endorsement of the thin ideal in turn predisposes them to disturbed eating attitudes and behaviors, and presumably in extreme cases, to eating disorders.

The adult cultural ideal of thinness becomes personally relevant during puberty (Hermes & Keel, 2003). Adolescence is typically characterized by a preoccupation with appearance and identity development, heightening susceptibility to pressures and influences from the media (Wertheim, Paxton, Schultz, & Muir, 1997). Teenagers are among the heaviest users of many forms of mass media, particularly magazines (Arnett, Larson, & Offer, 1995). It therefore hardly seems surprising that adolescence is the peak onset period for eating disorders.

Media influences, however, constitute only one avenue for the transmission of sociocultural messages. Teenagers tend to be extremely sensitive about appearance-related comments (Striegel-Moore, & Kearney-Cooke, 1994). Also, peer pressure peaks during adolescence (Heaven, 1991). Adolescent girls often talk about dieting and weight issues, and the peer group's degree of weight concerns influences and predicts a girl's own behavior (Paxton, 1996). Girls who sacrifice their health to present a proscribed, desired body shape are paying a high price to fulfill a group requirement, give the group what it needs, seek approval, and avoid being discounted. Conforming to a group ideal of thinness to the extent that an eating disorder develops can in itself therefore be regarded as an expression of pathological altruism.

Concern for appropriateness is no doubt both environmentally and genetically based. It has been found to be associated with a vasopressin receptor AVPR1A promoter region microsatellite (Bachner-Melman et al., 2005b), and the same microsatellite was found to be associated with disordered eating (Bachner-Melman et al., 2004). Assuming a link between concern for appropriateness and pathological altruism, the vasopressin receptor gene may be contributing risk for anorexia, at least in part, via pathological altruism. This line of investigation should be further explored in future research.

One major anomaly in the association between pathological altruism and eating disorders deserves some explanation. Freud defined altruism as "the opposite of egoism" (Freud, 1957, p. 418), and indeed, the term is commonly used as an antonym of selfishness or narcissism. Yet, despite eating-disordered individuals' frequent surrender to others, they often describe themselves as narcissistic and selfish. Core symptoms of eating disorders such as self-destructive starvation, binge-eating, purging, defiant self-sufficiency, noncommunication, and social isolation appear manipulative, controlling, and self-centered—so far removed from altruism, in fact, that they invariably trigger hostile reactions and earn eating-disordered patients a reputation of being notoriously difficult to understand and treat (Kaplan & Garfinkel, 1999). Indeed, narcissism is a frequently documented characteristic of eating-disordered patients (Johnson, 1991; Riebel, 2000; Steiger, Jabalpurwala, Champagne, & Stotland, 1997). Rather than fulfilling full criteria according to the *Diagnostic and Statistical Manual of Mental Disorders, 4th Edition* (DSM-IV) for narcissistic personality disorder, eating-disordered patients tend to fit Gabbard's (1989) description of "hypervigilant narcissists," about whom he writes: "At the core of their inner world is a deep sense of shame related to their secret wish to exhibit themselves in a grandiose manner.... Attention is continually directed toward others . . . they study others intensely to figure out how to behave." So, if pathological altruism is a characteristic of eating disorders that needs to be addressed in treatment and recovery, how can it be reconciled with undeniable narcissism?

It seems that, in the eating disorders, as in other pathology, narcissism and altruism represent two sides of the same coin. With the onset of an eating disorder, frustration at constantly giving so much, sacrificing so much of self, comes to a peak. One thing that can be possessed and held on to is food intake and a low weight. An eating disorder makes it legitimate to express the wish to be the center at least of a narrowly defined world. Unmet grandiose needs and wishes break through and gratification is obtained in a disguised way (Goodsit, 1984). Symptoms of weight loss, remaining thin despite overeating, "rising above" natural appetite, maintaining a dangerously low weight, and/or purging without becoming ill (Riebel, 2000) create the grandiose illusion of being empowered, special, and superior to others. When they first start to lose weight, women with anorexia report feeling "delighted, inspired, triumphant, proud, and powerful . . . special, superior, and deserving of the respect and admiration of others" (Bemis, 1986, quoted in Vitousek & Ewald, 1993). This initial "high" could conceivably be connected with changes in levels of endorphins, associated with a feeling of elevation in runners (Huebner, 1993) and in levels of the neurotransmitter dopamine, associated with reward (Bachner-Melman et al., 2007; Barry & Klawans, 1976; Levitan et al., 2004).

We have seen that, in the eating disorders, food consumption is viewed as selfish, whereas self-starvation is experienced as depriving, selfless, and therefore paradoxically nourishing, satisfying, and commendable. Fasting is, in most religions, a means of drawing close to the Divine. In eating disorders, as in extreme forms of religion, self-indulgence and pleasures of the flesh tend to be shunned (Mogul, 1980; Lelwica, 2009; Vandereycken & van Deth, 1990). Freedom from body and bodily needs can lead to a feeling of immortality, omnipotence, spiritual purity, and moral superiority (Green, 2001). It is evident that a sense of satisfaction and superiority is achieved, paradoxically, via self-deprivation. A sense of triumph is achieved by relinquishing parts of oneself (Green, 2001). When autonomy and self-sufficiency are valued (after thinness) above all else, giving to others becomes, despite its high price, one of the only permissible sources of pleasure.

The functions of the narcissism described above are primarily defensive. Although eating disorders may appear to stem from an egotistical desire to improve one's appearance, motivation to improve body shape stems from a sense of being ugly and inadequate. Feeling strengthened and superior to others is an antidote for feelings of weakness and inefficacy (Goodsit, 1984). Grandiose fantasies of omnipotence and invulnerability coexist with and protect against a terrifying awareness of helplessness and vulnerability that characterizes a poorly defined identity (Tobin, 1993).

To conclude, the pathological altruism seen in conjunction with eating-disorder symptomatology has important implications for recovery, treatment, and prevention. Concerning recovery, cross-sectional research has shown levels of selflessness and concern for appropriateness in women completely recovered from anorexia to be similar to those of women with no history of an eating disorder (Bachner-Melman, Zohar, Ebstein, & Bachar, 2007; Bachner-Melman et al., 2009). Pathological altruism therefore may be an aspect of an eating disorder that, thankfully, can heal with recovery from eating and weight symptoms.

> Pathological altruism may be an aspect of an eating disorder that, thankfully, can heal with recovery from eating and weight symptoms.

Concerning treatment, therapy provides an unfamiliar experience for eating-disordered patients: an opportunity to focus on their needs and not those of others. One potential trap for therapists lies in the character of pathological altruism itself; patients may be hypersensitive to the therapists' reactions, expectations, and narcissistic needs, and respond "appropriately" instead of exploring and expressing genuine feelings and lacks. Important objectives in therapy include learning to recognize and fulfill authentic needs, developing and consolidating a sense of identity, learning to distinguish and respect clear boundaries between self and other, developing the courage to differ, and learning to buffer vulnerability and counteract negative messages from the media, teachers, friends, and family (Piran, 1997). Family therapy is often helpful for younger patients, since family roles can be shifted to relieve the eating-disordered child from the responsibility of constantly serving others.

> Much anecdotal, clinical, narrative, and empirical evidence suggests that pathological altruism may be a precursor of, and therefore a risk factor for, eating disorders.

The overlap between pathological altruism and eating disorders also has potential implications in the field of prevention. Further research should examine and clarify whether, and how specifically, pathological altruism predicts the emergence of an eating disorder as opposed to other psychopathology such as depression or obsessive-compulsive disorder. In the meantime, much anecdotal, clinical, narrative, and empirical evidence suggests that pathological altruism may be a precursor of, and therefore a risk factor for, eating disorders. Parents, teachers, coaches, doctors, and the public at large should be educated to be on the lookout for overly giving, self-sacrificing children and teenagers, and awareness should be increased that such individuals may be experiencing serious and undetected distress. Pathological altruism, if detected early enough, could provide a valuable warning about the threat of an impending eating disorder. Such a sign, together with other risk factors, such as specific personality traits and genetic markers to be determined by prospective research, could form the basis of a recognized risk profile for eating disorders. If high risk can be recognized, preemptive interventions such as individual psychotherapy, family therapy, nutritional guidance, psychoeducation, assertiveness training, or changes in social or study environment may be able to prevent the enormous pain and suffering inflicted by an eating disorder, and possibly even save lives.

References

Arnett, J. J., Larson, R., & Offer, D. (1995). Beyond effects: Adolescents as active media users. *Journal of Youth and Adolescence, 24*, 511–518.

Asbury, K., Dunn. J., Pike, A., & Plomin, R. (2003). Nonshared environmental influences on individual differences in early behavioral development: A monozygotic twin differences study. *Child Development, 74*, 933–43.

Bachar, E. (1998). The contributions of self psychology to the treatment of anorexia and bulimia. *American Journal of Psychotherapy, 52*, 147–165.

Bachar, E., Canetti, L., Latzer, Y., Gur, E., Berry, E., & Bonne, O. (2002). Rejection of life in anorexic and bulimic patients. *International Journal of Eating Disorders, 31*, 42–47.

Bachar, E., Gur, E., Canetti, L., Berry, E., & Stein, D. (2010). Selflessness and perfectionism as predictors of pathological eating attitudes and disorders: A longitudinal study. *European Eating Disorders Review, 18*(6),496–506.

Bachar, E., Kanyas, K., Latzer, Y., Canetti, L., Bonne, O., & Lerer, B. (in press). Depressive tendencies and lower levels of self-sacrifice in mothers, and selflessness in their anorexic daughters. *European Eating Disorders Review*.

Bachar, E., & Samet, Y. (in press). Self psychology in the treatment of anorexia nervosa and bulimia nervosa. In: Y. Latzer, J. Merrick, & D. Stein (Eds.), *Understanding eating disorders: Integrating culture, psychology and biology*. New York: Nova Science.

Bachner-Melman, R., Gritsenko, I., Nemanov, L., Zohar, A.H., Dina, C., & Ebstein, R.P. (2005a). Dopaminergic polymorphisms associated with self-report measures of human altruism: A fresh phenotype for the dopamine D4 receptor. *Molecular Psychiatry, 10*(4), 333–335.

Bachner-Melman, R., Lerer, E., Zohar, A. H., Kremer, I., Elizur, Y., Nemanov, L., et al. (2007). Anorexia nervosa, perfectionism and dopamine D4 receptor (*DRD4*). *American Journal of Medical Genetics Part B (Neuropsychiatric Genetics), 144*(6), 748–756.

Bachner-Melman, R., Zohar, A. H., Bacon-Shnoor, N., Elizur, Y., Nemanov, L., Gritsenko, I., & Ebstein, R. P. (2005b). Linkage between vasopressin receptor AVPRIA promoter region microsatellites and measures of social behavior in man. *Journal of Individual Differences, 26*(1), 2–10.

Bachner-Melman, R., Zohar, A. H., Ebstein, R. P., & Bachar, E. (2007). The relationship between selflessness levels and the severity of anorexia nervosa symptomatology. *European Eating Disorders Review, 15*, 213–220.

Bachner-Melman, R., Zohar, A. H., Elizur, Y., Kremer, I., Golan, M., & Ebstein, R. P. (2009). Protective self-presentation style: Association with disordered eating and anorexia nervosa mediated by sociocultural attitudes to appearance. *Eating and Weight Disorders, 14*(1), 1–12.

Bachner-Melman, R., Zohar, A. H., Elizur, Y., Nemanov, L., Gritsenko, I., Konis, D. & Ebstein, R.P. (2004). Association between a vasopressin receptor AVPRIA promoter region microsatellite and eating behavior measured by a self-report questionnaire (Eating Attitudes Test) in a family-based study of a non-clinical population. *International Journal of Eating Disorders, 36,* 451–460.

Barry, V. C., & Klawans, H. L. (1976). On the role of dopamine in the pathophysiology of anorexia nervosa. *Journal of Neural Transmission, 38,* 107–122.

Bearden, W., & Rose, R. (1990). Attention to social comparison information: An individual difference factor affecting consumer conformity. *Journal of Consumer Research, 16,* 473–481.

Bemis, K. (1986). *A comparison of the subjective experience of individuals with eating disorders and phobic disorders.* Unpublished doctoral dissertation, University of Minnesota, Minneapolis, MN.

Boskind-Lodahl, M. (1976). Cinderella's stepsisters: A feminist perspective on anorexia nervosa and bulimia. *Journal of Women in Culture and Society, 2,* 342–356.

Bruch, H. (1973). Eating disorders: Obesity, anorexia nervosa and the person within. London: Routledge and Kegan Paul.

Bruch, H. (1978). *The golden cage: The enigma of anorexia nervosa.* Cambridge, MA: Harvard University Press.

Bulik, C. M., Hudson, J. I., Pope, H. G. Jr., Laird, N. M., Reichborn-Kjennerud, T., & Javaras, K. N. (2008). Familiarity and heritability of binge eating disorder: Results of a case-control family study and a twin study. *International Journal of Eating Disorders, 41,* 174–179.

Claude-Pierre P. (1997). The Secret Language of Eating Disorders. Sydney: Bantam.

Cloninger, C. R. (1987). A systematic method for clinical description and classification of personality variants. *Archives of General Psychiatry, 44,* 573–588.

Fineman, M. A. (2005). *The autonomy myth: A theory of dependency.* New York: New Press.

Freud, S. (1957). Introductory lectures on psychoanalysis: The libido theory and narcissism. In J. Strachey (Ed. and Trans.), *The standard edition of the complete psychological works of Sigmund Freud* Vol. 16 (pp. 412–430). London: Hogarth Press. (Original work published 1917)

Gabbard, G. O. (1989). Two subtypes of narcissistic personality disorder. *Bulletin of the Menninger Clinic, 53,* 527–532.

Geist, R. (1989). Psychological reflections on the origins of eating disorders. In J. R. Bemporad & D. B. Herzog (Eds.), *Psychoanalysis and eating disorders* (pp. 5–27). New York: American Academy of Psychoanalysis.

Geist, R. (1998). Self psychological reflections on the origins of eating disorders. *Journal of the American Academy of Psychoanalysis, 17,* 5–28.

Geller, J., Cockell, S. J., Goldner, E. M., & Flett, G. L. (2000). Inhibited expression of negative emotions and interpersonal orientation in anorexia nervosa. *International Journal of Eating Disorders, 28,* 8–19.

Gilligan, C., Rogers, A. G., & Tolman, D. L. (1991). *Women, girls and psychotherapy.* New York: Haworth Press.

Goodsitt, A. (1984). Self psychology and the treatment of anorexia nervosa. In D. M. Garner, & P. E. Garfinkel (Eds.), *Handbook of psychotherapy for anorexia nervosa and bulimia* (pp. 55–82). New York: Guilford Press.

Goodsitt, A. (1997). Eating disorders: A self psychological perspective. In D. M. Garner, & P. E. Garfinkel (Eds.), *Handbook of psychotherapy for eating disorders* (pp. 205–228). New York: Guilford Press.

Green, A. (2001). *Life narcissism death narcissism*. London: Free Association Books.

Heaven, P. C. L. (1991). *Contemporary adolescence: A social psychological approach*. Melbourne, Australia: Macmillan.

Hermes, S. F. & Keel, P. K. (2003). The influence of puberty and ethnicity on awareness and internalization of the thin ideal. International Journal of Eating Disorders, *33*: 465–467.

Holland, A., Sicotte, N., & Treasure, J. (1988). Anorexia nervosa: Evidence for a genetic basis. *Journal of Psychosomatic Research, 32*(6), 561–571.

Huebner, H. F. (1993). *Endorphins, eating disorders and other addictive behaviors*. New York: Norton.

Johnson, C. L. (1991). Treatment of eating-disordered patients with borderline and false-self/narcissistic disorders. In C. L. Johnson (Ed.), *Psychodynamic treatment of anorexia and bulimia* (pp. 165–193). New York: Guilford.

Johnson, M. A. (1989). Concern for appropriateness scale and behavioral conformity. *Journal of Personality Assessment, 53*, 567–574.

Kaplan, A. S. & Garfinkel, P. E. (1999). Difficulties in treating patients with eating disorders: A review of patient and clinician variables. *Canadian Journal of Psychiatry, 44*(7), 665–670.

Kohut, H. (1968). The psychoanalytic treatment of narcissistic personality disorders. *Psychoanalytic Study of the Child, 23*, 86–113.

Kohut, H. (1971). *The analysis of the self*. New York: International Universities Press.

Lelwica, M. (2009). *The religion of thinness: Satisfying the spiritual hungers behind women's obsession with food and weight*. Carlsbad, CA: Gürze Books.

Lennox, R. D., & Wolfe, R. N. (1984). Revision of the self-monitoring scale. *Journal of Personality and Social Psychology, 46*, 1349–1364.

Levitan, R. D., Masellis, M., Basile, V. S., Lam, R. W., Kaplan, A. S., Davis, C., et al. (2004). The dopamine-4 receptor gene associated with binge eating and weight gain in women with seasonal affective disorder: An evolutionary perspective. *Biological Psychiatry, 56*(9), 665–669.

Mazzeo, S. E., Mitchell, K. S., Bulik, C. M., Aggen, S. H., Kendler, K. S., & Neale, M. C. (2009). A twin study of specific bulimia nervosa symptoms. *Psychological Medicine, Oct 12*, 1–11. doi:10.1017/S003329170999122X

Minuchin, S., Rosman, B.L., Baker, L. (1987). *Psychosomatic Families: Anorexia nervosa in context*. Cambridge (MA): Harvard University Press.

Modell, A. H. (1965). On having the right to a life: An aspect of the superego's development. *International Journal of Psycho-Analysis, 46*, 323–331.

Mogul, S. L. (1980). Asceticism in adolescence and anorexia nervosa. *Psychoanalytic Study of the Child, 35*, 155–175.

Paxton, S. J. (1996). Prevention implications of peer influences on body image dissatisfaction and disturbed eating in adolescent girls. *Eating Disorders, 4*, 334–347.

Piran, N. (1997). Prevention of eating disorders: Directions for future research. *Psychopharmacology Bulletin, 33*, 419–423.

Riebel, L. (2000). Hidden grandiosity in bulimics. *Psychotherapy: Theory, research, practice, training, 37*, 180–188.

Schlenker, B. R. (1982). *Impression Management: The self-concept, social identity and interpersonal relations*. Belmont, CA: Brooks/Cole.

Schupak-Neuberg, E., Nemeroff, C. (1993). Disturbances in identity and self-regulation in bulimia nervosa: Implications for a metaphorical perspective of "body as self." *International Journal of Eating Disorders, 13*, 335–347.

Seelig, B. J., & Rosof, L. S. (2001). Normal and pathological altruism. *Journal of the American Psychoanalytic Association, 49*, 933–959.

Selvini Palazzoli, M. (1978). *Self starvation.* New York: Jason Aronson.

Steiger, H., Jabalpurwala, S., Champagne, J., & Stotland, S. (1997). A controlled study of trait narcissism in anorexia and bulimia nervosa. *International Journal of Eating Disorders, 22,* 173–178.

Stone, M.H. (2000). Normal narcissism: An etiological and ethological perspective. In C. F. Ronningstam (Ed.), *Disorders of narcissism* (pp. 7–28). Northvale, NJ: Jason Aronson.

Striegel-Moore, R. H., Kearney-Cooke, A. (1994). Exploring parents' attitudes and behaviors about their children's physical appearance. *International Journal of Eating Disorders, 15,* 377–385.

Strober, M. (1991). Disorders of the self in anorexia nervosa: An organismic-developmental paradigm. In C. Johnson (Ed.), *Psychodynamic treatment of anorexia nervosa and bulimia* (pp. 354–373). New York: Guilford Press.

Strober, M., Freeman, R. N., Lampert, C., Diamond, J., & Kaye, W. (2000). Controlled family study of anorexia nervosa and bulimia nervosa: Evidence of shared liability and transmission of partial syndromes. *American Journal of Psychiatry, 157*(3), 393–400.

Tobin, D. L. (1993). Psychodynamic psychotherapy and binge eating. In C. G. Fairburn & G. T. Wilson (Eds.), *Binge eating: Nature, assessment, and treatment* (pp. 287–313). New York: Guilford.

Vandereycken, W., & Van Deth, R. (1990). *From fasting saints to anorexic girls: The history of self-starvation.* New York: University Press.

Vitousek, K., & Ewald, L. (1993). Self-representation in eating disorders: A cognitive perspective. In Z. Segal, & S. Blatt (Eds.), *The self in emotional disorders* (pp. 221–257). New York: Guildford Press.

Wechselblatt, T., Gurnick, G., & Simon, R. (2000). Autonomy and relatedness in the development of anorexia nervosa: A clinical case series using grounded theory. *Bulletin of the Menninger Clinic, 64,* 91–123.

Wertheim, E. H., Paxton, S. J., Schultz, H. K., & Muir, S. L. (1997). Why do adolescent girls watch their weight? An interview study examining sociocultural pressures to be thin. *Journal of Psychological Research, 42,* 345–355.

Winnicott, D. W. (1965). *The maturational process and the facilitating environment: Studies in the theory of emotional development.* New York: International Universities Press.

CHAPTER 8

ANIMAL HOARDING

How the Semblance of a Benevolent Mission Becomes Actualized as Egoism and Cruelty

Jane N. Nathanson and Gary J. Patronek

KEY CONCEPTS

- In animal hoarding, animals are used to support the hoarder's own emotional needs with respect to intimacy, self-esteem, control, identity, and fear of abandonment.
- Self- versus other-centeredness in animal hoarding reflects a lack of empathy and often leaves the true needs of animals unmet.
- Precipitating factors for animal hoarding likely include failure to develop functional attachment styles during childhood as a result of caregiver unavailability, neglect, or abuse.
- A hoarder's feeling of being a savior of animals is not the same as actually saving those animals. Although believing they are animals' saviors, rescuer hoarders fail to provide for the animals' basic life requirements.

THIS CHAPTER EXPLORES how a superficially benevolent and altruistic mission to save animals can fail to achieve its stated goal and instead follow a degenerative course that is egotistically self-serving and even criminal. The specific behavior to be discussed is animal hoarding, which was first defined in 1999 (Patronek, 1999), and is typified by the following characteristics:

1. Failure to provide minimal standards of sanitation, space, nutrition, and veterinary care for the animals
2. Inability to recognize the effects of this failure on the welfare of the animals, human members of the household, and the environment
3. Denial or minimization of problems and living conditions for people and animals
4. Obsessive attempts to accumulate or maintain a collection of animals in the face of progressively deteriorating conditions

A typology of animal hoarding has been described on the bases of the hoarder's motivation, level of insight, degree of defensive entrenchment, and the potential for intervention to remediate the highly problematic conditions (Patronek, Loar, & Nathanson, 2006). For the purpose of this chapter, the examples we present focus on one of these types, the *rescuer-hoarder*, since this type is most closely associated with pathological altruism. Rescuer-hoarders fervently profess that their mission is the saving of animals' lives by way of rescuing, sheltering, and caring for animals who are unwanted, homeless, and potentially to be euthanized in animal shelters. A visual description of how pet-hoarding behavior unfolds is summarized in Figure 8.1.

To an outsider, unaware of the deplorable conditions of animals kept by a hoarder, it is easy to believe the hoarder is acting benevolently and that the behavior is benign in intent and outcome. Indeed, the power of professing an altruistic motivation and goal can affect media accounts of these cases, especially when there are contributing statements from unsuspecting neighbors or people who have given animals to the hoarder. Rescuer-hoarders may act alone or in concert with a network of enablers who are either hoarders themselves or who have allowed themselves to become convinced that they are involved in altruistic behavior. In some cases, hoarders have either hijacked the efforts of a legitimate nonprofit animal welfare organization, or have set up their own nonprofit endeavor to further their seemingly altruistic actions.

The reality of animal hoarding is quite different from the picture painted by the hoarder. Animals are grossly neglected, starving, ill from infectious disease

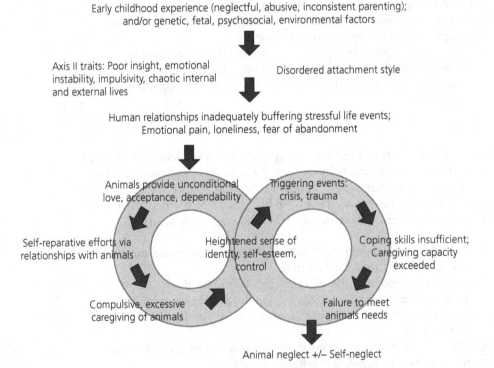

FIGURE 8.1
Proposed explanatory model for animal hoarding.

or chronic health conditions, dying, or dead. Living areas may no longer be able to serve the function for which they were intended, and basic utilities (e.g., water, electricity, sewer) or appliances (refrigerator, stove) may be nonfunctional. For human inhabitants, the conditions often meet the criteria for declaring a dwelling unfit for habitation, thereby resulting in condemnation of the home. Neighborhood residents and the community in general are adversely affected, not only with regard to safety and health, but also in terms of the costs associated with the municipality's intervention.

Childhood Experience as It Relates to Animal Hoarding and Pathological Altruism

Our clinical experience with animal hoarders frequently indicates that the person's relationship with companion animals began in a functional manner, often during childhood. However, at some point, the person develops a pattern in which animals are used as a form of emotional support. Understanding this developmental trajectory, and how it deteriorates into a self-reparative relationship in adulthood, is crucial in this discussion of pathological altruism. For example, rescuer-hoarders frequently report that in childhood their primary caregivers were unavailable, neglectful, or even physically or emotionally abusive. As we previously noted (Patronek & Nathanson, 2009), these early childhood experiences and how a child responds to other traumatic events play an important role in shaping beliefs and future interactions with animals.

This "hidden trauma of caregiver unavailability" (Lyons-Ruth et al., 2006, p. 70) may be the basis for the hoarder's unhealthy emotional attachment with companion animals. As pioneered by Bowlby (1980, 1988), attachment is such an essential biological and psychological drive that when primary caregiver attachment fails, the child may attempt to develop a relationship with a secondary attachment figure. In Nathanson's casework, the majority of animal hoarders report early childhood trauma or unsatisfactory bonding with primary caregivers. The unconditional acceptance and love derived from animals provided a buffer to help the child cope with unfulfilled needs for attachment to parents (or guardians). This child–animal relationship is normally a healthy attachment. However, it can turn into a disordered attachment style when the child's positive sense of self and worthiness of being loved is fundamentally undermined. As adults, the lives of these individuals may be characterized by chronic conflict between a longing for intimacy and a paralyzing fear of rejection. One of Nathanson's rescuer-hoarder cases presented the following background:

> Case 1: Susan reported that her mother was a college professor who was either preparing lectures, conducting classes, or mentoring individual students throughout the day; during evenings, the mother was preoccupied with grading student papers or engaged in research and writing activities. Susan's father was absent for long periods on business trips, and when at home he drank heavily. Susan conveyed that she was an only child who felt she was left to fend for herself most of the time. Considered to be "odd" by her peers, Susan stated that her lack of friends compounded her feelings of loneliness and "not being good enough" to merit more attention from her parents. According to her account, Susan's "best friends" and "playmates" were her neighbor's two dogs. She explained that, unlike her parents and peers, her animal companions were always ready to demonstrate acceptance and affection.

Disordered attachment is empirically linked to addictive-type behavior and efforts to self-repair (Flores 2004; Patronek & Nathanson, 2009). Flores (2004) comparatively describes this link:

> It is as if a person with a wide open gastric fistula were trying to still his hunger through eating. He may obtain pleasurable taste sensations by his frantic inges-tion of food but, since the food does not enter that part of the digestive system where it is absorbed into the organism, he continues to starve.

The insatiable need to repeatedly acquire and control animal dependents highlights the futility of this or any addictive behavior as a means of self-repair. Nevertheless, excessive or compulsive caregiving remains a hallmark of animal hoarding. Initially, some animals may benefit from the behavior, but such behav-ior ceases to be benign when the animals' needs for food, sanitation, comfort, socialization, exercise, and medical care become neglected in the hoarder's search for safety, self-esteem, security, and identity. This is illustrated in Case 2:

> Case 2: Paul's animal hoarding behavior developed after his wife divorced him and gained full custody of their three teenage children. Paul was an assistant manager at a pet store, where regular customers would frequently tell him about their own or others' pets who were no longer wanted and were going to be surrendered at shelters. Paul became increasingly aware of how readily and favorably animals of all types responded to him. According to his account, Paul would volunteer "I can give him/her a home." Since Paul was unable to set limits on his desire to help animals in need, every room of his small home became filled with cages of rabbits, ferrets, guinea pigs, and birds. With only narrow pathways of free space, the 35 cats and five dogs were severely restricted. He was unable to afford veterinary care for all these animals; consequently, illnesses and injuries often went untreated. Nonetheless, Paul said he believed he was doing the right thing by way of giving the animals a home. "Once the first needy and traumatized animal came into my life," he noted, "I got a huge feeling of fulfill-ment helping him and giving him a new life of his own. From there, I forgot how to say no, and the mutual love played a part. I truly didn't count—I only saw a need."

> The insatiable need to repeatedly acquire and control animal dependents highlights the futility of pet hoarding or any addictive behavior as a means of self-repair.

Hoarders often report social histories charac-terized by dysfunctional human relationships from adolescence into adulthood. According to Nathanson's clinical work, animal hoarders frequently note their attraction to girl/boyfriends, partners, and spouses whom they knew to be troubled or needy. They are unable to see the con-nection between their partners' apparent needi-ness and propensity to become highly dependent upon them and their own need to achieve relational security through their care-giving role. Case 3 presents a frequent pattern:

> Case 3: Carol reported that, as a child, she always felt she was a disappointment to her parents. The mother was a beautician prior to starting a family. The father, an artist, was frequently out of work, and financial difficulties were often the cause of her parents' arguments. At times, the father became physically abusive

to Carol's mother and verbally abusive to Carol. Carol felt her younger brother was the "favorite"—he excelled both academically and in competitive sports. Carol stated she was always criticized by her parents for numerous shortcomings in appearance, intelligence, or lack of "social graces." As a teenager, Carol sought attention from the popular "bad boys" at school. From late adolescence throughout adulthood, Carol had relationships with men she thought were "needy" (often being substance abusers, chronically unemployed, or emotionally unstable). Most relationships ended after about 2 years due to her partners' infidelity and "having taken up with other women."

Triggering Events Precipitate Hoarding

In our experience, the onset of hoarding behavior tends to be sudden and triggered by the loss of a significant, stabilizing relationship or a highly stressful, dramatic change in status, health, or lifestyle conditions. Often, a hoarder's reaction to this loss or trauma is one of "complicated grief." Distinct from normal bereavement, complicated grief is a pathological grief reaction having symptoms resembling posttraumatic stress disorder and is often associated with fears of abandonment. A triggering event frequently appears to have turned the tide from having functional relationships with animals to an abnormal dependency on an extreme level of control to temper a paralyzing fear of abandonment or insecurity. Thus, the apparent altruism arises more out of a need to self-repair in response to a trauma than from an inherent desire to selflessly assist others. It has been suggested that persons with attachment disturbances and personality traits suggesting self-regulatory defects may be at increased risk of complicated grief following loss (Prigerson et al., 1997). It is typical to observe affective instability, intense and unstable interpersonal relationships, and even dissociative symptoms in hoarders. Thus, childhood history may interact with loss to create even more difficult challenges in coping, which predisposes hoarders to pursue compulsive animal "caregiving" as an avenue of self-repair.

> Case 4: After the death of her first husband, Amanda was left to raise their only child. Her second marriage ended in divorce when she was in her forties. She maintained her career into her fifties, until the time her daughter, a divorced mother of two, was killed in a car accident. Amanda relocated to become a guardian to her grandchildren, both of whom had significant developmental disabilities. She stated the children already had a cat at the time, and although she didn't initially even like cats, she began to be aware of numerous strays or ferals in the area, some of which were very ill or pregnant, and she felt compelled to take them in. When the litters were born, Amanda said "the helplessness of the kittens got to me." Neighbors also brought unwanted cats and kittens to her, knowing she would give them a home. When the cat population grew to over 50, Amanda acknowledged that she needed "to find a way of saying no," as she realized the home had become extremely unsanitary with cat excrement and noxious odors. She feared that public health and child protection agencies might intervene and possibly condemn the home, causing her to lose custody of the children. Yet, she was unwilling to take the cats to kill shelters, and there was only one no-kill shelter in this remote, rural environment. Amanda acknowledged that, even if the no-kill shelter had available space to take any surrendered animals, she felt a deep internal conflict, noting, "They are members of my family, they provide physical attention and are a source of affection and touching not available elsewhere."

Hoarders appear to become enmeshed in a pattern of excessive need to acquire, possess, and control. Perceived unconditional love from animals serves as a path, albeit a futile one, toward healing (Patronek & Nathanson, 2009). In a tragic paradox, a hoarder's animals are denied some of the very healing efforts (compassion, comfort, empathy) sought by the hoarder. In a worst-case scenario, the hoarder acquires a healthy animal and fails to provide for its basic needs. After a terrible and lengthy period of neglect, the animal dies of preventable causes such as malnutrition, dehydration, untreated injuries, or acquired diseases.

Unselfish Versus Selfish Motivation

Although rescuer-hoarders profess unselfish motives, they themselves derive the benefit from the human–animal relationship. When asked, "Why have you become mission-bound to rescue unwanted, homeless animals?," rescuer-hoarders consistently express that their motivation is to love and care for helpless and deserving animals. While this well-intentioned motivation or concern for animals is understandable and may hold true at times or in specific cases, it is important to explore a deeper level for this motivation, which is the identification the hoarder is most likely making with helpless animals.

> While well-intentioned motivation or concern for animals is understandable . . . it is important to explore a deeper level for this motivation, which is the identification the hoarder is most likely making with helpless animals.

Brown's examination of selfobject theory (2007, 2009) provides a window into the selfishness of the relationship between a hoarder and his or her animals. Selfobject theory holds that people need certain responses from the environment around them to maintain and promote a sense of self (Brown, 2007). These responses can be provided by people, animals, things, experiences, or even ideas that promote a sense of empathy, soothing, affirmation, or calm. Brown (2007) has hypothesized that a human may come to regard an animal as a selfobject, because the animal may provide self-cohesion, self-esteem, calmness, soothing, and acceptance. With reference to Wolf (1988), Brown explains how animal selfobjects may be of one or more of three distinct types: mirroring, twinship, or idealized. Citing Wolf (1988, p. 329) she presents the mirroring and twinship functions to be most often associated with the human–animal relationship. "Mirroring selfobjects build the self by providing acceptance and affirmation of the goodness of the self. Twinship selfobjects sustain the self by providing an essential likeness of another's self."

As Case 1 described, Susan was a solitary, lonely child, adolescent, and adult. Her animal hoarding began when she moved from her family home to live independently. Susan's explanation for why she was continuously bringing in one cat after another was, "I would think that the ones I already have would want to see a new face." She was taken by surprise when Nathanson presented information about cat colonies in the wild being self-limiting; that she was creating an "artificial" colony that was in fact violating the animals' environmental needs and behaviors. Nathanson asked Susan, "Do you think that you may be the one who would like to see a new face?" Susan was so taken aback by the question that she became unable to respond in her customary defensive manner.

Failure to Recognize Others as Distinct from Self

As Brown notes, awareness of another, as well as empathy to perceive the other's needs, is required for altruism (Brown, 2009). Citing Hagman (1997, p. 10), she points toward two levels of selfobject function—archaic and mature. Archaic selfobject function, as the inability to perceive that others have "needs and lives separate and different from their own," demonstrates "self-centeredness versus other-centeredness." Empathy that relates to mature selfobject function is, therefore, "other-centeredness" and recognizes the other's perspective. If people are relating to companion animals as archaic selfobjects, they would see animals as part of themselves and therefore be unable to empathize with how the animals feel or to understand what they need apart from what the hoarder requires for herself. In functioning at the archaic level and so failing to take the perspective of the animal and behave on the animal's behalf, animal hoarders by definition fail to meet the key criteria for altruism: acting on behalf of another without expectation of self-benefit (Figure 8.2).

In animal hoarding cases, animal neglect is not uncommonly comorbid with self-neglect (Nathanson, 2009). Many animal hoarders exist in squalor, inattentive to personal and home care, and often untreated for physical and mental health problems. The rescuer-hoarders Nathanson has counseled typically explain that the accumulation of animal excrement, the toxic environment, the lack of clean facilities, and the filthy personal or home conditions are not at all objectionable to them. Several hoarders tacitly remarked, "Well, it's just a little dirty;" others commented that they didn't consider animal excrement (which covered floors, furniture, eating surfaces) to be unclean or unhealthy. Their perspective becomes, "If it's okay for me, it's okay for them," or "If I'm not concerned about it, neither are the animals." With this in mind, the hoarder does not acknowledge the distinction between oneself and others. The hoarder is not contradicted; as Brown (2009) notes : "Animals are unable to disagree with a human's interpretation of how they feel or what they want. People can believe animals feel and think exactly like them whether they actually do or not."

Rescuer-hoarders' apparent obliviousness to their animals' deplorable conditions may be conveyed by way of defensiveness, minimizing, denial, or dissociation. This lack of empathy belies any altruistic behavior or motivations. By seeing their animals as extensions of themselves, hoarders fail to acknowledge or understand whether or how their animals might have needs that are distinct from their own. In other words, by failing to acknowledge and appropriately respond to the animals as "others," rescuer-hoarders become, essentially, self-serving. Therefore, it would be erroneous to conclude that the hoarder's state of self-neglect is self-sacrificing—that is, that they are unselfishly foregoing their own needs in order to provide for their animals—and their motivation and actions cannot be rightly viewed as demonstrating the altruistic criteria of an unselfish concern for others.

Further supporting how hoarders are not self-sacrificing is their tendency to reject or strongly resist intervention to improve their personal and home conditions. These cases of self-neglect are frequently reported to Adult Protective Services (APS), as this resource is generally called upon to intervene and

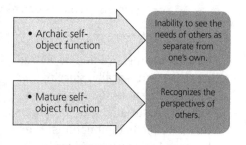

- Archaic self-object function → Inability to see the needs of others as separate from one's own.

- Mature self-object function → Recognizes the perspectives of others.

FIGURE 8.2
Archaic versus mature selfobject function.

facilitate resolution of the problems of gross deficiencies in both personal and home care practices. For the most part, the self-neglecting animal hoarder refuses all services, or at best is reluctant to acknowledge there is any need for improvement. When family members of animal hoarders have consulted with Nathanson regarding a parent, sibling, or other relative's self-neglecting behaviors, they have conveyed sincere consternation that the hoarder has refused offers of financial or hands-on assistance to remediate the hoarder's poor nutrition, physical/mental health care, unclean or insufficient clothing, home repair needs, and the like. Nathanson's casework with animal hoarders has found that, even when individuals independently have sufficient finances or community resources to provide satisfactorily for themselves, they have little or no desire to do so.

The Unattained Goal of Welfare

Channeling their excessive caregiving tendencies and energies toward the rescue and shelter of animals, rescuer-hoarders are prone to experiencing a "caregiver's high" as needy animals are in ever-abundant supply, and the hoarder derives a sense of being a savior—contrary to the reality that their animals experience. As Bonas et al. have noted, because the pet cannot verbally express an opinion of its owner, the owner may project whatever interpretation he or she wishes on the pet's behavior, and do so without fear of contradiction (Bonas, McNicholas, & Collis, 2005).

Animal hoarders tend to persist in their assertion that if they did not possess the animals, the animals would be homeless or die. However, given the severe neglect of their essential needs, animals in hoarding conditions are deprived of an environment that is in keeping with their species, and consequently they exist in prolonged states of deprivation, disease, pain, and suffering. Despite animal hoarders' expressed motivation to save animals' lives, we may well ask: "Is any life better than no life?" (Nathanson 2009). In some cases, this contradiction extends to denying death itself, with the hoarders simultaneously professing their intent to save animals from death as they step over the bodies of animals that have died as a result of their lack of care.

Rescuer-hoarders cannot be viewed as acting altruistically, since the animals are subjected to pain and suffering associated with conditions that are alien to their natures. The hoarders' professed goal to improve animal welfare fails. Especially disconcerting is the hoarder's vehement insistence or certitude, which persists even when animal protection and veterinary professionals inform the hoarder of the disease, pain, and suffering that the animals are experiencing.

If the hoarders do become affected by authoritative intervention, their response remains defensive—perhaps acknowledging that the conditions may not be "ideal," but excusing any deficiencies by remarking, in effect, that "at least they are loved, not homeless or fated to be euthanized."

> Rescuer-hoarders cannot be viewed as acting altruistically, since the animals are subjected to pain and suffering associated with conditions that are alien to their natures. The hoarders' professed goal to improve animal welfare fails.

Conclusion

Our research and casework have indicated that, prior to becoming animal hoarders, individuals reported having relationships with animals that were initially functional or beneficial, as both the human and animal(s) have served one another's needs for trust and safety, comforting responsiveness, and healthy interactions. Animals came to represent a reliable and continuous source from which a child, adolescent, or adult was able to cultivate a sense of identity, self-esteem, and control—heightened all the more when there were chronic problematic relationships with humans. The development of dysfunctional relationships with animals appears to have evolved from a trajectory of attachment disorder; related excessive caregiving behavior; codependency; and a triggering event, such as a major loss and/or trauma with subsequent complicated grief, followed by a pattern of animal acquisition and attachment in an effort to achieve self-repair. Rescuer-hoarders essentially create an exclusive domain with animals within which they strive to fulfill their own needs to feel highly valued, loved, and secure. Despite their professed altruistic motivations, ostensible goals of animal welfare, and even against their self-perception as saviors, animal hoarders fail to provide for the animals' basic requirements. Fundamentally, animals are being held captive under deplorable conditions as rescuer-hoarders deny the problem and refuse intervention to help them.

We conclude that the behavior of rescuer-hoarders is a demonstration of pathological altruism, as there is failure to fulfill the criteria of unselfish motivation, concern for other(s) distinct from self, and the goal of welfare.

References

Bonas, S., McNicholas, J., & Collis, G. (2005). Pets in the network of family relationships: An empirical study. In A. L. Podberscek, E. S. Paul, & J. A. Serpell (Eds.). *Companion animals & us.* (pp. 209–236). Cambridge, U. K.: Cambridge University Press.

Bowlby, J. (1980). *Attachment and loss:* Vol. 3. *Loss: sadness and depression.* New York: Basic Books.

Bowlby, J. (1988). *A secure base: Parent-child attachment and human development.* Great Britain: Routledge Publishing Co.

Brown, S. E. (2007). Companion animals as selfobjects. *Anthrozoos, 20,* 329–343.

Brown, S. E. (2009) (in press). Self psychological theoretical constructs of animal hoarding. *Society & Animals, Journal of Human-Animal Studies.*

Flores, P. J. (2004). *Addiction as an attachment disorder.* Latham, MD: James Aronson.

Hagman, G. (1997). Mature selfobject experience. In A. Goldberg (Ed.),. *Progress in self psychology* (Vol 13, pp. 85–107). Hillside, NJ: The Analytic Press.

Lyons-Ruth, K., Dutra, L., Schuder, M. R., & Bianchi, I. (2006). From infant attachment disorganization to adult dissociation: relational adaptations or traumatic experiences? *Psychiatric Clinics of North America* (Vol 29, pp. 63–86).

Nathanson, J. N. (2009). Animal hoarding: Slipping into the darkness of co-morbid animal and self-neglect. *Journal of Elder Abuse & Neglect, 21,* 307–324.

Patronek, G. J., Loar, L., & Nathanson, J. N. (Eds.). (2006). *Animal hoarding: Structuring interdisciplinary responses to help people, animals and communities at risk.* Retrieved January 2, 2010 from www.tufts.edue/vet/cfa/hoarding/

Patronek, G. J., & Nathanson, J.N. (2009). A theoretical perspective to inform assessment and treatment strategies for animal hoarders. *Clinical Psychology Review, 29,* 274–281.

Prigerson, H. G., Shear, M. K., Bierhals, A. J., Pilkonis, P. A., Wolfson, L., Hall, M., et al. (1997). Case histories of traumatic grief. *Omega-Journal of Death and Dying, 35,* 9–24.

Wolf, E. S. (1988). *Treating the self: Elements of clinical self psychology.* New York: The Guild Press.

CHAPTER 9

EVERYONE'S FRIEND? THE CASE OF WILLIAMS SYNDROME

Deborah M. Riby, Vicki Bruce, and Ali Jawaid

KEY CONCEPTS

- Williams syndrome illustrates how atypical development can affect social functioning.
- Individuals with the disorder are often referred to as caring, empathetic, and hypersociable.
- The Williams syndrome style of social engagement occurs alongside high levels of anxiety and social vulnerability in adults.

CHILDREN WITH THE genetic disorder Williams syndrome are often interested in interacting with other people. Despite this, adults with the syndrome are often socially isolated, in part because of their overly friendly style of interaction. Williams syndrome contrasts with autism, and both disorders illustrate how atypical neurobiological development can affect social functioning.

Here, we analyze components of the Williams syndrome social phenotype to better understand atypicalities of social orientation and interpersonal empathy. We also probe the neuronal mechanisms that underlie the atypical social phenotype. Understanding the pathology of overfriendliness in the disorder may also provide a better understanding of these traits in the general population. These findings may have important implications in medicine, sociology, and law.

The Williams Syndrome Social Phenotype

Williams syndrome is a genetic disorder with a prevalence of 1 in 20,000; it is caused by the deletion of approximately 25 genes on chromosome 7 (7q11.23; Donnai & Karmiloff-Smith, 2000). This neurodevelopmental disorder creates mild to moderate learning difficulty that occurs with more impaired nonverbal (visuospatial) processing than verbal processing. A clear example of this dissociation between verbal and nonverbal abilities was given by Bellugi and colleagues (1999) when they required individuals with Williams syndrome to both describe and draw an elephant. The verbal description was lengthy and detailed, but the drawing revealed poor linkage between the elephant's component parts.

Of particular interest in relation to this volume is the Williams syndrome social phenotype. A range of behaviors is displayed that may indicate extreme or pathological empathy—those with the disorder might best be characterized as "hypersociable" (Jones et al., 2000). Their behavior demonstrates a "social stimulus drive" (Frigerio et al., 2006) that can compel them to interact in an overly friendly fashion not only with those they know well, but even with strangers. This atypical behavior is very different from the social withdrawal shown by individuals with autism (Frith, 1989). Both autism and Williams syndrome, in their distinctly differing ways, illustrate the impact of atypical development on social expertise (Brock, Einav, & Riby, 2008).

Meeting and engaging with a person who has Williams syndrome can be a paradoxical experience. Williams syndrome individuals are usually characterized as outgoing and friendly, so whether you know the person or not, you will probably be greeted with open arms (Udwin & Yule, 1991; Udwin, Yule, & Martin, 1987). Both children and adults with the syndrome seem to enjoy social engagement, however, their open and engaging demeanor may hide underlying problems with social relationships and can have widespread implications for everyday functioning (Dykens, 2003; Mervis & Klein-Tasman, 2000).

> The behavior of those with Williams Syndrome demonstrates a "social stimulus drive" that can compel them to interact in an overly friendly fashion not only with those they know well, but even with strangers.

Children with the disorder are often referred to as "people-oriented," "sensitive," "empathetic," "affectionate," and "friendly" (Gosch & Pankau, 1997; Klein-Tasman & Mervis, 2003; Tager-Flusberg & Sullivan, 2000; Tomc, Williamson, & Pauli, 1990). Yet, Williams syndrome children experience unstable relationships and problematic interactions with peers, so that interactions with adults come to be preferred (Davies, Udwin, & Howlin, 1998). Anecdotal reports even go so as far as to suggest that children with the syndrome restrict their empathetic or affectionate behaviors to their interactions with adults. Irrespective of the course of social development, however, adults with the disorder often experience social isolation.

Other children may simply be less accommodating than adults of the social interaction styles characteristic of individuals with Williams syndrome. For example, peers may find the intense and prolonged gaze behavior that characterizes Williams syndrome off-putting (Mervis et al., 2003; Riby & Hancock, 2008, 2009). They may also be wary of the Williams syndrome style of readily approaching both familiar and unfamiliar people (Frigerio et al., 2006; Jones et al., 2000). Studies employing rating scales have noted that, in some circumstances, those with Williams syndrome show an increased rating of approachability to unfamiliar faces (Frigerio et al., 2006; Jones et al., 2000; Martens, Wilson, Dudgeon, & Reutens, 2009; but see Porter, Coltheart, & Langdon, 2007). Notably this atypical approachability can be reduced if the individual with Williams syndrome is able to accurately infer the emotion of the face they are judging (Porter et al., 2007). Increased approach ratings have important implications if extrapolated to the real world.

The long-term implication of atypical social behaviors is that about 73% of adults with Williams syndrome experience social isolation (Davies et al., 1998). Communication, independence, and socialization are clear problems for adults with the disorder (Howlin, Davies, & Udwin, 1998). For a population characterized by a friendly, caring, and empathetic manner, this level of social isolation is dramatic and has practical consequences.

Emotional Understanding

Children with Williams syndrome are described as sensitive, caring, and empathetic. These traits suggest that those with Williams syndrome may have a heightened emotional understanding of others, and they would be particularly good at interpreting emotional cues. This expectation would seem particularly appropriate given the increased attention to faces shown by those with the disorder, which could be hypothesized to provide heightened access to emotional signals. However, a range of dysfunction is seen when individuals with the disorder recognize, discriminate, and sort even the most basic facial expressions. Instead of being exceptionally good at interpreting emotional cues, those with Williams syndrome only perform at a level predicted by the mental, and not chronological, age. As individuals with the disorder are often characterized by mild-moderate learning difficulties, performance at mental age level implies that performance is well below what we might expect for someone of the same age who does not have Williams syndrome.[1]

Real-life social communication often involves a range of complex mental states that go far beyond basic facial expressions, so it would seem that perhaps those with Williams syndrome lack skill in theory of mind (ToM). Although some studies have suggested that those with the disorder show relatively intact ToM skills compared to their other intellectual abilities, in fact, when sensitive assessments have been used, performance is shown to be as expected from their mental age (again, the presence of learning difficulties means this is lower than expected for the age of the individual with Williams syndrome).[2] There is certainly no concrete evidence that individuals with Williams syndrome show strong, or even heightened, ToM ability.

Summing up, a contradiction exists between performance on emotional recognition and mental state interpretation tasks, and the everyday empathetic behavior that has been widely reported for Williams syndrome. If those with the syndrome have such clear problems interpreting basic as well as complex emotions from faces, how does this link to reports of highly empathetic and caring behavior in everyday encounters? This dissociation may map on to the dissociable components of empathetic behavior that have been suggested (e.g., Decety & Jackson, 2004). Although many different definitions of empathy exist, it seems logical that this is a multidimensional construct whereby separate components relate to (a) knowing what a person is feeling and (b) responding to another person (e.g., in times of distress). Although much work remains to be done in unraveling the difference between performance on emotion/mental state perception tasks and everyday empathetic behavior, this contradiction could provide insights into pathological empathy and may even extrapolate to individuals with atypicalities of empathetic behavior who do not have Williams syndrome.

Research has shown that when individuals with Williams syndrome show high levels of anxiety (which is frequent), they are often concerned about the well-being of other people (Dodd, Schniering, & Porter, 2009). This suggests those with Williams syndrome not only respond to other people in an empathetic manner, but that sometimes they show more concern for others than for themselves. It will be important to determine whether individuals with the disorder show care and concern for others due to purely altruistic tendencies or because they have difficulty understanding their own feelings as opposed to those of other people. Although speculative, it could be proposed that individuals with Williams syndrome have difficulty understanding the boundaries between themselves and others. In this manner, when other people are hurt, they take it as themselves being hurt and respond with heightened empathy. Future research might profitably focus on how those with Williams syndrome understand their own emotions and feelings. After all, to understand what another person is feeling well enough to respond empathetically, it is important to be able to feel and interpret those very same emotions oneself.[3]

> Individuals with Williams syndrome may have difficulty understanding the boundaries between themselves and others. When others are hurt, they may take it as themselves being hurt and respond with heightened empathy.

Another important area for future work is to understand how individuals with Williams syndrome relate to the actions and emotions of others, especially if there is preliminary evidence of high levels of empathy and altruistic tendencies in everyday situations. The mirror neuron system—the double-duty system that fires not only when a person performs an action, but also when another person is witnessed performing the action—may be implicated here. The mirror neuron system is thought to involve the prefrontal cortex, inferior parietal cortex, amygdala, and insular cortex. This system is important to ToM skill, early language development, and understanding of intentions and empathy (Schulte-Rüther, Markowitsch, Fink, & Piefke, 2007). As described earlier, Williams syndrome individuals show atypicalities in all these behaviors. In the future, functional imaging tasks involving empathetic abilities may reveal atypicalities of the mirror neuron system. If this is true, it will imply that Williams syndrome individuals are not only "overly friendly," but are true friends in the sense that they even "feel" the pain of others in an exaggerated manner, which may in turn contribute to exaggerated psychopathology.

Smooth running social interactions require interpretation of cues from other people with one critical source of information being the human face. Research suggests that, in typical development, adults possess a dedicated neural network for the interpretation of faces and other socially relevant information (Haxby, Hoffman, & Gobbini, 2000). Haxby and his colleagues note the importance of the superior temporal sulcus in the perception of communicative and changeable face cues. This region plays an important role in the visual analysis of such cues; it interacts with the extended brain, including the amygdala and limbic system as a whole, as well as with the anterior temporal regions. The role of the amygdala is particularly important when processing information of social and emotional importance (Adolphs, Tranel, Damsio, & Damasio, 1994). As noted below, it is likely that the amygdala will also play an important role in the social behaviors associated with Williams syndrome.

Williams Syndrome as Compared to Down Syndrome and Other Developmental Disorders

One question regarding all the issues raised so far is how the social phenotype of Williams syndrome is unique and syndrome-specific, particularly compared to other disorders of social engagement. We have already mentioned clear differences between Williams syndrome and autism, but another developmental disorder that affects social behavior is Down syndrome. As with Williams syndrome, Down syndrome is characterized by increased empathy and social orientation. Individuals with Down syndrome have been described as charming, social, friendly, and engaging (Dykens, Hodapp, & Finucane, 2000), and children with the disorder show concern and empathy when the person they are interacting with pretends to hurt him- or herself (Kasari et al., 1990). Children with Down syndrome also use other people as an important tool for social referencing and show more interest in attending to the person playing with them than to the toys at their disposal (Kasari et al., 1990, 1995). It could therefore be suggested that the social behaviors seen in Williams syndrome are somewhat mirrored in Down syndrome. However, differences of social behavior appear when individuals with these disorders are directly compared.

Gosch and Pankau (1996) reported that children with Williams syndrome were less reserved with strangers than children with Down syndrome (importantly, both disorders are associated with learning difficulty, as previously mentioned in relation to Williams syndrome). The Williams syndrome group was also more tearful and anxious. This finding also relates to reports by Rosner and colleagues (2004) that individuals with Williams syndrome were less socially capable than those with Down syndrome. In summary, it has been proposed that, compared to groups of individuals with other forms of intellectual difficulty and neurodevelopmental disorders, children with Williams syndrome are less reserved toward strangers, more approaching, more curious, more extroverted, and more overly affectionate (Gosch & Pankau, 1997; Tomc et al., 1990). There is therefore evidence of a syndrome-specific impact upon social behavior in Williams syndrome.

Psychopathological Implications

Individuals with Williams syndrome show outgoing social behaviors that might lead one to believe that they are not likely to experience social anxiety. But recent research suggests that individuals with Williams syndrome may show anxiety during social interactions, as well as heightened nonsocial anxiety.[4] These psychopathological characteristics are likely to be linked to the social behaviors reported in this chapter; the increased social drive that occurs in parallel with high levels of social worry and adult social isolation. The pathological empathy and socialization that characterizes the disorder may therefore have an unhealthy long-term impact. Inappropriate social orientation of individuals with Williams syndrome, along with limited cognitive abilities, are likely to be implicated in an alarmingly high rate of alleged sexual abuse (20%, according to Davies et al, 1998). Although a direct comparison has not been made, these rates appear to be higher than those reported for children and adolescents with mild to moderate intellectual disabilities (5%–14%, according to Pan, 2007 and Balogh et al., 2001). Importantly, these unhealthy social experiences, coupled with the limited social independence and general developmental delay, are likely to relate to additional underreported psychopathology in this disorder, as for example with posttraumatic stress disorder or substance abuse.

The Hunt for Underlying Neural Mechanisms

The neurobiological underpinning of the Williams syndrome social phenotype has been a topic of considerable recent research. Performing conventional neuropsychological testing has proved somewhat difficult because of the level of general intellectual functioning that accompanies the disorder. Instead, studies investigating neuroanatomical localization of hypersociability have focused on approachability tasks and imaging modalities. Two neuroanatomical foci have recently been proposed as central to the Williams syndrome phenotype; namely, the amygdala and the frontal lobes.

Two neuroanatomical foci have recently been proposed as central to the Williams syndrome phenotype: the amygdala and the frontal lobes.

A Role for the Amygdala

Individuals with Williams syndrome show abnormalities of amygdala structure and functioning that are probably related to atypical social functioning.[5] This is not surprising, as the amygdala is critical to the perception of facial expressions, and individuals with amygdala damage have difficulty interpreting complex emotions in much the same way as seen in Williams syndrome. The abnormalities also extend to amygdala–prefrontal connectivity, as shown by Meyer-Lindenberg and his colleagues (2006) using functional magnetic resonance imaging (fMRI) techniques. This study revealed that when adults with Williams syndrome attend to angry and fearful facial expressions, they experience reduced amygdala activation. Similar findings have been suggested by measurement of galvanic skin response and evidence of general hypoarousal, an amygdala-mediated measure. Plesa-Skwerer et al. (2009) reported hypoarousal when individuals with Williams syndrome attend to emotionally expressive faces, whereas Doherty-Sneddon et al. (2009) reported hypoarousal during one-to-one interactions.[6]

Involvement of the amygdala is also implicated by comparison with other populations known to show atypicalities of amygdala functioning and atypical social behavior. The Williams syndrome social phenotype is closely related to that of "SM," an individual diagnosed with Urback-Weithe syndrome who had isolated bilateral calcification of the amygdala (Bellugi et al., 1999). SM and other individuals with isolated bilateral amygdala impairment exhibit deficits in the recognition of negative emotions (anger, fear; Adolphs et al., 1994). They also show increased approachability to faces typically deemed inapproachable (Adolphs, Tranel, & Damasio, 1998). The link to the social characteristics associated with Williams syndrome is clear (for a discussion see Jawaid et al. (2010)). Interestingly, one previous study focusing on atypical approachability in Williams syndrome revealed a correlation between right amygdala volume and approachability ratings for negative faces (Martens et al., 2009). However, it is difficult to accommodate divergent approachability findings in the current Williams syndrome literature with *direct* links to amygdala atypicality. Porter et al. (2007) report that Williams syndrome approachability behavior is not typical of isolated amygdala impairment. Moreover, there is no evidence suggesting *selective* deficits in the ability to correctly identify expressions of anger and untrustworthiness. Therefore, the heterogeneity of the existing approachability data and the lack of selective emotional recognition deficits seen in Williams syndrome suggest involvement of additional neuroanatomical mechanisms. Importantly, however, it is likely that these additional atypicalities exist alongside those seen for the amygdala.

Involvement of the Frontal Lobes

Researchers have suggested that the hypersociable characteristics of individuals with Williams syndrome result from an inability to suppress impulses toward social interactions. A fundamental aspect of this hypothesis is that individuals with Williams syndrome do know the difference between "good" and "bad"; however, they exhibit exaggerated approachability due to an inability to control impulses as a consequence of frontal lobe dysfunction (Porter et al., 2007). The strongest evidence for this comes from an approachability study showing that "normal" approachability ratings were given to faces in which the Williams syndrome participant could correctly label the expressed emotion (e.g., happy, sad, angry). Porter and colleagues suggest that other reports of increased approachability could actually be due to impaired response inhibition (Porter et al., 2007).

More general frontal lobe impairment, measured through the ability to control attention, has also been reported in Williams syndrome. Thus, the syndrome's effects are not restricted to social behaviors. Lincoln, Lai, and Jones (2002) reported problems in those with Williams syndrome in alternating attention between an auditory and a visual target. Similarly, Cornish, Scerif, and Karmiloff-Smith (2007) noted that infants and toddlers with Williams syndrome differed from infants with fragile X syndrome due to problems in disengaging attention in a visual search task. Indeed, Williams syndrome patients show widespread difficulties in the control and modulation of attention. It is likely that problems in shifting and modulating attention exist throughout the developmental spectrum of Williams syndrome and are likely to play a role in both socially and nonsocially relevant information processing (see Rhodes et al., 2010.

> Amygdala dysfunction might lead to altered social judgment, which might manifest as an atypical autonomic response, while the frontal lobes might modulate attention and approach behaviors based on these signals.

Given the heterogeneity of evidence, it is not currently possible to posit an isolated neuronal localization of hypersociability in Williams syndrome. The amygdala and frontal lobes are both implicated at different levels in the heightened salience toward social information. Amygdala dysfunction might lead to altered social judgment, which might manifest as an atypical autonomic response, while the frontal lobes might modulate attention and approach behaviors based on these signals. Although speculative, the authors hypothesize that social cognition in primates is governed by complex neuronal circuitry, akin to a Papez circuit[7] for memory storage. The amygdala and frontal lobes may be the two interlinked regulators of this proposed circuit. The distinct Williams syndrome social phenotype could be a result of deviance within this complex circuit, which may occur either due to frontal lobe dysfunction, amygdala impairment, or both.

Conclusion

We have used the genetic disorder Williams syndrome to illustrate the impact of atypical development on social behavior, with a particular focus on the empathetic nature of individuals with the disorder. Although at a gross level individuals with the disorder seem highly engaging and appear sociable and empathetic, the Williams syndrome social phenotype shows much atypicality (as evidenced in Figure 9.1). These atypicalities play a role in problems forging peer friendships during childhood, and in the emergence of social anxieties or isolation later in life. Recent research has focused on the neural underpinnings of this

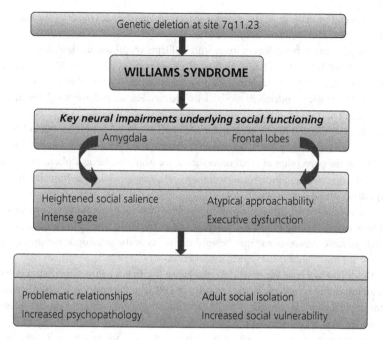

FIGURE 9.1
A descriptive account of the social domain of Williams syndrome.

social behavior and identified the possible involvement of the amygdala and the frontal lobes. There is still a great deal of work to be done in understanding the exact nature of the neural underpinnings of social behavior shown by those with the syndrome.

Notes

1. For descriptions of the sensitive, caring, and empathetic nature of those with Williams syndrome, see Klein-Tasman and Mervis (2003), Tager-Flusberg and Sullivan (2000), and Gosch and Pankau (1997). For an analysis of recognition see Gagliardi et al. (2003); Plesa-Skwerer, Verbalis, Schofield, Faja, and Tager-Flusberg (2006); and Porter, Coltheart, and Langdon (2007). For discrimination, see Karmiloff-Smith, Klima, Bellugi, Grant, and Baron-Cohen (1995). For heightened attention to faces in those with Williams syndrome, see Mervis et al. (2003) and Riby and Hancock (2008, 2009). Finally, for a general review of an emotional understanding of others, see Decety and Jackson (2004).

2. Theory of mind skill relates to the ability to understand feelings and thoughts expressed by other people—it is critical to social expertise and empathy (Baron-Cohen, 1995). For findings of relatively intact theory of mind in Williams syndrome patients, see Karmiloff-Smith, Klima, Bellugi, Grant, and Baron-Cohen (1995) and Tager-Flusberg, Boshart, and Baron-Cohen (1998). For assessment of mental age level performance in Williams syndrome, see Plesa-Skwerer et al. (2006).

3. Interestingly, research has indicated similar problems in understanding one's own feelings and emotions in individuals with Asperger syndrome and related syndromes of alexithymia (a disorder of the ability to identify and describe feelings). A number of studies have reported a correlation between Asperger syndrome and alexithymia, especially type II alexithymia, in which emotions are consciously experienced, but there

exists no cognitive capacity to describe those feelings (Berthoz & Hill, 2005; Fitzgerald & Bellgrove, 2006; Hill, Berthoz, & Frith, 2004).

4. Outgoing social behaviors of those with Williams syndrome are described by Doyle et al. (2004) and Jones et al. (2000). Nonsocial anxieties are described by Mervis and Klein-Tasman (2000); the higher incidence of nonsocial anxieties over social anxieties is described by Leyfer, Woodruff-Borden, Klein-Tasman, Fricke, and Mervis (2006) and Dodd et al. (2009).

5. For atypical social functioning and the relation to amygdala functioning in Williams syndrome, see Haas et al. (2009). See Adolphs et al. (1994) for the importance of the amygdala in the perception of facial expressions. See Adolphs, Baron-Cohen, and Tranel (2002) for a discussion of individuals with amygdala damage and their difficulty in interpreting complex emotions.

6. It should be noted that galvanic skin response involves more than the amygdala—the prefrontal cortex and the brainstem also play a role. Therefore, atypicality measured through galvanic skin response may be an abnormality of the autonomic nervous system and may not solely indicate amygdala dysfunction.

7. Described by James Papez in 1937, the Papez circuit is a neurocortical circuit that plays an important role in the storage of memories. The initial pathway is described as hippocampal formation → fornix → mamillary bodies → mamillothalamic nuclei → anterior thalamic nucleus → genu of internal capsule → cingulate cortex → cingulum → parahip-pocampal gyrus → entorhinal cortex → perforant pathway → hippocampus. Recent evidence suggests that prefrontal cortex and amygdala may make important contributions to the circuit as well.

References

Adolphs, R., Baron-Cohen, S., & Tranel, D. (2002). Impaired recognition of social emotions following amygdala damage. *Journal of Cognitive Neuroscience, 14,* 1264–1274.

Adolphs, R., Tranel, D., Damasio, H., & Damasio, A. (1994). Impaired recognition of emotion in facial expressions following bilateral damage to the human amygdala. *Nature, 372,* 669–672.

Adolphs, R., Tranel, D., & Damasio, A. R. (1998). The human amygdala in social judgment. *Nature, 393,* 470–474.

Balogh, R., Bretherton, K., Whibley, S., Berney, T., Graham, S., Richold, P., et al. (2001). Sexual abuse in children and adolescents with intellectual disability. *Journal of Intellectual Disability Research, 45,* 194–201.

Baron-Cohen, S. (1995). *Mindblindness: An essay on autism and theory of mind.* Cambridge, MA: MIT Press.

Bellugi, U., Lichtenberger, E., Mills, D., Galaburda, A., & Korenberg, J. R. (1999). Bridging cognition, brain, and molecular genetics: Evidence from Williams syndrome. *Trends in Neuroscience, 5,* 197–208.

Berthoz, S., & Hill, E. L. (2005). Reliability of the Bermond-Vorst Alexithymia questionnaire. Data from adults with autism spectrum disorder, their relatives and normal controls. *European Psychiatry, 20,* 291–298.

Brock, J., Einav, S., & Riby, D. M. (2008). The other end of the spectrum? Social cognition in Williams syndrome. In V. Reid, & T. Striano (Eds.) *Social Cognition: Development, neuroscience and autism.* Oxford: Blackwell.

Cornish, K., Scerif, G., & Karmiloff-Smith, A. (2007). Tracing syndrome-specific trajectories of attention across the lifespan. *Cortex, 43,* 672–685.

Davies, M., Udwin, O., & Howlin, P. (1998). Adults with Williams syndrome. Preliminary study of social, emotional and behavioral difficulties. *British Journal of Psychiatry, 172*, 273–276.

Decety, J., & Jackson, P. L. (2004). The functional architecture of human empathy. *Behavioral and Cognitive Neuroscience Reviews, 3*, 71–100.

Dodd, H. F., Schniering, C. A., & Porter, M. A. (2009). Beyond behaviour: Is social anxiety low in williams syndrome? *Journal of Autism and Developmental Disorder, 39*, 1673–1681.

Doherty-Sneddon, G., Riby, D., Calderwood, L., & Ainsworth, L. (2009). Stuck on you: Face-to-face arousal and gaze aversion in Williams syndrome. *Cognitive Neuropsychiatry, 14*, 510–523.

Donnai, D., & Karmiloff-Smith, A. (2000). Williams syndrome: From genotype through to cognitive phenotype. *American Journal of Medical Genetics, 97*, 164–171.

Doyle, T. F., Bellugi, U., Korenberg, J. R., & Graham, J. (2004). "Everybody in the world is my friend" Hypersociability in young children with Williams syndrome. *American Journal of Medical Genetics, 124A*, 263–273.

Dykens, E. M. (2003). Anxiety, fears, and phobias in persons with Williams syndrome. *Developmental Neuropsychology, 23*, 291–316.

Dykens, E. M., Hodapp, R. M., & Finucane, B. M. (2000). *Genetics and mental retardation syndromes: A new look at behavior and interventions.* Baltimore: Brookes.

Fitzgerald, M., & Bellgrove, M. A. (2006). Letter to the editor: The overlap between alexithymia and Asperger's syndrome. *Journal of Autism and Developmental Disorders, 36*, 573–576.

Frigerio, E., Burt, D. M., Gagliardi, C., Cioffi, G., Martelli, S., Perrett, D. I., & Borgatti, R. (2006). Is everybody always my friend? Perception of approachability in Williams syndrome. *Neuropsychologia, 44*, 254–259.

Frith, U. (1989). *Autism: Explaining the enigma.* Oxford: Blackwell.

Gagliardi, C., Frigerio, E., Burt, D. M., Cazzaniga, I., Perrett, D. I., & Borgatti, R. (2003). Facial expression recognition in Williams syndrome, *Neuropsychologia, 41*, 733–738.

Gosch A., & Pankau R. (1996). Psychologische aspekte beim Williams-Beuren syndrom. *Forum Kinderarzt, 9*, 8–11.

Gosch, A., & Pankau, R. (1997). Personality characteristics and behavior problems in individuals of different ages with Williams syndrome. *Developmental Medicine and Child Neurology, 39*, 527–533.

Haas, B. W., Mills, D., Yam, A., Hoeft, F., Bellugi, U., & Reiss, A. (2009). Genetic influences on sociability: Heightened amygdala reactivity and event-related responses to positive social stimuli in Williams syndrome. *Journal of Neuroscience, 29*, 1132–1139.

Haxby, J. V., Hoffman, E. A., Gobbini, M. I. (2000). The distributed human neural system for face perception. *Trends in cognitive sciences, 4*, 223–233.

Hill, E. L., Berthoz, S., & Frith, U. (2004). Cognitive processing of own emotions in individuals with autistic spectrum disorder and their relatives. *Journal of Autism and Developmental Disorders, 34*, 229–235.

Howlin, P., Davies, M., & Udwin, O. (1998). Cognitive functioning in adults with Williams syndrome. *Journal of Child Psychology and Psychiatry, 39*, 183–189.

Jawaid, A., Riby, D. M., Egridere, S., Schmolck, H., Kass, J. S., & Schulz, P. E. (2010). Approachability in Williams syndrome. *Neuropsychologia. 48*, 1521–1523.

Jones, W., Bellugi, U., Lai, Z., Chiles, M., Reilly, J., Lincoln, A., & Adolphs, R. (2000). Hypersociability in Williams syndrome. *Journal of Cognitive Neuroscience, 12*, 30–46.

Karmiloff-Smith, A., Klima, E., Bellugi, U., Grant, J., & Baron-Cohen, S. (1995). Is there a social module? Language, face processing, and theory of mind in individuals with Williams syndrome. *Journal of Cognitive Neuroscience, 7*, 196–208.

Kasari, C., Mundy, P., Yirmiya, N., & Sigman, M. (1990). Affect and attention in children with Down syndrome. *American Journal on Mental Retardation, 95,* 55–67.

Kasari, C., Freeman, S., Mundy, P., & Sigman, M. (1995). Attention regulation by children with Down syndrome: Coordinated joint attention and social referencing looks. *American Journal on Mental Retardation, 100,* 128–136.

Klein-Tasman, B. P., & Mervis, C. B. (2003). Distinctive personality characteristics of children with Williams syndrome. *Developmental Neuropsychology, 23,* 271–292.

Leyfer, O. T., Woodruff-Borden, J., Klein-Tasman, B. P., Fricke, J. S., & Mervis, C. B. (2006). Prevalence of psychiatric disorders in 4 to 16-year olds with Williams syndrome. *American Journal of Medical Genetics, 141,* 615–622.

Lincoln, A., Lai, Z. & Jones, W. (2002). Shifting attention and joint attention dissociation in Williams syndrome: Implications for the cerebellum and social deficits in autism. *Neurocase, 8,* 226–232.

Martens, M. A., Wilson, S. J., Dudgeon, P., & Reutens, D. C. (2009). Approachability and the amygdala: Insights from Williams syndrome. *Neuropsychologia, 47,* 2446–2453.

Mervis, C. B., & Klein-Tasman, B. P. (2000). Williams syndrome: Cognition, personality, and adaptive behavior. *Mental Retardation & Developmental Disability Research Reviews, 6,* 148–158.

Mervis, C. B., Morris, C. A., Klein-Tasman, B. P., Bertrand, J., Kwitny, S., Appelbaum, L. G., & Rice, C. E. (2003). Attentional characteristics of infants and toddlers with Williams syndrome during triadic interactions. *Developmental Neuropsychology, 23,* 243–268.

Meyer-Lindenberg, A., Mervis, C. B., & Berman, K. F. (2006). Neural mechanisms in Williams syndrome: A unique window to genetic influences on cognition and behavior. *Nature Reviews Neuroscience, 7,* 380–393.

Pan, S. M. (2007). Prevalence of sexual abuse of people with intellectual disabilities in Taiwan. *Intellectual Development and Disability, 45,* 373–379.

Plesa-Skwerer, D., Verbalis, A., Schofield, C., Faja, S., & Tager-Flusberg, H. (2006). Social-perceptual abilities in adolescents and adults with Williams syndrome. *Cognitive Neuropsychology, 23,* 338–349.

Plesa-Skwerer, D., Borum, L., Verbalis, A., Schofield, C., Crawford, N., Ciciolla, L., & Tager-Flusberg, H. (2009). Autonomic responses to dynamic displays of facial expressions in adolescents and adults with Williams syndrome. *Social Cognitive and Affective Neuroscience, 4,* 93–100.

Porter, M. A., Coltheart, M., & Langdon, R. (2007). The neuropsychological basis of hypersociability in Williams and Down syndrome. *Neuropsychologia, 45,* 2839–2849.

Rhodes, S. M., Riby, D. M., Park, J., Fraser, E., & Campbell, L. E. (*2010*). Executive neuropsychological functioning in individuals with Williams syndrome. *Neuropsychologia.* 48, 1216–1226.

Riby, D. M., & Hancock, P. J. B. (2008). Viewing it differently: Social scene perception in Williams syndrome and Autism. *Neuropsychologia, 46,* 2855–2860.

Riby, D. M., & Hancock, P. J. B. (2009). Looking at movies and cartoons: Eye-tracking evidence from Williams syndrome and autism. *Journal of Intellectual Disability Research. 53,* 169–181.

Rosner, B. A., Hodapp, R. M., Fidler, D. J., Sagun, J. N., & Dykens, E. M. (2004). Social competence in persons with Prader-Willi, Williams and Down's syndrome. *Journal of Applied Research in Intellectual Disability, 17,* 209–217.

Schulte-Rüther, M., Markowitsch, H. J., Fink, G. R., & Piefke, M. (2007). Mirror neuron and theory of mind mechanisms involved in face-to-face interactions: A functional magnetic resonance imaging approach to empathy. *Journal of Cognitive Neuroscience, 19,* 1354–1372.

Tager-Flusberg, H., Boshart, J., & Baron-Cohen, S. (1998). Reading the windows to the soul: Evidence of domain-specific sparing in Williams syndrome. *Journal of Cognitive Neuroscience, 10,* 631–639.

Tager-Flusberg, H., & Sullivan, K. (2000). A componential view of theory of mind: Evidence from Williams syndrome. *Cognition, 76,* 59–89.

Tomc, S. A., Williamson, N. K., & Pauli, R. M. (1990). Temperament in Williams syndrome. *American Journal on Medical Genetics, 36,* 345–352.

Udwin, O., & Yule, W. (1991). A cognitive and behavioural phenotype in Williams syndrome. *Journal of Clinical and Experimental Neuropsychology, 13,* 232–244.

Udwin, O., Yule, W., & Martin, N. (1987). Cognitive abilities and behavioural characteristics of children with idiopathic infantile hypocalcaemia. *Journal of Child Psychology and Psychiatry and Allied Disciplines, 28,* 297–309.

PART III

SOCIETAL IMPLICATIONS OF PATHOLOGICAL ALTRUISM

CHAPTER 10

PATHOLOGICAL CERTITUDE

Robert A. Burton[1]

In *Les Miserables*, Victor Hugo describes the policeman, Javert, whose role is
to embody "justice"—or, to be precise, "the law":

> Probity, sincerity, candor, conviction, the sense of duty, are things which
> may become hideous when wrongly directed; but which, even when hideous,
> remain grand: their majesty, the majesty peculiar to the human conscience,
> clings to them in the midst of horror; they are virtues which have one
> vice—error. . . . Nothing could be so poignant and so terrible as . . . the
> *evil of the good.* (Hugo, 1862)

KEY CONCEPTS

- Believing that you are acting in another's best interest is not synonymous
  with acting in another's best interest. It is a belief, not a fact.
- Moral judgments, such as "good intentions," arise out of basic
  biological drives, not out of inherent goodness or evilness.
- Justifications of behavior such as "I'm just trying to help," should be
  used with great restraint and viewed with great skepticism.

DR. X., A prominent oncologist widely known for his aggressive approach to
treatment of even the most terminal patients, has asked me to do a spinal tap on
an elderly man with advanced widespread cancer. "He's not as mentally clear as
he was yesterday. Maybe he has an infection—meningitis, a brain abscess—
something treatable." I've known Dr. X. for years and have no doubt about his
clinical skills and his utter dedication to his patients. Medicine is his life; he's
available 24/7, and, when all fails, he even attends his patients' funerals. And yet,
I dread working with him. Driven by a personal, unshakable ethic of what a
good doctor *must do* for his patients, he wears his mission on his rolled-up
sleeves, his full-steam-ahead attitude challenging and often shaming those of us
who favor palliative care over prolongation of a life at any cost. He has the
intense, uncompromising look of someone with a calling.

Upon entering the room, spinal tap tray in hand, I am confronted by the
patient's family. "Please, no more," they say in unison, backed up by the frail

patient's silent nodding. "Could you talk with Dr. X, tell him that we're all in agreement?"

I page Dr. X and explain the family's wishes. "No, I want the spinal tap done now," he says. "And don't try to tell me how to practice medicine. I know what's best for my patients."

"Please," the wife pleads, her hand gripping my arm. She'd overhead Dr. X on the phone. "I know that he cares, but it's not what we want." But moments later, Dr. X rushes in with his characteristic air of urgency, and explains why the test is necessary. No one really believes him, not the patient, not the family, and certainly not the nurse who turns away to hide her look of "how could you?" And yet, the family accedes. Even the patient agrees to the test, resigning himself to more poking and prodding, pain and suffering, in order not to offend his doctor. I, too, give in.

The spinal tap is difficult and painful, and reveals nothing treatable. The patient has a post-spinal tap headache that lasts until he lapses into coma and dies 3 days later. Afterward, in talking with Dr. X, it's clear that he's learned nothing from this experience. "It could have been something; you can't know if you don't look. End of discussion."

Sadly, the exuberant healer who unintentionally harms his patients (and, indirectly, their families and caretakers) is all too common. One need only think of the doctors who recommend back surgeries such as spinal fusions, despite knowing that there is no convincing evidence of a lasting benefit, and that a significant percentage of patients will incur more pain and disability as a result of the surgery (Deyo, Nachemson, & Mirza, 2004; Leape, 1989). Worse, these same surgeons are well aware of the diagnosis specifically designed to categorize patients with a bad surgical outcome—*failed back surgery syndrome* (Harutyunyan, 2009).

When wondering why physicians promote unnecessary, even harmful treatments, we tend to think of negative psychological mechanisms ranging from greed and avarice to ignorance, arrogance, and indifference. Perhaps the most oft-quoted explanation/accusation is that "doctors think they're gods." Yet, often, these physicians are motivated by nothing more than a judgment clouded by an excessive sense of obligation to help others (Browne, 2003).

> Despite the fact that a moral conviction feels like a deliberate, rational conclusion to a particular line of reasoning, it is neither a conscious choice nor even a thought process.

Many of the chapters in this book present evidence that a significant component of "altruistic" behavior is biologically mediated. But altruistic behavior may result from the mixing and matching of seemingly unrelated desires and motivations. A combination of fear of humiliation, a rigid upbringing that requires strict adherence to religious precepts, and a desire not to stand out as different, might produce the same "altruistic" behavior as someone with an empathic "pureness of generosity" that approaches saintliness.

Although motivations will vary, the thread linking all altruistic behavior is a profound sense of conviction that one's actions are both morally correct and serve an ultimate good. Yet, despite the fact that a moral conviction feels like a deliberate, rational conclusion to a particular line of reasoning, it is neither a conscious choice nor even a thought process. Certainty and similar states of "knowing what we know" arise out of primary brain mechanisms that, like love or anger, function independently of rationality or reason (Burton, 2008a, 2008b).

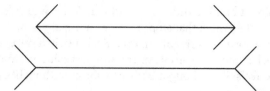

FIGURE 10.1
Line length optical illusion; both lines are the same length.

To get a feeling for this separation between objective and "felt" knowledge, look at the Muller-Lyer optical illusion in Figure 10.1.

Even when we can accurately determine that these two horizontal lines are the same length, we experience the simultaneous disquieting sensation that this thought—the lines are of equal length—is not correct. Our objective, conscious measurements are in conflict with unconscious elements of visual perception that judge comparative lengths based upon additional cues, such as the shape of objects.

With this example, you get a palpable sense of how we can have different and conflicting forms of knowledge—the strictly conscious determinations that can be easily verified, and unconsciously mediated mental sensations. (William James coined the phrase "felt knowledge" to describe this feeling of knowing that occurs in the absence of any awareness of actively thinking).

This sensation can vary in intensity. On one end of the spectrum would be the tip-of-the-tongue sense that you know a name that you can't directly recall, or the subtle feeling that you recognize someone but can't place her. At the other end is the profound sense of understanding—the "a-ha" or "Eureka, I've got it" moment when a difficult puzzle or problem suddenly "makes sense." For simplicity, I have chosen to lump together the closely allied feelings of certainty, rightness, conviction, correctness, and recognition under the all-inclusive term, the *feeling of knowing.*

It is easy to speculate on why our brain might have developed such a potentially misleading sensation. Foremost would be the role in learning. All thoughts need a reward—a sense that you have made the right choice, or at least are on the right track. This intimate relationship between thought and reward is best seen in the imaging and detailed anatomic studies, as well as microelectrode implantations, that demonstrate extensive connections between the regions of the brain responsible for pleasure–reward systems, affect and emotion, and opioid peptides (endorphins) (Schultz et al., 2008). This *mesolimbic dopamine system* extends from the upper brainstem (the ventral tegmental area) to regions that integrate emotion and cognition, including portions of the limbic system, orbitofrontal cortex, and the nucleus accumbens (Shidara & Richmond, 2002).

Second, the feeling of knowing also provides a very clever evolutionary adaptation to the age-old metaphysical problem that no thought can permanently and absolutely confirm another. As an isolated system, thought is doomed to the perpetual "yes, but" that arises out of not being able to know what you don't know. The first time you escape a charging lion by running up a tree, reason will tell you that this is an excellent strategy. But, eventually, you learn from experience that great strategies sometimes fail miserably and that there might be better options that you haven't considered. The best that reason can do in the way of confirmation of the strategy is to declare that climbing the tree was effective *this time.*

Without a circuit breaker, indecision and inaction would rule the day. What is needed is a mental switch that stops infinite ruminations and calms our fears of missing an unknown superior alternative. Such a switch can't be a thought, or we would be back at the same problem. The simplest solution would be to evolve a sensation that feels like a thought but isn't subject to thought's perpetual self-questioning.

This feeling of knowing also serves as a moment-to-moment guide to our perceptions. Consider a scenario in which you've been invited to dinner at Joe Blow's. It's been 20 years since you've been to his home. It's a dark and stormy night; none of the street addresses is visible. You trust your memory to tell you which is Joe's place. You drive past row upon row of houses without any prompting a sense of familiarity. Then, without you having any particular thought, you have the distinct feeling that a particular house is Joe's.

At a basic perceptual level, a bevy of interconnected neural networks have scanned myriad aspects of each house—color, shape, size, pattern of window placement, number of stairs, etc.—comparing the incoming image with the previously stored image of Joe's place. When the networks sense a good match, the feeling of recognition is triggered. The closer the match, the stronger will be this feeling of knowing that the house is Joe's. Seen in this light, the feeling of knowing is the mental sensation that corresponds to our unconscious calculation of the likelihood of correctness.

To clarify this intimate relationship between unconscious perception and how we sense something is correct, let me borrow a term, "hidden layer," from the artificial intelligence (AI) community.

By mimicking the way the brain processes information, AI scientists have been able to build artificial neural networks (ANNs) that can play chess and poker, read faces, recognize speech, and recommend books at Amazon.com. Unlike a fixed computer program, the ANNs are initially devoid of any specific information or guidance. For example, when you first go to Amazon, it has no recommendations for other books. But as soon as you purchase books, Amazon will begin to learn your preferences. Each additional purchase will further refine what recommendations the AI program makes. These recommendations result from calculations made in the hidden layer—a theoretical hub interposed between inputs and outputs in which resides the set of equations that weighs all incoming information in order to generate the names of those books that you are most likely to buy.

With an ANN, the hidden layer is conceptually located within the interrelationships between all the incoming information and the mathematical code used to process it. In the human brain, the hidden layer isn't a discrete interface or specific anatomic structure; rather, it functions within the connections between all neurons involved in any neural network.

The hidden layer offers a powerful metaphor for the way the brain processes information. It is in the hidden layer that our unique traits, from genetic predispositions to neurotransmitter variations and fluctuations, and past experience, whether remembered or long-forgotten, shape incoming information into our conscious perceptions and thoughts. It is the anatomic crossroad where nature and nurture intersect and individual personalities emerge. It is why your red is not my red, your idea of beauty isn't mine, why eyewitnesses offer differing accounts of an accident, or why we don't all put our money on the same roulette number.

In addition to creating sensory perceptions and thoughts, the hidden layer lets us know the likelihood that these outputs are correct. These hidden layer calculations occur outside of awareness and our direct control. If the hidden layer determines that it has recognized Joe Blow's house, it sends up into consciousness the feeling of knowing that we are looking at Joe's place. *Without a doubt* is nothing more than an involuntary sensation of a perfect match. But objective verification depends on who answers the door. If it's Joe, the feeling of knowing is justified. But the feeling can be completely misleading, as when a total stranger answers and curtly tells you that Joe lives four doors down the street.

Now, apply this same line of reasoning to conceptualizing a thought. Imagine a colleague asking you, "How should one live the good life?" Before you even understand what you are being asked (the time necessary for conscious auditory perception), the question will have been inputted to those neural networks that you've previously established for considering life's meaning and purpose. Like members of a vast committee, each personal influence weighs in, bringing up everything from subtle genetic tendencies for risk-taking, empathy, and altruism to advice from parents, teachers, friends, and yes, enemies. Powerful prior encounters with memorable role models will cast their votes. So will aphorisms and one-liners from long-forgotten comic book heroes and fortune cookies. The final tally (output from the networks) will determine what your initial approach to the question will be. The first phrase that pops into your mind will be nothing more than a verbalization of what the hidden layer has sent up into consciousness as its first approximation of a response.

Suppose that your initial response to the best way to lead the good life is "to be kind to others." The stronger the accompanying feeling of correctness, the greater the likelihood that this answer will become a guiding principle in how you treat others.

But here's the rub. What feels like a conscious life-affirming moral choice—*my life will have meaning if I help others*—will be greatly influenced by the strength of an unconscious and involuntary mental sensation that tells me that this decision is "correct." It will be this same feeling that will tell you the "rightness" of giving food to starving children in Somalia, doing every medical test imaginable on a clearly terminal patient, or bombing an Israeli school bus.

It helps to see this feeling of knowing as analogous to other bodily sensations over which we have no direct control. At the simplest level, we can't stop a cut forearm nerve from creating the sensation of numbness and tingling in our hand. At a more complex level, we cannot sidestep unjustified sensations that arise out of involuntary brain mechanisms. Consider the example of phantom limb pain. A man's arm is accidentally amputated. The region of brain that previously received sensory inputs from the now-missing arm undergoes changes that cause it to misfire. The tragic result is the ghostly and often painful recreation of the missing arm—the so-called phantom limb. As with the forearm nerve injury, in which you cannot will away the numbness, the amputee can clearly see that the arm is missing, yet cannot stop the disturbing phantom limb sensations. All the amputee can do is learn to cope, beginning with the recognition that the sense of the presence of his arm is a perceptual illusion.

Although the study of the evolutionary roots of morality is in its infancy, evidence to date strongly supports a major biological role underlying our moral choices (Glausiusz, 2007). For example, how you view suspected terrorist interrogation techniques such as water-boarding would be subliminally influenced by your degree of innate empathy for the victim, general level of squeamishness, tendency toward paranoia, or phobia of drowning. Of course, personal experiences such as losing a close friend in the World Trade Center bombing would also play a role. All of these personality traits and memories can be conceptualized as being voting members of the hidden layer committee that prods us to advocate or decry water-boarding.

But there is a compounding problem. Given that the feeling of knowing is the reward for a thought, the more important the question, the greater the pleasure will seem. For example, it's certainly satisfying to figure out which is Joe's house, or solve a math problem, but consider how much more powerful would the reward feel if it represented an answer to such a profound question as how best to live your life.

Talk to an insistent know-it-all who refuses to consider contrary opinions and you get a palpable sense of how the feeling of knowing can create a mental state akin to an addiction. "My mind is made up; don't bother me with facts" is the garden-variety expression of the power of "knowing" to resist contrary evidence. If the sense of pleasure in being certain about mundane opinions, such as one's political affiliation, prevents an open mind, imagine the profound effect of feeling certain that you have ultimate answers, such as the meaning of life and how best to achieve this sense of meaning. Relinquishing such strongly felt personal beliefs would require undoing or lessening major connections with the overwhelmingly seductive pleasure–reward circuitry. Think of such a shift of opinion as producing the same type of physiological changes as withdrawing from drugs, alcohol, or cigarettes.

> Talk to an insistent know-it-all who refuses to consider contrary opinions and you get a palpable sense of how the feeling of knowing can create a mental state akin to an addiction.

The strength of a moral decision can be seen, at least in part, as the synergistic action of unconscious cognition, involuntary feelings reflecting the rightness of this decision, and a powerful sense of pleasure in knowing that this decision is correct. It isn't in our nature to willfully abandon feelings of rightness and sense of purpose, especially when you add in the moral dimension of such actions making you "a good person."

I cannot imagine a more powerful recipe for potentially misguided "good behavior." The only defense is the understanding that we can't know with any objective or even reasonable certainty that what we consider an act of altruism is actually of overall benefit to others.

Back to Dr. X. Despite many attempts on the part of other medical staff, Dr. X continued to his dying day working nonstop to help his patients—whether or not they wanted his help. No contrary or tempering advice sunk in. At his memorial service, I sat through an outpouring of poignant testimonials to his dedication and devotion. No one spoke for those patients who suffered from his well-meaning excesses. Years later, I remember Dr. X mainly for what he taught me about uncritical acceptance of believing that you "are doing good."

For me, acting altruistically is like prescribing a medication. Believing that you are helping isn't enough. You must know, to the best of your ability, the potential risks as well as benefits. And, you must understand that the package insert as to the worth of the medication (your altruistic act) was written by your biased unconscious, not by a scientific committee who has examined all the evidence.

In the 1950s, Reinhold Niebuhr, the prominent Protestant theologian said, "The pretensions of virtue are as offensive . . . as the pretensions of power.

Pretension blinds nations to "the ambiguity of all human virtues and competencies . . . ." (Niebuhr, 2008).

Note

1. Copyright 2009, Robert Burton, all unassigned rights reserved.

References

Browne, A. (2003). Helping residents live at risk. *Cambridge Quarterly of Healthcare Ethics, 12*(1), 83–90.

Burton, R. (2008a). The certainty epidemic. *Salon*, Feb 29. Retrieved from http://www.salon.com/life/mind_reader/2008/02/29/certainty/index.html

Burton, R. (2008b). *On being certain: Believing you are right even when you're not.* New York: St. Martin's Griffin.

Deyo, R., Nachemson, A., & Mirza, S. (2004). Spinal-fusion surgery—The case for restraint. *New England Journal of Medicine, 350*(7), 722.

Glausiusz, J. (2007). Discover interview: Is morality innate and universal? *Discover Magazine*. Retrieved from http://discovermagazine.com/2007/may/the-discover-interview-marc-hauser

Harutyunyan, R. (2009). Unnecessary spinal surgery will waste billions in 2009. *EmaxHealth*. Retrieved from http://www.emaxhealth.com/2/45/28350/unnecessary-spinal-surgery-will-waste-billions-2009.html

Hugo, V. (1862). *Les Miserables.* Retrieved from http://www.classicreader.com/book/268/68/

Leape, L. L. (1989). Unnecessary surgery. *Health Services Research, 24*(3), 351–407.

Niebuhr, R. (2008). *The irony of American history.* Chicago, IL: University of Chicago Press.

Schultz, W., Preuschoff, K., Camerer, C., Hsu, M., Fiorillo, C., Tobler, P., et al. (2008). Explicit neural signals reflecting reward uncertainty. *Philosophical Transactions B, 363*(1511), 3801.

Shidara, M., & Richmond, B. (2002). Anterior cingulate: Single neuronal signals related to degree of reward expectancy. *Science, 296*(5573), 1709.

CHAPTER 11

ALTRUISM AND SUFFERING IN THE CONTEXT OF CANCER

Implications of a Relational Paradigm

Madeline Li and Gary Rodin

If I am not for myself, who will be for me?
If I am not for others, what am I?
And if not now, when?
Rabbi Hillel (Jewish Scholar and Theologian, 30 BC–9 AD)

KEY CONCEPTS

- Individuals who disavow their own need for support may be vulnerable to distress in the context of medical illness, both as patients themselves and as caregivers to others.
- The term "pathological altruism" has heuristic appeal, but is problematic in the context of life-threatening illness in that:
  - The term "pathology" in this circumstance implies a categorical external judgment of behavior and motivation, based on an arbitrary threshold that does not necessarily account for the social or relational context or the degree of suffering of the other.
  - The concept of altruism implies a dichotomy, often false, between the interests of self and those of the other.
  - Humans are relationally organized, such that acts of caregiving, particularly toward family members or loved ones, are often intrinsically rewarding and therefore not purely altruistic.
- The multiple determinants of altruism in the cancer caregiving context challenge us to develop a new nosology of such behavior and concern, informed by biological, social, and psychodynamic theory.

ALTRUISM HAS BEEN defined as "unselfish concern for the welfare of others" (Neusner & Chilton, 2005). This definition implies that concern for self and concern for other are distinct psychological states and, indeed, that the psychological boundary between self and other can be demarcated. This chapter will challenge this implicit assumption, as well as those about the degree of altruism that is pathological in the face of the suffering of another to whom one is emotionally and even biologically linked.

Pathological altruism can be divided into three broad types, based on its motivation and consequences. The first is concern for others that may be beneficial to its recipients but which incurs an inordinate cost to the presumed altruist, who may then have difficulty living a "normal life." The second type is misdirected altruism, in which actions that are motivated by the wish to benefit others are ineffective or counterproductive in their impact on the intended beneficiary. The third type of altruism, dramatically illustrated with suicide bombing, is characterized by destructive intent, albeit with the ultimate goal of improving the world, or at least the community of the perpetrator. Caregiving to individuals with cancer may represent either the first or second type of pathological altruism, when the caregiving is either self-damaging to the caregiver or unwanted by or aversive to the recipient. However, a clear demarcation between motivation that is self-directed and that which is other-directed can rarely be identified in these situations. Consequently, any threshold above which altruism is considered pathological seems arbitrary and difficult to justify.

> Any threshold above which altruism is considered pathological seems arbitrary and difficult to justify.

Defining Altruism: Can the Interests of Self and Other Be Separated?

The definition of "altruism" implies that the motives of self-interest and concern for others are mutually exclusive. However, Homant and Kennedy (Chapter 14) emphasize that all behavior is motivated by some reward for the actor. In the case of altruism, this reward is primarily derived from the perception of benefiting others. Homant and Kennedy distinguish altruism that is empathic (motivated by the desire to relieve perceived distress in another) from that which is 1) normative (based on adherence to internalized religious or cultural norms of self-sacrifice); 2) reciprocal (linked to expectation of future reciprocated good will); 3) egoistic (motivated more by the need to bolster self-esteem than to relieve distress in others); and, 4) situational (determined by social cues that are independent of the disposition of the actor). All these forms of altruism may generate positive feelings in the altruist, thereby exposing the logical flaw in the argument that altruism represents a unilateral benefit for the other.

Modern thinking in psychoanalysis and social psychology recognizes that humans are fundamentally relational in nature and that the intrapsychic motivations of self-interest and concern for others cannot be clearly demarcated. This is consistent with gene-centered evolutionary theory, which proposes that seemingly altruistic behavior is mediated by so-called "selfish genes" (Dawkins, 2006). This potential neurobiological basis for altruism, which has been well described in this volume (see Chapters 9, 22, 25–28), includes its presumed mediation by genetically determined variants in the expression of multiple neurotransmitters (e.g., serotonin, dopamine, prolactin, oxytocin, etc.), with variations in the capacity for empathy partly determined by the functioning of mirror neurons (Cattaneo & Rizzolatti, 2009; Iacoboni, 2009). There is also evidence of social benefit from altruism, since generosity in social situations has the greatest likelihood of eliciting cooperation from others (Klapwijk & Van Lange, 2009).

A biological basis for the impulse toward caregiving is not unexpected. After all, altruism is an evolutionarily adaptive trait in mammals, whose newborns depend for their survival on a prolonged period of caregiving. According to gene-centered evolutionary theories, the reward for altruism is a selection benefit for the altruist's genes (Baschetti, 2007). Thus, altruism and selfishness may represent complementarities, rather than polarities, in both the biological and intrapsychic domains. Benefit to the self derived from altruistic acts is enhanced when such acts are directed to those with a close genetic relationship to the actor. For this reason, it is difficult to disentangle the genetic interests of self from those of the other, particularly when the other is a family member. This has particular relevance in the context of caregiving in cancer, since the care provided to close family members suffering from distressing, disabling, and life-threatening illness may be essential to their well-being or survival. In these circumstances, the interests of self and other become indistinguishable.

Symbiosis may be a more fitting term to capture the nature of the relationship between the caregiver and the care recipient in the cancer context. This term is used to refer to an interdependent relationship between two persons, in which the interests of self and other are linked, either beneficially or detrimentally (Douglas, 1992). Symbiotic relationships can be categorized as mutualistic (both benefit), commensal (one benefits, the impact on the other is neutral), amensal (one is unaffected, the other is harmed), parasitic (the actor benefits, the other is harmed), or competitive (both harmed) (Table 11.1) (Paszkowski, 2006). Caregiving in the context of cancer is often mutualistic or commensal, but may be considered amensal, parasitic, or competitive when it is misdirected or exceeds the capacity of the caregiver. The latter may also be understood as a failure to optimize mutuality in a symbiotic relationship.

What Is Pathology?

The term *pathology*, rooted in the categorical concept of disease, implies that norms can be established to distinguish what is normal from what is abnormal or harmful. However, in the context of cancer caregiving, norms for the amount or type of appropriate caregiving are difficult or impossible to establish. Cutpoints used to establish what is pathological are likely to be influenced by personal and culturally based values and attitudes of the observer. In that regard, there may be a greater tendency in Western cultures to emphasize self-interest and contractual obligations compared to the value placed on altruism and collectivist attitudes in Eastern cultures (Keller, Edelstein, Schmid, Fang, & Fang, 1998; see also Traphagan, Chapter 21). Concern that altruism may be pathological is reflected in legal requirements in the United Kingdom (Potts, 2009) that psychiatric

TABLE 11.1   SYMBIOTIC RELATIONSHIPS

		Partner A		
		Benefit	Neutral	Harm
	Benefit	Mutualistic	Commensal	Parasitic
Partner B	**Neutral**	Commensal		Amensal
	Harm	Parasitic	Amensal	Competitive

illness be ruled out in cases of proposed altruistic organ donation to nonfamily members. In any case, we argue that the dichotomization of a continuous dimension of human behavior into nonpathological and pathological categories is artificial and arbitrary. If such a dichotomy were to be made, the threshold for pathology should, at the least, be raised in the context of caregiving for individuals with cancer who may face extreme suffering.

Caregiving and Suffering in Cancer

The diagnosis and treatment of cancer is universally associated with significant physical and psychological suffering related to the disease, as well as anticipation of worse yet to come. Distressing physical symptoms, such as pain, nausea, fatigue, and physical disability, are common and have a powerful impact. The disease may result in changes in bodily appearance and functioning, restrictions in occupational and recreational activities, and alterations in family role functioning and intimate relationships. Existential concerns related to the foreshortened life trajectory, and fears about the loss of autonomy and independence can lead to depression, anxiety, and loss of the will to live (Lo, Li, & Rodin, 2008; Rodin et al., 2009).

Disease- and treatment-related factors typically amplify the relationship needs of cancer patients. As the disease progresses, family members often must assume primary caregiving roles at significant personal cost. These caregivers not only share the impact of the cancer itself, but also must often contend with the simultaneous demands of caregiving, managing a household, and their own employment. These multiple responsibilities may leave little time for caregivers to take care of themselves (Grunfeld et al., 2004; Lutgendorf & Laudenslager, 2009). Not surprisingly, we and others have found equal or higher levels of depressive symptoms in cancer caregivers as in their ill family members (Braun, Mikulincer, Rydall, Walsh, & Rodin, 2007; Hodges, Humphris, & Macfarlane, 2005; Matthews, 2003).

It has been suggested that caregivers at the greatest risk of distress are those who disregard their own needs while attending to their loved ones (Goldstein et al., 2004; Schumacher, Stewart, & Archbold, 2007). Such consummate caregivers may also have great difficulty accepting a dependent role when they become ill themselves. The inability of these individuals to attend to their own needs increases the likelihood they will become distressed, neglect their own health, and delay seeking help for their own physical and emotional needs (Rohleder, Marin, Ma, & Miller, 2009). Further, cancer patients who have previously been consummate caregivers may have difficulty being in a dependent position and may perceive themselves as a burden to others (McPherson, Wilson, Lobchuk, & Brajtman, 2007). Their tendency to reject help may further increase their risk of disability, depression, and even suicide (Filiberti et al., 2001).

Self-perceived burden to others is a multidimensional construct that reflects guilt and distress in care recipients about the requirements of their dependency, and often includes a sense of responsibility for their caregivers' hardship. It may be often found in those who more usually assume the caregiving role in relationships. Qualitative research in cancer patients indicates that self-perceived burden to others consists of two

> Consummate caregivers may have great difficulty accepting a dependent role when they become ill themselves.

interrelated categories: *Concern for Others* and *Implications for Self* (McPherson, Wilson, & Murray, 2007). *Concern for Others* refers to the awareness of specific physical, social, and emotional burdens that patients worry that they may impose on others. *Implications for Self* refers to the alterations in self-concept evoked by the requirement of dependency and associated feelings of guilt and shame. The difficulty some patients experience accepting help from others may arise from the view that relationships with others are contingent on providing, rather than receiving help (McPherson, Wilson, & Murray, 2007; Rodin, Walsh et al., 2007). Such individuals may engage in strategies to minimize burden to others by concealing their needs for care, providing emotional reassurance to their caregivers, and even by desiring a hastened death. The desire to die in such individuals may be motivated by the wish to avoid dependency and to minimize the burden and suffering of others (Rodin, Zimmermann et al., 2007).

> The difficulty some patients experience accepting help from others may arise from the view that relationships with others are contingent on providing, rather than receiving help.

Professional caregivers in the field of cancer care may also be at risk of psychological morbidity as a result of the continuous demands of caregiving. Individuals who tend to be empathic may be more likely to choose work of this kind, motivated either by a desire to help others (i.e., empathic altruism) or as a result of personal life experience with cancer (i.e., empathic or egoistic altruism). When such caregiving is extreme or is unbalanced by appropriate self-interest, it can lead to *compassion fatigue*, a syndrome characterized by insomnia, depression, and "burn-out" (see Klimecki and Singer, Chapter 28 in this volume, and Najjar, Davis, Beck-Coon, and Carney Doebbeling [2009]). Such caregivers may be misattuned to their own needs, which they may come to perceive as unimportant compared to the needs of others. They may experience what has been termed "pathogenic empathy-based guilt" about the validity or appropriateness of their own legitimate needs, which causes them to neglect or discount these needs (see O'Connor et al., Chapter 2). When such unbalanced empathy is present in oncology physicians, nurses, or social workers, it can lead to caregiving that is not only unprofessional and intrusive in the lives of patients, but is depleting and damaging to their own personal lives.

> Unbalanced empathy can lead to caregiving that is not only unprofessional and intrusive, but is depleting and damaging to the life of the caregiver.

In the case of health care professionals with egoistic altruism, the inordinate need for validation of their own sense of competence can lead them to deliver ineffective and even harmful interventions, as described in the case of Dr. X, in Chapter 10 (by Robert Burton). Similarly, egoistic altruism in a family caregiver can result in care that is experienced as aversive when it is misattuned to the patient's needs and primarily motivated by the needs of the caregiver. Examples include pressured, intrusive, and futile feeding of an anorexic and cachectic patient or unhelpful overprotectiveness of cancer patients that actually compromises quality of life and interferes with autonomous and informed treatment decision making.

Although the term *pathological altruism* has dramatic appeal, we prefer the term *problematic caregiving* to refer to states of altruism that are experienced as disturbing either to the object of the altruism or to the altruist. This functional terminology does not require external judgment about the degree of caregiving that is pathological in this extraordinary circumstance, being based instead on the experience of the caregiving by both parties. The complexity of this issue is perhaps best illustrated through case examples.

> Although the term *pathological altruism* has dramatic appeal, we prefer the term *problematic caregiving* to refer to states of altruism that are experienced as disturbing.

Problematic Caregiving: Case Examples

Pathological Altruism in a Cancer Patient-cum-Caregiver?

Mr. A was a lawyer in his mid-30s, single with no children, whose vocational interest involved disadvantaged groups and social equality. He was referred for psychiatric assessment because of disabling anxiety related to the diagnosis of colon cancer, but his main concern was the impact of his illness on his friends and family.

Mr. A was a self-described consummate caregiver. He provided support in most relationships in his life, showing no apparent desire or need for reciprocity. When his cancer brought needs of his own, Mr. A found himself without a social support network upon which he could draw for practical assistance or for emotional support to buffer his sadness, anxiety, and disturbing fears. He withdrew from friends, who seemed unable or unwilling to support him in his time of need. The culmination of this process was the end of his relationship with a romantic partner whom he felt was unwilling to support him during his cancer treatment. However, Mr. A. did not seek support from those who were more likely to provide it, and usually rejected offers of support that were made. Mr. A shielded his parents and his siblings from his distress because he perceived them as preoccupied with their own difficulties. He reflexively regarded his cancer as a stressor that should be borne alone and therefore he did not inform others of worrisome test results and complications, so as not to burden them.

Mr. A completed cancer treatment and, with professional psychosocial support and treatment, gained insight into the imbalances in the relationships in his life. He established new and meaningful friendships within the cancer survivor movement, eventually devoting much of his time to fund raising and other activities intended to improve the process of care for other cancer patients. These activities and relationships were still colored by Mr. A's altruistic inclinations, although there was, at least initially, much greater reciprocity than before.

Even after several years of disease remission, Mr. A was still cautious about engaging in new romantic relationships. He doubted that he could be of benefit to a new partner, in view of his cancer-related disabilities and potential disease recurrence. He was sceptical about whether he had undergone psychological growth and was puzzled when other cancer survivors referred to so-called "post-traumatic growth." Such growth is thought by some to be precipitated by illness or other trauma (Cordova & Andrykowski, 2003; Wong, Ussher, & Perz, 2009). This hypothesized transformation is characterized by an enhanced focus on the present, reorganization of goals, direction of attention to meaningful activities, and an increased importance assigned to personal authenticity. The latter is both a philosophical and psychological term that denotes giving priority to one's internal spirit or desire, rather than to external pressures (Cunningham, 2003). However, personal authenticity remained elusive for Mr. A.

Mr. A later became a cancer caregiver when his mother was diagnosed with advanced ovarian cancer. He became her primary caregiver and, out of concern for their frailty, moved both of his parents into his home. Mr. A became preoccupied with his mother's cancer care, insisting that he be the family member who accompanied her to all her medical appointments and treatments. This led to absenteeism and declining work performance, thereby compromising his advancement opportunities at an early and critical stage of his career. When his mother was eventually admitted to a palliative care unit, Mr. A orchestrated a 24-hour circle of care at her bedside. He coordinated visits from her friends and other family members and even attempted to orchestrate the precise dialogue that he felt should occur between his mother and her medical team and between his mother and her visitors. As a result of rules and requirements that Mr. A imposed for the 24-hour care of his mother, his father, siblings, and his mother's friends began to withdraw, feeling both restricted and overwhelmed by the investment of time Mr. A was requesting. The palliative care team were concerned about Mr. A's intense involvement and suggested that he seek individual psychiatric assessment because of his visible and evidently profound symptoms of anxiety and depression.

When interviewed, Mr. A spoke of feeling consumed by thoughts of his mother's illness and imminent death. He felt unable to engage in pleasurable activities, such as having a drink with colleagues, exercising, or even laughing, believing that he should not experience any form of enjoyment while his mother was suffering. He established a 24-hour circle of care for his mother because he said that he found it unbearable to contemplate her being alone at the time of her death. He slept with vigilance, anxiously awaiting the telephone call that would herald her death and precipitate his rush to the hospital. He was driven by the belief that, as a cancer survivor and the only unmarried sibling in his family, he had a unique ability and responsibility to care for his mother and a desire to spare his father and siblings from the burden of such care. His compulsive caregiving was not modified by the expressed concern of his mother about his own psychological state, nor by her sadness about her reduced contact with other family members and friends, and the rising tensions among her children. Unlike Mr. A himself, his mother and other family members were confident about the ability of the palliative care staff to provide excellent end-of-life care.

Mr. A's problematic caregiving may reflect several types of altruism—empathic, normative, reciprocal, and egoistic—all problematic in terms of contributing to his own emotional breakdown. His empathy-based guilt reflected an unusual sensitivity to his mother's suffering, together with an exaggeration of his unique responsibilities and capacities as a caregiver for her. Survivor guilt plagued him and enhanced his need to care for his mother. The vicarious distress he experienced in response to his mother's suffering activated an extreme and compulsive form of caregiving that became problematic for him, his mother, and other caregivers. Through counseling, Mr. A realized he had been attempting to manage his own anxiety by exerting control over his mother's care, and that he had taken on more responsibility than was feasible, necessary, or desired. He eventually relinquished some of his role as primary caregiver and directed attention to his own needs after being informed that taking care of himself would allow him to better care for his mother. His self-interest and that of his mother nevertheless remained inextricably intertwined.

Was Elisabeth Kübler-Ross a Pathological Altruist?

Examination of the life of a famous and public professional caregiver may also illustrate the benefits and hazards of extreme devotion to altruistic activities. Details in this case report have been extracted from documentary and written biographies of Elisabeth Kübler-Ross (EKR; Figure 11.1) (Gill, 1982; Haupt, 2002). All interpretations presented are based solely on published biographical material rather than personal or professional knowledge of EKR, and represent only the personal opinions of the authors.

EKR, 1926–2004, a psychiatrist and thanatologist, was the first modern health care professional to demonstrate that dying patients can be helped by contemplating and talking about death. This work culminated in the publication of her seminal book, *On Death and Dying* (1969) (Kübler-Ross, 1970), in which she elaborated her five-stage theory of the psychological adaptation to death, in which the last stage was death acceptance. EKR was a celebrated writer, authoring over 20 books and receiving 23 honorary doctorates and numerous awards and recognitions for her selfless devotion to the terminally ill. She is credited with encouraging the hospice movement in North America; she also cofounded the American Holistic Medical Association. However, despite these accomplishments, EKR's academic career was fraught with controversy, and her personal life was compromised by her devoted need to serve others. Several biographies and reviews of her life have been published, but none has reflected on her life from the perspective of pathological altruism.

EKR had an inherent drive to help others. She ranked Mahatma Gandhi and Carl Gustav Jung among the people she would most like to meet upon her death. Born in Zurich, Switzerland, her formative experiences included talking with terminally ill neighbors in her youth and then volunteering as a teenager to work with Polish refugees in Swiss hospitals after the German invasion. At the age of 19, she joined the International Volunteers for Peace and was profoundly influenced both by the human suffering and the indomitable spirit of the victims

FIGURE 11.1
Elisabeth Kübler-Ross provides counseling to a terminally ill patient. *Louise and Elisabeth Kübler-Ross.* From *To Live Until We Say Good-Bye,* Copyright ©1978 by Elisabeth Kübler-Ross Family LP and Mal Warshaw. Reprinted by arrangement with Mal Warshaw and The Barbara Hogenson Agency. All rights reserved.

whom she observed when visiting Nazi concentration camps. She went on to complete a medical degree from Zurich University, marry fellow medical student Emanual Robert Ross, and then obtain specialist qualifications in psychiatry at the University of Colorado. She began her work with dying patients at Billings Hospital in Chicago. There, she developed her techniques, delivering ground-breaking seminars and allowing students to view interviews with dying patients from behind a one-way mirror.

EKR's work was immensely popular. It was featured in *Life Magazine* in 1969, and Kübler-Ross herself was named Woman of the Year in Science and Research in 1977, and Woman of the Decade by the *Ladies' Home Journal* in 1979. However, colleagues criticized EKR's work as ghoulish and exploitive; her position was eventually terminated by Billings for lack of scholarly activity. Her apparently altruistic devotion to patient care precluded her spending sufficient time to conduct the research or other academic activity necessary to advance her academic career.

At her own personal expense, EKR provided extraordinary care to her patients, often personally paying for ambulances, against medical advice, to transport dying children home for Christmas. In 1977, she established Shanti Nilaya, a self-funded healing center for the dying in Escondido, California. There, EKR obsessively devoted her time to her patients, becoming consumed by her work and essentially living at the healing center so as to be available to her patients at all times. She also began to have paranormal experiences, claiming to see the ghosts of her patients, which led her to begin investigating life after death. It was during this period that EKR fell victim to the so-called psychic channeler, Jay Barham, who was revealed, amidst a sexual scandal, to be a fraud. The damage to her reputation as a result of these activities was extensive, but EKR refused to give up on her new theories and continued to expound on her controversial statement that "death is an illusion." Eventually, her husband became disturbed by her endless preoccupation with her work; he asked her to spend more time with him and their two children. Faced with this choice between work and family, EKR chose work, disappointing her husband and family and receiving a harsh judgment by the divorce court, which ruled against her in custody proceedings.

In 1990, EKR transferred her work to her own family farm in Headwater, Virginia, where she established a facility to train health care professionals to work with terminally ill patients. This work continued until 1995, when a series of strokes left her partially paralyzed and increasingly paranoid. Alone, despairing, and despondent, media reports remarked on "the death and dying lady who can't seem to manage her own death." EKR's altruism mirrored that of her mother, whom she described as someone who "gave and gave and gave her entire life. There was one thing she couldn't do. That was to take or receive." EKR said that her mother's greatest fear was to be left "vegetating," and "not really being alive." Unfortunately, her mother suffered precisely that fate after a stroke left her paralyzed and unable to speak for 4 years.

Tragically, the end of life of EKR's mother foreshadowed that of EKR herself, who was unable to find the comfort she had helped so many others in that state to achieve. EKR faced the end of life without a sense of inner peace; she instead yearned for a hastened death. In her last documentary biography, EKR remarked "I told God last night that he's a damned procrastinator." "Sitting in a chair, 18 hours a day, that's not living, it's just vegetating. Every now and then, a medical student comes by. It makes me feel better when I can contribute something; I'm not used to such dependency." At the end, EKR did obtain some relief from a therapist who urged her to "learn to love myself" and to "surrender." Ultimately, EKR learned to question the ideals she was raised with: "You are only a valuable human being if you work. This is utterly wrong. Half working, half dancing—that is the right mixture. I myself have danced and played too little."

EKR's altruism might be seen as problematic, with obsessive caring for dying patients provided at great cost to herself—financially, professionally, and personally. EKR was also victimized by a charlatan, an outcome that is associated with altruism (Homant & Kennedy, Chapter 14). However, the greatest cost to EKR of her consummate need to be a caregiver was that it denied her what she had valued so highly—a good death. EKR's altruism gave her life meaning and therefore served self-interest, but it might equally be argued that it reflected unbridled and problematic altruism. The "hyperempathy" she shared with her mother reflected a familial, and perhaps genetic, inheritance that may have predisposed both of them to this problem (see Baron Cohen, Chapter 26).

Psychobiological Determinants

The motivation for all human behavior, including altruism, is multidetermined, arising out of genetic, biological, sociocultural, and developmental factors that may operate both independently and interactively (Organization, 1979; Strain, 2005). For example, genetic predisposition and developmental factors in the childhood environment are now understood to be neither mutually exclusive nor independent (Dodge, 2004). In fact, recent trends in genetic research include a focus on gene × environment interactions (Hodgins-Davis & Townsend, 2009), in which environmental factors influence phenotypic expression (Turner, 2009), and genotypes shape an individual's environmental exposure (Kendler & Baker, 2007). These interactions may all play a role in explaining the origins of problematic caregiving.

A number of social psychology theories, such as pathogenic empathy-based guilt (Chapters 2, 25, 27), pathological certitude (Chapter 10), or self-righteous addiction (Chapter 5), have been postulated in this volume to explain pathological altruism. Genetic vulnerability may include variations in neurotransmitter expression or neuronal functioning that result in personality traits that predispose to high levels of empathy and altruism (see Widiger & Presnall, Chapter 6). Environmental influences include social developmental factors that contribute to psychodynamic processes that may also underlie problematic caregiving behavior.

Anna Freud first described "altruistic surrender" in 1946 (Freud, 1946) as a defensive and pathological solution to conflict about self-gratification or self-interest Her formulation, which became widely accepted, proposed that individuals who are guilt-ridden and therefore inhibited in their own desires may gratify themselves vicariously by satisfying the wishes of others. Pseudoaltruism is another postulated defensive solution in which guilt about feelings of aggression and envy is relieved by the self-induced punishment of suffering and victimization (Seelig & Rosof, 2001). These classical psychoanalytic views are of value to explain some forms of pathological altruism. However, they fail to take into account the potential adaptive value of altruism and that the capacity for altruistic surrender may represent an important developmental accomplishment. Further, although traditional psychoanalytic metapsychology considered the secondary influence of the present relational surround on motivation, it did not take into account its potential influence as a primary motivating factor.

Turvey (Chapter 13) proposes a motivational typology for pathological altruism that is based on both classical psychodynamic theories and on newer approaches (Seelig & Rosof, 2001). It includes classical defensive forms of altruism arising from a need to avoid or resolve intrapsychic conflict related to self-interest, aggression, or envy. It also includes malignant (controlling or punishing others through self-sacrificing acts) and protective (self-image or identity is tied to being a hero or protector) forms of altruism. The latter is closer to more contemporary self-psychological views that have emphasized the centrality of self-experience and the motivation to engage in behaviors that bolster or maintain the sense of self (Kohut, 1977).

Self-psychology theory helps to explain egoistic altruism, in which other-directed behavior is engaged in primarily to bolster a defective or fragile sense of self (i.e., Turvey's *protective altruism*). In some cases, this heightened attunement to the needs of others is associated with a lack of awareness of, or attention to, one's own personal feelings and needs. This phenomenon has been identified as a pathogenic factor in the genesis of eating disorders in young women (see Bachner-Melman Chapter 7, and de Groot & Rodin, 1994). It is also consistent with Alice Miller's view that a fragile sense of self may arise from a hypersensitive awareness of children to their parents' needs, and a corresponding repression of their own desires, which are perceived as unacceptable to the parents (Miller, 1996; see also Zahn-Waxler & Van Hulle, Chapter 25). Similarly, "moral masochism" has been described as an individual's denial of personal need or pleasure arising from a childhood experience of themselves as a painful burden, rather than a source of pleasure to a parent perceived as suffering and self-sacrificing (Markson, 1993). Those who grow up with this experience may come to idealize painful self-sacrifice as a familiar identification with a weary parent who is viewed as both a victim and an aggressor.

Neither conflict-based nor self-psychology theories fully take into account the extent to which the self-experience is continuously determined by a reciprocal relationship. Relational theory (Aaron, 1996; Mitchell, 2000) posits that the self is intrinsically relational, and therefore that empathy and altruism are fundamentally and intrinsically rewarding. This is consistent with the view that self-interest and altruism cannot be demarcated, thereby complicating assumptions about pathological altruism. From a relational point of view, problematic caregiving might be understood to arise during early development as a result of an implicit requirement that a relationship with a caregiver depends on the sacrifice of the individual's developmental needs and psychological distinctness. The latter has been described as a system of pathological accommodation (Brandchaft, 2007) in which the needs of the parental figure must take precedence, in order to protect against intolerable pain and isolation that would occur as a result of losing this relationship. This is akin to the "silencing of the self" considered by Zahn-Waxler and Van Hulle to increase the risk for pathological altruism and depression in women (Chapter 25).

An attachment theory perspective would describe problematic caregiving as a compulsive-caregiving attachment style (Bowlby, 1977). Bowlby was the first to consider attachment in evolutionary and ethological terms, describing how infants seek proximity to an attachment figure to survive in the face of danger (Goldberg, 2000). Attachment behaviors are thus instinctually activated to ensure protection, the nature of the care provided by the attachment figure determining the particular attachment style of an individual. Attachment patterns or styles are thought to become organized early in life and are "activated" in times of stress, such as is often associated with medical illness (Tan, Zimmermann, & Rodin, 2005). Attachment styles can be described as secure—in which individuals are able to rely on both themselves and others in times of stress—or as insecure in one of several different ways. Compulsive-caregiving is an insecure attachment style that develops from early childhood parentification, in which care is provided to a parental figure in order to maintain security and proximity to him or her. In adults, a compulsive-caregiving attachment style can be manifest in caregiving behaviors that are misattuned because they are driven more by the needs of the actor than the care recipient.

> Insecure attachment styles, such as may be seen in compulsive-caregiving attachment, may result from early relational trauma and disorganization of right brain cortical–subcortical limbic–autonomic circuits.

The interplay of biological, social, and psychological factors in the development of the human attachment bond has been elegantly articulated by Allan Schore (2009) His work in neuropsychoanalysis has contributed to significant interdisciplinary paradigm shifts in the psychological and biological sciences. Schore describes self-organization of the infant's developing brain as emerging in the context of a relationship with another self and another brain—those of the maternal attachment figure. Communication in this infant–maternal relationship is based on implicit, nonverbal, unconscious body language (e.g., mutual eye gaze, touch, tone of voice, facial expression, etc.), which impacts limbic and cortical neuronal development of the right cerebral hemisphere.[1] Sophisticated neuroimaging and social science experiments demonstrate experience-dependent maturation of right brain systems. These systems mediate the visual-spatial, auditory-prosodic, and tactile-gestural affective communications that are the psychobiological substrates for empathy. Through their empathic mirroring, maternal attachment figures serve to provide homeostatic emotional balance to their infants. Preverbal 6- to 10-month old infants have been shown to demonstrate social evaluation and moral judgement (Hamlin, Wynn, & Bloom, 2007). These observations are consistent with the view that social relatedness and the concern for others develop early in life, shaped by the unconscious emotional processing of danger signals and attachment behaviors in the right brain.

Schore further hypothesizes that insecure attachment styles, such as may be seen in compulsive-caregiving attachment, result from early relational trauma and disorganization of right brain cortical–subcortical limbic–autonomic circuits. He suggests that this primes the hypothalamic-pituitary-adrenal (HPA) stress axis for hyperarousal, thereby predisposing to the emergence of posttraumatic stress disorder (PTSD) in response to future stressors. In support of this hypothesis, prior trauma in Holocaust survivors has been shown to induce epigenetic changes in glucocorticoid pathways that persistently render the neuroendocrine system acutely responsive to environmental stressors (Yehuda, 2006). This HPA axis hyperarousal is heritable, predisposing the offspring of Holocaust survivors to PTSD (Yehuda & Bierer, 2008). Animal models have also implicated epigenetic DNA methylation changes in the glucocorticoid receptor gene in response to inadequate maternal care, leading to alterations in HPA axis function that parallel those in PTSD (Weaver et al., 2004; Weaver, Szyf, & Meaney, 2002). Maternal programming of the stress response illustrates how epigenetic changes are one mechanism by which social factors can affect biological processes such as gene expression and neurodevelopment, ultimately mediating attachment behaviors.

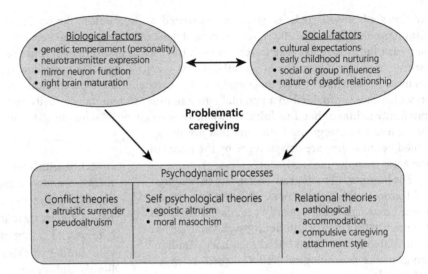

FIGURE 11.2
The biopsychosocial model for problematic caregiving behavior includes reciprocal interactions between biological and social factors that contribute to the development of several possible individual psychodynamic processes.

These interdisciplinary interactions underpin the biopsychosocial model of psychiatric case formulation in understanding human behavioral pathology.

Case Formulations

The psychodynamic explanations of altruism can be applied to the histories of both EKR and Mr. A, to develop a formulation of the evolution and persistence of their problematic caregiving. Mr. A was the youngest of four children, and his problematic caregiving may have been related to hostility, emotional overinvolvement, and criticism (Barrowclough & Hooley, 2003). He described his father as an "exceptional" man who was a world-class chess player and athlete but who was dominating, competitive, and "threatened by the success of his own children." His mother was described as "irritable, angry, and non-nurturing" during Mr. A's childhood. Mr. A and his mother developed a much closer relationship in his adult years; he came to understand that his mother's emotional unavailability to him in childhood was linked to his father's domineering behavior. Mr. A was a gifted student, with high emotional intelligence who excelled academically, although he believes that his success prompted competitiveness among his siblings for attention and praise from his parents.

Mr. A's altruistic behavior may be understood, in part, to arise from an inherently strong capacity for empathy, together with a role reversal in his relationship with his mother. The latter contributed to a protective or egoistic form of altruism, in which his caregiving served to ensure his special place and unique role with his mother. He experienced her other relationships as a threat to his tie to her, which had always seemed tenuous. As a result of her marital difficulties, his mother's emotional well-being and capacity for caregiving were compromised; consequently, she required Mr. A to assume the role of a caregiver for her. Mr. A's caregiving was rewarding to him and to his mother, but also represented a form of pathological accommodation and compulsive-caregiving that limited the development of his own sense of autonomy and self-worth.

Returning to EKR, her developmental history was most significantly marked by being one of triplet girls, which she felt interfered with her individual identity. She believed that the several weeks she spent in hospital at the age of 4, in isolation for pneumonia, were formative in terms of her later interest in humanizing and personalizing medical care. Her mother's consummate caregiving also suggests the possibility of both a genetic and learned predisposition to altruistic behavior. EKR's father, on the other hand, was a stern and cruel man who once had her pet rabbit butchered and then forced her to join the family as they ate her pet for dinner. He also opposed her desire to be a doctor, demanding that she work as a secretary in his business. EKR's childhood memories suggest an experience of nonrecognition and unresponsiveness to her individual needs, which may have contributed to her difficulty in attending to her own needs in adult life.

EKR's altruistic concern for the suffering of others may have reflected her identification with the suffering of others and her sensitive capacity for empathy and responsiveness to others. Her caregiving, which may be regarded as compulsive, appears to have simultaneously served her own needs and those of others who were in need of comfort and support. This life of extraordinary altruism was undoubtedly meaningful to EKR, although it appears to have been associated with a lack of attunement to her own relational needs and perhaps to her inner life. Such a lack of attunement may have contributed to her being deceived by a fraud and to her relinquishment near the end of her life of the relationships that had been important to her. Further, as she became ill, EKR was no longer able to care for others or find another way of having her own needs met. We may wonder whether it was her altruism or the loss of the capacity for altruism that contributed most to her difficulty in adjusting to the end of life.

Treatment

Understanding the motivation of problematic caregiving, particularly from a social and psychodynamic perspective, can help to inform therapeutic assistance. Addressing this behavior is important because of its potential harm to the emotional and physical well-being of the actor. Mate (2003) suggests that inattention to one's needs and emotions may contribute to physical illness via biological pathways.

> We may wonder whether it was Elisabeth Kubler-Ross's altruism, or the loss of the capacity for altruism that contributed most to her difficulty adjusting to the end of life.

Although theoretically possible (Zachariae, 2009), such hypotheses are unproven. However, there is evidence to suggest that a lack of emotional support is associated with worse health outcomes in medical populations (Li & Rodin, 2009) and with more severe symptoms of depression in patients with metastatic cancer (Rodin et al., 2009).

The two case studies presented here illustrate the potential risks and benefits that come from problematic caregiving, and demonstrate that so-called pathological altruism serves self-interest as much as it does the interest of others. However, despite the potential adverse effects of problematic caregiving, this behavior is difficult to change, because it is usually ego-syntonic (i.e., in harmony with an individual's sense of self and belief systems). Treatment may be

> Despite the potential adverse effects of problematic caregiving, this behavior is difficult to change, because it is usually in harmony with an individual's sense of self and belief systems.

sought only when the burden of this behavior or its adverse effects on others produce significant psychological distress or interpersonal conflict.

The cornerstone of the treatment for problematic caregiving is insight-oriented psychotherapy, in which the needs of the individual can be identified and legitimized and in which the problem of mutuality and reciprocity can be understood and addressed. Further, the experience of a secure tie to a therapist in which the patient can be the recipient of care can itself be transformative. The psychological benefit of psychotherapy may be profound and has even been associated with metabolic changes in limbic and cortical brain regions (Goldapple et al., 2004). However, the conundrum in individuals with problematic caregiving is that treatment may not be pursued because its initiation requires them to accept a personal anathema—becoming a recipient of care. This may be allowed by them only when a breakdown has occurred within themselves or their social system. As in the case of EKR, treatment may begin only when the pain of isolation threatens to replace the burden of altruism.

Note

1. Such nonverbal affective communication is also well described in mediating affiliative behavior that may underlie pathological altruism in adults (see Pessin, Chapter 28).

References

Aaron, L. (1996). *A meeting of minds. Mutuality in psychoanalysis.* Hillsdale, NJ: The Analytic Press, Inc.

Barrowclough, C., & Hooley, J. M. (2003). Attributions and expressed emotion: A review. *Clinical Psychology Review, 23*(6), 849–880.

Baschetti, R. (2007). Evolutionary, neurobiological, gene-based solution of the ideological "puzzle" of human altruism and cooperation. *Medical Hypotheses, 69*(2), 241–249.

Bowlby, J. (1977). The making and breaking of affectional bonds. *British Journal of Psychiatry, 130,* 201–210.

Brandchaft, B. (2007). Systems of accommodation and change in psychoanalysis. *Psychoanalytic Psychology, 24,* 667–687.

Braun, M., Mikulincer, M., Rydall, A., Walsh, A., & Rodin, G. (2007). Hidden morbidity in cancer: spouse caregivers. *Journal of Clinical Oncology, 25*(30), 4829–4834.

Cattaneo, L., & Rizzolatti, G. (2009). The mirror neuron system. *Archives of Neurology, 66*(5), 557–560.

Cordova, M. J., & Andrykowski, M. A. (2003). Responses to cancer diagnosis and treatment: posttraumatic stress and posttraumatic growth. *Seminars in Clinical Neuropsychiatry, 8*(4), 286–296.

Cunningham, A. J. (2003). The return to authenticity. *Advances in Mind-Body Medicine, 19*(2), 8–9.

Dawkins, R. (2006). *The selfish gene: 30th anniversary edition.* New York, New York: Oxford University Press.

de Groot, J., & Rodin, G. (1994). Eating disorders, female psychology and the self. *Journal of the American Academy of Psychoanalysis, 22,* 299–316.

Dodge, K. A. (2004). The nature-nurture debate and public policy. *Merrill Palmer Quarterly, 50*(4), 418–427.

Douglas, A. (1992). *Symbiotic interactions.* Oxford: Oxford University Press.

Filiberti, A., Ripamonti, C., Totis, A., Ventafridda, V., De Conno, F., Contiero, P., et al. (2001). Characteristics of terminal cancer patients who committed suicide during a home palliative care program. *Journal of Pain Symptom Management, 22*(1), 544–553.

Freud, A. (1946). *The ego and the mechanisms of defense.* New York: International Universities Press.

Gill, D. L. T. (1982). *Quest: The life of Elisabeth Kübler-Ross:* Ballantine Books.

Goldapple, K., Segal, Z., Garson, C., Lau, M., Bieling, P., Kennedy, S., et al. (2004). Modulation of cortical-limbic pathways in major depression: Treatment-specific effects of cognitive behavior therapy. *Archives of General Psychiatry, 61*(1), 34–41.

Goldberg, S. (2000). *Attachment and development.* London: Arnold Publishers.

Goldstein, N. E., Concato, J., Fried, T. R., Kasl, S. V., Johnson-Hurzeler, R., & Bradley, E. H. (2004). Factors associated with caregiver burden among caregivers of terminally ill patients with cancer. *Journal of Palliative Care, 20*(1), 38–43.

Grunfeld, E., Coyle, D., Whelan, T., Clinch, J., Reyno, L., Earle, C. C., et al. (2004). Family caregiver burden: results of a longitudinal study of breast cancer patients and their principal caregivers. *Canadian Medical Association Journal, 170*(12), 1795–1801.

Hamlin, J. K., Wynn, K., & Bloom, P. (2007). Social evaluation by preverbal infants. *Nature, 450*(7169), 557–559.

Haupt, S. (Writer, Director). (2002). *Facing Death. Elisabeth Kübler-Ross.* USA: First Run Features.

Hodges, L. J., Humphris, G. M., & Macfarlane, G. (2005). A meta-analytic investigation of the relationship between the psychological distress of cancer patients and their carers. *Social Science and Medicine, 60*(1), 1–12.

Hodgins-Davis, A., & Townsend, J. P. (2009). Evolving gene expression: From G to E to GxE. *Trends in Ecology and Evolution, 24*(12), 649–658.

Iacoboni, M. (2009). Imitation, empathy, and mirror neurons. *Annual Review of Psychology, 60,* 653–670.

Keller, M., Edelstein, W., Schmid, C., Fang, F. X., & Fang, G. (1998). Reasoning about responsibilities and obligations in close relationships: A comparison across two cultures. *Developmental Psychology, 34*(4), 731–741.

Kendler, K. S., & Baker, J. H. (2007). Genetic influences on measures of the environment: a systematic review. *Psychological Medicine, 37*(5), 615–626.

Klapwijk, A., & Van Lange, P. A. (2009). Promoting cooperation and trust in "noisy" situations: the power of generosity. *Journal of Personality and Social Psychology, 96*(1), 83–103.

Kohut, H. (1977). *The restoration of the self.* New York: International Universities Press, Inc.

Kübler-Ross, E. (1970). *On death and dying.* Great Britain: Tavistock Publications Ltd.

Li, M., & Rodin, G. (2009). Chapter 8 depression. In J. L. Levenson (Ed.), *Textbook of psychosomatic medicine* (2nd ed., pp. in press). Arlington, VA: American Psychiatric Publishing.

Lo, C., Li, M., & Rodin, G. (2008). The assessment and treatment of distress in cancer patients: overview and future directions. *Minerva Psichiatrica, 49,* 129–143.

Lutgendorf, S. K., & Laudenslager, M. L. (2009). Care of the caregiver: Stress and dysregulation of inflammatory control in cancer caregivers. *Journal of Clinical Oncology, 27*(18), 2894–2895.

Markson, E. R. (1993). Depression and moral masochism. *International Journal of Psychoanalysis, 74,* 931–940.

Mate, G. (2003). *When the body says no: The cost of hidden stress.* Toronto: Knopf Canada.

Matthews, B. A. (2003). Role and gender differences in cancer-related distress: A comparison of survivor and caregiver self-reports. *Oncology Nursing Forum, 30*(3), 493–499.

McPherson, C. J., Wilson, K. G., Lobchuk, M. M., & Brajtman, S. (2007). Self-perceived burden to others: Patient and family caregiver correlates. *Journal of Palliative Care, 23*(3), 135–142.

McPherson, C. J., Wilson, K. G., & Murray, M. A. (2007). Feeling like a burden: Exploring the perspectives of patients at the end of life. *Social Science and Medicine, 64*(2), 417–427.

Miller, A. (1996). *Prisoners of childhood: The drama of the gifted child and the search for the true self.* New York: Basic Books.

Mitchell, S. (2000). *Relationality: From attachment to intersubjectivity.* Northvale, N J: The Analytic Press.

Najjar, N., Davis, L. W., Beck-Coon, K., & Carney Doebbeling, C. (2009). Compassion fatigue: A review of the research to date and relevance to cancer-care providers. *Journal of Health and Psychology, 14*(2), 267–277.

Neusner, J., & Chilton, B. D. (Eds.). (2005). *Altruism in world religions.* Washington, DC: Georgetown University Press.

Paszkowski, U. (2006). Mutualism and parasitism: The yin and yang of plant symbioses. *Current Opinion in Plant Biology, 9*(4), 364–370.

Potts, S. (2009). Transplant psychiatry. *Journal of the Royal College of Physicians Edinburgh, 39,* 331–336.

Rodin, G., Lo, C., Mikulincer, M., Donner, A., Gagliese, L., & Zimmermann, C. (2009). Pathways to distress: The multiple determinants of depression, hopelessness, and the desire for hastened death in metastatic cancer patients. *Social Science and Medicine, 68*(3), 562–569.

Rodin, G., Walsh, A., Zimmermann, C., Gagliese, L., Jones, J., Shepherd, F. A., et al. (2007). The contribution of attachment security and social support to depressive symptoms in patients with metastatic cancer. *Psychooncology, 16*(12), 1080–1091.

Rodin, G., Zimmermann, C., Rydall, A., Jones, J., Shepherd, F. A., Moore, M., et al. (2007). The desire for hastened death in patients with metastatic cancer. *Journal of Pain Symptom Management, 33*(6), 661–675.

Rohleder, N., Marin, T. J., Ma, R., & Miller, G. E. (2009). Biologic cost of caring for a cancer patient: Dysregulation of pro- and anti-inflammatory signaling pathways. *Journal of Clinical Oncology, 27*(18), 2909–2915.

Schore, A. N. (2009). Relational trauma and the developing right brain: An interface of psychoanalytic self psychology and neuroscience. *Annals of the New York Academy of Science, 1159,* 189–203.

Schumacher, K. L., Stewart, B. J., & Archbold, P. G. (2007). Mutuality and preparedness moderate the effects of caregiving demand on cancer family caregiver outcomes. *Nursing Research, 56*(6), 425–433.

Seelig, B. J., & Rosof, L. S. (2001). Normal and pathological altruism. *Journal of the American Psychoanalytic Association, 49*(3), 933–959.

Strain, J. J. (2005). Psychiatric diagnostic dilemmas in the medical setting. *Australian and New Zealand Journal of Psychiatry, 39*(9), 764–771.

Tan, A., Zimmermann, C., & Rodin, G. (2005). Interpersonal processes in palliative care: An attachment perspective on the patient-clinician relationship. *Palliative Medicine, 19*(2), 143–150.

Turner, B. M. (2009). Epigenetic responses to environmental change and their evolutionary implications. *Philosophical Transactions of the Royal Society London B Biological Sciences, 364*(1534), 3403–3418.

5

Weaver, I. C., Cervoni, N., Champagne, F. A., D'Alessio, A. C., Sharma, S., Seckl, J. R., et al. (2004). Epigenetic programming by maternal behavior. *Nature Neuroscience, 7*(8), 847–854.

Weaver, I. C., Szyf, M., & Meaney, M. J. (2002). From maternal care to gene expression: DNA methylation and the maternal programming of stress responses. *Endocrine Research, 28*(4), 699.

Wong, W. K., Ussher, J., & Perz, J. (2009). Strength through adversity: Bereaved cancer carers' accounts of rewards and personal growth from caring. *Palliative Support and Care, 7*(2), 187–196.

World Health Organization. (1979). *Workshop on psychosocial factors affecting health: Assessment classification and utilization.* Geneva: World Health Organization.

Yehuda, R. (2006). Advances in understanding neuroendocrine alterations in PTSD and their therapeutic implications. *Annals of the New York Academy of Science, 1071,* 137–166.

Yehuda, R., & Bierer, L. M. (2008). Transgenerational transmission of cortisol and PTSD risk. *Progress in Brain Research, 167,* 121–135.

Zachariae, R. (2009). Psychoneuroimmunology: A bio-psycho-social approach to health and disease. *Scandinavian Journal of Psychology, 50*(6), 645–651.

CONSIDERING PATHOLOGICAL ALTRUISM IN THE LAW FROM THERAPEUTIC JURISPRUDENCE AND NEUROSCIENCE PERSPECTIVES

Michael L. Perlin

KEY CONCEPTS

- Therapeutic jurisprudence and neuroimaging are valuable tools when considering the treatment of pathological altruism in the law, in cases of organ donations to strangers and cases raising "cultural defenses."
- Therapeutic jurisprudence gives us a benchmark by which we can assess whether the pathological altruist (if, indeed, the altruist is pathological) has sacrificed her dignity to do the putatively pathologically altruistic act, an assessment process that can also illuminate whether the underlying behavior is irrational, harmful to others, or self-harming.
- Neuroimaging gives us new tools to potentially assess whether the pathological altruist is a rational moral agent in doing such acts.

ONE OF THE most important legal theoretical developments of the past two decades has been the creation and dynamic growth of therapeutic jurisprudence (see e.g., Wexler 1990, 2008; Wexler & Winick, 1996; Winick, 2005). Initially employed in cases involving individuals with mental disabilities, but subsequently expanded far beyond that relatively narrow area, therapeutic jurisprudence presents a new model for assessing the impact of case law and legislation, recognizing that, as a therapeutic agent, the law that can have therapeutic or antitherapeutic consequences. The ultimate aim of therapeutic jurisprudence is to determine whether legal rules, procedures, and lawyer roles can or should be reshaped to enhance their therapeutic potential, while not subordinating due process principles (Perlin, 2003a, 2005, 2008).

Therapeutic jurisprudence "asks us to look at law as it actually impacts people's lives" (Winick, 2009, p. 535) and focuses on the law's impact on emotional life and psychological well-being (Wexler, 2000, in Stolle, Wexler, & Winick, 2000). In recent years, scholars have considered a vast range of topics through a therapeutic jurisprudence lens, including, but not limited to, all aspects of mental disability law, domestic relations law, criminal law and procedure, employment law, gay rights law, and tort law (Perlin, 2002–2003). As Ian Freckelton has noted, "it is a tool for gaining a new and distinctive perspective utilizing socio-psychological insights into the law and its applications" (Freckelton, 2008, p. 582).

One of the central principles of therapeutic jurisprudence is a commitment to dignity. Ronner describes the "three Vs": voice, validation, and voluntariness (2008, p. 627), arguing:

> What "the three Vs" commend is pretty basic: litigants must have a sense of voice or a chance to tell their story to a decision maker. If that litigant feels that the tribunal has genuinely listened to, heard, and taken seriously the litigant's story, the litigant feels a sense of validation. When litigants emerge from a legal proceeding with a sense of voice and validation, they are more at peace with the outcome. Voice and validation create a sense of voluntary participation, one in which the litigant experiences the proceeding as less coercive. Specifically, the feeling on the part of litigants that they voluntarily partook in the very process that engendered the end result or the very judicial pronunciation that affects their own lives can initiate healing and bring about improved behavior in the future. In general, human beings prosper when they feel that they are making, or at least participating in, their own decisions. (Ronner, 2002, pp. 94–95; see generally, Ronner, 2010)

At the same time, legal scholars have also turned their attention to the relationship between neuroscience and the law, mostly in the context of criminal law and procedure, but also in civil matters such as trauma suffered by victims of brain injuries, testamentary capacity disability claims, toxic tort exposure, and the relationship between violent behavior and video games (Moriarty, 2008; Perlin, 2009b, 2009c). Scholars have begun to investigate (by way of an example to which I will return in a later part of this chapter) the relationship between brain functioning and the nature of human aggression (Archer, 2009; Siegel & Victoroff, 2009).

Articles by legal scholars about altruism-related issues encompass civil and criminal law, as well as private and public law. Topics include, but are not limited to, cases involving organ donation law[1] and the potential exculpatory impact of sociobehavioral syndromes known as "cultural defense cases" on criminal responsibility (these are further described in the section "Cultural Defenses and Pathological Altruism"). The altruism in these cases may potentially be characterized as posing questions of *pathological altruism*.[2,3]

In this chapter, I will first discuss the basic principles of therapeutic jurisprudence, which then leads to consideration of the relationship between neuroimaging and the law.[4] Then I will consider the connection between organ donation and pathological altruism, and subsequently, between a "cultural defense" and pathological altruism. This will lead to a discussion of the interplay between therapeutic jurisprudence and pathological altruism, and between neuroimaging and the law and pathological altruism. Finally, I will offer some modest suggestions for scholars and policy makers.

Therapeutic Jurisprudence

As previously mentioned, therapeutic jurisprudence seeks to enhance values of "voice, validation, respect, and self-determination" and "voluntary participation." Importantly, it accomplishes this task in an interdisciplinary manner. (Waldman, 2008). Wexler summarizes:

> Generally, therapeutic jurisprudence looks at the traditionally underappreciated area of the law's impact on emotional life and psychological well-being. It recognizes that, whether we know it or not, whether we like it or not, the law is a social force with consequences in the psychological domain. Also, therapeutic jurisprudence examines the role of the law as a therapeutic agent and its enormous potential to heal. Therapeutic jurisprudence looks not merely at the law on the books but rather at the law in action—how the law manifests itself in law offices, client behavior, and courtrooms around the world. The underlying concern is how legal systems actually function and affect people. (Wexler, 2008, p. 20)

Much of therapeutic jurisprudence's strength comes from this commitment to dignity[5] and the awareness of those who write from a therapeutic jurisprudence perspective of the potential for humiliation inherent in the legal process. Authors have contextualized therapeutic jurisprudence in a wide range of legal issues, including criminal prosecution (Winick, 2009), child abuse and neglect proceedings (Salisbury, 2005), involuntary civil commitments (Winick, 1999), law in relation to terrorism (Rotman, 2008), international human rights (Winick, 2002), *Miranda* warnings (Ronner, 2002), and problem-solving courts (Winick, 2003). Authors underscore that therapeutic jurisprudence upholds human dignity and rejects humiliation as a legal tool (Freckelton, 2008) and that it empowers participants in the legal process (King, 2009). As Bruce Winick tells us: "If people are treated with dignity . . . and generally treated in ways that they consider to be fair, they will experience greater satisfaction and comply more willingly with the ultimate outcome of the proceedings, even if adverse to them" (Winick, 2003, p. 1089).

Some of the most important criticism of therapeutic jurisprudence flows from what is perceived—incorrectly, in my view—as its willingness to subordinate civil libertarian concerns to therapeutic interests (Kahn, 2002).[6] Indeed, some of the enthusiasm that therapeutic jurisprudence has engendered may flow implicitly from the assumption that therapeutic interests will take precedence over due process (that is, legal) interests. Wexler and Winick, however, stress that therapeutic jurisprudence cannot and must not "trump" civil libertarian interests (e.g., Perlin, 2000; Wexler, 1993), as for example by refusing to allow a competent but institutionalized individual to refuse the involuntary imposition of antipsychotic medication (see e.g., Perlin, 2005).

It makes sense, then, to consider this book's central topic, pathological altruism, through a therapeutic jurisprudence lens. In this way, we may better understand why people sometimes act, at least at first blush, to their own detriment. A therapeutic jurisprudence filter gives us clues both about the source of this behavior and how the legal system should construe it. Several scholars have considered the link between therapeutic jurisprudence and altruism in the past.

For example, Susan Daicoff (1999) has argued that therapeutic jurisprudence is particularly well suited for lawyers with personality traits atypical of lawyers in general, such as altruism (see also, Perlmutter, 2005). But none have considered the interrelationship between therapeutic jurisprudence and pathological altruism until now. The question will be framed this way: To what extent does the sort of behavior that is at the core of these subject matters—a willingness to donate organs to strangers, or to passively allow a criminal assault on the part of a domestic partner—reflect (or reject) therapeutic jurisprudence's commitment to dignity and the "three Vs"—voice, validation, and voluntariness?

Neuroimaging

Although neuroimaging is fraught with uncertainties (Roberts, 2006, p. 266, n. 155), and the steps used in the production and presentation of neuroimaging evidence are not only not standardized but easily manipulated by a person with the knowledge of the technology (Reeves, Mills, Billick, & Brodie, 2003), it is clear is that the *existence* of neuroimaging techniques has nonetheless changed the contours of the courtroom playing field (Perlin & McClain, 2009a, pp. 5–6).

Proponents of neuroimaging characterize it as "an *objective*, non-invasive *quantifiable* image, which can provide useful information, especially when the clinical examination may otherwise be normal" (Baskin et al., 2007, p. 247). Further, they argue that neuroscience seems "advanced enough to enter forensic psychiatry" (Witzel, Walter, Bogerts, & Northoff, 2008, p. 115), and claim "advances in neurobiological research methods allow one to address the nature and biological basis of human behavior" (Muller et al., 2008, p. 131) Some of those skeptical about wider admissibility of neuroimaging evidence in the court process note that a "brain image is the *vivid* representation of anatomy or physiology through a pictorial or graphic display of data" (Reeves et al., 2003, p. 89), and fear that this vividness "might lead unwitting fact-finders to believe that the story told by the neuroimaging picture is susceptible to only one interpretation" (Perlin, 2009b, p. 890). Opponents of the wider admissibility of such testimony argue the ambition of cognitive neuroscientists is "to use the claims of their discipline and the new powers conferred by neuroimaging to overthrow retributive justice as a legitimate justification for criminal sanctions" (Snead, 2007, p. 1316), and that neuroimaging may be simply a "neo-phrenological fad." (Marks, 2007, p. 492, quoting Uttal, 2003). Jurors may be inappropriately swayed by what they perceive as the evidence's "nonfalsifiability"—because it appears to be *vivid, objective, quantifiable,* and *advanced* (Perlin, 2009b, 2009c). On the question of how neuroscientific evidence may inappropriately sway juries in insanity defense cases by leading them to focus on questions not relevant to the legal question before them, see Batts (2009).

There are other issues of importance in relation to neuroimaging evidence. Most important, from a legal perspective, is whether such evidence is admissible at a trial. In *Daubert v. Merrill Dow Pharmaceuticals* (1993), the Supreme Court ruled that jurors could hear evidence and weigh facts from experts whose testimony included novel scientific theories—even if those theories had not gained "general acceptance" in the scientific community—as long as the testimony was "relevant" and "reliable." In construing relevance and reliability, the Court specified consideration of five factors: (1) whether the expert's hypothesis has been tested, (2) whether peer review and publication of the methodology has occurred, (3) the frequency of erroneous results, (4) standards controlling the technique's operations, and (5) acceptance of the methodology in the scientific community.[7]

Empirical studies have consistently demonstrated the stark disparity in judicial decision making in *Daubert* cases. In criminal cases, the prosecutor's position is sustained (either in support of questioned expertise or in opposition to it) vastly more often than is defense counsel's (Risinger, 2000, pp. 105–108). By way of example, in 67 cases of challenged government expertise, the prosecution prevailed in 61. Out of 54 complaints by criminal defendants that their expertise was improperly excluded, the defendant lost 44. Contrarily, in civil cases, 90% of *Daubert* appeals were by the defendants, who prevailed two-thirds of the time.[8] This disparity must be kept in mind when we seek to "tease out" the ways that neuroimaging testimony will (or will not) be accepted as evidence at trial.

In an earlier paper on neuroimaging and the law, I sought to capture the ambivalence that surrounds the relationship between this evidence and the judicial process:

> Neuroimaging is (or isn't) hard science. It is (or isn't) relatively easy for jurors to interpret. It is (or isn't) immune to falsification efforts. It is (or isn't) objective. It will (or won't) lead jurors to "better" verdicts in insanity cases. It will (or won't) be used disproportionately in *Action News*-friendly cases. It will (or won't) "trump" jurors' inherent suspicion of the insanity defense. It does (and here there is no contradictory or antipodal position) raise a variety of important and provocative legal, behavioral, and social issues, none of which has received nearly enough attention by the courts or by commentators. (Perlin, 2009b, p. 915)

How does this ambiguity apply to the matter at hand? Although some scholars have begun to examine how neuroscience advances may illuminate the roots of altruistic behavior[9] there has so far, to the best of my knowledge, been no such focus on its relationship to pathological altruism.[10] Although we are still barely at the speculative stage here, multiple questions arise: Might neuroimaging provide a better understanding of not only altruism, but also pathologies of altruism?[11] Might it offer clues when a party alleges that a certain action was altruistically motivated, when, in fact, that might not be so? And, most importantly for these purposes, if neuroimaging does appear to offer these answers, and the testing in question is offered in a court proceeding, how will courts construe it?[12]

Organ Donation and Pathological Altruism

Michele Goodwin, one of the most prominent critics of the current organ donation system, charges that the altruistic model is socially taxed "beyond its capacity" (Goodwin, 2004, p. 308), that "altruism . . . is a losing battle" (p. 311; p. 311, n. 20), and concludes that "the success of altruism relies on the macabre" (p. 319) Other scholars have described the ethical propriety of academic scholarship programs that might stimulate the donation of organs by the living (Cherry, 2009; Graham & Livingson, 2009; Linford, 2009).

The title of an article about the motivations of organ donors asks: "The Living Anonymous Donor: Lunatic or Saint?" (Henderson et al., 2003). The authors of the piece, which focused on kidney donations, note that some critics argue that such altruism "appears by definition as either irrational or pathological" (p. 203).[13] The results of the authors' empirical study demonstrate that this is not the case: "there is a significant number of psychologically stable, altruistically motivated individuals who want to donate a kidney anonymously to a stranger and seek no material compensation in return" (p. 208).[14] Yet, there is no question that many commentators consider such altruistic acts to reflect "a defensive cloak for sadomasochism," in some instances flourishing as "psychotic altruism, manifest[ing] in bizarre forms of . . . behavior and associated self-denial based in delusion" (Baskin, 2009, p. 378).[15]

Cultural Defenses and Pathological Altruism

A cultural defense allows a defendant to seek a reduction in the level of a criminal charge because he was ostensibly acting according to his culture's norms and expectations in cases in which he may not have had time to assimilate or understand American cultural values (Goldstein, 1994; Suri, 2000).[16] Although this defense has been offered on rare occasions as a form of insanity defense (thus making the claim of nonresponsibility), it is more often relied on in support of claims of mistake of fact, diminished capacity, "heat of passion," self-defense, or in support of a reduced sentence (DePalma, 2009; Goldstein, 1994).[17] Relevant to the context of this chapter are cultural defense claims raised in cases in which (1) defendants kill their unfaithful wives (or wives perceived to be unfaithful), and (2) mothers kill their children in response to spousal infidelity (Lee, 2007).[18]

This has led scholars to grapple with related questions of how the law should deal with (a) victims who voluntarily participate in activities that meet statutory criteria for criminality but might be acceptable behavior in the victim's native culture,[19] where, perhaps, victims accept the "externalizing of blame" (Wang, 1996, p. 156) or "subscribe . . . to [the culture's] tenets" (Li, 1996, p. 787);[20]and (2) defendants whose crimes are attributed to altruistic motives in this context.[21] This literature should be read in tandem with the writings of feminist scholars such as Robin West, who suggest that the altruistic behavior we encourage in women is often a "gender-specific harm" (McClain, 2001, p. 1707, discussing West, 1997) and that we need to distinguish altruism rooted in care from altruism rooted in fear (Sheehan, 2000, p. 93, n. 37, discussing West, 1997, p. 123).[22] These insights have led to great debates among scholars as to whether the cultural defense conflicts with or can stand aligned with the battered spouse syndrome (Suri, 2000; Volpp, 1994). [23] In this context, Hannah Crockett has observed:

> The cultural defense promotes stereotypes by reinforcing "false, anachronistic" images of a defendant's culture. The cultural defense "reinforces Western notions of a primitive, not quite autonomous 'other' who is too culture-bound to make reasoned judgments . . . [D]iscussions of foreign cultures in the context of the defense assume those cultures to be static and rigid, unlike the presumably ever-changing, fluid [dominant culture of the] West." The cultural defense, rather than counteracting prejudice, may actually promote contempt for minority culture groups. (2006, p. 684)[24]

People v. Kimura (1985) has received great attention in the academic literature. In this case, a married Japanese-American woman in her 30s, the mother of a young child and an infant, intended to commit parent–child suicide (*oyako-shinyu*) after learning her Japanese-American husband had been keeping a mistress for many years. The children drowned, but the mother was rescued by a passerby. The prosecution charged her with first-degree murder. However, the Japanese-American community petitioned the court to reduce the charge, emphasizing that parent–child suicide was at the root of her culture behavior, and she should be judged within the context of Japanese standards. (Perlin & McClain, 2009a, 2009b; see Goel, 2004, p. 455; petitions with more than 25,000 signatures were submitted to the sentencing court). Her psychiatric diagnosis was "brief reactive psychosis," including major depression (Chiu, 2006, p. 1356, n. 156). As a result of input from both the experts and the community, the homicide was reduced to voluntary manslaughter and the defendant was sentenced to 1 year in custody and 5 years probation with psychiatric counseling recommended (Perlin & McClain, 2009a).[25]

One commentator has discussed the *Kimura* case in the context of what she characterizes as "altruistic" filicide, the suicidal parent believing murder to be an altruistic act because she either cannot abandon the child or wishes to alleviate the child's suffering, either real or imagined (Wu, 2003, p. 1013, n. 277). Society's response to such cases may mirror that of infanticidal mothers who plead the insanity defense: "Unlike the typical insanity-pleading defendant (who fills jurors with fear and loathing), these defendants puzzle jurors: 'How could this defendant have committed such an inexplicable and irrational crime? She must have been crazy!'" (Perlin, 2003, p. 19; see generally, Oberman, 2004).[26] As Daina Chiu explains, women are "assumed to be inherently passive, gentle, and tolerant; and mothers are assumed to be nurturing, caring, and altruistic. It is an easy step, therefore, to assume that a 'normal' woman could surely not have acted in such a way" (Chiu, 1988, p. 1118).

These cases are perplexing to criminal law and procedure scholars for many reasons, not least of which because they involve conflicting stereotypes and conflicting heuristics.[27] Several years ago, I wrote this in an article about the use of the insanity defense in infanticide cases (focusing especially on neonaticide cases):

> This area of the law is especially incoherent even when compared to [other] insanity defense cases . . . . On one hand, we are especially punitive towards such defendants because they have violently violated our precepts of motherhood. On the other, we are more willing to find some of these defendants not guilty by reason of insanity than we are in cases involving almost any other kind of insanity pleader (again, almost in a way that imitates nullification verdicts) as a reflection of our desire to maintain an inviolate image of "mother love." (Perlin, 2003, p. 6)

The use of the cultural defense in cases involving pathological altruism—either in which the pathological altruist is the willing victim (as with an acquiescent wife in culturally sanctioned wife abuse) or the perpetrator (as with a woman killing her children to save them from shame, often caused by the perpetrator's husband's infidelity)—causes us to reconsider these conflicts. It forces us to confront how our preexisting sets of biases shape and distort our thinking and decision making in this area of law and social policy. It is another reason why we must now turn to therapeutic jurisprudence as a potential solution.[28]

Therapeutic Jurisprudence and Pathological Altruism

Interestingly, therapeutic jurisprudence scholars have underscored the relationship between therapeutic jurisprudence and altruism, and contrarily, the *disconnect* between altruism and the law-and-economics model (Slobogin, 1995, p. 95).[29]

Miller argues that therapeutic jurisprudence "legitimizes preventive law by providing it with an altruistic motivation" (Miller, 2009, p. 275; see also Stolle et al., 2000); Shuman questions whether "plaintiffs experience a sense of altruism based upon a belief that the lawsuit has prevented this injury from happening to others?" (Shuman, 1993, p. 756; see also, Binder, Trimble, & McNiel, 1991). Daicoff uses psychological data on the personality traits of lawyers to argue that therapeutic jurisprudence is particularly well suited for lawyers with altruistic personality values (Daicoff, 1999; see also Shuman, 1993).[30] But there is no mention in the therapeutic jurisprudence literature about its relationship—if there is one—to pathological altruism, and about what it might have to say about behavior reflecting the "willingness of a person to irrationally place another's perceived needs above his or her own in a way that causes self-harm." It is considered, interestingly, in Goodwin's work on organ donation, which argues that "dignity, trust, and autonomy [*not* altruism] are the more relevant values to be preserved and promoted in organ transplantation" (Goodwin, 2009, p. 34).

A related issue is whether organs may ever be harvested from persons who are, at the time, legally incompetent. One author has concluded that such harvests should be "categorically prohibited" (Cheyotte, 2000, p. 469).[31] Similar issues are raised in cases involving donations by adolescents (Hartman, 2008). There is an important parallel here in the discussion of whether a person of fluctuating competency[32] is capable of giving informed consent to biomedical research. Bruce Winick has noted:

> Another potential use for advance directive instruments is in the area of participation in biomedical or behavioral research. Under ethical and legal requirements for human experimentation, the informed consent of the individual is required and consent may be revoked at any time. This latter requirement may be problematic for people suffering from mental disorders that cause fluctuating periods of incompetency. Should such individuals, therefore, be barred from participation in research? Can they enter into advance directive instruments agreeing to participate in research and appointing surrogates who can revoke their consent to participate on their behalf during a period of incompetency? If so, what safeguards need to be built into such advance directive instruments so that they may protect the rights of research participants and allow investigators to accept their participation consistent with ethical and legal requirements? (Winick, 1998, p. 602)

To what extent, then, does the sort of pathological altruism that is reflected in "stranger" organ donation cases or in cultural defense cases honor Ronner's principles of therapeutic jurisprudence—"voice, validation, and voluntariness"?[33] Empirical studies of such donations suggest they are empowering for many of the donors (for discussions, see Henderson et al., 2003; Landolt et al., 2001; Spital, 2001), as long as the donor is competent to make the donation decision on his or her own (Cheyotte, 2000; Henderson et al, 2003; Winick, 1998). Such behavior, then, might not be "irrational" under my definition, and might not, under that definition, "interfere with rational social behaviors."[34]

On the other hand, it is much more difficult to find a therapeutic jurisprudence basis for the behaviors of acquiescent victims in the cultural defense cases. If Patricia Hernandez is correct when she states that victimization reflects "the cross that God has sent me"(2003, p. 865), and if this putatively altruistic behavior is regularly rooted in fear (e.g., Sheehan, 2000; West, 1997), then it appears that the dignity that is a core underpinning of therapeutic jurisprudence (e.g., Winick, 2003, p. 1089) is wholly absent in this self-harming and irrational behavior.

Neuroimaging and Pathological Altruism

Neuroimaging may offer important insights into the neural roots of empathy and trust (DeMartino, Kumaran, Seymour, & Dolan, 2006; Shirtcliff et al., 2009) and the biological bases of both human decision making (Knabb, Welsh, Ziebell, & Reimer, 2009) and moral judgments (Green et al., 2001). Scholars and researchers have made significant progress in employing neuroimaging tools to learn more about the etiology of altruism.[35] Some go as far as to say that, from an anthropological perspective, neural "wiring" makes some decision making inevitable (Schreiber, 2009). Recent research argues that functional magnetic resonance imaging (fMRI) scans can be strongly predictive of a person's likelihood for altruistic behavior (Parker, 2007), and that positron emission tomography (PET) scans indicate a signature reflective of the decision of game players to mete out altruistic punishments to cheaters (Parker, 2004).

It appears reasonably certain that neuroimaging is capable of revealing some of the roots of altruistic behavior. But this leads to another question: To what extent would such evidence be admissible in court proceedings that relate to the underlying issues? On the surface, neuroimaging might illuminate competency issues that are relevant to some organ donation questions, as well as mental state issues that are relevant to some cultural defense questions (on the need for those doing neuropsychological forensic assessments to be culturally competent, see Judd, 2005; on how the expanded use of neuroimaging techniques "manifest larger cultural concerns about . . . medical expertise," see Aggarwal, 2009, p. 241). However, as mentioned earlier, there are ongoing threshold obstacles to the introduction of neuroimaging evidence, and it is not at all clear that, in the decision making process, courts are rendering their decisions in bias-free ways (Perlin, 2009c; Risinger, 2000; Rozelle, 2007). On this point, then, my conclusion is simply that, although I believe that neuroimaging might have much to tell us about the root causes of some behaviors of some pathological altruists, we may not yet be at the point at which the legal system is ready to embrace such testimony.

> Therapeutic jurisprudence gives us a benchmark by which we can assess whether the pathological altruist (if, indeed, the altruist is pathological) has sacrificed her dignity to do the putatively pathologically altruistic act, an assessment process that can also illuminate whether the underlying behavior is irrational or self-harming.

Conclusion

Both therapeutic jurisprudence and neuroimaging are valuable tools when considering the treatment of pathological altruism in the law, in the scenarios discussed in this chapter. Therapeutic jurisprudence gives us a benchmark by which we can assess whether the pathological altruist (if, indeed, the altruist is pathological) has sacrificed her dignity to do the putatively pathologically altruistic act, an assessment process that can also illuminate whether the underlying behavior is irrational or self-harming. Neuroimaging and neuroscience give us new tools to potentially assess whether the pathological altruist is a rational moral agent in doing such acts. These tools may help illuminate our further and deeper understanding of these issues, and may give us new insights into why people do engage in such actions even when they appear to be self-defeating as well as self-destructive.

A robust body of therapeutic jurisprudence literature has grown over the past two decades (see Perlin & Cucolo, 2009, §2D-4, listing articles), and in the past several years, scholars have begun to grapple with the full range of issues related to the use of neuroimaging evidence in the court system (see Perlin, 2009b, 2009c, citing articles). Yet, there has been virtually no attention paid to the issues that I seek to address in this chapter. My hopes are that scholars who write and do empirical research in both fields will now turn their focus to these questions in an effort to illuminate some of the underlying issues.

In my writings about the insanity defense, I have always tried to focus on the perplexing question of "why do we feel the way we do about these people?" (e.g., Perlin, 1999, p. 17, referring to those who plead the insanity defense). More recently, in a piece on neuroimaging and the law, I noted difficulties in the criminal justice process involving cases of "defendants with mental disabilities who commit, on-the-surface, inexplicable acts" (Perlin, 2009b, p. 909). To many of us, the acts committed by those discussed in this chapter—stranger organ donors and cultural defense pleaders/victims—are equally inexplicable, with an inexplicability that is intertwined with both societal and judicial stereotypes (see Maguigan, 1995, p. 66, n. 103). I believe that the application of the therapeutic jurisprudence lens and filter[36] to these cases will make the debate far richer, and that if neuroscience scholars turn their attention to these questions, we may have increasing confidence in the fairness of the disposition of cases involving these issues.

Acknowledgments

The author wishes to thank David Wexler for his helpful comments and suggestions, Naomi Weinstein for her impeccable research assistance, and Barbara Oakley for her superb editorial suggestions. He is saddened that Bruce Winick, who offered so much aid and encouragement, did not live to see the publication of this volume.

Notes

1. See Part IV. A recent simple WESTLAW search of "organ donation" in the ALLCASES database yielded a total of 136 cases (search conducted December 15, 2009).

2. For a historical review of the psychoanalytic explanation of pathological altruism, see McWilliams (1984). For subsequent consideration, see Seelig and Rosof (2001).

3. For the purposes of this chapter, I am adopting a modified version of pathological altruism used elsewhere in this volume by Michael McGrath and Barbara Oakley: I define it as the willingness of a person to irrationally place another's perceived needs above his or her own in a way that causes self-harm. Put another way, it involves an excessive expression of empathy demonstrated in ways that can interfere with rational social behaviors (Eisenberg, 1984).

4. On the potential relationship between therapeutic jurisprudence and neuroimaging, see Perlin (2009a).

5. On how therapeutic jurisprudence presupposes the protection of and shares the values of dignity, see Rotman (2008); on its use as a tool for the restoration of dignity, see Salisbury (2005) and Perlin (2009a).

6. For example, see Petrila (1993, p. 893) discussing "the assumption that in virtually all circumstances the legal system should defer to the prescriptions of treaters"—in other words, that courts should be exceedingly deferential to institutional decision making in cases involving persons residing in psychiatric facilities.

7. *Daubert* was decided under the Federal Rules of Evidence and is binding in all federal cases. In addition, many states have chosen to follow *Daubert*'s guidance. Other states continue to adhere to the earlier rule set down in *Frye v. United States* (1923) allowing judges to exclude evidence from expert witnesses if it has not been "generally accepted."

8. Susan Rozelle is blunt: "The game of scientific evidence looks fixed" (2007, p. 598).

9. Ben Seymour and his colleagues, by way of example (2007, p. 309), posit that altruistic punishment is a strategy employed by humans to promote the cooperation needed for the maintenance of human societies. Stacey Tovino (2007, p. 418) asks, "Can fMRI reveal whether an individual is racially prejudiced, deceitful or altruistic?"; see also generally, Kuklin (2008).

10. For a parallel inquiry into the relationship of the *Daubert* test to the admissibility of transcranial magnetic stimulation (TMS) evidence in deception detection, see Luber et al. (2009).

11. On the question of whether there is a genetic predisposition for altruism, see Knafo et al. (2007, 2009). On the mechanisms of cultural transmission that result in "positive selection pressures on rules mandating beneficent behaviors," see Allison (1992–1993, p. 295).

Scholars have also begun to explore the religious roots of excessive altruism (Wilson, 2007) and the patriotic roots of manipulated altruism (Rushton, 1989, p. 516). On altruism exemplified by actions based on a sense of duty and moral obligation, see Harrison (1986, p. 1326).

12. This is especially relevant in that it is unclear that neuroimaging results in these cases would meet the teleological preconceptions of the factfinder (see Perlin, 1994, p. 262): "The legal system selectively—teleologically—either accepts or rejects social science evidence depending on whether or not the use of that data meets the a priori needs of the legal system"; see generally, Appelbaum (1987). On how therapeutic jurisprudence might combat the inappropriate use of teleology by courts in insanity defense cases (see Perlin, 2009b, p. 913).

13. Cf. Rushton (1989, p. 503), who notes: "In extreme form, altruism involves self-sacrifice."

14. See also Baskin (2009) on the positive value of altruistic donation, and Schwartz et al. (2003), describing how altruistic social behaviors are positively associated with better mental health. Henderson and his colleagues conclude that the evidence is "sufficiently compelling to consider developing [anonymous donor] programs nationally and internationally" (Baskin, 2009, p. 208; Henderson, 2003). Other studies reveal that about a quarter of surveyed respondents would be willing to donate a kidney to a stranger (Landolt et al., 2001, p. 1694 [29%]; Spital, 2001, p. 1061 [24%]). Other research suggests that donors may be motivated by a heightened altruistic sense of civic duty (see Blumkin & Margalioth, 2008).

15. For the standard psychoanalytic interpretation of the narcissistic bases of such altruism, see Seelig and Rosof (2001) and Garrett(1983); on the putatively altruistic acts that reflect "self-loathing," see Jansen (2009, p. 27); on the psychological roots of some "selfish altruism," see Shapiro and Gabbard (1994) and Atkinson (1999); for altruism's relationship to social Darwinism, see Goodenough (2006).

On the specific role of religious-based altruism in the "Jesus Christian" religious community, see Mueller et al. (2008); on religion and altruism more generally in this context, see Dixon and Abbey (2000).

16. Certain "culture-bound syndromes" are included in the American Psychiatric Association's *Diagnostic and Statistical Manual of Mental Disorders*. For a discussion in this context, see King (1999).

17. On the relationship between the cultural defense and the "ignorance of the law defense," see Power (2007, discussing the defense's potential application to cases from the Pitcairn Islands involving sex with minors).

18. Omitted from this chapter for reasons of space is the third category discussed by Professor Lee, men who claim "marriage by capture" as part of the Hmong tradition. See generally, Evans-Pritchard and Renteln (1995); see also Goel (2004, p. 457, n. 59), discussing *People v. Moua* (1985) (finding defendant guilty of forcible confinement rather than kidnapping and rape based on the traditional Hmong practice of marriage by capture; defendant argued that he mistook the victim's resistance for the ritual resistance required by the traditional ceremony, and therefore reasonably believed that the victim was actually consenting). Cynthia Lee (2007, p. 959) argues "the persuasiveness of a defendant's cultural claims may turn on the extent to which the claims converge with the dominant subtexts of racism and sexism."

19. See Harvard Note (1986, p. 1309): "A cultural defense should more readily be admitted when the crime is limited to persons capable of meaningful consent who belong to that culture and subscribe to its tenets"; see also Villareal (1991).

20. See Goozner (1994) quoting the director of a Japanese psychiatric research institution, who characterizes battered Japanese women as being afflicted with "pathological altruism." Hernandez (2003, p. 865) argues that, in Latin American culture, domestic violence victimization often leads to acceptance as "the 'cross that God has sent me.'"

21. For example, see Wu (2003, p. 1013, n. 277): "The most common motive for parents killing their children was what the parent believed to be altruism: the suicidal mother or father who thinks that they cannot abandon the child, or who kills to alleviate the child's suffering, whether real or imagined."

22. Notes West (1997, p. 119): "Women's inclination toward private or intimate altruism—particularly in the home—is also, many times, and in many ways, the measure of the harms such women have distinctively sustained." See McClain (1999, p. 499), discussing West (1997, p. 119), describing how women's altruistic acts are often driven by "fear and insecurity." On how women are expected to be more altruistic than are men, see West (1997, p. 109; see also, West, 1988, discussed in Kell, p. 367, n. 64). On how women are assigned a "disproportionate responsibility for care," see McClain (2001, p. 1707).

23. Compare Lee (2007, p. 939: "successful cultural defenses often reinforce racial or ethnic stereotypes"), to Renteln (2004, p. 65: "A serious objection to the cultural defense is the worry it will reinforce stereotypes about groups. It is important that the cultural question be handled with sensitivity, so that the case does not convey the erroneous impression that just because one individual followed a tradition, everyone within a particular cultural community behaves in a way that violates the law"). For a comprehensive defense of the cultural defense, see Renteln (1993).

24. On how the use of such a defense can pathologize cultural difference, see Tseng, Matthews, and Elwyn (2004, pp. 181–182).

25. See generally, Lee (2007), Goldstein (1994), Goel (2004), Hoeffel (2006, p. 331), MacGuigan (1995); see also Wu (2003, p. 1002, n. 192), discussing the infanticide case of *People v. Wu* (1991), and see id. at p. 1015, n. 290, suggesting the link between immigrant mothers in Southern California who killed their children was not culture, but rather

that they "suffered depression from pressure and stress of adjusting to a new life in a new land."

26. On the impact of psychosis on maternal filicide, see Lewis and Bunce (2003).

27. See Perlin (2009a, p. 887, footnote omitted):

> Thus, when we consider . . . the impact of neuroimaging evidence on juror decision making in insanity defense cases[,] we need to recalibrate our focus so as to incorporate other questions that are as essential (most likely more essential) to the resolution of the underlying dilemma: . . . (2) will [the] "falsifiability issue" even matter to jurors whose personal values/moral codes reject the notion of any non-responsibility verdict because it is dissonant with their heuristics-driven, false "ordinary common sense"[?]

28. See Perlin (2010, on the use of therapeutic jurisprudence as a tool to remedy the incoherence of the insanity defense.

29. Compare Brady (2008, p. 559) who argues that law and economics "largely ignores altruism," with Menkel-Meadow (1992, p. 387), who describes the proscriptions and prescriptions of the codes of lawyers' ethical conduct as antithetical to the ethos of therapeutic jurisprudence. On how judicial altruism flies in the face of the rational choice approach associated with law and economics, see Stout (2002 p. 1610).

30. See also Landsman and McNeel (2004), who note that preference for altruistic law practice predicts law students' moral judgment scores; Chamlin and Cochran (1997) describe the beneficent behaviors of social altruism; Ronel et al. (2009) write on the significance of perceived altruism.

31. See Cheyotte (2004, p. 508): "Imputing the psychological benefits of altruistic behavior to individuals who, because of age, cognitive ability, and circumstances cannot make altruistic choices, is myopic." For a fascinating dialogue on the consideration and construction of competency in an altruistic organ donation case, compare Spike (1997) to Silverman (1997).

32. Competency is not a fixed state but may fluctuate as a natural course of an individual's illness, or in response to treatment or psychodynamic factors (Johns, 2004).

33. Compare this with Yuille (2007, 392, n. 5), who notes: "The concept of 'altruistic pathology' is meant to distinguish between the moral, social, and legal norms that pathologize outsider groups for the purpose of—or that have the effect of enabling—oppression and the pathology that characterizes outsiders' abnormality as a justification for special, supposed positive treatment."

34. On the related question of the rationality of appearance-enhancing cosmetic surgery, see for example Ruel (2007, p. 125, quoting, in part, Sullivan, 2000, p. 28):

> Whether a woman elects cosmetic surgery because of the social norms expressed in centerfolds, swimsuit issues, or the workplace, the inescapable conclusion remains that the decision is "a rational response to prevailing cultural values that reward those considered more attractive" and penalizes the ugly or less attractive.

35. For example, see Damasio (2007) and Tankersley et al. (2007). For the neural bases of altruism, see Rilling (2008, 2009).

36. See Perlin (2005, p. 754): "A therapeutic jurisprudence lens should regularly be applied to this entire area of the law, and courts should begin to consider the issues discussed here through a therapeutic jurisprudence filter."

References

Aggarwal, N. K. (2009). Neuroimaging, culture, and forensic psychiatry. *Journal of the American Academy of Psychiatry and Law, 37,* 239–244.

Allison, P. D. (1992). The cultural evolution of beneficent norms. *Social Forces, 71,* 279–301.

Appelbaum, P. (1987). The empirical jurisprudence of the United States Supreme Court. *American Journal of Law & Medicine, 13,* 335–350.

Archer, J. (2009). The nature of human aggression. *International Journal of Law and Psychiatry, 32*(4), 202–208.

Atkinson, R. (1999). Liberating lawyers: Divergent parallels in "Intruder in the Dust" and "To Kill a Mockingbird." *Duke Law Journal, 49,* 601–748.

Baskin, J.H. et al. (2007). Is a picture worth a thousand words? Neuroimaging in the courtroom, *American Journal of Law and Medicine, 33,* 239–269.

Baskin, J. H. (2009). Giving until it hurts? Altruistic donation of solid organs. *Journal of the American Academy of Psychiatry and Law, 37,* 377–379.

Baskir, C. E. (2009). Fostering cultural competence in justice system "gatekeepers." *Judicature, 92,* 232–237.

Batts, S. (2009). Brain lesions and their implications in criminal responsibility. *Behavioral Sciences & Law, 27,* 261–272.

Binder, R. L., Trimble, M. R., McNiel, D. E. (1991). Is money a cure? Follow-up of litigants. *Bulletin of the American Academy of Psychiatry & Law, 19,* 151–160.

Blumkin, T., & Margalioth, Y. (2008). On terror, drugs, and racial profiling. *International Review of Law & Economics, 28,* 194–203.

Brady, K. L. (2008). The value of human life: A case for altruism. *Natural Resources Journal, 48,* 541–562.

Chamlin, M. B., & Cochran, J. K. (1997). Social altruism and crime. *Criminology, 35,* 203–228.

Cherry, M. J. (2009). Embracing the commodification of human organs: Transplantation and the freedom to sell body parts. *St. Louis University Journal of Health Law and Policy, 2,* 359–377.

Cheyotte, C. (2000). Organ harvests from the legally incompetent: An argument against compelled altruism. *Boston College Law Review, 41,* 465–515.

Chiu, D. C. (1988). The cultural defense: Beyond exclusion, assimilation, and guilty liberalism. *California Law Review, 83,* 1053–1125.

Chiu, E. M. (2006). Culture as justification, not excuse. *American Criminal Law Review, 43,* 1317–1374.

Crockett, H. Y. (2006). Cultural defenses in Georgia: Cultural pluralism and justice—can Georgia have both? *Georgia State University Law Review, 22,* 665–688.

Cruz, E. (2008). Through the clinical lens: A pragmatic look at infusing therapeutic jurisprudence into clinical pedagogy. *Thomas Jefferson Law Review, 30,* 463–485.

Daicoff, S. (1999). Making law therapeutic for lawyers: Therapeutic jurisprudence, preventive law, and the psychology of lawyers. *Psychology, Public Policy & Law, 5,* 811–844.

Damasio, A. (2007). Neuroscience and ethics: Intersections. *American Journal of Bioethics, 7,* 3–7.

Daubert v. *Merrill Dow Pharmaceuticals, Inc.,* 509 U.S. 579 (1993).

DeMartino, B., Kumaran, D., Seymour, B., & Dolan, R. (2006). Frames, biases, and rational decision-making in the human brain. *Science, 313,* 600–601.

DePalma, A. R. (2009). I couldn't help myself–my culture made me do it: The use of cultural evidence in the heat of passion defense. *Chicana/o-Latina/o Law Review, 28,* 1–18.

Dixon, D. J. & Abbey, S. E. (2000). Religious altruism and organ donation. *Psychosomatics*, *41*, 407–411.

Evans-Pritchard, D. & Renteln, A. D. (1995). The interpretation and distortion of culture: A Hmong "marriage by capture" case in Fresno, California. *Southern California Interdisciplinary Law Journal*, *4*, 1–48.

Freckelton, I. (2008). Therapeutic jurisprudence misunderstood and misrepresented: The price and risks of influence. *Thomas Jefferson Law Review*, *30*, 575–591.

Frye v. United States, 293 Fed. 1013 (D.C. Cir. 1923).

Garet, R. R. (1983). Communality and existence: The rights of groups. *Southern California Law Review*, *56*, 1001–1075.

Goel, R. (2004). Can I call Kimura crazy?: Ethical tensions in the cultural defense. *Seattle Journal of Social Justice*, *3*, 443–460.

Goldstein, T. F. (1994). Cultural conflicts in court: Should the American criminal justice system formally recognize a "cultural defense"? *Dickinson Law Review*, *99*, 141–168.

Goodenough, O. (2006). Cultural replication theory and law: Proximate mechanisms make a difference. *Vermont Law Review*, *30*, 989–1004.

Goodwin, M. (2004). Altruism's limits: Law, capacity, and organ commodification. *Rutgers Law Review*, *56*, 305–407.

Goodwin, M. (2009). Confronting the limits of altruism: A response to Jake Linford. *Saint Louis University Journal of Health Law & Policy*, *2*, 327–345.

Goozner, M. (1994, July 24). Japan finally comes to grips with reality of domestic violence. *Buffalo News*, A4.

Graham, W. K., & Livingston, J. P. (2009). Perspectives on financial incentives to induce live kidney donation: Scholarships in exchange for the gift of life. *St. Louis University Journal of Health Law and Policy*, *2*, 347–358.

Greene, J. D., Sommerville, R. B., Nystrom, L. E., Darley, J. M., & Cohen, J. D. (2001). An fMRI investigation of emotional engagement in moral judgment. *Science*, *293*, 2105–2108.

Harrison, J. L. (1986). Egoism, altruism, and market illusions: The limits of law and economics. *UCLA Law Review*, *33*, 1309–1363.

Hartman, R. G. (2008). *Gault's* legacy: Dignity, due process, and adolescents' liberty interests in living donation. *Notre Dame Journal of Law, Ethics & Public Policy*, *22*, 67–106.

Henderson, A. J. Z., Landolt, M. A., McDonal, M. F., Barrable, W. M., Soos, J. G., Gourlay, W., et al. (2003). The living anonymous kidney donor: Lunatic or saint? *American Journal of Transplantation*, *3*, 203–213.

Hernandez, P. M. (2003). The myth of machismo: An everyday reality for Latin American women. *Saint Thomas Law Review*, *15*, 859–882.

Hernandez- Truyol, B. E. (2008). The gender bend: Culture, sex, and sexuality–a critical human rights map of Latina/o border crossing. *Indiana Law Journal*, *83*, 1283–1331.

Hernandez, P. M. (2003). The myth of machismo: An everyday reality for Latin American women. *Saint Thomas Law Review*, *15*, 859–882.

Hoeffel, J. C. (2006). Deconstructing the cultural defense debate. *University of Florida Journal of Law and Public Policy*, *17*, 303–344.

Jansen, L. A. (2009). The ethics of altruism in clinical research. *Hastings Center Report*, *39*, 26–36.

Johns, A. F. (2004). Older clients with diminishing capacity and their advance directives. *Real Property, Probate & Trust Journal*, *39*, 107–134.

Judd, T. (2005). Cross-cultural forensic neuropsychological assessment. In K. Barrett, & W. George (Eds.), *Race, culture, psychology and law* (pp. 141–162). Thousand Oaks, CA: Sage Publications.

Kahn, M. (2002). Jurisprudential countertransference. *Touro Law Review, 18*, 459–477.

Kell, W. A. (1998). Ties that bind? Children's attorneys, children's agency, and the dilemma of parental affiliation. *Loyola University Chicago Law Journal, 29*, 353–376.

King, M. (2009). *Restorative justice, therapeutic jurisprudence and the rise of emotionally intelligent justice.* Research Paper No. 2009/11, Faculty of Law, Monash University, Victoria, AU. Retrieved from http://ssrn.com/abstract=no.1498923=

King, N. A. (1999). The role of culture in psychology: A look at mental illness and the "cultural defense." *Tulsa Journal of Comparative & International Law, 7*, 199–225.

Kivivuori, J. (2007). Crime by proxy: Coercion and altruism in adolescent shoplifting. *British Journal of Criminology, 4*, 817–833.

Knabb, J. J., Welsh, R. K., Ziebell, J. G., & Reimer, K. S. (2009). Neuroscience, moral reasoning, and the law. *Behavioral Sciences and the Law, 27*, 219–236.

Knafo, A., Israel, S., Darvasi, A., Bachner-Melman, R., Uzefovsky, F., Cohen, L., et al. (2007). Individual differences in allocation of funds in the dictator game associated with length of the arginine vasopressin 1a receptor RS3 promoter region and correlation between RS3 length and hippocampal mRNA. *Genes, Brain and Behavior, 7*, 266–275.

Knafo, A. et al (2009) *Heritability of children's prosocial behavior and differential susceptibility to parenting by variation in the Dopamine D4 Receptor (DRD4) gene.* (Submitted to Development and Psychopathology special issue on differential susceptibility to environmental influences.)

Kuklin, B. (2008). The morality of evolutionarily self-interested rescues. *Arizona State Law Journal, 40*, 453–521.

Landolt, M. A., Henderson, A. J., Barrable, W. M., Greenwood, S.D., McDonald, M.F., Soos, J. G., and Landsberg, D.N. (*2001*). *Living anonymous kidney donation: What does the public think? Transplantation, 71*, 1690–1696.

Landsman, M. & McNeel, S. P. (2004). Moral judgment of law students across three years: Influences of gender, political ideology and interest in altruistic law practices. *South Texas Law Review, 45*, 891–919.

Lee, C. (2007). Cultural convergence: Interest convergence theory meets the cultural defense. *Arizona Law Review, 49*, 911–959.

Lewis, C. F. & Bunce, S. C. (2003). Filicidal mothers and the impact of psychosis on maternal filicide. *Journal of the American Academy of Psychiatry & Law, 31*, 459–470.

Li, J. (1996). The nature of the offense: An ignored factor in determining the application of the cultural defense. *University of Hawaii Law Review, 18*, 765–796.

Linford, J. (2009). The kidney donor scholarship act: How college scholarships can provide financial incentives for kidney donation while preserving altruistic meaning. *St. Louis University Journal of Health Law and Policy, 2*, 265–325.

Luber, B., Fisher, C., Appelbaum, P. S., Ploesser, M., & Lisanbyet, S. H. (2009). Non-invasive brain stimulation in the detection of deception. Scientific challenges and ethical consequences. *Behavioral Sciences & Law, 27*, 191–208.

Maguigan, H. (1995). Cultural evidence and male violence: Are feminist and multiculturalist reformers on a collision course in criminal courts? *New York University Law Review, 70*, 36–99.

Marks, J. H. (2007). Interrogational neuroimaging in counterterrorism: A "no-brainer" or human rights hazard, *American Journal of Law and Medicine, 33*, 483–502.

McClain, L. C. (1999). The liberal future of relational feminism: Robin West's "Caring for Justice." *Law & Social Inquiry, 24*, 477–516.

McClain, L. C. (2001). Care as a public value: Linking responsibility, resources, and republicanism. *Chicago-Kent Law Review, 76*, 1673–1731.

McWilliams, N. (1984). The psychology of the altruist. *Psychoanalytic Psychology, 1,* 193–213.

Menkel-Meadow, C. (1992). Is altruism possible in lawyering? *Georgia State University Law Review, 8,* 385–419.

Miller, D. (2009). Applying therapeutic jurisprudence and preventive law to the divorce process: Enhancing the attorney-client relationship and the Florida practice and procedure form "Marital settlement agreement for dissolution of marriage with dependent or minor child(ren)." *Florida Coastal Law Review, 10,* 263–297.

Moriarty, J. (2008). Flickering admissibility: Neuroimaging in the U.S. courts, *Behavioral Sciences & Law, 26,* 29–49.

Mueller, P. S., Case, E. J., & Hook, C. C. (2008). Responding to offers of altruistic living unrelated kidney donation by group associations: An ethical analysis. *Transplantation Reviews, 22,* 200–205.

Muller, J. L., Sommer, M., Dohnel, K., Weber, T., Schmidt-Wilcke, T., & Hajak, G. (2008). Disturbed prefrontal and temporal brain function during emotion and cognition interaction in criminal psychopathy, *Behavioral Sciences and the Law, 26,* 131–150.

Note (1986). The cultural defense in the criminal law. *Harvard Law Review, 99,* 1293–1311. (Harvard Note).

Oberman, M. (2004). Mothers who kill: Coming to terms with modern American infanticide. *DePaul Journal of Health Care Law, 8,* 3–107.

Parker, R. (2004). Brain rewards for carrying out altruistic punishment. *FuturePundit: Brain Altruism Archives.* Retrieved from http://www.futurepundit.com.archives.cat_brain_altruism.html

Parker, R. (2007). Altruistic people differ in brain scans. *FuturePundit: Brain Altruism Archives,* Retrieved from http://www.futurepundit.com.archives.cat_brain_altruism.html

People v. *Kimura,* No. A-091133 (Cal. Sup Ct., LA County, April 24, 1985).

People v. *Moua,* No. 315972-0 (Cal. Super. Ct. Fresno County Feb. 7, 1985).

People v. *Wu,* 286 Cal. Rptr. 868 (App. 1991) (depublished).

Perlin, M. L. (1994). The sanist lives of jurors in death penalty cases: The puzzling role of "mitigating" mental disability evidence. *Notre Dame Journal of Law, Ethics & Public Policy, 8,* 239–279.

Perlin, M. L. (1997). "The borderline which separated you from me": The insanity defense, the authoritarian spirit, the fear of faking, and the culture of punishment. *Iowa Law Review, 82,* 1375–1426.

Perlin, M. L. (1999). "Half-wracked prejudice leaped forth": Sanism, pretextuality, and why and how mental disability law developed as it did. *Journal of Contemporary Legal Issues, 3,* 14–36.

Perlin, M. L. (2000). A law of healing. *University of Cincinnati Law Review, 68,* 407–433.

Perlin, M. L. (2002-2003). "Things have changed": Looking at non-institutional mental disability law through the sanism filter. *New York Law School Law Review, 46,* 535–546.

Perlin, M. L. (2003). "She breaks just like a little girl": Neonaticide, the insanity defense, and the irrelevance of ordinary common sense. *William & Mary Journal of Women and Law, 10,* 1–34.

Perlin, M. L. (2005). "And my best friend, my doctor, won't even say what it is I've got": The role and significance of counsel in right to refuse treatment cases. *San Diego Law Review, 42,* 735–755.

Perlin, M. L. (2008). "Everybody is making love/or else expecting rain": Considering the sexual autonomy rights of persons institutionalized because of mental disability in forensic hospitals and in Asia. *University of Washington Law Review, 83,* 481–508.

Perlin, M. L. (2009a). A therapeutic jurisprudence inquiry into the roles of dignity and humiliation in the law. *Human Dignity and Humiliation Studies*. Retrieved from http://www.humiliationstudies.org/whoweare/annualmeeting14.php

Perlin, M. L. (2009b). "His brain has been mismanaged with great skill": How will jurors respond to neuroimaging testimony in insanity defense cases? *Akron Law Review, 42,* 885–916.

Perlin, M. L. (2009c). "And I see through your brain": Access to experts, competency to consent, and the impact of antipsychotic medications in neuroimaging cases in the criminal trial process. *Stanford Technology Law Journal, 2009, 4.*

Perlin, M. L. (2010). "Too stubborn to ever be governed by enforced insanity": Some therapeutic jurisprudence dilemmas in the representation of criminal defendants in incompetency and insanity cases. *International Journal of Law and Psychiatry, 33,* 475–481.

Perlin, M. L., & Cucolo, H. E. (2009 Cum. Supp.). *Mental disability law: Civil and criminal* Vol. 1 (2nd ed.). Newark, NJ: Lexis-Nexis Publ.

Perlin, M. L., & McClain, V. (2009a). Unasked (and unanswered) questions about the role of neuroimaging in the criminal trial process. *American Journal of Forensic Psychology, 28,* 5–22.

Perlin, M. L., & McClain, V. (2009b). "Where souls are forgotten": Cultural competencies, forensic evaluations, and international human rights. *Psychology, Public Policy & Law, 15,* 257–277.

Perlmutter, B. (2005). George's story: Voice and transformation through the teaching and practice of therapeutic jurisprudence in a law school child advocacy clinic. *Saint Thomas Law Review, 17,* 561–621.

Petrila, J. (1993). Paternalism and the unfulfilled promise of "Essays In Therapeutic Jurisprudence." *New York Law School Journal of Human Rights, 10,* 877–905.

Power, H. (2007). Pitcairn Island: Sexual offending, cultural difference and ignorance of the law. *Criminal Law Review,* 609–629.

Reeves, D., Mills, M. J., Billick, S. B., & Brodie, J. D. (2003). Limitations of brain imaging in forensic psychiatry. *Journal of the American Academy of Psychiatry and the Law, 31,* 89–96.

Renteln, A. D. (1993). A justification of the cultural defense as partial excuse. *Southern California Review of Law & Women's Studies, 2,* 437–526.

Renteln, A.D. (2004). The use and abuse of the cultural defense. *Canadian Journal of Law and Society, 20,* 47–67.

Rilling, J. K. (2008). Neuroscientific approaches and applications within anthropology. *Yearbook of Physical Anthropology, 51,* 2–32.

Rilling, J. K. (2009). The neurobiology of cooperation and altruism. *Context and the evolution of mechanisms for solving collective action problems.* Paper, Indiana University. Retrieved from http://ssrn.com/abstract=1368881

Risinger, D. M. (2000). Navigating expert reliability: Are criminal standards of certainty being left on the dock? *Albany Law Review, 64,* 99–152.

Roberts, A. (2007). Everything new is old again: Brain fingerprinting and evidentiary analogy. *Yale Journal of Law & Technology, 9,* 234–272.

Ronel, N., Haski-Leventhal, D., Ben-David, B. M., & York, A. S. (2009). Perceived altruism: A neglected factor in initial intervention. *International Journal of Offender Therapy & Comparative Criminology, 53,* 191–209.

Ronner, A. (2002). Songs of validation, voice, and voluntary participation: Therapeutic jurisprudence, Miranda and juveniles. *University of Cincinnati Law Review, 71,* 89–120.

Ronner, A. (2008). The learned-helpless lawyer: Clinical legal education and therapeutic jurisprudence as antidotes to Bartleby syndrome. *Touro Law Review, 24,* 601–664.

Ronner, A. (2010). *Law, literature and therapeutic jurisprudence.* (Durham, NC: Carolina Academic Press).

Rotman, E. (2008). Therapeutic jurisprudence and terrorism. *Thomas Jefferson Law Review, 30,* 525–545.

Rozelle, S. (2007). *Daubert,* Schmaubert: Criminal defendants and the short end of the science stick. *Tulsa Law Review, 43,* 597–606.

Ruel, M. D. (2007). "Vanity tax": How New Jersey has opened Pandora's box by elevating its moral judgment about cosmetic surgery without consideration of fair health care policy. *Journal of Legal Medicine, 28,* 119–134.

Rushton, J. P. (1989). Genetic similarity, human altruism, and group selection. *Behavioral and Brain Sciences, 12,* 503–559.

Salisbury, C. S. (2005). From violence and victimization to voice and validation: Incorporating therapeutic jurisprudence in a children's law clinic. *Saint Thomas Law Review, 17,* 623–676.

Schreiber, D., et al. (September, 2009). *Red brain, blue brain: Evaluative processes differ in democrats and republicans.* Paper presented at the American Political Science Association, Toronto, ON. Retrieved from http://papers.ssrn.com/Sol3/papers.cfm?abstract_id=1451867

Schwartz, C., Meisenhelder, J. B., Ma, Y., & Reed, G. (2003). Altruistic social interest behaviors are associated with better mental health. *Psychosomatic Medicine, 65,* 778–785.

Seelig, B. J., & Rosof, L. S. (2001). Normal and pathological altruism. *Journal of the American Psychoanalytic Association, 49,* 933–959.

Seymour, B., Singer, T., & Dolan, R. (2007). The neurobiology of punishment, *Nature Reviews Neuroscience, 8,* 300–311.

Shapiro, Y., & Gabbard, G. O. (1994). A reconsideration of altruism from an evolutionary and psychodynamic perspective. *Ethics & Behavior, 4,* 23–42.

Sheehan, K. C. (2000). Caring for deconstruction. *Yale Journal of Feminism, 12,* 85–142.

Shirafi, M. (2008). "Justice in Many Rooms" since Galanter: De-romanticizing legal pluralism through the cultural defense. *Law and Contemporary Problems, 71,* 139–146.

Shirtcliff, E. A., Vitacco, M. J., Graf, A. R., Gostisha, A. J., Merz, J. L., & Zahn-Waxler, C. (2009). Neurobiology of empathy and callousness: Implications for the development of antisocial behavior. *Behavioral Sciences and the Law, 27,* 137–171.

Shuman, D. W. (1993). Making the world a better place through tort law? Through the therapeutic looking-glass. *New York Law School Journal of Human Rights, 10,* 739–752.

Siegel, A., & Victoroff, J. (2009). Understanding human aggression: New insights from neuroscience, *International Journal of Law and Psychiatry, 29,* 209–215.

Silverman, H. (1997). The role of emotions in decisional competence, standards of competency, and altruistic acts. *Journal of Clinical Ethics, 8,* 171–175.

Slobogin, C. (1995). Therapeutic jurisprudence: Five dilemmas to ponder. *Psychology, Public Policy & Law, 1,* 193–219.

Snead, O. C. (2007). Neuroimaging and the "complexity" of capital punishment. *New York University Law Review, 82,* 1265–1337.

Spike, J. (1997). What's love got to do with it? The altruistic giving of organs. *Journal of Clinical Ethics, 8,* 165–170.

Spital, A. (2001). Public attitudes toward kidney donation by friends and altruistic strangers in the United States. *Transplantation, 71,* 1061–1064.

Stolle, D. P., Wexler, D. B. & Winick, B. J. (2000). *Practicing therapeutic jurisprudence: Law as a helping profession.* Durham, NC: Carolina Academic Press.

Stout, L. A. (2002). Judges as altruistic hierarchs. *William & Mary Law Review, 43,* 1605–1627.

Sullivan, D. A. (2000) *Cosmetic surgery: The cutting edge of commercial medicine in America*. New Brunswick, NJ: Rutgers University Press.

Suri, S. K. (2000). A matter of principle and consistency: Understanding the battered woman and cultural defenses. *Michigan Journal of Gender and Law, 7,* 107–139.

Tankersley, D., Stowe, C. J., & Huettel, S. A. (2007). Altruism is associated with an increased neural response to agency. *Nature Neuroscience, 10,* 150–151.

Tovino, S. (2007). Functional neuroimaging information: A case for neuro exceptionalism? *Florida State University Law Review, 34,* 415–486.

Uttal, W. (2003). *The new phrenology: The limits of localizing cognitive processes in the brain*. London, UK: The MIT Press.

Villareal, C. (1991). Culture in lawmaking: A Chicano perspective. *University of California Davis Law Review, 24,* 1193–1242.

Volpp, L. (1994). (Mis)identifying culture: Asian women and the "cultural defense." *Harvard Women's Law Journal, 17,* 57–101.

Waldman, E. (2008). Therapeutic jurisprudence: Growing up and looking forward. *Thomas Jefferson Law Review, 30,* 345–349.

Wang, K. (1996). Battered Asian American women: Community responses from the battered women's movement and the Asian American community. *Asian Law Journal, 3,* 151–184.

West, R. (1997). *Caring for justice*. New York City: New York University Press.

Wexler, D. B. (Ed.). (1990). *Therapeutic jurisprudence: The law as a therapeutic agent*. Durham, NC: Carolina Academic Press.

Wexler, D. B. (1993). Therapeutic jurisprudence and changing concepts of legal scholarship. *Behavioral Sciences & Law, 11,* 17–29.

Wexler, D. B. (2000). Practicing therapeutic jurisprudence: Psycholegal soft spots and strategies. In D. P. Stolle, D. B. Wexler, & B. J. Winick (Eds.), *Practicing therapeutic jurisprudence: Law as a helping profession* (pp. 45–68). Durham, NC: Carolina Academic Press.

Wexler, D. B. (2008). *Rehabilitating lawyers: Principles of therapeutic jurisprudence for criminal law practice*. Durham, N.C.: Carolina Academic Press.

Wexler, D. B. (2008). Two decades of therapeutic jurisprudence. *Touro Law Review, 24,* 17–28.

Wexler, D. B. & Winick, B. J. (Eds.). (1996). *Law in a therapeutic key: Recent developments in therapeutic jurisprudence*. Durham, NC: Carolina Academic Press.

Wilson, L. T. (2007). The beloved community: The influence and legacy of personalism in the quest for housing and tenant's rights. *John Marshall Law Review, 40,* 513–538.

Winick, B. J. (1998). Foreword: Planning for the future through advance directive instruments. *Psychology, Public Policy & Law, 5,* 579–608.

Winick, B. J. (1999). Therapeutic jurisprudence and the civil commitment hearing. *Journal of Contemporary Legal Issues, 10,* 37–56.

Winick, B. J. (2002). Therapeutic jurisprudence and the treatment of people with mental illness in Eastern Europe: Construing international human rights law, *New York Law School Journal of International & Comparative Law, 21,* 537–572.

Winick, B. J. (2003). Therapeutic jurisprudence and problem solving courts. *Fordham Urban Law Journal, 30,* 1055–1084.

Winick, B. J. (2005). *Civil commitment: A therapeutic jurisprudence model*. Durham, NC: Carolina Academic Press.

Winick, B. J. (2009). Foreword: Therapeutic jurisprudence perspectives on dealing with victims of crime. *Nova Law Review, 33,* 535–541.

Witzel, J., Walter, M., Bogerts, B., & Northoff, G. (2008). Neurophilosophical perspectives of neuroimaging in forensic psychiatry-giving way to a paradigm shift? *Behavioral Sciences and the Law, 26*, 113–130.

Wu, M. W. C. (2003). Culture is no defense for infanticide. *American University Journal of Gender, Social Policy, and the Law, 11*, 975–1022.

Yuille, L. K. (2007). Nobody gives a damn about the gypsies: The limits of Westphalian models for change. *Oregon Review of International Law, 9*, 389–430.

CHAPTER 13

PATHOLOGICAL ALTRUISM
Victims and Motivational Types

Brent E. Turvey

KEY CONCEPTS

- Healthy forms of altruism and pathological altruism are distinguished by the compulsion to be altruistic coupled with a maladaptive outcome.
- Pathological altruism may be found in association with criminal behavior, in which the altruist may be the victim, the victimizer, or both.
- Pathological altruism may be viewed as a manifestation of cognitive distortions resulting from genetic, chemical, environmental, or developmental factors acting alone or in concert.
- Pathologically altruistic behavior can be classified into four major types: *protective*, *defensive*, *masochistic*, and *malignant*, each having both psychotic and nonpsychotic incarnations.

IN MID-OCTOBER OF 2009, Linda Brown, 44, arrived at the Columbus, Ohio, Burlington Coat Factory in a rented stretch Hummer limousine. She had won the lottery, she announced, and she intended to pay for all purchases at the store, all day long, up to $500.00 per customer. She also encouraged everyone to call friends and family to join them at the store. During an interview with the local TV station, Brown explained she had suffered hardship all of her life. She didn't want the lottery money—instead, she had a strong desire to help people. When Brown's credit card reached a $5,000.00 limit, she left, explaining she was going to the bank to get more money.

The store continued to ring up charges for customers on her behalf, and an impatient crowd gathered. Concerned employees soon called the police. Ms. Brown returned, but without any money. Her driver handed her over to authorities upon realizing she couldn't pay for the Hummer rental. By the time merchants realized Brown was unable to pay, it was too late; people had their "free" clothing in hand—they felt entitled to it.

Police eventually dispersed the now angry crowd. The shopping spree was cancelled. Brown had not won the lottery—instead, she was arrested for previous outstanding warrants related to aggravated menacing, misuse of a 911 system, and causing false alarms—all unrelated to the Burlington Coat

Factory incident. Her family came forward to explain that Brown had a long history of mental illness; when she went off her medication, she was prone to fits of extravagance. As of this writing, Brown faces a charge of inducing a public panic, among other charges, all pending a mental health evaluation.

In this case of altruism gone wrong, many questions arise. The first is *why*? Mental disorder? Chemical imbalance? Attention-seeking behavior, or the need to be a celebrity or hero? Determining the cause of such behavior is crucial in understanding what happened, as well as in determining whether such behavior will happen again and how it should be handled by authorities.

As will be discussed, cases of altruism gone wrong, or *pathological altruism*, are not uncommon and can often be found in association with criminal activity. As a consequence, behavioral scientists (psychologists, sociologists, and criminologists) have an obligation to understand what pathological altruism is, what it can mean, and how to identify it when encountered in casework. In this chapter, we will take a criminological approach to pathological altruism, oriented to understanding behavior and relationships as opposed to origins or treatment.

In essence, this chapter proposes a behaviorally oriented motivational typology of pathological altruists. The goal is to define the range of pathological altruism, and to help characterize the nature of relevant relationships. Each type includes a discussion of underlying traits, motives, and psychodynamics, along with specific case examples. (See Table 13.1 for a quick overview.) Readers will come to appreciate that the continuum of pathological altruism is very diverse—it is not just confined to those who continually give too much of themselves out of distorted or masochistic benevolence.

> The continuum of pathological altruism is very diverse—it is not just confined to those who continually give too much of themselves out of distorted or masochistic benevolence.

Altruism

Altruism refers to unselfish behavior that promotes the happiness, survival, and welfare of others at a personal cost. Thus, it is more than compassion, pity, and the performance of good works. Altruism is characterized by a self-sacrificing alignment with the well-being of other people. For example, when the wealthy donate money, it is considered generous; however, only when they regularly sacrifice their time or other irreplaceable resources are their actions altruistic.

Pathological altruism refers to the habitual, maladaptive, and/or compulsive pursuit of the welfare of others (see generally Seelig & Rosof, 2000). This refers to irresistible and even uncontrollable patterns of altruism that do not ultimately help or promote healthy relationships. More specifically, pathological altruism involves excessive or extreme behaviors that go beyond self-sacrificing. They are a self-destructive set of actions based on distorted thinking. Although pathological altruists seek to put others first, they do so while inflicting and suffering different levels of harm. Pathological altruism victimizes the altruists themselves, as well as those in their path.

Pathological altruism does not exist as a fixed state in each of those afflicted with psychodynamic uniformity. It is more a pattern of self-destructive behavior that manifests itself within a spectrum of traits across a continuum of motivational variation and intensity. It is dependant upon individual biology, chemistry, personal development, emotional associations, and psychological needs.

Types of Pathological Altruists	Examples	
	Nonpsychotic	Psychotic
A *protective* altruist voluntarily places him- or herself directly in harms' way for the explicit benefit of others out of some form of deep personal commitment, such as love, friendship, family, service, or a strong sense of community.	A police officer who plants evidence	Some obsessive stalkers; parents who kill their own children to protect them from "evil"; animal hoarders
Defensive altruism involves pleasure or satisfaction from the success, pleasure, and/or welfare of others. However, unlike protective altruism, it is reactive and rises out of the need to resolve conflict. It is referred to as "defensive" because of its self-preserving nature in response to confrontation and hostility.	Staying in an abusive relationship "for the kids"; codependency involving support of a drug addict; parents who continually protect teens from the consequences of their behavior	Elderly person of strong religious conviction who regularly drains his or her bank account making donations to apocalyptic evangelists professing their money is needed to fight evil
Masochistic altruism refers specifically to a maladaptive need to suffer or be the victim, compensating for profound envy, jealousy, anger, aggression, and/or low self-esteem and thoughts of inadequacy. Masochistic altruists seem to be characterized by a pattern of self-sacrifice in which altruism is a coping mechanism for masking inner negativity and conflict. Unlike the defensive altruist who seeks to resolve or move past conflict, the masochistic altruist is compensating for and concealing it. Masochistic altruism often involves the conscious or subconscious belief that one does not deserve to be happy.	"Professional victims" who enjoy being the martyr; compulsive care taking of others	The psychotic manifestations of masochistic altruism are essentially the same as the nonpsychotic. The major difference is that the psychotic altruist may experience inner negativity and conflict regarding events that did not actually occur (e.g., hallucinations, delusions, or paranoia).
Malignant altruism refers to pleasure or satisfaction gained from controlling or punishing others with self-sacrificing acts, including any resulting displays of suffering.	The controlling parent who gives generously to a child, but uses sacrifice, martyrdom, and punishment to achieve compliance with specific wishes	In psychotic cases of malignant altruism, the pathological altruist is detached from the real world by the influence of drugs or a mental disorder. As with masochistic altruism, the psychotic manifestations of malignant altruism are essentially the same as the nonpsychotic. The major difference is that the psychotic altruist may experience or misperceive wrongs that did not actually occur (e.g., hallucinations, delusions, or paranoia).

Victimity

> Pathological altruism victimizes the altruists themselves, as well as those in their path.

Before we discuss the victims of pathological altruism and pathological altruists, we must first understand what victimity is. As explained in Turvey (2009, p. 34), *victimity* refers to "the state, quality, or fact of being a victim." A victim, in the most general sense, refers to anyone who has experienced loss, injury, or hardship due to the actions of another (see generally Petherick & Turvey, 2009).

The role of the victim is not always cut and dry; one can be victimized, the victimizer, or both.[1] Moreover, victimity is not a state of moral superiority, as many believe. That is to say, victims do not naturally possess the moral high ground in a situational vacuum.

The term *victim* is criminological in nature, and is meant to denote loss, harm, or suffering. Its use throughout this chapter is not intended to convey a moral judgment. It describes a relationship and the impact of actions by one that harm the other—intentional and otherwise.

As we will demonstrate, pathological altruism can harm would-be altruists, as well as those in their path. Sometimes this is by design, sometimes it is incidental, and sometimes it is precisely the opposite of what is intended. These relationships and consequences must be investigated and established, not assumed.

Pathological Altruism as a Cognitive Distortion

Pathological altruism is found in any pattern of altruistic behavior that results in severe harm to oneself or others. However, the pathological altruist's thinking is also irrational and distorted. That is to say, his or her thinking appears to be characterized by a suspension of logic and reason with respect to the outcomes of their actions.

Pathological altruism is not necessarily a discrete psychological condition unto itself—instead, it might be best viewed as a mental disturbance symptomatic of deeper underlying issues. It is helpful to regard it as a defense mechanism for a mind in conflict with itself; a compromised way of thinking that protects or defends against the full awareness of emotionally painful or otherwise harmful realities. As explained in Bowins (2004, p. 1):

> Psychological defense mechanisms represent a crucial component of our capacity to maintain emotional homeostasis. Without them the conscious mind would be much more vulnerable to negatively charged emotional input, such as that pertaining to anxiety and sadness. Fear and anxiety occur within the context of threat and danger. Loss is the most common circumstance producing sadness and depression. Fear/anxiety, sadness, and other emotions arise from unconscious and conscious cognitive activating appraisals [references cited in the original source have been deleted here].

Within the spectrum of psychological defense mechanisms, pathological altruism is perhaps best understood as a form of *cognitive distortion* (i.e., exaggerated and irrational thoughts). Bowins (2004) provides that (p.7):

> This class of psychological defense mechanism in effect places a sugar coating on events, making an individual's experience of the world more palatable. It refers

to the tendency of people to place a self-enhancing spin on experience and alter the perception of unfavorable events in a positive way to lessen the impact. Distortion in this context is equivalent to an alteration, modification, or transformation. The tendency to distort experience cognitively in a manner that is positive and enhancing to the self is extremely common [references cited in the original source have been deleted here].

In psychodynamic theory, many different forms of cognitive distortion may be evident in different pathological altruists, depending on individual etiology. For one example, in the mind of some pathological altruists, the relatively mature and healthy defense mechanism of altruism (Bowins, 2004) may become a neurotic *reaction formation*. In such cases, the individual feels one thing and expresses the opposite in an excessive or exaggerated manner to compensate for, and even conceal, the negative emotions that the original feeling causes. Among the most common reaction formations are those that involve overcompensating for feelings of dislike toward someone by acting exceedingly friendly—standard behavior in most offices or other places of work where collegiality is necessary to maintain employment and productivity despite politics and the backstabbing that goes along with it. Others include the latent homosexual who marries, has five kids, and crusades against homosexual rights; or the overly religious sex-addict who preaches chastity and attempts to make others do the same by picketing adult bookstores.

An example of this type of behavior might be the mother of an unwanted child who overcompensates to conceal feelings of guilt by spoiling the child and being excessively uncritical and overprotective. Here, altruistic displays are an effort to convince everyone (e.g., the child, her spouse, herself) that she is a good mother despite not wanting the child in the first place. She may be consciously aware of the effort, or she may suffer from a metacognitive deficit that prevents her from this level of self-awareness. Every case must be examined closely to make independent determinations regarding mental defects, psychodynamics, and motive, without which a theory as to causes and origins is less than informed.

> Within the spectrum of psychological defense mechanisms, pathological altruism is perhaps best understood as a form of *cognitive distortion.*

In the same way that pathological altruism involves cognitive distortions, it may also involve metacognitive failure, or what the author refers to as *metacognitive dissonance*. *Metacognition* refers to "the ability to know how well one is performing, when one is likely to be accurate in judgment, and when one is likely to be in error" (Krueger & Denning, 1999, p. 1121). At a fundamental level, metacognition can be conceived of as thinking about thinking. It is essentially our ability to estimate how well we are performing, when we are likely to be accurate, and when we are likely to be in error (Turvey, 2008). Metacognitive dissonance refers specifically to the false belief that one is (Turvey, 2008, p. 71) "capable of recognizing one's own errors in thinking, reasoning, and learning, despite either a lack of evidence or overwhelming evidence to the contrary."

The use of this terminology does not imply a particular cause or origin. Such irrational thinking may be the result of genetic, chemical, environmental, or developmental factors acting alone or in concert. That is also to say that pathological altruism may be the result of psychotic origins (a lack of contact with reality), or it may be the result of a combined absence of logic, reasoning, awareness, and foresight. Again, each case must be examined independently.

Pathological Altruism: A Motivational Typology

Although not all-inclusive, or even exclusive within individuals, the typology provided here may be used to characterize the behavioral and motivational components behind the major incarnations of pathological altruism. Seelig and Rosof (2000, p. 934) warn: "Because human behavior is complex and multidetermined, it is often difficult to categorize." The author agrees, and notes that individuals exhibiting multiply motivated types of pathological altruism should not be a surprise. People do different things for similar reasons, and often do the same thing for different reasons. The goal of this analysis is not to cram altruists into a single box, but rather to understand the psychodynamic aspects of their relationships and reasoning.

Although this typology has roots in Seelig and Rosof (2000), it is better conceived as developing their work further rather than relying on it uncritically. For example, Seelig and Rosof provide a motivational typology that delineates (p. 934) five distinct categories of altruism, including the *psychotic altruist*. In fact, "psychotic" is not a discrete category, but rather a mental state characterized by lack of contact with reality.

In accordance with Seelig and Rosof's work, as informed by the author's own practical experience in criminology and victimology, pathological altruism might best be classified into four major types: *protective*, *defensive*, *masochistic*, and *malignant*. Each type of pathological altruism might be thought of as having both psychotic and nonpsychotic incarnations. These will be explained and clarified by example.

Protective Altruism

The *protective* altruist voluntarily places himself or herself directly in harms' way for the explicit benefit of others out of some form of deep personal commitment, such as love, friendship, family, service, or a strong sense of community. Nonpathological manifestations of protective altruism are often characterized by single events, in which the cost is fully understood and the benefit is clearly defined. In such cases, the cost is reasonably understood to be commensurate to an expected gain, generally without intentional harm to others. Typical examples would include acts of heroism, such as rescuing someone from a capsized boat in stormy seas or from a burning building; or intentionally suffering harmful consequences meant for another, such as being fired to protect a colleague, going to jail to protect a child or younger sibling, or taking a bullet to protect a friend or brother-in-arms.

Pathological (e.g., obsessive, diseased) manifestations of protective altruism are characterized by a pattern of behavior in which the cost is not fully realized or acknowledged, and the outcome ranges from lacking clear benefit to being outright harmful to those it is intended to help. Such pathologically altruistic acts are planned in advance, with strong cognitive bias or impairment, and are also proactive. Individuals evincing this behavior are doing what they believe to be morally right—they further believe their actions will be beneficial, even though these actions are actually harmful, at a much higher cost than they can acknowledge or appreciate.

A pathological subtype of the protective altruist is the *pseudoaltruist*; one who deliberately and repeatedly creates or stages a crisis, so that he or she can save the day. Such behavior does not involve true altruism or sacrifice, as harm or suffering is being caused in order to be revered as the hero. Examples of pseudoaltruism would include some firemen who set fires in order to put them out and those suffering from Munchausen by proxy.[2]

Nonpsychotic

In nonpsychotic cases of pathological "protective" altruism, one's self-image, identity, and happiness are intertwined with being a hero, a protector, or a philanthropist. There is often an acute and even distorted concern over criticism by others; those afflicted feel, for whatever reason, they have a lot to live up to or give back. This often bears out in their vocation or volunteer activities, which are characterized by obsession and excess. Moreover, extreme measures may be taken to ensure their image is secured, even if it takes violent crime to secure it.

Examples would include EMTs, law enforcement officers, firemen, or soldiers who choose their high-risk, crisis-oriented profession out of a distorted sense of duty. They can become unable to maintain a healthy level of self-esteem unless they are perceived as heroic protectors (e.g., a police officer who regularly plants evidence or lies in his or her reports to help convict those who he believes to be guilty; a fireman who drives around looking for fires).

Example: Joseph Rodriguez

Consider the following example of 27-year-old Joseph Rodriguez, a Manhattan transit police officer. After 9/11, he had become depressed. His supervisors put him on modified duty shortly after, working a desk without a gun. He was also scheduled to be retired on a psychological disability pension. He had lost his gun, authority, and self-image. To regain it, he felt he had to be hero.

On July 19, 2004, Mr. Rodriguez placed a pipe bomb in a Times Square subway station. Initially hailed as a hero for his efforts in rescuing others from the "attack," he was subsequently arrested. At first, he denied any involvement. As reported in Brick (2004):

> Mr. Rodriguez was the only person injured when the pipe bomb exploded just after the evening rush on July 19 on the mezzanine in the station leading to the A, C, and E lines. But the bomb, inside a bag and packed with black powder and pellets, panicked riders who feared another terrorist attack, and shut down train service in one of the city's largest and busiest stations. That night, the police credited Mr. Rodriguez, who had just finished a shift at the Manhattan Transit Task Force in the Times Square station, with discovering the device, warning people away, and calling for backup. Mr. Rodriguez was injured in the leg when the pipe bomb exploded.
>
> Within a day, though, he became the subject of the police investigation. The shift Mr. Rodriguez had completed that evening was already set to be the penultimate one in his four-year career; he was being retired on a psychological disability pension. He had been assigned to modified duty, working at a desk without a gun, since the end of 2001, when his superiors decided that he seemed too disturbed by the terror attack of Sept. 11 to function on patrol duty.

In December 2005, Mr. Rodriguez pled guilty to reckless endangerment for setting the bomb. He claimed that he was depressed and traumatized as the result of 9/11, and was now receiving religious counseling to fill the voids in his life. He was sentenced to 1–3 years in prison.

Mr. Rodriguez had undeniable mental health issues; however, they were far short of psychosis. He was apparently victimized emotionally by 9/11, and then felt victimized by the NYPD. He further victimized himself physically and with the loss of his career by setting the pipe bomb. The potential for civilian casualties was also quite high.

Mr. Rodriguez's behavior appears compensatory; his motive appears to have been restoration of his power, authority, and image via pseudoaltruistic behavior—a distorted pattern of obsessive thought regarding an altruistic self-image. In this case, pathological altruism appears to be a result of cognitive distortion. This would include his obvious cognitive dissonance (the uncomfortable feeling caused by holding two contradictory ideas simultaneously), an overvalued idea regarding his self-image (a false or exaggerated belief sustained beyond reason or logic—but not completely believed, as with a delusion), and resulting compartmentalization (separating two distinct parts of oneself that are in moral conflict, in this case the bomber and the hero).

It should also noted that there is not enough historical information to determine whether this is a case of job-related stress causing self-image issues and mental disorder, or whether the foundation was there before he became a police officer.

Psychotic

In psychotic cases of pathological protective altruism, pathological altruists are detached from the real world. They wrongly persist in the belief that their obsessive and excessive behavior is heroic, protective, or philanthropic, when instead it stems from attachment to a nonexistent reality. As a consequence, they do not understand and may not foresee the harm that their actions can cause—even when confronted directly with the consequences.

Examples would include parents who kill their children or entire family to protect them from evil or demonic possession; stalkers who threaten, harass, and even kill those they purport to be protecting; and individuals who collect and hoard animals, believing that they are saving them from euthanization or starvation while being unable to care for, feed, or provide them with healthy living conditions.

Example: Elizabeth Brown

Consider the following example of Elizabeth Brown, a 64-year-old woman with a history of mental problems from Paxton, Illinois. As reported in Warren (2009):

> Brown, 64, was arrested Jan. 25, 2008, by Will County police and charged with cruelty to animals, a felony. . . . A few days before her arrest and on one of the coldest days of the year, humane society investigators and Will County police seized 18 starving dogs—animals that belonged to Brown—from two locations. Most were in an unheated barn in Manhattan Township, and the others were in the yard of the empty house on Loganberry Lane. One dog lost part of an ear to frostbite. Another had a baseball-sized tumor and glaucoma. Authorities later removed 10 cats from inside the same unheated Joliet Township home.

According to Warren (2009), Brown has a history of charges and convictions relating to animal hoarding in other counties around the state. She pled guilty and was ordered by the judge to cease owning or living with any animals ever again.

As noted in Chapter 8, it is common for animal hoarders to have dozens of animals breeding uncontrollably in their home, sometimes dying of starvation or disease—all unnoticed. These individuals often believe they are entitled to keep as many animals as they wish, that they are in fact protecting the animals from harm or death. They are emotionally incapable of letting their animals go.

The pathological altruist in this case would appear to suffer from a form of mental illness that leads to a limited contact with reality. The altruist is both the victim of her own mental illness and a victimizer, with respect to harming the animals in her care by creating an unhealthy environment. She repeats her criminal behavior despite unequivocal warnings, has no sense of time, no clear understanding of the harm she is causing, and does not appear able to take responsibility for her actions. In this case, pathological altruism would be a symptom of psychosis.

Defensive Altruism

Defensive altruism involves pleasure or satisfaction from the success, pleasure, and/or welfare of others. However, unlike protective altruism, it is reactive and rises out of the need to resolve conflict. It is referred to as "defensive" because of its self-preserving nature in response to confrontation and hostility. Nonpathological manifestations of defensive altruism are characterized by adaptive compromise, in which another's pleasure acts as a proxy for one's own when conflict is resolved or avoided.

Pathological manifestations of defensive altruism are characterized by a pattern of self-sacrifice in which continued avoidance, denial, compromise, and overcompromise lead to the inability to experience joy for oneself. In extreme cases, attempting to engage in pleasurable activity in the absence of altruistic sacrifice appears to cause this pathological altruist to experience severe emotional and even physical distress. The most common emotional consequence for the defensive altruist is guilt for not having sacrificed enough, even when they have given everything they can.

Nonpsychotic

In nonpsychotic cases of pathologically manifested defensive altruism, the perceived conflict is very real. Moreover, these individuals suffer from an emotional inability to deal with its negative consequences. They will do anything and give up everything to simply make it through another day or another "fight." However, their sacrifices actually fuel the problem by enabling a continuation of what has essentially become a toxic relationship.

Examples would include the parent who remains in a relationship with an abusive spouse "for the kids"; codependent relationships involving an addict manipulating a family member or significant other with guilt in order to continue financial and emotional support of his or her addiction; those who give of their time, emotions, and financial resources to a relationship in which there is no emotional or financial reciprocation, to the point of financial ruin; and parents who continually protect defiant teens from the consequences of their behavior without providing boundaries or guidance.

Example: Jerri Gray

Consider the case of Jerri Gray, a 49-year-old mother from South Carolina who was arrested for criminal neglect related to the care of her son, Alexander.

Under her care, he weighed 555 lbs by the age of 14. As reported in Barnett (2009):

> Authorities in South Carolina say that what went wrong was Gray's care and feeding of her son, Alexander Draper. Gray, 49, of Travelers Rest, S.C., was arrested in June and charged with criminal neglect. Alexander is now in foster care . . . .
>
> "This is not a case of a mother force-feeding a child," [Gray's attorney, Grant] Varner says. "If she had been holding him down and force-feeding him, sure, I can understand. But she doesn't have the means to do it. She doesn't have the money to buy the food to do it . . . ."
>
> The arrest warrant in the Gray case alleges that her son's weight was "serious and threatening to his health" and that she had placed him "at an unreasonable risk of harm."
>
> Virginia Williamson, counsel for the South Carolina Department of Social Services, says her agency sought custody of Alexander "because of information from health care providers that he was at risk of serious harm because his mother was not meeting his medical needs."

Although it is unclear whether this is the case in this particular situation, it is common for cases of super morbidly obese teens to involve codependency. Families in many cultures view the preparation and eating of food as signs of love and affection. Failure to accept the food may even be met with a sense of rejection. For some, this can lead to obesity, an unhealthy appetite, and "hunger pangs" that result in continued pleas for food. Once a child is bedridden or physically disabled by obesity, the mother can become mired in a cycle of working to buy food, preparing it, and then returning to work. In such a case, the mother may even take on extra shifts and forgo personal relationships to meet the constant demand.

This pattern of overall self-sacrifice resulting from the confusion of food with love and acceptance is a clear form of defensive pathological altruism. By continuing to feed the super morbidly obese teen, everyone gets to feel good, and conflict is avoided. However, the end result is an unhealthy child who is unable to care for him- or herself, and at risk of death.

Psychotic

In psychotic cases of pathologically manifested defensive altruism, the pathological altruist is detached from the real world. Under these circumstances, either perception of the conflict is false, or understanding of reciprocation is out of step with reality. That is to say, the pathological altruist is behaving altruistically to resolve imagined conflicts, or believes his or her sacrifice is being appreciated or reciprocated when that is not in fact the case. In such situations, the pathological altruist is a victim of his or her own mental disturbance, often being preyed upon by another.

One example would be an elderly parent with a mental disorder who continually rescues an adult child with respect to legal or financial failures, believing that there has been no failure on their child's part whatsoever (or that each time is the first time). A more common example would be an elderly person of strong religious conviction who regularly drains his or her bank account by making donations to apocalyptic evangelists professing their money is needed to fight evil.

Example: Lucinda Bennett

Consider the case of Lucinda Bennett, a 37-year-old heiress from Palm Beach, Florida. When her great-grandmother died at the age of 92, Bennett inherited more than $2 million in cash and assets. Over the next ten months, Bennett donated that and more to various religious causes associated with her church (Musgrave, 2007).

In the eventual lawsuit filed against Rev. Keith Thomas, Ms. Bennett alleges she was mentally ill at the time she made these donations. The result was her financial ruin. As reported in Musgrave (2007):

> In a lawsuit expected to go to trial in the next month, there is no dispute that over 11 months in 2000 Bennett gave the bulk of her inheritance to the wealthy church and a former pastor who regularly told the faithful of the blessings they would receive if they embraced biblical teachings to tithe . . . .
>
> To attorneys representing the church and its former head pastor, the Rev. Keith Thomas, Bennett was merely exercising her First Amendment right to religious freedom when she wrote checks to the church, Thomas, and at least one other former pastor who now teaches at Palm Beach Atlantic University.
>
> To Bennett, who goes by the name Cinda, she was systematically manipulated by people who knew she was rich and easy prey.

The church argued that they had no idea how much money she was actually giving, or that she was mentally ill. Ms. Bennett, on the other hand, argued that there was no way for the church and its representatives not to know. This case was settled in March 2008, with a confidential agreement.

The pathological aspects of altruism in this case may be found in the overly generous nature of Ms. Bennett's ongoing charitable donations, and the fact that giving so much money left her in financial ruin. She believed she was giving money to the church and those associated with its good works. She further believed this was the right thing to do to help the church's spiritual cause. The conflict she sought to resolve may have been guilt related to her inheritance, or a strong belief in fighting evil by doing good works. Or, it may have been related to her mental illness: She was convinced, and continually reassured, that the more she gave, the more good would come back to her—from God. As someone suffering from depression at the very least, she may have believed she could pay off the Almighty to simply feel good about herself—to make it through the day and feel valued as a person in a group that made her feel special and needed. Whatever the precise origins, her conflict was such that she was looking to buy her way out.

In any case, Ms. Bennett reportedly suffered from ongoing mental illness that prevented an appreciation of the financial consequences of her generosity. Additionally, she appeared to have an unrealistic view of the return she would gain from her benevolence, beyond that of a reasonably informed person. This is evidenced by the attempts of some church members to intervene when they saw what was happening to her (Musgrave, 2007). So, while she was apparently the victim of her own mental disorder, which manifested in a religious fervor that placed her out of touch with reality, she was also targeted and exploited by her church.

Masochistic Altruism

Masochism refers to experiencing pleasure from receiving pain, suffering, and humiliation—often at the hands of a love object. This is commonly found in sexual contexts, but may extend beyond intimate activities. Although generally harmful and maladaptive, the psychodynamics and consequences of masochistic tendencies in consenting relationships have not been adequately studied to determine whether this must always be the case.

Masochistic altruism, however, refers specifically to a maladaptive need to suffer or be the victim, compensating for profound envy, jealousy, anger, aggression, and/or low self-esteem and thoughts of inadequacy. Masochistic altruists seem to be characterized by a pattern of self-sacrifice in which altruism is a coping mechanism for masking inner negativity and conflict. Unlike the defensive altruist who seeks to resolve or move past conflict, the masochistic altruist is compensating for conflict and concealing it. Masochistic altruism often involves the conscious or subconscious belief that one does not deserve to be happy. In extreme cases, there is no genuine pleasure in actions that result in the success or pleasure of others, and there is a severe constriction of, or inability to, experience pleasure or joy of any kind.

This classification is drawn from *pseudoaltruism* as described by Seelig and Rosof (2000). However, the author views their terminology as misleading, given that the prefix "pseudo" implies that the altruism is phony, when this is not the case. This pathological altruist's self-sacrifice is real, as is the pleasure experienced by some of those who may receive it. That the altruists experience no joy as a consequence of their altruism is irrelevant, as altruism does not require it—especially the pathological forms.

Moreover, Seelig and Rosof (2000) inappropriately fused sadism and masochism into the same type, referring to (p. 934) "underlying sadomasochism." This term has come to reference a relationship between a sadist and a masochist, in which the first party achieves sexual gratification from inflicting pain (psychological or physical), while the second party achieves sexual gratification from receiving it. Not only is this an inappropriate descriptor for a solely masochistic type, but Seelig and Rosof (2000) fail to provide any discussion of those pathological altruists who revel in their self-sacrifice in order to harm or control others. This type will be discussed in the next section, the Malignant Altruist.

Nonpsychotic

In nonpsychotic cases of masochistic altruism, inner negativity and conflict appear to be the product of a history of abuse suffered by the pathological altruist. This includes negligence, violence, mental abuse, excessive criticism, problems with physical appearance, inadequate achievements, long-term unemployment, and other negative experiences. Such individuals feel worthless, hurt, ugly, depressed, and/or angry—and they have no idea how resolve these feelings. Their masochism is often an attempt to beat the world to the punch. Many of them are seeking to inflict damage on themselves before anyone else can, and they gravitate toward destructive individuals who can help.

Some suffer in silence, projecting a false mask of enjoyment, while others martyr themselves openly and embrace the role of victim. Those who are in essence "professional victims" can also elicit anger or resentment from those in their lives, as their fits of martyrdom are recurring and emotionally manipulative to the point of abuse.

Nonpsychotic manifestations of masochistic altruism include compulsive care taking of others with obsessive self-denial; extreme martyrdom; and self-destructive pattern of volunteering to suffer abuse, humiliation, and/or debasement for the pleasure of others. This chronic self-denial, self-destruction, and unsolicited compensatory self-sacrifice may be associated with sexual activity, but not necessarily so.

Psychotic

In psychotic cases of masochistic altruism, the pathological altruist is detached from the real world by the influence of drugs or a severe mental condition. In some cases, the psychotic altruist will have a history of negative experiences that leads to substance abuse or facilitates a mental disorder as a coping mechanism. In others, conversely, the onset of substance abuse or mental disorder has led to real or perceived negative experiences.

Interestingly, the psychotic manifestations of masochistic altruism are essentially the same as the nonpsychotic. The major difference is that the psychotic altruist may experience inner negativity and conflict regarding events that did not actually occur (e.g., hallucinations, delusions, or paranoia). The emotional result and its behavioral manifestation, however, are difficult to distinguish.

Example: Jan Hasegawa

In 2008, the author examined, and subsequently gave expert testimony in, a death penalty case for the defense involving the murder of Jan Hasegawa, 48, by her long-time boyfriend, Jack Henry Lewis, 39. Their relationship was characterized by a history of domestic violence and drug abuse, including methamphetamine abuse. She regularly capitulated to his violent behavior and sexual requests, eventually joining in his use of drugs during sexual activity. He also regularly choked, bit, punched, slapped, and pulled her hair during sex.

The sexual asphyxia in this case included choking Hasegawa during climax. Family members asserted she had told them Lewis had choked her to the point of unconsciousness during sex more times than she could count. She also told friends that he was violent, but she truly believed he would change if she could just love him more.

On September 8, 2005, Hasegawa's nude body was discovered by police officers responding to multiple anonymous 911 calls. She was found deceased, face up on her bedroom floor with a bowl of unmelted ice cubes next to her head. She had suffered more than 150 blunt force injuries that were in varying stages of healing; chunks of her hair had been pulled out; fecal matter was on towels and smeared on the walls; and she had suffered manual strangulation. Additionally, a miniature flashlight was discovered on the bed. It was smeared with Lewis's fecal matter consistent with its insertion into his rectum.

Within 48 hours, her domestic partner of a dozen years, Jack Lewis, turned himself in to authorities and made statements implicating himself in her death. Both Hasegawa and Lewis also tested positive for methamphetamine, and there was testimony that this may have contributed to her death. In August 2008, Lewis was convicted of first-degree murder; however, the jury did not give him the death penalty.

The masochistic altruism in this case is reflected in Hasegawa's long-term relationship with Lewis. It involves a pattern of total self-sacrifice with respect to her physical and sexual submission. In order to keep and maintain the relationship, she apparently held the distorted belief that his anger would eventually transform into love. Although it did not start out as a psychotic manifestation of masochistic altruism, rooted in her pathological low self-esteem, it became psychotic once she started using methamphetamine. As explained in Hunt, Kuck, and Truitt (2006; p.44):

> The immediate methamphetamine rush is followed by an extended high that can last 4 to 24 hours. During this period, the user is overly stimulated, shows rapid flights of ideas and speech, is highly assertive or confident, but may also display suspicious or paranoid behaviors.

Moreover, chronic use of methamphetamine can cause violent behavior, anxiety, confusion, insomnia, auditory hallucinations, mood disturbances, delusions, and paranoia (National Institute on Drug Abuse, 1998).

Malignant Altruism

Malignant altruism refers to pleasure or satisfaction gained from controlling or punishing others with self-sacrificing acts, including any resulting displays of suffering. It is intended to service feelings of impotence, or punish others for real or perceived wrongs that have been suffered. It is commonly characterized by dramatic displays of martyrdom and even some traits associated with malignant narcissism (a disorder that includes narcissistic and antisocial behaviors). Malignant altruism is by definition harmful, either to the altruist or the person on the receiving end. In many cases, the malignant altruist has two faces: the benevolent, self-sacrificing victim portrayed outwardly, and the malevolent, insecure tormentor experienced inwardly and even subconsciously.

Nonpsychotic

In nonpsychotic cases of malignant altruism, the altruism is genuine. That is to say, such altruists believe what they are doing is necessary and helpful. They give time, money, and emotional support in ways that are truly beneficial, and often unsolicited. However, secondary to altruistic acts, and often because of inner feelings of impotence and conflict, these individuals may be compelled to lash out. Malignant altruists are prone to coerce, manipulate, and attempt control over those they have helped, either because they believe they are entitled to do so, or because they believe their sacrifice is not adequately appreciated. Malignant altruists are commonly found in a continuous cycle of sacrifice, martyrdom, and punishment.

The malignant altruist is generally unaware of this vindictive cycle, as most lack genuine insight into their behavior and motives. The ability to self-reflect is often limited by a distorted, egotistic view, and may be the result of profound metacognitive dissonance.

Psychotic

In psychotic cases of malignant altruism, the pathological altruist is detached from the real world by the influence of drugs or a mental disorder. As with masochistic altruism, the psychotic manifestations of malignant altruism are essentially the same as the nonpsychotic. The major difference is that the psychotic altruist may experience or misperceive wrongs that did not actually occur (e.g., hallucinations, delusions, or paranoia).

Example: The Controlling Parent

One of the most common forms of malignant altruism is the controlling parent. Such individuals give to their children generously and to a fault. However, generosity is expressed with the subconscious expectation of a particular form of gratitude or compliance with specific wishes. When the controlling parent does not get what they want, the cycle of sacrifice, martyrdom, and punishment kicks in until they do, or until the child is driven away. Such instances can have both psychotic and nonpsychotic manifestations.

Conclusion

Pathological altruism refers to the habitual, maladaptive, and/or compulsive pursuit of the welfare of others. Rather than being an isolated condition with a clear etiology, it is actually a symptom of deeper personal and psychological issues. It is best conceived as a form of cognitive distortion; a product of one's biology, personal toxicology (e.g., drug and alcohol abuse), and environment.

The pathological altruist is not necessarily a victim, a victimizer, or a criminal. He or she may be any combination of these. The criminologist must examine each individual occurrence and its component parts in order to determine which is the case.

The typology provided in this chapter represents an exploration of the vast behavioral landscape encompassed by the various incarnations of pathological altruism. Each has its own underlying psychodynamics, patterns, and motivations. Although not all-inclusive, it presents a new perspective on the complex, difficult-to-understand set of behaviors seen when altruism shades from healthful to harmful.

Notes

1. See generally, the research cited in Weaver, Borkowski, and Whitman (2008).

2. *Munchausen by proxy syndrome* refers to cases in which a caregiver, such as a parent or childcare worker, exaggerates, fabricates, or induces illness or symptoms of illness in a child. This is done in order to receive the attention and sympathy of friends, family, intimates, medical personnel, and sometimes the public in general. Such individuals get satisfaction from the sympathy, from being the center of attention, and from successfully deceiving those around them.

References

Barnett, R. (2009). S.C. case looks on child obesity as child abuse. But is it? *USA Today*, July 23.

Bowins, B. (2004). Psychological defense mechanisms: A new perspective. *The American Journal of Psychoanalysis*, 64(1), 1–26.

Brick, M. (2004). Officer charged in bomb blast at subway. *New York Times*, August 1. url: http://www.nytimes.com/2004/08/01/nyregion/officer-charged-in-bomb-blast-at-subway.html

Hunt, D., Kuck, S., & Truitt, L. *Methamphetamine use: Lessons learned*. USDOJ: Document No. 209730, Award Number 99-C-0February 08, 2006.

Krueger, J., & Dunning, D. (1999). Unskilled and unaware of it: How difficulties in recognizing one's own incompetence lead to inflated self-assessments. *Journal of Personality and Social Psychology, 77*(6), 121–134.

Musgrave, J. (2007). Heiress accuses W. Palm church of exploiting her mental illness. *Palm Beach Post*, April 1. Retrieved from http://www.palmbeachpost.com/localnews/ content/local_news/epaper/2007/04/01/s1a_FIRST_BAPTIST_0401.html

National Institute on Drug Abuse. 1998. *Methamphetamine: Abuse and addiction.*

Petherick, W., & Turvey, B. (2009) *Forensic Victimology.* San Diego: Elsevier Science.

Seelig, B., & Rosof, L. (2000). Normal and pathological altruism. *Journal of the American Psychoanalytic Association, 49*(3), 933–959.

Turvey, B. (2008). *Criminal profiling: An introduction to behavioral evidence analysis* 3rd ed. San Diego: Elsevier Science.

Turvey, B. (2009). Victimity: Entering the criminal justice system. In W. Petherick, & B. Turvey (Eds.), *Forensic victimology.* San Diego: Elsevier Science.

Warren, S. (2009). Woman gets probation for cruelty to animals. *The Southtown Star*, September 27.

Weaver, C., Borkowski, J., & Whitman, T. (2008). Violence breeds violence: Childhood exposure and adolescent conduct problems. *Journal of Community Psychology, 36*,(1), 96–112.

CHAPTER 14

DOES NO GOOD DEED GO UNPUNISHED? THE VICTIMOLOGY OF ALTRUISM

Robert J. Homant and Daniel B. Kennedy

KEY CONCEPTS

- Pathological altruism can be briefly summarized as altruism that:
  - is unnecessary or uncalled for
  - has consequences that cause the actor to complain, yet the actor continues doing it anyway
  - is motivated by values or needs within the altruist that are irrational or are symptoms of psychological disturbance
  - is of no real benefit to anyone, and a reasonable person would have foreseen this
- The higher the level of altruistic behavior reported by subjects, the higher their level of criminal victimization.
- Self-reported altruism has been found to be a significant predictor of both property and personal crime victimization.
- The relationship between altruism and victimization has been found to be especially due to *risky altruism*, which in turn is correlated with the basic personality trait of sensation seeking.

"NO GOOD DEED goes unpunished"—a quip attributed to Clare Boothe Luce—is a contrarian take on the extra work and hassle that often result from being helpful. More seriously, psychologists have recently paid attention to the maladaptive aspects of generally positive traits (Widiger, Costa, & McCrae, 2002). For example, altruism is a trait that may increase the probability that one's "routine activities" will intersect with motivated offenders (Felson, 2002), thus increasing the probability of being the victim of a crime. In this chapter, we examine altruism from the perspective of victimology. We report results from our exploratory research testing the hypothesis that engaging in altruistic behavior makes some people more susceptible to criminal victimization. The Five-Factor Model of personality is then employed to better understand the association between altruism and victimization.

Defining Altruism

By *altruism* we mean behaviors that are engaged in primarily for the benefit of another, with no evident benefit and at least some cost to the actor. This is not to say that there is *no* benefit; we assume that all behavior is engaged in because of some reward or expectation of reward. With altruism, however, the main reinforcement is directly related to the perception of some benefit to the person being helped. Many different explanations have been offered for exactly how and why a perception of benefit to the other is reinforcing. These different reasons may be used to distinguish various types of altruism (Dovidio, Piliavin, Schroeder, & Penner, 2006). Five main types of altruism are of interest to us here (Table 14.1).

Empathic altruism is often considered "true altruism" (Dovidio et al., 2006; Lamm, Batson, & Decety, 2007). The perception of distress in another person directly triggers the motivation to help the person in distress. There is increasing evidence for and acceptance of the idea that humans as a species, have selected for a set of genes that predispose us to empathy (Bachner-Melman et al., 2005; Ebstein, 2006; Preston & de Waal, 2002; Rushton, Bons, & Hur, 2008). Empathy here refers to the ability to feel what another is feeling, not simply in the calculating sense of deducing the feeling but in the sense of actually sharing in the feeling. The perception of emotional cues in the body language and paralinguistics of the other may well establish a kind of resonance in the observer, so that some representation of the other's feelings is established in the self (Preston & de Waal, 2002).

Normative altruism refers to selfless behavior that is engaged in because the actor has internalized various religious or cultural norms of self-sacrifice and love of neighbor. Just as there is biological selection for empathy, there is cultural selection for beliefs and values that increase the probability of a culture being transmitted to future generations (Gibson, McKelvie, & de Man, 2008). The willingness to die for one's country, one's religion, one's group, or simply one's friends and family reflects culture-based values, or memes, that increase the probability of a culture (and any ethnic group that carries that culture) being successful.

Reciprocal altruism is helping behavior that the actor engages in because of a more or less vague expectation that the person being helped, or others in society, will be willing to help the actor in the future, should help be needed (Gouldner, 1960). Although such behavior may well be related to underlying feelings of empathy and supported by cultural values, a person with no particular feelings for others and no sense of value-based obligation to the community may well behave altruistically simply in the expectation that the good will that is being established will pay off.

TABLE 14.1	TYPES OF ALTRUISM
Empathic	Motivated by the desire to relieve perceived distress in another
Normative	Based on internalized religious or cultural norms of self-sacrifice
Reciprocal	Linked to expectation of future reciprocated good will
Egoistic	Motivated more by the need to bolster self-esteem than to relieve distress in others
Situational	Determined by social cues that are independent of the disposition of the actor

Egoistic altruism refers to behavior engaged in to make oneself feel better, not because one is distressed over the misfortune of others but because it is seen as a way of increasing one's own sense of self-esteem (Penner, Dovidio, Piliavin, & Schroeder, 2005). This can be similar to normative altruism, in that the reinforcement may involve positive feedback from others, but here the need for this feedback lies in perceived deficits in the self. Examples would be the attempt to relieve guilt feelings by sacrificing for others, playing the martyr role to get sympathy from others, or doing good deeds as a way of gaining emotional control over others.

Finally, *situational altruism* refers to behavior that is relatively independent of the personality and dispositions of the actor. Much of the early work on altruism focused on social cues that facilitated or inhibited altruism (Darley & Latane, 1968). The classic case of Kitty Genovese exemplified a situation in which virtually no one helped, or at least this was the original understanding (Dovidio et al., 2006, p. 19). In contrast, some research situations were found in which *all* subjects behaved altruistically (Staub, 1974). In such "strong" situations, the underlying traits or dispositions of the actor are basically irrelevant (Dovidio et al., 2006).

Maladaptive Altruism

The types of altruism just described are differentiated based on the motivation involved. One may also characterize behavior in terms of whether it represents positive or negative adjustment for the actor. This chapter has been written specifically for a book dealing with *pathological altruism*, one definition of which is "such a solicitousness for the concerns of others, on an ongoing basis, that the person involved has difficulty living a normal life." In other words, it is altruism that has been carried too far.

The idea of "too much of a good thing," although common enough in everyday discourse, is relatively rare in descriptions of personality disorder. Mental illness and various psychosocial adjustment problems are typically seen as the negative pole of a continuum, such as antisocial as opposed to prosocial personality. This difference is also reflected in the psychological tests typically used to measure adaptive versus maladaptive personality traits.

> One definition of pathological altruism is "such a solicitousness for the concerns of others, on an ongoing basis, that the person involved has difficulty living a normal life." In other words, it is altruism that has been carried too far.

Of special relevance to us here is the Five-Factor Model of personality. There seems to be increasing acceptance of the idea that the "Big Five" of openness (to experience), conscientiousness, extraversion, agreeableness, and neuroticism (giving the acronyms OCEAN or CANOE) provide a very useful model for organizing personality traits (Goldberg, 1981, 1993). Each of the Big Five factors has been further subdivided into six facets; altruism, for example, is one of the facets of Agreeableness, along with trust, straightforwardness, compliance, modesty, and tender-mindedness (Widiger, Costa, & McCrae, 2002). With the exception of Neuroticism, tests that measure the five factors, such as the NEO-PI-R (Costa & McCrae, 1992), are generally measures of positive traits.

Although generally considered a positive trait (Dovidio et al., 2006), altruism may also be maladaptive. The *Diagnostic and Statistical Manual of Mental Disorders, 4th Edition, Text Revision* (DSM-IV-TR), for example, lists excessive helpfulness as one of the characteristics of Dependent Personality Disorder.

Widiger, Costa, and McCrae (2002) have proposed that the Five-Factor Model can be used to organize the Axis II personality disorders of the DSM. They maintain that all 30 facets (five factors, each with six facets) have a maladaptive aspect that is not simply a low score on the trait in question. For example, maladaptive altruism is defined as: "Is excessively selfless and sacrificial; is often exploited, abused, or victimized due to a failure to consider or be concerned with his or her own needs or rights" (Widiger et al., 2002, p. 441).

In a direct test of the idea of maladaptive variants of positive traits, Haigler and Widiger (2001) altered item wordings on the NEO-PI-R to reflect maladaptive behavior. With respect to measuring altruism, for example, one item's original wording was: "I think of myself as a charitable person." This was changed to: "I am so charitable that I give more than I can afford" (p. 347). Thus altered, both the original and the revised NEO-PI-R, along with the Minnesota Multiphasic Personality Inventory (MMPI) and other diagnostic tests, were given to 86 outpatients. The two versions of the NEO-PI-R correlated well with each other, demonstrating that the same basic traits were being measured. However, only the revised version showed strong and meaningful correlations with the various psychiatric diagnoses found in the sample and verified by the MMPI-2 and other tests. With respect to agreeableness, the standard NEO-PI-R was completely unpredictive of a diagnosis of dependent personality. With the revised version, however, with the extreme wording for altruism and its other facets, agreeableness correlated $+0.66$ ($p < 0.01$) with MMPI-2 scores for dependent personality disorder. This finding provides strong support for the hypothesis that altruism can be maladaptive.

Distinguishing Pathological Altruism

We believe that any of the types of altruism we have identified above—other than situational—could become pathological in the sense of causing maladjustment. A problem arises, however, in the case of what might be called "heroic altruism" in extreme or emergency situations. For example, those individuals who helped save Jews and others from the Nazi Holocaust often took extreme risks that sometimes resulted in their own death. The well-known case of Swedish diplomat Raoul Wallenberg comes to mind (Oliner & Oliner, 1988; Staub, 2003). His altruism apparently led to years spent in the Soviet Gulag—ironically, as a result of Stalinist paranoia rather than being caught by the Nazis; here is certainly an extreme case of being a crime victim as a result of one's altruistic behavior. Whether or not Wallenberg was fully aware of the risks, we would term such altruism "heroic" rather than "pathological." Or, consider the more recent case of New York City firefighters rushing into the collapsing World Trade Center. Granted, this was a single act rather than ongoing behavior, at what point does such risky behavior, if done over time, become pathological? The case of Father Damien working with the lepers of Molokai until he finally caught the disease himself provides an example of such ongoing risky altruistic behavior (Stewart, 2000). We know of no objective way of determining whether such altruism is pathological. Nevertheless, we can offer the following guidelines.

In distinction to heroic altruism and self-sacrifice, we suggest that pathological altruism is likely to be characterized by the following:

- It is likely to be unnecessary or uncalled for. Either the distress in the other is not sufficient to warrant the costs or risks to the actor, or there are better ways of meeting the other's needs.

- The actor is likely to complain about the consequences of the altruism, yet continues doing it anyway.
- The values or needs within the altruist that motivate the behavior may themselves be irrational, or symptoms of psychological disturbance.
- The altruism is of no real benefit to anyone, and a reasonable person would have foreseen this.

Applying any of the above criteria, especially the fourth, would entail a very subjective judgment. We do not maintain that pathological altruism must have all of the above characteristics; these are simply heuristics that can be used to identify probable instances of pathological altruism.

Victimology

To understand how altruism may be a factor in crime victimization, we need to look briefly at how criminologists have classified crime victims. One common classification involves the degree to which a victim makes it easier for a crime to occur. Victimologists distinguish various levels of victim involvement in a crime ranging from no contribution to provocation (Karmen, 2004; Turvey & Petherick, 2009). For purposes of exploring the relationship between altruism and victimization, we believe four degrees of victim involvement should be distinguished: random victimization, victim characteristics, victim facilitation, and victim precipitation.

By *random victimization*, we refer to those cases in which the offender cannot articulate a reason for picking the target; it was simply time to commit a crime. Because the social nature of altruism may cause one to be out and about more than the average person, one's routine activities may simply increase the probability of encountering a motivated offender in the absence of a "capable guardian" (Felson, 2002).

Victim characteristics refers to socially normal aspects of the victim that attract a particular offender. A sex offender may target women of a certain appearance. A mugger may size up a person's defensive abilities. Some stranger rapists have been found to target a helpful, friendly appearing woman as opposed to a cold, unfriendly one. Since there is clear evidence that altruists are more sociable and outgoing (Penner et al., 2005), this aspect of their character may make them more likely targets.

Victim facilitation refers to behavior by the victim that in some way makes things easier for the criminal. This typically involves some level of carelessness by the victim, either out of ignorance or more or less normal thoughtlessness. Because altruists have more empathy and concern for others, they may be inclined to be overly trusting or to discount risks, which in turn would make them attractive targets for criminals.

In *victim precipitation,* the victim's behavior instigates the offender's aggression. This may include provoking a criminal response in an otherwise not criminally motivated offender (Wolfgang, 1958), or behaving so recklessly that one is too good a mark not to be taken advantage of.

Altruism and Victimization

An argument can be made in either direction as to how altruism might affect victimization. One might expect altruists to experience less victimization because altruism is associated with a variety of prosocial behaviors: altruists have been found to have higher self-esteem, to be more successful in business and personal relationships, and to live longer. Furthermore, altruists are less likely to exhibit many kinds of behavior that are associated with both criminal and victim behavior: they are lower on drug and alcohol abuse, delinquent behavior, early pregnancy, and arrest (Penner et al., 2005).

On the other hand, behaving altruistically might increase one's vulnerability simply because it involves additional routine activities (Cohen & Felson, 1979; Felson, 2002). This would represent an increased risk either for random or characteristics-based victimization. Also, altruistic behavior might help to identify someone as helpful and trusting, and therefore as a suitable target for certain types of victimization, especially frauds. Helping others may also entail risks in that one may be more inclined to help strangers, especially in circumstances where there are few observers (Darley & Latane, 1968). It is a matter of social judgment to determine the point at which being trusting and friendly progresses from a normal "victim characteristic" to a level of risk that could be termed facilitation or even precipitation.

An Exploratory Study of Altruism and Victimization

We were unable to find any research that directly examined the question of whether altruism might facilitate crime victimization. Therefore, we conducted an exploratory survey for this chapter using college students from various sociology and criminal justice courses. This survey, which we refer to as Study I, supported the hypothesis that altruism correlates with an increased risk of victimization but raised questions as to the reason for that relationship. Hence, a follow-up survey was conducted to clarify the nature of the relationship between altruism and crime victimization. This second survey, Study II, shows that it is specifically "risky altruism" rather than simple risk taking that explains the link between altruism and victimization.

Study I

In Study I, which was designed to explore some of the initial questions discussed in this chapter, 100 subjects filled out a questionnaire in which they described their criminal victimization history and responded to items taken from the Prosocial Personality Battery (Penner, Fritzche, Craiger, & Freifeld, 1995). Subjects also responded to a 14-item altruism scale adapted by Penner et al. from a scale by Rushton, Chrisjohn, and Fekken (1981). As depicted in Table 14.2, a positive correlation exists between the extent of subjects' helping behavior and the likelihood that they will be victimized by property and personal crimes.

As established through analysis of variance, the level of a subject's victimization differed according to type of altruism (empathic, normative, egoistic, and mixed). However, no one type of altruism could be identified as significantly more related to being victimized. Therefore, we formed two subscales within the Altruism scale: a six-item scale measuring what we termed "Risky Altruism" ($\alpha = 0.70$) and an eight-item scale measuring "Safe Altruism" ($\alpha = 0.71$). The six altruism items correlated with victimization all involved some level of risk taking with a stranger, such as: "I have made change for a stranger" and "I have given a stranger a lift in my car." In contrast, the eight items that did not correlate with victimization involved very-low-risk altruism. For example, "I have offered to

TABLE 14.2   CORRELATIONS BETWEEN ALTRUISM AND VICTIMIZATION

	Victimization Type		
Predictor Variable	*Property*	*Personal*	*Total*
Full-scale Altruism	0.22*	0.25*	0.21*
Safe Altruism	0.06	0.13	0.06
Risky Altruism	0.37***	0.34***	0.35***

$N = 100$ throughout. * $p < 0.05$; *** $p < 0.001$.

help a handicapped or elderly stranger across a street," "I have allowed someone to go ahead of me in a line," or "I have donated goods or clothes to a charity."[1]

It should be noted that the full Altruism scale had an α of 0.82, and there was nothing in the interitem correlations to indicate two separate factors. (The difference in α between 0.82 and 0.71, or 0.70, is due to the differences in scale length and not an indication that the subscales are less homogeneous.) The Risky Altruism items had a mean of 2.38, compared to 3.04 for the Safe Altruism items, indicating that subjects as a group engaged in lower levels of the Risky Altruism, as one would expect.

The difference between Risky and Safe Altruism as predictors of victimization was dramatic. As shown in Table 14.2, the relationship between altruism and victimization was due almost entirely to the contribution of Risky Altruism; Safe Altruism had only very small and nonsignificant correlations with victimization.

Actual Differences in Victimization

To obtain a more concrete picture of what the correlation between risky altruism and crime victimization implies, we compared victimization experiences for subjects as a function of their Risky Altruism scores. Table 14.3 shows the huge differences in victimization experienced by subjects who had different levels of risky altruism. There is a very evident difference in victimization experiences between those with high versus low scores on risky altruism. Subjects with the highest risky altruism scores reported about 3.5 times more property crime victimization than did those who avoided all risky altruism. With respect to personal crime, 21 times more crime per capita was reported by the highest risk-taking altruists! This is somewhat overstated because of the near zero rate of personal victimization in the low-risk group: only 2 of the 21 lowest-risk subjects reported *any* personal crime, compared to 6 of the 13 highest-risk subjects.

TABLE 14.3   MEAN VICTIMIZATION ACCORDING TO LEVEL OF RISKY ALTRUISM

	Level of Risky Altruism				
Victimization	*Very Low (21)**	*Low (20)*	*Medium (28)*	*High (18)*	*Very High (13)*
Property	1.19	1.45	1.96	3.88	4.08
Personal	0.08	0.50	0.50	1.50	1.69
Total	0.92	1.60	1.89	3.22	3.23

* Number of subjects in each group is given in parentheses. Complete explanations of all data analyses are available from the first author at homantr@udmercy.edu.

More important than the per capita differences of the two extreme subgroups is the fact that the trends of the mean victimization scores are very consistent across the five subgroups. With one minor exception (a tie), the level of victimization increases with each step up in risky altruism.

Summary of Study I

In summary of Study I, self-reported Altruism was a significant predictor of both property and personal crime victimization. The strength of the relationships held with all demographic variables controlled for. When scores on the Altruism scale were subdivided into Risky Altruism and Safe Altruism, it was clear that most of the relationship between victimization and altruism was due to what we now term "risky altruism."

Although we cannot rule out the possibility that victimization leads to increased altruism, two considerations make this unlikely. First, we did find a handful of cases—one in particular—in which altruistic behavior clearly facilitated the victimization. Second, the relationship between victimization and altruism was largely accounted for by risky altruism. If being a victim increased one's altruism, this should also have been true for safe altruism. Still, we cannot rule out the possibility of reciprocal causality: Granted that risky altruism leads to victimization, it may also be that repeated experiences as a crime victim might make one more willing to take a chance on helping others. As Study II will suggest, however, certain personality factors are more likely to explain altruism than would a history of victimization.

Study II : Risky Altruism, Victimization, and the "Big Five"

The strong correlation between risky altruism and victimization raises the issue of whether victimization is a consequence of a specific trait involving helping strangers in ways that increase one's vulnerability, or whether a more general risk-taking trait is predictive of both the risky altruism and other risk-taking behaviors that increase one's vulnerability to crime. Such general risk taking might involve carrying large amounts of money, attending events in high-crime areas without taking suitable precautions, leaving one's car parked on the street without any antitheft devices, engaging in casual sex with strangers, and the like. In other words, it might be simply a general risk-taking trait that accounts for the correlation between risky altruism and victimization.

These considerations led us to do a follow-up study that focused on a basic measure of risk taking. Our hypothesis was that risk taking would account for some of the relationship between risky altruism and victimization, but even with risk taking controlled for we expected that there would still be some association between risky altruism and victimization.

Measuring the Personality of Altruists

To understand the nature of risky altruism, we used Zuckerman's (2002) measure of Impulsive Sensation Seeking (ISS). For further understanding of subjects' personalities, we also included John et al.'s (2008) Big Five Inventory as a measure of basic traits. We were able to measure these personality traits for 67 of the original 100 subjects. (Missing subjects had either dropped the class, been absent for the follow-up, or had not given enough information to allow for

TABLE 14.4 CORRELATIONS BETWEEN PERSONALITY TRAITS AND ALTRUISM AND VICTIMIZATION

Personality Traits	Altruism			Victimization		
	Total	*Risky*	*Safe*	*Total*	*Personal*	*Property*
Openness	0.32**	0.26*	0.31*	0.37**	0.29*	0.21
Conscientiousness	0.14	0.10	0.15	0.10	0.05	0.07
Extraversion	0.40***	0.33**	0.39***	0.02	0.12	−0.03
Agreeableness	0.06	0.11	0.01	0.04	0.00	−0.06
Neuroticism	0.02	0.02	0.01	−0.14	−0.26*	0.06
Sensation Seeking (ISS)	0.30*	0.34**	0.21	0.16	0.25*	0.11

N is 67 throughout.
* *p* < 0.05; ** *p* < 0.01; *** *p* < 0.001 (all *p* values are two-tailed)

matching with the original questionnaire.) The follow-up sample did not differ from the total sample on any variables.

The critical question for the follow-up study was whether Risky Altruism was a function of sensation seeking. As shown in Table 14.4, ISS is a strong predictor of Risky Altruism (r = +0.34, p = 0.005) and has only a nonsignificant relationship with Safe Altruism (r = +0.21, p = 0.084). This supports our analysis in Study I that identified two subscales within altruism and concluded that risk-taking altruism was the main correlate of victimization.

Predicting Altruism

Table 14.4 also shows how the three altruism measures correlate with the Big Five personality traits. Extraversion has a +0.40 correlation with Altruism (p <0.001). Openness also shows a significant relationship with altruism: r = +0.32 (p = 0.009).[2] Both of these correlations make sense. With respect to extraversion, altruism is primarily an interpersonal activity; and Openness has been linked to idealism and adventurousness (John et al., 2008).

However, there is no meaningful correlation between altruism and Agreeableness (r = +0.06, p = 0.648). As mentioned above, altruism is generally considered to be a facet of Agreeableness, and the Five-Factor Model would clearly expect a much larger positive correlation here (Costa & McRae, 1992; John et al., 2008). We attribute the low correlation between altruism and Agreeableness to the homogeneity of our sample, who were mostly high on Agreeableness; we believe that a more heterogeneous sample would show a much higher correlation.

A Model of Risky Altruism and Victimization

The results shown in Table 14.4 supported our conclusion that a particular type of altruism, risky altruism, is associated with criminal victimization. Risky altruism, in turn, is a product of a combination of interacting personality variables. To rule out the possibility that our findings were the result of correlations with demographic variables, we entered all of our data into a series of multiple regression equations. This analysis led to two main findings.

First, risky altruism is best explained as resulting from a combination of Sensation Seeking, Extraversion, and Openness to experience. Low Neuroticism also plays a role—probably by making one less anxious or cautious.

Second, with all other personality and demographic variables taken into account, risky altruism remained a significant predictor of victimization. All variables combined attained an R of +0.510 with total victimization; risky altruism by itself showed a *partial r* of +0.354 (all other variables controlled for; $p < 0.01$).

To sum up our findings, a variety of personality dispositions, namely Impulsive Sensation Seeking, Extraversion, and Openness to Experience, predispose people to engage in risky altruism. Independently of the underlying motivation for engaging in risky altruism, such behavior either in itself, or together with other lifestyle variables that encourage risky altruism, serves to facilitate criminal activity and renders the person significantly more likely to become a crime victim. We believe that the following model (Figure 14.1) best captures our findings.

The arrows indicate significant ($p < 0.05$) zero-order correlations. The direction of the arrows is a matter of theory, not evidence, for which a longitudinal study would be needed. Thus, it makes sense to say that Openness and Extraversion lead to Sensation Seeking, Sensation Seeking (along with other variables) leads to Risky Altruism, and Risky Altruism leads to Personal and Property crime victimization. Even with Risky Altruism controlled for, however, both Openness and Neuroticism still correlated with victimization. We believe that an unmeasured variable, routine activities, accounts for the relationships between Openness and Neuroticism with Victimization when Risky Altruism is controlled for.[3]

In interpreting this model, several points should be made. First, the nature of "risky altruism" is clearly the key to the model. Risky Altruism (and not Safe Altruism) correlated significantly with sensation seeking (ISS); and when all of the personality correlates of Risky Altruism were controlled for, that scale remained a strong predictor of both personal and property crime victimization.

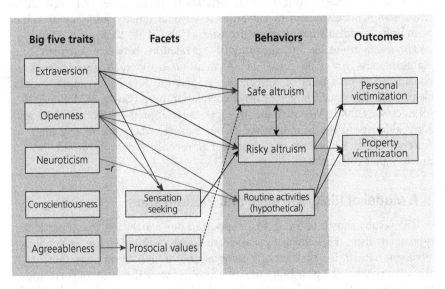

FIGURE 14.1
Risky altruism as a link between personality and victimization.

Finally, it should be stressed that a complete model of the relationships between altruism and victimization would include two additional features. One would be a variable inserted between Behaviors and Outcomes, indicating the routine activities of "motivated offenders." This would indicate all of the ways that offenders interact with the safe altruist and the risky altruist. Such a variable would indicate whether it was the helpful behavior of the altruist that made him or her more vulnerable, whether the offender merely used the helpfulness as a marker to indicate someone to target, or whether the helpfulness was part of a general tendency (toward risk taking or naïve trust) that made the person more vulnerable in other ways.

Also, a complete model should consider the likelihood of feedback loops. In line with Staub and Vollhardt's (2008) concept of "altruism born of suffering," the experience of victimization may loop back to make safe and/or risky altruistic behaviors more or less likely. Likewise, the underlying personality traits that we have identified should not be considered totally fixed or unalterable. On the one hand, there is a consensus that such traits are heritable, and relatively high heritability coefficients have been found, generally in the neighborhood of 0.40 to 0.60 (Widiger & Lowe, 2007; Zuckerman & Kuhlman, 2000). Significant changes in these traits over the lifespan, however, have also led to the conclusion that an individual's experiences, especially in the "nonshared" environment, i.e., outside of one's immediate family, significantly affect these basic traits (Srivastava, John, Gosling, & Potter, 2003; Zuckerman, 2002). In other words, if you experience enough victimization as a consequence of your helpfulness, you are likely to become somewhat less outgoing and sociable.

Conclusion

In summary, we have put forth a theory as to how altruistic behavior might result in victim facilitation of crime. We conducted an exploratory study in which we found a significant correlation between subjects' self-reported level of altruism and their level of personal and property crime victimization. Further analysis of the measure of altruism led to the conclusion that it was composed of two subscales, which we termed safe and risky altruism. A follow-up study on the original subjects provided confirming evidence that it was indeed risky altruism that was related to crime victimization; this altruism was found to be a function of Sensation Seeking, Openness, and Extraversion. The failure of the full-scale altruism measure to correlate with Agreeableness was the only major result that did not "fit" our expectations. Risky Altruism was a significant predictor of victimization with all other personality and demographic variables controlled for, suggesting that there was something about the altruistic behavior itself (and not just the sensation seeking and other related activities that led up to it) that facilitated victimization. These relationships were put in the larger context of the Five-Factor Model of personality, and it was suggested that, besides Risky Altruism, factors such as Neuroticism and Openness had their own negative and positive links, respectively, to victimization.

> Risky Altruism was a significant predictor of victimization with all other personality and demographic variables controlled for, suggesting that there was something about the altruistic behavior itself (and not just the sensation seeking and other related activities that led up to it) that facilitated victimization.

Pathological Altruism

Have we, then, found one form of pathological altruism? Even assuming that our results stay substantially the same under cross-validation, we would not say that behaviors measured in the Total Altruism scale qualify as "pathological." Most of these items do not go much beyond common courtesies. The assumption underlying the Altruism Scale, of course, is that someone who *very frequently* lends things of value, gives rides to strangers, and the like will be more likely to help in all situations, even where prudence would dictate caution. There was at least some anecdotal evidence for this in some subjects' descriptions of a few of their victimizations. Also, the high level of victimization reported by the highest levels of risky altruism (Table 14.3) certainly supports the term "maladaptive," if "pathological" seems too strong.

Notes

1. As a rather extreme example of risky altruism, one subject took two troubled teenagers into his home. In one case, the teenager stole from his home. In the second case, the teenager stole his car. Both teens were initially strangers to this Samaritan and were introduced by his friends and relatives.

2. On standard measures of the Big Five, such as the NEO-PI-R and the BFI used here, "sensation seeking" is seen as a facet of Extraversion. In our data, ISS correlated +0.349 ($p = 0.004$) with Extraversion and +0.331 ($p = 0.006$) with Openness. This also helps account for the correlations of those variables with altruism. Notice, however, that it is only ISS that has a *higher* correlation with Risky Altruism than with either Total or Safe Altruism.

3. An example might be visiting a new city on business. Someone high on Openness would be likely to explore the city; someone high on Neuroticism would likely stay put in a hotel or only venture out with a group. The routine activity of walking through an unknown neighborhood may result in an encounter with an opportunist criminal, thus facilitating a street robbery. Sensation Seeking might also result in such exploration, but more because one is attracted by risk than because of intellectual curiosity.

References

Bachner-Melman, R., Gritsenko, I., Nemanov, L., Zohar, A. H., Dina, C., & Ebstein, R. P. (2005). Dopamine polymorphisms associated with self report measures of human altruism: A fresh phenotype for the dopamine D4 receptor. *Molecular Psychiatry, 10,* 333–335.

Cohen, L., & Felson, M. (1979). Social change and crime rate trends: A routine activities approach. *American Sociological Review, 44,* 588–608.

Costa, P. T., & McCrae, R. R. (1992). *Revised NEO Personality Inventory (NEO-PI-R) and NEO Five-Factor Inventory (NEO-FFI) professional manual.* Odessa, FL: Psychological Assessment Resources.

Darley, J. M., & Latane, B. (1968). Bystander intervention in emergencies: Diffusion of responsibility. *Journal of Personality and Social Psychology, 8,* 377–383.

Dovidio, J. F., Piliavin, J. A., Schroeder, D. A., & Penner, L. A. (2006). *The social psychology of prosocial behavior.* Mahwah, NJ: Lawrence Erlbaum.

Ebstein, R. P. (2006). The molecular genetic architecture of human personality: Beyond self-report questionnaires. *Molecular Psychiatry, 11,* 427–445.

Felson, M. (2002). *Crime and everyday life.* Thousand Oaks, CA: Sage.

Gibson, K. L., McKelvie, S. J., & de Man, A. F. (2008). Personality and culture: A comparison of Francophones and Anglophones in Quebec. *The Journal of Social Psychology, 148*, 133–165.

Goldberg, L. R. (1981). Language and individual differences: The search for universals in personality lexicons. In L. Wheeler (Ed.), *Review of personality and social psychology* Vol. 2 (pp. 141–165). Beverly Hills: Sage.

Goldberg, L. R. (1993). The structure of phenotypic personality traits. *American Psychologist, 48*, 26–34.

Gouldner, A. W. (1960). The norm of reciprocity: A preliminary statement. *American Sociological Review, 25*, 161–178.

Haigler, E. D., & Widiger, T. A. (2001). Experimental manipulation of NEO-PI-R items. *Journal of Personality Assessment, 72*, 339–358.

John, O. P., Naumann, L. P., & Soto, C. (2008). Paradigm shift to the integrative Big Five trait taxonomy: History, measurement, and conceptual issues. In O. P. John, R. W. Robins, & L. A. Pervin (Eds.), *Handbook of personality* (3rd ed., pp. 114–158). New York: Guilford.

Karmen, A. (2004). *Crime Victims* (5th ed.). Belmont, CA: Wadsworth.

Lamm, C., Batson, C. D., & Decety, J. (2007). The neural substrate of human empathy: Effects of perspective-taking and cognitive appraisal. *Journal of Cognitive Neuroscience, 19*, 42–48.

Oliner, S. P., & Oliner, P. M. (1988). *The altruistic personality: Rescuers of Jews in Nazi Europe*. New York: Free Press.

Penner, L. A., Dovidio, J. F., Piliavin, J. A., & Schroeder, D. A. (2005). Prosocial behavior: Multilevel perspectives. *Annual Review of Psychology, 56*, 365–392.

Penner, L. A., Fritzsche, B. A., Craiger, J. P., & Freifeld, T. S. (1995). Measuring the prosocial personality. In J. N. Butcher, & C. D. Spielberger (Eds.), *Advances in personality assessment* Vol. 12 (pp. 147–163). Hillsdale, NJ: Erlbaum.

Preston, S. D., & deWaal, F. B. M. (2002). Empathy: Its ultimate and proximate bases. *Behavioral and Brain Sciences, 25*, 1–72.

Rushton, J. P., Bons, T. A., & Hur, Y. -M. (2008). The genetics and evolution of the general factor of personality. *Journal of Research in Personality, 42*, 1173–1185.

Rushton, J. P., Chrisjohn, R. D., & Fekken, G. C. (1981). The altruistic personality and the self-report altruism scale. *Personality and Individual Differences, 2*, 293–302.

Srivastava, S., John, O. P., Gosling, S. D, & Potter, J. (2003). Development of personality in early and middle childhood: Set like plaster or persistent change? *Journal of Personality and Social Psychology, 84*, 1041–1053.

Staub, E. (1974). Helping a distressed person: Social, personality, and stimulus determinants. In L. Berkowitz (Ed.), *Advances in experimental social psychology*, Vol. 7 (pp. 293–341). New York: Academic Press.

Staub, E. (2003). *The psychology of good and evil: Why children, adults, and groups help and harm others*. New York: Cambridge University Press.

Staub, E., & Vollhardt, J. (2008). Altruism born of suffering: The roots of caring and helping after victimization and other trauma. *American Journal of Orthopsychiatry, 78*, 267–280.

Stewart, R. (2000). *Leper priest of Molokai*. Honolulu: University of Hawaii Press.

Turvey, B. E., & Petherick, W. (2009). *Forensic victimology: Examining violent crime victims in investigative and legal contexts*. Boston: Elsevier.

Widiger, T. A., Costa, P. T., & McCrae, R. R. (2002). A proposal for Axis II: Diagnosing personality disorders using the five-factor model. In P. T. Costa, & T. A. Widiger (Eds.), *Personality disorders and the five-factor model of personality* (pp. 431–456). Washington, DC: American Psychological Association.

Widiger, T. A., & Lowe, J. R. (2007). Five-Factor Model assessment of personality disorder. *Journal of Personality Assessment, 89,* 16–29.

Wolfgang, M. (1958). *Patterns in criminal homicide.* Philadelphia: University of Pennsylvania Press.

Zuckerman, M. (2002). Zuckerman-Kuhlman Personality Questionnaire (ZKPQ): An alternative five-factor model. In B. de Raad, & M. Perugini (Eds.), *Big Five assessment* (pp. 377–396). Seattle: Hogrefe & Huber.

Zuckerman, M., & Kuhlman, D. M. (2000). Personality and risk-taking: Common biosocial factors. *Journal of Personality, 68,* 999–1029.

CHAPTER 15

SUICIDE ATTACK MARTYRDOMS

Temperament and Mindset of Altruistic Warriors

Adolf Tobeña

"You have atomic bombs, but we have suicide bombers."
—*New York Times Reporter* David Rohde,
quoting his Taliban captors. (Rohde, 2009)

"The predictors of terrorism are unclear."
—Alan Krueger and Jitka Malecková, in their *Science* article
"Attitudes and action: Public opinions and international terrorism."
(Krueger & Malecková, 2009)

KEY CONCEPTS

- Suicide attacks are a combative tactic arising from a lethal, nonpathological altruism in some warfare contexts.
- Altruism is the only widely agreed upon temperamental attributes of suicide attackers.
- Strong altruistic dispositions are increasingly being found to have underlying biological mediators.
- Understanding the neurocognitive underpinnings of willingness to commit extreme altruistic acts may help us understand suicide attacks.

RECOGNITION THAT SOCIOECONOMIC conditions are not reliable predictors of terrorism is good news (Derin-Gure, 2009: Krueger & Malecková, 2003, 2009). It helps us realize how ignorant we are about the source of recent "suicide" war tactics that have galvanized politics and research efforts worldwide. After all, the study of terrorism sociopsychology is based primarily on anecdotal observations and subjective interpretations; most studies and theories fail to take into account the heterogeneity of terrorists' backgrounds, temperaments, and mentalities (Victoroff, 2005). Researchers seem particularly lost when dealing with the motives of suicide bombers.

Social scientists have tried to make sense of suicide missions by gathering sound statistical records and making detailed analyses of the phenomenon, but with little success (Gambetta, 2006). Since suicide attacks depend ultimately on conviction—that is, on events that occur in the mind/brain of an individual—it may be useful to consider such behavior from a neurobiological perspective.

The Exceptional Motivation of Suicide Attackers

The core problem in understanding violent martyrdoms is, How do suicide attackers arrive at and commit themselves to their deadly and extreme decisions? Motivations of suicide attackers customarily include the following (Atran, 2003; Elster, 2006; Kruglanski, Crenshaw, Post, & Victoroff, 2008):

- *Belief systems*, including ideological reasons such as a struggle against perceived oppression, resistance to occupation or marginalization, or attempts to ensure the supremacy of a political or religious creed
- *Revenge* for previous personal harm or humiliation; retaliation in response to earlier misdeeds
- *Ties* between members of a combative, highly cohesive group such as brothers-in-arms
- *Ambition* to gain status amid comrades and sympathizers (glory craving)

All of these motivations are likely to fuel a drift toward combativeness in insurgencies, although they don't explain why *some* individuals make the extraordinary decision to kill themselves while killing as many enemies as possible. The first domain—belief systems—appears most important in legitimizing lethal actions. The latter three domains, on the other hand, appear to nurture each person's mindset within their fighting cells or units, as they turn toward willingness to sacrifice through violent martyrdom. Ultimately, however, the driving weight and the particular sequence of vectors behind suicidal attacks have not been established. The proposal of a *martyrdom disposition*—a constellation of distinctive personality traits that may fuel proneness to martyrdom acts in warfare contexts particularly—has not yet received empirical support, in no small part because it is tough to find subjects (Tobeña, 2004, Victoroff, 2005). In fact, the only attribute for which there is full consensus between scholars who have approached the sociopsychology of suicide attacks is a temperamental one: altruism (Atran, 2006; Gambetta, 2006; Kruglanski et al., 2008; Pedazhur, Perliger, & Weinberg, 2003; Sageman, 2004, Victoroff, 2005), although such consensus has not resulted in further studies.

> The only attribute for which there is full consensus between scholars who have approached the sociopsychology of suicide attacks is a temperamental one: *altruism*.

However, consideration of violent martyrdom as a tool—one of many in the "strategic arsenal" of intergroup conflicts—has proven helpful in understanding and countering such tactics (Ashworth, Clinton, Meirowitz, & Ramsay, 2008; Bernmelech & Berrabi, 2007; Pape, 2003, 2005). What is commonly known as "kamikaze terrorism" (to accentuate its rarity and implausibility) appears to be a rational option when a weak insurgent group is opposing a very powerful one—a military superpower, for instance. Violent martyrdom is thus not necessarily the desperate conduct of marginalized gangs, but an extreme option for publicity that undergirds a firm ambition to prevail (Gambetta, 2006). From a psychological standpoint, the damage inflicted in the attacks does not matter so much as the intimidation of the powerful, even as the base of the insurgencies gains strength and support. Dying for a cause is also a powerful recruiting tool because it reinforces the narrative of the weaker party. After all, how can one remain passive while others give their very lives? In fact, the inspiring and imitation-arousing impact of martyrdom is not new: It has been cultivated by religious, political, and military leaders throughout the ages—whenever combat's outcome hangs in the balance.

What is more, the exaltation of martyrdom can set off increasing competition between groups: During the worst years of the second Intifada, there was an escalation of suicide actions between Hamas, Jihad, Martyrs of Al-Aqsa, and Fatah in an apparent one-upmanship propaganda race of atrocities (Ricolfi, 2006). These extreme actions provoke an exaggerated response from the enemy—which ultimately creates more victims on the terrorists' own side. This, of course, helps with both recruitment and retaliatory enthusiasm. In all of these ways, then, suicide attacks tactics may indeed function as a bootstrapping option in highly unequal combats.

The Statistics of Suicide Attacks

The proliferation of suicide attacks created deep apprehension in Western countries at the turn of the century, a fear that peaked after the September 11, 2001 attacks in New York and Washington. Anxiety faded over the years as it became clearer that Islamic guerrillas could not shake the status and military strength of the major powers. Figure 15.1 depicts the worldwide number of suicide attacks in

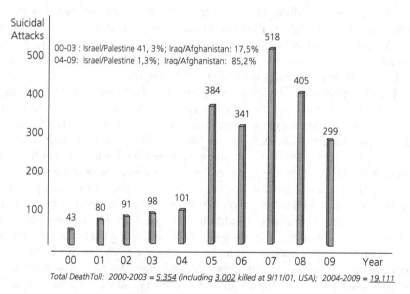

FIGURE 15.1
Worldwide scores of suicidal attacks from 2000 to 2009. Numbers on top of bars indicate the total figure of attacks per year. Elaborated from Atran, S. (2004). *Science, 304,* 47–48 (Sup. materials:sciencemag.org/cgi/content/full//304/5667/47/DC1), and the Worldwide Incidents Tracking System, U.S. Government (wits.nctc.gov/reports/analytical/). As noted in these sources, the calculations are approximate as the definition of suicide attack varies across databases and because of difficulties arising at the recording sites. The descending trend initiated at 2009 was consolidated along 2010, approaching the scores of 2004.

the present decade. The year 2003 was a turning point. Before that time, suicide attacks appeared primarily in Israel/Palestine, Chechnya, Kashmir, and Sri Lanka (77% of attacks in these regions). After that date, attacks erupted in Iraq, Afghanistan, and Pakistan, escalating the number of incidents by five and the total fatalities by three.

The wars that the United States and its allies launched on Afghanistan (2002) and Iraq (2003) were followed by insurgent responses (with varying delays) that changed the map of suicide bombings. Such attacks have almost disappeared in Israel/Palestine, Chechnya, Kashmir, and Sri Lanka. Meanwhile, the cities and roads of Iraq, and later Afghanistan and Pakistan, have felt the near daily brunt of suicide attackers targeting foreign patrols and their local allies and recruits, or more commonly, civilian assemblies in mosques, markets or administrative offices (90,7% of attacks in these three regions). Suicide attacks have attained unprecedentedly high numbers in Iraq and Afghanistan/Pakistan. These numbers have required thousands of guided volunteers who are prepared for the supreme sacrifice of suicide. Thus, although the recruitment base for these extreme tactics may be small, it cannot be as restricted as usually supposed (Gambetta, 2006). Apparently, tens of thousands of individuals are eager for violent sacrifice, particularly during severe conflicts.

Earnest reaction and efficient counterterrorism measures orchestrated by some governments have resulted in an almost complete halt of suicide launchings in some regions (Israel/Palestine, Chechnya). On the other hand, Iraq and Afghanistan have witnessed the deployment of foreign armies and associated logistic bodies dedicated to rebuilding the shattered countries—these have provided a perfect niche for the deadly proliferation of suicide attacks. The recent surge in suicide attacks in Pakistan (25% of the total 2009 figure) is an apparent result of at least two different causes: the extension of the Afghanistan war to tribal areas within Afghani-Pakistani border regions, and longstanding enmity and local grievances between insurgencies. Last, some domestic conflicts—Sri Lanka, for instance—have been characterized by punctuated waves of activity, with a complete absence of suicidal killings during truces.

The changing trends depicted on Figure 15.1 reinforce an obvious, although often neglected, fact—suicide attacks are a war tactic. They are one of the tactics— a commando or a "lone warrior" mission—of guerrilla warfare (Bohórquez, Gourley, Dixon, Spagat, & Johnson, 2009). Many analysts of terrorism have been confused by the nature of suicide guerrilla tactics. But the links between the historical battles of the zealots-sicarii and those of modern kamikazes and "islamikazes" provide evidence of the following: At critical points in history, insurgent factions or armies have been either cornered or perceive the contest as deeply asymmetrical—although changeable by courageous determination. As a consequence, they have opted for converting the bodies of combatants into murderous weapons (bombs or vehicle-driven "missiles") to inflict harm upon the enemy, with the main aim of intimidating and shattering his nerve (Gambetta, 2006). The military importance of suicide attacks is clear for Japanese kamikazes or the Black Tigers of Sri Lanka (Gambetta, 2006), but the highly charged religious rhetoric, aloofness, and futility that have characterized some islamikaze missions have created confusion about their military attributes. Suicide attacks can take a variety of forms and sometimes kill no one except the attacker, but the propaganda effects are never negligible. It is fair to say, nevertheless, that some social analysts have firmly asserted the military attributes of suicide missions: Holmes (2006), in his dissection the Al-Qaeda team who mounted and executed the raids of September 11, 2001, or Biggs (2006), in his analysis of immolations without killing.

Commonalities of Suicide Attacks

Sociological records and studies have been helpful in establishing common traits that characterize people, organizations, circumstances, and narratives involving in suicide missions (Gambetta, 2006).

However, after detailed dissection of incidents, goals, consequences, and historical trends across regions and organizations, there has been no convincing explanation of the roots behind the willingness to accept an engagement in suicide missions. The commonalities listed in Table 15.1 permit only a general description: Suicide attacks appear to be a cost-effective weapon for insurgents in highly asymmetrical contests, provided a suitable recruitment line can be found and fostered. This is important, although it counts only as an a posteriori strategic description. It says nothing of substance about the personal attributes of the many recruits eager to participate in suicidal attacks. The crucial requirement of their missions (the death of the weapon carriers) puts these individuals nearer to

> Suicide attacks appear to be a cost-effective weapon for insurgents in highly asymmetrical contests, provided a suitable recruitment line can be found and fostered.

TABLE 15.1 COMMONALITIES IN SUICIDE ATTACKS WORLDWIDE

- Suicide launchings appear in highly asymmetrical conflicts when the weaker factions preserve a capacity and determination to intimidate.
- Perpetrators are primarily self-recruited volunteers.
- Young males form the preponderance of actors (male-to-female ratio around 8:2, although less disparate figures are seen in some regions).
- Organizations serve as providers, helpers, and handlers in providing weapons and transportation. Much less often, the organizations deliver extensive and narrow coaching in closed cells.
- Perpetrators have a full spectrum of sociodemographic and economic origins, with a trend toward middle-class in some regions.
- Weapons have high comparative efficacy—five to 15 times higher than those of ordinary guerrilla fighters.
- Restricted recruitment base is available, although sufficient to supply plentiful volunteers from population tails (often from far from the particular contest/region).
- Different motivations exist for perpetrators (suicide agents) versus organizers/handlers (commanders).
- Religious/ideological accelerants of bellicosity are apparent against enemies (fanaticism) in otherwise common people regarding other, nonideological, beliefs and values.
- Preponderance of secular-oriented as opposed to religious-oriented organizations is noted.
- Contagion appears to play a role—there are waves with distinguishable peaks and lulls during which periods of strong activity alternate with apparent silence.
- Perpetrators see themselves as soldiers fulfilling a high-esteem mission for their nation or creed.
- Suicide martyrdom is usually practised within the context of a particular hotspot or battlefield with long-lasting grievances, but with prominent outliers (U.S., London, Madrid*).

---

*The Madrid, November 3, 2004 bombings (199 deaths and 1,000 wounded) are usually excluded from records of suicide attacks because the commandos left the explosive backpacks on the trains and ran. The terrorist cell, however, had a further agenda with suicide as an option—3 weeks later, seven members blew themselves up, killing an officer and destroying a building when they were surrounded by police (Rodriguez, 2004). Those who escaped blew themselves up later in Iraq.

no-escape or high-risk missions in ordinary wars than to self-immolation tactics during campaigns of protest.

The regularities listed in Table 15.1 thus help to provide a plausible context for the conditions in which suicidal launchings appear. But there is still no answer regarding why these fighting tactics arise only at particular historical points and why some individuals are eager to abruptly close their personal future by participating in suicidal attacks. As mentioned previously, the only attribute for which there is full consensus between scholars who have approached the sociopsychology of suicide attacks is a temperamental one: altruism (Atran, 2006; Gambetta, 2006; Kruglanski et al., 2008; Pedhazur et al., 2003; Sageman, 2004, Victoroff, 2005). In seeking an explanation for such extreme warrior acts, it may be useful to explore the biological roots of altruism, because if it does indeed play a pivotal role in such attacks, then violent martyrs themselves might best be characterized as gullible souls with a "beneficent" disposition that nevertheless fails to prevent them from leaving a host of victims. It should be pointed out, however, that Machiavellian leaders or handlers do not usually give their lives for their group. Their gift for simulating altruism is used for their own gain.

> Machiavellian leaders or handlers do not usually give their lives for their group. Their gift for simulating altruism is used for their own gain.

Neurogenetics of Strong Altruism

"You never lose by being too generous," Robert M. May (as quoted by Nowak, 2008, p. 579).

Findings from economic games (Fehr & Fischbacher, 2003; Fehr & Camerer, 2007) involving real gains and losses in cash have shown that there are pockets of individuals eager to:

- Punish defectors or violators of social norms despite detrimental consequences
- Reject unfair though valuable offers
- Punish unfair treatments when observing them as neutral and uninvolved third parties
- Invest in strangers at a risk of losing.

I have previously characterized suicide attacks as a form of *lethal altruism*, a highly damaging drift away from humanity's more generous tendencies (Tobeña, 2004a, 2009). Lethal altruism is related to the concept of *strong altruism*, which requires generous deeds at a significant personal cost, as well as to *costly altruism*, which involves the punishment of defectors or norm violators at significant personal cost.

Individual variability in strong altruism can be measured either with psychometric scales or economic games; the search for plausible genetic markers has already borne fruit. This should serve as a starting point to study any possible "martyrdom disposition" since the trait implies there will be pockets of *extreme altruists* among all populations—that is, those willing to make high-cost investments in genetically unrelated others. Attempts to measure the heritability of altruism as measured by self-report scales in twins have been contradictory, since genetic effects have varied from 50% to none (Koenig, McGue, Krueger, & Bouchard, 2007; Krueger, Hicks, & McGue, 2001; Rushton, Fulker, Neale, Nias, & Eysenck, 1986). Studies in large samples of twins using fair–unfair decisions in economic games have been more consistent. In a study of 658 Swedish twins (comparing 71 dizygotic pairs with 253 monozygotic pairs), more than 40% of rejection of unfair offers in the Ultimatum Game was explained by genetic effects (Wallace, Cesarini, Lichtenstein, & Johansson 2006). In a subsequent work combining the Swedish twins and an American sample recruited at a large twin gathering, investments on strangers during trials of the Trust Game provided heritabilities ranging from 0.2 to 0.32 (Cesarini, Dawes, Fowler, Jojansson, Lichtenstein, & Wallace 2008).

An Israeli study showed an association between large allocations (generosity) in the Dictator Game with the AVP1a vasopressin receptor gene long-repeat polymorphisms at promoter region RS3 (Knafo, Israel, Darvasi, Bachner-Melman, Uzefowski, Cohen, Feldmann, Lerer, Laiba, Raz, Nemanov, Gritsenko, Dina, Agam, Dean, Bornstein and Ebstein et al., 2008). The same group had previously demonstrated an association between dopamine receptor DRD4 variants with self-reported altruism (Bachner-Melman, Gritsenko., Nemanov., Zohar., Dina, & Ebstein et al., 2005). Variants of oxytocin receptors have also been associated with empathy and prosocial behaviors (Ebstein, Israel, Lerer, Uzefovsky, Shalev, Gritsenko, Riebold, Salomon & Yirmiya et al., 2009; Rodrigues, Saslow, Garcia, John, & Keltner, 2009). Moreover, the disruption of serotonin (5-HT) function through tryptophan depletion selectively alters reactions to unfairness without affecting mood or judgement (Crockett, Clark, Tabibnia, Lieberman, & Robbins, 2008): A transitory drop of serotonin was found to be accompanied by increased rejection of unfair offers (righteous indignation). A parallel study measured serotonin content in platelets (Emanuele, Brondino, Bertona, Re, Geroldi, 2008): Volunteers with low serotonin function had higher rejection of unfair offers. Both results support previous data showing affiliative/agonistic modulation by serotonergic systems. Moreover, the agonistic effects of testosterone have been replicated in the Ultimatum Game: In males, high basal androgenic levels enhance rejection and retaliation toward unfairness (Burnham, 2007).

Neuroimaging studies have identified several brain regions preferentially implicated in modulating costly options and reactions in games for real money. Neural areas and circuits have been found that seem to process fair versus unfair/unequal/disgusting outcomes in social interactions (De Quervain et al., 2004; Sanfey, Rillings, Aronson, Nystrom, & Cohen, 2003). The functioning of all these neural systems can be modified by pharmacological interventions (Baumgartner, Heinrichs, Volanthen, Fischbacher, & Fehr, 2008; Kosfeld, Heinrichs, Zak, Fischbacher, & Fehr, 2005; Zak, Stanton, & Ahmadi, 2007). It seems safe to conclude, then, that traits behind costly altruistic behaviors are under a substantial biological influence that manifests itself through a variety of neurohormonal pathways and mechanisms that have only just begun to be understood.

Altruistic and Parochial Martyrs

The association between altruism and parochialism (hostility toward outgroup members) probably feeds the agonistic side of loyalty among comrades when confrontations arise against rival bands or parties. Showing swift, automatic preferences for known (in-group) individuals is a well-known phenomenon (Hammond & Axelrod, 2006), but demonstrating a willingness to punish at a cost those strangers who act unfairly, particularly when the victims of the unfairness are comrades, seems even more relevant to explain exceptional in-group investments.

This is precisely what was found in a study (Bernhard, Fischbacher, & Fehr, 2006) with pairs of 195 individuals (17–60 years old) drawn from two Papua-New Guinea small-scale societies who had to play the Third Party Punishing Game. A neutral third party had to spend his money to punish unfair "dictators" for violations of egalitarian sharing of gifts (10 units of money) with unknown "recipients" in one-shot decisions. Punishing appeared on every condition if dictators opted not to share, or gave a blatantly ungenerous split. Costly sanctions were much higher when the three players were from same group or when the recipient and third party were also comrades, than when either the third party was an outsider (so viewing the unfairness from a detached frontier), or the recipient was the outsider (contemplating the unfairness applied to a foreigner).

Parochialism is a new word for the old notions of sectarianism or ethnocentrism. The concept is beginning to illuminate Darwinian selection mechanisms that may underlie warfare between tribes or bands in ancient human populations (Bowles, 2009). Choi and Bowles (2007) used a long-range evolutionary simulation to find that altruistic and parochial (that is, sectarian, ethnocentric, or tribal-like) traits could have evolved jointly by promoting war between groups. The simulation ran for 50,000 generations and allowed for interactions between 20 groups, each with 26 members. There were opportunities for trade, war, or no contact, and fitness outcomes, all depending on the relative frequencies of two alleles (A/NA: altruists/selfish; P/T: parochial/tolerant) at two different loci, resulting in four possible "genomes": PA (parochial altruists), TA (tolerant altruists), TNA (tolerant selfish), PNA (parochial selfish). Only two stable populations evolved, which were dominated either by parochial altruists (patriots thriving with frequent or at least occasional wars) or tolerant selfish (merchants devoted to profiting trade). Minor numbers of bullies (parochial selfish) or philanthropists (tolerant altruists) survived under the warrior or trader regimes, but never predominated.

> Perhaps surprisingly, political partisanship is a type of parochialism.

Perhaps surprisingly, political partisanship is a type of parochialism. In this regard, the strength (although not the direction) of partisanship has been shown to be heritable in a sample of American twins, with a heritability of about 45% (Settle, Dawes, & Fowles, 2009). This fits with cohering twin data showing that genetic mediation of in-group favoritism requires both a mechanism for unespecified groupal affiliation alongside with focused systems for processing salient cues such as those heralding race, ethnicity or religion (Lewis and Bates, 2010). There are also indirect data showing that people who self-identify as parochial altruists are more willing to participate in violent political action and are also readier to contemplate martyrdom as an option in fighting for collective interests (Ginges & Atran, 2009). Hence, costly altruism—that is, altruism at a high price and without guaranteed return—may occur because it tends to promote biological yields, not only for the recipients of help but also for the giver's relatives and comrades. (Azam 2003; Bowles, 2006, 2009; Choi & Bowles, 2007).

A Temperamental Workspace for Martyrdom

Altruistic parochialism thus seems to be a precondition for risky aggression toward foes in group contests, although it cannot be the full story. Such altruism

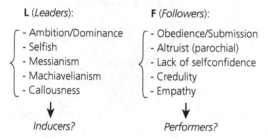

(A) **Combative activists: Self-recruitment of people with extreme scores on traits**

Venturesome (↑ extreme-risk fondness)
Impulsive (↓ ponderation)
Bold (↓ fearfulness)
Dominant (↑ masculinity)
Aggressive (↑ agonistic bursts)
Callousness (↓ empathy, compassion)

Common to Leaders(L) and Followers(F)?

(B)
Temperamental clusters associated to different roles in martyrdom

L (*Leaders*):
- Ambition/Dominance
- Selfish
- Messianism
- Machiavelianism
- Callousness

Inducers?

F (*Followers*):
- Obedience/Submission
- Altruist (parochial)
- Lack of selfconfidence
- Credulity
- Empathy

Performers?

FIGURE 15.2
Common and distinctive temperamental traits for leaders and followers within combat units in partisan conflicts. **A:** Common personality traits. **B:** Differential profiles for leaders (inducers) and followers (performers) of high-risk missions. From Tobeña, A. (2004a). *Mártires mortíferos: Biología del altruismo letal*. Valencia (Spain): PUV-Bromera Ed., with permission of the publisher.

should be understood in conjunction with other traits linked to prosocial/antisocial tendencies. Figure 15.2 depicts several traits that appear to fuel the agonistic high-risk lifestyles that are typically pursued by self-recruited volunteers entering violent gangs. These can be gangs motivated by either territorial or profit-making feuds, or by politico-religious goals (Tobeña 2004a; Wrangham & Peterson 1997). Bold, ambitious, dominant, adventurous, and callous young males form a characteristic cluster in recruits of combative groups in both apes and humans (Wrangham & Peterson, 1997, Wrangham & Wilson, 2004; Wrangham, Wilson, & Muller, 2006). Combatants in insurgencies and rebellious factions, whether male or female, appear to share these masculine tendencies (Van Vugt, 2009). By adding to such agonistic traits the personality dimensions of selfishness-to-altruism and Machiavellianism-to-gullibility, distinctions can hypothetically be drawn between leaders and followers within combative bands. Figure 15.3 depicts a dimensional space outlined to distinguish between clusters of potential inducers and performers of martyrdoms depending on the weights placed on three traits: selfishness versus altruism, dominance versus submission, and empiricism versus credulity.

I selected these dimensions because there is a solid tradition of measuring dominance/leadership versus submission/conformity in personality research (Duckit et al., 2007; Van Vugt, Hogan, & Kaiser, 2008), as well as doctrinairism/empiricism either as such or in the form of Machiavellianism–gullibility or tough–soft-mindedness (Wilson, Near, & Miller, 1996). Leadership heritability,

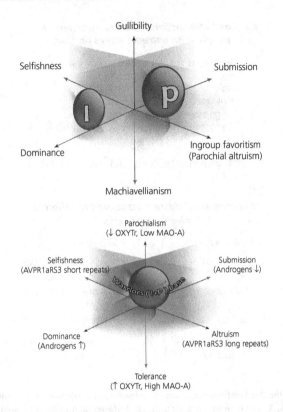

FIGURE 15.3
A temperamental workspace to distinguish warriors' proneness to martyrdom. *Top*: Hypothetical space for agonistic clusters defining combative activists across three temperamental traits: dominance–submission, Machiavellianism–gullibility, and selfishness–altruism. *Bottom*: Neurohormonal and genetic polymorphisms that may foster temperamental attributes encompassing distinctive clusters of warriors: Relative distributions along these biological traits would distinguish between generous warriors (*P*) and selfish warriors (*I*) who put themselves near or far away, respectively, from the high-risk/martyrdom frontier. I, inducer; P, performer; OXYTr, oxytocin receptor; MAO-A, monoamine oxidase A; AVPr, vasopressin receptor variants. Arrows denote activity. From Tobeña, A. (2004a). *Mártires mortíferos: Biología del altruismo letal*. Valencia (Spain): PUV-Bromera Ed., with permission of the publisher.

for instance, has been calculated to be around 0.3 in studies of large samples of twins. Comparisons have also shown that leadership abilities depend more on social dominance and achievement ambition than on other temperamental characteristics (Arvey, Rotundo, Jonhson, Zhang, & McGue et al., 2006; King, Johnson, & Van Vugt, 2009). The dimensional space outlined in Figure 15.3 is just a conjecture—it shows a visual metaphor for understanding the spectrum of traits involving dominance–submission, Machiavellianism–gullibility, and selfishness–altruism, although other dimensions may be required. Callousness–empathy would also be a relevant trait, possibly related to Machiavellianism–gullibility. Existing scales conflate different tendencies, so sensitive and consistent measures, particularly regarding parochialism and selfishness–altruism, would be critical in any analysis (Koenig, McGue, Krueger & Bouchard et al., 2007).

Studies in this area might use either hormonal/physiological signatures or genetic markers, along the lines of a previous study of political preferences

(Fowler, Baker, & Dawes, 2008). Alternatively, neuroimaging and neurotracking methods of temperaments could be used (Chiao, Mathur, Harada, & Lipke, 2009; Oxley, Smith, Alford, Hibbing, Miller, Scalora, Hatemi & Hibbing et al., 2008; Zink, Tong, Chen, Bassett, Stein, & Meyer-Lindenberg, et al., 2008). Clues to target relevant human genetic polymorphisms may also be derived from studies of social behavior in animals (Donaldson & Young, 2008; Clutton-Brock, T. (2009); Ebstein, Israel, Chew, Zhong, & Knafo (2010).

In-group Morality and Out-group Amorality—Potential Areas for Research

Teaching soldiers to suppress empathy for adversaries has long been an important tactic. Thus, it isn't a surprise to find that violent martyrs often view those they kill as somehow less than human. In fact, violent martyrs plan and carry out massacres with the utter conviction that they are doing good—they kill in the name of supreme justice and duty. Suicide bombers are a spectacular example of an impregnable morality toward one's own group that coexists, without contradiction, alongside a radical amorality toward members of another group. The intergroup barrier closes the domain of moral obligations. The immediate family of the martyr may have honors or advantages bestowed upon them (Atran, 2006), yet those who sacrifice themselves have no firm guarantees that this will be the case, even when they act under contract.

Research is needed to address the paradoxical coexistence of benumbing and moral exaltation of those prone to sacrifice themselves for the good of their comrades (Tobeña, 2007). Data is required, for example, on empathic perception with regard to the suffering of members of in- versus out-groups. Economic games are helpful in studying how neural systems process in-group versus out-group reactions. There are already plausible candidates for neuroimaging analysis. The anterior insula, for example, plays a prominent role in the rejection of unfair offers in the Ultimatum Game (Sanfey et al., 2003). The ventral striatum appears to be related to gratifying vengeance involving monetary sanctions to unfair players at the Trust Game (De Quervain et al., 2004) or involving inflicting pain (faked electric shocks) to unfair players in relation to a Public Goods Game (Singer, Seymour, O'Doherty, Stephan, Dolan, & Frith. et al., 2006). The dorsal and ventral section of the medial prefrontal cortex (mPFC) are each implicated in varying fashion with retaliatory activities in administering mechanical pain to unfair opponents, with the ventral section linked in particular to differences in callousness (Lotze, Veit, Anders, & Birbaumer, 2007).

> It isn't a surprise to find that violent martyrs often view those they kill as somehow less than human. In fact, violent martyrs plan and carry out massacres with the utter conviction that they are doing good—they kill in the name of supreme justice and duty.

The hostility side of altruistic parochialism can be explored from another perspective by examining the subtleties of prejudices and stereotypes toward outsiders. For example, previous studies have shown that when students viewed pictures of out-group members, patterns on functional magnetic resonance imaging (fMRI) brain activations differed depending on the specific attributes of outsiders (Harris & Fiske, 2006). Pictures of extreme out-group persons situated on a low warmth–low competence quadrant (i.e., disgusting homeless and drug addicts) activated the anterior insula and amygdala but not the medial pre-frontal cortex (mPFC), meaning the threat–aversion brain systems are highly reactive but devoid of the signature of interaction with another person, which is a mPFC-modulated function. Extreme out-groups are thus automatically dehumanized during social interaction routines. Whether similar automatic dehumanizing occurs with foreign "enemies," seen by comparing fMRI activa-tions of parochial altruists versus selfish tolerants, is yet to be explored. Another interesting avenue for exploration involves differences in the strength and per-sistence of learned fear memories depending on racial in-group/out-group aver-sive cues (white and black faces) (Olsson, Ebert, Banaji, & Phelps, 2005). Finally, orbito-frontal mediation of social norm compliance appears to be related to Machiavellianism scores (Spitzer, Fischbacher, Herrnberger, Grön, & Fehr, 2007), which provides yet another intriguing area for further investigation.

Other areas of research related to morality and brain function might involve people who show heightened scores for traits such as credulity and radicalism in addition to strong altruism. Links between markers of group parochialism and certain mechanisms of neurocognitive bias (Efferson, Lalive, & Fehr, 2008; Tobeña, Marks, & Dar, 1999) are also of interest, as this interdependence can be taken advantage of by doctrinal creeds to widen the gap between one group and another. Subtle effects of subliminal priming with conspicuous parochial signals (the Israeli, Italian, U.S., or Russian flags, for instance) upon attitudes and deci-sions of citizens differing in nationalistic attitudes, have already been shown (Hassin, Ferguson, Shidlovski, & Gross, 2007; Hassin et al., 2009). Moreover, while responding to moral dilemmas, only the Spaniards whose personal identi-ties were completely fused with their national group showed a willingness to sacrifice their lives for comrades that exceeded their will to perish for outsiders (Swan, Gómez, Dovidio, Hart, & Jetten, 2010). The changes on intragroup coop-eration of synchronic motoric rituals like marching or singing together might form another fruitful area for investigation (Wiltermuth & Heath, 2009).

Sympathizers of Suicide Combatants: Beware Adult Temple-Goers and Combative Youths

Suicide attackers often share their morals not only with their comrades-in-arms, but often with the community at large. It is well known that passionate belief in a doctrine widens the gap between groups, a gap that serves to strengthen and limit feelings of solidarity. Fanatical sectarianism takes root within tiny pockets of society, but these pockets can help intensify the beliefs of large communities. Polls have reflected sustained support for suicide missions within some societies (Atran, 2006), support that has been laid at the feet of religious fanaticism. In this respect, findings from surveys of Palestinian students and Israeli settlers have shown that religious devotion by itself does not relate to support for suicide attacks. It is reli-gious-driven social cohesion (measured by attendance to mosque, synagogue, or church) that fosters support for intergroup conflict and the lethality of suicide attacks (Ginges & Atran, 2009). The dangerousness of fanaticism does not spring from intimate feelings of transcendence or the depth of religious beliefs, but from the in-group loyalty and combativeness that religions sometime convey. It is paro-chialism again: the well-known ability of religious or secular ideologies to trigger ethnocentric and patriotic tendencies (God, King, country, people).

Findings from questionnaires provided to 52 adolescent boys from the Gaza strip are also relevant in gaining a deeper understanding of the characteristics of the larger population from which suicide martyrs are drawn (Victoroff, Qouta, Celinska, Abu-Safieh, Adelman, & Stern et al., 2006). Twenty-two of the boys could tell stories of close relatives who were imprisoned, wounded, or killed by Israeli troops. The questionnaires measured psychological distress and evaluated feelings of political oppression, religiosity, interest in politics, and sympathy with terrorist activities. Samples of saliva were also taken once a week over 4 weeks to test cortisol and testosterone levels. Results showed that precarious living in a refugee camp amid an armed conflict was reflected in distressed mood, although aggressiveness only predicted perceived oppression: The greater the aggressiveness, the more feelings of oppression. Perhaps surprisingly, cortisol levels (physiological stress) did *not* predict sympathy for suicide missions, although depression did. For the whole sample, testosterone levels did not correlate with aggressiveness, sympathies for terrorism, or with the perceived oppression. But when the eight boys with the highest testosterone levels were compared with the eight with the lowest figures, the results became very different—maximum expressions of sympathy for suicide terrorism and the maximum oppression was perceived in the boys with higher androgenic levels. Hence, among adolescents sympathizing with insurgencies, those with marked androgenic activation seem to be the most belligerent, regardless of their living conditions, confirming the agonistic vector discussed earlier.

All of this is valid only for a subsample (valuable, but restricted) of sympathizers in a particular location. It says nothing, or very little, about the vectors leading to suicide martyrdom attacks. It must again be stressed that being a sympathizer or supporter, or even simply helping groups that practice suicide terrorism is one thing, but lending oneself to be the human bomb is quite another. Howewer, data gathered in Israeli prisons from "failed suicide bombers" as well as from organizers/handlers of Palestinian suicide attacks (Merari, Diamant, Bibi, Broshi, & Zakin (2010) have provided depictions of distinctive temperamental profiles which complement the abovementioned findings from sympathizers: failed martyrs tended to be submissive, dependent, influenceable and moderately depressed whereas organizers were self-assured and combative individuals though reluctant to enlist themselves as suicide bombers.

> Among adolescents sympathizing with insurgencies, those with marked androgenic activation seem to be the most belligerent, regardless of their living conditions.

Conclusion

The recurrent suicide campaigns that have tragically punctuated conflicts in the Middle East and South Asia during the last decades have taught insurgency leaders that they can count on sustained pipelines of recruits. There appears to be no shortage of volunteers offering themselves for extreme sacrifice. This means suicide missions can be treated as simply one among a number of tactical options for an organization.

No one knows how long the Islamic and non-Islamic guerrillas who use suicide fighters as weapons will persevere (Bohórquez, Gourley, Dixon, Spagat, & Johnson, et al., 2009). But we do know that violent martyrdom used systematically in repeated waves has never been as widely seen as in the present period. This has puzzled Western public opinion and experts alike, nurturing fears that "outliers"—shocking major attacks far from usual hotspot regions—may be attempted again. Suicide fighters are an invaluable type of weaponry because deterrence is difficult, making counterterrorism measures a tricky business indeed.

At the individual level, warrior acts that call for absolute certainty of death are both extravagant and puzzling; they have defied understanding by scholars. As Elster (2006) notes, the final mindset, motivators, and beliefs of suicide attackers is an enigma: A true and full understanding of states of mind that are extraordinary but ephemeral may prove, in the end, to be impossible to achieve. In this chapter, I've attempted a simpler goal—to link the exceptional decisions and mindset of martyrs to common, if no less singular, traits of "warrior" temperament. There is already solid terrain to begin the search for empirical grounds of these challenging dispositions and behavioral options. I suspect there will be progress at identifying the crucial propensities that put some self-selected individuals near the point of ultimate sacrifice in war.

References

Arvey, M. D., Rotundo, M., Jonhson, W., Zhang, Z., & McGue, M. (2006). The determinants of leadership occupancy: Genetics and personality factors, *The Leadership Quarterly, 17*, 1–20.

Ashworth, S., Clinton, J. B., Meirowitz, A., & Ramsay, K. W. (2008). Design, inference and the strategic logic of suicide terrorism. *American Political Science Review, 102*(2), 1–5.

Atran, S. (2003), Genesis of suicide terrorism. *Science, 299*, 1534–1539.

Atran, S. (2006). The moral logic and growth of suicide terrorism. *The Washington Quarterly, 29*, 127–147.

Atran, S., Axelrod, R., & Davis, R. (2007). Sacred barriers to conflict resolution. *Science, 317*, 1039–1040.

Azam, J. P. (2003). Suicide-bombing as an inter-generational investment. IDEI Working Papers *234*. Toulouse: Institut d'Économie Industrielle (IDEI).

Bachner-Melman, R., Gritsenko, I., Nemanov, L., Zohar, A. H., Dina, C., & Ebstein, R. J. (2005). Dopaminergic polymorphisms associated with self-report measures of human altruism: a fresh phenotype for the dopamine D4 receptor. *Molecular Psychiatry, 10*, 333–335.

Baumgartner, T., Heinrichs, M., Volanthen, A., Fischbacher, U., & Fehr, E. (2008). Oxytocin shapes the neural circuitry of trust and trust adaptation in humans. *Neuron, 58*, 639–650.

Bernmelech, E., & Berrabi, C. (2007). Attack assignments in terror organizations and productivity of suicide bombings. *Working paper 12910*. Cambridge MA: National Bureau of Economic Research.

Bernhard, H., Fischbacher, U., & Fehr, E. (2006). Parochial altruism in humans. *Nature, 442*, 912–915.

Bohórquez, J. C., Gourley, S., Dixon, A. R., Spagat, M., & Johnson, N. F. (2009). Common ecology quantifies human insurgency. *Nature, 462*, 911–914.

Biggs, M. (2006). Dying without killing: Self-immolations, 1963–2002. In D. Gambetta (Ed.), *Making Sense of Suicide Missions* (pp.173–208). New York: Oxford University Press.

Bowles, S. (2006). Group competition, reproductive leveling and the evolution of human altruism. *Science, 314*, 1569–1572.

Bowles, S. (2009). Did warfare among ancestral hunter-gatherers affect the evolution of human social behaviors? *Science, 324*, 1293–1298.

Burnham, T. C. (2007). High-testosterone men reject low ultimatum game offers, *Proceedings of the Royal Society-B, 274*, 2327–2330.

Cesarini, D., Dawes, C. T., Fowler, J. H., Jojansson, M., Lichtenstein, P., & Wallace, B. (2008). Heritability of cooperative behaviour in the trust game. *Proceedings of the National Academy of Sciences, 105*, 10, 3721–3726.

Chiao, J., Mathur, V. A., Harada, T., & Lipke, T. (2009). Neural basis of preference for human social hierarchy versus egalitarianism. In S. Atran, A. Navarro, K. Ochsner, A. Tobeña, & O. Vilarroya (Eds.), Values, empathy and fairness across social barriers. *Annals New York Academy of Sciences, 1167* 174–181.

Choi, J. K., & Bowles, S. (2007). The coevolution of parochial altruism and war. *Science, 318*, 636–640.

Clutton-Brock, T. (2009). Cooperation between non-kin in animal societies. *Nature, 462*, 51–57.

Crockett, M. J., Clark, L., Tabibnia, G., Lieberman, M. D., & Robbins, T. W. (2008). Serotonin modulates behavioural reactions to unfairness. *Science, 320*, 1739.

De Quervain, D. J. F., Fischbacher, U., Treyer, U., Schellhammer, M., Schnyder, U., Buck, A., & Fehr, E. (2004). The neural basis of altruistic punishment. *Science, 305*, 1254–1258.

Derin-Gure, P. (2009). *Does terrorism have economic roots?* Boston, MA: Boston University (working papers).

Donaldson, Z. R., & Young, L. J. (2008). Oxytocin, vasopressin and neurogenetics of sociality. *Science, 322*, 900–904.

Duckitt, J. (2007). Differential effects of right wing authoritarianism and social dominance orientation on outgroup attitudes and their mediation by threat from and competitiveness to outgroups. *Personality and Social Psychology Bulletin, 32*, 5, 684–696.

Durkheim, E. (1970). *Suicide: A study in sociology.* London: Routledge and Kegan Paul. (Original published in 1897).

Ebstein, R. P., Israel, S., Lerer, E., Uzefovsky, F., Shalev, I., Gritsenko, I., et al. (2009). Arginin vasopressin and oxytocin modulate human social behavior. In S. Atran, A. Navarro, K. Ochsner, A. Tobeña, & O. Vilarroya (Eds.), Values, empathy and fairness across social barriers. *Annals New York Academy of Sciences, 1167*, 87–102.

Ebstein R.P.; Israel S.; Chew S.H.; Zhang S, & Knafo, A. (2010) Genetics of human social behavior, *Neuron, 65*, 831–844.

Efferson, C., Lalive, R., & Fehr, E. (2008). The coevolution of cultural groups and ingroup favoritism. *Science, 321*, 1844–1849.

Elster, J. (2006). Motivations and beliefs in suicide missions. In D. Gambetta (Ed.), *Making sense of suicide missions* (pp. 231–258). New York: Oxford University Press.

Emanuele, E., Brondino, N., Bertona, M., Re, S., & Geroldi, D. (2008). Relationships between serotonin content in platelets and rejections of unfair offers in the ultimatum game. *Neuroscience Letters, 437*, 158–161.

Fehr, E., & Camerer, C. F. (2007). Social neuroeconomics: The neural circuitry of social preferences. *Trends in Cognitive Sciences, 11*(10), 419–427.

Fehr, E., & Fischbacher, U. (2003). The nature of human altruism. *Nature, 425*, 785–791.

Fowler, J. H., Baker, L. A., & Dawes, C. T. (2008). Genetic variation in political participation. *American Political Science Review, 102*(2), 233–248.

Gambetta, D. (Ed.). (2006). *Making sense of suicide missions.* New York: Oxford University Press.

Ginges, J., & Atran, S. (2009). What motivates participation in violent political actions: Selective incentives or parochial altruism? In S. Atran, A. Navarro, K. Ochsner, A. Tobeña, & Vilarroya, O. (Eds.), Values, empathy and fairness across social barriers. *Annals New York Academy of Science, 1167*, 115–123.

Ginges, J., Hansen, I., & Norenzayan, A. (2009). Religion and support for suicide attacks, *Psychological Science, 20*(2), 224–230.

Hammond, R. A., & Axelrod, R. (2006). The evolution of ethnocentrism. *Journal of Conflict Resolution, 50*(6), 926–936.

Harris, L. T., & Fiske, S. T. (2006). Dehumanizing the lowest of the low: Neuroimaging responses to extreme outgroups. *Psychological Science, 17*(10), 847–853.

Hassin, R., Ferguson, M. J., Shidlovski, D., & Gross, T. (2007). Subliminal exposure to national flags affects political thought and behavior. *Proceedings of the National Academy of Sciences, 104*(50), 19757–19761.

Hassin, R., Fergusson, M. J., Kardosh, R., Porter, S. C., Carter, T. J., & Dudareva, V. (2009). Precis of implicit nationalism. In S. Atran, A. Navarro, K. Ochsner, A. Tobeña, & O. Vilarroya (Eds.), Values, Empathy and Fairness across Social Barriers. *Annals New York Academy of Sciences, 1167*, 135–145.

Henrich, J., McElreath, M., Barr, A., Ensminger, J., Barrett, C., Bolyniatz, A., et al. (2006). Costly punishment across human societies. *Science, 312*, 1767–1770.

Holmes, S. (2006). Al-Qaeda, September 11, 2001. In D. Gambetta (Ed.), *Making Sense of Suicide Missions* (pp. 131–172). New York: Oxford University Press.

King, A. J., Johnson, D. D. P., & Van Vugt, M. (2009). The origins and evolution of leadership. *Current Biology, 19*(19), R911–R913.

Knafo, A., Israel, S., Darvasi, A., Bachner-Melman, R., Uzefowski, F., Cohen, L., et al. (2008). Individual differences in allocation of funds in the dictator game associated with length of arginin vasopressin 1a receptor RS3 promoter region and correlation of RS3 and hippocampal mRNA. *Genes, Brain and Behavior, 7*(3), 266–275.

Koenig, L. B., McGue, M., Krueger, R. F., & Bouchard, T. J. (2007). Religiousness, antisocial behavior and altruism; genetic and environmental mediation. *Journal of Personality, 75*(2), 265–290.

Kosfeld, M., Heinrichs, M., Zak, P. J., Fischbacher, U., & Fehr, E. (2005). Oxytocin increases trust in humans. *Nature, 435*, 673–676.

Krueger, A. B., & Malecková, J. (2003). Education, poverty, political violence and terrorism: Is there a causal connection? *Journal of Economic Perspectives, 17*(4), 119–144.

Krueger, A. B., & Malecková, J. (2009). Attitudes and action: Public opinions and international terrorism. *Science, 325*, 1534–1536.

Krueger, R. F., Hicks, B. M., & McGue, M. (2001). Altruism and antisocial behavior: Independent tendencies, unique personality correlates, distinct etiologies. *Psychological Science, 12*, 397–402.

Lehmann, L., Rousset, F., Roze, D., & Keller, L. (2007). Strong reciprocity or strong ferocity? A population genetic view of the evolution of altruistic punishment. *The American Naturalist, 170*(1), 21–36.

Lewis GJ and Bates TC (2010) Genetic evidence for multiple biological mechanisms underlying in-group favoritism, *Psychological Science*, 21 (11), 1623–1628.

Lotze, M., Veit, R., Anders, S., & Birbaumer, N. (2007). Evidence for a different role of the ventral and dorsal medial prefrontal cortex for social reactive aggression: An interactive fMRI study. *Neuroimage, 34*, 470–477.

Merari, A., Diamant, I., Bibi,A, Broshi. Y., & Zakin, G. (2010) Personality characteristics of "selfmartyrs/suicide bombers" and organizers of suicide attacks, *Terrorism and Political Violence*, 22, 87–101.

Nowak, M. (2006). Five rules for evolution of cooperation. *Science, 314*, 1560–1563.

Nowak, M. (2008). Generosity: A winner's advice. *Nature, 456*(7222), 579.

Olsson, A., Ebert, J. P., Banaji, M. R., & Phelps, E. A. (2005). The role of social groups in the persistence of learned fear. *Science, 309*, 785–787.

Oxley, D. R., Smith, K. B., Alford, J. R., Hibbing, M. V., Miller, J. L., Scalora, M., et al. (2008). Political attitudes vary with physiological traits. *Science, 321*, 1667–1670.

Pape, R. (2003). The strategic logic of suicide terrorism. *American Political Science Reviews, 97*, 343–361.

Pape, R. (2005). *Dying to win: The strategic logic of suicide terrorism.* New York: Random House.

Pedazhur, A., Perliger, A., & Weinberg, L. (2003). Altruism and fatalism: The characteristics of Palestinian suicide terrorists. *Deviant Behavior: An Interdisciplinary Journal, 24*, 405–423.

Ricolfi, L. (2006). Palestinians, 1981–2003. In D. Gambetta (Ed.), *Making Sense of Suicide Missions* (pp. 77–129). New York: Oxford University Press.

Rodrigues, S. M., Saslow, L. R., Garcia, N., John, O. P., & Keltner, D. (2009). Oxytocin receptor variation relates to empathy and stress reactivity in humans. *Proceedings of the National Academy of Sciences.* /106, /50, 21437-21441//

Rodriguez, J. A. (2004). La red terrorista del 11-M. *Revista Española de Investigaciones Sociológicas, 107*, 155–179.

Rohde, D. (2009, October 19). Held by the Taliban. Part Three. 'You have atomic bombs, but we have suicide bombers'. *New York Times.* Retrieved from http://www.nytimes.com/2009/10/20/world/asia/20hostage.html

Rushton, J. P., Fulker, D. W., Neale, M. C., Nias, D. K., & Eysenck, H. J. (1986). Altruism and aggression: The heritability of individual differences. *Journal of Personality and Social Psychology, 50*(6), 1192–1198.

Sageman, M. (2004). *Understanding terror networks.* Philadelphia: University of Pennsylvania Press.

Sanfey, A. G., Rilling, J. K., Aronson, J. A., Nystrom, L. E., & Cohen, J. D. (2003). The neural basis of economic decision-making in the ultimatum game. *Science, 300*, 1755–1758.

Settle, J. E., Dawes, C. T., & Fowles, J. H. (2009). The heritability of partisan attachment. *Political Research Quarterly, 63*(3), 601–613.

Singer, T., Seymour, B., O'Doherty, J. P., Stephan, K. E., Dolan, R. J., & Frith.Ch. D. (2006). Empathic neural responses are modulated by the perceived fairness of others. *Nature, 439*, 466–469.

Spitzer, M., Fischbacher, U., Herrnberger, B., Grön, G., & Fehr, E. (2007). The neural signature of social norm compliance. *Neuron, 56*, 185–196.

Swan W.B.; Gómez, A.; Dovidio, J.F.; Hart, S. & Jetten, J. (2010) Dying and killing for one's group: identity fusion moderates responses to intergroup versions of the trolley problem, *Psychological Science, 21*(8), 1176–1183.

Tobeña, A. (2004). Individual factors in suicide attacks. *Science, 304*(5667), 47.

Tobeña, A. (2004a). *Mártires mortíferos: Biologia del altruismo letal.* Valencia (Spain): PUV-Bromera Ed.

Tobeña, A. (2007). Benumbing and moral exaltation in deadly martyrs: A view from neuroscience. In O. Vilarroya, & F. Forn-Argimon (Eds.), *Social brain matters: Stances on the neurobiology of social cognition* (pp. 83–99). New York: Rodopi.

Tobeña, A. (2009). Lethal altruists: Itineraries along the dark outskirts of moralistic prosociality. In S. Atran, A. Navarro, K. Ochsner, A. Tobeña, & O. Vilarroya (Eds.), Values, empathy and fairness across social barriers. *Annals New York Academy of Sciences, 1167*, 5–15.

Tobeña, A., Marks, I. M., & Dar, R. (1999). Advantages of bias and prejudice: An exploration of their neurocognitive templates. *Neuroscience and Biobehavioral Reviews, 23*, 1047–1058.

Van Vugt, M., Hogan, R., & Kaiser, R. B. (2008). Leadership, followership and evolution: Some lessons from the past. *American Psychologist, 63*(3), 182–196.

Van Vugt, M. (2009). Sex differences in intergroup competition, aggression and warfare: The male warrior hypothesis. In S. Atran, A. Navarro, K. Ochsner, A. Tobeña, & O. Vilarroya (Eds.), Values, Empathy and Fairness across Social Barriers. *Annals New York Academy of Sciences, 1167*, 124–134.

Victoroff, J. (2005). In the mind of a terrorist: A review and critique of psychological approaches. *Journal of Conflict Resolution, 49*(1), 3–42.

Victoroff, J., Qouta, S., Celinska, B., Abu-Safieh, R., Adelman, J., & Stern, N. (2006). Sympathy for terrorism: Possible interactions between social, emotional and neuroendocrine factors. In J. Victoroff (Ed.), *Tangled roots: Social and emotional factors in the genesis of terrorism* (pp. 227–234). Amsterdam: IOS Press.

Wallace, B., Cesarini, D., Lichtenstein, P., & Johansson, M. (2006). Heritability of ultimatum game responder behavior. *Proceedings of the National Academy of Sciences, 104*, 15631–15634.

Wilson, D. S., Near, D., & Miller, R. R. (1996). Machiavellianism: A synthesis of the evolutionary and psychological literature. *Psychological Bulletin, 119*(2), 285–299.

Wiltermuth, S. S., & Heath, C. (2009). Synchrony and cooperation. *Psychological Science, 20*(1), 1–5.

Wrangham, R., & Peterson, D. (1997). *Demonic males: Apes and the origins of human violence*. New York: Houghton Mifflin.

Wrangham, R. W., & Wilson, M. L. (2004). Collective violence: Comparisons between youths and chimpanzees. In J. Devine, J. Gilligen, K. A. Miczek, R. Shaikh, & D. Pfaff (Eds.). Youth Violence: Scientific Approaches to Prevention. *Annals of the New York Academy of Science, 1036*, 233–256.

Wrangham, R. W., Wilson, M. L., & Muller, N. M. (2006). Comparative rates of violence in chimpanzees and humans. *Primates, 47*, 14–26.

Zak, P. J., Stanton, A., & Ahmadi, S. (2007). Oxytocin increases generosity in humans. *PloS ONE, 2*, e1128.

Zink, C. F., Tong, Y., Chen, Q., Bassett, D. S., Stein, J. L., & Meyer-Lindenberg, A. (2008). Know your place: Neural processing of social hierarchy in humans. *Neuron, 58*, 273–283.

CHAPTER 16

GENOCIDE

From Pathological Altruism to Pathological Obedience

Augustine Brannigan

KEY CONCEPTS

- Low self-control, which is a major covariate of criminal behavior, appears early in life and is relatively stable over the life course.
- Levels of self-control may vary across historical periods as people become more sensitive to socially intrusive behavior.
- The perplexing levels of obedience in major genocides do not reflect deficiencies in self-control but suggest the oversocialization of the internal executive function by external social hierarchies.

THIS CHAPTER PROPOSES an explanation of genocide based on a pair of pathologies: pathological altruism and pathological obedience. Pathological altruism is reflected in the pursuit of mass murder to further the aspirations of political elites. In the 1994 Rwandan case, the senior Hutu politicians and generals planned the total physical destruction of the Tutsi minority, ostensively to protect the beleaguered Hutus from the feudal repression of the traditional Tutsi chiefs (Dallaire 2003; Melvern 2006). The "liberation of the oppressed masses" resulted in the murder of approximately 500,000 to 1 million Rwandans (Brannigan & Jones 2009). However, the pathological altruism would not have been possible without the ready cooperation of the rank and file of the civil service and the political followers who implemented the genocidal policies. I call this pathological obedience. Without such complicity, the policies would fail. On the issue of elite motivation, Barbara Oakley (2008) has advocated a neuroscientific and genetically based model to explain the motives of lethal leaders such as Hitler, Milosevic, and Stalin, who are described as high-functioning manipulative individuals with subclinical symptoms of borderline and antisocial personality disorders.

This chapter complements Oakley's analysis by focusing on the mass mobilization and ready cooperation of people who are obviously not psychopathic but who participate in mass murder nonetheless. In their studies of German police battalions, Browning (1992) referred to the perpetrators as "ordinary men," whereas Goldhagen (1996) called them "ordinary Germans." Both pointed to the mobilization of rank-and-file masses in the Nazi scheme to decimate the European Jews. Where Goldhagen emphasized extreme "eliminationist anti-Semitism" in the minds of the perpetrators, Browning offered a more nuanced account based of the variability of motives among the perpetrators (also see Pendas, 2006, p. 295).

This compliance was explained by Stanley Milgram in a disturbing series of experiments analyzing the obedience of ordinary subjects to an authority figure. Milgram argued that individuals who joined a bureaucracy under the supervision of an authority figure entered an "agentic state" in which they automatically surrendered their autonomy and individual responsibility. Milgram (1974, p. 133) speculated that this "alteration of attitude" from self-directed autonomy to a form of automatism had a biological foundation: "there is certainly an alteration in the internal operations of the person, and these, no doubt, reduce to shifts in patterns of neural functioning." At the time when he wrote, tools did not exist to explore such processes. Our contemporary understanding of the development of neural executive functions makes it unlikely that such a radical loss of autonomy or self-control is based primarily on situational pressures. Nonetheless, the problem of the agentic state remains.

My proposal is based on one of the most important perspectives in contemporary criminology—*control theory* (Gottfredson & Hirschi, 1990). Control theory argues that crime is suppressed by teaching children self-control, and that in the absence of effective socialization, children will be more likely to resort to the use of aggression and fraud in the pursuit of self-interest as they grow older. Evidence suggests that differences in self-control are inculcated early in life, persist over the life-course and, once established, are stable and highly resistant to further change (Moffitt, 1993). Persons who do *not* acquire self-control early in life are unlikely to acquire it as adults. The criminological literature makes a bolder claim regarding self-control that is outlined in the work of Norbert Elias (1996). Elias argues that societies differ in the extent to which they inculcate self-control, and that such differences shed light on the mobilization problem at the heart of the scope, speed, and effectiveness of genocide.

> Societies differ in the extent to which they inculcate self-control—such differences shed light on the mobilization problem at the heart of the scope, speed and effectiveness of genocide.

In this chapter, I proceed as follows. First, I describe Elias's theory of the civilizing process and its relationship to changing levels of self-control in European societies. Second, I summarize his later analysis of the rise of the Nazis and the roots of "barbarism" in German national development that represents, for Elias, a reversal of the civilizing process. Third, I apply the model to the 1994 Rwandan case. Fourth, I examine the significance of the concept of *habitus*, which permits us to understand how levels of self-control could change across history while being relatively stable over the life cycle. Finally, I propose that Milgram's agentic state be reexamined, not as a universal psychological condition, but as a specific historical development that sheds light on pathological obedience.

Elias on Civilization and Changes in Levels of Self-control

At the individual level, Elias argues that, over the last seven or eight centuries, Europeans became increasingly governed by *impulse control*. As the social structures changed, Europeans became more prone to feelings of delicacy, sensitivity, and courtesy—reflecting the cultural impact on the brain's executive function and attentional mechanisms (Han & Northoff 2007). At the collective level, Elias tracks changes in the rise and evolution of societies from feudalism to the Renaissance and modern sovereign states. The power struggles over this period resulted in the monopolization of the right to use force by the absolute monarch. The absorption of the warrior classes during feudalism into the courts of the major feudal lords was associated with a "pacification" of emotional life. Force was increasingly replaced by diplomacy; sexual frankness by romantic love; and lust, pillage, and mayhem by the cultivation of taste, music, and poetry. Likewise, the initial conflicts between knights, the town bourgeoisie, and the emerging monarchs were superseded by deeper forms of social integration that were achieved by the adoption of courtly, that is, *courteous* behavior. Economic and political cooperation was intensified by the money economy. This increasing interdependency created an imperative to transfer impulse control from courtly society increasingly down to the masses of the population. This took centuries.

What, then, is the importance of Elias's theory of self-control? What we treat today as a normal level of self-control is a socially inculcated habit that has evolved gradually and almost imperceptibly over time. As Garland (1990, p. 222) observes, "the civilizing process produces individuals of heightened sensibilities whose psychological structures are heavily loaded with restraints, self-controls and inhibitions"—the same factors that are thought to be critical in crime prevention in children today. For Elias, the course and direction of conduct toward civilization was not inexorable and could be subject to reversals. In his second major work, *The Germans* (1996), Elias examined how the Holocaust could have occurred in one of the most cultured nations of Europe.

> What we treat today as a normal level of self-control is a socially inculcated habit that has evolved gradually and almost imperceptibly over time.

Barbarism and *The Germans*

Elias argues that every modern European nation's history becomes incorporated to some degree in the emotional life of its citizens as they are weaned on memories of their collective victories and defeats. Kuperman (2001) argues similarly that tribal identities and their histories are more salient than national identities in modern African countries, presumably because they have no collective memories of acting as nations. Both suggest that history becomes embedded in personality. The Germans were initially united in the first *reich* after the establishment of the Holy Roman Empire. However, unlike French and English societies, the unification of the German-speaking peoples was delayed until late in the 19th century. In addition, the unification was erected on a tradition of Prussian militarism marked by antagonism to democratic institutions and values. The German's first national achievement in modern times *as Germans* was the conquest of France in 1871. Elias described the victory of the German armies over France as "at the same time a victory of the German nobility over the German middle class" (1996, p. 145). By this, he meant the political development of 19th-century Germany was largely conservative or reactionary. Prussian military traditions were idealized, and not only among the middle classes. The university student societies cultivated dueling, and facial scars from such honor contests were worn with pride. Max Weber noted (1968, p. 211): "It is well known that the student fraternities constitute the typical social education of aspirants for nonmilitary offices, sinecures, and the liberal professions of high social standing. The 'academic freedom' of dueling, drinking, and class cutting stems from a time when other kinds of freedoms did not exist in Germany."

After the Great War, the Allies enforced a humiliating peace treaty on the Germans. Many were traumatized. The democratic government created in the post-war Weimar republic was openly opposed by the *freikorps*, who assassinated liberal politicians by the hundreds and undermined the democratization of the republic (Brenner, 2001, p. 72). Hitler's promise of a "third reich" based on racial purity replaced the unifying attraction of the German aristocracy. Having a strong man in charge reverberated well with a tradition in which militaristic ideals dominated the emerging middle class. Making the Germans masters of all of Europe was a political fantasy that appealed to a people whose historical prestige was a distant memory.

What was the average German's emotional outlook after the defeat? Political autonomy and individual self-control were eschewed in favor of external or social control. Elias argues that: "Many Germans cheerfully shed the burden of having to control themselves and shoulder the responsibility for their own lives" (1996, p. 383). State control inhibited the full development of self-control (p. 384). In the Nazi state, there was little overt opposition to racial politics since the "self-control of the mass of the German people in all matters of public concern, remained highly dependent on the state" (p. 386). "The Germans never ceased to obey" (p. 387). The Fuhrer became like a shaman who took the burden of failure off the shoulders of the German masses and promised them historical fulfillment. Where England and France increasingly had made heightened levels of self-control a prerogative of the individual, in Elias's view, German development placed autonomy in the hands of elites.

This explains the paradox of Browning's findings in *Ordinary Men*. Compliance in mass murder did not require that the perpetrators of mass murder be ideological extremists. The perpetrators of genocide were more likely to comply with orders to kill because of their sense of obligation to their immediate comrades and superiors, because they did not want to appear as weak and effeminate, and because killing was a duty required to protect the Reich from its enemies. This is consistent with the impoverished sense of autonomy that was created over decades by German political institutions, and which was reinforced by the Nazi dictatorship. It did not matter that the Order police who carried out the final solution in Poland came to political maturity *before* the Nazis; they had the same mentality as the young men who joined the student fraternities before the Great War and the soldiers who formed the *freikorps* after it. As Browning (1998 Afterword) notes, being anti-Semitic was equivalent to being antidemocratic, antimodern, and anticosmopolitan. A specific animosity against the Jews was not required. Nor was it necessary to secure obedience through fear of retribution. If Elias is correct, history had created a mentality that valorized militarism and state violence. Can Elias's model of collective social control apply elsewhere?

We explore evidence from Rwanda based, in part, on the author's fieldwork in 2004–2005.

Rwanda: Historical Continuities in Social Dependency

René Lemarchand (1994) noted the highly obedient nature of Hutus during the 1972 genocide in Burundi. Well-educated Hutus were summoned to Tutsi police stations for questioning. Despite the fact that these Hutus were known to go missing, others continued to comply with orders to appear. In this fashion, some 200,000 Hutus were murdered by Tutsi police and army units. Is this simple obedience of the Milgram variety? My view is that Milgram's "agentic state" had historical origins both in Germany and Rwanda.

> The perpetrators of genocide were more likely to comply with orders to kill because of their sense of obligation to their immediate comrades and superiors, because they did not want to appear as weak and effeminate, and because killing was a duty required to protect the Reich from its enemies.

There had been a history of obligatory relationships in the Rwandan kingdom linking Hutu peasants and Tutsi rulers prior to colonial contact that may help explain this level of compliance. Tutsi aristocrats would extend largesse in the form of cattle to Hutu farmers in exchange for their loyalty. These client–sponsor relationships took many forms of exchange and were aptly characterized in the title of Newbury's (1988) history of the period, *The Cohesion of Oppression*. Newbury described a tightly knit set of hierarchical interrelationships based on mutual gifts and service that had the effect of oppressing the bottom rung of those who entered into them. The Belgium colonial powers used these client relationships under colonial rule to administer the colony. Tutsi power over the Hutu would be exploited to promote Hutu participation in unpaid or *corvée* labor. The 1920s and 1930s were "the time of whips" (Jefremovas, 2002, p. 68), when exploitation of the Hutu intensified, and when the boundaries between Tutsis and Hutus were defined immutably by the identity cards that fixed everyone's lineage. With the transfer of colonial rule to the postcolonial republic, the Tutsi chiefs were routed. They were replaced by a tight hierarchy of Hutu chiefs and administrators. The obedience noted by Lemarchand earlier had a long institutional history. The patron–client dependency had become a feature of tribal identity extending back into the 19th century (Table 16.1).

The administrative system was further refined by President Habyarimana in the second republic (1973–1994). The political consequences of the hierarchical system were profound. Under the presidency, the country was divided into ten provinces administered by préfects or governors appointed by the president. The provinces were subdivided into sous-préfectures, each combining four or five communes and run by sous-préfects. These were divided into communes (counties) each run by a mayor or burgomaster. (Twagilimana, 2003, p. 161). The counties were divided into sectors governed by an elected councilor. Below the sector was the "cell" or hamlet governed by a group of five residents, one of whom was designated the head or the "responsible" who reported to the sector council. As a result, there was a tight vertical integration of power from the president to the individual hamlets. Every political position represented the president. According to Mamdani (2001, p. 144) "the prefect was like the colonial chief: he decided how many acres of coffee should be cultivated in each commune. . . . He alone was responsible for public order and tranquility." The burgomasters were like colonial subchiefs demanding "gifts in return for administrative

TABLE 16.1   A SELECTIVE CHRONOLOGY OF RWANDA

Date	Condition
Second half of the 1800s	Emergence of a unified state under Tutsi feudal control over Hutu and Twa populations
1899	German colonial presence is established; replaced by Belgium in 1916.
1924–1935	Belgium administrative reforms reduce traditional Hutu obligations of service and gifts to Tutsi chiefs and replaces these with a head-tax and obligations of service to the colonial authorities represented by the traditional chiefs.
1927 onwards	Government introduces widespread planting of coffee trees to create an export crop. These are later supplemented by widespread cultivation of tea and sisal. Plantation, road construction, and irrigation control requires mandatory service from Hutus.
1935	Registration of population by lineage crystallizes the caste division of Rwandan society. Hutu social advancement is effectively blocked.
1957	The *Hutu Manifesto* challenges the social, economic, and political monopoly of the minority Tutsi.
1959	Open rebellion of Hutu against the Tutsi chiefs. Thousands of Tutsi huts are burned and tens of thousands flee the country. A state of emergency is declared.
1960	Twenty-two thousand Tutsis are displaced by conflict and exiled. The Tutsi king is deposed, and the nation becomes a republic.
1961	Provisional government of Hutus established without any representation of minority Tutsis.
1962	Exiled Tutsis strike back across borders from Burundi and Uganda. Two thousand Tutsis are massacred in retaliation.
1963	Up to 20,000 Tutsis are massacred in retaliation for further cross-border raids.
1972	Up to 200,000 Hutus are massacred in neighboring Burundi by Tutsi police and security forces.
1973	New massacres of Tutsis. A *coup d'état* by Juvenal Habyarimana replaces the first Hutu dictator, Grégoire Kayibanda.
1990	Tutsi led-RPF invades Rwanda from Uganda. Four hundred Tutsis massacred in retaliation in Kibilira; 10,000 suspects arrested nation-wide.
1991	Between January and March, up to 1,000 Bagogwe Tutsi are massacred in northern Rwanda.
1992	In March hundreds (if not thousands) of Tutsis are massacred at Bugesera by mobs and policemen. In August, several hundred Tutsis were massacred in Kibuye.
1993	In February, several hundred Tutsis were massacred in Gisenyi.
1994	Beginning in April, an estimated 800,000 were massacred across Rwanda.
1994	In July, the RPF defeated the national army. This resulted in an exodus of some 2 million Hutus into Zaire, Burundi, Uganda, and Tanzania.
1996–2002	Incursions by the RPF into Zaire/Congo resulted in several million further deaths, primarily of Hutus.

Based on Dorsey, Learthen (1994). *Historical dictionary of Rwanda*, Lantham MD: Scarecrow Press; and Twagilimana, A. (2007). *A historical dictionary of Rwanda*, Lanham MD: Scarecrow Press.

services, from settling a case to penning a signature" (Mamdani, 2001). Anyone living on one of the traditional hills required the mayor's permission to apply for a job or school outside the commune (Twagilimana, 2003, p. 162). The burgomaster was a gatekeeper for individual advancement through education and employment. As a result of the administrative structure, dependency was the paramount feature of Rwandan society. Rwandan society was totalitarian, but obedience was not enforced by terrorism or fear of reprisal, but by the ingrained supervisory hierarchy (Figure 16.1).

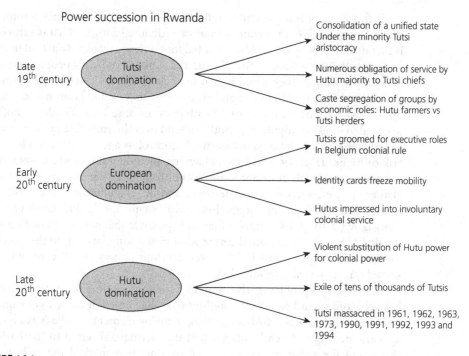

Power succession in Rwanda

Late 19th century — Tutsi domination
- Consolidation of a unified state Under the minority Tutsi aristocracy
- Numerous obligation of service by Hutu majority to Tutsi chiefs
- Caste segregation of groups by economic roles: Hutu farmers vs Tutsi herders

Early 20th century — European domination
- Tutsis groomed for executive roles In Belgium colonial rule
- Identity cards freeze mobility
- Hutus impressed into involuntary colonial service

Late 20th century — Hutu domination
- Violent substitution of Hutu power for colonial power
- Exile of tens of thousands of Tutsis
- Tutsi massacred in 1961, 1962, 1963, 1973, 1990, 1991, 1992, 1993 and 1994

FIGURE 16.1
Three major periods characterize Rwandan political control: those in which the Tutsis, Europeans, and finally, the Hutus, were dominant.

The consequences of this were startling in terms of the population's mobilization. Given the tight vertical administration of the population, it was virtually unthinkable for individuals to refuse the demands from commune and hamlet politicians to pick up machetes and to "uproot the cockroaches." The perpetrators were told where to assemble in the mornings and where to undertake searches of the marshes and mountains for fleeing Tutsis. At the end of the day, they were summoned back from the killing with whistles by officials who were ever-present to organize the slaughter (Hatzfeld, 2005). Most accounts report that the period of killing lasted 3 months and ended with the occupation of Kigali, the capital city, by the Rwanda Patriotic Front under the command of General Kagame. However, evidence suggests that in most places the killing was completed much more quickly. Ibuka (1991), the national survivor's association, reports that 80% of those murdered were actually dispatched *within 2 weeks* of the destruction of Habyarimana's plane on April 6. Most people were already dead before the United Nations passed its first resolution to deal with the situation on April 21. For the events to have proceeded so quickly, the level of popular participation in the killings was necessarily massive. Rwanda had become an "agentic state."

Reports of the *gacaca* courts designed to try perpetrators in their own communities suggest that, by 2008, over 1,000,000 prosecutions had been initiated (Musoni, 2009). This also gives some indication of the extent of the mobilization. When the Hutus were told to join the exodus with the Hutu government and armed forces into Zaire, they obeyed and departed *in their millions*—setting the stage for a much larger genocide against Hutus by the Tutsi and Congo armies between 1996 and 2002 (Lemarchand, 2009, p. 69ff).

At this point, it is important to reflect on the nature of the crimes committed during the genocide, and crimes of a more individual nature. What is surprising is that ordinary people could be recruited for enormously bloody acts of murder and rape, that they were recruited from the ranks of ordinary people, and that, generally speaking, they could return to society, like the German perpetrators after World War II, without apprehension that they would continue to offend. These observations are inconsistent with patterns of serious offenders who, due to elevated levels of impulsivity, tend to offend over the entire life cycle. Evidence suggests that people who do not learn self-control by age 8 or 10 have a life-long risk of higher levels of impulsive behaviour, including misconduct. These patterns are notoriously resistant to interventions later in life that are designed to change such preferences (i.e., deterrence and/or rehabilitation). The reason for this is that child–parent interactions help "shape the brain." Goldberg and Bougakov (2010, p. 408) suggest that "it is possible that social stimulation is to the development of the frontal cortex what visual stimulation is to the development of the occipital cortex." Whatever develops by way of self-control is preserved due to neural myelinization.

There are two problems. The main explanation of crime in control theory— low self-control and *persistent impulsiveness*—has little relevance to our understanding of genocidal obedience. Also, a major element of Elias's later work appears incorrect. When he alleges that the Germans reverted to "barbarism," this is not the spontaneous, emotional conduct that marked the early feudal period, nor is it the infantilism of an unsocialized child. It is my hypothesis that the ease with which the Rwandans and the Germans entered the agentic state suggests, not a failure of socialization (the usual control approach) but that they are/were *over*socialized. Pathological obedience appears to be based on the development of a mentality that reflects long-term patterns of affiliation that inculcate a suppression of self-control in which the executive function cedes its autonomy to external sources of direction.

> Pathological obedience appears to be based on the development of a mentality that reflects long-term patterns of affiliation that inculcate a suppression of self-control in which the executive function cedes its autonomy to external sources of direction.

I suspect this is a cultural achievement, but it likely has neurological implications since the brutality entailed by genocidal behavior does not appear to arouse the same levels of anxiety that would attend violence that is personally initiated. The peculiarity of the emotional state of the *génocidaires* in Rwandan prisons was their general lack of contrition, remorse, or guilt. Pendas noted the same reaction among the Auschwitz guards during their trials. Milgram seems to be thinking of this when he noted that "for a man to feel responsible for his actions, he must sense that the behavior has flowed from 'the self'. . . subjects have precisely the opposite views of their actions" (1973, p. 146). They murder out of loyalty and duty. In this view, the agentic state is not a failure of socialization or a reversion to barbarity but an oversocialization in which the actor cedes self-control and the executive function to a "superego."

Habitus: Changing Second Nature

The term *habitus* is used by social theorists to connote regularities in social habits that "go without saying," or (in Elias's use of the term), which form a group's "second nature." These patterns of behavior typically present without reflection and appear natural, but can change dramatically over time—such as the level of impulse control required by society. Such control of behavior operates below the level of consciousness. The medieval period that Elias describes was marked by a spontaneity that would become inappropriate in bourgeois or town society.

Elias's observations are reminiscent of Daly and Wilson's (1988, p. 123ff) descriptions of "trivial altercations" among unmarried, unemployed young males—the leading cause of male-on-male homicide in contemporary society. Persons known to one another exchange verbal insults, a fight ensues, a weapon appears, and someone is killed. Often, the deaths are victim-precipitated. The outcomes are unpredictable, and the conflicts are typically unplanned. This form of emotional spontaneity was legion in the English feudal towns in the 13th and 14th centuries and resulted in levels of homicide many times higher than those found today. The evidence for this was meticulously catalogued by Ted Gurr (1981), who based his findings on about 30 historical estimates of homicide recorded in court records and coroner reports in various cities, towns, and counties in England over the period 1200–1900. Manuel Eisner (2003, p. 95ff) updated Gurr's database with 390 estimates of homicide from Europe over the same period. Consistent with Elias's analysis of self-control, patterns of homicide declined dramatically from about 20 homicides per 100,000 population in the 13th century to about 2 per 100,000 by 1800.

It seems reasonable to infer that the evidence of stability in low self-control offenders, and the versatility of that misconduct, implies, as noted earlier, some nontransitory change in the prefrontal cortex that "fixes" the level of self-control. This mechanism appears to be one of inhibition since low self-control or impulsiveness and spontaneity are the consequences that arise from a failure to inculcate habits of self-restraint (Gottfredson & Hirschi, 1990, pp. 94–97). Self-control inhibits the spontaneity of hedonism and cultivates "executive control" that permits the person to anticipate the future, respond to changes in the environment, and develop self-awareness (Goldberg & Bougakov, 2010, p. 404).

If neocortical development explains the stability of self-control over the life cycle, I would suggest a different process explains the changes in levels of self-control over time: *habitus*. It is not necessary to speculate on genetic changes across generations that explain changing levels of self-control. The changing mechanisms for self-control over the last seven or eight centuries *do* imply ontogenetic changes in the brain's biological structure, particularly as a result of the process of the child's mimicry and identification with parents. The preference for self-restraint, or for changes in how restraint is manifested, could reproduce itself as a *meme* (Dawkins, 1976) and would survive across successive generations due to the *short-term* social advantages it conferred. Memes associated with self-control are precarious because they do not have a genotypic continuity across successive generations.

The spread of a meme related to changes in self-restraint obviously depends on a number of factors, including the development and teaching of beliefs and practices designed to inculcate habits of self-regulation. Wilson (1985, pp. 229–233) argues that in early 19th-century North America, the migrant European society invested in social institutions designed to create "character." He refers to the Second Great Awakening, the Sunday school movement, the YMCA, and most important of all, the Temperance Movement (what Wilson refers to as "the single most important attempt to fundamentally change social behavior according to a plan"). There was a dramatic decline in per capita consumption of beverage alcohol throughout the 19th century, and a longer-term decline in homicide that reached its nadir in the United States by the middle of the 20th century. Eisner's European data show a similar trough in homicide around 1950 (Eisner, 2003, p. 88). Wilson (1985, pp. 234–240) and Eisner suggest that the long-term decline in homicide was largely a result of social investments in self-restraint.

Conclusion

This chapter proposed an explanation of genocide based on a pair of pathologies: pathological altruism and pathological obedience. Genocide may be advanced as an elite policy undertaken to defend a race or a nation (the Aryans or the Hutus) and hence advocated for altruistic reasons. I argued that, typically, such policies advance the careers and aspirations of the political elite. The paradox is that the magnitude of the crime of genocide requires significant mobilization of people who may not share the elite's political views—what I've called pathological obedience. I have explored a hypothesis for pathological obedience grounded in control theory.

My conclusions here are based on case studies of specific societies. They do not preclude the examination of self-control mechanisms that arise in other cultures that may be more (or less) stringent that the Eliasian model. Elias argued that the civilizing processes at the collective and historical level are subject to what he described as reversions to "barbarity." We rejected this model since the "reversions" have none of the spontaneity of action attributed to feudal violence, nor do they appear infantile. On the contrary, the rigid patterns of mass mobilization suggest that such persons are oversocialized.

> Societies that host genocide seem to experience overdevelopment of dependency on external, hierarchical sources of control that make significant portions of the population vulnerable to recruitment to mass murder with minimum moral reservations.

This analysis suggests that, in each case, the societies that hosted the genocide had experienced overdevelopment of dependency on external, hierarchical sources of control that made significant portions of the population vulnerable to recruitment to mass murder with minimum moral reservations. The *habitus* of Nazi Germany and the Rwandan Republic after decolonization removed the solution of intergroup conflict from the scope and capacity of individuals in favor of the political decisions of the elite. As a result, there was massive participation in genocidal murder without much evidence of individual guilt, remorse, or contrition. If anything, mass murder appears to be undertaken as a duty and carried out with righteousness, not as sullen submission to authority.

By way of illustration, Hatzfeld (2005) records the celebrations in Rwanda during the time of mass killings in which the killers spent their evenings drinking beer and dining on the goats and cows of those they had killed. In *The Good Old Days* Klee, Dressen, and Riess (1996) record the celebrations of the mass murderers in the German officers' clubs. Bruchfeld and Levine (1998, p. 3) record the last day of 20 Scandinavian children in April 1945 who had been used in medical experiments in the Neuengamme concentration camp in Hamburg. They were hanged with their French caregivers from the plumbing pipes in the cellar of their school. "When all the children were dead, schnapps and cigarettes were doled out to the SS men present. Then it was time for the next group to be hanged—this time 20 Soviet prisoners of war."

References

Brannigan, A., & Jones, N. (2009). Genocide and the legal process in Rwanda: From genocide amnesty to the new rule of law. *International Criminal Justice Review, 19*(2), 192–207.

Brenner, A. D. (2001). *Emil J. Gumbel: German pacifist and professor.* Boston: Brill Academic Publishing.

Bruchfeld, S., & Levine, P. A. (1998). *Tell Ye Your Children: A book about the Holocaust in Europe 1933–1945.* Stockholm: Swedish Ministry of Education.

Browning, C. (1992, Afterword 1998). *Ordinary men: Reserve police battalion 101 and the final solution in Poland.* New York: Harper Collins.

Dallaire, R., & Beardsley, B. (2003). *Shake hands with the devil. The failure of humanity in Rwanda.* Toronto: Random House.

Daly, M., & Wilson, M. (1988). *Homicide.* New York: Aldine de Gruyter.

Dawkins, R. (1976). *The selfish gene.* Oxford UK: Oxford University Press.

Dorsey, L. (1994). *Historical dictionary of Rwanda.* Lantham MD: Scarecrow Press.

Eisner, M. (2003). Long-term historical trends in violent crime. In M. Tonry (Ed.), *Crime and justice: Annual review of research* Vol. 30 (pp. 83–142). Chicago: University of Chicago Press.

Elias, N. (1996). *The Germans: Power struggles and the development of habitus in the nineteenth and twentieth centuries.* (E. Dunning, & S. Mennell, Trans., Eds.). New York: Columbia University Press.

Elias, N. (2000). *The civilizing process: Sociogenetic and psychogenetic investigations* (Rev. ed.). E. Dunning, & S. Mennell (Trans., Eds.). London: Wiley-Blackwell.

Garland, D. (1990). *Punishment and society: A study in social theory.* Chicago: University of Chicago Press.

Goldberg, E. M., & Bougakov, D. H. (2010). Goals, executive control, and action. In B. J. Baars, & N. M. Gage (Eds.), *Cognition, brain and consciousness* (Rev. 2nd ed., pp. 401–420). London: Academic Press.

Goldhagen, D. (1996). *Hitler's willing executioners: Ordinary Germans and the Holocaust.* New York: Knopf. (Re-published in 1997 with an afterward).

Gottfredson, M., & Hirschi, T. (1990). *A general theory of crime.* Stanford, CA: Stanford University Press.

Gurr, T. R. (1981). Historical trends in violent crime: A critical review of the evidence. In M. Tonry, & N. Morris (Eds.), *Crime and justice: An annual review of research,* Vol. 3 (pp. 295–353). Chicago: University of Chicago Press.

Han, S., & Northoff, G. (2007). Culture-sensitive neural substrates of human cognition: A transcultural neuroimaging approach. *Molecular Systems Biology, 3,* 137.

Hatzfeld, J. (2005). *Machete season.* New York: Farrar, Straus and Giroux.

Ibuka (1991). *The Kibuye dictionary project.* Kigalia, Rwanda: Ibuka Survivors.

Jefremovas, V. (2002). *Brickyards to graveyards: From production to genocide in Rwanda.* Albany, NY: State University of New York Press.

Klee, E., Dressen, W., & Riess, V. (1996). *"The good old days": The Holocaust as seen by its perpetrators and bystanders.* (D. Burnstone, Trans., Ed.). Old Say, CT: Konecky and Konecky.

Kuperman, A. J. (2001). *The limits of humanitarian intervention: Genocide in Rwanda.* Washington, DC: Brookings Institution Press.

Lemarchand, R. (1994). *Burundi: Ethnic conflict and genocide*. New York: Cambridge University Press.

Lemarchand, R. (2009). *The dynamics of violence in Central Africa*. Philadelphia: Pennsylvania University Press.

Mamdani, M. (2001). *When Victims Become Killers* Princeton NJ: Princeton University Press.

Melvern, L. (2006). *Conspiracy to murder: The Rwandan genocide* London: Verso.

Milgram, S. (1974). *Obedience to Authority: An Experimental View* New York: Harper and Row.

Moffitt, T. (1993). Adolescence-limited and life-course-persistent antisocial behavior: A developmental taxonomy. *Psychological Review, 100*, 674–701.

Musoni, E. (2009, March 12). Gacaca courts to close in June. *The New Times(Kigali)*. Retrieved from *http://allafrica.com/stories/200903130267.html*

Newbury, C. (1988). *The cohesion of oppression: Clientship and ethnicity in Rwanda 1860–1960*. New York: Columbia University Press.

Oakley, B. (2008). *Evil genes: Why Rome fell, Hitler rose, Enron failed and my sister stole my mother's boyfriend*. New York: Prometheus Books.

Pendas, D. (2006). *The Frankfurt Auschwitz trial 1963–65: Genocide, history and the limits of the law*. Cambridge UK: Cambridge University Press.

Twagilimana, A. (2003). *The debris of Ham: Ethnicity, regionalism and the 1994 Rwandan genocide*. Lanham, MD: University Press of America.

Twagilimana, A. (2007). *A historical dictionary of Rwanda*. Lanham MD: Scarecrow Press.

Weber, M. (1968). The Prussian Junkers. In S. N. Eisenstadt (Ed.), *Max Weber on charisma and institution building* (pp. 209–244). Chicago, IL: University of Chicago Press.

Wilson, J. Q. (1985). *Thinking about crime* (Rev. ed.). New York: Vintage Books.

CHAPTER 17

TOO MUCH OF A GOOD THING? FOREIGN AID AND PATHOLOGICAL ALTRUISM

Guruprasad Madhavan and Barbara Oakley

There is a proper time and proper mode in charity; just as the vigorous
warrior goes to battle so is the man who is able to give.
—From the *Sayings of Buddha* (1957)

KEY CONCEPTS

- Altruism and emotional contagion have a powerful capacity to mobilize financial and humanitarian aid to impoverished nations.
- Although external economic assistance has been helpful for many countries, a large number of altruistic, nonstrategic, foreign aid programs over the past several decades have failed—worsening the very situation they were meant to help. Many other humanitarian programs have also been ineffective at enormous cost.
- Altruistic efforts for social improvements must be guided, not purely by emotion, but with a well thought out objective strategy and endpoint.
- Neuroscience is allowing us to understand how default emotional approaches to helping others can backfire and cripple otherwise noble intentions.
- Public policies and interventions that have incorporated smart, strategic, and tempered altruism may be effective in alleviating poverty and stimulating economic development.
- There may be value in recruiting a new breed of nontraditional talent that is capable of reframing the way development assistance is carried out.

"YOU ARE OUR God," said the young orphan to Madonna. It was October 2009, and the pop queen was visiting Mchinji, Malawi, to help her charity, "Raising Malawi."

"Where could we have been without you?" the orphan continued. Madonna looked bemused—one observer noted she "seemed cool with it" (US Magazine, 2009).

Since establishing her charity in 2006, Madonna has spent millions of dollars to alleviate poverty, poor health, illiteracy, and malnourishment in Malawi. Writing in the *Huffington Post*, Madonna explained how her charity is "dedicated to ending poverty." She beseeched the world to help her "literally transform the future of an entire generation" (Madonna, 2009).

An analogous hyperaltruistic tone can be found in the concluding words of former President Bill Clinton's book *Giving: How Each of Us Can Change the World*: "So much of modern culture is characterized by stories of self-indulgence and self-destruction . . . . There's a whole world out there that needs you, down the street or across the ocean. Give" (Clinton, 2007). Through various partnerships, Mr. Clinton and his foundation are helping to channel $100 million over the next ten years toward Malawi and Rwanda's development. Financial altruism toward Africa has grown with additional funds from the Bill and Melinda Gates Foundation, which announced a $10 billion commitment at the 2010 World Economic Forum (Bill and Melinda Gates Foundation, 2010). More recently, Bill Gates and Warren Buffett have pressed their mega-rich peers to give away at least half of their total assets to charity (Guth & Banjo, 2010).

The Economist magazine's Matthew Bishop and coauthor Michael Green describe this burgeoning phenomenon of charity as "philanthrocapitalism" (Bishop & Green, 2009). The 2009 figures show that the net official development aid from the United States alone was close to $30 billion—a more than 5% increase from 2008 (Organisation for Economic Co-operation and Development [OECD], 2010). Although financial contributions from wealthy donor nations have declined slightly in the post-Lehman Brothers economy, the foreign aid industry has continued to benefit from the involvement of super-rich celebrity donors.

The Faster They Run, the Behinder They Fall

Besides the emerging industry of philanthrocapitalism, foreign aid has been delivered via several means: through government-to-government transfers or via intergovernmental organizations (for example, the World Bank, the International Monetary Fund) or other cumbersome public–private partnerships. In more recent years, the United Nations' Millennium Development Goals (MDG) have brought public attention to the role and effectiveness of foreign aid in development. An international set of commitments agreed upon by all countries, the eight MDGs consisted of eradicating extreme poverty and hunger; achieving universal primary education; promoting gender equality and empowering women; reducing child mortality; improving maternal health; combating HIV/AIDS, malaria, and other diseases; ensuring environmental sustainability; and developing a global partnership for development by 2015.

However, recent reports are beginning to show that achieving the MDGs could be nearly impossible. Even countries like Malawi, which are receiving financial help from several different sources—including Madonna's much-touted charity—are still not achieving, or even approaching, the MDGs (Manda, 2009; MDG Monitor, 2010).

> Financial altruism detached from strategic and objective thinking has been shown time and again to have detrimental consequences at exorbitant costs.

U.N. Secretary-General Ban Ki-Moon in his 2010 report *Keeping the Promise* expressed worries that progress in several nations has been uneven and "without additional efforts several of the [MDGs] are likely to be missed in many countries" (United Nations, 2010). He cautioned that falling short of achieving the MDGs "would be an unacceptable failure from both the moral and the practical standpoint. If we fail, the dangers in the world—instability, violence, epidemic diseases, environmental degradation, runaway population growth—will all be multiplied."

The question of why MDGs seem increasingly impossible to meet is an important one. Were the goals not realistic, logical, or pragmatic enough? Were the methods employed to meet them too "pathologically altruistic?" Are there insufficient monetary resources to accomplish the MDGs? Have governments failed in implementing the needed changes? Or, was it a combination of these and other factors? The answer, at this point, is unclear.

The Irony of Foreign Aid

We are not against foreign aid. We are for *prudent* aid. Not all aid is bad. For example, foreign aid driven design and delivery of oral rehydration treatment for diarrhea helped avert hundreds of thousands of deaths in the 1960s. The program was successful because of the effective use of financial resources coupled with well-trained staff to administer the therapy in Egypt and dozens of other countries. Foreign aid has also helped African countries such as Mozambique to rekindle their basic educational system: since 1998, the country has quintupled the enrollment of children in its secondary schools (Lapper, 2010). Aid supported by good technical and ground-level management strategies also helped China manage tuberculosis, Bangladesh reduce its fertility rate, Morocco to control trachoma, and more than 50 countries to eradicate polio and smallpox, all over the last three decades (Levine, 2007).

But all too often, even programs that initially seem effective eventually end up being counterproductive. One frequently cited success story, for example, is India's use of foreign aid to change from a "begging bowl" to a "bread basket" in the 1960s. And in fact, a smart blending of agricultural technologies and financial assistance helped India in the short term. But, in ensuing years, the country's agricultural productivity tumbled largely due to poor soil health and defocused government policies. Ultimately, it was the liberal policy reforms of early 1990s—*not* foreign aid—that gave India the escape velocity for an economic take-off. It is successes and failures such as these that have sparked continued debate regarding the efficacy of foreign aid—that is, whether massive investments alone are of any use.

> Not all aid is bad. But debate has continued regarding the efficacy of foreign aid—that is, whether massive investments are of any use.

In a 1958 *Yale Law Review* essay, economist Milton Friedman prophetically critiqued the principles of foreign aid (Friedman, 1995):

> The objectives of foreign economic aid are commendable. The means are, however, inappropriate to objectives. Foreign economic aid, far from contributing to rapid economic development along democratic lines, is likely to retard improvement in the well-being of the masses, to strengthen the government sector at the expense of the private sector, and to undermine democracy and freedom. The proponents of foreign aid have unwittingly accepted a basic premise of the Communist ideology that foreign aid is intended to combat. They have accepted

the view that centralized and comprehensive economic planning and control by government is an essential requisite for economic development. This view is contradicted by our own experience and the experience of every other free country. An effective program must be based on our own ideology, not on the ideology we are fighting.

Building further on the prescient warnings of economist Peter Bauer in 1970s (1976), this discussion has begun to seep into the popular media thanks in part to the hard-hitting arguments of several recent books: *The White Man's Burden* by New York University's William Easterly (2006), *Dead Aid* by former Goldman Sachs executive Dambisa Moyo (2009), and *The Crisis Caravan* by investigative journalist Linda Polman (2010). The latter book provides compelling evidence that aid actually induces atrocities as warlords vie with one another to deliberately produce the worst atrocities so as to attract foreign intervention. (See also (Gourevitch, 2010).)

There have been decades of work by generous donor organizations, the World Bank, and governmental agencies worldwide, at a cost of over a trillion dollars, yet the 300 million people of Africa are still living at virtually the same level of poverty they were at in 1960. In that same time period, East Asia's gross domestic product has *quintupled* (Rees, 2009).

Further, there appears to be a fundamental communication hurdle between donors and recipients as more and more cash is dispatched: Poor countries typically don't understand what rich countries are trying to do to help them. A recent research survey carried out by the Center for Effective Philanthropy and the Bill and Melinda Gates Foundation noted: "Many of our grantee partners said we are not clear about our goals and strategies, and they think we don't understand their goals and strategies" (Gates Foundation Grantee Perception Report, 2010). This is discouraging news, especially when donors are pouring more money into development work. For example, financial contributions toward tackling infectious diseases and supporting local health sectors have more than tripled from $5.6 billion to $21.8 billion between 1990 and 2007, with the United States being the lead contributor (Ravishankar et al., 2009). A recent *Lancet* study found that in all developing countries, government domestic spending on health between 1995 and 2006 in U.S. dollars rose by 100%; support from the International Monetary Fund increased by 120% and the World Health Organization by 88% (Lu et al., 2010). This study also raises questions concerning the outright harmful aspects of foreign aid: how some developing countries reduce their domestic spending on development issues and route the received funds to projects that are untraceable.

Balancing Empathy and Objectivity

There is never going to be a single panacea that ensures uniformly effective policies and programs for development. But it is helpful to remind ourselves that effective development should be designed and deployed with a balanced mix of empathy and objectivity. A surprisingly relevant theory is *Empathizing-Systemizing* (E-S) theory, which was developed by autism research expert Simon Baron Cohen of Cambridge University (see Chapter 26). *E-S* theory hypothesizes that individuals tend toward empathizing or systemizing: two opposite poles of personality. Empathizing can be thought of as ways of thinking that help make sense of the living world—especially other human beings. Systemizing, in contrast, is the drive to objectively analyze and operate complex systems. From an evolutionary standpoint, these two abilities in their yin–yang fashion have driven human advancement—each is obviously vital. Underlying this theory is a deeper one—that "the human brain makes a fundamental distinction between the living and nonliving world, and that distinct cognitive networks and rule systems operate when processing subjects and objects" (Von Horn, Bäckman, Davidsson, & Hansen, 2009; see also Herrmann, Call, Hernandez-Lloreda, Hare, & Tomasello, 2007). As psychiatrist Iain McGilchrist explains in his masterful *The Master and His Emissary*, asymmetry in hemispheric function of the brain underlies what Baron-Cohen terms "systemizing" and "empathizing." McGilchrist explains:

> I suggest that there are two opposing ways of dealing with the world that are both vital but are fundamentally incompatible, and that therefore, even before humans came on the scene, required separate treatment, even neurological sequestration from one another. One tendency, important for being able to get things from the world for one's own purposes, involves isolation of one thing from the next, and isolation of the living being, perceived as subjective, from the world, perceived as objective. The drive here is toward manipulation, and its ruling value is utility. It began in my view by colonising the left hemisphere. . . The other tendency was centripetal, rather than centrifugal: towards the sense of the connectedness of things, before reflection isolates them, and therefore towards engagement with the world, towards a relationship of 'betweenness' with whatever lies outside the self. With the growth of the frontal lobes, this tendency was enhanced by the possibility of empathy, the seat of which is the right frontal expansion in social primates, including humans (McGilchrist, 2010).

Also relevant is Jules Lobel and George Loewenstein's theory that "human behavior is the product of at least two neural systems that operate according to different principles and often clash with one another" (Lobel & Loewenstein, 2004). The first of the two is an evolutionarily ancient system that underpins emotion—aptly dubbed the "emote control" system. The second system relates to the rational capabilities and deliberate thought of the prefrontal cortex. It would be a stretch to say that the "empathizing" of Baron-Cohen's E-S theory, or McGilchrist's "right brain" approach, are equivalent to Lobel and Loewenstein's "emote control"; or that systemizing or "left brain" approaches are equivalent to rational capabilities. But clear analogies exist between the theories—right down to the idea that overly heavy systemizing ("rational") abilities and lack of emotion (one aspect of which is empathy) should result in developmental disorders such as those seen in autism. Conversely, overdependence on empathy may result in amorphous syndromes such as codependency (see Chapter 4 by Michael McGrath and Barbara Oakley).

> To be effective, development assistance policies and programs must be designed and deployed with a balanced mix of empathy and objectivity.

As it turns out, the default mode for most human thinking—particularly in emotionally fraught situations—is emote control. Staring at pictures of starving children can, in some sense, hijack the analytical portions of the brain. Perhaps it is this that results in some of the ineffectual and pathologically altruistic behavior that characterizes many foreign aid policies and programs. Although the underlying intent of many of these policies and programs may be driven by crass political motives or to reap publicity bonanzas, the public may more easily acquiesce to the giveaways in part because their emote control is hijacked by heartbreaking images.

E-S theory lends itself to yet another pragmatic theory of social interaction. If empathy is somewhat analogous to trust, and systemizing to verification, we find ourselves, only half tongue-in-cheek, recommending an E-S approach to foreign aid that is analogous to "trust but verify."

A New Path Forward

But there is intriguing research that may point toward new avenues for dealing with these issues. A 2007 study by Taiwanese neuroscientist Yawei Cheng and colleagues shows how physicians are able to "change their brain" to reduce empathy so as to avoid overreacting to other's pain (Cheng et al., 2007). In response to watching a needle inserted into another person for example, expert acupuncturists increase "top-down" executive control—associated with activity in the medial and superior prefrontal cortices—while also ramping up portions of the temporoparietal lobe, an area that allows a person to conceptualize him- or herself as physically distinct from others. Counter intuitively, it seems that developing dispassion—the ability to displace ourselves emotionally from a situation that arouses our primal, emote control responses—is vital in being able to help others. In a related vein, developing the ability to use our rational brain to feel compassion for others—*without mirroring their emotions*—is important in preventing the compassion fatigue or burnout often seen in those who care for the suffering (see Chapter 29 by Klimecki and Singer).

Correspondingly, we suggest that foreign aid programs might explore counterintuitive training activities that emphasize the development of dispassion. Training of the leaders themselves would be critical. After all, top-down control of development assistance programs by the executives of aid organizations is in some sense analogous to top-down control over emotions by the executive control system of the brain.

In conjunction with such training activities, we believe it is important to encourage governments, and inter- and nongovernmental foreign-aid organizations to recruit more systemizers to advise, run, and audit their development assistance programs and aid effectiveness research. Engineers especially, it seems, self-select for this characteristic, which is enhanced by their training, but many others, from doctors to judges to police, also possess hard-earned abilities to step back and act dispassionately—and, as importantly, to be inquisitive and skeptical.

Relevant here are the observations of Michael Hammer, one of the founders of the management theory of business process reengineering and co-author of the landmark *Reengineering the Corporation: A Manifesto for Business Revolution* (2003). "Crucially," Hammer noted, "engineers are taught that design matters; that most things are part of a system in which everything interacts; that their job is to worry about trade-offs; and that they must continually be measuring the robustness of the systems they set up. Such a frame of mind . . ., fosters innovation. It may be no coincidence that many of the greatest corporate leaders in America, Europe and Japan, past and present, trained first as engineers" (*Economist*, 2004).

One may argue that a number of systemizers preexist in the development community—usually in the form of economists. Economists, truly so, have long dominated the doctrines of development assistance and top ranks of aid organizations. More recently, however, there has been a growing desire and unrest—even *within* the economics community—to cultivate new thinking and policy frameworks that span beyond traditional, rigid theories to propel economic growth.

> Foreign aid programs and policies could benefit from the development of counterintuitive training activities that emphasize the development of dispassion.

Another possible argument is that we are presupposing that foreign aid agencies, intergovernmental organizations, and private philanthropies are currently driven by empathetically and emotionally impulsive people with a propensity for nonstrategic charity. That is not the case. Our fundamental suggestion is this: Recruit a new breed of nontraditional talent that is capable of reframing the way development assistance is carried out. Furthermore, infusing a new breed of systemizers into development work would introduce fresh thinking to what Clark Gibson and colleagues call a "collective action" situation in their 2005 book *Samaritan's Dilemma*. (Gibson, Andersson, Ostrom, & Shivakumar, 2005) In short, a collective action situation is one that could benefit from different skills, nontraditional inputs, and diverse view points. This makes sense—after all, we don't want donors to simply temporarily infuse funds or jobs without an objective approach to the development challenge. That the systemizers may be armed with an innate neural capacity to calibrate their empathy and objectivity could be fundamentally useful toward designing interventions for situations especially vulnerable to moral emotions and despair.

"Desperation deforms judgment, and not just among victims" notes *Time*'s Nancy Gibbs (Gibbs, 2010). She continues:

> After the 2004 tsunami, aid poured in from all over the world. But it included tons of outdated or unneeded medicines that Indonesian officials had to throw out. People sent Viagra and Santa suits, high-heeled shoes, and evening gowns. A year later, after an earthquake in Pakistan, so much unusable clothing arrived that people burned it to stay warm. It may make us feel good to put together children's care packages with cards and teddy bears—but whose needs are we trying to meet? . . . It may not feel glorious, but often the greatest good is accomplished quietly, invisibly. Either way, the same principle holds in helping as in healing: First, do no harm.

Altruism is a powerful instrument that can help as well as cause harm. Altruism also has complex underpinnings: people display it to gain what Nobel-winning economist Gary Becker termed "psychic income." Or a "warm glow." Or simply a self-serving advantage. As *New York Times* columnist Nicholas Kristof observes: "while charity has a mixed record helping others, it has an almost perfect record of helping ourselves. Helping others may be as primal a human pleasure as food or sex" (Kristof, 2010).

To help ourselves by helping others, foreign aid policies and interventions must be time-bound, finite, focused, limited, and have a clear exit plan. Financial altruism detached from strategic and objective thinking has been shown time and again to have detrimental consequences at exorbitant costs. Historical lessons—and mistakes—should therefore help motivate us to balance empathy and objectivity. In more straightforward terms, we should take a step back before opening up our wallets: be it to give a dollar to a homeless person, contemplate complex, exotic international "climate aid" policies, or when attempting—like Madonna—to fill God's shoes. Assuming the mantle of dispassion and pragmatism allows us to follow a prudent, not pathological, path toward altruism.

Acknowledgments

The authors would like to thank, in particular, Bradley Sawyer, Sujai Shivakumar, Stephen Merrill, Kevin Finneran, Daniel Mullins, Joshua Brandoff, Subbiah Arunachalam, and David Koon for their useful comments.

References

Bauer, P. (1976). *Dissent on development*. Cambridge: Harvard University Press.
Bishop, M., & Green, M. (2009). *Philanthrocapitalism: How giving can save the world*. New York: Bloomsbury Press.
Cheng, Y., Lin, C., Liu, H., Hsu, Y., Lim, K., Hung, D., et al. (2007). Expertise modulates the perception of pain in others. *Current Biology, 17*(19), 1708–1713.
Clinton, B. (2007). *Giving: How each of us can change the world*. New York: Knopf.
Easterly, W. (2006). *The white man's burden: Why the west's efforts to aid the rest have done so much ill and so little good*. New York: Penguin Press.
Friedman, M. (1995). *Foreign Economic Aid: Means and objectives, essays in public policy No. 60*. Stanford, CA: Hoover Institution on War, Revolution, and Peace.
Gates Foundation. (2010, January 29). *Bill and Melinda Gates Pledge $10 Billion in Call for Decade of Vaccines* [Press release].
Gates Foundation and the Center for Effective Philanthropy Survey. (2010). *Grantee Perception Report Summary*. Retrieved from www.gatesfoundation.org/learning/Pages/grantee-perception-report.aspx.
Gibbs, N. (2010, February 22). There is no point in doing good badly. *Time*.
Gibson, C., Andersson, K., Ostrom, E., & Shivakumar, S. (2005). *Samaritan's dilemma: The political economy of development aid*. New York: Oxford University Press.
Gourevitch, P. (2010, October 11). Alms dealers: Can you provide humanitarian aid without facilitating conflicts? *The New Yorker*.
Guth, R., & Banjo, S. (2010, June 16). Gates, Buffett goad peers to give billions to charity. *The Wall Street Journal*.
Hammer, M., & Champy, J. (2003). *Reengineering the corporation: A manifesto for business revolution*. New York: HarperBusiness Essentials.
Herrmann, E., Call, J., Hernandez-Lloreda, M., Hare, B., & Tomasello, M. (2007). Humans have evolved specialized skills of social cognition: The cultural intelligence hypothesis. *Science, 317*(5843), 1360.
Kristof, N. (2010, January 16). Our basic human pleasures: Food, sex and giving. *The New York Times*.
Lapper, R. (2010, June 1). Mozambique typifies aid dilemma. *The Financial Times*.
Levine, R. (2007). *Millions saved: Proven successes in global health*. Washington, DC: Jones & Bartlett.
Lobel, J., & Loewenstein, G. (2004). Emote control: The substitution of symbol for substance in foreign policy and international law. *Chicago Kent Law Review*, 80.
Lu, C., Schneider, M., Gubbins, P., Leach-Kemon, K., Jamison, D., & Murray, C. (2010). Public financing of health in developing countries: a cross-national systematic analysis. *Lancet, 375*(9723), 1375–1387.
Madonna. (2009, October 28). Raising Malawi: Will you join me? *The Huffington Post*.
Malawi Orphan to Madonna. (2009, October 28). "You are our god." *US Magazine*.

Manda, M. (2009). *Water and sanitation in urban Malawi: Can they meet the millennium development goals? A study of informal settlements in three cities.* London: International Institute for Environment and Development.

McGilchrist, I. (2010). *The Master and his emissary: The divided brain and the making of the modern world.* New Haven, CT: Yale University Press, pp. 127–8.

MDG Monitor: Tracking the Millennium Development Goals, United Nations Development Program. Retrieved from www.mdgmonitor.org, accessed April 2010.

Moyo, D. (2009). *Dead aid: Why aid is not working and how there is another way for Africa.* New York: Farrar, Straus and Giroux.

Organisation for Economic Co-operation and Development. (2010, April 14). *Development Aid Rose in 2009 and Most Donors Will Meet 2010 Aid Targets* [Press release].

Polman, Linda, (2010), *The crisis caravan: What's wrong with humanitarian aid?* New York: Metropolitan Books.

Ravishankar, N., Gubbins, P., Cooley, R., Leach-Kemon, K., Michaud, C., Jamison, D., et al. (2009). Financing of global health: Tracking development assistance for health from 1990 to 2007. *Lancet, 373*(9681), 2113–2124.

Rees, M. (2009, March 17). When help does harm. *The Wall Street Journal.*

Sayings of Buddha. (1957). New York: Peter Pauper Press.

The Economist. (2004, April 24). Special Report, Business Innovation: Don't laugh at gilded butterflies, 71–73.

United Nations, Report of the Secretary-General. (2010). *Keeping the promise: A forward-looking review to promote an agreed action agenda to achieve the millennium development goals by 201,5* Report No. A/64/665.

Von Horn, A., Bäckman, L., Davidsson, T., & Hansen, S. (2009). Empathizing, systemizing and finger length ratio in a Swedish sample. *Scandinavian Journal of Psychology, 51*(1), 31–37.

CHAPTER 18

WAS GANDHI A "PATHOLOGICAL ALTRUIST"?

Arun Gandhi

KEY CONCEPTS

- Finding Truth was Gandhi's ultimate objective.
- Nonviolence is a key means for obtaining Truth.
- Nonviolence can, on occasion, become a pathologically altruistic enterprise, unnecessarily hurting others, and it cannot be dogmatically followed if the greater good of Truth is to be attained.

THE EDITORS' INVITATION to explore the idea that my grandfather Mohandas K. Gandhi's philosophy of nonviolence was based on "pathological altruism" has prompted a great deal of thought. After much discussion with my collegial Gandhian scholars, we concluded that it was not necessarily nonviolence Gandhi was altruistic about, but Truth. For Gandhi, the relentless pursuit of Truth could not be compromised in any way. He said: "Finding Truth is my ultimate objective and nonviolence is the way to achieve this." For Gandhi, Truth was God, and finding God, and thereby the meaning of life, had to be pursued with single-minded devotion and dedication. It might be argued that since truth and nonviolence are so closely connected, and since Gandhi also believed that means and ends are as closely related as the seed and a tree, that the pursuit of God through nonviolence makes both nonviolence and the search for Truth altruistic enterprises.

> It was not necessarily nonviolence Gandhi was altruistic about, but Truth.

During his years in South Africa, from 1893 to 1914, Gandhi struggled with the concept of how ordinary people could apply ancient Jain philosophy to everyday life. To help better understand these issues, Gandhi corresponded extensively with Raychandbhai, a well-known Jain Guru in India. Gandhi was aware that the Jain community in India followed the teachings of Lord Mahavir, who had started a nonviolent branch of Hinduism 2,500 years before after being appalled by the animal sacrifice in Hindu temples that became a norm. It is debatable whether Lord Mahavir categorically supported the concept of

"Total Nonviolence" as practiced by Jains today, or whether this is a subsequent misinterpretation of the religion's original precepts, as has happened with other world religions.

In this correspondence, Raychandbhai maintained that all human beings must attempt to attain total nonviolence at all times, under any circumstances. Jain priests can often be seen walking with a mask over their mouths in order not to breathe in microbes, and a fly switch in their hands to sweep away little insects when they walk. The fact that only priests do this and not all Jains must be construed to mean that the practice is impractical. After all, such practices, if generally followed, would mean Jains should not ride automobiles or other vehicles that are likely to kill insects, birds, or animals.

In one letter, Gandhi expressed his concern with deadly snakes. He had just established his first ashram, the Phoenix Settlement, which was infested with some of South Africa's deadliest snakes. These included black and green mambas and puff adders that could spit deadly venom straight into your eyes and blind you immediately. Gandhi asked Raychandbhai what he would do if a deadly snake was about to attack his loved one. Would he let the snake attack and escape, or would he kill the snake? Raychandbhai's response was that a true Jain would sacrifice their beloved and let the snake escape unharmed. Gandhi considered this very difficult to accept and profess.

Diaries of the settlers on Phoenix Settlement talk about daily encounters with these snakes. They tried their best not to harm the snakes or other deadly wildlife. But when it became inevitable, they valued human life more than the life of a reptile or animal. The concept of total nonviolence, the settlers claimed, was difficult to practice.

Distortions and misinterpretations are more readily followed today by believers of all the different religions than is the Truth that Gandhi sought. This becomes possible since scriptures are ambiguously worded and lend themselves to different interpretations. Gandhi's search for that Truth from the Jains, as from all other religions, was honest and open.

Gandhi wrote later that some violence is inevitable in life, but that one should attempt constantly to come as close to total nonviolence as possible. Gandhi also expanded the concept of nonviolence from non-killing and non-hurting to improving relationships, building respectful communities, and living a compassionate life style. Gandhi urged those who lived with him in the ashrams in South Africa and in India to understand the many ways in which we practice violence. He defined the two forms of violence as one in which physical force is used, and the other in which no physical force is used, yet people are still hurt, either directly or indirectly, emotionally and otherwise. It is not enough that we avoid physical violence and continue to practice passive violence. The best way to avoid passive violence, Gandhi said, was to ask yourself: "If the action you contemplate will help someone or hurt them." In modern times, passive violence is also practiced in religious institutions that compete with or denounce one another.

Gandhi was once assaulted in South Africa by fellow Indians who did not understand his intentions when he signed an agreement with the South African Government. Gandhi's eldest son, Harilal, who was then eagerly trying to understand and practice his father's philosophy of nonviolence, asked: What should I have done nonviolently to help you if I was present at the time these people attacked you? Gandhi's said: You must always protect fellow human beings even if it means using a limited amount of violence.

Of course, it must be understood that Gandhi's philosophy kept evolving during his lifetime. In fact, he was once criticized as being inconsistent. Gandhi's response was that he could not remain dogmatically wedded to a theory that appeared to be the truth at that time. Truth is ever changing, as is our understanding of it. Gandhi thought the problem with modern society was that we approach all philosophy dogmatically because that is the academic approach. A philosophy, to be meaningful, must be living and vibrant.

> Truth is ever changing, as is our understanding of it.

What Gandhi said to his son in South Africa in the early years of his transformation into a nonviolent activist is today taken to mean that he supports wars. This is not necessarily true. Gandhi viewed each case independently and based his reaction according to his understanding of the situation. He supported the action taken by the Indian Government in 1947, when Pakistan attacked Kashmir, because this was an aggressive act and the people of Kashmir sought India's protection. Yet, there is no doubt that he abhorred all violence—especially wars. He had long come to realize that the only way wars and violence could be avoided was by building communities and nations that respected each other and lived in cooperation and compassion. The important question was not about violent versus nonviolent approaches, but about how nonviolent approaches could be viable amidst human cultures that are so dominated by violence. After all, violence is everywhere—in our language, our behavior, our relationships, our economics, and even our sports.

Gandhi clarified his ideas by referring to cultures of violence versus cultures of nonviolence. Thus, he would say, living in a culture of violence is like living in a snake pit with millions of creepy crawly reptiles threatening your very existence. If you want to be secure in a culture of violence, your only option is to build a fortress around you, and then hope the snake doesn't get in. If the snake *does* get in, your only option is to kill it or be killed yourself. But there is another option—that is, not to live in a snake pit, but rather, to create a culture of nonviolence around you so that there is an atmosphere of respectful coexistence where no one is a threat to anyone else. This can be achieved if we rebuild a society where love, respect, understanding, appreciation, and compassion would supersede the existing suspicion, hate, prejudice, intolerance, and exploitation.

While the philosophy of nonviolence was still in its developmental stage during his years in South Africa, Gandhi was torn between his duties as a faithful, law-abiding citizen of the British Empire and as a nonviolent pacifist. In 1899, when the British declared war against the descendants of Dutch settlers, the Boers, this mental turmoil came to the fore. Should he support the war, or denounce it and have nothing to do with it? He chose not to support the fighting, and instead created an ambulance corps of volunteers who would take care of the injured and dead. His consequent close proximity with violence repulsed him—he saw within it the destruction of human civilization.

Ultimately, the 1906 war between the British and the Zulus, which was sparked by an unjust tax levy, convinced Gandhi that radical measures were in order. Although the Boer war was "give and take" in the sense that both sides were equally armed and equally vicious, the Zulu war showed Gandhi the inhumanity of the British, whom he had once held in high esteem for their sense of justice and fair play.

During the Zulu conflict, Gandhi's band of mostly Indian volunteers ministered to the wounded and often walked 20 to 40 miles a day carrying the wounded and the dead on stretchers on their shoulders. More fatefully, Gandhi saw well-armed British soldiers chasing after fleeing Zulus armed with sticks and spears and shooting them down. Ninety percent of the Zulus were shot in the back. The question as to whether this form of savagery could or should be tolerated in a civilized society began to nag. It was during this time that his war against all forms of violence took root.

At the core of much of the violence, Gandhi realized, was materialism that bred capitalism, which in turn bred selfishness. The culmination of all this was either passive or physical violence. Civilizations were built on exploitation, and the measure of success was the material wealth of a society or an individual. Gandhi was convinced that materialism and morality had an inverse relationship—when one increases, the other tends to decrease. Since the world is today obsessed with material pursuits, it is evident that morality is fast eroding. The morality we profess rather than practice is superfluous and meaningless. The more that Gandhi witnessed this worldwide erosion in human values and ethics, the more he was convinced that nonviolence cannot simply be a philosophy or a tool for conflict resolution, but that it must instead become a way of life, deeply embedded in a culture that exposed and nourished the inherent goodness in every human being.

The culture of violence that dominates human societies everywhere has convinced us that violence is human nature and that there is nothing we can do to change that reality. Gandhi discarded this notion as being absurd. He said, if violence is human nature, then why do we need military academies and martial arts institutions to teach us to fight and kill? Why are we not born with these instincts as other animals are? What is a part of human nature is anger, not violence. Anger (as Gandhi told me when I was 12 years old) is like electricity. It is very useful when used intelligently or very destructive if abused. Anger, in fact, is to humans what fuel is to automobiles. Unfortunately, instead of using anger intelligently, we have learned to abuse it and cause violence. Gandhi concluded that violence is insidious—it is destructive and must be treated as a cancer that is destroying human civilization. He refuted the argument that, because we cannot practice total nonviolence, we should not attempt to reduce the level of violence that consumes us. If we diagnose a cancer in the human body do we just live with it? Of course not! We do everything in our power to cure our body of the cancer even when the doctor says that we may not be able to eradicate it totally. So, Gandhi would ask today, if violence is a cancer that is destroying human society, why are we helplessly watching the erosion? Why are we not taking any radical steps to destroy it?

Does one have to be a resolute dogmatic to understand and practice nonviolence? I think Gandhi would say no. He would instead insist that we be honest, sincere, and committed to follow nonviolent means to ultimately achieve true human civilization. To Gandhi, nonviolence was not the end in itself, it was the means

> Although Gandhi swore by nonviolence, he also understood that nonviolence can become a pathologically altruistic enterprise; it cannot be dogmatically followed if the greater good of Truth is to be attained.

to understand the ultimate Truth, or God. Gandhi would say one must be dogmatic in his or her search for Truth but not necessarily in the way one reaches that understanding. Although he swore by nonviolence, he also understood that nonviolence can become a pathologically altruistic enterprise; it cannot be dogmatically followed if the greater good of Truth is to be attained.

CHAPTER 19

A CONTRARIAN PERSPECTIVE ON ALTRUISM

The Dangers of First Contact[1]

David Brin

KEY CONCEPTS

- Much of what is called "altruistic" behavior in nature can have self-serving, kinship, or game-based roots that we should not ignore simply out of aesthetic Puritanism.
- Unselfish altruism can emerge out of satiability, satiation, empathy, and sympathy, as well as cultural and individual values. Although sometimes implemented in ways that are ill-conceived or pathological, this trait is viewed as a high feature of intelligence.
- Occasionally, altruism *between* species seems to be unleashed by full bellies and sympathy, along (sometimes) with enlightened self-interest in the long-term survival of an entire world.
- Modern Western society disavows the notion that ideas are inherently dangerous or toxic, or that an elite should guide gullible masses toward correct thinking. However, virtually every other culture held the older, prevalent belief in "toxic memes." As yet, there is no decisive proof supporting one side over the other.
- Western assumptions color the search for extraterrestrial intelligence (SETI) just as previous "first-contact" events were driven by cultural assumptions of past eras. Especially pervasive—and unwarranted—is the belief that all advanced civilizations will automatically be altruistic.

Altruism in the Natural World: Advantage and Satiation

Contact with "alien" others is not so uncommon as one might think. After all, animals from cephalopods to dogs to dolphins are in some sense alien—as are people who were raised in very different cultures. Past "first-contact" events between diverse societies—for example, when expansionist Europeans met native peoples of Africa, Asia, and the Americas—illustrate how highly intelligent groups with different backgrounds can have severe difficulties establishing a relationship of mutual understanding A clear-eyed view of our human past may help us remain agile if we ever encounter others from beyond our planet.

Reciprocally, thought experiments about contact with alien (nonhuman) cultures may prove edifying to those wanting a fresh angle on interhuman interactions. Specifically, the search for extraterrestrial intelligence (SETI) provides an interesting case study—not so much of extraterrestrials, but of our own current Western attitudes toward how to approach a novel encounter between civilizations. Reflecting their almost entirely Western-liberal value system, supporters of SETI have generally taken for granted the axiom that altruism—a selfless imperative to assist others without expectation of reward—is likely to be a supreme attribute among advanced technological civilizations. The implication is that humanity should strive to display this attribute in communicating with extraterrestrial life forms who may be many centuries (or much more) ahead of us in development. Along these lines, a recent series of workshops[2] on how to craft and send a deliberate message from Earth into space was based on the supposition that we can dismiss any substantial likelihood of danger or bad outcomes from transmitting messages into space.[3]

Are these altruistic assumptions warranted? Or, do they reflect the personal inclinations and wishes of a narrow group arising from a particular culture and era?

I, for one, would feel more confident in the inevitability of alien altruism if that beneficent trait appeared more often in nature.

> I, for one, would feel more confident in the inevitability of alien altruism if that beneficent trait appeared more often in nature.

Overall, we know that kinship altruism is one of the strongest forces in nature. However, science acknowledges important exceptions to the curve relating generosity to genetic payoff. The human ability to extend "kinship" in abstract (as with patriotic self-sacrifice) can be prodigious. We have all seen well-publicized examples in which mothers of one species seemed impelled to adopt and nurse surrogate offspring from another. Dolphins have pushed human castaways toward boats or islands. And today, upon hearing word that whales are stranded on some shore, modern people are frequently known to drop everything and race down to the beach with the same alacrity and eagerness that their ancestors would have shown upon hearing the same news. The purest form of altruism—in which individuals sacrifice advantage to benefit others without hope of recompense—does not at first appear to have anything to do with a cost–benefits game matrix.

But pause for a moment and consider that example of human beings racing toward stranded whales. The vigor and speed of response has remained constant. Today, the aim of those hurrying to the beach is to gently rescue rare, precious creatures. During most of our past, people hearing the same news would have rushed to the surf line with a different purpose in mind . . . lunch (Figure 19.1).

The difference is clearly based on two transformations—*education* and *satiation*. We now know more about cetaceans and can thus identify with them far more easily. But above all, we no longer need their flesh to feed our hungry young. Satiation (acting upon the necessary, preexisting trait of satiability) appears to be a critical element in the rising movement of Western nations to include animals within the protection of law, and to elevate altruism above other

THE FAR SIDE®   By GARY LARSON

"Calm down, Edna. ... Yes, it's some giant, hideous insect ... but it could be some giant, hideous insect in need of help."

FIGURE 19.1

culturally promoted ideals, such as tribal patriotism and glory-at-arms, that our ancestors considered paramount. Note that not all human cultures have made such an agile shift from predation to inclusion. Not only satiation and knowledge, but also cultural elements—for example, a habit and readiness to practice inclusive "otherness" in defining people who are different as deserving of tribal protection—are also necessary. Indeed, some other cultures consider this Western quality to border on madness.

Group dynamics can play a major role. We all recognize the emotions we feel when faced with discourteous or selfish public behavior. Along this vein, it has long been known that both animals and humans will often find ways to ensure that generosity is a widely exhibited trait by either overtly or subtly reproving or disciplining those who behave selfishly. These behaviors have been dubbed *altruistic punishment* or *costly punishment*. In a game situation, for example, the violation of certain rules can result in players ganging up, en masse, on defectors who play selfishly or fail to meet minimal standards of cooperation or beneficence. This occurs even when the act of punishing the defector adds costs and no benefits to the other players, and when any resulting altered behavior will help some other, later team, and not themselves (Fehr & Gächter, 2002; Henrich et al., 2006).

Is beneficent behavior that takes place in the shadow of altruistic punishment classifiable as true altruism? Uncomfortable to ponder, this question adds one more reason to worry about the oversimplification performed by those who simply assume that generosity will be universal, amid the stars. At present, those pushing this assumption in the SETI community are largely idealistic astronomers and their eager fans, whereas the quite different and more cynical field of exobiology is composed of biologists, who know that evolution does not predispose living creatures toward truly selfless altruism any more than it does toward aesthetics. It may be that our bent for altruism is instead a quirky, emergent property of our background as gregarious, exogamous, and cooperative apes.

And yet, even if it is largely absent from the natural world, that fact alone does not render pure altruism irrelevant. I just mentioned emergent properties. Complexity theory describes how new forms of order arise as systems gain intricacy. It may be no accident that the most complex society created by the most complex species on Earth has elevated altruism from a rare phenomenon to an ideal—something to be striven toward across the present and into future years. Furthermore, in another ironic twist, it is entirely by these recent, higher standards that we now project an even higher level of altruism upon those we hope to find more advanced than ourselves.

On the other hand, perhaps our present fixation on altruism is chauvinistic and humanocentric. For contrast, consider what kind of moral systems you might expect to arise if lions independently developed sapience. Or solitary and suspicious tigers. Bears are omnivores, like ourselves, and yet their consistent habit of male-perpetrated infanticide seems deeply rooted. Meta-ursine moralists might later view this inherited tendency as an unsavory sin and attempt to cure it by preaching restraint. Or else, perhaps they would rationalize and sacralize it, writing great literature to portray and justify the beauty of their way, just as we romanticize many of our own most emotion-laden traits. Anyone who doubts that intolerant or even murderous habits can be romanticized should study the religious rites of the ancient Aztecs and baby-sacrificing Carthaginians. If we are capable of rationalizing and even exalting brutally unaltruistic behaviors, might advanced extraterrestrials also be capable of such feats of mental legerdemain? Especially if their evolutionary backgrounds predispose them?

For this reason—in a spirit of cordial, contrarian questioning—let me offer to play devil's advocate. I suggest that it may be foolish for us to beam any messages from this planet until we know a lot more. To do so will be like ignorant children, screaming "Hello!" at the top of their lungs, in the middle of a dark, unknown jungle.

Physical and Biological Contact

> Beaming messages from this planet is like ignorant children screaming "Hello!" at the top of their lungs, in the middle of a dark, unknown jungle.

To start with, I would like to narrow the focus of discussion onto first contact itself—the day we might learn we aren't alone. What dangers should we consider during the following days and months? What possibilities should we keep in mind while seeking neighbors among the stars?

The first question has to be, will first contact be made in person? Or, will it be a mere exchange of greetings and information by radio? It is the latter scenario most SETI scholars predict. But let's begin by briefly considering dangers that might arise if we met alien beings face to face.

Conquest and plunder—the grist of lurid movies—might be set aside to the "rather unlikely" shelf. But perhaps one of the most fearsome possibilities might be disease. Until our recent acquired immune deficiency syndrome (AIDS) epidemic, the concept of plague had grown strange to modern Westerners. Yet, history shows that infection was a major element in countless first contacts between human cultures. Often, it played a crucial role. Anthropologist Alfred W. Crosby points out that the European conquest of the Americas and Oceanea was facilitated by such Eurasian diseases as measles and smallpox—sometimes introduced intentionally, but more often quite inadvertently and, ironically, often quite soon after both sides shook hands over treaties of friendship!

Some claim alien physiologies would be too incompatible . . . that extraterrestrial parasites would be unable to prey upon human organisms, and our pathogens would certainly fail against our guests. But there is wide disagreement about this among biologists.

Stanley Miller, one of the premier experts on the origins of life, offered a different opinion. Miller held that biological chemistry throughout the universe probably involves the same small set of amino acids and nucleic bases that Earth life forms use. Those chemicals happen to be the most stable—the best at forming complex structures of enzymes and proteins.

On the other hand, arguing from earthly experience, it seems that cross-infection follows a curve not too dissimilar to that of interspecies altruism. The more genetically remote a given species is from us, the less likely it is to transmit a parasite to us. A lot of the most lethal agents (for example, human immunodeficiency virus [HIV] and monkey B virus) seem to have started off in other primates, albeit in modified form. But, as you move away on the genetic continuum, these events are fewer. Once you leave mammals, you have parrot fever and various flu viruses from birds, and little or nothing from amphibians, reptiles, or fish. Insects, which make up most of the eukaryotic biomass of the planet, serve as carriers for a few things like malaria, but these are more vectors than hosts. If you assume that ET is very far from us genetically, the likelihood of cross-infection seems low.

Suppose our extraterrestrial guests pass successfully through quarantine. There are still reasons to be nervous. For example, how are we to guarantee their safety? Would you risk letting alien tourists walk unguarded down our city streets? Ninety-nine percent of the population may welcome them gladly. But most people also liked John Lennon of the Beatles. Human diversity is one of our treasures. Alas, it also means our mad fringe will be a persistent danger to visitors from space. This may be hard for guests to understand if they come from a homogeneous species or society.

And what about diversity among the extraterrestrials themselves? In both SETI and science fiction, we tend to envision each type as uniform in characteristics, with little variation—a bad habit that is related to the evils of racism, sexism, and stereotyping others by class. It is, in fact, quite possible that the first exemplars of communicating aliens that we meet may be atypical. Moreover, they may have reasons not to convey this fact to us. How do you know whether you're dealing with a council of elders that have high tolerance and a low fear level, or a disaffected alien teenager?

In the past, several human societies found themselves plunged into calamitous wars against European powers, precipitated by a few local hot-heads acting against the wishes of wise and cautious local chiefs, or else by unscrupulous occidental traders seeking short-term advantage. This will be a source of danger in any future contact situation, as well. Of that you can be sure.

Propagation as Information

We have only touched lightly on the range of possible outcomes and drawbacks from direct physical contact between ourselves and extraterrestrials. But let us move on, putting aside that category for now (it is highly unpopular among SETI enthusiasts, who almost universally deride interstellar travel as impossible even while they avidly pursue contact with aliens; the ironies can be delicious). Let us concentrate instead on what most scholars consider the more likely eventuality—communication with other worlds solely via radio or light waves, exchanging only information.

Only information? Surely no harm can come to either side from such an encounter!

Well, we shouldn't be too certain about that. One has only to look again at the history of first contact between human cultures to see how much pain sometimes came about, not from conquest or disease, but when one civilization encountered another's ideas. What are some of the mistakes we might make, if ever we encounter someone out there with something to say?

What if a government manages to slap a TOP SECRET classification on the discovery, sequestering knowledge of contact for the benefit of some group or nation here on Earth. We cannot know for certain that this hasn't already happened! Just because an idea has been worked to death in bad dramas doesn't mean that it's completely impossible. America's National Security Agency (NSA) is just one group already possessing far more sophisticated listening apparatus than all of the world's SETI teams put together. If SETI discovers a point source in some portion of the sky next week, can we know for certain that the NSA did not pick it up first, perhaps many years ago?

Sequestration of information is a clear danger to be guarded against. But now—in the spirit of contrarian criticism—I want to turn around and warn about the opposite trend, the growing assumption that absolutely everything about first contact should automatically and unquestionably be released right away, into the direct spotlight of mass media.

This extreme, too, could cause severe problems.

Take, for instance, the way the press turns some events into media circuses. During the early phases of a discovery—while scientists are still trying to verify that it is indeed "contact" and not some fluke or natural phenomenon—premature media attention could do great harm. What if a mistake was made?

I am reminded of the events surrounding detection of the first pulsar, which was initially thought to be an interstellar beacon because of its uncannily regular radio pulsation. If there had been an Internet back then, perhaps that false alarm might have aborted the entire SETI enterprise! How many false alarms can a program survive before it turns into a laughing stock? For this reason, we must expect some caution while responsible researchers triple check their data and discreetly seek verification from colleagues around the world.

Also, we must remember, researchers are people, with families and obligations. Their employers—for instance, NASA—may have operational rules and internal procedures that scientists are expected to follow before any public announcement might be made. It would be unfair to shout "coverup!" just because a little bureaucratic paperwork delays the big press conference by a few days.

This may mean the first announcement won't be made by responsible, careful scientists, but by a person on the periphery, perhaps a lurker in the rumor loop, someone with an appetite for headlines. Those who grab the front pages may not be the ones most qualified or deserving to represent us during the critical stages of first contact.

We should recall that it is only very recently that a few cultures began ascribing to the notion of freely exchanging ideas. Throughout history, nearly every tribe or nation held instead to the more traditional notion—that some concepts are too dangerous (or valuable) to be let loose among common folk. Were all those cultures entirely wrong to believe this? (See box below)

I happen to think they were. I hold to my own culture's central tenet that openness is good. The best way to protect people from bad ideas is to let them experience the entire range of human concepts, so they can learn for themselves to judge wheat from chaff. But then, honesty compels me also to admit I might be wrong. My culture's central assumption could be mistaken. Every other human culture may have been right instead, when they posited that ideas in are inherently dangerous.

It is the height of arrogance not to at least ponder this possibility, instead of simply assuming that a very recent set of upstart principles are automatically and obviously true. The possibility of receiving information that could—in its own right—prove dangerous is exemplified by the ease by which our computers are infected by software viruses. But a prudent civilization might well pay some attention to how humans, themselves, can also host infectious memes.

How much worse might these problems be if the extraterrestrials are responding to an ill considered message of our own? Whether they do so inadvertently, or out of deliberate malice, it will be within the power of alien communicators to use words and symbols in unhelpful ways. History suggests caution.

But let's return again to the topic of dangerous ideas. Is it possible that *we* may be the infectious ones? Before dismissing the idea out of hand, consider that the apparent silence out there could have any number of possible reasons. We who

---

TOXIC IDEAS: *CHOOSE WHICH STATEMENT COMES CLOSEST TO YOUR BELIEF*

- Many ideas are inherently dangerous or toxic. People are easily misled. An elite should protect or guide gullible masses toward correct thinking. (*Memic Frailty.*)
- Children can be raised with openness and skepticism to evaluate concepts on their merits. Citizens can pluck useful bits even from bad images or ideologies, discarding the rest on their own. (*Memic Maturity.*)

If you believe in the second proposition, how do you explain the fact that nearly every other human culture held to the first? Were they all wrong? Can you prove it?

are so new to understanding the depth and potential of syntactical information flow—are we the best judges of what is possible, let alone dangerous, to others? Would it really hurt to spend a little while advancing our knowledge in those areas, before ecstatically and impulsively shouting (or "sneezing") in all directions?

How about those wonders of technology we hope to acquire once we begin learning under the remote tutelage of our wise, beneficent predecessors? There has been talk about solving many of the problems that dog us—including the energy crises, disease, and unsafe transportation—by sharing solutions that might have been discovered long ago by alien others. They might even know answers to biological and sociological quandaries that today threaten our very survival.

Suppose we do start receiving a wad of generous schematics for all sorts of wonders. What if they are technologies we're not ready for? Like a simple way to make antimatter using common household materials and wall current? Ninety-nine point nine percent of the population may behave responsibly and refrain from blowing us up. The remaining 0.1% would kill us all.

Many Westerners believe in the free competition of ideas—letting the fittest survive in open argument. We tend—quite rightly—to see any attempt to restrict that openness as a direct threat. And yet, returning to an earlier point, there may be ways, quite conceivable ways, in which information from the stars could prove harmful, as in "virus" computer codes that infect a mainframe or microcomputer, proceeding to gobble up memory space, ruin data, and then spread to other hosts. So far, most inimical programs have proved fairly primitive—nothing compared to the voracious, computer-eating monsters depicted in some science fiction stories. And yet, those stories *were* correct in predicting computer viruses in the first place. And these viruses are getting more sophisticated all the time.

A software "invader" needn't be intentional. On Earth, there are endless stories of programs interfering destructively with other programs. What, then, of sophisticated code from an alien culture, taken in through our antennas and suddenly introduced into a data-handling system for which it wasn't designed? Any message from the stars is likely to include error correction modules, designed to repair damage done to the message during transit through the dust and plasma of interstellar space. Once the code is embedded in an active computing medium, such modules would "wake up"—much like a hibernating animal aroused from sleep—and would then begin using available computing resources to restore the integrity and function of the message.

As bizarre as this concept may sound at first, it isn't science fiction. Far from it. This is how the world's best information specialists say *they* would design any complex code meant to beam at the stars! Moreover, consider how each of these dangers should be considered in the *opposite* direction, as we prepare potential messages to transmit. Our own coding assumptions may have unexpected side effects when they enter the medium of an alien information system.

Under normal circumstances, an extraterrestrial message may be completely harmless. But what is "normal" for alien software? There is no guarantee such a program won't inadvertently take over more of an unfamiliar host system than anyone ever imagined. This accident might be made even worse if the program suffered "mutation" in transit.

Giving It All Away

Today, SETI scientists worry far more about lurid headlines ("SCHOLARS THINK EXTRATERRESTRIAL PROGRAMS MIGHT EAT US!") than about warding off infection by self-replicating alien software. And they are right. After all, nobody believes virus codes really represent a high-probability hazard to us or our civilization. But the wrong type of publicity, even misquoted, is a sure way to see your grant slashed. With that far more imminent danger always looming nearby, it's no wonder that talk of potential hazards from first contact rates far down most researchers' lists of priorities.

And yet, is it wise to go into this enterprise simply assuming there's no danger at all? That's called *success-oriented planning*; it was used extensively by the U.S. Space Shuttle Program. Need I say more?[4] In this modern world, we keep coming up with low-probability but huge-outcome situations that challenge the normal practice of risk analysis. Even if each individual scenario seems very unlikely, the sheer number of these "black swans" almost guarantees that a few of them (and some we haven't yet imagined) will come true (Taleb, 2007). Finding a mature and prudent way to deal with such quandaries—without stifling human progress—will be a challenge for this and coming generations.

But even if first contact turns out to be "safe," that wouldn't mean that we could relax. For, even in a civilized setting, life can still be dangerous if you don't know the rules. (Don't believe me? Try investing in Wall Street without any experience!)[5]

What, after all, is the most common peaceful enterprise of human beings? Commerce, of course. And what is likely to be the main commodity—perhaps the only commodity—of commerce on an interstellar scale?

> Even in a civilized setting, life can still be dangerous if you don't know the rules.

It will almost certainly be information.

Not the malign, dangerous information we spoke of earlier, but useful information—neat inventions and brilliant innovations, even—especially—art and literature. Anything novel and original. Whatever's fresh and new.

How will most of you respond if the first thing we're asked by aliens is, "Send us your music and your art!" The Voyager spacecraft carry disk recordings of samples of Earth culture, along with graphic instructions on how to read the information. In the spirit of the United Nations, it simply never occurred to any of the people planning this gesture that the album should have carried a price tag, as well.

It's all very well to speak of altruism and of the joys of free exchange. But we should always remember that is a very recent concept in human affairs. *Quid pro quo* is a more venerable theme. Throughout human history, in most of our daily lives, and even among the higher animals, the real rule for civilized relations is not "be generous."

It is "be fair."

And make no mistake, there is a difference!

Nice as they may be, our extraterrestrials will almost certainly engage in trade. And their stock in trade will be information. We may seek from them the answers to our ultimate questions. They, in turn, may reply, "Great. We've got some answers. But surely you have something to offer in exchange?"

> The real rule for civilized relations is not "be generous." It is "be fair." And make no mistake, there is a difference!

What can we offer? All we may have is ourselves—our art, our music, our books, and drama. Forget physical resources. The true wealth of humanity lies in our culture. That is what we have to trade. It is our treasure.

And it is also the very first thing we are likely to beam to the stars, in giga-bytes, within days after first contact! Given the spirit of the times, and our ecstatic enthusiasm for contact, it's what would seem only natural as we eagerly seek to "share with" (or impress) our newfound neighbors.

And that very admirable rush to share—proving our altruism in an orgy of transmission—might turn out to be the worst mistake of all time.

They may be nice. They may operate under rules we would call fair. But nobody expects to pay for a free gift! It could be that history will speak of no worse traitors to humanity than those who, with all the best intentions, cast out to the skies our very heritage, asking nothing in return, thereby impoverishing us all.

Let me reiterate this point: Nature is mostly tooth-and-claw.

At the opposite end of the spectrum, there are genuine glimmers of altruism, exhibited by dolphins now and then, an occasional dog, plus a large number of recent human beings who want to be much better than they are. Our great opportunity for improvement shines at this end. I hope we make it. But as yet there is no guarantee. There is hardly even a trend.

What is more firmly based in both nature and human experience is some-thing that lies midway between the extremes—our concept of fairness in dealing with each other on a basis of quid pro quo. Many animals seem to understand the basic notion of exchanging favors, tit-for-tat, making a deal.

Unlike pure altruism, pragmatic cooperation stands on much firmer ground, rooted solidly in observed nature, halfway along the road from predation to total beneficence. Moreover, one can easily imagine how to portray fair trade in a message. There is every chance that intelligent aliens will understand this con-cept, even if they find "altruism" incomprehensible.

Because of this, let me humbly suggest that a fair and open approach based on cautious quid pro quo should be our central theme as we take measured steps toward contact, while all the time remembering that we are new and small and weak in a vast universe that seems mysterious—especially in its chilling silence.

If aliens truly are benignly altruistic, they will forgive us this precaution, this vestige of pragmatic self-interest. Noble beings will bear in mind our recent dif-ficult experience. They will understand.

Conclusion

Optimistic scholars may be right in saying that we have nothing to fear from that eventual encounter with wise beings from the stars. Still, we cannot be reminded often enough to look back on our own history of contact among humans here on Earth, a litany of dire cautionary tales. We are, all of us, descended—only a few generations back—from folk who suffered horribly because they weren't ready for the challenges brought on by new vices, new tech-nologies, new diseases, new ideas, new opportunities, new people. And those ancestors were the lucky survivors! Many peoples and cultures—including every species of hominids other than our own—left no descendants at all.

In this chapter, I've only touched on just a few of the dangers conceived by various gloomy thinkers and writers over the years. I could go on, but a complete listing isn't necessary. What matters is the general lesson of circumspection and caution. The worst mistake of first contact, made throughout history by indi-viduals on both sides of every new encounter, has been the unfortunate habit of making assumptions.

Notes

1. Originally submitted to a conference on "Encoding Altruism: The Art and Science of Interstellar Message Composition," Paris, France, March 23–24, 2003, and finally published in shorter and somewhat different form online at www.setileague.org/iaaseti/brin.pdf.

2. *Encoding Altruism* conferences, 2002, 2003. See http://publish.seti.org/art_science/2003/ Accessed September 6, 2009.

3. The reader should be aware of an ongoing international tussle over METI—or Messages to Extraterrestrial Intelligence—also called "Active SETI." At least a dozen narrow, extremely powerful beamed massages have already been briefly transmitted, vastly brighter, at-target, than our normal radio, television, and radar signals, which have been shown to fade into background beyond about 1 light year. Those who have embarked upon these exercises dismiss all concerns or pleas for prediscussion, citing untested assumptions such as the one discussed here—universal altruism. Concern over METI was raised by the science journal *Nature* in an editorial in October 2006, which commented on a recent meeting of the *International Academy of Astronautics* SETI study group. The editor said, "It is not obvious that all extraterrestrial civilizations will be benign, or that contact with even a benign one would not have serious repercussions" (*Nature 4* (43), 12, 06 p. 606). This author offers a summary view of the imbroglio at http://lifeboat.com/ex/shouting.at.the.cosmos

4. Success-oriented planning is actually the most reasonable thing to do in many cases in which there isn't a large asymmetry or irreversibility in the payoff matrix. First contact with an unknown life form does not meet the criterion, however. Potential downsides of failure are immense and irreversible. This makes success-oriented planning truly irresponsible.

5. The most effective con artists are the least rapacious-seeming folks you will probably ever have the misfortune to meet. Kenneth Galbraith once said that we experience big financial cons about every 20 years because we let our guard down. We can afford several-year setbacks every 20 years. What we can't afford is a millennia-scale setback, simply because we didn't argue about something for a while before responding.

References

Brin, G. D. (1983). The great silence: 100 tentative explanations for our lack of contact with extraterrestrial intelligence. *Quarterly Journal of Royal Astronomical Society, 24,* 283–309.

Fehr, E., & Gächter, S. (2002). Altruistic punishment in humans. *Nature, 415*(6868), 137–140.

Henrich, J., McElreath, R., Barr, A., Ensminger, J., Barrett, C., Bolyanatz, A., et al. (2006). Costly punishment across human societies. *Science, 312*(5781), 1767–1770.

Taleb, N. N. (2007). *The Black Swan: The impact of the highly improbable.* New York.

CHAPTER 20

IS PATHOLOGICAL ALTRUISM ALTRUISM?

Bernard Berofsky

KEY CONCEPTS

- Ethical altruism can be defined either as the view that we have obligations to others or that altruism is a virtue. Ethical egoists believe that we have obligations only to ourselves and that altruism is not a virtue.
- Psychological egoists deny that there are altruists. Since altruism is characterized by intention rather than outcome, and there are people who act with the intention to help others at their own expense, psychological egoism seems clearly false.
- Since a conscious intention to help can conceal an unconscious motivation to harm, one can redefine psychological egoism more plausibly as the view that no one is really motivated to sacrifice his or her own interests to help others.
- If the psychological egoist is right and there are no altruists, how can there be pathological altruists?
  - First answer: Pathological types have some common characteristics—compulsiveness, destructiveness, ignorance of motivation.
  - Second answer: More importantly, the pathological altruist's altruistic *intention* is an essential expression of his self-regarding *motivation*. He must intend to help in order to serve his own destructive needs.

FOOL'S GOLD IS not gold; but red jellybeans are jellybeans. Is pathological altruism an impaired form of altruism, or is it not altruism at all? Before we begin to answer this question, some preliminaries are in order.

Altruism has two very different dimensions, ethical and psychological. Since our topic is pathological altruism, we want first to situate altruism in a broader context. We begin by looking at a challenge to the conventional view that altruism is both (psychologically) possible and (morally) commendable. The challenge is known as egoism and it has two dimensions (Figure 20.1).

FIGURE 20.1
Opposing positions.

Ethical Egoism

Ethical egoism can be defined as the view that we have no obligations to others (alternatively, we ought always to be motivated by self-interest) or as the view that altruism is not a virtue or not meritorious.[1] But even ethical altruists will usually draw some line between acts we have a duty to perform for others and genuinely heroic acts. The latter—for example, surrendering one's life for another—are normally deemed praiseworthy or noble, but are not morally required.

Those who reject ethical egoism are ethical altruists. Thus, they believe either that we have obligations to others or that altruism is meritorious. On the former definition, the ethical altruist must draw a line between obligation and heroism (sometimes called *supererogation*), and many moral philosophers do not accept conventional views as to the location of the line. Some who are disturbed by the enormous discrepancy in the world between rich and poor believe, in the name of global justice, that people who are well off ought to share their excess wealth with the poor. Others come down on the other end of the spectrum and view conventional morality itself as overly demanding. Peter Singer (1994) has recently argued that parents of children born with severe defects should not be expected to care for them and ought morally to be allowed, in certain cases, to let them die.

An egoist might reject any line, arguing not just that we have no obligations to others, but also that one who sacrifices himself for others is a fool rather than a hero. This negative character assessment obviously implies that altruism is not really a virtue. We turn then to the conception of ethical altruism as the view that altruism is a virtue.

Due to Aristotle's influence, we generally reserve the term "virtue" for character traits, which are general dispositions. Generosity and compassion are character traits; a generous or compassionate person is generally disposed to act a certain way (generously, compassionately) under appropriate conditions. Although it is a bit odd to talk of altruistic persons, we do say that a person can be self-sacrificing, that is, prone to sacrifice his or her interests for the sake of another. So, we may include altruism in the same group of virtues as compassion and generosity. (Aristotle called this group the "moral virtues" in contrast with the "intellectual virtues," such as practical reason and intuitive wisdom.) So, the position that altruism is a virtue is better presented as the more general doctrine that what we normally call virtues (compassion, generosity) are not genuine virtues. It is one way in which to reject conventional morality. This is the view associated with Ayn Rand and her followers (1964). Friedrich Nietzsche (1966) is another revisionist moral philosopher; but, in one sense, it is misleading to call him an ethical egoist. He certainly abhorred Christian charity and its associated "virtues"; but the ultimate morality is to be defined by the *Ubermensch*, the ideal human toward which human evolution is leading, whose "moral" stance is left intentionally indefinite. If one is "beyond good and evil,"[2] it is unpredictable at this pre-Ubermensch stage to predict how he will act. Nietzsche tells us that he will act out of power, unconstrained by limits that are not self-imposed; but it does not follow that his acts are never intended to help others. After all, Zarathustra (Nietzsche, 2005) was interested in transmitting his wisdom to others.

There would be little point to worrying about the ethical status of altruism if no one is really an altruist. But before we consider this position—psychological egoism—we should understand more carefully what altruism would be if it were possible.

Psychological Egoism

Altruistic behavior is defined by intent, not outcome. The actions of an altruistic agent may backfire. See Guruprasad Madhaven and Barbara Oakley's account (Chapter 17) of the harm suffered by the beneficiaries of our altruistic foreign aid policy.[3] In general, people (nations) can be incompetent, ignorant, and worse. Thus, an altruistic action may benefit no one. A soldier sacrifices his life for his buddies, who are killed anyway.[4] Conversely, evil, self-serving people can incidentally help others. During World War II, when concern about their oral health led high-ranking Nazi officials to retain Jewish dentists, their actions benefited the dentists by keeping them from the gas chambers. The officials were clearly not acting altruistically, for their intentions were hardly altruistic.[5]

> If "altruism" applies to intentions, it is undeniable that altruism is a fact. People form intentions to benefit others at their own expense.

If "altruism" applies to intentions, it is undeniable that altruism is a fact. People form intentions to benefit others at their own expense. (This remains true even if there are unclear cases, such as the agent who happens to be a beneficiary of his own action as well, but believes that he would have acted the same way even if the action would have harmed him.) Most adults have life insurance policies, instruments designed to benefit others that incur the penalty to the purchaser of their cost. Yet, there are people who defend psychological egoism, the view that we are always motivated by self-interest. Assuming for the moment that we identify motives with intentions, psychological egoism appears to be obviously wrong. If so, where did it go wrong? Bishop Joseph Butler had an answer. As he pointed out in *Fifteen Sermons Preached at the Rolls Chapel* (1726), the egoist may be confusing motive as a psychological state, an internal thing, with the object of the motive, say, food, an external thing. I am moved by hunger, an internal state; but the object of my hunger is the food out there. The altruist may similarly be moved by the subjective desire for the good of others. Although the desire and its satisfaction are subjective states, what satisfies the desire is external to the person: the good of others, a condition distinct from the desiring person.

We must recognize the distinction between motive and object, for there are cases in which motive exists and object does not: I seek the Holy Grail. My seeking is a genuine activity; but since the Holy Grail does not exist, there is no object of my seeking. I seek to get into medical school and fail, in which case, in spite of the actual seeking, there is no object "my getting into medical school."

Now, it may be true that we never act without some motive. I would not seek food if I were not hungry; I would not seek the good of others if I did not desire to help others. But it is still true that my desiring is different from what I desire, even if the satisfaction of my desire is a pleasant consequence of my realizing my desire (securing food, improving someone's lot). This remains true even if we would not act without this desire (just as we would not seek food if it does not satiate hunger). Thus, if "we are always motivated by self-interest" means "we are always moved to act by some motive or desire," it may be true; but if "we are always motivated by self-interest" means "the object of every motivation is the self-interest of the person with the motive," it is false.

If the egoist insists that the *real* object is the satisfaction of the motive, that the altruist wants only the satisfaction of his altruistic desire, then he is saddled with the following case:

Fred is a blissfully happy man. He believes that he possesses all the best that life can offer: a loving wife, children who adore him, an important job that is personally fulfilling, employers that boost his self-esteem by frequent expressions of high praise, and a huge trust fund bequeathed to him by his father. He dies in peace. In truth, everyone despised him, including his family and colleagues, but they artfully maintained this deception throughout Fred's life—a monumental task, to be sure—to insure rewards from his will. Moreover, Fred's work was, unbeknownst to him, worthless; but his employers had to keep him happy in the hopes that they, too, would benefit at his death. According to the psychological egoist, Fred received everything in life that he wanted, for all that Fred really wanted was psychological satisfaction, not the love, esteem, or the doing of important work.

The psychological egoist may bite the bullet and agree with the immediately preceding sentence, or he may counter by insisting upon a distinction between intention and motive and conceding intention to the believer in altruism. Let us pursue the latter alternative. Yes, people form altruistic intentions, intentions directed to the securing of another's benefit at one's own expense, and then carry them out. So, on a superficial, conscious level, intentions are a part of the causal process. Yet they provide little in the way of explanation. Imagine a baseball hurtling toward home plate. At a certain point in time, it will be 30 feet from home plate. Why that position? The answer, that a split second before, it was 45 feet from and headed toward that spot, is a minimal explanation although, like the forming of an intention, it is part of the causal process. The answer, that the pitcher was trying to strike out the batter with a low, inside pitch, is far more illuminating. Similarly, if you ask me why I gave up my seat and stood throughout the performance, it would not be erroneous for me to tell you that I formed the intention to do so shortly before I proceeded with the gesture. It tells you at least that it was not an accident, that I did not get up just to stretch my legs for a minute, unaware that you would quickly pounce. But it would be far more illuminating (if true) for me to tell you that I did it in order to make you feel guilty, so that I could later extract a favor from you. An important difference between motive and intention is that it is difficult to challenge an agent's honest report of his or her intentions, whereas we readily allow that a person who honestly reports that he was moved to act out of concern for the other may well be mistaken. In the example, I may be unaware that I was not moved by altruistic motives.

Of course, if I did have this selfish motive, I could not truly say that I did it for your sake. Whether or not I know my real motives, this statement would be false. It misidentifies the motive that led me to form the intention.

This argument does not prove that motives themselves cannot be altruistic, even if it responds to a simple argument for altruism. It opens a possibility for the radical position of psychological egoism, characterized now as the view that we are always *motivated* by self-interest. In a way, the egoist's argument is similar to one directed against advocates of the paradigm case argument. Let me explain.

The twentieth century saw the linguistic turn in philosophy. The intense focus on language, together with the belief that, with the unraveling of its mysteries, there would as well issue solutions (or dissolutions) of central philosophical problems, culminated in ordinary language philosophy, centered in Oxford. To the nonphilosopher, it appeared that the queen of the sciences had been relegated to a lowly place within the intellectual pantheon, performing scullery duty for scientists, who were the true truth-seekers. But the philosophers contended that, through ordinary language analysis, they really were solving traditional philosophical problems. For example, some of them contended that one can prove the reality of free will through the "paradigm case argument." To simplify the argument: the absence of free will in some people makes sense only through contrast with clear cases (paradigms) of positive application of the concept. So, Jones lacks free will because he is being compelled or is psychologically deranged or is ignorant of crucial facts or is the victim of posthypnotic suggestion, etc. But then Smith must *have* free will because he is not acting under compulsion, is emotionally healthy, is knowledgeable, is not a victim of posthypnotic suggestion, etc. Thus, the concept must have application. Some people must have free will.

The way these simple solutions failed is similar to the way the simple proof that there must be altruistic behavior fails. Concepts in general, and especially ones like free will and altruism, do not apply to the world on the basis of simple, assumption-free, determinate observations (like "red"). If there is a distinction between purely observational concepts, ones whose application is guaranteed when proffered by a normal observer under normal conditions of observation, and theoretical concepts, ones whose application depends in part on theoretical assumptions whose refutation would undermine even an ideal observational judgment, surely a concept such as free will must fall on the side of the theoretical. Those who worry about the destruction of our power to do otherwise by determinism believe that the proper application of "free" presupposes a breach in the causal scheme posited by determinism, and they are not to be assuaged by the existence of ordinary, "correct" uses of "she did it of her own free will." So, even in so-called paradigm cases, if determinism reigns, we are wrong in attributing free will. The distinction in ordinary discourse between "free" and "unfree" conceals a background assumption (the rejection of determinism) that is open to challenge. Whether the challenge succeeds or not, the idea of a simple proof of free will fails. Analogously, devotees of psychological egoism are not to be assuaged by the fact that people form intentions to help others at the expense of their own interests. The real issue must be addressed at the deeper level of motives. And motives are not directly accessible to the person with the motive and, a fortiori, to others. Thus, the performer can be mistaken in attributing altruistic motives to himself. And, once we concede the possibility of error at the level of motivation, the psychological egoist is thereby equipped with a tool for undermining any claim of altruistic motivation.

It is again important to note that these thoughts do not *establish* psychological egoism. Psychological evidence is needed for that. The role of the philosopher is restricted to determining whether any a priori limits render psychological egoism impossible. The above discussion lends support to the position that there are none, and if that is right, the question can be turned over to the empirical scientists.

Suppose that the psychological egoist is right We are always moved by self-interest, even if self-interest leads us to form altruistic intentions, intentions to help others, viewed as means to promote our own self-interest. Thus, in a deep sense, there is no altruism. But then, if there is no altruism at all, how can there be pathological altruism, altruism gone awry? A partial answer may be found through reflection on the following analogy.

Psychological Egoism and Pathological Altruism

Compare the relation between altruism and pathological altruism with the relation between robbery and kleptomania. Both the ordinary thief and the kleptomaniac form intentions to steal; but the motive of the thief is typically the securing of some desirable object. Kleptomaniacs, on the other hand, generally steal objects that are regarded as having little objective worth, indicating that their motives are different in nature from those of the normal thief. But, independently of motivation, there are other important differences. Kleptomania, as a pathological condition, possesses some generic traits of pathology in general, such as compulsiveness and lack of self-knowledge (probably in the form of self-deception).

> We are always moved by self-interest, even if self-interest leads us to form altruistic intentions, intentions to help others, viewed as means to promote our own self-interest. Thus, in a deep sense, there is no altruism. But then, if there is no altruism at all, how can there be pathological altruism, altruism gone awry?

Similarly, we may invoke general pathological syndromes to set off the pathological altruist from others; compulsiveness, loss of control, distorted thinking, and self-destructiveness (that goes beyond the self-sacrificing component built into the "altruistic" character of the performance itself), to name a few.

We can also find differences between the simple altruist and the pathological altruist by revisiting the area of motivation. For, even if the psychological egoist is right and there are no altruistic motives, we can distinguish normal self-interest from pathologies of motivation. A man who knowingly spends a lot of money on a bauble designed to lower the resistance of his wife to his purchase of an expensive sports car may be conniving or naïve, but he is not pathological. A person who forms an altruistic intention as part of a defense mechanism designed to avoid painful realities or as a device to sustain a relationship that is both self- and other-destructive is pathological. A child who assumes greater than her share of familial responsibilities may be unconsciously attempting to control her siblings through the creation of guilt feelings in them.

In elaborating on the above, we can highlight yet a third way to distinguish altruism from pathological altruism. Pathological altruism is not only self-destructive; it is also destructive to others. One can, as we just said, engage in self-sacrifice in order to control or punish another human being, perhaps by inducing guilt. Earlier, I noted that altruistic acts can have destructive consequences because of the ineptitude or ignorance of the performer. But there is a big difference in this respect between normal and pathological altruism. The unfortunate consequences in the case of the former arise either from garden-variety lack of foreknowledge or from other nonpathological failings. Ignorance, culpable or not, and ineptitude are common human failings, unrelated to pathology. The destructive consequences of the need to control or punish others, on the other hand, arise out of the very pathological motivation itself. Unlike the bungler's failures, those of the pathological altruist are intrinsic to his pathology. We will later elaborate on this important feature: that is, the special manner in which the motivation guides the process in ways that render it pathological.

Thus, even if there is no normal altruism, there are ways to distinguish what appears to be altruism from pathological altruism. Pathological altruism can be identified whether or not there are normal altruists. But other conceptual hurdles remain.

Altruism and Pathological Altruism

If we assume psychological egoism, then there is no altruism. There are altruistic intentions; but we have concluded that an altruist must be motivated by altruism, that altruism at the level of intention only is shallow. Well, if there is no altruism, then it is not surprising that the pathological altruist is not really an altruist. He cannot be—there are no altruists.

But we cannot just assume psychological egoism. We have not argued for it, only against some poor reasons for denying it. So, let us, at this point, adopt a neutral stance. There may then be normal altruists, people driven by the desire to help others at the expense of themselves.

If we characterize altruistic behavior in terms of motivation—and we have argued that we should—what becomes of pathological altruism if there is such a thing as normal altruism? If we look at the motives of the pathological altruist— guilt, the avoidance of pain (or the confronting of painful realities), the avoidance of conflict, the desire to control others, the desire to punish others—it turns out that pathological altruism is not altruism at all *even allowing that normal altruism exists*. Perhaps then "pathological altruism" is an oxymoron. It is related to altruism in the way that fool's gold is related to gold. The creators of this anthology need not be alarmed, since it does not follow that there is no such thing as pathological altruism. (Fool's gold is real; so are mock battles and counterfeit money.) We suggested that, as a pathology, it can be identified through features found in pathologies in general. The individual acts compulsively, and his motivation is difficult or impossible to access consciously. Hence, he loses rational control over his own behavior and his thought processes themselves exhibit irrationality.

But we need a way to distinguish this pathology from others, and it is clear what that way is. If there is normal, nonpathological altruism, the intention to help another flows naturally from the desire or motive to do so. We usually don't bother even to distinguish intention from motive. To be sure, motivation is complex and possibly mixed. Perhaps a genuine desire to help another is commingled with a more self-regarding one. And, if we dig more deeply into the unconscious roots of motivation, we may find genetic or genetic/cultural grounds—Marc D. Hauser (Chapter 29) suggests that ingroup favoritism is a crucial evolutionary factor—that can appear to be in tension with the idea of an individual or personal origin. Indeed, considerations such as these may form part of the basis of the blanket denial of altruism.

But, whatever obtains in the individual who is supposedly a normal altruist, we know that the basic difference between him and his pathological cousin, beyond the generic pathological elements, is the distortion that takes place as motive is converted to intention. Whatever the nature of that distortion, the altruism component of the pathological altruist is constituted by the intention, a component that is superficial in the normal case, yet crucial in a sense to be specified for the pathological case.

Although the pathological altruist is not *really* altruistic, she would not be what she is without the altruistic intention. That is what is meant by "crucial." The very nature of her condition requires that she form an altruistic intention. This is most obvious in the case of malignant altruism (see Turvey, Chapter 13, this volume). One sort of malignant altruist feels hurt by the real or perceived wrongs she has suffered and desires to punish the guilty party. She (intends to and) performs an act that benefits this party, but results in great harm to herself. The self-sacrifice is intended to elicit feelings of guilt on the part of the recipient, guilt that is magnified by the (perhaps unconscious) recognition that she, the recipient, once wronged the performer. The malignant altruist may also wish to exert control over the other party through this manipulative mechanism. There are, of course, a variety of ways to induce guilt in or gain control over others. So, people have a variety of pathologies to "choose" from. But the pseudoaltruism of the malignant altruist plays an essential role in the mechanism of this individual. Guilt on the part of party B is enhanced by the exquisite combination of the conferral of a benefit on B combined with the suffering or martyrdom required by A to achieve this end.

The fact that altruistic intentions play an essential role in pathological altruism enables us to distinguish this case from sociopathy. A con man may form altruistic intentions as a way to soften his mark. If he lets the target experience early wins, it will be easier later to pull in the big haul. But if he can achieve the final goal without appearing to benefit the target, he will do so. The pathological altruist does not have this luxury. He needs to appear as the savior or martyr.

Conclusion

In the end, then, "pathological altruism" is an appropriate label in spite of the fact that it is not altruism. For an altruistic intention is essential to the underlying mechanism, even though that mechanism is in fact other- (and self-) destructive. The pathological altruist must appear to be motivated by altruism at the same time she that is destroying the other.

In a normal person, this intention is a sign of an actual altruistic motive, the criterion of genuine altruism. Since signs are not always reliable, psychological egoism emerges as a possibility. (We must again be reminded, however, that defenses of this position may require the overcoming of other conceptual hurdles and certainly do require the marshaling of empirical evidence.) To be sure, the psychological egoist's position is more radical, since he believes that the "sign" in the case of apparently altruistic behavior is *never* reliable. He would probably argue that the seductions of altruism arise from the fact that we generally move easily from intention to underlying motive, from declaring an intention to give to charity to really wanting to give to charity. Indeed, the closeness of the link between intention and motive is a hallmark of rationality. People who form intentions that never match their real motives are barely rational agents. The psychological egoist is not, however, contemplating such an extreme. Since she supposes a breakdown *in the special case* in which the interests of the other are at stake, we are not contemplating divergence between intention and motive for all human action. So, the breakdown in the linkage in the *special case* of altruism does not jeopardize rationality in general.

However the perennial debate between the egoist and the altruist is resolved, we have found a place in the conceptual scheme of things for pathological altruism. We may coherently identify persons as pathological altruists without having to suppose that they are altruists at all.

Notes

1. Aristotle thought of virtue as excellence of character. So, the virtues are a set of character traits whose possession confers excellence upon one and warrants praise from others.

2. The title of (and lead character in) one of Nietzsche's books, in which he repudiates traditional morality.

3. One cannot talk about these issues without talking about benefit and harm, and there is no space for a full-fledged discussion of these concepts. My inclination is to initiate a characterization of harm to an individual in terms of what the individual herself finds harmful. This first stab would have to be amended to take into account ignorance, neuroticism, and irrationality. A person may not know what is helpful or harmful to her, or she may refuse to recognize some harm or benefit out of some neurotic need. So, the revised account would talk of what the individual finds harmful *if* she were knowledgeable, rational, mentally healthy, etc.

Some may object to the failure to incorporate social and cultural elements into the definition. In fact, these elements have not played a role in my discussion, although I acknowledge their importance in characterizing the very concept of altruism. In this connection, I have learned a great deal from other authors in this volume, such as John W. Traphagen.

4. Take my brother-in-law, please. (Apologies to Henny Youngman.) He would give you the shirt off his back. But it would have a big hole in it.

5. An action that benefits both the performer and the recipient may be an altruistic action if the intent is the benefit of the recipient. The latter obtains if the performer would have performed the action even if it had harmed herself, the performer. Of course, this counterfactual is often difficult to evaluate, and even the performer of the prima facie altruistic action may be ignorant or even self-deceived as to the genuine altruism of her own action. Also, although the term "altruistic" is used only for intentions to benefit persons, a case can be made that it should be extended to intentions designed to benefit an ideology or an institution. People have certainly sacrificed their interests, indeed, their lives, on behalf of these impersonal entities.

References

Butler, J. (1726). Sermon IX: Upon the love of our neighbor. In *Fifteen sermons preached at the Rolls chapel* (London).

Nietzsche, F. (2005). *Thus spoke Zarathrusta* trans. G. Parkes. Oxford: Oxford University Press. (Original work published 1909).

_____ (1966). *Beyond Good and Evil*, trans. Walter Kaufmann. New York: Random House. (Original work published 1885).

Rand, A. (1964). *The virtue of selfishness*. New York: Signet.

Singer, P. (1994). *Rethinking life and death: The collapse of our traditional ethics*. New York: St. Martin's Press.

CHAPTER 21

ALTRUISM, PATHOLOGY, AND CULTURE

John W. Traphagan

KEY CONCEPTS

- Altruism and pathology are concepts that do not necessarily translate well from one culture to another; this raises questions for how biological and cultural aspects of these concepts influence behavior.
- Certain features of altruistic behavior may be relatively consistent across different cultures, but nuances of meaning vary, necessarily implying that deviation from the "norm" will vary as well.
- Pathological altruism is behavior that deviates from norms of action that shape concepts of altruism in particular cultures, but those acts themselves have no moral value and are not necessarily parallel from one culture to another.

IN HER FASCINATING study, *Evil Genes*, Barbara Oakley (2007, p. 33) makes an interesting observation—that if emerging genetic research is right, the concept of "psychopathic" behavior may be rather simplistic and that "evil" behavior may be not merely a result of nasty parenting or bad breaks in life, but could well have a genetic basis. Oakley argues convincingly that genes influence our behavior in general and our capacity for bad behavior in particular. But her work also points to an important question she does not address: To what extent are concepts like "moral," "right," "wrong," "evil," "good," "altruism," or "psychopathic" value-neutral?

Philosophers such as Kant have proposed an objective and universal human dignity with an associated moral good—true morality is out there to be found and should not be a matter of cultural convention. If Kant is right, this would seem to align nicely with the idea that there is a universal genetic basis that contributes to how humans conceptualize right and wrong. Nonetheless, Kant's approach has been rejected by other philosophers (Rorty, 1983; Wong, 1984), who have argued, to paraphrase Richard Rorty, that the "moral self" is nothing more than a network of interlocking beliefs, desires, and emotions that are shaped by a particular cultural and political context with no objective foundation (Rorty, 1983, p. 583). In other words, for moral relativists, right and wrong are entirely a matter of convention; there is no objective spiritual, biological, or natural basis for determining if an action is right or wrong. In general, the empirical evidence drawn from ethnographic research tends to support the relativist position, while research from other areas of the social sciences, such as psychology and biological sciences, such as Oakley's discussion of evil genes, tend to lean in the other direction.

This leaves us with something of a conundrum when thinking about the relationship between biology and morality: How can there be a fundamental biological basis for moral action, or even some type of biological foundation that shapes our ideas about right and wrong, when human interpretation of moral action is not universally agreed upon and, in

> To what extent are concepts like "moral," "right," "wrong," "evil," "good," "altruism," or "psychopathic" value-neutral?

fact, can exhibit very contradictory ideas about right and wrong across different cultures? If, in society A, for example, it is considered morally wrong and evidence of psychopathology to attempt (or commit) suicide, but in society B suicide is considered an honorable form of death—even a moral good in certain circumstances—how do we identify a linkage between genes that are universally evident in human bodies and moral concepts that are not? If pathological behavior has a genetic foundation, how do we respond to the fact that the same behavior can be pathological in one society and not in another?

In this chapter, I explore and unpack meanings associated with concepts of altruism and pathology. The issue here stems in part from a tendency in the discipline of anthropology, and more broadly in the social and behavioral sciences, to drift in the direction of methodological extremes that treat humans either as primarily biological beings or cultural beings, and the concomitant tendency to think about human behavior in terms of cultural determinism or biological determinism. In anthropology, this problem has exhibited itself in rifts deep enough to split departments between the biological and cultural elements of a discipline that has historically prided itself on its holistic approach; more generally, a similar split can be seen in the departmental organization of universities that normally (at least in the United States) fragment along the lines of natural and social sciences. Cultural anthropologists and other scholars who tend to see humans as fundamentally cultural beings have often provided important critiques of the biological approach, noting that cultural biases generate assumptions about language, behavior, and biology itself that can significantly influence the methodology and interpretation of results (Strier, 2003). Unfortunately, this important point has at times been expressed in an intellectualized and reductionistic politics of antiscience, in which the proposition of a genetic basis to human behavior becomes a warped imagining of hegemonic Western white male intellectual culture (cf. Calcagno, 2003, p. 10).

Nonetheless, ethnographic data suggest extreme care is needed in thinking about what may be universal in human behavior, how behavior is shaped by biology as opposed to culture, and the potential influence culturally shaped assumptions about behavior may have on scientific research. There are reasonable questions to be considered about the extent to which contemporary neuroscientists

> If pathological behavior has a genetic foundation, how do we respond to the fact that the same behavior can be pathological in one society and not in another?

are working, not independently of their own cultures, but are shaped when thinking about "social values" or moral values by the very cultures in which they operate—largely those of the West. For example, anthropologists have found a variety of structural forms that appear to be universal—all human societies appear to develop some way of reckoning kin relationships and also appear to have developed something that can be considered religious behavior (depending upon how one defines religion). A good example of universality in human behavior is the incest taboo. Humans, like animals in the wild, appear to have a general tendency toward avoidance of incest (Brown, 1991, p. 118). However, culture significantly influences what this means for different groups of people. In societies that raise children in peer groups, such as Israeli *Kibbutzim*—rather than nuclear families—social sanctions toward incestual behavior are relatively indifferent, in part because there is little interest in incestual sex among members (Brown, 1991, p. 120). We might argue, as does McCabe (1983), that this supports the idea that intimate proximity as children are reared inclines them toward avoidance of sexual activity and, thus, indexes a biological disinclination toward incest. The problem here arises in determining what counts as incest; in the case of the *kibbutzim*, although while the children raised together tend to avoid sexual intimacy, many of the children are not biologically related, which could weaken the argument that there is any biological basis for the incest taboo—on the one hand, it may be that proximity kicks-in a genetically based discomfort with sex among kin, but it may equally be the result of a cultural cause, or some combination of culture and biology acting together (in my view, the most likely answer).

A further problem is one of meaning. One need only look at U.S. state laws on incest to see that variation exists in how the behavior is interpreted. In some states (e.g., Alabama) sibling incest includes sexual relations with a brother or sister of whole or half-blood or by adoption. In others, adoption is not an issue (e.g., Alaska) or includes sexual relations between adoptive ancestors or descendents (e.g., Missouri). When it comes to first-cousin marriage, U.S. states vary considerably; 30% of U.S. states prohibit first-cousin marriage, while the remainder either allow it or allow it in a restricted manner, such as provided the couple cannot produce children.

In Arab countries, there is a preference for patrilineal parallel cousin marriage (marriage of a man to his father's brother's daughter). Although McCabe argued that the intimate familial association in childhood leads to sexual distancing, several scholars have rejected her conclusions (McCabe, 1983, p. 50; Dodd & Prothro, 1985, p. 135). And Kopytoff (1984) argues that McCabe's data suggest the potential institutional viability of sibling marriage. In short, there has been quite a bit of debate within anthropology about the extent and nature of the incest "taboo" among human societies, but what seems relatively clear is that, although most humans avoid sexual relations between primary kin, considerable variation exists in what counts as primary kin, and in some cases, sibling marriage is actually expected, making it difficult to claim a universal *prohibition* on incest because the meaning of incest varies among different cultures (McCabe, 1985, p. 135).

In fact, translation of the term is, itself, extremely difficult, as Ager (2005, p. 1–2) points out in her study of Ptolemaic incest, noting that the Latin *incestum* implies impurity and pollution, but in ancient Greek there was no word to describe marriage or intercourse with overly close kin, while in Chinese the term *luan lun* implies a disorder in social relationships rather than impurity or pollution. In short, both ethnographic and historical research have shown that it is very difficult to claim a single, universal prohibition on incest, due to the fact that meanings and interpretations vary (significantly) from one culture to another.

Analysis of terms such as incest in cross-cultural perspective raises a fundamental problem in understanding moral behavior, particularly when considering behaviors that appear to be human universals, as it often has been pursued from the perspective of biology. Put simply, it is not unusual for scientists (both social and natural) to draw upon Western philosophical ideas to ground their assumptions about human nature while ignoring a wide body of ethnographic data suggesting strongly that Western philosophical constructs about morality and human nature are very much products of the cultures in which they arose, despite their tendency to be presented as universal. Rather than assuming that human nature is an objective thing to be found, and that certain moral notions, such as altruism, are a priori elements of that nature, it may be more prudent (and fruitful) to ask questions such as: What does it *mean* to be altruistic, and how does that meaning vary among different groups of humans? This question, in turn, raises another question central to this volume: What does it *mean* to be pathologically altruistic? To address these types of questions, we need to embark upon a deconstruction of the cultural assumptions that are implicit in the terms altruism and pathology; this type of deconstruction should be an important component of thinking about how to pursue research on the genetic basis for moral reasoning. In the remainder of this chapter, I will argue that this process of deconstructing meaning is essential to explaining how what Hauser (2006, p. 36) refers to as the (universal) human moral faculty—the biologically endowed capacity to evaluate actions and behaviors in terms of (non-universal) principles of right and wrong—is expressed and used by people in different societies. When we think about altruism or pathology, we are contemplating a set of behaviors that are not only executed, but also interpreted within a cultural context that shapes the development and structure of the brains within that context.

> It is not unusual for scientists (both social and natural) to draw upon Western philosophical ideas to ground their assumptions about human nature while ignoring a wide body of ethnographic data suggesting strongly that Western philosophical constructs about morality and human nature are very much products of the cultures in which they arose, despite their tendency to be presented as universal.

Is Altruism Always Altruism?

Recent research in neuroscience has made use of magnetic resonance imaging (MRI) and functional MRI (fMRI) technologies to explore the neural foundations of moral reasoning. Two important questions underlie much of this research: How did a sense of a moral conscience that appears to be evident in the majority of humans, and which some argue differentiates us from other animals, emerge (Tobeña, 2007, p. 84)?[1] And, how does the brain construct, interpret, and communicate the moral conscience, the moral/social values that operate in a particular person? The published work stemming from this important research on the one hand seems to provide fairly strong quantitative evidence for the idea that, among research subjects, certain parts of the brain are activated when individuals are presented with words, problems, or ideas that are viewed as having moral content. However, much of this work relies on a set of assumptions—either explicit or implicit—about the nature of moral conscience in humans and about the consistency of moral reasoning across different cultural contexts. It also works from a perspective, when generalized to human behavior, that morally charged terms can, in fact, be translated into other languages without significant loss of meaning.

For example, Jorge Moll and several of his collaborators have produced ground-breaking work using fMRI technologies to show what parts of the brain are activated when their subjects are presented with specific problems that the researchers deem moral in nature. They have found that "social values" are related to a neural architecture that "provides the basis for our ability to communicate about the meaning of social values across cultural contexts without limiting our flexibility to adapt their emotional interpretation" (Zahn et al., 2008, p. 276). Given the human penchant for conflict and war, one can question just how effectively humans manage to communicate about the meanings of social values across cultures or even within cultural groupings. Indeed, Moll and other neuroscientists tend to rely upon a conceptualization of human moral reasoning and social attachment that works from a set of assumptions that humans universally have an intuitive and innate sense of concern for others, a sense of what constitutes fair and equitable action, and consistently observe and adhere to cultural norms of behavior and moral right (Moll & Schulkin, 2008, p. 456). Working from such assumptions, these scholars directly or tacitly index the works of Western moral philosophy, with its own assumptions about the nature of human being. Moll, in particular, draws upon the ideas of 18th-century moral philosophers Kant and Smith to buttress his idea that at some objective (and acultural) level, all humans who do not have pathological tendencies share at least basic notions of right and wrong that are tied to a fundamental brain/cognitive structure that is a product of human evolution and generates a universal sense of morality.

This approach ignores the wealth of ethnographic evidence showing, quite to the contrary of the assumption taken by Moll and others, that humans do not necessarily show concern for other humans whom they do not deem as persons—in other words, if an entire group of biologically human beings is deemed by another group to be either nonhuman or subhuman, then it becomes quite possible to eschew empathetic responses to the situation of that group or of individuals within that group. Conceptualizations of personhood are cultural categories articulated within the confines of largely agreed upon social values operating in a particular community, but these are not necessarily extended to members of other communities (Morris, 1994, p. 11). Benedict showed more than 75 years ago that many tribal societies, such as the Zuni or Dene, use terms of self-reference that mean "people" or "human beings" that set themselves morally apart from their neighbors (Benedict, 1934, p. 5). Although they may recognize other groups as consisting of human-like animals, from the perspective of moral value, there is an implication of genuine personhood only for the in-group and non or diminished personhood for others (Morris, 1994, p. 11). This, of course, is not limited to tribal societies; one need only look at institutionalized behaviors such as slavery, Nazi concentration camps, or the treatment of prisoners at Abu Ghraib to recognize that dehumanizing other groups is far closer to the norm for modern nation-states than it is an exception. At the same time, some Native American societies extended the notion of personhood far beyond that normally posited by contemporary Westerners, recognizing nonhuman animals as persons equivalent to humans and deserving of equal treatment and consideration (Martin, 2001).

In some Native American groups, such as Iroquoian peoples, recognition of the humanity, or at least the value, of outsiders could be tied to evidence apparent through a series of ritual tortures that ended in a capturing group eating a captured individual who had shown his bravery (and his value as a human) as a

> Humans do not necessarily show concern for other humans whom they do not deem as persons.

means of embodying the other's power (Traphagan, 2008). Cases like the Iroquoian example raise odd questions for ethnographers and historians—is it possible, for example, that ingesting the enemy "other" was perceived as an altruistic act among the group eating him? Certainly, they were honoring that individual, despite his identity as enemy, because he honored himself during the ritual tortures. What did cannibalizing the enemy *mean* for the Iroquoians who engaged in that type of activity?

In fact, when it comes to daily use, we rarely give much thought to what terms like altruism mean in our own societies, let alone in other societies with different, and at times even repugnant, values. The term *altruism* derives from the Latin word *alter* meaning "other." Altruism is defined in English-speaking contexts as unselfish concern or devotion to the well-being and welfare of others, and can refer to behavior by a human or nonhuman animal that benefits others while potentially harming oneself. This meaning, however, does not necessarily map into other languages. For example, several words in Japanese can be translated as altruism when placed into English, including *aitashugi, taai, ritashugi,* and *orutoruezumu.* The easiest of these to translate is the last, *orutoruezumu,* which is written in Japanese as follows: オルトルイズム. If the reader pronounces the Romanized version of the word, it becomes evident that this term is borrowed from English; indeed, the fact that it is written in the katakana syllabary tells us that it is a loan word. Since there are other words for this concept in Japanese, one is left wondering why the word would be imported into the Japanese language. Although it is not possible to determine the exact reason, it seems likely that the word, like many other loan words from English, came into usage in part because it reflects meaning not inherent to related words of native origin.

Native Japanese terms share meanings with the English term altruism, some important differences also exist, particularly when one unpacks the specific meanings of each kanji character that composes the words. Below, each term is displayed in its Japanese form using kanji and then Romanized using hyphens to separate the sound associated with each character.

愛他主義　　ai-ta-shu-gi
他愛　　　　ta-ai
利他主義　　ri-ta-shu-gi

All of these terms imply some sense of selfless behavior, and an additional term, *ritatekikoui* (利他的行為), implies a sense of self-sacrifice that is not immediately evident in the other three. Considering the definitions of these terms used in Japanese language dictionaries is illuminating. The term *ritashugi,* for example, is defined in the *Shogakukan Japanese Language Dictionary* as the antonym of egoism and as a principle that considers the happiness of others over one's own happiness. And *aitashugi* is defined as an impulse or a feeling of consideration (for others), or a behavior based on that consideration. In *Longman's English-Japanese Dictionary*, altruism is translated as *ritashugi*, which is defined as unselfish behavior or behavior like a "warning voice" (警告声 けいこくせい) that what one does will be disadvantageous to one's self, but will give a benefit to one's fellows. Although the *Longman's* definition indexes some sense of self-sacrifice associated with the term, it is important to recognize that this is a translation of the English "altruism" into a native Japanese term—in the *Shogakukan* dictionary, which is not a translation dictionary, there is no direct referencing of the notion of self-sacrifice.

While these words represent meanings as coherent wholes and should be understood in that way, it is instructive to recognize that each kanji character that comprises part of a particular word also represents specific meanings; when a Japanese person sees a word, he or she can understand not only the meaning of the compound of characters, but also the specific meanings of individual characters that make up the compound. This is akin to understanding Latin roots in English, although in Japanese this is much stronger because each kanji character represents an immediately identifiable meaning in pictorial form that is included in other words and also likely represents a word on its own. In the above list, the first word, *aitashugi*, contains characters that mean love or affection (*ai*); other(s) (*ta*); master (*shu*); and justice, righteousness, honor, and loyalty (*gi*). Taken together, the second pair of characters make the compound word *shugi*, which means doctrine, rule, or principle. Thus, if we translate the word *aitashugi* into English literally, it means "doctrine or principle of love for others."

The second word, *taai*, includes characters that mean love of other(s) (plural and singular are not normally differentiated in the Japanese language), just as found in the term *aitashugi*, although the order of these characters is reversed in *taai*, which influences the meaning. *Taai* indicates a love for others or a cherishing of the matters of others, but there is a subtle nuance of romance associated with the term. And the third word combines the characters for master and justice, righteousness, honor, loyalty with characters that mean profit, advantage, or benefit (*ri*) and the same term for other or others (*ta*). Again, the *shugi* portion of the word means doctrine, rule, or principle; thus, the term *ritashugi* can be translated as "doctrine or principle of profit or benefit to others."

It should be immediately evident that when dissecting the compounds, the notion of these actions as being "selfless" does not appear in the kanji that make up any of the native Japanese terms, although because selflessness is highly valued in Japanese society, we can assume that Japanese people would include this by implication in contemplating the meaning of these terms. At the same time, several concepts are included that do not appear in the English term altruism. Both words *aitashugi* and *ritashugi* reference social hierarchy, because the term *shugi* includes meanings related to honor, loyalty, and justice (which are closely related concepts in Japanese culture) and master or chief. In other words, these concepts contain a sense of love for others, shaped within the confines of hierarchical structures that themselves are conceptualized in terms of loyalty and honor, rather than in terms of selflessness.

This variation in meaning has implications for behavior, particularly when it intersects with other values in Japanese culture, such as a tendency to organize individual identities around values of belongingness that, in turn, create relatively strong notions of in- and out-group membership. Indeed, as Chiao et al. note in Chapter 22, at least at an ideological level, Japanese tend to emphasize interdependence over independence when they contemplate appropriate social relatedness. Care is needed, however, in unpacking this emphasis, because although Japanese do have an ideology of interdependence, they also can be strongly individualistic; Zen, which has had a profound influence on Japanese society, particularly when it comes to pedagogies associated with practices such as the martial arts, tea, or pottery making, is a highly inner-focused form of practice that aims at generating intense concentration, which outside of Zen monasteries tends to have very practical applications associated with attainment of a high level of skill.[2]

Chaio et al. make the important point that the way in which people think about their relationships to others significantly influences how they conceptualize altruistic behavior. Although Japanese can certainly recognize and respond to an altruistic act, far more important than the idea of altruistic action is the idea of actions that promote *harmony* among members of a group and society in general, which interestingly enough may have a biological basis. The functional magnetic resonance imaging (fMRI) research conducted by Freeman et al. (2009, p. 358) with a group of 17 Japanese and 17 Americans suggests that culture shapes mesolimbic responses to signals related to dominance and subordination. The value placed upon exhibiting dominant as opposed to subordinate behavior varies significantly in American and Japanese ideologies of social hierarchy and, thus, are conceptualized differently in terms of positive and negative meaning by many Japanese and Americans. The work of Freeman et al. indicates that not only is there cross-cultural variation in mesolimbic response to signals of dominance and subordination, but this corresponds to how their subjects self-report their own behaviors.

What does this mean for understanding altruism? It would seem reasonable to argue that different culturally shaped attitudes (and biological responses) to evidence of dominant behavior would influence how people conceptualize behaviors such as altruism. In fact, notions of harmony and belongingness (and subordination of personal desires in some cases) for Japanese also involve expectations about reciprocal obligations associated with doing things for others, and these obligations can actually operate as a brake on altruistic actions. An individual may choose not to help a stranger, for example, because the act of helping creates the implication of a relationship that will require ongoing reciprocal responses in terms of actions and gift giving (and often ever-increasing responses) on the part of both parties, as an act of kindness to another can also imply the creation of a social bond that is closely linked to notions about social and cosmic order (Daniels, 2009, p. 388; Traphagan, 2004b).

Examining contexts such as Japan raises important theoretical questions for understanding the interaction between culture and biology. Although we may be able to identify genetic bases for the evolution of both altruism and pathological altruism, the expression of altruistic tendencies needs to be understood as significantly shaped by two environments. The first is the cultural context in which individuals are raised and socialized into thinking about human relationships and their own specific relationships to other individuals and groups. Second, the brain itself should be understood as an environment whose neural pathways are shaped by cognitive development within a cultural context: The meaning or importance of "altruism" as it is expressed in culturally shaped brains necessarily will vary in relation to the contexts of valuation in which those brains mature and integrate values into patterns of behavior. In other words, whatever altruism means to an individual is co-constructed with a wide array of other

The meaning or importance of "altruism" as it is expressed in culturally shaped brains necessarily will vary in relation to the contexts of valuation in which those brains mature and integrate values into patterns of behavior.

variables that are also culturally constructed. These environments interact in individuals to generate both idiosyncratic and culturally shaped expressions of empathy, kindness, and caring for others as the meaning of acts and ideas—and the concomitant meaning of altruism—that are socially and culturally constructed among groups of people and in individual brains.

What Is Pathology?

Imagine the following situation: An elderly person in your neighborhood takes ill and increasingly becomes a burden to the members of his family and community. At the request of that elder, his son-in-law enters his room one evening and stabs him in the heart with a knife (cf. Glascock, 1990, p. 47). Has a crime been committed? Does the son-in-law, or the father, exhibit signs of an abnormal, or pathological, mental condition? Or, was the action of the son-in-law one of altruism?

Among some preindustrial societies, death-hastening practices have long been common both for unproductive and burdensome elderly and infants who are either unwanted or deformed. The above behavior was observed early in the 20th century among the Chukchee people living in northeastern Siberia. The Lau people in Polynesia in the mid-20th century were known to take old and feeble members of their community to a lagoon where they were abandoned—anthropologists observed a cave with skeletal remains of those who had been taken there over time. And elderly in some groups, such as the Bororo in the Amazonian forest, were denied food or, as with the Yakut in Siberia, denied all support or beaten by children and ejected from their own households—in both cases, these behaviors led to the death of the elder (Glascock, 1990, pp. 47–48). In his research comparing death-hastening practices related to the elderly, Glascock found that ethnographic literature identifies more than 20 preindustrial societies that exhibited some form of death-hastening practice, ranging from direct killing to abandonment or forsaking of the individual. In other societies, including modern industrial societies, myths associated with the aging process and the usefulness of the elderly to society are not uncommon; in Japan, the legend of Obasuteyama—mountain for discarding granny—is widely known and has been the subject of two motion pictures in the last 60 years (Traphagan, 2000). In fact, there is an actual mountain by this name in Nagano Prefecture. Although it is unclear as to whether the custom ever actually was practiced, the content of the legend does not necessarily paint the story in a negative light. In both movie versions, as the son carries his mother to the top of the mountain to be abandoned, he cries and resists, but after he leaves her there and it begins to snow (white being symbolic of purity and goodness), he realizes that it was the right thing to do.

It would be difficult, when considering culture, to take any of these actions as pathological, despite the fact that in American society patricide would strongly suggest the need for psychological evaluation. Similarly, self-killing is not uniformly seen as pathological in non-Western societies (or even within Western societies, for that matter). One need only consider the so-called "suicide" bombers in the Middle East to recognize that entirely different notions of suicide, pathology, and altruism are operating. For Americans, these actions are seen as murder–suicides and fundamentally immoral. Although debated by Islamic religious and legal scholars (al-Atawneh, 2008), for the bombers and their associates these are seen as a form of sacrifice and martyrdom (Patkin, 2004, p. 79)—in other words, the actions of suicide bombers are closely aligned with the moral good and, therefore, carry an image of altruistic behavior. They represent acts of ultimate self-sacrifice for a greater good—the service of Allah. Indeed, the difficulty in aligning the action with meaning is evident in the fact that in the Arab press suicide bombers are referred to as "human bombs," while for a period of time following 9/11 the Bush Administration encouraged the press to use the term "homicide bombers" (Patkin, 2004, p. 79).

Attacks that involve taking of one's own life are not new, of course. The Japanese employed similar tactics during World War II in the use of kamikaze and other similar techniques for killing the enemy. Japan represents an excellent example of the complexities of meaning inherent to actions of self-killing that are deemed as having moral content. The term normally translated as suicide in Japanese—*jisatsu* (自殺)—is only one of several words that represent acts of self-killing. These include *ikkanshinju* (family suicide), *shinju* (lovers' suicide), and several others. None of these terms includes characters that refer to *jisatsu*, and in my own ethnographic research I have found that Japanese are uncomfortable in applying the term *jisatsu* to actions like *hara-kiri* or those of the kamikaze, as these do not represent suicides, per se, in the minds of my informants, despite the fact that they are recognized as forms of self-killing (Traphagan, 2004a, pp. 319–320; Traphagan, 2010).

Perhaps the most striking example of how differently Japanese can conceptualize the notion of self-killing is found in the word *gyokusai,* which refers to the wave-style attacks used by the Japanese Imperial Army during World War II. Although Japanese recognize this as a form of self-killing, the term means "honorable defeat" or "honorable death." However, upon reading the kanji that make up the term, it is clear that the characters 玉砕 imply an aesthetic sense or a sense of sad beauty. The literal translation of the word is "shattered jewel," and the term references a sense of deep beauty in the collapse of something that is itself beautiful—one might imagine fireworks as an example such a feeling. This is closely connected to another moral idea in Japanese known as *mono no aware,* which refers to a powerful aesthetic sense associated with the fleeting nature of beauty and the pathos of things.

These examples raise important questions for considering what we define as pathologies represented in the form of antisocial personality disorders. Spitzer et al. (2007, p. 185) argue that, because there is evidence of peer punishment as a significant means of establishing social control and generating compliance with social norms (which themselves establish the limits of social and antisocial behavior), it is reasonable to think that humans have developed neural mechanisms that encourage norm compliance—in other words, alignment of behavior with established norms of moral right. This is an important conjecture, because it suggests that a neural basis exists for *adherence* to established moral norms in any given cultural context,[3] which is a result of evolutionary advantages of norm compliance, rather than working from an idea that humans have evolved to universally agree upon some notion of what represents fair or equitable behavior.

> What is considered pathological must be understood as a product of the interaction between cultural context and the biology of brains.

This also suggests that what is considered pathological must be understood as a product of the interaction between cultural context and the biology of brains. In other words, that which is "pathological" is not universal, but closely tied to the definition of social norms within a given cultural context. For Japanese, some forms of self-killing are pathological, while others are not.[4] Indeed, for Japanese during World War II, certain types of self-killing, such as the actions of the kamikaze or *gyokusai* soldiers, were seen as having a sense of beauty and moral goodness. Self-killing behavior is not inherently pathological, but is pathological as it relates to the norms of killing that operate in a particular context, and, as is true in the case of Japan during World War II, the same basic action can have multiple and complex meanings. When asked, several of the people with whom I've spoken have ambivalent feelings about self-killing by individuals such as business leaders who jump out of buildings to take responsibility for the corrupt activities of their subordinates (or themselves). In such cases, some Japanese are not sure if the action aligns best with *jisatsu* or something more akin to the actions soldiers in World War II. The meaning, and the relationship of the act to social norms (which are themselves unclear in this case), is muddled (cf. Traphagan, 2010). And, in the example of suicide bombers in the Middle East, the social norms themselves are contested—there is not a clear consensus on how to think about the suicide bombers, because religious and legal scholars have yet to come to a consensus on whether the actions are examples of homicides, suicides, or sacrificial martyrdom (al-Atawneh, 2008).

Conclusion

Culture and Pathological Altruism

The preceding discussion of culture's influence on moral reasoning and feeling does not refute the importance of biology and evolutionary processes in shaping moral behavior; rather, it points out the complexities, and necessity, of including culture in the equation. Figure 21.1 depicts the relationship between four key elements that contribute to the structure and shape of any moral concept in a given social context: culture, biology, values, and actions. Both culture and biology permeate the context in which people encounter the world and process what they have encountered (interpretation), develop moral responses to that environment (values), and act upon those values (agency). There is a strong aspect of feedback in this system. Biology shapes and limits the capacity of humans to "do culture"—to create cultural contexts. In other words, our cognitive processes and our bodies themselves shape the manner in which culture is formed and expressed. Culture, in turn, shapes the creation of values, which then limits the scope and nature of the actions that we consider to be normal, or even possible, in a given cultural context. Beyond this, our actions shape our biology—biomedicine being a prime example of culturally shaped, value-laden contexts out of which particular actions (genetic engineering, for example) can shape the very nature of our biology. In more subtle ways, our physical bodies are shaped by cultural context—how we hold our postures, where we point when we index self, etc. are drawn from cultural assumptions, such as the idea that sitting up straight is a good thing. Each of these features is mediated by ongoing interpretation. Humans interpret biological and cultural expressions of self and society (concepts like race, for example, which are highly meaningful from a cultural perspective, but are not very meaningful at a biological level, despite the

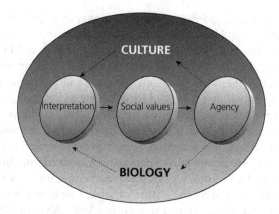

FIGURE 21.1
Values and action understood as products of and feedback into culture and biology, mediated by continuous interpretive activity.

fact that race is normally interpreted as a biological category). They also interpret values and actions that stem from both their biology and from the cultural contexts in which they live. Our understanding of the world is *entirely* drawn from this interpretive action; thus, our understanding of the world is inherently mediated.

The implication of this approach is the recognition that concepts like altruism and pathology are closely tied to cultural context, although in somewhat different ways. The nature of altruistic behavior itself varies from one culture to another—it may be a form of supreme altruism to blow oneself up in order to expel imperialist infidels from one's homeland in one place, although representing a form of psychological pathology in the form of homicide and suicide in another. Furthermore, the meaning of "altruism" is itself variable in relation to culture—in the Japanese context, words that are associated with what is termed altruistic behavior among English speakers also includes nuances of meaning that are quite different—implying in addition to selflessness, notions of love (even romantic), and indexing notions of social hierarchy that are not evident in the English word.

This means that the nature of what is defined as pathological behavior is shaped by the social norms and values that are operating in a particular society. Hauser's notion that humans are endowed with an innate moral faculty is quite helpful here. Human societies vary enormously in what they determine to be right and wrong, but the manner in which we construct moral systems is similar to the manner in which we construct systems of communication (language); it is based upon a "universal moral grammar that enables each child to grow in a narrow range of possible moral systems" (Hauser, 2006, pp. 419–420). This means, as Hauser has argued, that the capacity to do and mutually understand morality, like the capacity to do and understand language, is grounded in biology. However, humans interact with their natural and cultural environments, and these are in a continual process of change. There may be fixed (and encoded in DNA) principles for doing moral reasoning, but there is no fixed manner in which those principles may be expressed, interpreted, constructed, and reconstructed in relation to particular environments. A tendency toward certain kinds of other-centered behaviors ("altruism") may well be encoded in our DNA as part of the basic moral grammar, but the manner in which the *meanings* of that type of behavior will be interpreted and enacted can vary enormously. This, in turn, means that, although there may be a universal moral facility, there is no universal morality. In other words, the moral self is not an objective thing, but is a fluctuating network of beliefs, desires, and emotions (Rorty, 1983, pp. 585–86)—a process that is limited by our basic moral facility, but that does not consist of principles that have any a priori quality of rightness or wrongness inherent in them. Altruism itself is neither good nor bad, any more than a left big toe is good or bad; it is a common, multiply interpreted and constructed mode of behavior based upon parameters that are derived from biology.

This understanding of morality implies that the nature of what constitutes *pathological* altruism, just as the nature of what constitutes normal altruism, necessarily varies from one context to another. And, although the pathological may have a basis in biology, the meaning and definition of a pathological form of behavior will be based upon cultural frameworks for determining values of right and wrong, normal and abnormal. This is not merely a matter of interpretation of concepts; like the capacity to do moral reasoning, the conceptualization of pathology involves an intricate interplay between culture and biology, because the sociocultural environment in which we are reared contributes to the formation of neural pathways in the brain. Indeed, as Wexler (2006, p. 39) notes, individuals and their environment are so completely intertwined that to talk of a relationship between the two seems to overstate the distinction. The body is in a constant process of exchanging gases and fluids with its surrounding environment; individual brains are also in a constant process of exchanging and interpreting a continual flow of input from the cultural environments they inhabit. The brain, which is completely dependent upon its environment as it develops, is structured at a neural level by the cultural context it inhabits—the perceptual structures of the brain are (physically) constructed in the brain by the contexts of meaning and interpretation in which we are reared, socialized, and continue to operate as adults (Wexler, 2006, p. 47). This suggests that, not only are the interpretations of notions such as pathology or altruism variable in relation to cultural context at the level of interpretation and meaning, but they may also be variably programmed into the minds of humans who inhabit those different contexts. Although certain features of altruistic behavior may be relatively consistent across different cultures, the nuances of meaning vary, necessarily implying that deviation from the "norm" will vary as well, and this may well be biologically encoded in those brains associated with that context.

> Pathological altruism represents behavior that deviates from norms of action that define the limits and structures of altruistic acts—but those acts themselves have absolutely no moral value and are not necessarily parallel from one culture to another.

In a sense, what is pathological is that which fails to align with the environment of beliefs, desires, and emotions that surrounds a particular individual or group of individuals. Humans embody rationality at a biological level both through encoding in our DNA and through the culturally circumscribed formation of our brains as we age. Although the moral self is a network of beliefs, desires, and emotions, it is important to recognize that it is a biologically encoded network. In this sense, both altruism and pathological altruism represent a meeting of the biological and cultural that, in fact, are not all that different. Hauser's notion of the moral facility of humans can be easily extended to be viewed as the cultural facility of humans, of which the moral facility is one element. Pathological altruism represents behavior that deviates from norms of action that define the limits and structures of altruistic acts—but those acts themselves have absolutely no moral value and are not necessarily parallel from one culture to another.

Notes

1. Although, as de Waal has noted, a priori assumptions rejecting the idea of cognitive and psychological continuities between human and nonhuman animals are highly problematic (de Waal 2009, p. 175).

2. It is important to be cautious in application of the work of Takeo Doi. Although, as Chiao et al. note, Doi has significantly influenced the study of Japanese culture and society, his work was published almost 40 years ago, and since that time, Japan has undergone considerable change. In addition, Doi's work has been critiqued by a variety of scholars on the extent to which it oversimplifies the importance of collectivism in Japan or even essentializes Japanese society around a single pattern of social interaction (see Long, 1999).

3. Experimental cross-cultural work in economics focused on the Ultimatum Game has raised interesting questions related to cultural variation in what is perceived as being fair. (The Ultimatum Game has subjects respond to proposed divisions of money as a way of measuring ideas about fairness.) In the meta-analysis of research on this topic by Oosterbeek, Sloof, and van de Kuilen (2004), response differences are observed that correlate to regions such as Asia and the United States. Oosterbeek and his colleagues do a good job describing some of the problems of cross-country studies, noting that culture and country do not necessarily align. However, culture is still treated in a simplistic way. For example, the authors group Japan, Mongolia, and Papua New Guinea together as "Asia." These are not societies that share common cultures. Japan, for example, is a highly industrialized society with extensive contact with the West (it has been occupied by U.S. forces for more than 50 years). Mongolia and Papua New Guinea, on the other hand, have each had very different histories and have been influenced by different value systems.

Noting that similarities exist between these Asian countries tells us very little, and is ultimately an arbitrary grouping based on Western notions of Asia and Asian culture. Detailed analysis of these societies would show significant cultural differences that test the extent to which they can be thought of as comparatively "Asian." Furthermore, culture is not monolithic, but is rather a process in which people manipulate and contest values and in which various subgroupings can play an important role. One is left wondering how a group of Zen monks in Japan would respond to the Ultimatum Game.

4. Sociologist Émile Durkheim (1897) long ago recognized that "suicide" is best understood if divided into various types, such as altruistic suicide or egoistic suicide, due to the fact that intention needs to be factored into the nature of the act.

References

Ager, S. L. (2005). Familiarity breeds: Incest and the Ptolemaic dynasty. *The Journal of Hellenic Studies, 125,* 1–34.

al-Atawneh, M. (2008). Shahada versus terror in contemporary islamic legal thought: The problem of suicide bombers. *Journal of Islamic Law and Culture, 10*(1),18–29.

Benedict, R. (1934). *Patterns of culture.* London: Routledge & Kegan Paul.

Brown, D. E. (1991). *Human universals.* New York: McGraw-Hill, Inc.

Calcagno, J. M. (2003). Keeping biological anthropology in anthropology, and anthropology in biology. *American Anthropologist, 105*(1), 6–15.

Daniels, I. (2009). The 'Social Death' of Unused Gifts: Surplus and value in contemporary Japan. *Journal of Material Culture, 14*, 384–409.

de Waal, F. B. M. (2009). Darwin's last laugh. *Nature, 460*, 175.

Dodd, P. C., & Terry Prothro, E. (1987). Comment on FDB marriage. *American Anthropologist, 87*, 133–135.

Durkheim, E. (1951). *Suicide*. (G. Simpson, & J. A. Spaulding, Trans.). New York: The Free Press. (Original work published 1897).

Freeman, J. B., Rule, N. O., Adams, R. B., Jr., & Ambady, N. (2009). Culture shapes a mesolimbic response to signals of dominance and subordination. *NeuroImage, 47*, 353–359.

Hauser, M. E. (2006). *Moral minds: The nature of right and wrong*. New York: Harper Perennial.

Glascock, A. P. (1990). By any other name, it is still killing: A comparison of the treatment of the elderly in american and other societies. In J. Sokolovsky (Ed.), *The cultural context of aging: Worldwide perspectives* (pp. 43–56). Westport: Bergin & Garvey.

Kopytoff, I. (1984). On the Viability of Sibling Marriages: A comment on mccabe's argument. *American Anthropologist, 86*(2), 407–408.

Long, S. O. (1999). *Lives in motion: Composing circles of self and community in Japan*. Ithaca, NY: Cornell East Asia Series.

Martin, J. (2001). *The land looks after us: A history of native american religion*. Oxford: Oxford University Press.

McCabe, J. (1985). FBD marriage, westermarck, and incest taboos: Replies to Dodd and Prothro, Graber, and Kopytoff. *American Anthropologist, 87*, 135–136.

McCabe, J. (1983). FBD Marriage: Further support for the Westermarck hypothesis of the incest taboo? *American Anthropologist, 85*, 50–69.

Morris, B. (1994). *Anthropology of the self: The individual in cultural perspective*. London: Pluto Press.

Oakley, B. A. (2007). *Evil genes: Why rome fell, hitler rose, enron failed, and my sister stole my mother's boyfriend*. Amherst, NY: Prometheus Books.

Oosterbeek, H., Sloof, R., & van de Kuilen, G. (2004). Cultural differences in ultimatum game experiments: Evidence from a meta-analysis." *Experimental Economics, 7*, 171–188.

Patkin, T. T. (2004). Explosive baggage: Female palestinian suicide bombers and the rhetoric of emotion. *Women and Language, 27*(2), 79–88.

Rorty, R. (1983). Postmodernist bourgeois liberalism. *The Journal of Philosophy, 80*(10), 583–589.

Spitzer, M., Fischbacher, U., Hernberger, B., Grön, G., & Fehr, E. (2007). The neural signature of social norm compliance. *Neuron, 56*, 185–196.

Strier, K. B. (2003). Primate behavioral ecology: From ethnography to ethology and back. *American Anthropologist, 105*(1), 16–27.

Tobeña, A. (2007). Benumbing and Moral Exaltation in Deadly Martyrs: A view from neuroscience. In O. Vilarroya, & F. Forn i Argimon (Eds.), *Social brain matters: Stances on the neurobiology of social cognition*. Amsterdam: Rodopi.

Traphagan, J. W. (2000). *Taming oblivion: Aging bodies and the fear of senility in Japan*. Albany: State University of New York Press.

Traphagan, J. W. (2004a). Interpretations of elder suicide, stress and dependency among rural Japanese. *Ethnology, 43*(4), 315–329.

Traphagan, J. W. (2004b). *The practice of concern: Ritual, well-being, and aging in rural Japan*. Durham, NC: Carolina Academic Press.

Traphagan, J. W. (2008). Embodiment, ritual incorporation, and cannibalism among the Iroquoians after 1300 C.E." *Journal of Ritual Studies, 22*(2), 1–12.

Traphagan, J. W. (2010). Intergenerational ambivalence, power, and perceptions of elder suicide in rural Japan. *Journal of Intergenerational Relationships. 8(1)*, *21–37*.

Wexler, B. E. (2006). *Brain and culture: Neurobiology, ideology, and social change.* Cambridge: MIT Press.

Wong, D. (1984). *Moral relativity*. Berkeley: University of California Press.

Zahn, R., Moll, J., Paiva, M., Garrido, G., Kreuger, F., Huey, E. D., & Grafman, J. (2008). The neural basis of human social values: Evidence from Functional MRI." *Cerebral Cortex*, *19*, 276–283.

PART IV

CULTURAL AND EVOLUTIONARY DIMENSIONS OF PATHOLOGICAL ALTRUISM

CHAPTER 22

CULTURE–GENE COEVOLUTION OF EMPATHY AND ALTRUISM

Joan Y. Chiao, Katherine D. Blizinsky, Vani A. Mathur, and Bobby K. Cheon

KEY CONCEPTS

- Western and East Asian cultures vary in individualism and collectivism, or cultural values that influence how people think about themselves in relation to others.
- Cultural differences in social behavior are associated with cultural differences in allelic frequency of serotonin transporter-linked polymorphic region v (*5-HTTLPR*) variants.
- Culture–gene coevolution between individualism–collectivism and the *5-HTTLPR* may influence brain regions associated with empathy and altruism.

The "please help yourself" that Americans use so often had a rather unpleasant ring in my ears before I became used to English conversation. The meaning, of course, is simply "please take what you want without hesitation," but literally translated, it has somehow the flavor of "nobody else will help you," and I could not see how it came to be an expression of good will. The Japanese sensibility would demand that, in entertaining, a host should show sensitivity in detecting what was required and should himself "help" his guests. (Doi, 1971)

In his pioneering work *The Anatomy of Dependence* (1971), Doi offered a candid window into the experience of culture shock, recounting events such as his arrival in the United States from Japan to perform his medical residency. Doi was fascinated in particular with what seemed to him to be contradictory ways in which people in the United States responded to the needs of others. Living in Japan, Doi was familiar with tacit societal expectations encouraging dependence on close others for help, a phenomenon known as *amae*. By contrast, Doi noticed that the Americans around him actively sought independence from others; in order to be a good friend or host to another was to support and encourage self-help, rather than offering one's own altruistic hand. How could such apparently incongruous cultural value systems have evolved? What was the origin and purpose of these divergent cultural traditions, and what was the influence of these cultural value systems on the human mind and brain?

Concepts such as *amae* bring to light fundamental yet subtle, ways in which cultural values, practices, and beliefs can vary across cultural contexts. In collectivistic cultures like Japan, helping others is an expected social norm, indicating closeness and trust between two individuals, whereas in individualistic cultures, such as the United States, helping others is seen as more extraordinary, arising from heightened empathic experience. No doubt, such cultural diversity in social standards of helping behavior can be traced to fundamental differences in how diverse cultures conceptualize the self and its relation to others, or self-construal style. In this chapter, we explore the role the cultural values of individualism and collectivism might have had on shaping complex social behaviors, including empathy and altruism, and examine the role that culture–gene coevolution may have played in the emergence and persistence of individualistic and collectivistic cultural norms across generations. In particular, we explore the notion that at least some kinds of pathological altruism can be viewed as byproducts of culture, whereby altruistic behavior can be seen as either adaptive or maladaptive (e.g., pathological), depending on the cultural context.

Cultural Values of Individualism and Collectivism

Evident from the writings of Socrates and Lao Tzu, cultural divergences in ancient Western and East Asian philosophical views of the self are thought to have emerged early in human history (Markus & Kitayama, 1991; Triandis, 1995). The manner in which people define themselves and their relation to others in their environment is referred to as self-construal style , and it is a fundamental way through which culture shapes human behavior (Markus & Kitayama, 1991; Triandis, 1995). Specifically, cultural psychologists have identified two primary modes of self-construal across cultures: individualism and collectivism (Markus & Kitayama, 1991; Triandis, 1995). Individualistic cultures encourage people to be considered as independent of each other. By contrast, collectivistic cultures endorse viewing people as highly interconnected to one another. Individualistic cultures emphasize self-expression and pursuit of individuality over group goals, while collectivistic cultures favor maintenance of social harmony over assertion of individuality (Markus & Kitayama, 1991; Triandis, 1995). Self-construal style affects a wide range of human behavior, including how people feel, think, perceive, and reason about people and objects in their environment (Kitayama & Cohen, 2007; Nisbett, 2003) and their underlying neural substrates (Chiao & Ambady, 2007; Chiao, 2009).

Cultural values of individualism and collectivism have been shown to affect the degree to which people empathize and help others. For instance, research has shown that people from collectivistic cultures have been shown to be more sensitive to other people's perspective during a communication game, collectivistic participants were shown to take their partner's perspective more often than their individualistic counterparts (Wu & Keyser, 2007). In fact, individualists were shown to sometimes ignore their partner's perspective all together, whereas collectivistic participants almost never did (Wu & Keyser, 2007). Another study found that bicultural people exhibit greater cooperative behavior toward close others when reminded of collectivistic values, suggesting that the degree to which a person helps a close other is affected by the extent to which they view themselves as highly interconnected to or autonomous from the close other (Wong & Hong, 2005). Taken together, these results demonstrate cultural variation in social norms regarding when and to what extent it is appropriate to empathize and help others.

Relative to individualistic cultures, collectivistic cultures are more likely to endorse social norms that encourage empathizing (e.g., perspective-taking) and helping others (e.g., cooperative behavior) close to oneself. Given these cultural differences in optimal frequency of displaying empathy and altruism, it is plausible that a typical empathic and altruistic response in a collectivistic culture may be perceived as pathological or maladaptive (e.g., too much empathy or altruism) to a person from an individualistic culture. Similarly, it is plausible that a typical empathic and altruistic response in an individualistic culture may be seen as pathological or maladaptive (e.g., too little empathy or altruism) to a person from a collectivistic culture. Revisiting Doi's example of culture shock, it is now easier to understand how being encouraged to "help yourself" at an American party could have been misinterpreted by Doi, a collectivist, as a sign of neglectfulness by the individualistic party host. The importance of individualism and collectivism in shaping social norms and social behavior is clear; yet, important questions remain. In the next section, we explore the role of culture–gene coevolutionary forces in the emergence and transmission of individualism and collectivism across the globe.

A Theory of Culture–Gene Coevolution

Conventional evolutionary biology theory posits that organisms adapt to their environment, and that over time, species develop favorable traits or characteristics that best enable them to survive and reproduce in their given environment through the process of natural selection (Darwin, 1859). The concept of natural selection has been enormously influential to the study of human behavior, chiefly in evolutionary psychology, which has emphasized that much of human behavior arises as a by-product of adaptive mechanisms in the mind and brain (Barkow, Cosmides, & Tooby, 1992). More recently, culture–gene coevolution has emerged as an influential theory to explain how human behavior is a product of two complementary and interacting evolutionary processes: genetic and cultural evolution (Boyd & Richerson, 1985; Cavalli-Sforza & Feldman, 1981; Lumsden & Wilson, 1981; Figure 22.1). This dual inheritance theory of human behavior proposes that cultural traits are adaptive, evolve, and influence the social and physical environments under which genetic selection operates (Boyd & Richerson, 1985). A central claim of culture–gene coevolutionary theory is that once cultural traits are adaptive, it is likely that genetic selection causes refinement of the cognitive and neural architecture responsible for the storage and transmission of those cultural capacities (Boyd & Richerson, 1985). A prominent example of dual inheritance theory is the culture–gene coevolution between cattle milk protein genes and human

> Relative to individualistic cultures, collectivistic cultures are more likely to endorse social norms that encourage empathizing and helping others close to oneself.

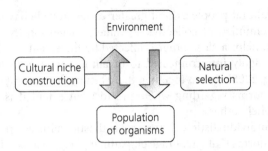

FIGURE 22.1
Model of two complementary evolutionary processes: natural selection and cultural niche construction, by which the environment exerts selective pressure on organisms, and organisms modify their environment in order to alter selection pressures exerted on them. Culture–gene coevolutionary theory further asserts that both genes and cultural traits may undergo selection pressure.

lactase genes (Beja-Pereira et al., 2003), whereby the cultural propensity for milk consumption in humans has led to genetic selection for milk protein genes in cattle and genes encoding lactase in humans. Although well-studied with computational modeling approaches (Smith, Kalish, Griffiths, & Lewandowsky, 2008), the study of culture–gene coevolutionary theory of human behavior has received less widespread empirical attention.

Culture-Gene Coevolution of Individualism-Collectivism and the Serotonin Transporter-Linked Polymorphic Region (*5-HTTLPR*)

Recently, Chiao and Blizinsky (2010) found evidence for culture–gene coevolution between the cultural values of individualism and collectivism and the serotonin transporter gene. The serotonin transporter gene (*SLC6A4*) contains a polymorphic region in its promotor, known as the 5-HTTLPR. The degenerate repeat region has a short (S) allele and a long (L) allele form that each result in differential serotonin (5-HT) expression and function (Hariri & Holmes, 2006; Lesch et al., 1996). The S allelic variant of the 5-HTTLPR is associated with increased negative emotion, including heightened anxiety (Munafo, Clark, & Flint, 2005; Sen, Burmeister, & Ghosh, 2004), harm avoidance (Munafo, Clark, & Flint, 2005), fear conditioning (Lonsdorf et al., 2009), attentional bias to negative information (Beevers et al., 2007), as well as increased risk for depression in the presence of environmental risk factors (Caspi et al., 2003; Taylor et al., 2006; Uher & McGuffin, 2008). Convergent evidence from endophenotypes indicates that activity in brain regions that are regulated by serotonergic neurotransmission and are critical to emotional behavior, such as the amygdala, varies as a function of 5-HT. Specifically, individuals carrying the S allele show greater amygdala response (Hariri et al., 2002; Munafo, Brown, & Hariri, 2008), which is likely due to increased amygdala resting activation (Canli, Omura, Haas, Fallgatter, & Constable, 2005) and decreased functional coupling between the amygdala and subgenual cingulate gyrus (Pezawas et al., 2005), relative to L allele carriers.

> Geographic regions characterized by cultural collectivism exhibit a greater prevalence of S allele carriers of the serotonin transporter gene.

Examining the relationship between self-construal style and prevalence of S allele for the serotonin transporter gene, Chiao and Blizinsky (2010) found that geographic regions characterized by cultural collectivism exhibit a greater prevalence of S allele carriers of the serotonin transporter gene, even when cultural regions rather than nations served as the unit of analysis (Figure 22.2). They also showed that global variability in historical pathogen prevalence predicted global variability in self-construal style due to genetic selection of the S allele of the serotonin transporter gene in regions characterized by high collectivism. Finally, Chiao and Blizinsky (2010) revealed a novel and surprising negative association between self-construal style, frequency of S allele carriers of the 5-HTTLPR, and global prevalence of anxiety and mood disorder. Across nations, both collectivism and allelic frequency of the S allele negatively predict global prevalence of anxiety and mood disorders. Taken together, these results indicated that greater population frequency of S allele carriers is associated with decreased prevalence of anxiety and mood disorders due to increased cultural collectivism and suggest a novel demonstration of culture–gene coevolution of human behavior. By emphasizing social norms that increase harmony and encourage the giving of social support to others, collectivistic cultures likely serve an "antipsychopathology" function by creating an ecological niche that lowers the prevalence of chronic life stress, protecting genetically susceptible individuals from environmental pathogens known to trigger negative emotion and psychopathology.

A central claim of culture–gene coevolutionary theory is that once cultural traits are adaptive, it is likely that genetic selection causes refinement of the cognitive and neural architecture responsible for the storage and transmission of those cultural capacities (Boyd & Richerson, 1985). Extending this logic to the current findings, we speculate that S and L allele carriers of 5-HTTLPR may possess information processing biases in the mind and brain that enhance their ability to store and transmit collectivistic and individualistic cultural norms, respectively. Recent behavioral evidence suggests that individuals carrying the

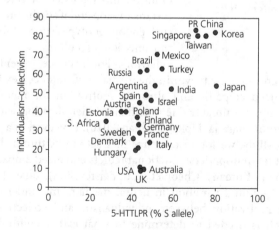

FIGURE 22.2

Culture–gene coevolution of individualism–collectivism and the serotonin transporter gene (*5-HTTLPR*). Adapted from Chiao, J.Y. & Blizinsky, K.D. (2010). Culture-gene coevolution of individualism-collectivism and the serotonin transporter gene (5-HTTLPR). *Proceedings of the Royal Society B: Biological Sciences, 277(1681)*, 529–537. Collectivistic nations showed higher prevalence of S allele carriers.

S allele exhibit stronger attentional bias for negative words (Beevers, Gibb, McGeary, & Miller, 2007), while individuals carrying the L allele demonstrate a stronger attentional bias toward positive, relative to negative, pictures (Fox, Ridgewell, & Ashwin, 2009). By extension, S allele carriers may be more likely to demonstrate sensitivity to negative information, such as expressions of pain and suffering in others, which may enhance collectivistic cultural norms of sensitivity to and interdependence with others, as well as tacit expectations to help when others are in need. By contrast, L allele carriers may be less sensitive to negative information, such as the pain and suffering of others and thus, may be more likely to maintain individualistic cultural expectations for people to help themselves and demonstrate autonomy.

Towards a Cultural Neuroscience of Empathy and Altruism

Neural activity within brain regions innervated by serotonergic neural pathways likely serve as another information processing mechanism involved in the storage and transmission of the cultural values of individualism and collectivism. Individuals carrying the S allele show greater amygdala response to emotional stimuli (Hariri et al., 2002; Munafo, Brown, & Hariri, 2008), which is likely due to increased amygdala resting activation (Canli et al., 2005) and decreased functional coupling between the amygdala and subgenual cingulate gyrus (Pezawas et al., 2005), relative to individuals carrying the L allele. Recent cross-cultural neuroimaging evidence demonstrates cultural specificity in amygdala response to fear faces (Chiao et al., 2008), as well as modulation of the medial prefrontal response during self-relevant processing as a function of individualistic and collectivistic cultural values (Chiao et al., 2009, 2010).

> Cultural variation has been revealed in the neural mechanisms underlying empathy and altruistic motivation across individualistic and collectivistic cultures.

Future research in cultural neuroscience may investigate the extent to which the cultural values of individualism and collectivism are associated with affective information processing biases and neural response within brain regions regulated by serotonergic neurotransmission and if so, the process by which such endophenotypes support the storage and transmission of cultural values and related behaviors. For instance, recently we found evidence that greater activity within the medial prefrontal cortex in Americans predicts enhanced empathy and altruistic motivation for members of one's own social group, presumably due to enhanced identification with own-group members (Mathur, Harada, Lipke, & Chiao, 2010). However, in a cross-cultural neuroimaging study, we found evidence that activity within a different brain region, the left temporoparietal junction, predicts enhanced empathy and altruistic motivation in Koreans (Cheon et al., under revision). Taken together, these findings reveal cultural variation in neural mechanisms underlying empathy and altruistic motivation between individualistic and collectivistic cultures. Future research is needed to determine to what extent cultural variation in empathic neural response arises due to specific kinds of cultural and genetic selection pressures. Another important direction for future studies is determining whether or not cultural variation in display rules, those regarding when and to what extent it is appropriate to empathize and help others, is supported by shared or distinct neural circuitry across cultures.

Conclusion

The current evidence demonstrates how cultural values, practices, and beliefs shape social norms regarding when and how people should experience empathy and express altruism toward others. The fundamental cultural dimension of individualism–collectivism, in particular, prescribes vastly distinct ways of interacting with others. Even in ordinary social situations, like dinner parties, social interactions and expectations can vary dramatically depending on whether one thinks of themselves as autonomous or highly connected and interdependent with others. Importantly, cultural differences in norms governing appropriate levels of empathy and altruism appear unarbitrary and constrained by culture–gene coevolutionary forces. Evidence indicates that geographic variability in environmental pressures, such as pathogen prevalence, have given rise to geographic variability in individualism–collectivism (Fincher et al., 2008) due to the adaptive nature of particular values in specific regions of the globe.

Given that cultural variation in prevalence of *amae* or empathic closeness between one's self and others likely has adaptive qualities, it is important to reconsider what it means for a particular helping behavior to be deemed *pathological altruism*. Certainly, it is likely that individual variability in human empathy and altruism exists in extremes that go beyond typical observed cultural variability. For instance, psychopaths who have theory of mind but lack empathy for others exhibit levels of antisocial behavior that go far beyond independent behaviors encouraged by individualistic societies (Crowe & Blair, 2008). Nevertheless, our review demonstrates the importance of culture–gene coevolutionary forces in shaping distinct cultural norms of empathy and altruism. Cultural differences in habits, like taking another's perspective or cooperating with close others, can naturally lead to cultural misunderstandings in everyday social situations, as Doi experienced, as well as larger-scale cultural conflicts related to how and when it is appropriate to help people from other social groups or even nation-states. By gaining a broader understanding of how culture–gene coevolutionary forces shape empathy and altruism-related mechanisms in the human mind and brain, we come closer to gaining insight into solving intercultural conflict and recognizing contexts in which different cultural standards of appropriate empathy and altruism may have adaptive, rather than maladaptive, value.

References

Barkow, J. H., Cosmides, L., & Tooby, J. (Eds.). (1992). *The adapted mind: Evolutionary psychology and the generation of culture.* New York: Oxford University Press.

Beevers, C. G., Gibb, B. E., McGeary, J. E., & Miller, I. W. (2007). Serotonin transporter genetic variation and biased attention for emotional word stimuli among psychiatric inpatients. *Journal of Abnormal Psychology, 11,* 208–212.

Beja-Pereira, A., Luikart, G., England, P. R., Bradley, D. G., Jann, O. C., Bertorelle, G., et al. (2003). Gene-culture coevolution between cattle milk protein genes and human lactase genes. *Nature Genetics, 35,* 311–313.

Boyd, R., & Richerson, P. J. (1985). *Culture and the evolutionary process.* Chicago: The University of Chicago Press.

Canli, T., Omura, K., Haas, B. W., Fallgatter, A., & Constable, R. T. 2005 Beyond affect: A role for genetic variation of the serotonin transporter in neural activation during a cognitive attention task. *Proceedings of the National Academy of Sciences USA, 102*(34), 12224–12229.

Caspi, A, Sugden K, Moffitt TE, Taylor A, Craig IW, Harrington H, McClay J, Mill J, Martin J, Braithwaite A, Poulton R. (2003). Influence of life stress on depression: moderation by a polymorphism in the 5-HTT gene. *Science, 301(5631)*: 386–9.

Cavalli-Sforza, L., & Feldman, M. (1981). *Cultural transmission and evolution: A quantitative approach.* Princeton, NJ: Princeton University Press.

Cheon, B. K., Im, D., Harada, T., Kim, J., Mathur, V. A., Scimeca,. . . Chiao, J. Y. (under revision). Cultural influences on the neural basis of intergroup empathy.

Chiao, J. Y. (2009). Cultural neuroscience: A once and future discipline. *Progress in Brain Research,* 178, 287–304.

Chiao, J. Y., & Ambady, N. (2007). Cultural neuroscience: Parsing universality and diversity across levels of analysis. In S. Kitayama, & D. Cohen (Eds.), *Handbook of cultural psychology* (pp. 237–254). New York: Guilford Press.

Chiao, J. Y., & Blizinsky, K. D. (2010). Culture-gene coevolution of individualism-collectivism and the serotonin transporter gene (5-HTTLPR). *Proceedings of the Royal Society B: Biological Sciences, 277(1681)*, 529–537.

Chiao, J. Y., Harada, T., Komeda, H., Li, Z., Mano, Y., Saito, D.N., et al. (2009). Neural basis of individualistic and collectivistic views of self. *Human Brain Mapping, 30(9),* 2813–2820.

Chiao, J.Y., Harada, T., Komeda, H., Li, Z., Mano, Y., Saito, D.N., Parrish, T.B., Sadato, N., Iidaka, T. (2010). Dynamic cultural influences on neural representations of the self. *Journal of Cognitive Neuroscience, 22*(1): 1–11.

Chiao, J. Y., Iidaka, T., Gordon, H. L., Nogawa, J., Bar, M., Aminoff, E., et al. (2008). Cultural specificity in amygdala response to fear faces. Journal of Cognitive Neuroscience, 20(12), 2167–2174.

Crowe, S. L., & Blair, R. J. (2008). The development of antisocial behavior: What can we learn from neuroimaging studies? *Developmental Psychopathology, 20*(4), 1145–1159.

Darwin, C. (1859). *On the origin of species by means of natural selection, or the preservation of favoured races in the struggle for life.* London: Murray.

Doi, T. (2001). *The anatomy of dependence.* New York: Kodansha America, Inc.

Fox, E., Ridgewell, A., & Ashwin, C. (2009). Looking on the bright side: Biased attention and the human serotonin gene. *Proceedings of the Royal Society B.* doi: 10.1098/rspb.2008.1788

Hariri, A. R., Mattay, V. S., Tessitore, A., Kolachana, B., Fera, F., Goldman, D., et al. (2002). Serotonin transporter genetic variation and the response of the human amygdala. *Science, 297*(5580), 400–403.

Hariri, A. R., & Holmes, A. (2006). Genetics of emotion regulation: The role of the serotonin transporter in neural function. *Trends in Cognitive Sciences,* 10, 182–191.

Kitayama, S., & Cohen, D. (2007). *Handbook of cultural psychology.* New York: Guilford Press.

Lesch, K. P., Bengel, D., Heils., S., Sabol, S. Z., Greenberg, B. D., Petri, S., et al. (1996). Association of anxiety-related traits with a polymorphism in the serotonin transporter gene regulatory region. *Science, 274,* 1527–1531.

Lonsdorf, T.B., Weike, A., Nikamo, P., Schalling, M., Hamm, A. O., & Ohman, A. (2009). Genetic gating of human fear learning and extinction: possible implications for gene-environment interaction in anxiety disorder. *Psychological Science, 20*(2), 198–206.

Lumsden, C. J., & Wilson, E. O. (1981). *Genes, Mind and Culture: The coevolutionary process.* Cambridge, MA: Harvard University Press.

Markus, H. R., & Kitayama, S. (1991). Culture and the self: Implications for cognition, emotion and motivation. *Psychological Review, 98,* 224–253.

Mathur, V. A., Harada, T., Lipke, T., & Chiao, J. Y. (2010). Neural basis of extraordinary empathy and altruistic motivation. *Neuroimage, 51*(4), 1468–1475.

Munafò, M. R., Clark, T., & Flint, J. 2005. Does measurement instrument moderate the association between the serotonin transporter gene and anxiety-related personality traits? A meta- analysis. *Molecular Psychiatry, 10*, 415–419.

Munafò, M. R., Brown, S. M., & Hariri, A. R. (2008). Serotonin Transporter (5HTTLPR) genotype and amygdala activation: A meta-analysis. *Biological Psychiatry, 63*(9), 852–857.

Nisbett, R. E. (2003). *The geography of thought.* New York: The Free Press.

Pezawas, L., Meyer-Lindenberg, A., Drabant, E. M., Verchinski, B. A., Munoz, K. E., Kolachana, B. S., et al. (2005). 5-HTTLPR polymorphism impacts human cingulate-amygdala interactions: A genetic susceptibility for depression. *Nature Neuroscience, 8*(6), 828–834.

Sen, S., Burmeister, M. L., & Ghosh, D. (2004). Meta-analysis of the association between a serotonin transporter promoter polymorphism (5-HTTLPR) and anxiety related personality traits. *American Journal of Medical Genetics. Part B, Neuropsychiatric Genetics, 127*(1), 85–89.

Smith, K., Kalish, M. L., Griffiths, T. L., & Lewandowsky, S. (2008). Cultural transmission and the evolution of human behaviour. *Philosophical Transactions of the Royal Society of London: B Biological Science, 363*, 3469–3476.

Taylor, S. E., Way, B. M., Welch, W. T., Hilmert, C. J., Lehman, B. J., & Eisenberger, N. I. (2006). Early family environment, current adversity, the serotonin transporter polymorphism, and depressive symptomatology. *Biological Psychiatry, 60*, 671–676.

Triandis, H. C. (1995). *Individualism and collectivism.* Boulder: Westview.

Uher, R., & McGuffin, P. (2008). The moderation by the serotonin transporter gene of environmental adversity in the aetiology of mental illness: Review and methodological análisis. *Molecular Psychiatry, 13*(2), 131–146.

Wong, R. Y., & Hong, Y. Y. (2005). Dynamic influences of culture on cooperation in the prisoner's dilemma. *Psychological Science, 16*(6), 429–434.

Wu, S., & Keysar, B. (2007). The effect of culture on perspective taking. *Psychological Science, 18*(7), 600–606.

THE MESSIANIC EFFECT OF PATHOLOGICAL ALTRUISM

Jorge M. Pacheco and Francisco C. Santos

KEY CONCEPTS

- Without additional mechanisms, cooperation is not an evolutionarily viable behavior, as the *tragedy of the commons* often emerges as the final doomsday scenario.
- In a black-and-white world in which individuals' actions are limited to cooperate or to defect, pathological altruists can be seen as obstinate cooperators, who go to all lengths to maintain their behavior.
- Pathological altruists cooperate indiscriminately, being unmoved by the temptations of greed and fear that lead to defection.
- A single pathological altruist can obliterate the evolutionary advantage of defectors, letting others ignore the temptation to cheat and become, themselves, cooperators. Hence, they generate a messianic effect, which spreads through the entire community.
- Pathological altruists catalyze social cohesion, as their presence benefits the entire community even when defection remains as the single rational option and individuals act in their own selfish interest.

HUMANS LIVE IN large societies characterized by exchange and cooperation between individuals who, in the majority of cases, are not kin-related. Close examination reveals that humans actually cooperate more often than would be expected from evolutionary game theory, as modeled in terms of the classic Prisoner's Dilemma (Axelrod & Hamilton, 1981; Hofbauer & Sigmund, 1998; Maynard-Smith, 1982). Prisoner's Dilemma is rooted on the assumption that the act of cooperation entails a certain cost c, which need not be a monetary cost. The recipient of a cooperative act receives a benefit b. Quantitatively, the magic of cooperation relies on the fact that $b > c$.

In a black-and-white world in which people can only behave as cooperators or defectors, one of only four possible outcomes takes place when two individuals interact. When both *cooperate* (C), each receives a benefit b but also experiences a cost c; hence each receives a net profit of $b - c$. When both *defect* (D), neither player receives cost nor benefit. Last, if one player cooperates while the other defects, then D receives a benefit without a cost, whereas C experiences a cost with no benefit. These four entries fill in what is known in game theory as the *payoff matrix*:

$$
\begin{array}{cc}
 & \begin{array}{cc} C & D \end{array} \\
\begin{array}{c} C \\ D \end{array} & \begin{pmatrix} R & S \\ T & P \end{pmatrix}
\end{array}
$$

with $R = (b - c)$, $T = b$, $S = -c$, and $P = 0$. These four entries satisfy the ranking order $T > R > P > S$, which is the hallmark of a Prisoner's Dilemma game. The fact that mutual cooperation is always better than mutual defection implies that $R > P$. When $T > R$, one may think of *greed*, as an individual is tempted to play D toward a C (Macy & Flache, 2002). Indeed, in the absence of *greed* ($T < R$), the dilemma is relaxed from a pure defector dominance game into a coordination game, termed the *Stag-Hunt Dilemma* (Skyrms, 2004). In this case, only the *fear* of being cheated on by a defector ($P > S$) provides a reason for defecting instead of cooperating (Macy & Flache, 2002). But there is yet another scenario—that in which *fear* is removed from the Prisoner's Dilemma, so that *greed* becomes the only reason to defect. This dilemma then becomes a coexistence game, known as the *Chicken, Hawk–Dove*, or *Snowdrift Dilemma* (Maynard-Smith, 1982).

In sum, then, Prisoner's Dilemma emerges as the most stringent of the social dilemmas captured in terms of symmetric, one-shot, two-player games. It is the stringent Prisoner's Dilemma, in its cost–benefit version (the parameterization above), that constitutes the hallmark of most studies carried out to date addressing the evolution of cooperation (Nowak, 2006a, 2006b; Taylor, Day, & Wild, 2007).

A Mathematical Model of Pathological Altruism

In keeping with such studies, we shall also adopt the Prisoner's Dilemma and consider a finite population, small enough to make it equally likely that anyone in the population could interact with anyone else (Dunbar, 2003). This is the commonly encountered *well-mixed assumption* (known as the *mean field approximation* in physics) (Hofbauer & Sigmund, 1998). Under such circumstances, cooperators are always at a disadvantage when compared with defectors, and natural selection favors the increase of Ds at the expense of Cs. This is related to the fact that the payoff for Cs (interpreted as fitness or social success in evolutionary game theory) is lower than that of Ds. For a population of size N with k Cs, the average payoff of Cs and Ds is

$$
\Pi_C(k) = \frac{k}{N}R + \frac{N-k}{N}S = \frac{k}{N}b - c
$$

(Equation 23.1)

$$
\Pi_D(k) = \frac{k}{N}T + \frac{N-k}{N}P = \frac{k}{N}b
$$

(Equation 23.2)

(for $R = (b - c)$, $T = b$, $S = -c$, and $P = 0$, ignoring residual self-interaction corrections), and since $T > R > P > S$, we immediately see that Cs do worse than Ds independently of k, which means Ds ultimately dominate unconditionally the evolutionary dynamics in Prisoner's Dilemma (see Figure 23.1d).

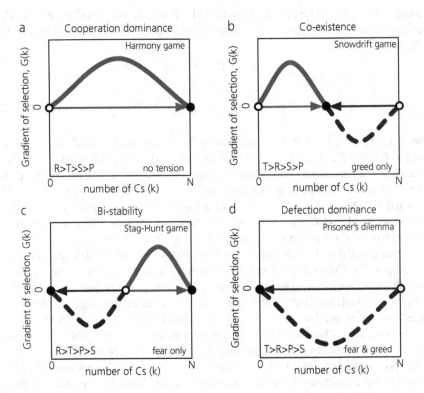

FIGURE 23.1

The behavioral dynamics of a population can be studied by analyzing the sign of the gradient of selection $G(k)$, defined as the difference between the probability of increasing in the number of cooperators, $T^+(k)$ versus that of decreasing, $T^-(k)$ for each value k of cooperators in a population of size N. Whenever $G(k) > 0$, cooperators will have an advantage over defectors, increasing their fraction in the population. On the contrary, if $G(k) < 0$, evolution will promote the increase of defectors. Here, we depict the dynamics of symmetric two-person one-shot dilemmas using gradients of selection. When cooperators have an advantage irrespectively of k, a Harmony Game is obtained (**A**). In this situation, individual and collective interests always coincide, and hence there is no dilemma. In the remaining three cases, individual and collective interests no longer coincide: *Co-existence* can be promoted (**B**) in situations in which a minority of individuals adopting a given behavior gain an advantage, losing this advantage when they become abundant. Hence, there is an *internal equilibrium* that is stable, represented in **B** by a solid circle. A *coordination dilemma* emerges whenever the opposite occurs (**C**)—the *internal equilibrium* becomes *unstable* (represented by an open circle in C). Finally, whenever cooperation is always a disadvantage we obtain a Prisoner's Dilemma situation in which cooperators have no chance to survive (**D**). The figure also illustrates how *greed* and *fear* operate in the various dilemmas. *Greed* alone (temptation to defect, $T > R$) results in a *stable equilibrium* (**B**). *Fear* alone (fear of being cheated upon, $P > S$) results in an *unstable equilibrium* (**C**). *Greed* and *fear* are both present as we move to **D**, with its combination of *stable* and *unstable equilibrium* points.

Besides individual fitness, evolutionary dynamics relies on a process by which individuals revise their strategic behavior. Here, we adopt a popular stochastic update known as the *pairwise comparison rule* (Szabó & Tőke, 1998; Traulsen, Nowak, & Pacheco, 2006): At each time step, an individual i will adopt the strategy of a randomly chosen individual in the population j with a probability that increases with the increase in payoff difference between j and i. Hence, successful behaviors will be imitated and spread in the population. This probability is conveniently written in terms of the so-called Fermi distribution (from statistical physics), $F\left[\Pi_j(k) - \Pi_i(k)\right] = \left[1 + e^{-\beta\left[\Pi_j(k) - \Pi_i(k)\right]}\right]^{-1}$, in which $\Pi_i(k)$ and $\Pi_j(k)$

are the payoffs of individuals i and j, respectively defined in Equations 23.1 and 23.2, and β (an inverse temperature in physics) translates here into noise associated with errors in decision making. For high values of β we obtain pure imitation dynamics commonly used in cultural evolution studies, whereas for $\beta \to 0$, selection becomes so weak that evolution proceeds by random drift.[1] Under such a stochastic dynamics, one can compute the probabilities $T^+(k)$ and $T^-(k)$ for the number of Cs in the population to grow or diminish by a single cooperator in a given time step. Assuming there are k Cs in a population of size N, we may write

$$T^+(k) = \frac{N-k}{N}\frac{k}{N}F[\Pi_C(k) - \Pi_D(k)]$$

(Equation 23.3)

$$T^-(k) = \frac{k}{N}\frac{N-k}{N}F[\Pi_D(k) - \Pi_C(k)]$$

(Equation 23.4)

such that the sign of the gradient of selection $G(k) = T^+(k) - T^-(k)$ indicates whether evolution favors the increase ($G(k) > 0$) or decrease ($G(k) < 0$) of Cs in the population. In Figure 23.1 we show the typical profile of $G(k)$ for the Prisoner's Dilemma and other social dilemmas. Given the stochastic nature of the dynamics introduced, combined with the finite size of the population, the end states of evolution are inevitably monomorphic; that is, populations will be entirely comprised of Cooperators only or Defectors only, which become absorbing states of the evolutionary dynamics. Only in infinite populations can polymorphic states become stable. Yet, as shown in Figure 23.1, even in finite populations natural selection may lead populations to spend most of their time in polymorphic states, associated with the internal roots of $G(k)$. Hence we employ, for finite populations, the same nomenclature that is strictly correct only in infinite deterministic dynamics, using an italic font to emphasize this association. With this proviso in mind, our discussion should cause no confusion.

What happens if we now introduce a small number of pathological altruists (*PA*) in this population? Unlike conventional Cs, *PA*s do not imitate or let themselves be influenced by anyone—they are *obstinate* Cs. Hence, and similar to Cs, they suffer the exploitation of Ds while benefiting from the cooperation of Cs (and other *PA*s, if present). Although they do not imitate anyone, their altruistic behavior can be imitated by others—those who do so will be Ds who become Cs, given that, from the outset, *PA*s and Cs are indistinguishable. Let $p \le N$ be the (fixed) number of *PA*s in the population. If $k = k' + p$, where k' is the number of "conventional" Cs in the population, then the payoff of Cs and Ds is still given by Equations 23.1 and 23.2, whereas the transition probabilities now read

$$T_{PA}^+(k) = \frac{N-k}{N}\frac{k}{N}F[\Pi_C(k) - \Pi_D(k)]$$

(Equation 23.5)

$$T_{PA}^-(k) = \frac{k-p}{N}\frac{N-k}{N}F[\Pi_D(k) - \Pi_C(k)]$$

(Equation 23.6)

where $0 \le p \le k \le N$

Evolutionary Dynamics of Pathological Altruists

Comparison of Equations 23.3 and 23.4 with Equations 23.5 and 23.6) shows a subtle difference rooted in the profound changes introduced by the existence of PAs in the population—no matter how few PAs are introduced. The prefactors of the Fermi function no longer coincide in Equations 23.5 and 23.6. Instead, the symmetry is broken by the appearance of an additional term in p, due to the presence of PAs. As we show below, this term is capable of disrupting the unconditional dominance of Ds portrayed in Figure 23.1d for the Prisoner's Dilemma. Indeed, this additional factor provides an overall net positive contribution to $G(k)$, with important consequences in the overall evolutionary dynamics of the population. Figure 23.2 provides a concrete example of the impact of PAs in a population of $N = 200$ individuals. In particular, the fact that

$$G(p) = \frac{p}{N} \frac{1-p}{N} \frac{1}{1+e^{-\beta c}} > 0 \quad \text{(for all } p > 0\text{)} \text{ means that a single } PA \text{ is sufficient to}$$

reverse the direction of natural selection, compared to the conventional Prisoner's Dilemma, to instead favor an increase in the number of cooperators when these are rare.

In essence, then, the presence of pathological altruists means that Cs no longer tend to go extinct, as in the standard Prisoner's Dilemma ($p = 0$ in Figure 23.2a). Instead, natural selection now drives the population into an internal *polymorphic equilibrium* characterized by the *coexistence* of Cs and Ds in the population. As Figure 23.1 revealed, such a *coexistence equilibrium* was possible due to *greed* alone, but the presence of PAs now renders *fear* and *greed* no longer sufficient to stop cooperators from surviving in a population in which at least one PA appears. In fact, for given values of c, β, and p, *equilibrium* is attained at

$$k^* = \frac{p}{1-e^{-\beta c}}$$

(Equation 23.7)

This is a remarkable result. The presence of p PAs induces an internal *stable equilibrium* in the evolutionary dynamics. More importantly, this *equilibrium* occurs for a value $k^* > p$, as shown in Figure 23.2b, a result that does not depend sensitively on the specific value of the *cost-to-benefit* ratio of cooperation. In other words, the presence of PAs catalyzes the appearance of standard cooperators in the population. It is also noteworthy that all this happens despite the fact that Cs and PAs have a lower fitness than Ds.

From a mathematical perspective, and to the best of our knowledge, this is the first time one obtains an evolutionary dynamics in a well-mixed population in which the *internal equilibria do not* coincide with the zeroes of $\Pi_D(k) - \Pi_C(k)$ For general symmetric two-person games, this difference depends on the number of k cooperators (pathological or not), and it is the possibility that this difference becomes zero that leads to the appearance of *internal equilibria, stable* or *not*. However, in the present case, and for the particular (so-called "benefit–cost") parameterization of the Prisoner's Dilemma adopted, $\Pi_D(k) - \Pi_C(k) = c$ for all k, and hence the evolutionary viability of Cs in the presence of PAs is due to the modified nature of the evolutionary dynamics, which no longer follows a standard replicator-like equation. This is easily understood when we take the (unrealistic) limit of infinite, well-mixed populations. To this end, we define, in the usual sense, $x = k/N$ as the fraction of Cs (and PAs), and $\phi = p/N \le x$ as the

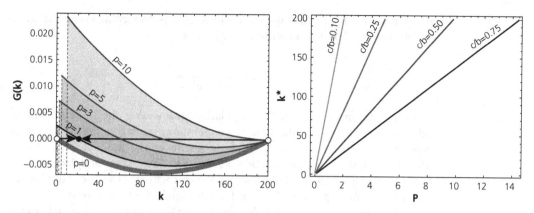

FIGURE 23.2

Left panel: Dynamics of cooperation under a Prisoner's Dilemma (c/b = 0.5) for different numbers of *PAs* in a population of N = 200 individuals. A single *PA* (p = 1) is able to transform the original Prisoner's Dilemma into a *co-existence* game with a *stable equilibrium* in the interval $p < k \leq N$ In this particular case, for p = 1 we obtain ($\beta = 0.1$) k* = 14 (see Equation 23.7 and right panel), whereas for p = 3, we obtain k* = 61. These results should be compared with the conventional dynamics corresponding to p = 0, in which case *Cs* are not evolutionary viable. The vertical dashed lines indicate the minimum value k = p. *Right panel:* Stable equilibria k* for the same conditions as in the left panel and different values of c/b and p. A small number of *PAs* is able to create a spectacular boost of cooperators in the population, providing evidence of the messianic effect of *PAs*, a process that occurs independently of the specific value of the cost-to-benefit ratio associated with the act of cooperation.

fraction of *PAs* in the population, such that the corresponding fraction of *Ds* becomes 1 − x Taking the limit $N \to \infty$ and maintaining both x and ϕ constant leads to the following differential equation (Traulsen et al., 2006):

$$\dot{x} = x(1-x)\tanh\left[\frac{\beta}{2}\left(\Pi_C(x) - \Pi_D(x)\right)\right] + \phi(1-x)F\left[\Pi_D(x) - \Pi_C(x)\right]$$

The first term on the right-hand side is nothing but the standard modified replicator dynamics equation resulting from the pairwise comparison rule (Traulsen et al., 2006), adopted for strategy update and governed by the fitness difference between *Cs* (and *PAs*), and *Ds*. The second term results from the presence of *PAs* in the population, and is due to the inability of the evolutionary dynamics to reach values of x satisfying $x \leq \phi$ More important, however, is the fact that $\dot{x}(\phi) > 0$ transforming $x = \phi$ into an *unstable fixed point*, promoting the appearance of *Cs* in the population.[2]

> The presence of "pathological" altruists catalyzes the appearance of standard cooperators in the population.

Discussion

The present model studies the impact of a fixed amount of *PAs* on the evolutionary dynamics of a finite, well-mixed population. *PAs* are obstinate cooperators who maintain their strategies irrespective of any stimuli to change that may surround them. We find that the presence of *PAs* in a population of size *N* leads the population to spend most of the time in a polymorphic composition in which the *equilibrium* number of Cs is given by

$$k_C^* = k^* - p = \frac{p}{e^{\beta c} - 1}$$

Hence, the more PAs in the population, the weaker the force of natural selection or the smaller the cost of cooperation, the larger the incidence of cooperators in the population. In fact, whenever the product βc satisfies $\beta c < -\ln(1 - p/N)$ natural selection will favor the extinction of defectors. This is a remarkable effect in what concerns the impact of PAs in the evolutionary dynamics of the population. What is the intuition behind this result?

As becomes clear from this discussion, the fitness of an individual results from his or her interaction with peers. These interactions clearly favor Ds, as individuals engage here in a Prisoner's Dilemma. However, the evolutionary dynamics of the strategies within the population depend only partially on individual fitness. Indeed, for obstinate PAs what difference does the fitness of others make if the PAs themselves will never deviate from their altruistic behavior? An easy means to disentangle the roles played by fitness and *strategy update* is to view the fate of individuals as proceeding along the links of one or more complex networks.

Under the well-mixed assumption, everyone is connected to everybody else and will freely interact with everybody. Hence, we can define an interaction network, illustrated at the bottom of Figure 23.3, associated with a bidirectionally complete graph, in which individuals occupy the nodes of the graph and the links between nodes define who interacts with whom. On the other hand, and inspired by the work described in Ohtsuki, Pacheco, and Nowak (2007) and Ohtsuki, Nowak, and Pacheco (2007), we can also define a second graph, the so-called reproduction, update, or imitation graph, represented on the top of Figure 23.3. Similar to the interaction network, individuals occupy nodes (the same nodes, as the individuals are the same in both graphs), but now the links are no longer bidirectional, as in this case some individuals may use another as a role model without the reverse being true. This is precisely the case of PAs, who may be role models of all non-PAs in the population, but accept no role models themselves. That is, PAs are effectively disconnected in the imitation network, although they remain fully connected with everybody else through the interaction graph.

Because of this peculiar topology of the imitation graph, the presence of PAs induces a symmetry breaking that is ultimately responsible for their *messianic effect* in the population as a whole, paving the way for cooperators to thrive. Depending on the value of the cost implicit in each act of cooperation, as well as on how strong natural selection leads individuals to change their strategy, the presence of rare (e.g., a single individual, see Figure 23.2) PAs may be enough to change the evolutionary dynamics from one in which Cs become extinct into another in which Cs dominate. This is a remarkable effect of PAs that can be rationalized in terms of their strong role in the imitation sector of the evolutionary dynamics. This is more so whenever selection is weak.

As argued elsewhere (Nowak, 2006a), the Prisoner's Dilemma game considered here is but one of the many evolutionary game theory games that "individuals" engage in. That is to say, in both game theory and real life, individuals have many interaction networks. And, in these different networks, and even in

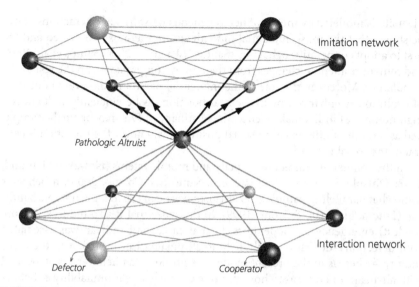

FIGURE 23.3
The figure illustrates a well-mixed population of seven individuals, in this case four *Cs* (*black*), two *Ds* (*gray*), and one *PA* (*dark gray*). The evolutionary dynamics is the result of (a) interactions between individuals, which proceed along the links of the interaction network (*bottom*, a complete graph of bidirectional links) and (b) behavior update, which proceeds along the links of the imitation network (*top*, a complete graph of bidirectional links except those that emerge from the single *PA*). Here, we adopt the notation that bidirectional links have no arrows, in contrast with directional links. Because links to *PAs* in the imitation network are *not* bidirectional, reflecting the obstinacy of *PAs* who never change behavior, the evolutionary dynamics of a population in the presence of *PAs* is profoundly affected by them: Their influence induces the emergence of *Cs*. As a visualization aid, nodes of the networks depicted have different sizes (bigger are meant to be closer) merely to induce a rudimentary sense of perspective to the picture.

the same network at different times, individuals play different games, some of which involve cooperation, some not. All of these interactions ultimately contribute to the fitness value of each individual. As such, when one concentrates on a single game, as we did here, it is natural to assume that fitness changes resulting solely from this game will be small or, equivalently, selection pressure due to this game alone will be weak. But this means, then, that random drift will dominate (or other games will be perhaps more important, which is not of interest here), and the weaker the effect of the game on fitness, the stronger the role of obstinate *PAs*. Hence, one expects *PAs* to introduce profound changes in the evolutionary dynamics of well-mixed communities.

In view of the discussion so far, the question remains regarding the origin of *PAs* and how they may actually emerge in a population. As we (Santos, Santos, & Pacheco, 2008; Van Segbroeck, Santos, Lenaerts, & Pacheco, 2009) and others (McNamara, Barta, Fromhage, & Houston, 2008; McNamara, Barta, & Houston, 2004) have argued at length, humans are prone to explore new forms of behavior, and behavior diversity is an attribute of most free human societies. Within the time scale of cultural evolution studied here, it is likely that some individuals may become "attached" to their behavior, perhaps as a result of genetic predisposition, or as a result of their beliefs, perhaps simply because they respond too slowly to external stimuli to change. In any of these cases, we may be confronted with the obstinacy that characterizes *PAs*. Interestingly, whenever social diversity is modeled by means of heterogeneous networks of interactions, it can be shown that the most influential individuals are the most connected and the first to adopt cooperative behaviors (Santos & Pacheco, 2006; Santos et al., 2008) and remain resilient to changes from then on by comparison with the rest of the population. Moreover, the role of the influential person in the overall outcome of evolution is enhanced by his central position, as he efficiently influences a high number of individuals. Hence, the obstinacy of PAs may be further amplified as a result of differences in social positions, whenever their location is central in the social network.

In the context of indirect reciprocity and moral systems (Nowak & Sigmund, 1998; Ohtsuki & Iwasa, 2004; Pacheco, Santos, & Chalub, 2006), a behavior somewhat paralleling pathological altruism has been called a phenotypic handicap (Lotem, Fishman, & Stone, 1999), in the sense that it also induces a (more modest) emergence of cooperators. In that case, the handicap was associated with defection—defectors would help to stimulate discrimination in the community—whereas in the present model, the immutable phenotype is associated with altruism. In both cases, however, one can view this immutability of behavior as maladaptive, which by no means implies that this type of individuals is rare. The result for PAs, as shown here, is that the appearance of a single such individual may have a spawning effect in the emergence of cooperation, a feature that would be unavailable until its appearance. The consequences can be devastating for defectors, as we have shown.

A related issue that remains to be investigated is what happens if such an obstinate maladaptation would occur with a defector, instead of a cooperator. The upshot is that the model could then be extended to incorporate pathological defectors ("cheaters," or "psychopaths") in the population. In a nutshell, pathological cheaters would act to increase the strength of natural selection toward defection. In the simultaneous presence of both pathological altruists and pathological cheaters, the latter would, at most, reduce the fraction of cooperators who optimally coexist with defectors in the population. But these pathological defectors would not be able to counteract the fundamental rift in symmetry introduced by pathological altruists, who would always open a window of viability for cooperation to be maintained in populations.

To summarize, pathological altruists—obstinate cooperators who never change their behavior toward others—introduce profound changes in the evolutionary dynamics of tight communities. In their presence, cheaters no longer push cooperators to extinction. Instead, the population evolves towards *a coexistence* of altruists and cheaters that characterizes its composition most of the time. Ironically, in the currency of cooperation, pathological altruists are very effective in allowing the population to avoid falling into the "tragedy of the commons" doomsday scenario referred to at the chapter's opening. This is done by securing the maintenance of cooperators in the population. In doing so, opportunity is also provided for cheaters to have cooperators to exploit.

Notes

1. Decreasing values of β may be thought of as increasing the likelihood that someone who actually wants to help fails to do so. For instance, someone comes across a beggar and wants to give him some money but realizes that has forgotten his purse. In other words, an example of a cooperator who fails to act accordingly. β is also related, indirectly, to the issue of bounded rationality—sometimes, just by chance, one does not do what one is

supposed to do rationally. Moreover, β measures errors in the imitation process related with the fact that often individuals face difficulties in assessing the success (or not) of others. This may lead individuals to change their behavior to something which is, in fact, worse than their previous choice.

2. Metaphorically, this might explain why dictators go to any lengths to purge and eliminate those who speak out against them. But, in those cases, so many factors contribute to such perversion that it is difficult to disentangle the effects of pathological altruists. In modern times, attempts to control the media by governments and the existence of those who resist such attempts parallels, to some extent, the classic dictator example.

References

Axelrod, R., & Hamilton, W. D. (1981). The evolution of cooperation. *Science, 211*(4489), 1390–1396.

Dunbar, R. I. M. (2003). The social brain: Mind, language, and society in evolutionary perspective. *Annual Review of Anthropology, 32*(1), 163–181.

Hofbauer, J., & Sigmund, K. (1998). *Evolutionary games and population dynamics.* Cambridge, UK: Cambridge University Press.

Lotem, A., Fishman, M. A., & Stone, L. (1999). Evolution of cooperation between individuals. *Nature, 400,* 226–227.

Macy, M. W., & Flache, A. (2002). Learning dynamics in social dilemmas. *Proceedings of the National Academy of Science U S A, 99*(Suppl 3), 7229–7236.

Maynard-Smith, J. (1982). *Evolution and the theory of games.* Cambridge: Cambridge University Press.

McNamara, J. M., Barta, Z., Fromhage, L., & Houston, A. I. (2008). The coevolution of choosiness and cooperation. *Nature, 451*(7175), 189–192.

McNamara, J. M., Barta, Z., & Houston, A. I. (2004). Variation in behaviour promotes cooperation in the Prisoner's Dilemma game. *Nature, 428*(6984), 745–748.

Nowak, M. A. (2006a). *Evolutionary Dynamics.* Cambridge, MA: Belknap/Harvard.

Nowak, M. A. (2006b). Five rules for the evolution of cooperation. *Science, 314*(5805), 1560–1563.

Nowak, M. A., & Sigmund, K. (1998). The evolution of indirect reciprocity by image scoring. *Nature, 393,* 573–577.

Ohtsuki, H., & Iwasa, Y. (2004). How should we define goodness?—Reputation dynamics in indirect reciprocity. *Journal of Theoretical Biology, 231*(1), 107–120.

Ohtsuki, H., Nowak, M. A., & Pacheco, J. M. (2007). Breaking the symmetry between interaction and replacement in evolutionary dynamics on graphs. *Physical Review Letters, 98,* 108106.

Ohtsuki, H., Pacheco, J. M., & Nowak, M. A. (2007). Evolutionary graph theory: Breaking the symmetry between interaction and replacement. *Journal of Theoretical Biology, 246*(4), 681–694.

Pacheco, J. M., Santos, F. C., & Chalub, F. A. (2006). Stern-judging: A simple, successful norm which promotes cooperation under indirect reciprocity. *PLoS Computational Biology, 2*(12), e178.

Santos, F. C., & Pacheco, J. M. (2006). A new route to the evolution of cooperation. *Journal of Evolutionary Biology, 19*(3), 726–733.

Santos, F. C., Santos, M. D., & Pacheco, J. M. (2008). Social diversity promotes the emergence of cooperation in public goods games. *Nature, 454*(7201), 213–216.

Skyrms, B. (2004). *The stag hunt and the evolution of social structure.* Cambridge, UK: Cambridge University Press.

Szabó, G., & Tőke, C. (1998). Evolutionary prisoner's dilemma game on a square lattice. *Physical Review E, 58*(1), 69–73.

Taylor, P. D., Day, T., & Wild, G. (2007). Evolution of cooperation in a finite homogeneous graph. *Nature, 447*(7143), 469–472.

Traulsen, A., Nowak, M. A., & Pacheco, J. M. (2006). Stochastic Dynamics of Invasion and Fixation. *Physical Review E, 74* 011090.

Van Segbroeck, S., Santos, F. C., Lenaerts, T., & Pacheco, J. M. (2009). Reacting differently to adverse ties promotes cooperation in social networks. *Physical Review Letters, 102,* 058105.

CHAPTER 24

BATTERED WOMEN, HAPPY GENES

There Is No Such Thing as Altruism, Pathological or Otherwise

Satoshi Kanazawa

> **KEY CONCEPTS**
>
> - Psychologically altruistic acts may not necessarily be evolutionarily altruistic.
> - Battered women and their violent mates have more sons than others.
> - Therefore, battered women's decision to stay with their abusers may be psychologically altruistic, but evolutionarily self-interested, as they gain the genetic benefit of producing violent sons.

MANY BEHAVIORAL SCIENTISTS regard altruism as a central theoretical problem, especially in microeconomics, game theory, and other fields that conceptualize the human actor as rational and self-interested. Why would such actors behave in ways that benefit others at a cost to themselves? There is also a significant interest in altruism in evolutionary biology and psychology (Barclay & Willer, 2007). If organisms are evolutionarily designed to maximize their own inclusive fitness, why would they behave altruistically toward genetically unrelated others?

Evolutionary Constraints and Limitations of the Human Brain

In my view, the theoretical attention still given to the problem of altruism is unwarranted, because I consider the problem to be resolved. There are at least two ways to explain altruism from an evolutionary psychological perspective. The first is to recognize the evolutionary limitations of the human brain. Pioneers of evolutionary psychology (Crawford, 1993; Symons, 1990; Tooby & Cosmides, 1990) all recognized that the evolved psychological mechanisms in the brain are designed for and adapted to the conditions of the environment of evolutionary adaptedness, not necessarily to the conditions of the current environment.

Kanazawa (2004a) synthesizes these observations into what he calls the *Savanna Principle*: The human brain has difficulty comprehending and dealing with entities and situations that did not exist in the ancestral environment. Burnham and Johnson (2005, pp. 130–131) refer to the same observation as the *evolutionary legacy hypothesis*, whereas Hagen and Hammerstein (2006, pp. 341–343) call it the *mismatch hypothesis*.

> **THE SAVANNA PRINCIPLE**
>
> The human brain has difficulty comprehending and dealing with entities and situations that did not exist in the ancestral environment

The Savanna Principle can potentially explain why individuals behave altruistically, both in laboratory experiments and naturalistic settings. For example, nearly half the players of one-shot Prisoner's Dilemma games make the theoretically irrational choice to cooperate with their partner (Sally, 1995). The Savanna Principle would suggest that this may possibly be because the human brain has difficulty comprehending completely anonymous social exchange and absolutely no possibility of knowing future interactions (which together make the game truly one-shot) (Kanazawa, 2004a, pp. 44–45). Neither of these situations existed in the ancestral environment; however, they are crucial for the game-theoretic prediction of universal defection.

Similarly, our ancestors spent nearly all of their time in evolutionary history living in small hunter-gatherer bands of about 50–150 related individuals. The Savanna Principle would therefore suggest that the human brain has difficulty comprehending large metropolises with millions of inhabitants who are genetically unrelated total strangers. Altruism among genetic kin and repeated exchange partners has already been well explained by inclusive fitness (Hamilton, 1964) and reciprocal altruism (Trivers, 1971), respectively. Contemporary humans may cooperate with genetically unrelated others, mistakenly (and unconsciously) thinking that they are kin or repeated exchange partners.

> Contemporary humans may cooperate with genetically unrelated others, mistakenly (and unconsciously) thinking that they are kin or repeated exchange partners.

Some are skeptical of the explanation of altruism and cooperation based on the Savanna Principle. In their critique of what they call "the big mistake hypothesis" (their name for the explanation of cooperation based on the Savanna Principle), Fehr and Henrich (2003), for example, suggest that one-shot encounters and exchanges might have been common in the ancestral environment. In their response to Fehr and Henrich, Hagen and Hammerstein (2006) point out that, even if *one-shot* encounters were common in the ancestral environment, *anonymous* encounters could not have been common, and the game-theoretical prediction of defection in one-shot Prisoner's Dilemma games requires both noniteration and anonymity. A lack of anonymity can lead to reputational concerns even in nonrepeated exchanges.

Psychological Versus Evolutionary Altruism

Another way to explain altruism and cooperation is to draw on Sober and Wilson's (1998) distinction between psychological altruism and evolutionary altruism. *Psychological altruism* refers to behavior that the actors believe would benefit others at the cost to themselves. *Evolutionary altruism* refers to behavior that increases the reproductive fitness of others at the cost of decreasing the actors' own reproductive fitness. From this perspective, some behavior that on the surface *appears* to be altruistic at the individual level may not truly be altruistic at the genetic level. Psychologically altruistic behavior may not necessarily be evolutionarily altruistic. There may be no such thing as altruism at the evolutionary level. One possible illustration of this is the "altruistic" decision of battered women to stay with their abusive partners.

The Puzzle

Domestic violence against women reduces their health and well-being tremendously. Occasionally, women are even killed by their abusive mates. Given the enormous health and somatic costs of spousal abuse, the question of why many battered women stay with their abusive husbands or boyfriends is a puzzling one. Although most battered women eventually leave their abusers, a substantial minority of them (estimates range from a quarter to a third) remain in their abusive relationships (Gondolf, 1988; Snyder & Sheer, 1981). LaBell (1979) notes that three-quarters of women living in a shelter have returned to their abusive mates at least once. Barnett and LaViolette (1993, p. 137) estimate that the average length of abusive relationships is no different from the average length of all marriages.

Why? Why do they stay, even temporarily? Are battered women who stay being pathologically altruistic to their abusive mates? If social sciences are branches of biology (Daly & Wilson, 1999; Kanazawa, 2004b; van den Berghe, 1990), and if nothing in biology makes sense except in the light of evolution (Dobzhansky, 1973), then an otherwise puzzling social phenomenon like why so many battered women stay in their abusive relationships might begin to make sense in light of evolutionary logic, in particular, in reference to the distinction between psychological and evolutionary altruism.

Spousal abuse exacts tremendous somatic costs to the abused women, and thus there is no question that their decision to stay with their abusers represents psychological altruism at the individual level. There is nothing that the abused women themselves (as individuals) gain by staying with their abusive partners. However, even such seemingly extreme acts of psychological altruism may nonetheless represent evolutionary self-interest; abused women may be "choosing" to stay with their abusive partners for the evolutionary benefit of their genes (including the benefit to their children with their abusers). Their decision to stay may *not* represent evolutionary altruism.

Battered Women Have More Sons

Earlier studies (Kanazawa, 2006, 2008) have shown that battered women and their violent mates have more sons than the general population. A meta-analysis of published studies of battered women and their children shows that the proportion of boys among the children of battered women is 0.5286, which is significantly ($p < 0.05$) higher than the population mean of 0.5122 (Kanazawa, 2006, Table 1). Further, an analysis of the National Child Development Study and the British Cohort Study in the United Kingdom shows that women who have had at least one abusive husband in their lives have significantly more sons on average than women who have never had any abusive husband

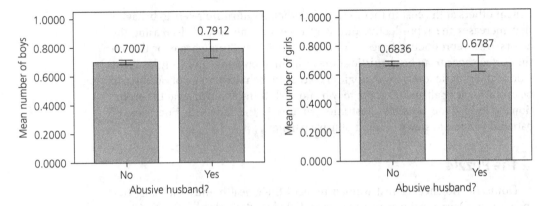

FIGURE 24.1
Mean number of boys and girls that women have, by whether they have ever had a physically abusive husband.
National Child Development Study/British Cohort Study.
(Note: Error bars represent 95% confidence intervals.)

(0.7912 vs. 0.7007). In sharp contrast, women who have had abusive husbands do not have any more daughters than women who have never had any abusive husband (0.6787 vs. 0.6836). Even after controlling for education, income, social class, and current marital status in a multiple regression analysis, the number of abusive husbands that women have had increases the number of boys that they have ($p < 0.001$), while it has no effect on the number of girls (Kanazawa, 2006, Table 2). The unstandardized coefficient for the number of abusive husbands in the multiple regression model ($b = 0.1324$) suggests that women have more than one-eighth of a boy for each abusive husband they have (Figure 24.1).

Clear individual differences exist in the extent to which men engage in violent behavior; some men are decidedly more aggressive and violent than others (Ellis & Walsh, 1997; Moffitt, 1993; Rowe, Vazsonyi, & Figueredo, 1997). Further, given the generality of violence and antisocial behavior (Gottfredson & Hirschi, 1990; Hirschi & Gottfredson, 1994), men who are violent in one context are expected to be violent in others. Thus, on average, men who physically abuse their wives and girlfriends should be more aggressive and violent toward their intrasexual rivals than are men who do not abuse their mates.

Aggression and violence, although they exact enormous physical tolls on the women in the context of spousal abuse, are at the same time important determinants of the outcome of male intrasexual competition, especially in the ancestral environment where most, if not all, dominance contests were at least partly physical. Even today, men's testosterone levels, which predict their aggression and violence (Booth & Osgood, 1993; Dabbs & Morris, 1990), also predict their dominance ranks in such a modern yet intrasexually competitive organization as the U.S. Army (Mueller & Mazur, 1996). *Ceteris paribus*, men who batter their wives on average would therefore have been intrasexually more competitive *in the ancestral environment* and would have attained higher dominance ranks than men who don't.

Given that (1) aggression and violence are conducive to dominance in the ancestral environment; (2) domestic violence is largely a function of men's testosterone levels (Soler, Vinayak, & Quadagno, 2000); (3) the tendency toward aggression and violence, measured by baseline testosterone levels, is highly heritable (Harris, Vernon, & Boomsma, 1998; Rushton, Fulker, Neale, Nias, & Eysenck, 1986); and (4) violent men are more likely to have sons than other men (Kanazawa, 2006), there are some evolutionary (reproductive) benefits for women to mating with abusive men. Such women can expect to have intrasexually competitive (if also wife-beating) sons, who will go on to dominate status hierarchies and garner many reproductive opportunities in their lifetimes. It may therefore be reasonable to posit that women may have been selected to tolerate a certain level of nonlethal violence in their mates in order to gain reproductive advantages by having violent sons.

There may be other reproductive advantages to staying with abusive mates. If the battered woman already has children with the batterer, she may not be able to find a superior alternative mate and father for her children, because stepfathers represent perhaps the greatest physical danger to children (Daly & Wilson, 1985). Thus, as terrible as living with a batterer might be for the physical welfare of the mother, the alternative (leaving him and living with another man who is not the genetic father of her children) may even be worse for the physical and reproductive welfare for her children (and thus her genes). In other words, her decision to stay with an abusive mate may represent *psychological altruism* (because it poses tremendous costs to the individual woman) but may not represent *evolutionary altruism* (because it has benefits for her genes). It may indeed be evolutionarily self-interested behavior.

The Big Irony

So, battered women's decision to stay with their abusive mates may represent an act of psychological altruism, but not evolutionary altruism. By staying in their abusive relationships, they may be advancing their reproductive goals at the genetic level, while personally suffering from tremendous somatic costs at the individual level.

> A woman's decision to stay with an abusive mate may represent psychological altruism (because it poses tremendous costs to the individual woman) but may not represent evolutionary altruism (because it has benefits for her genes).

The big irony, however, is that battered women may *not* be advancing their reproductive interests at the genetic level today after all. As noted above, the Savanna Principle states that the human brain, just like any other body part of any other species, is designed for and adapted to the conditions of the ancestral environment, not necessarily to those of the current environment. The disjuncture between the ancestral environment, to which our brain is adapted, and the current environment, in which we now live, may mean that many of the psychologically altruistic, evolutionarily selfish acts, like staying with an abusive mate, may not lead to evolutionary benefits today. In the ancestral environment, aggressive and violent men were more likely to win intrasexual competition and attain higher status. This may not necessarily be the case in the current environment.

Dabbs (1992) finds a negative correlation between testosterone and men's occupational achievement in the United States, and Figueredo (Figueredo & McCloskey, 1993; Figueredo et al., 2001) shows that physically abusive men in the United States and Mexico are "competitively disadvantaged." In most civilized societies, spousal abuse is a felony, for which the men go to jail for a long time, physically separated from their mates and thereby unable to reproduce and pass on their violent tendencies to their sons. So, in the current environment, women's unconscious desire to stay with their abusive mates may ultimately be maladaptive, and may inadvertently represent evolutionary altruism as well as psychological altruism. This observation does not detract from, but instead adds to, the evolutionary psychological explanation of why some battered women choose to stay in their abusive relationship, and the conclusion that there may be no such thing as altruism at the evolutionary level. It may be a consequence of psychologically altruistic, evolutionarily selfish act misapplied in the evolutionarily novel environment.

References

Barclay, P., & Willer, R. (2007). Partner choice creates competitive altruism in humans. *Proceedings of the Royal Society of London, Series B, 274,* 749–753.

Barnett, O. W., & LaViolette, A. D. (1993). *It could happen to anyone: Why battered women stay.* Newbury Park, CA: Sage.

Booth, A., & Osgood, D. W. (1993). The influence of testosterone on deviance in adulthood: Assessing and explaining the relationship. *Criminology, 31,* 93–117.

Burnham, T. C., & Johnson, D. D. P. (2005). The biological and evolutionary logic of human cooperation. *Analyse & Kritik, 27,* 113–135.

Crawford, C. B. (1993). The future of sociobiology: Counting babies or proximate mechanisms? *Trends in Ecology and Evolution, 8,* 183–186.

Dabbs, J. M., Jr. (1992). Testosterone and occupational achievement. *Social Forces, 70,* 813–824.

Dabbs, J. M. Jr., & Morris, R. (1990). Testosterone, social class, and antisocial behavior in a sample of 4,462 men. *Psychological Science, 1,* 209–211.

Daly, M., & Wilson, M. (1985). Child abuse and other risks of not living with both parents. *Ethology and Sociobiology, 6,* 197–210.

Daly, M., & Wilson, M. (1996). Homicidal tendencies. *Demos, 10,* 39–45.

Daly, M., & Wilson, M. I. (1999). Human evolutionary psychology and animal behaviour. *Animal Behaviour, 57,* 509–519.

Dobzhansky, T. (1973). Nothing in biology makes sense except in the light of evolution. *American Biology Teacher, 35,* 125–129.

Ellis, L., & Walsh, A. (1997). Gene-based evolutionary theories in criminology. *Criminology, 35,* 229–276.

Fehr, E., & Henrich, J. (2003). Is strong reciprocity a maladaptation? On the evolutionary foundations of human altruism. In P. Hammerstein (Ed.), *Genetic and cultural evolution of cooperation* (pp. 55–82). Cambridge, MA: MIT Press.

Figueredo, A. J., & McCloskey, L. A. (1993). Sex, money, and paternity: The evolutionary psychology of domestic violence. *Ethology and Sociobiology, 14,* 353–379.

Figueredo, A. J., Corral-Verdugo, V., Frías-Armenta, M., Bachar, K. J., White, J., McNeill, P. L., et al. (2001). Blood, solidarity, status, and honor: The sexual balance of power and spousal abuse in Sonora, Mexico. *Evolution and Human Behavior, 22,* 295–328.

Gottfredson, M. R., & Hirschi, T. (1990). *A general theory of crime.* Stanford, CA: Stanford University Press.

Gondolf, E. W. (1988). The effect of batterer counseling on shelter outcome. *Journal of Interpersonal Violence, 3,* 275–289.

Hagen, E. H., & Hammerstein, P. (2006). Game theory and human evolution: A critique of some recent interpretations of experimental games. *Theoretical Population Biology, 69,* 339–348.

Hamilton, W. D. (1964). The genetical evolution of social behaviour. *Journal of Theoretical Biology, 7*, 1–52.

Harris, J. A., Vernon, P. A., & Boomsma, D. I. (1998). The heritability of testosterone: A study of Dutch adolescent twins and their parents. *Behavior Genetics, 28*, 165–171.

Hirschi, T., & Gottfredson, M. R. (Eds.) (1994). *The generality of deviance.* New Brunswick, NJ: Transaction Publishers.

Kanazawa, S. (2004a). The Savanna Principle. *Managerial and Decision Economics, 25*, 41–54.

Kanazawa, S. (2004b). Social sciences are branches of biology. *Socio-Economic Review, 2*, 341–360.

Kanazawa, S. (2006). Violent men have more sons: Further evidence for the generalized Trivers-Willard hypothesis (gTWH). *Journal of Theoretical Biology, 239*, 450–459.

Kanazawa, S. (2008). Battered woman have more sons: A possible evolutionary reason why some battered women stay. *Journal of Evolutionary Psychology, 6*, 129–139.

LaBell, L. S. (1979). Wife abuse: A sociological study of battered women and their mates. *Victimology: An International Journal, 4*, 257–267.

Moffitt, T. E. (1993). Adolescence-limited and life-course-persistent antisocial behavior: A developmental taxonomy. *Psychological Review, 100*, 674–701.

Mueller, U., & Mazur, A. (1996). Facial dominance of West Point cadets as a predictor of later military rank. *Social Forces, 74*, 823–850.

Rowe, D. C., Vazsonyi, A. T., & Figueredo, A. J. (1997). Mating-effort in adolescence: A conditional or alternative strategy. *Personality and Individual Differences, 23*, 105–115.

Rushton, J. P., Fulker, D. W., Neale, M. C., Nias, D. K. B., & Eysenck, H. J. (1986). Altruism and aggression: The heritability of individual differences. *Journal of Personality and Social Psychology, 50*, 1192–1198.

Sally, D. (1995). Conversation and cooperation in social dilemmas: A meta-analysis of experiments from 1958 to 1992. *Rationality and Society, 7*, 58–92.

Snyder, D. K., & Scheer, N. S. (1981). Predicting disposition following brief residence at a shelter for battered women. *American Journal of Community Psychology, 9*, 559–566.

Sober, E., & Wilson, D. S. (1998). *Unto others: The evolution and psychology of unselfish behavior.* Cambridge, UK: Cambridge University Press.

Soler, H., Preeti, V., & Quadagno, D. (2000). Biosocial aspects of domestic violence. *Psychoneuroendocrinology, 25*, 721–739.

Symons, D. (1990). Adaptiveness and adaptation. *Ethology and Sociobiology, 11*, 427–444.

Tooby, J., & Cosmides, L. (1990). The past explains the present: Emotional adaptations and the structure of ancestral environments. *Ethology and Sociobiology, 11*, 375–424.

Trivers, R. L. (1971). The evolution of reciprocal altruism. *Quarterly Review of Biology, 46*, 35–57.

van den Berghe, P. L. (1990). Why most sociologists don't (and won't) think evolutionarily. *Sociological Forum, 5*, 173–185.

PART V

THE DEVELOPMENT AND UNDERLYING BRAIN PROCESSES OF PATHOLOGICAL ALTRUISM

CHAPTER 25

EMPATHY, GUILT, AND DEPRESSION

When Caring for Others Becomes Costly to Children

Carolyn Zahn-Waxler and Carol Van Hulle

> That we often derive sorrow from the sorrow of others is a matter
> of fact too obvious to require any instances to prove it.
> —Adam Smith, 1853

KEY CONCEPTS

- Empathy emerges early in life and often motivates caring, prosocial actions toward others. This leads to social competence and healthy emotional development.
- Children's empathy can lead to pathogenic guilt, anxiety, and a sense of personal failure when early family environments require too much of them.
- Parental depression contributes to pathogenic guilt in children which, in turn, creates conditions conducive to risk for developing depression.
- Genetic and environmental factors combine to determine why some children, especially girls, are likely to develop empathy-based pathogenic guilt and depression.

Overview

In most, if not all societies, females more often than males engage in voluntary activities that provide physical and emotional care for others. They also are more often involved in the helping professions and education of children. These roles require a deeply ingrained sense of personal responsibility for resolving the problems and distresses of others. Empathic proclivities of females facilitate these processes. Under certain conditions, however, caring for others becomes draining and debilitating. It is common to hear of burnout and compassion fatigue in adults (Chapter 28, by Klimecki and Singer), as well as depression. Here, we consider children's empathy from the first years of life through childhood and adolescence. We focus on family conditions that expose children to chronic, pervasive suffering and can compromise their development.

The Nature of Empathy and Altruism

Altruism is commonly defined as unselfish regard or concern for the welfare of others. It includes voluntarily helping others without external reward. It also may involve risk and self-sacrifice. Because underlying motives and intentions are hard to discern in children, altruistic acts are more commonly referred to as *prosocial behaviors*; that is, helping, sharing, comforting, protecting, defending, and cooperation. Here, we use the terms altruism, caring acts, and prosocial behaviors interchangeably. We emphasize actions that we believe can involve risk and self-sacrifice, as children take on the burdens of others at their own expense. Scientists also focus on the role of empathy in motivating altruistic acts. The capacity to emotionally experience the distress of the other (as described in the quote by Adam Smith) can lead to sympathy and compassion. These are hallmarks of positive human morality. Indeed, the idea of pathological empathy and altruism in children is an anathema to many. Yet, some children show concern for others that may be detrimental to their well-being.

> The idea of pathological empathy and altruism in children is an anathema to many. Yet, some children show concern for others that may be detrimental to their well-being.

Empathy, Guilt, and Depression

Despite its adaptive nature, empathy may contribute to depression under certain conditions (Zahn-Waxler, Cole, & Barrett, 1991). O'Connor and her colleagues (2007) describe depression in adults (more often women) as a disorder of Concern for Others. The moral system is on overdrive; empathy becomes coupled with pathogenic guilt and anxiety, culminating in submission and depression. We propose that these processes begin in early childhood and provide an explanatory model. High empathy is not necessarily a risk factor for depression. But when coupled with biological/genetic leanings toward sadness and depression and/or family environments that involve parental suffering, it may contribute to depression. Empathic over-arousal can begin in the first years of life when children try to help and care for their parents. *Role-reversal* is defined as a relationship disturbance in which a parent looks to a child to meet that parent's need for comfort, parenting, intimacy, or play, and the child attempts to meet those needs. Another term used is "compulsive caregiving." This "grown-up" behavior likely masks insecurities as children begin to suppress their own needs. Patterns of codependency between parent and child can develop.

Sex Differences in Depression and Related Emotions

Women are two to three times more likely than men to experience unipolar depression, as seen in both community-based and clinically referred samples (Kessler, McGonagle, Swartz, & Blazer, 1993; Nolen-Hoeksema, 1990). Sex differences in depression emerge in adolescence, but processes that create risk (more often for girls) can begin much earlier, and prodromal signs may go unnoticed. Normatively, girls show more internalizing emotions (sadness, anxiety, guilt, and shame) related to depression than boys early in development (Zahn-Waxler, 2000).

Anxiety is more common in girls than boys, even in the preschool years (Zahn-Waxler, Shirtcliff, & Marceau, 2007). Depression often co-occurs with anxiety (Angold, Costello, & Erkanli, 1999), and this comorbidity is much more common in girls (Lewinson, Rohde, & Seeley, 1995). Anxiety typically develops earlier than depression. Because it involves dysregulation of limbic, vegetative, and autonomic systems, this high arousal eventually taxes these systems, causing a person to shut down, withdraw, and become depressed. Thus, anxiety may be one early antecedent of depression. Children who are overwhelmed by their parents' needs are likely to experience anxiety.

Guilt, especially pathogenic guilt (O'Connor, Berry, Weiss, & Gilbert, 2002; O'Connor et al., 2007; Chapter 2 by O'Connor, Berry, and Lewis) is also implicated in depression. For many years, young children were viewed as incapable of guilt and depression. Both were thought to be based on the ability to be self-critical, which required advanced cognitive skills. We now know that depression occurs in preschool children (Luby et al., 2009). These children also show maladaptive guilt and shame, both of which are central to feelings of unworthiness and depression.

Sadness, too, is relevant both to empathy and depression. When children feel the sorrow of another person, they enter into that emotional state to some degree. In fact, sadness is an element of empathic concern that is inferred from facial expressions (downturned mouth, oblique brow) and vocalizations (drop in pitch). In adults, sadness as an element of concern predicts prosocial behavior (Eisenberg & Eggum, 2009).

Early Empathy: Alternative Outcomes

Figure 25.1 presents different processes that can stem from early empathy and lead to different developmental outcomes. One pathway is adaptive. When empathy leads to concern and sympathy for another, this can motivate caring acts that reflect social competence and help to create a sense of well-being.

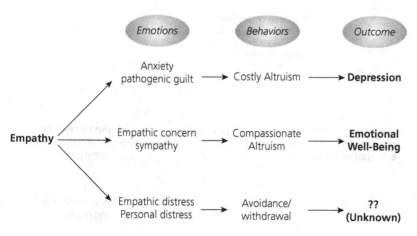

FIGURE 25.1
Alternative pathways and developmental outcomes of early empathy.

Positive socialization experiences (Eisenberg & Fabes, 1998; Hastings, Utendale, & Sullivan, 2007) and a minimum of environmental adversity also contribute to this pathway, by which empathy transitions into sympathy, compassionate altruism, and adaptive developmental outcomes. Another pathway occurs when empathy results in empathic distress or personal distress. Here, children become highly aroused and emotionally dysregulated; they focus on their own pain, turn away from others' distress, withdraw, and become avoidant. Theory and research with adults and children (see Batson & Shaw, 1991; Eisenberg & Fabes, 1998) have emphasized these two pathways.

However, there is an unexplored third pathway, also indicated in Figure 25.1 and elaborated in Figure 25.2. This occurs when children become distressed by the distress of others but are unable to turn away, thus creating costly altruism that can eventually lead to depression. This can happen when children with an emotionally distressed caregiver try to care for that parent. Here, empathy is likely to create anxiety, sadness, and eventually guilt as the child starts to develop negative cognitions and self-attributions of blame. Pathogenic guilt follows from these cognitive errors as the child begins to assume a causal role in the parent's depression. This creates a vicious cycle; negative cognitions and internalizing emotions become exaggerated, children engage in costly altruism, and forerunners of clinical and subclinical anxiety and depression emerge.

Many factors will determine particular outcomes. Biological child factors include gender, genes, neural circuitry, hormones, central and autonomic arousal, and temperament. Socialization reflects the roles of society, culture, institutions, and family. For young children, socialization operates primarily within the home setting. Children experience parents' personalities and mental health problems, family emotional climates, and child-rearing practices. Biological and social processes are not fully separable or mutually exclusive; they operate synergistically with interactive effects.

Here, we focus on early family experiences and parental characteristics that may transform children's early empathy into pathogenic guilt, which then creates risk for depression. These factors are identified in Figure 25.3. Biological/child factors include gender, genes, hormones, and temperament. These factors

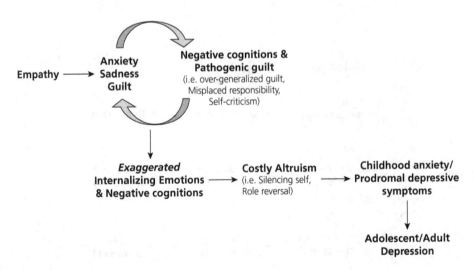

FIGURE 25.2
How early empathy leads to costly altruism and risk for depression.

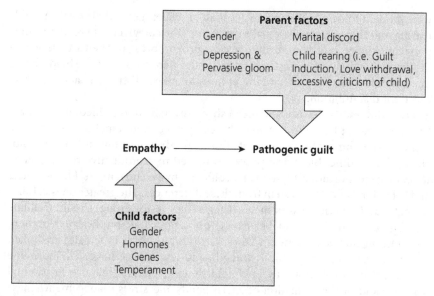

FIGURE 25.3
Parental factors that transform early empathy into pathogenic guilt.

are thought to create risk when present in family environments that include parental depression, marital discord, a negative global affective environment, and child-rearing practices that emphasize guilt-induction, love-withdrawal, and criticality. Parents' gender and genes also contribute to these processes. In the remainder of the chapter, we consider theoretical and empirical evidence for the pathway by which children's concern for others becomes costly and detrimental to adaptive development.

Biological Bases for Sex Differences in Empathy and Depression

An Evolutionary Perspective

MacLean (1985) proposed that empathy is a quality we share with other mammals. It evolved from parental care for the young, whose distress cries required responsive caregiving if the species was to survive. MacLean proposed that empathy was based on interconnections between the limbic system and the prefrontal cortex, linked originally to parental concern for the young. These neural connections between brain areas involving emotion and foresight made the expression of a broader sense of responsibility possible: Parental concern for the young generalized to other members of the species through the higher reaches of the brain.

In virtually all species of mammals, females are primarily responsible for feeding, nurturing, and protecting the young, so that parental concern in MacLean's theory more properly refers to maternal concern. Early in civilization, sex roles were differentiated based largely on biological differences. Females bore and reared the offspring, while males hunted and fended off foes. Bjorklund and Kipp (1996) proposed that inhibition mechanisms evolved from the need to control social and emotional responses in small groups of humans for the purposes of cooperation, affiliation, and group cohesion. Pressures for inhibition were thought to be greater on females than on males, given their roles in child-rearing and their greater parental investment. The caregiver role requires emotion regulation as mothers are often in close proximity to (and hence experience) the distress of their offspring. In contrast, males were required to be bold, skilled in exploration and combat, and impervious to others' distress; all activities that called for disinhibition.

Over time, sex roles became increasingly diversified, modified by socialization, and (except for child-bearing) shared by males and females. However, the fact of sexual dimorphism, implicated in these early divisions of labor, has not changed over time. Biological processes related to reproductive roles, notably the endocrine (hormonal) systems, still differ for males and females. Physiological and behavioral effects also stem from these differences. The greater physical size, strength, and muscle mass of males (triggered by testosterone) should facilitate disinhibitory emotions and behaviors (e.g. aggression, physical exploration, competition, and achievement). Lower testosterone levels in females are linked to smaller stature, less physical strength, and less muscle mass. The hormone oxytocin plays a role not only in childbirth and lactation, but also in parental behavior and in the formation of social bonds and stress management. These hormonal patterns in females should facilitate inhibitory emotions and behaviors (e.g., squelching aggressive impulses), social finesse, and communal activities (e.g., nurturing, caregiving, fostering of group cohesion). Recent theories of stress and coping also emphasize biological, hormonal sex differences (Taylor et al., 2000); for example, the "fight-or-flight" stress response is more common to males (as testosterone-based) and the "tend-and-befriend" response is more common to females (as oxytocin-based).

It is hardly coincidence that behaviors reflecting the different roles assumed by men and women are faithfully mirrored in the different play activities of boys and girls (see review by Zahn-Waxler, Shirtcliff, & Marceau, 2007). Consistent with Taylor et al. (2000), the most robust sex differences observed include greater physical aggression in boys (Coie & Dodge, 1998) and more prosocial, caring behaviors in girls (Eisenberg & Fabes, 1998).

Genes

Genes play a role in depression (see review by Zahn-Waxler, Race, & Duggal, 2005). Children's (and particularly girls') susceptibility to internalizing emotions (anxiety, guilt, sadness) prior to the appearance of depression also may be heritable.

Hormones and Brain Development

Circulating testosterone in the intrauterine environment masculinizes the brains of male infants. Differences in brain structure and function are thought to result from higher levels of testosterone in males than females. Geschwind and Galaburda (1985) and Baron-Cohen (2002) have argued that excessive testosterone contributes to delayed maturation, neurodevelopmental problems, and problems related to disinhibition, seen more often in males than females. In this view, the extreme male brain is also associated with empathy deficits (Baron-Cohen, 2002). Empathy surfeits more common to females (i.e., an extreme female brain) originally were not seen as problematic. More recently (Chapter 26, by Baron-Cohen) speculates that extremes of empathy may reflect a form of pathological altruism, noting that this hypothesis remains to be tested. We will report supportive evidence for the view that heightened empathy contributes to problems more common to females (anxiety and mood disorders).

> Evidence suggests that heightened empathy contributes to problems such as anxiety and mood disorders.

Baron-Cohen's theory emphasizes lack of testosterone as contributing to higher empathy in females. Low fetal testosterone is associated with higher empathy in both boys and girls (Chapman, et al., 2006). Oxytocin and vasopressin (known to differ in males and females) also are also implicated in empathy and altruism, at least in adults (Knafo et al., 2008; Rodrigues, Saslow, Garcia, John, & Keltner, 2009). Just as delayed maturation may signal risk (more for boys) for disinhibitory problems associated with deficient social awareness and empathy, so too may early maturity in young children may signal risk (more for girls) for inhibitory problems linked to heightened social awareness and empathy (Zahn-Waxler et al., 2007).

Neural Activity

Neuroimaging and electroencephalogram (EEG) studies show greater activation of parts of the pain matrix relevant to empathy in adult females' than males' responses to others' pain or distress (Schulte-Ruther, Markowitsch, Shah, Fink, & Piefke, 2008; Singer, 2006; Yang, Decety, Lee, Chen, & Cheng, 2008). These sex differences in neural resonance to others' emotions confirm commonly observed behavioral sex differences. Our ability to share affective states is based on phylogenetically old structures that develop very early in ontogeny (Singer, 2006). Neural resonance relies on limbic and paralimbic structures that are present in infancy. The greater observed resonance (contagious crying) of female than male infants to distress cries of other infants (Hoffman, 1977) likely reflects greater neural resonance as well. This is consistent with evolutionary explanations of biologically based preparedness of females to nurture and care for the young. A review of sex differences from infancy through adolescence indicates a right hemisphere advantage for females for processing emotional cues (McClure, 2000). (For further review of neural processes and empathy see Chapter 2 by O'Connor, Berry, and Lewis, and Decety & Meyer, 2008).

Temperament: Sociability, Effortful Control, and Social Sensitivity

Sociability refers to friendliness and affiliation—the desire to be in the company of others. Sociable children are likely to intervene on behalf of someone in distress. Affiliation and close dyadic relationships are more common in girls than boys. Regulation of emotion also is central to empathic concern and caring acts (Eisenberg & Fabes, 1998). The temperament quality of *effortful control* is a component of emotion regulation. Effortful control includes the ability to concentrate and inhibit dominant responses. It involves the ability to delay gratification, resist temptation, and to easily stop when told "no."

These qualities are more common in girls than boys and support a view of girls as more compliant, well-behaved, eager to please, and easier to socialize than boys. Social sensitivity reflects a keen awareness of the social world, emotional attunement, and the ability to read others' emotions. It is probably related both to effortful control and sociability. It is linked as well to suppression of anger and aggression. All these qualities reflect inhibitory processes described by Bjorkland and Kipp (1996) that are relevant to girls' later roles as caregivers. Inhibition may create greater risk for heightened empathy and depression, especially if it occurs in troubled family environments.

> Inhibition may create greater risk for heightened empathy and depression, especially if it occurs in troubled family environments.

The Environment and Sex Differences in Empathy and Depression

Neopsychoanalytic and Psychodynamic Theories

Early ideas about causal links between empathic overinvolvement, pathogenic guilt, and depression came from clinical work with adult patients, mainly women who were, and still are, more likely than men to seek treatment. The moral emotions—guilt in particular—were first implicated in adult depression by Freud, who emphasized childhood precursors seen in harsh superego development and internalization of criticism and blame. Neopsychoanalysts later posited links between empathy and guilt in childhood that could culminate in adult depression. Modell (1965) and Friedman (1985) proposed that guilt has an underlying altruistic motive; genuine caring and love for others becomes exaggerated under some conditions.

These theorists used concepts of survivor guilt and separation guilt to describe the long-term consequences of growing up in disturbed families. Survivor guilt initially referred to survivors of disasters in which others have died. But its meaning was extended to children living with a dysfunctional parent. Separation guilt is the belief that developing autonomy would damage the parent. Guilt may result from behaving in ways that may be seen as disloyal, or that hinder, worry, or sadden the parent (Friedman, 1985). Parents may reinforce children's feelings of responsibility by conveying that they are capable of determining the parents' fate. Repeated experiences of blame in childhood may lead to pervasive feelings of responsibility that later in life make one vulnerable to depression.

> Repeated experiences of blame in childhood may lead to pervasive feelings of responsibility that later in life make one vulnerable to depression.

According to Bush (1989), superego development begins at 2 or 3 years of age and could become the basis for later depression. Children develop ideas about how they are to blame for traumas they (or other family members) experience. These internal representations may become repressed in the course of development and lead to (a) distorted conceptions of children's power to hurt others, (b) a sense of being bad and undeserving, and (c) pathological symptoms and defenses linked to themes of self-punishment and restitution.

Bergman (1982) described ways in which mothers who are depressed and dissatisfied with their own lives impose their problems on their children, particularly their daughters. A parent with many unmet needs may unwittingly try to assuage them through the child (Miller, 1979, 1981). Children may often assume an understanding and caring role, but at the expense of authentic personal growth and identity formation. Later, they may draw others into their own service because of earlier unmet needs. This inability to develop a "true self" is seen as a precursor to depression.

A related theory from the clinical arena regarding roots of female depression emphasizes the importance of relationships for women and the costs of "silencing the self" (Jack, 1991). Depression results from the tensions between sacrificing needs to preserve a relationship and acting on needs at the risk of losing the relationship. Women learn to censor themselves, devalue their experience, repress anger, and remain silent—all of which require inhibition and self-control. This downside of the relational self may begin in childhood when girls, especially, begin to place their parents' needs before their own. When females are ambivalent or uncertain about their goals for autonomy, especially in adolescence and early adulthood, they often construe separation and individuation as aggressive acts (Gilligan, 1982) and are likely to internalize distress.

Cognitive Attributional Theories of Depression

Depression is characterized by overwhelming feelings of both helplessness and responsibility. In Seligman's (1975) model of depression, learned helplessness develops when there is no contingency between one's responses and outcomes. When individuals learn that events are uncontrollable, they give up and become depressed. Beck's (1967) cognitive model postulates that depressives often interpret interactions as instances of failure. They assume personal responsibility for events with negative outcomes, producing guilt, self-blame, self-deprecation, and depressed mood. In this view, the self is seen as worthless; the world as unfair; and the future as hopeless. In reformulated attribution theory, Abramson and Sackheim (1977) merged the two theories to explain why people blame themselves for outcomes they know they didn't cause and which they cannot control.

Cognitive attributional theories originally were developed to explain the emergence of depression in adults. However, the framework can be extended readily to explain how children could develop inconsistent simultaneous beliefs about responsibility and helplessness, and also in how they develop negative views of the self, the world, and the future. Many children with a distressed caregiver may both attempt to create a more effective parent and come to believe that they have caused the damage. They fundamentally cannot help the parent, which would lead to feelings of failure and helplessness. The belief, however, that they can create change would be intermittently reinforced by their occasional successful efforts, so they keep trying. Overinvolved young children could experience depression-like symptoms of helplessness and responsibility early and repeatedly, eventually to assume unrealistic, generalized responsibility for others. There is reason to believe that (a) girls will be more affected than boys, and (b) this will more likely occur when a parent is depressed.

Parental Depression and Marital Discord: The Affective Environment

A substantial body of research exists on the generally adverse effects for children of having a depressed parent (Beardslee, Versage, & Gladstone, 1998; Downey & Coyne, 1990; Goodman & Gotlib, 1999; Zahn-Waxler, 2002).

> Over involved young children could experience depression-like symptoms of helplessness and responsibility early and repeatedly, eventually to assume unrealistic, generalized responsibility for others.

Because depression is heritable to some degree, it is commonly assumed that the children are at increased risk for genetic reasons. However, the *experiences* of children with a depressed parent also differ markedly.

Depressed parents are, on average, less reciprocal, attuned, and engaged in interactions with their children, even as early as infancy, when compared to well mothers. In addition to sadness and anhedonia, depressed parents also express a greater range and intensity of negative emotions, including anxiety, guilt, irritability, and anger. Often, marital conflict exists, so that the children are likely to observe parental arguments. Children exposed to negative emotions associated with parental depression may experience these same emotions via contagion and imitation. Even infants in the first months of life are sensitive to emotional states of caregivers, trying to repair interactions or reengage the mother if she is withdrawn or depressed (Cohn, Campbell, Matias, & Hopkins, 1990).

Child Rearing Practices of Depressed Parents

Several child-rearing practices also could draw children into parental distress in ways that "facilitate" empathically based guilt (see review by Zahn-Waxler, 2002). Depressed parents are prone to make critical comments, directing them to their children, as well as to themselves. They often model helpless, passive styles of coping and tend to use discipline methods that are either ineffectual or too coercive. Guilt-induction and love-withdrawal are particularly damaging to self-worth and are seen more often in depressed than in well parents (Donatelli, Bybee, & Buka, 2007). In guilt-induction, the parent directs unwarranted, inappropriate blame and responsibility toward the child—expressing disappointment, self-sacrifice, and the burden created by the child. Depressed mothers also talk more about sadness and distress with their preschool children than do well mothers, and both groups do so more with daughters than sons (Zahn-Waxler, Ridgeway, Denham, Usher, & Cole, 1993).

Early Development of Empathy and Prosocial Behavior

Normative Development

Here, we consider the typical development of empathic concern and caring acts. This provides a comparative base for the empirical review that follows of children and adolescents who become overly involved in the problems of their parents. From birth onward, human infants respond to distress cries of others. Newborns show contagious crying when they hear other infants cry, and this response is stronger than to equally aversive nonsocial sounds. We are wired to be responsive to other humans (Hoffman, 1977). Attachment and bonding with the caregiver during the first year prepares the child for later empathy. It evolves from a complex interplay and sharing of emotions, as well as from cooperation and turn-taking in parent–infant social interactions.

During the first and second years of life, the reflexive distress in response to others' distress gradually gives way to more modulated emotion. Children show caring acts of physical comforting (pats, hugs) around their first birthday (Zahn-Waxler, Radke-Yarrow, Wagner, & Chapman, 1992). Prosocial acts directed toward someone in distress (e.g., crying, frightened, sad, injured) increase during the second year of life. They also become more nuanced and attuned to the specific nature of the other's distress. Often, but not always, caring acts are directed to familiar persons. By 2 years of age, children help, share, give physical comfort, and verbal sympathy, and protect and defend victims. Empathic concern can be seen in facial expressions and sympathetic sounds.

Prosocial acts occur, on average, a third of the time. Although young children vary widely in the extent of their prosociality toward persons in distress, it is extremely rare to see a child who never responds. When someone is in less dire straits (e.g., has dropped something), most toddlers provide spontaneous help that seems intrinsically motivated (Warneken & Tomasello, 2008). Caring for others is a major developmental milestone.

Here is one mother's account of a strong caring response in her 18-month-old daughter, Julie.

> A neighbor asked me to take care of her baby. After she left, the baby began to shriek. He was very upset by my efforts to comfort him, so I put him in a high chair and gave him a cookie. As soon as he began to cry, Julie looked very startled and worried. Her body stiffened. She bent toward him and cocked her head, reaching toward him. He began to throw the cookies. She tried to return them, which surprised me because usually she tries to eat everyone's cookies. She put the pieces on the tray and looked worried. Her eyebrows were up and her lips were pursed. She hovered around him whimpering herself and looking at me. I put him back in the playpen, and he continued to cry. She continued to look anxious and cry once in a while. She reached into the playpen, patted his shoulder, and began to stroke his hair. I could hear her cooing and making concerned sounds. Then she came into the kitchen, took my hand and led me to the living room. She kept looking at me with a very concerned, worried look. Then she took my hand and tried to put it on top of Brian's head.

Julie showed empathic concern that underlies several different kinds of caring behaviors, a remarkable constellation of caring acts in a child so young. If she was simply bothered by the crying and wished for it to stop, she could have left the room. No one exerted pressure on her to intervene. Rather, she urged her mother to act when her own efforts failed, and tried to get her mother to help. Julie's responses were voluntary and impelled from within. Her empathic concern for the baby and her personal distress (i.e., whimpering and crying) existed side by side. We have observed this fluid interplay in other studies, particularly in young girls (Zahn-Waxler & Robinson, 1995).

Five years later, in a longitudinal follow-up, Julie was observed to take off her sandals and give them to a younger barefoot child as they walked together across the hot beach sands. Julie appeared predisposed to show strong concern for the welfare of others. Both her responses typified her more general style of response to others in distress. It is difficult to view these reactions as anything other than adaptive. (i.e., beneficial to both parties).

Connections Between Empathy and Guilt in Young Children

However, young children with propensities for empathic acts of caring could be at risk in troubled home environments. They are still immature in terms of other aspects of cognitive, physical, and social development. They can be vulnerable to early socialization experiences that keep them overly involved with the family and interfere with their ability to join a wider social world of playmates and friends, teachers, and other role models, and eventually adult partners.

Empathy may become compromised if suffused with anxiety and guilt, and if it involves too much sadness.

Children frequently see and hear others in distress. Sometimes they are innocent bystanders (e.g., a hungry sibling cries), and sometimes they cause the distress (e.g., the child hurts a sibling). Children show empathic concern and caring acts in both types of situations. When the child has caused the distress, these reactions are thought to reflect guilt/remorse and reparation. In Hoffman's theory of moral development (1982), guilt is viewed as a special case of empathy. We conducted longitudinal research on 1- to 3-year-old children's responses to distresses they witnessed as bystanders and those they caused (Zahn-Waxler et al., 1992). Children showed empathic concern and prosocial actions similarly in witnessed and caused distresses. Their responses increased with age for both types of situations. Empathic concern and guilt were highly correlated, as were prosocial and reparative acts. These responses were often more common in girls than boys, consistent with other studies (see Eisenberg & Lennon, 1983; Zahn-Waxler, 2000).

Young children sometimes became confused as to whether or not they had caused distress in another person. There were instances of "misplaced responsibility." That is, some children responded as if they had caused distress when they had not. Upon seeing their mother cry, for example, they asked apologetically, "Did I make you sad?" or "Sorry, I be nice." They were also more likely to show remorse when they caused distress in another person (i.e., they seemed more guilt-prone in general). These children also showed more guilt than their counterparts 5 years later, suggesting the early origins of an enduring pattern (Cummings, Hollenbeck, Iannotti, Radke-Yarrow, & Zahn-Waxler, 1986).

Socialization Experiences That Heighten Early Guilt

Children's guilt-proneness was enhanced by certain child-rearing practices and forms of discipline (Zahn-Waxler, Radke-Yarrow, & King, 1979). Mothers who frequently explained to the child the consequences of his or her harmful actions for the victim had children who more often showed remorse and tried to make amends. This was particularly true when explanations were embellished with judgmental reactions, strong convictions, and disappointment; for example, adopting a moralistic stance against harming others ("You must *never* hurt anyone! It is a very bad thing to do"). Sometimes these mothers also used love withdrawal (e.g., walking away from the child after saying, "That really hurt—and I don't want to be near you when you act like that").

This is the moral system on overdrive (O'Connor et al., 2007), seen here in a moralistic approach to child-rearing. The term "moral system on overdrive" typically refers to the berating of the self by a depressed person. But depressed mothers also berate their children, creating guilt and a potential mechanism for transmission of depression across generations. Some mothers also dramatized expressions of pain "inflicted" on them by their children (e.g., if the child accidentally bit the mother while nursing). The message to the child is "see how your behavior hurts me" as the mother takes on the role of victim.

Costly Empathy and Guilt in Young Children

Empathic overarousal in children can occur under a number of environmental conditions. However, research has focused on families with a depressed parent, mostly mothers, and where there is marital discord. Under these conditions, suffering often is chronically present in the home, and children may readily be drawn into the process.

Children's Early Responses to Marital Discord

In one of our first studies, children as young as 2 years became emotionally aroused and intervened when their parents argued (Cummings, Zahn-Waxler, & Radke-Yarrow, 1981). Fights between parents were mainly verbal, with occasional shoving and throwing. Children from high-conflict homes showed distress and anger during the fights. They also tried to stop parents from fighting, to comfort one of them, or to get them to make up. Parents were often remarkably uninsightful about the negative fallout for their children of being drawn into problems of grown-ups, sometimes expressing pride in the child's ability to comfort them. One mother who cried after a fight with her husband stated that her 21-month-old "Came over and sat on my lap, hugged me, and kissed me on the forehead. That cleared up all my depression, and I reached over and hugged her, and then she began to smile and looked relieved."

These children were seen again at ages 6 to 7 years (Cummings, Hollenbeck, Iannotti, Radke-Yarrow & Zahn-Waxler, 1986), and role-reversal was again evident (e.g., "Take it easy, Dad. Calm down. Be quiet. It will be all right"—said to a father who comes in shouting at his wife. And, "Now come on Mom. If Dad says that you never say you're sorry, it's your turn to say you're sorry"—said to parents having a fight). Such responses reflect precocious involvement that is likely to be detrimental.

Children's Early Responses to Diagnosed Maternal Depression

We observed preschool age children's responses in a natural setting and also when mothers simulated sadness (crying in response to a sad newspaper story; Radke-Yarrow, Zahn-Waxler, Richardson, Susman, & Martinez, 1994). We compared children of mothers diagnosed with depression and those of well mothers. Caring acts were most frequent in children who had a depressed mother, particularly if the children were also anxious and had a close relationship with the mother. Girls were more prosocial than boys, whether or not the mother was depressed. These data supported the idea that young children (especially girls) with a depressed parent may become overly involved in another's distress.

In a study of 2- to 3-year-old children exposed to potential guilt-inducing experiences (Cole, Barrett, & Zahn-Waxler, 1992), children with depressed mothers often made special efforts to behave well, suppressing tension and frustration in situations in which such responses would be expected. These children may have muted their frustration so as not to concern their mothers. In a third study, 2-year-olds with depressed mothers were reluctant to harm others, relative to children of well mothers who showed normative levels of aggression (Denham, Zahn-Waxler, Cummings, & Iannotti, 1991). By age 5, these children were *less* likely to be prosocial with a playmate than children of well mothers. Children's early efforts to be caring and well-behaved at home can prove costly to the quality of their interpersonal relationships in a widened social world.

> Children's early efforts to be caring and well-behaved at home can prove costly to the quality of their interpersonal relationships in a widened social world.

In children's narratives and symbolic play in hypothetical situations of conflict and distress, preschool children of depressed mothers showed more themes of interpersonal responsibility (empathy and guilt) than children of well mothers (Zahn-Waxler, Kochanska, Krupnick, & McKnew, 1990). By middle childhood, however, children of well mothers showed more themes of responsibility. Precocious expressions of empathy and guilt are likely to place burdens on young children; internalized themes of interpersonal responsibility are more consistent with socialization expectations for older children. Girls showed more responsibility than boys, regardless of age and maternal depression. Also, empathy and guilt were linked with self-distress and relationship concerns only for girls.

Children of depressed mothers showed narrative themes that were often exaggerated, complex, and unresolved (Zahn-Waxler et al., 1990). In neopsychoanalytic theories, this is viewed as pathogenic guilt. As an example of an unusually heightened sense of responsibility, one child said "The mom's leaving home because the boy wouldn't eat his peas." This readiness to claim responsibility for another's plight can reflect a pathogenic belief that unwanted outcomes could be prevented if one were a different (better) person.

Some narratives reflecting pathogenic guilt were particularly poignant. One child told a story about a mother who was sad because a robber came into the house and stole all her lights—an apt metaphor for the dullness and darkness that characterizes deep depression. He went on to say that someone had called her a bad mother. He then quickly rushed to her defense, saying it wasn't true. His overinvolvement in the mother's depression suggests that he would be a candidate for developing anxiety and depression Although we did not examine children's internalizing symptoms here, children's pathogenic guilt assessed in another study using parallel procedures was related to their internalizing symptoms (Fergusson, Stegge, Miller, & Olson, 1999).

Girls of depressed mothers also showed more unassertive, submissive ways of coping with conflict than did boys (and girls of well mothers) (Hay, Zahn-Waxler, Cummings, & Iannotti, 1992). These girls may submerge their own interests and goals for the sake of their parents. In three studies of preschool children, when girls were aggressive, they made greater efforts to repair their transgressions than did boys (Zahn-Waxler, 2000). Other studies as well show more guilt/reparation and compliance in young girls than boys (Kochanska, Gross, & Nichols, 2002; Zahn-Waxler, 2000).

Children who appear competent and helpful to their parents, who are well-behaved and compliant, may also experience considerable internal distress that could lead to later internalizing problems. Girls are more adept than boys at masking disappointment and frustration, by smiling and assuming a cheerful demeanor (Cole, 1986). In childhood, girls show far fewer behavior problems than do boys, supporting the myth that they generally experience benign childhoods (Zahn-Waxler, 1993). Higher rates of depression and anxiety in females than males do not emerge until adolescence. Thus, most scientists have not studied childhood precursors of sex differences in depression. However, our data suggest that the roots of these differences can begin quite early.

Depression in Children and Youth: Costs of Caring

The Role of Parental Depression

We also now know that empathic overarousal and pathogenic guilt are linked to depression in middle childhood and adolescence, especially in girls from distressed family environments. The dynamics undoubtedly become even more complex as parents begin to treat older children as confidants with secrets to be kept. Girls are typically more susceptible than boys to the influences of maternal depression (e.g., Boyle & Pickles, 1997; Conger et al., 1993). There are long-term effects of maternal depression on later development of depression in daughters, but not sons (Davies & Windle, 1997; Duggal, Carlson, Sroufe, & Egeland, 2001; Fergusson, Horwood, & Lynsky, 1995). Depression increased over time in adolescent daughters, but not sons, who provided comfort and suppressed their aggression (Davis, Sheeber, Hops, & Tildesley, 2000). Submissive coping during conflict with the mother also predicted increases in depressive symptoms a year later for adolescent daughters but not sons (Powers & Welsh, 1999), consistent with proposed deleterious effects of self-silencing.

Adolescent daughters more than sons provided active support to their depressed mothers, and also expressed more sadness, worry, withdrawal, and feelings of responsibility (Klimes-Dougan & Bolger, 1998). Daughters may be more susceptible to their mothers' unhappiness because they spend more time with them and have stronger emotional ties (Gurian, 1987). Although children of depressed parents say they are more prosocial than those of well parents, their parents are *less* likely to see them in this light (Hay & Pawlby, 2003). This mismatch may lead to feeling devalued and unappreciated.

Observed empathy in 6- to 8-year-olds has been associated with maternal (but not paternal) depression and with the child's own depressive symptoms (Van Hulle, Schreiber, Goldsmith, & Zahn-Waxler, 2009). In a community sample of Finnish 12-year-olds' (Solantaus-Simula, Punamaki, & Beardslee, 2002) responses to low parental mood, girls tended to empathize and cheer up mothers more than did boys. Boys were less worried and more avoidant, whereas girls showed more emotional overinvolvement. Overinvolved children of unhappy parents were also likely to feel angry, scared, guilty, and self-deprecating. Girls reported greater depressed mood than boys; overinvolvement was linked to the highest levels of depressed mood.

These findings are consistent with earlier research suggesting that it is the overinvolvement in parents' unhappiness that creates risk. Beardslee and Podorefsky (1988) identified a small group of resilient adolescents with parents with major depression who functioned well over a 2.5-year period. They showed clear self-understanding, a deep commitment to relationships, and individuation from their parents (although many took care of their ill parents). We do not know, however, how these youth fared later (e.g., after they married and had their own children).

The Role of Parental Discord/Divorce

Parental conflict and divorce also are implicated in children's depression and here, too, caring orientations in offspring create risk.

> It is the overinvolvement in parents' unhappiness that creates risk.

Adolescent girls exposed to family conflict and discord were more likely than boys to develop depression and related problems (Aseltine, 1996; Crawford, Cohen, Midlarsky, & Brook, 2001; Dadds, Atkinson, Turner, Blum, & Lendich, 1999; Formoso, Gonzales, & Aiken, 2000; Garnefski, 2000; Vuchenich, Emery, & Cassidy, 1988). Girls showed higher levels of interpersonal caring and involvement in others' problems (particularly mothers) than did boys, which contributed to girls' higher rates of depressed mood (Gore, Aseltine, & Colton, 1993). Davies and Lindsay (2004) found a similar pattern; for girls only, elevated levels of communion partly accounted for greater reactivity to parental conflict and internalizing problems. Communion consists of interpersonal connectedness and empathic concern, as indexed by items such as "I care what happens to others" and "When someone's feelings are hurt, I try to make them feel better." Even before adolescence, girls felt more fearful and blameworthy than boys (Davies & Lindsay, 2004). Aube et al. (2000) found that unassertive girls who felt overly responsible for others were more depressed than boys.

In summary, parental depression and marital discord are linked with higher levels of concern and caring, guilt and responsibility, and internalizing problems, particularly in girls, from early childhood through adolescence. Cumulatively, these findings provide substantial support for early clinical theories based on observations of adult patients.

Gender, Empathy, Guilt, and Depression: A Developmental Model

We now consider further some of the ways in which biology and socialization contribute to consolidation of internalizing emotions, more often in girls, to later become reflected in depression. Dienstbier (1984) proposed that different temperaments might lead to different emotion-attributional styles and levels of guilt. Early proneness to emotional tension should result in internal discomfort and distress following transgressions (both real and imagined). The child is then likely to experience links between tension and transgression, and come to experience anticipatory anxiety (the knot in the stomach). Anxious children may develop "affective maps" or "somatic markers" of their experiences (Derryberry & Reed, 1994; Damasio, Tranel, & Damasio, 1991). This physiological reactivity may facilitate early, rapid development of mechanisms related to conscience, such as guilt and restraint from wrongdoing. It may also facilitate feelings of responsibility in encounters that do not involve transgressions (i.e., when children are bystanders to distress). Because girls normatively experience more internalizing emotions (empathy, guilt, anxiety, sadness), they are more likely to be more influenced than boys.

Heightened internalizing emotions in girls and actions that stem from these feelings in early childhood are not necessarily problematic. These qualities are part and parcel of social skills and sensitivity. This includes awareness of the consequences of one's actions on others (both positive and negative) and the ability to adapt appropriately. If girls' greater sensitivity makes them more prone to develop somatic markers that help them internalize norms than boys, this can provide many advantages. Biological factors do not *necessarily* create greater empathic overarousal or pathogenic guilt in girls than boys.

It is when empathy is present in troubled family environments (e.g., depressed and maritally distressed parents) that empathic overarousal and pathogenic guilt are likely to occur. Moreover, when these parents also use child-rearing practices that involve love-withdrawal, guilt-induction, and criticality, children's internalized distress is likely to become even more intense, sustained, and corrosive. Because girls are more emotionally responsive to problems of others than are boys, they are likely to react to a wider range of others' negative emotions and con-

> It is when empathy is present in troubled family environments (e.g., depressed and maritally distressed parents) that empathic overarousal and pathogenic guilt are likely to occur.

flicts. Girls are more often in close proximity to caregivers than are boys, influencing the extent to which a gloomy family climate and negative child-rearing experiences become ingrained in memory. Ruminative scripts (i.e., dwelling on problems) are likely to develop in girls from unhappy families—these scripts lead to more generalized anxiety and depression. The higher rates of rumination seen in adolescent and adult females compared to their male counterparts are known to contribute to females' higher rates of depression. The presence of ruminative themes in girls in middle childhood raises the possibility that the links between rumination and depression in fact have earlier origins. Boys are not necessarily immune to these processes, but their greater avoidance of family distress and conflict helps create a protective distance from depression and anxiety.

Discussion and Conclusions

Parental depression is a prototype of parental suffering that is chronically present in some children's lives. Parental suffering has many faces, parental depression being just one. It is also important to recognize there are depressed mothers who still provide the requisite care for their children and engage in sensitive child-rearing practices that facilitate healthy emotional and psychological development in their offspring (Zahn-Waxler et al., 1990). This is most likely to occur when the mothers also have a social support network and are financially comfortable.

Other parental mental health problems also may lead to empathic overinvolvement in children. Schizophrenia, severe anxiety, personality disorders, and addictions also translate into helplessness, vulnerability, and extreme emotional distress in parents. Economic problems dramatically alter the family landscape as the parents experience chronic distress. In addition, there are many parents who apparently function well in the world at large, but who place unrealistic demands on their children. Still other parents struggle to find their place in the world and try to fulfill their own dreams and ambitions through their children. These children, too, are likely to experience strong guilt and feel unworthy if they fail to meet parental expectations.

Only a subset of children responds to parental depression with empathy and caring actions. Another group reacts with anger and aggression, and is low on empathy (e.g., Jones, Field, & Davalos, 2000); and yet another group becomes avoidant. High (di)stress home environments are likely to evoke different extreme responses in children with different temperaments. Moreover, depression is not uniformly manifested. Some depressed mothers also are angry and hostile with their children. It would be harder for children to empathize with these mothers and easier to become angry. Several factors may contribute to greater anger-proneness in some depressed mothers: little education, single parenthood, poverty or low income, few material resources, limited reliable social networks, and unsafe neighborhoods.

Biology and socialization work in concert to incline girls, on average, more toward empathy, affiliation, and prosociality even as boys, on average, are more inclined toward independence, dominance, and aggression. When higher socialization demands are placed on girls than boys early in development, the effects can be particularly pernicious, especially since girls in general are already more responsible, empathic, and emotionally regulated than boys. Similarly, parents more often tolerate impulsive, aggressive behavior in young boys than girls. Boys also are taught to be stoic, as for example when they are encouraged not to cry in public, which may further disconnect them from more tender emotions. It is ironic at best and deeply problematic at worst, when parents, societies, and cultures encourage boys and girls to be more extreme in the sex differences they already show. It would be more productive to lessen demands for responsible behavior in girls who already show heightened receptivity to these socialization messages and increase socialization efforts for responsible interpersonal behavior in boys who act out.

Beardslee and colleagues emphasize the importance of interventions that include depressed parents and their children. One key element includes helping children understand that they are not responsible for their parents' problems (Beardslee & Gladstone, 2001). Beardslee, Gladstone, Wright, and Cooper (2003) conducted a family-based intervention with depressed parents and their children. It was administered either by a clinician to individual families or in group lectures to help parents deal with marital and family problems that may affect their children. Although both interventions were effective, participants in the clinician-based intervention had more favorable outcomes.

Ultimately, children's well-being and self-fulfillment will be best enhanced by helping the parents' achievement of the same. Many approaches can help parents regulate their negative emotions, for example, medication, psychotherapy, parent education, and relaxation practices, including meditation. This improved regulation, in turn, can help create less aversive home milieus for their children. At best, it would enhance all their capacities to feel valued, loved, and sufficient. Everyone would benefit from social relationships that are more joyful and less marred by sorrow, fear, and anger. Helping children to reduce their anxiety, guilt, and overinvestment in others' lives is one important step in this direction.

Just as we are wired to care for others, we are also biologically prepared to turn away from them. It is too simplistic to state that excessive concern for others is a female problem, whereas excessive disregard is a male problem. Males also care deeply for others, and females can be indifferent, even abusive, to offspring. But sex differences in concern and disregard do exist and are linked with sex differences in psychopathology. The study of these differences provides a way to study causal mechanisms of problems that occur in both sexes but that are more common to one sex than the other.

Empathy and guilt, at their core, are adaptive, affective states that support positive attachments and interpersonal connections, acts of caring and compassion, restraint from harming others, and acts of restitution and mending of relationships following antisocial acts. These are qualities that must survive and thrive for the sake of family, culture, society, and civilization. This is why it is so important to understand conditions that support these processes, as well as those that interfere to create further suffering.

References

Abramson, L. Y., & Sackheim, H. A. (1977). A paradox in depression: Uncontrollability and self-blame. *Psychological Bulletin, 84,* 838–851.

Angold, A., Costello, E., & Erkanli, A. (1999). Comorbidity. *Journal of Child Psychology and Psychiatry, 40*(1), 57–87. doi:10.1111/1469-7610.00424

Aube, J., Fichman, L., Saltaris, C., & Koestner, R. (2000). Gender differences in adolescent depressive symptomatology: Towards an integrated social-developmental model. *Journal of Social and Clinical Psychology, 19,* 297–313.

Aseltine, R.H. (1996). Pathways linking parental divorce with adolescent depression. *Journal of Health and Social Behavior, 37,* 133–148.

Baron-Cohen, S. (2002). The extreme male brain theory of autism. *Trends in Cognitive Sciences, 6,* 248–254.

Batson, C.D. & Shaw, L. L. (1991). Evidence for altruism: Toward a pluralism of prosocial motives. *Psychological Inquiry, 2,* 107–122.

Beardslee, W., & Gladstone, T. (2001). Prevention of childhood depression: Recent findings and future prospects. *Biological Psychiatry, 49,* 1101–1110. doi:10.1016/S0006-3223(01)01126-X

Beardslee, W. R., Gladstone, T. R., Wright, E. J., & Cooper, A. B. (2003). A family-based approach to the prevention of depressive symptoms in children at risk: Evidence of parental and child change. *Pediatrics, 112,* 119–131.

Beardslee, W. R., & Podorefsky, D. (1988). Resilient adolescents whose parents have serious affective and other disorders. *American Journal of Psychiatry, 145,* 63–69.

Beardslee, W. R., Versage, E., & Gladstone, T. (1998). Children of affectively ill parents: A review of the past ten years. *Journal of the American Academy of Child and Adolescent Psychiatry, 37,* 1134–1141.

Beck, A. T. (1967). *Depression: Clinical, experimental and theoretical aspects.* New York: Hoeber.

Bergman, A. (1982). Considerations about the development of the girl during the separation-individuation process. In D. Mandell (Ed.), *Early female development: Current psychoanalytic views.* New York: Spectrum.

Bjorkland, D. F., & Kipp, (1996). The role of immaturity in human development. *Psychological Bulletin, 122,* 153–169.

Boyle, M. H., & Pickles, A. (1997). Maternal depressive symptoms and ratings of emotional disorder symptoms in children and adolescents. *Journal of Child Psychology and Psychiatry, 38,* 981–992.

Bush, M. (1989). The role of unconscious guilt in psychopathology and psychotherapy. *Bulletin of the Menninger Clinic, 53,* 97–107.

Chapman, E., Baron-Cohen, S., Auyeung, B., Knickmeyer, R., Taylor, K., & Hackett, G. (2006). Fetal testosterone and empathy: Evidence from the Empathy Quotient (E.Q.) and the "Reading the Mind in the Eyes" test. *Social Neuroscience, 1*(2), 135–148.

Cohn, J., Campbell, S.B., Matias, R., & Hopkins, J. (1990). Face-to-face interactions of postpartum depressed and nondepressed mother-infant pairs at 2 months. *Developmental Psychology, 26,* 15–23.

Coie, J., & Dodge, K. (1998). Aggression and antisocial behavior. In W. Damon, & N. Eisenberg (Eds.), *Handbook of child psychology* (5th ed.): Vol. 3. *Social, emotional, and personality development* (pp. 779–862). Hoboken, NJ: John Wiley & Sons Inc.

Cole, P. M. (1986). Children's spontaneous control of facial expression. *Child Development, 57,* 1309–1321.

Cole, P. M., Barrett, K. D., & Zahn-Waxler, C. (1992). Emotion displays in two-year-olds during mishaps. *Child Development, 63,* 314–324.

Conger, R. D., Conger, K. J., Elder, G. H., Lorenz, F. O., Simons, R. L., & Whitbeck, L. B. (1993). Family economic stress and adjustment of early adolescent girls. *Developmental Psychology, 29,* 206–219.

Crawford, T. N., Cohen, P., Midlarsky, E., & Brook, J. S. (2001). Internalizing symptoms in adolescents: Gender differences in vulnerability to parental distress and discord. *Journal of Research on Adolescence, 11,* 95–118.

Cummings, E. M., Hollenbeck, B., Iannotti, R. J., Radke-Yarrow, M., & Zahn-Waxler, C. (1986). Early organization of altruism and aggression: Developmental patterns and individual differences. In C. Zahn-Waxler, E. M. Cummings, & R. J. Iannotti (Eds.), *Altruism and aggression: Biological and social origins* (pp. 165–188). New York: Cambridge University Press.

Cummings, E. M., Zahn-Waxler, C., & Radke-Yarrow, M. (1981). Young children's responses to expressions of anger and affection by others in the family. *Child Development, 52,* 1274–1282.

Dadds, M. R., Atkinson, E., Turner, C., Blums, G. J., & Lendich, B. (1999). Family conflict and child adjustment: Evidence for a cognitive-contextual model of intergenerational transmission. *Journal of Family Psychology, 13,* 194–208.

Damasio, A. R., Tranel, D. & Damasio, H. (1991). Somatic markers and the guidance of behavior: Theory and preliminary testing. In H. S. Levin, H. M. Eisenberg, & A. L. Benton (Eds.), *Frontal lobe function and dysfunction* (pp. 217–229). New York: Oxford University Press.

Davis, B., Sheeber, L., Hops, H., & Tildesley, E. (2000). Adolescent responses to depressive parental behaviors in problem-solving interactions: Implications for depressive symptoms. *Journal of Abnormal Child Psychology, 5,* 451–465.

Davies, P. T. & Lindsay, L. L. (2004). Interparental conflict and adolescent adjustment: Why does gender moderate early adolescent vulnerability? *Journal of Family Psychology, 18,* 160–170.

Davies, P. T., & Windle, M. (1997). Gender-specific pathways between maternal depressive symptoms, family discord, and adolescent adjustment. *Developmental Psychology, 33,* 657–668.

Decety, J., & Meyer, M. (2008). From emotional resonance to empathic understanding: A social developmental neuroscience account. *Development and Psychopathology, 20,* 1053–1080.

Denham, S. A., Zahn-Waxler, C., Cummings, E. M., & Iannotti, R. J. (1991). Social competence in young children's peer relations: Patterns of development and change. *Child Psychiatry and Human Development, 22,* 29–44.

Derryberry, D., & Reed, M. A. (1994). Temperament and the self-organization of personality. *Development and Psychopathology, 6,* 653–676.

Dienstbier, R. A. (1988). The role of emotion in moral socialization. In C. Izard, J. Kagan, & R. Zajonc (Eds.), *Emotions, cognition and behavior* (pp 484–514). New York: Cambridge University Press.

Donatelli, J., Bybee, J., & Buka, S. (2007). What do mothers make adolescents feel guilty about? Incidents, reactions, and relation to depression. *Journal of Child and Family Studies, 16,* 859–875. doi:10.1007/s10826-006-9130-1

Downey, G., & Coyne, J. C. (1990). Children of depressed parents: An integrative review. *Psychological Bulletin, 108,* 50–76.

Duggal, S., Carlson, E. A., Sroufe, L. A., & Egeland, B. (2001). Depressive symptomatology in childhood and adolescence. *Development and Psychopathology, 13,* 141–162.

Eisenberg, N., & Eggum, N. D. (2009). Empathic responding, sympathy, and personal distress. In J. Decety, & W. Ickes (Eds.), *The social neuroscience of empathy.* Cambridge, MA: MIT Press.

Eisenberg, N., & Fabes, R. A. (1998). Prosocial development. In W. Damon (Series Ed.), & N. Eisenberg (Vol. Ed.), *Handbook of child psychology* Vol. 3. *Social, emotional, and personality development* (pp. 701–778). New York: John Wiley.

Eisenberg, N., & Lennon, R. (1983). Sex differences in empathy and related capacities. *Psychological Bulletin, 94*, 100–131. doi:10.1037/0033-2909.94.1.100

Fergusson, D. M., Horwood, L. J., & Lynsky, M. T. (1995). Maternal depressive symptoms and depressive symptoms in adolescents. *Journal of Child Psychology and Psychiatry and Allied Disciplines, 36*, 1161–1178.

Fergusson, T., Stegge, H., Miller, & Olson, M. E. (1999). Guilt, shame, and symptoms in children. *Developmental Psychology, 35*, 347–357.

Formoso, D., Gonzales, N. A., & Aiken, L. S. (2000). Family conflict and children's internalizing and externalizing behavior: Protective factors. *American Journal of Community Psychology, 28*, 175–199.

Friedman, M. (1985). Toward a reconceptualization of guilt. *Contemporary Psychoanalysis, 21*, 501–547.

Garnefski, N. (2000). Age differences in depressive symptoms, antisocial behavior, and negative perceptions of family, school, and peers among adolescents. *Journal of the American Academy of Child and Adolescent Psychiatry, 39*, 1175–1181.

Geschwind, N., & Galaburda, A. M. (1985). Cerebral lateralization: Biological mechanisms, associations, and pathology: I. A hypothesis and a program for research. *Archives of Neurology, 42*, 428–459.

Gilligan, C. (1982). *In a different voice: Psychological theory and women's development.* Cambridge, MA: Harvard University Press.

Gore, S., Aseltine, R. H., & Colten, M. E. (1993). Gender, social-relational involvement, and depression. *Journal of Research on Adolescence, 3*, 101–125.

Goodman, S. H., & Gotlib, I. H. (1999). Risk for psychopathology in the children of depressed mothers: A developmental model for understanding mechanisms of transition. *Psychological Review, 106*, 458–490.

Gurian, A. (1987). Depression in young girls: Early sorrows and depressive disorders. In R. Formanek, & A. Gurian (Eds.), *Women and depression: A lifespan perspective. Springer Series: Focus on women* Vol. 11 (pp. 57–83). New York: Springer Publishing Co.

Hastings, P. D., Utendale, W. T., & Sullivan, C. (2007). The socialization of prosocial development. In J. E. Grusec, & P. D. Hastings (Eds.), *Handbook of socialization: Theory and research.* New York: The Guilford Press.

Hay, D., & Pawlby, S. (2003). Prosocial development in relation to children's and mothers' psychological problems. *Child Development, 74*, 1314–1327.

Hay, D. F., Zahn-Waxler, C., Cummings, E. M., & Iannotti, R. J. (1992). Young children's views about conflict with peers: A comparison of the daughters and sons of depressed and well women. *Journal of Child Psychology and Psychiatry, 33*, 669–683.

Hoffman, M. (1982). Development of prosocial motivation: Empathy and guilt. In N. Eisenberg (Ed.), *The development of prosocial behavior* (pp. 281–313). New York: Academic Press.

Hoffman, M. (1977). Sex differences in empathy and related behaviors. *Psychological Bulletin, 84*, 712–722.

Jack, D. C. (1991). *Silencing the self: Women and depression.* Cambridge, MA: Harvard University Press.

Jones, N. A., Field, T., & Davalos, M. (2000). Right frontal EEG asymmetry and lack of empathy in preschool children of depressed mothers. *Child Psychiatry and Human Development, 39*, 189–204.

Kessler, R., McGonagle, K., Swartz, M., & Blazer, D. (1993). Sex and depression in the National Comorbidity Survey: I. Lifetime prevalence, chronicity and recurrence. *Journal of Affective Disorders, 29*(2–3), 85–96. doi:10.1016/0165-0327(93)90026-G

Klimes-Dougan, B., & Bolger, A. (1998). Coping with maternal depressed affect and depression: Adolescent children of depressed and well mothers. *Journal of Youth and Adolescence, 27*, 1–15.

Knafo, A., Israel, S., Darvasi, A., Bachner-Melman, R., Uzefovsky, F., Cohen, L., et al. (2008). Individual differences in allocation of funds in the dictator game associated with length of the Arginine vasopressin 1a receptor RS3 promoter region and correlation between RS3 length and hippocampal mRNA. *Genes, Brain, and Behavior, 7*, 266–275.

Kochanska, G., Gross, J. N., & Nichols, K. E. (2002). Guilt in young children: Development, determinants, and relations within a broader system of standards. *Child Development, 73*, 461–482.

Lewinsohn, P. M., Rohde, P., & Seeley, J. R. (1995). Adolescent psychopathology 3: The clinical consequences of comorbidity. *Journal of the American Academy of Child and Adolescent Psychiatry, 34*, 510–519.

Luby, J., Belden, A., Sullivan, J., Hayen, R., McCadney, A., & Spitznagel, E. (2009). Shame and guilt in preschool depression: Evidence for elevations of self-conscious emotions in depression as early as age 3. *Journal of Child Psychology and Psychiatry and Allied Disciplines, 50*, 1156–1166.

MacLean, P. D. (1985). Brain evolution relating to family, play, and the separation call. *Archives of General Psychiatry, 42*, 405–417.

McClure, E. B. (2000). A meta-analytic review of sex differences in facial expression processing and their development in infants, children and adolescents. *Psychological Bulletin, 126*, 424–453.

Miller, A. (1979). Depression and grandiosity as related forms of narcissistic disturbances. *International Review of Psycho-Analysis, 6*(1), 61–76.

Miller, A. (1981). *Prisoners of childhood. The drama of the gifted child and the search for the true self.* New York: Basic Books.

Modell, A. H. (1965). On having the right to a life: An aspect of the superego's development. *International Journal of Psychoanalysis, 46*, 323–331.

Nolen-Hoeksema, S. (1990). *Sex differences in depression.* Stanford, CA: Stanford University Press.

O'Connor, L. E., Berry, J. W., Weiss, J., & Gilbert, P. (2002). Guilt, fear, submission, & empathy in depression. *Journal of Affective Disorders, 71*, 19–27.

O'Connor, L., Berry, J., Lewis, T., Mulherin, K., & Crisostomo, P. (2007). Empathy and depression: The moral system on overdrive. In T. Farrow, & P. Woodruff (eds). *Empathy in mental illness* (pp. 49–75). New York: Cambridge University Press.

Powers, S., & Welsh, D. (1999). Mother–daughter interactions and adolescent girls' depression. In M. Cox, & J. Brooks-Dunn (Eds.), *Conflict and cohesion in families: Causes and consequences* (pp. 243–281). Mahwah, NJ: Lawrence Erlbaum Associates Publishers.

Radke-Yarrow, M., Zahn-Waxler, C., Richardson, D. T., Susman, A., & Martinez, P. (1994). Caring behavior in children of clinically depressed and well mothers. *Child Development, 65*, 1405–1414.

Rodrigues, S., Saslow, L. R., Garcia, N., John, O. P., & Keltner, D. (2009). Oxytocin receptor genetic variation relates to empathy and stress activity in humans. *Proceedings of the National Academy of Sciences, 106*(50), 21437–21441. doi:10.1073/pnas.0909579100

Schulte-Ruther, M., Markowitsch, H. J., Shah, N. J., Fink, C. R., & Piefke, M. (2008). Gender differences in brain networks supporting empathy. *Neuroimage, 42*, 393–403.

Seligman, M. (1975). *Helplessness: On depression, development, and death.* New York: W H Freeman/Times Books/Henry Holt & Co.

Singer, T. (2006). The neuronal basis and ontogeny of empathy and mindreading: Review of literature and implications for future research. *Neuroscience and Behavioral Reviews, 30*, 855–863.

Smith, A. (1853). *The theory of moral sentiments.* London: Henry.

Soulantaus-Simula, T., Punamaki, R., & Beardslee, W. R. (2002). Children's responses to low parental mood. 1: Balancing between active empathy, overinvolvement, indifference, and avoidance. *Journal of the Academy of Child and Adolescent Psychiatry, 41*, 278–286.

Taylor, S., Klein, L. C., Lewis, B. P., Gruenewald, T. L., Gurung, R. A. R., & Updegraff, J. A. (2000). Biobehavioral response to stress in females: Tend and befriend, not fight-or-flight. *Psychological Review, 107*, 411–429.

Van Hulle, C. A., Schreiber, J. E., Goldsmith, H. H., & Zahn-Waxler, C. (2009). *Parental psychopathology, empathy, and depression in middle childhood.* SRCD Biennial Meeting, Denver, CO.

Vuchinich, S., Emery, R., & Cassidy, J. (1988). Family members and third parties in dyadic family conflict: Strategies, alliances, and outcomes. *Child Development, 59*(5), 1293–1302. doi:10.2307/1130492

Warneken, F., & Tomasello, M. (2008). Extrinsic rewards undermine altruistic tendencies in 20 month-olds. *Developmental Psychology, 44*, 1785–1788.

Yang, C., Decety, J., Lee, S., Chen, C., & Cheng, Y. (2008). Gender differences in the mu rhythm during empathy for pain: an electroencephalographic study. *Brain Research, 1251*, 176–184.

Zahn-Waxler, C. (1993). Warriors and worriers: Gender and psychopathology. *Development and Psychopathology, 5*, 79–89.

Zahn-Waxler, C. (2002). Children of depressed mothers. In B. S. Zuckerman, A. F. Lieberman, & N. A. Fox (Eds.), *Emotion regulation and developmental health: Infancy and early childhood* (pp. 203–219). Johnson & Johnson Pediatric Roundtable Monographs.

Zahn-Waxler, C. (2000). The development of empathy, guilt, and internalized distress: Implications for gender differences in internalizing and externalizing problems. In R. Davidson (Ed.), *Anxiety, depression, and emotion* (pp. 222–265). New York/Oxford, England: Oxford University Press.

Zahn-Waxler, C., Cole, P. M., & Barrett, K. C. (1991). Guilt and empathy: Sex differences and implications for the development of depression. In J. Garber, & K. A. Dodge (Eds.), *Emotional regulation and dysregulation.* Cambridge, England: Cambridge University Press.

Zahn-Waxler, C., Iannotti, R. J., Cummings, E. M., & Denham, S. (1990). Antecedents of problem behaviors in children of depressed mothers. *Development and Psychopathology, 2*, 271–291.

Zahn-Waxler, C., Kochanska, G., Krupnick, J, & McKnew, D. (1990). The development of guilt in children of depressed and well mothers. *Developmental Psychology, 26*, 51–59.

Zahn-Waxler, C., Race, E., & Duggal, S. (2005). Mood disorders, syndromes and symptoms: The development of depression in girls. In D. Bell, S. L. Foster, & E. J. Mash (Eds.), *Behavioral and emotional problems in girls* (pp. 25–77). New York: Kluwer Academic/Plenum.

Zahn-Waxler, C., Radke-Yarrow, M., & King, R. A. (1979). Child rearing and children's prosocial initiations toward victims of distress. *Child Development, 50*, 319–330.

Zahn-Waxler, C., Radke-Yarrow, M., Wagner, E., & Chapman, M. (1992). Development of concern for others. *Child Development, 63,* 126–136.

Zahn-Waxler, C., Ridgeway, D., Denham, S., Usher, B., & Cole, P. (1993). Pictures of infants' emotions: A task for assessing mothers' and young children's verbal communications about affect. In R. Emde, J. Osofsky, & P. Butterfield (Eds.), *Parental perception of infant emotions. Clinical Infant Report Series* (pp. 217–236).

Zahn-Waxler, C., & Robinson, J. (1995). Empathy and guilt: Early origins of feelings of responsibility. In K. Fisher, & J. Tangney (Eds.), *Self-conscious emotions: Shame, guilt, embarrassment, and pride* (pp. 143–173). New York: Guilford Press.

Zahn-Waxler, C., Shirtcliff, E. A., & Marceau, K. (2007). Disorders of childhood and adolescence: Gender and psychopathology. *Annual Review of Clinical Psychology, 4,* 1–29.

CHAPTER 26

AUTISM, EMPATHIZING-SYSTEMIZING (E-S) THEORY, AND PATHOLOGICAL ALTRUISM

Simon Baron-Cohen

KEY CONCEPTS

- Empathy involves two very different neural processes: affective (feeling an emotion appropriate in response to another person's thoughts and feelings) and cognitive (also called Theory of Mind—that is, being able to imagine someone else's thoughts or feelings).
- The ability to empathize forms one pole of a personality-related dimension; the opposite pole is the ability to systemize. (Put briefly, systemizing is the drive to create and understand systems, for example, the mechanical system of an old-fashioned clock).
- On average, empathizing is stronger in females, whereas systemizing is stronger in males.
- Empathizing-Systemizing theory can be used to quantify people's drive to empathize and systemize. More importantly, it makes predictions regarding the origins of conditions such as autism, which involves intact or even strong systemizing alongside difficulties in empathy.
- Empathizing-Systemizing theory also predicts that some individuals will have difficulties systemizing, but an intact or even a strong drive to empathize. These "hyper-empathizers" may escape clinical notice.

CLASSIC AUTISM AND Asperger syndrome involve problems in social interactions and communication, and also manifests in the display of narrow interests and repetitive actions. It is thought that children with autism and Asperger syndrome may be delayed in developing a *theory of mind* (ToM)—that is, their ability to understand the thoughts and feelings of others (Baron-Cohen, 1995; Baron-Cohen, Leslie, & Frith, 1985). These children may also have difficulty in themselves evincing, or in understanding others' emotions (Davis, 1994; Grandin, 1996). Empathizing-systemizing (E-S) theory has been proposed to help explain some of these behavioral syndromes.

The Empathizing-Systemizing (E-S) Theory

E-S theory explains the social and communication issues seen in autism and Asperger syndrome in connection, on the one hand, to delays and deficits in *empathizing*. The strengths in assimilating narrow areas of interest, on the other hand, involve an intact or even superior skill in *systemizing*[1] (Baron-Cohen, 2002, 2008, 2009; Lawson, Baron-Cohen, & Wheelwright, 2004).

E-S theory predicts five different "brain types" (as noted in Baron-Cohen, 2008):

- *Type E (E > S)*: individuals whose empathy is stronger than their systemizing
- *Type S (S > E)*: individuals whose systemizing is stronger than their empathy
- *Type B (S = E)*: individuals whose empathy is as good (or as bad) as their systemizing. (*B* stands for "balanced.")
- *Extreme Type E (E >> S)*: individuals whose empathy is above average, but who are challenged when it comes to systemizing
- *Extreme Type S (S >> E)*: individuals whose systemizing is above average, but who are challenged when it comes to empathy.

The E-S model predicts that females will tend toward type E, whereas males will tend toward type S. This, in fact, jibes with actual results, which show that the majority of males (54%) test as type S, whereas the majority of females (44%) test as type E (Baron-Cohen, 2009).

The Extreme Female Brain: Pathological Altruism?

Laying out the main brain types in the E-S theory raises the question as to why the fifth possibility has not been previously discussed. This is the profile *E >> S*, in which an individual may have below-average systemizing, alongside intact or even superior empathy. Mapping the E-S space predicts such individuals should exist, and indeed our questionnaire study using the Empathy and Systemizing Quotients (*EQ* and *SQ*) identified that such individuals do exist (Goldenfeld et al., 2005; see Figure 26.1). To date, no lab has called in such individuals for in-person testing, but it is worth considering what they should be like. First, we should expect more females than males to show this profile; the Goldenfeld et al. (2005) dataset confirms this prediction. Second, their sex ratio should be the mirror image of the autism sex ratio; again the Goldenfeld et al. (2005) dataset confirms this prediction.

In terms of everyday functioning, we would expect high-E individuals to avoid systemizing subjects such as science, technology, mathematics, or engineering at school, university, or on the job. At the same time, these high-E individuals would find subjects or jobs that involve empathy, such as listening, communicating, socializing, or supporting others, trivially easy. Consequently, high-E individuals would be drawn toward people-centered occupations such as counselling, working with children, teaching, and social work. This latter prediction has never been tested, but it would be straightforward to do so. This group should constitute an extreme of the female brain, using the earlier terminology. More descriptively, it should also constitute an extreme of type E.

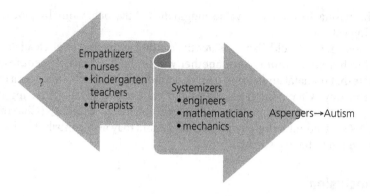

FIGURE 26.1
Just as we can divide people up by their tendencies toward extroversion or introversion, we can also divide people up by their tendencies to *empathize* or *systemize*. Empathizers are more interested in people—what they feel and why they think what they think. Systemizers are people who like to figure out the rules embedded in systems such as car engines, train time-tables, dance routines, or stamp collections. Illustration courtesy of Barbara Oakley.

Relevant to this book is the question of whether such individuals would have clinically significant difficulties, and what they would look like on an altruism dimension. One view is that such a profile need not lead to any clinical difficulties. Autism features empathy difficulties that form a high-risk factor for clinical difficulties such as social isolation. But in the case of the extreme type E profile, strong empathy may well be protective, since social networks may be easier to form and maintain, such that the individual is not isolated. The individual with an extreme type E profile has difficulties with systemizing, and this may simply mean that occupations such as engineering or mathematics would be avoided. In this view, such individuals may not come to the attention of researchers because they do not find their way to clinics. They may well be more likely to empathize with others' difficulties, and so take on other people's problems more than others might. Whether such "altruism" might become pathological would need to be investigated. Indeed, it raises the question of the optimal limit of altruism. At one extreme are individuals who are so self-centered that their altruism is minimal, and at the other extreme are individuals who devote most of their time and attention to others rather than to themselves. Missing from this model is any sense of where on this continuum behaviour becomes pathological. Presumably, when someone is so other-focused that they neglect their own basic needs for food, money, and other resources linked to survival, one can talk of pathology. But if people are comfortable devoting themselves to others, or using their high levels of empathy in altruistic ways, it

> We would expect high-E individuals to avoid systemizing subjects and be drawn instead toward people-centered occupations.

> Autism has a high risk for clinical difficulties such as social isolation. But strong empathy may well be protective, since social networks may be easier to form and maintain such that the individual is not isolated.

may be wrong to impose a value judgment on the behaviour by labelling it pathological.

In closing, we should also consider the causal factors that might lead an individual to have one brain type or another within the E-S space. Recent research suggests that prenatal androgens are one candidate factor that influences a child's later empathy (Chapman et al., 2006) and systemizing levels (Auyeung et al., 2006), and that genetic polymorphisms also correlate with *EQ* (Chakrabarti et al., 2009). Undoubtedly, environmental factors may also contribute, although these remain to be investigated.

Conclusion

In this chapter, we have considered a psychological theory of autism spectrum conditions (the E-S theory) and its link to typical sex differences in the general population. It was argued that E-S theory may not only be useful as a way of explaining the very broad range of features of autism spectrum conditions, but also for considering the mirror image of these disorders. Future research should focus on the extreme opposite of autism—that is, on individuals with excellent empathy but impaired systemizing—to understand if this is associated with any necessary clinical consequences.

Note

1. Major kinds of systems include the following (as noted in Baron-Cohen, 2002):

   - *Collectible* systems (distinguishing between types of stones or wood)
   - *Mechanical* systems (a video-recorder or a window lock)
   - *Numerical* systems (a train time-table or a calendar)
   - *Abstract* systems (the syntax of a language, or musical notation)
   - *Natural* systems (the weather patterns, or tidal wave patterns)
   - *social* systems (a management hierarchy, or a dance routine with a dance partner)
   - *Motoric* systems (throwing a Frisbee or bouncing on a trampoline).

References

Baron-Cohen, S. (1995). *Mindblindness: An essay on autism and theory of mind.* MIT Press/Bradford Books: Boston.

Baron-Cohen, S. (2002). The extreme male brain theory of autism. *Trends in Cognitive Science, 6,* 248–254.

Baron-Cohen, S. (2008). Theories of the autistic mind. *The Psychologist, 21,* 112–116.

Baron-Cohen, S. (2009). Autism: The empathizing–systemizing (ES) theory. *Annals of the New York Academy of Sciences, 1156,* 68–80.

Baron-Cohen, S., Leslie, A. M., & Frith, U. (1985). Does the autistic child have a "theory of mind"? *Cognition, 21,* 37–46.

Davis, M. H. (1994). *Empathy: A social psychological approach.* Colorado: Westview Press.

Goldenfeld, N., Baron-Cohen, S., & Wheelwright, S. (2005). Empathizing and systemizing in males, females, and autism *Clinical Neuropsychiatry, 2*(6), 338–345.

Grandin, T. (1996). *Thinking in pictures.* Vancouver, WA: Vintage Books.

Lawson, J., Baron-Cohen, S., & Wheelwright, S. (2004). Empathising and systemising in adults with and without Asperger syndrome. *Journal of Autism and Developmental Disorders, 34*(3), 301–310.

CHAPTER 27

SEDUCTION SUPER-RESPONDERS AND HYPER-TRUSTERS

The Biology of Affiliative Behavior

Karol M. Pessin

KEY CONCEPTS

- People are social animals who go to great lengths to belong—a need that may be rooted in biology. This behavior and biology directed toward social belonging may result in heightened altruism toward some and diminished empathy toward others.
- Whether altruism is pathological depends on its context, as empathy may be selective toward particular individuals or one's own in-group, at the expense of other individuals or groups.
- Oxytocin and vasopressin systems, structurally flexible and capable of rapid changes, appear to be key in understanding social behaviors in rapidly changing human societies.
- A "seduction super-response" may be rooted in biological systems for how receptive one is to social signals, such as vocalizing. Similarly, impaired sensitivity to social signals may lead to "hyper-trust" in failing to detect social threats.
- More broadly, social signals are transmitted through groups; a seduction super-response or undue hyper-trust may be a response to social contagions involving neurosensory or chemosensory means yet to be discovered.

IF SOCIAL NEUROSCIENCE had a mascot, it would be the prairie vole. Social neuroscientists follow these animals into mating laboratories with video cameras—not as vole voyeurs, but to learn about the biology of social behavior.

Prairie voles are living proof that social behavior has biological controls. In substantial contrast to meadow or montane voles, prairie voles are, broadly speaking, monogamous—they mate for life, a relatively rare characteristic occurring only in about 5% of mammals. Prairie voles spend about 50% of their time

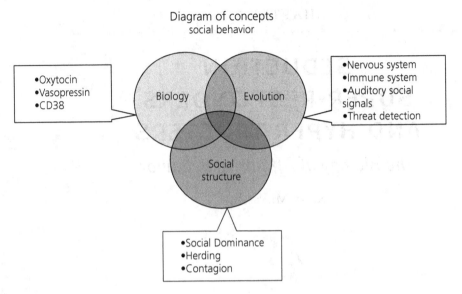

FIGURE 27.1
Interplay of biology, evolution, and social structure on altruistic behaviors.

grooming, socializing, and mating. Meadow voles and montane voles spend only about 5% of their time socializing, and even that 5% is spent mostly mating or fighting (see Young & Wang, 2004, review). Armed with genetic tools, those who study voles point to the significance of the brain peptides oxytocin and vasopressin, along with their receptors and regulatory molecules, as particularly relevant to social behaviors. Prairie voles have particular vasopressin variants (Young & Wang, 2004; also further explained below), and blocking or augmenting the vasopressin system results directly in behavioral changes. Prairie voles are emblematic of how biology can influence affiliative behavior, and studying their biology has much broader implications in human societies.

This chapter focuses on the two types of behaviors and the possible biology behind them: "seduction super-response" and "hyper-trust." *Seduction*, or being lead astray,[1] is used here in the context of being overly responsive to social signals such that one is led astray, away from one's own purposes, for the purpose of another. One may be seduced ostensibly for altruistic purposes, but such altruism may ultimately serve no prosocial purpose. Cults, religious or political authoritarians, even interpersonal relations can seduce, and there are some who may be biologically more predisposed to receive the message. The flip side, that is, being less sensitive to social signals, may result in hyper-trust—misplacing trust in those who are untrustworthy. Biological systems relating to being less predisposed to receiving social signals and missing social threats are also explored here.

Either way, biology can relate to how one receives social signals and responds to them. But, individuals are not altruistic in a vacuum. Because altruism as a notion is relative, it must be considered in the context of social behaviors—how individuals relate to a group, and how groups relate to each other. Where social behavior is distorted—perhaps due to biology—altruism may be distorted as well.

Distorted Social Behavior as Pathological Altruism

The social contract relies on predictability, yet human behavior is rarely purely rational (e.g., Bennis, Medin, & Bartels, 2009). As a consequence, societies create social norms to instill some degree of stability. Social norm compliance, often by punishing violators, is essential to large-scale cooperation (e.g., Marlowe et al., 2008). Although there are those who are *paid* social norm enforcers, such as policemen, why would anyone *voluntarily* punish social norm violators? Are social vigilantes altruistic? Perhaps. Or, depending on one's perspective, social norm enforcers may be *pathologically* altruistic.

Observing Bushman, a performance artist at San Francisco Fisherman's Wharf, is instructive. Bushman, not unlike mimes and other street performers, has a schtick: He crouches down low, covering himself in branches (as a bush), and jumps out in front of unsuspecting tourists exclaiming something like, "Ugga Bugga!" For this, he then he seeks nonobligatory payment.[2] Although occasionally charged with a misdemeanor in response to complaints from out-of-town tourists, Bushman is usually acquitted by a jury of local residents.

> **PATHOLOGICAL ALTRUISM**
>
> Even behavior that is objectively altruistic requires determining the subjective intent of the actor: Was the actor's intent to benefit others? Where this intent objectively violates social norms, such as those who murder an abortion doctor to prevent further abortions, or weaponize airplanes to bring down a society ostensibly deemed violative of a religion, the actor's intent is no longer prosocial—here, the actor seeks to dominate and impose will. (One could argue *what* social mores apply; however, moral relativism arguments are beyond the scope of this chapter.) This section, therefore, relies on a definition of pathological altruism that is really a proxy for "pathology of the subjectively altruistic actor as determined by objectively antisocial motives."

In San Francisco, earning one's livelihood by jumping out from a pile of branches yelling "Ugga Bugga!" complies with the social norms. So, why would the out-of-town tourists seek to punish Bushman? Why not just go back to the Midwest? There is an element of self-righteousness, of having been humiliated by the surprise and not knowing how to act, perhaps. The same rationale—ostensibly altruistic punishment—taken to an extreme could apply to those who seek to enforce extremist political or religious beliefs on those who are different. (Self-Addiction and Self-Righteousness, Chapter 5, by Brin).[3]

Two motives for this ostensible altruistic punishment stand out: Justice and anger. Arguably, these conflate to a single *ubermotive*: social dominance. Justice and fairness argue for punishing free riders, those who exploit the generosity of the group without reciprocity. Correcting this unfairness may activate the neural appetitive (reward) pathway (as well as the insula; e.g., Singer & Steinbeis, 2009). Punishing unfairness, as in altruistic punishment, may be predominantly impulsive – as opposed to an exercise of self-control – as demonstrated by serotonin depletion studies (Crockett et al., 2010). Anger, too, may be a primary motivator for altruistic punishment (Seip, van Dijk, & Rotteveel, 2009), and punishment may be a form of dogmatic aggression—that is, use of aggression against those holding a different cultural belief (Crowson, 2008, 2009). In a roiling brew of impulsivity mixed with cognitive motivation, the need to assert one's self, it seems, froths to the top.

Superiority is implicit (Saucier & Webster, 2010), and social vigilantes may be those who view the world in social dominance orientation. If one is only concerned with domination—whether at the PTA meeting or of a nation-state—one has a difficult time being empathetic with those for whom subordination is sought (see Chiao, Mathur, Harada, & Lipke, 2009 and references cited therein). Here, *lack* of empathy (toward the object of the punishment) can turn altruistic punishment into *pathologically altruistic* punishment: punishment for the sole purpose of social dominance in imposing one's social mores on an unwilling other.

What is the biology behind a pathological need for social dominance? In nature, red in tooth and claw so to speak, animal groups have hierarchical organization: The term "alpha male" is part of ordinary vocabulary. In animal hierarchies, social dominance and aggression are associated with vasopressin-type molecules and receptors, for example in trout (Backström & Winberg, 2009), mice (Caldwell & Young, 2009), clownfish social rank (Iwata, Nagai, & Sasaki, 2008), zebrafish (Larson, O'Malley, & Melloni, 2006), and chickens (Wirén, Gunnarsson, Andersson, & Jensen, 2009). Humans attempt domination in any number of ways, from blunt force, to subtle and finely tuned Machiavellianism. The affiliative biology systems reflect this continuum. Particular vasopressin receptor variants are reported, for instance, to be associated with generosity, aggression, or social stress, sometimes by what seems to be a direct result, and other times by a circuitous route involving other neural pathways (discussed below; see also Ebstein et al., 2009; Ebstein, Salomon, Chew, Zhong, & Knafo, 2010 and references cited therein).

Collectively, our individual biology may have more global effects. Consider a prominent economist who failed to warn about the financial crisis beginning in 2007–2008:

> In my position on the panel [of economic advisors for the Federal Reserve Bank of New York], I felt the need to use restraint. While I warned about the bubbles I believed were developing in the stock and housing markets, I did so very gently, and felt vulnerable expressing such quirky views. *Deviating too far from consensus leaves one feeling potentially ostracized from the group, with the risk that one may be terminated.* [Italics added.]
>
> Dr. Robert J. Shiller, professor of economics and finance at Yale University; former member economic advisory panel, Federal Reserve Bank of New York[4]

As Professor Shiller confesses, the *threat* of social ostracism is sufficiently painful to keep one's mouth shut in the face of pending financial doom. Social exclusion *is* painful (Eisenberg, Liberman, & Williams, 2003), and even *anticipated* social exclusion is painful (Spitzer, Fischbacher, Herrnberger, Grön, & Fehr, 2007); yet again, vasopressin receptor variants may be associated with sensitivity to social stress (Ebstein et al., 2009, 2010).[5] Perhaps, in addition to financial retaliation, the *anticipated pain of social exclusion* sets the biological stage for would-be whistleblowers who fail to speak up, and why, if they do, they should be viewed with higher credibility than those who otherwise have nothing to lose.

Punishing Bushman or (potentially) Professor Shiller serves no prosocial useful function—except to the punisher, that is. That seems to be the seductive calling: social dominance over others., Professor Shiller, as a consequence, seems to be led astray by his need, perhaps biological, to avoid being outcast from the group.

Oxytocin, discussed further below, may modulate this very human need for a sense of group belonging. Consider altruism toward one's in-group—to *favoring* one's in-group over an out-group, or *parochial* altruism (Choi & Bowles, 2007; Cikara et al. 2010). For instance, in an economic decision-making study involving male participants, those who received a nasal spray of oxytocin self-sacrificed in favor of their in-group more frequently than did those receiving placebo. Further, the oxytocin participants had a stronger tendency to preemptively punish competing group members by making decisions that would take money away from them when there was a *possibility* that this "out-group" could choose to punish first (De Drue et al., 2010). Thus, oxytocin may modulate not only the social need to be true to one's school, so to speak, but also to preemptively attack outsiders in *anticipation* of a threat.

Thus, one may view pathological altruism through a lens of parochial altruism, in which selective empathy toward one's own group is made at the expense of those considered "others." Further, empathy itself is a social behavior. As pointed out by Baron-Cohen (Chapter 26), pathological altruism can be also be viewed as a matter of degree, on a spectrum from extreme forms of empathizing behavior through systematizing thought processes and behaviors characteristic of individuals with autistic spectrum conditions. Zahn-Waxler and Van Hulle (Chapter 25) point to altruism contextually, as in situations where children empathize with depressed parents, to the point at which the children themselves are burdened, anxious, and depressed. Whether altruism is pathological, then, seems to be contextual, with regard to group and individual behavior, and may be a matter of degree, particularly as it relates to empathy.

Why or how one bestows empathy on another is the subject of much exploration in the biological sciences. As with the prairie vole, oxytocin, vasopressin, and related molecules seem to be instrumental. Looking to how this biology evolved, in view of social structures, informs an understanding of the underpinnings of social behavior.

Oxytocin and Vasopressin Genetic Instability: Response-ready Social Biology

People may not be as wired for social dominance as wolves in a pack or chickens in a pecking order, but it seems we all have our biologically determined "social set-point." The two social peptide systems mentioned above, for oxytocin and vasopressin, seem to have profound effects on social behavior. In humans, these evolutionarily archaic small proteins are part of a highly flexible system seemingly adapted for rapid response to all the twists and turns of modern human life. The genetics for oxytocin, vasopressin, their receptors and their regulatory molecules has built in instability that actually favors flexibility, a key advantage for "response-ready" adaption to the messy, imperfect world of human social organizations.

Oxytocin and vasopressin are cousins: each is nine amino acids long, and each has a sulfur bridge connecting two cysteines; the proteins differ by two amino acids, with oxytocin being neutrally charged and vasopressin being basic. Each molecule has a six amino acid ring with a three amino acid "tail" as in Figure 27.2.

As one can surmise from the structural similarity, the molecules are thought to be evolutionarily related, with the theory being that, of the two, oxytocin evolved later (Gwee, Tay, Brenner, & Venkatesh, 2009). Oxytocin is thought to have evolved along with giving live birth, and oxytocin production is associated with maternal bonding; females produce oxytocin when mating, giving birth,

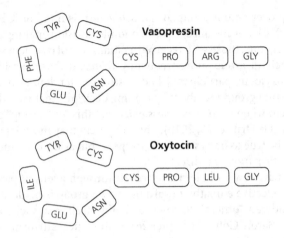

FIGURE 27.2
Vasopressin, oxytocin, and their receptors play a role in altruistic behaviors.

and nursing. For instance, oxytocin is released in nursing mammals in bursts synchronized with infant sucking rhythms (Hatton & Wang, 2008), and oxytocin's function extends to other aspects of giving birth, such as tissue and bone remodeling (Tamma et al., 2009, bone remodeling). Vasopressin, in mammals, acts as an antidiuretic and vasopressor (modulating blood pressure). Vasopressin also regulates aspects of thirst and appetite (Aoyagi et al., 2009), and relatedly, modulates body fluid tonicity (see generally, Young & Wang 2004; also, Donaldson & Young 2008, both review articles).

Just as Darwin's moth changed from white to gray in the soot of the industrial revolution, one can speculate that social "environmental" stressors produce changes in the oxytocin- or vasopressin-related DNAs. Structurally, the DNAs encoding these social peptide receptors are wobbly and readily changeable; the DNA changes can be intergenerational, or can even occur within the lifetime of a single individual. Epigenetic modulation may relate to oxytocin receptor expression patterns; vasopressin receptor DNA has microsatellite areas, lending instability but also leading to rapidly changeable expression patterns (Ebstein et al., 2009, 2010 and references cited therein). Rapid genetic adaptation is a clear advantage when moving about from group to group—or even mate to mate—and DNA structural instability may provide response-ready genetic adaptability.

There is a third-party intervenor in the system: Oxytocin production in the brain, surprisingly, is regulated by a molecule involved in immunity–CD38. (Salmina et al. 2010, review article). CD38 is a molecule normally found on the cell membrane, particularly at the junction between immune cells or between neurons. Digging a little deeper into the biology, CD38 also has another function: It makes potent synapse-signaling agents (Ca^{2+} mobilizing agents, cADPR and NAADP+). CD38 is a single molecule with (at least) two socially potent functions: oxytocin release from synapses and synaptic firing.

Consider the potential for CD38 as a love potion (or lust potion, perhaps). Oxytocin production is well known during human mating (e.g., Young & Wang, 2004, and reference cited therein). Synapses firing in synchrony are a sign of focused attention, particularly to socially salient signals, and oxytocin enhances recognition of biological movement (Keri & Benedek 2009; Perry et al. 2010). One may hypothesize that a mother gazes intently into the eyes of her infant as CD38, in the neural network for lactation, induces oxytocin expression and neural signals through calcium signaling. Hypothesizing further, the "look of love," as referenced in the Bert Bacharach song, is in the eyes, but could also be in the CD38 calcium signaling regulating oxytocin release.

Particular CD38 variants are associated with autistic spectrum conditions (see, Ebstein et al., 2009, Table 3). Some propose that autistic spectrum conditions, having selective attentional biases, may include calcium signaling dysfunctions (e.g., Palmieri et al., 2010). This logic follows easily: The fewer the calcium mobilizers, the fewer the calcium-mediated signals, and the fewer the neurotransmitters released, thus, lower synaptic activity. Or, CD38 expression patterns may relate to where synapses communicate and release oxytocin. If the oxytocin system relates to one's social perceptions, perhaps CD38, instrumental in calcium ion signals necessary for synaptic communication, is also involved.

> The "look of love," as referenced in the Bert Bacharach song, is in the eyes, but may also be in the CD38-related calcium signaling regulating oxytocin release.

Innumerable oxytocin/vasopressin/CD38 variants and expression patterns, along with their wobbly genetic structures, seem to reflect all the different kinds of human social groups, from peaceful agricultural villages to Visigoths, from large patrilineal families to lone scribes. Although research is still very early, the genetic variety is correlated with some of the behavior that one can see every day. For instance, some people have a vasopressin receptor RS3 long form microsatellite variant associated with high generosity and low stress. A different vasopressin microsatellite variant, an RS1 short form, is associated with autistic spectrum conditions (see Ebstein et al., 2009, 2010; Knafo et al., 2009; Meyer-Lindenberg et al., 2009). Yet another variant of the long form, RS3 334, is reportedly associated with a lack of monogamy: Men with two copies of the allele had twice the risk of experiencing marital dysfunction, with a threat of divorce during the last year, compared with men carrying one or no copies (Wallum et al., 2008). Particular oxytocin receptor variants are associated with generosity (Israel et al., 2009; see Ebstein et al., 2010 for a review of the genetics of human social behavior), and oxytocin may have a distorted expression pattern in autistic spectrum individuals (Ebstein et al., 2009, 2010; see also, Knafo et al., 2007; Levin et al., 2009; Gregory et al., 2010 [epigenetic changes]; see Wray, 2007 for a discussion of *cis*-regulatory variations).

Pathological Altruism: Hyper-Trust as Lack of Social Threat Detection

In contrast to those with hyper-empathy (Chapter 26 by Baron-Cohen), those with autistic spectrum conditions may behave in ways with reduced empathy and social awareness toward other people. When one is limited in social awareness, one may miss the signals for threat and place trust in those who are untrustworthy, for instance. The other extreme, as Baron-Cohen points out, is hyper-empathy; that is, caring about others *too* much, to the harm of oneself or innocent third parties. Either can be a path to altruism that, in context, is pathological, as shown in Figure 28.4.

Consider oxytocin's role in social awareness. Autistic spectrum conditions (characterized by distorted or impaired social awareness) are sometimes

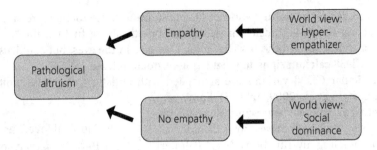

FIGURE 27.3
Proposed pathways to pathological altruism.

correlated with relatively low production of oxytocin; further, there may be associated a relatively low number of oxytocin receptors to receive whatever oxytocin is available (Gregory et al., 2010 [oxytocin receptor epigenetics]; see also Ebstein et al., 2009, Table 3, for CD38 variants that may relate to reduced oxytocin upregulation). One study reports that intranasal oxytocin enhances social behavior, such as eye gaze and social awareness, in high-functioning autistic spectrum individuals (Andari et al., 2010; see generally, Donaldson & Young, 2008 for a review). Perhaps low oxytocin levels, or low ability to use whatever oxytocin there is, impair one's ability to perceive social signals. (A full discussion on the densely complicated subject of autism genetics is beyond the scope of this chapter.)

Trust and threat are two sides of the same neural coin: interpreting a social signal. Oxytocin seems to play the role of making social salience come alive; that is, amplifying both positive and negative social vibes. This is not surprising, given oxytocin's role in maternal bonding: Think of the mother bear guarding the cubs. Any new social contact will be thoroughly examined with the threat-detection system on high alert.

In the movie, *The Big Lebowski*,[6] the two main characters illustrate the extremes of the threat detection–hyper-trust continuum. Dude, a middle-aged hippie living at the beach, is laid back and always doing favors for others; he is hardly startled when his home is invaded by Teutonic neo-Nihilists who throw a ferret in the bathtub with him. Perhaps part of this character's motivation involves the vasopressin variants associated with generosity; these variants are also associated with higher prepulse inhibition; that is, the more generous, the less startled by an unexpected noise (Levin et al., 2009). In contrast, Walter, a Viet Nam veteran, is uptight, pulling a gun at the bowling alley where he believes another player's foot went over the fault line. Biology also relates to misinterpreting such social cues, resulting in a bias toward interpreting intentions as hostile (see, e.g., Almeida et al., 2009, discussing individuals with bipolar disorders; Manuk et al., 2010, testosterone levels and androgen polymorphism predict heightened amygdala reactivity in men; see also Rodrigues et al., 2009, oxytocin variants associated with sensitivity to stress).

Walter and Dude notwithstanding, oxytocin and vasopressin, although not modulating hostility per se, seem to permit one to home in on salient social cues. *Lack* of oxytocin, on the other hand, is reportedly associated with more broad-brush aggressive behavior, particularly in men. Oxytocin levels in cerebral spinal fluid were found to be inversely correlated with a history of aggression (Lee, Ferris, van de Kar, & Coccaro, 2009), and testosterone, possibly as an oxytocin inhibitor, makes men stingier and more likely to use their own money to punish others—spiteful, aggressive behavior (Zak et al., 2009).

Selective aggression, moreover, seems to be a behavior enhanced by oxytocin, particularly preemptive, defensive aggression of a perceived out-group (De Dreu et al., 2010, discussed above). Interestingly, oxytocin enhances envy and gloating (Shamay-Tsoory et al., 2009). Undue envy, although not *directly* aggressive, can be viewed as a distorted response to the desire to secure resources to take care of offspring—a "super-response" of maternal aggression.

Pathological altruism therefore can be viewed as a distorted response to social salience. Although some may be hyper-empathizers, overloaded on oxytocin (say) with selective empathy to the detriment of innocent others, others may be hyper-trusters, perhaps lacking sufficient oxytocin machinery to adequately pick up on socially salient cues and having a faulty social threat-detector, so to speak.[7]

Seduced by the Group: The Biological Basis of Being Talked Into (or Out of) Something

One can't be altruistic alone. Altruism requires context—and how one perceives social context may relate to biological systems for sensory perception.

For instance, talking (auditory communication with language) is a fundamental tool for persuading others, and, alas, persuasion can seduce one to be led astray from one's original intentions. Being talked into something is an excuse commonly used to explain, although rarely justify, unwanted behavior. We hear the regrets of those who were talked into falling in love or talked out of something—usually money—perhaps by the same person. Biology, influencing our perception of what we think we hear, may lie at the heart of whether one is easily duped.

The oxytocin/vasopressin systems are associated with auditory communication—music, singing, or vocalization, and even dance (not strictly auditory, but in response to tempo). In frogs, extra frog vasopressin (vasotocin) increases the number of mating calls, although too much makes male mating calls unattractive to females (Kime, Whitney, Ryan, Rand, & Marler, 2010). In singing mice, the more vocal the mouse, the more pronounced the vasopressin receptors (Campbell, Ophir, & Phelps, 2009). In people, vasopressin (and its receptors) is associated with singing or musical ability (Ukkola, Onkamo, Raijas, Karma, & Järvelä, 2009). Creative dance (Bachner-Melman et al., 2005) is similarly associated with vasopressin protein variants, and dancing, at least traditionally, is directly tied to mating: One study reports that, of French married couples surveyed, one in four met while dancing (Bozon & Heran, 1989; this was true for mostly working-class French people, upper-class French people surveyed mostly met in smaller clubs and closed environments). People with Williams syndrome, a condition caused by a chromosomal deletion, are hypersociable and have a keen appreciation for music (e.g., Levitin, 2005; see Riby, Bruce, & Jawaid, Chapter 9, for a full review of Williams syndrome).

Singing enhances the feeling of well-being, and after a singing lesson, blood oxytocin levels increase and peripheral tumor necrosis factor (TNF)-α (an inflammatory protein) decreases (Grape, Sandgren, Hansson, Ericson, & Theorell, 2003; this feel-good effect is reported for amateurs, not professionals). Perhaps this is why karaoke is popular. It is worth noting that Queen's "Bohemian Rhapsody," with complicated words and harmonies, is consistently in the top 10 of karaoke songs.[8] We experience emotion, bound with music, giving rise to "chills"—physiologic pleasure states resulting from increased sympathetic arousal (Salimpoor, Benovoy, Longo, Cooperstock, & Zatorre, 2009). A mother's voice induces oxytocin and reduces stress hormones (Seltzer, Ziegler, & Pollack, 2010). Music sharing—ring tones, or even mothers singing to soothe their babies to sleep, makes perfect biological sense (Cf., Soley & Hannon, 2010, infants prefer musical meter of their own culture).

Cadence—the beat or rhythm—instills particular group bonding. The famous Snowball, a sulfur-crested cockatoo who dances in precise time to Backstreet Boys, may be neurally in sync with the rhythms (Patel, Iverson, Bregman, & Schultz, 2009 and related media showing Snowball "dancing" to Backstreet Boys "Everybody"). Consider, too, the military march or team fight song: the strong, predictable rhythm generates group cohesion. Musical expectation—knowing what pitch or rhythm is coming next—instills a sense of connectedness or synchronization, so that everyone can act the same way at the same time (see Large & Snyder, 2009).

Given the connection between auditory stimulus and affiliative neural networks, one can perhaps become seduced when the system is co-opted. Infomercials for "golden oldies" music may co-opt the emotions of one's youth—perhaps the music engenders an oxytocin response. Similarly, the television pitchman is fast talking and uses a particular cadence—he has the gift of gab, and also, perhaps, the gift of zeroing in on auditory-affiliative networks, making those cleaning supplies look irresistible.

> The television pitchman has the gift of gab—and maybe the gift of zeroing in on auditory affiliative networks.

Recall that oxytocin is not only associated with in-group bonding, but also intergroup preemptive aggression (De Dreu et al., 2010; see Choi & Bowles, 2007, for a discussion of parochial altruism and war). As group members bond with a team song or as nation-state citizens bond with nationalistic rituals, perhaps endogenous oxytocin production fuels hostility toward outsiders, inflaming passions and enhancing the likelihood of intergroup conflict.

Yet, some of the strongest forces for group bonding involve no sensory information, really. Electronic communication is a powerful force for creating group bonding of individuals who may never be in physical contact, only bonding in a virtual world. Electronic communication and the written word seem to have no immediate connection with affiliative peptides. Yet, somehow, people are connected by the common thread of an idea.

Seduced by the Group: Herding and Social Contagion

Seduction super-responders may be responding for the reason your parents probably said was no reason at all: Everyone else is doing it. Had you known about social neuroscience, you could have responded, "Yes, but it's a social contagion under whose spell I'm powerless. I get a pass."

That may not have helped with your parents, but it may be a valid excuse. Stability and predictability are the social glue providing cohesion for societal functions, and law, with its jurisprudence, generally follows prevailing social mores. A legal defense of "but everyone else was doing it" is not typically exculpatory, but evolving societal customs and beliefs can be a basis on which to change laws. Beheading, for instance, is an accepted criminal punishment in some jurisdictions and viewed as a medieval horror in others.

Groups exert a powerful influence on transmitting ideas, even without any coercion or propaganda. Consider the classic *Candid Camera* episode, in which three confederates enter an elevator and turn to face the back. The "victim," previously facing the front, sees the three others, and conforms—facing the back. Was the victim merely complying to avoid rejection? Was this mimicry and somehow biologically based? Did some kind of imperceptible chemosensory information waft in and make conforming to the group an irresistible urge?

Pattern-based analysis indicates patterns of people "catching" the behavior of others. The noted Framingham Heart Study population brings pattern-based behavior analysis into high relief. For instance, there are clusters of happy people in that "[a] person is 42% more likely to be happy if a friend who lives less than half a mile away becomes happy. The effect is only 22% for friends who live less than 2 miles away" (see Raafat, Chater, & Frith, 2009, citing Fowler & Christakis, 2008). Another study reports an increased likelihood of divorce when the subject has friends, siblings, or coworkers who divorce (McDermott, Christakis, & Fowler, 2009). Somewhat ironically, loneliness occurs in clusters (Cacioppo et al., 2009). In a different population, Las Vegas residents are reported to have 50% more suicides than those in surrounding counties, and leaving Las Vegas results in a 20% drop in suicide rates (Wray, Miller, Gurvey, Carroll, & Kawachi, 2008). Social contagion patterns perhaps can be seen in real time during televised congressional investigative hearings, in which industry executives point fingers at others for their own failures—the "blame game" may be socially contagious, particularly among members of one's own in-group (Fast & Tiedens, 2010).

Pattern-based analysis also points to transmitting ideas even without any physical contact at all. Geographic proximity alone isn't even necessary: After all, Facebook is known to make music or books popular (see Christakis & Fowler, 2009, including discussions of emotional contagion through Facebook and other social networks; also, Penenberg 2010, anecdotal report that tweeting boosted oxytocin and reduced stress hormones). Nor does social contagion last indefinitely: Social contagion can be "depleted," so to speak. Observing another person's extreme self-control is exhausting for the observer who is taking the perspective of the actor. When one is observing dispassionately, however, one may be encouraged to act (Ackerman, Goldstein, Shapiro, & Bargh, 2009). Thus, after being involved in watching a reality show about eating bugs for money, we may feel worn out. But, dispassionately watching volunteers assisting in disaster relief in a news report may encourage us to volunteer.

Pattern-based analysis shows that people act in "herds," but *why* this is so is unknown. Nonetheless, biological forces for group contagion—including emotional contagion and chemosensory information—may play a role.

Seduction Super-Response and Emotional Contagion

"Herding" in humans may be basic reflex, having a biological basis (see generally, Hatfield et al., 2009). Some propose a type of mirror neuron system, in which observation triggers a matching neural pathway in the beholder (see generally, Bastiaanson, Thioux, & Keysers, 2009).

Such reflexive, nondeliberative contagion is illustrated by contagious yawning. People normally "catch" yawns, and dogs catch human yawns from a live human experimenter (Joly-Mascheroni, Senju, & Shepherd, 2008), but not from watching a video of humans yawning (Harr, Gilbert, & Phillips, 2009). One study reports that, in addition to visual perception, *hearing* someone yawn not only increases a person's urge to yawn, but also activates brain areas believed involved in hearing and executing mouth actions as well as brain areas thought necessary for recognizing the actions of others (Arnott, Singhal, & Goodale 2009). Other studies report that children with autistic spectrum conditions exhibit no contagious yawning watching video clips unless they gaze at the eyes of the yawner (Giganti & Esposito Ziello, 2009; Senju et al., 2009a).

Eye gaze seems key to some reflexive acts, and oxytocin seems to increase eye gaze (see Frith & Frith, 2010 for a review; Senju et al., 2009a; Senju, Southgate, White, & Frith, 2009b; and Riby et al., Chapter 9, discussing intense eye gaze in individuals with Williams syndrome; see also Andari et al., 2010 for a report that oxytocin promotes social behavior, including eye gaze, in those with autistic spectrum condition). After all, with eye gaze, one can tell the difference between a person and an inanimate object. If eye gaze ignites social contagion, then perhaps oxytocin provides the spark.

Seduction Super-Response and Chemosensory Contagion

But, vision isn't the only, or necessarily the best, sensory perception for social communication. One of the oldest ways to send a seductive signal is with perfume. A scent evokes a memory, and vasopressin-producing cells in the part of the olfactory bulb that has branches to other parts of the brain may commit a scent to memory (Tobin et al., 2010). Perfume advertisements artfully depicting black-and-white dream-type sequences may be, then, sort of a "user's guide" for creating neural wiring that does the job of associating the romance with the scent.

Scent may not be the only chemosensory signal in the air. Probably adding to the delight of perfume advertising executives everywhere, chemosensory (sometimes called pheromonal) communication sends all sorts of social signals in mammals. What, exactly, is transmitted, and how it is received has been subject to much study, as human vomeronasal systems are much less apparent than those of other mammals.

Not unlike fine French perfumes, both feces and sweat are known to send social signals—but fear and anxiety are probably not the message intended by perfume makers. Rats find the smell of butyric acid aversive, for example, but the smell of fox feces makes them afraid (Endres & Fendt, 2009; 2,4,5-trimethyl-3-thiazoline (TMT) an odorant widely used to induce fear in rodents). Another recent report correlates body aroma and earwax. The degree to which one has pheromones wafting along with aroma from underarm sweat may be associated with particular genetic variants for a certain transporter protein, ABCC11, a protein also associated with whether one has earwax of the "wet" or "dry" variety (Preti & Leyden, 2010). A loss-of-function ABCC11 allelic variant is associated with unscented sweat and dry-type ear wax (Toyoda et al., 2009; also Ohashi, Naka & Tsuchiya, 2011, ABCC11 dry ear wax variant possible adaptation to cold). Another study reports that women who smelled men's armpit extracts had reduced activity in their serotonin transport protein, and, correspondingly, increased behavioral impulsivity (Marazziti et al., 2010). One can speculate that men with dry ear wax may find pheromone-laden cologne particularly worth the expense (should such product become available) when seeking to induce impulsivity in females. But, all sweat is not the same, and different kinds of sweat evoke different reactions. One study involved sweat from nervous people and, separately, sweat from people performing athletics. Test subjects smelled each kind of sweat under a brain scanner. Only the nervous sweat activated pathways involved in empathy (Prehn-Kristensen et al., 2009). Chemosensory perception of another's anxiety may act as a threat detector, in addition to visual and auditory social information.

Understanding and parsing chemosensory neural pathways may give clues to our ability to give off signals of vulnerability. If anxiety evokes empathy in another, does that mean humans can "smell" fear? And what does anxiety evoke in those who are incapable of affective empathy? One study reports that the more highly one ranked on a psychopathy checklist, the more white matter microstructure deficits in a region connecting the limbic system to the frontal lobes (Craig et al., 2009). This neural pathway is involved in empathic response. Does this mean that those who are not wired for empathy (because of the white matter deficits) perceive chemosensory "anxiety," but, instead of responding empathically, respond by exploiting this vulnerability? On the other hand, womens' emotional tears reportedly send chemosensory information associated with reduced male testosterone (among other effects, Gelstein et al. 2011). Could crying reducing aggression in others and enhance affiliative bonding? Perhaps chemosensory social signals are exploited, resulting in inadvertent pathological altruism.

Conclusion

Social Implications for Pathological Altruism

People are social creatures. We go to great lengths to avoid being alone; we also go to great lengths to ensure our belonging to a group. Human biology reflects this; many innate biological systems are adapted for social behavior. If pathological altruism is viewed as a distorted social behavior, such as a seduction super-response or undue hyper-trust, perhaps the biology, originally rooted in preserving group membership, is co-opted. Altruism, in its pathological form, then, perhaps is a distorted response to the biology that has served the animal kingdom so well.

Acknowledgment

Ms. Pessin wishes to acknowledge the assistance of Michelle R. Carney, an undergraduate student in cognitive science, at the University of California, Berkeley.

Notes

1. Definition from Wiktionary, http://en.wiktionary.org/wiki/seduce, retrieved May 23, 2010.

2. Matier, P., Ross, A. (2004). "Bushman" the boogeyman not so bad jury decides. *SF Gate* March 24, 2004. (Retrieved January 3, 2010 from http://articles.sfgate.com/2004–03-24/bay-area/17415587_1_bushman-tourists-tv-cameras); see also media, "2007 Bushman at San Francisco Fisherman's Wharf." Retrieved January 3, 2010 from http://www.youtube.com/watch?v=E0Zd8yz4a5c.

3. Taken to the extreme, social norm violation enforcement can involve blackmail: The threat to expose a social norm violation if one doesn't otherwise comply with the wishes of the punisher, and the motivation would seem to be greed, rather than social vigilantism (see Robinson, Cahill, & Bartels, 2009 for implications in the criminal law arena).

4. Shiller, R. (November 2, 2008) "Challenging the Crowd in Whispers, Not Shouts." *New York Times*. Retrieved January 17, 2010 from: http://www.nytimes.com/2008/11/02/business/02view.html, emphasis added. This view was corroborated in the Federal Open Market Committee meetings, with comments from Mr. Greenspan, indicating that dissent should not be transparent to the public. FOMC transcript March, 16, 2004, p. 90 ("We run the risk, by laying out the pros and cons of a particular argument, of inducing people to join in on the debate, and in this regard it is possible to lose control of a process that only we fully understand …"); retrieved May 23, 2010 from . http://www.federalreserve.gov/monetarypolicy/files/FOMC20040316meeting.pdf.

5. The biology of social stress and, relatedly, the biology of fairness, both subjects of intense research, are beyond the scope of this paper but important related concepts. Testosterone administration, for example, is also reported to decrease generosity, and, moreover, men with elevated testosterone were more likely to use their own money punish those who were ungenerous toward them. Zak et al. 2009. Other relevant biological agents include μ opioid receptor variants (associated with increased sensitivity to social rejection Way, Taylor, & Eisenberger, 2009) and serotonin-related molecules (Chapter 22, by Chiao et al.). One study reports that enhancing serotonin made subjects more likely to judge harmful actions as forbidden, but only in cases where harms were emotionally salient. Crockett, M.J., Clark, L. Hauser, M.D., and T.W. Robbins (2010).

6. Bevan, T., Fellner, E., Cameron, J., Coen, E. (Producers), Coen, J. (Director). (1998). *The Big Lebowski*. [Motion picture]. PolyGram Filmed Entertainment, Inc.

7. There may also be those who are hyper-threat detectors, perhaps with androgen or other hormonal influences, and maybe with neuroanatomical biases, such as a hair-trigger amygdala, resulting in an overactive social threat detection; see Chapter 22, by Chiao et al., for a discussion of recent work on the serotonin system.

8. *Telegraph*, UK. (December 5, 2009). "Official: Top 25 karaoke songs." Retrieved from http://www.telegraph.co.uk/news/6736491/Official-Top-25-karaoke-songs.html.

References

Ackerman, J. M., Goldstein, N. J., Shapiro, J. R., & Bargh, J. A. (2009). You wear me out: The vicarious depletion of self-control. *Psychological Science, 20,* 326–332.

Almeida, J. R., Mechelli, A., Hassel, S., Versace, A., Kupfer, D. J., & Phillips, M. L. (2009). Abnormally increased effective connectivity between parahippocampal gyrus and ventromedial prefrontal regions during emotion labeling in bipolar disorder. *Psychiatry Research, 174,* 195–201.

Andari, E., Duhamal, J. -R., Zalla, T., Herbrecht, E., Lebover, M., & Sirigu, A. (2010). Promoting social behavior with oxytocin in high-functioning autism spectrum disorders. *Proceedings of the National Academy of Science, 107,* 4389–4394.

Aoyagi, T., Kusakawa, S., Sanbe, A., Hiroyama, M., Fujiwara Y., Yamauchi, J., & Tanoue, A. (2009). Enhanced effect of neuropeptide Y on food intake caused by blockade of the V(1A) vasopressin receptor. *European Journal of Pharmacology, 622,* 32–36.

Arnott, S.R., Singhal, A., & Goodale, M.A. (2009). An investigation of auditory contagious yawning. Cognitive, *Affective & Behavioral Neuroscience 9,* 335–342.

Bachner-Melman, R., Dina, C., Zohar, A. H., Constantini, N., Lerer, E., Hoch, S., et al. (2005). AVPR1a and SLC6A4 gene polymorphisms are associated with creative dance performance. *PLoS Genetics, 1,* e42.

Backström T, & Winberg, S. (2009). Arginine-vasotocin influence on aggressive behavior and dominance in rainbow trout. *Physiology and Behavior, 96*, 470–475.

Bastiaansen, J. A., Thioux, M., & Keysers C. (2009). Evidence for mirror systems in emotions. *Philosophical Transactions of the Royal Society of London. B. Biological Sciences, 364*, 2391–2404.

Bennis, W. M., Medin, D. L., & Bartels, D. M. (2009). The costs and benefits of calculation and moral rules. Perspectives on Psychological Science, forthcoming. Retrieved from SSRN: http://ssrn.com/abstract=1462467

Bozon, M., & Heran, F. (1989). Finding a spouse: A survey of how French couples meet. *Population, 44*, 90–121.

Cacioppo, J. T., Fowler, J. H., & Christakis, N. A. (2008). Alone in the crowd: The structure and spread of loneliness in a large social network. *Journal of Personality and Social Psychology, 97*, 977–991.

Caldwell, H. K., & Young, W. S., III. (2009). Persistence of reduced aggression in vasopressin 1b receptor knockout mice on a more "wild" background. *Physiology and Behavior, 97*,131–134.

Campbell, P., Ophir, A. G., & Phelps, S. M. (2009). Central vasopressin and oxytocin receptor distributions in two species of singing mice. *Journal of Comparative Neurology, 516*, 321–333.

Chiao, J. Y., Mathur, V. A., Harada, T., & Lipke, T. (2009). Neural basis of preference for human social hierarchy versus egalitarianism. *Annals of the New York Academy of Science, 1167*, 174–181.

Choi, J. -K., & Bowles, S. (2007) The coevolution of parochial altruism and war. *Science, 318*, 636–640.

Christakis, N., & Fowler, J. (2009). *Connected: The surprising power of our social networks and how they shape our lives.* New York: Little, Brown.

Cikara M., Farnsworth R.A., Harris L.T., Fiske S.T. (2010). On the wrong side of the trolley track: neural correlates of relative social valuation. Social, *Cognitive and Affective Neuroscience 5*,404–13.

Craig, M. C., Catani, M., Deeley, Q., Latham, R., Daly, E., Kanaan, R., et al. (2009). Altered connections on the road to psychopathy. *Molecular Psychiatry, 10*, 946–53, 907.

Crockett, M. J., Clark, L. Hauser, M. D., Robbins T. W. (2010). Serotonin selectively influences moral judgment and behavior through effects on harm aversion PNAS - USA, *107*, 17433–17438.

Crockett, M. J., Clark, L., Lieberman, M. D., Tabibnia, G., Robbins, T.W. (2010). *Emotion 10*, 855–62.

Crowson, H. (2008, July 09). *Cultural and economic conservatism: Relationships with epistemic beliefs and motives, death anxiety, and dogmatic aggression.* Paper presented at the annual meeting of the ISPP 31st Annual Scientific Meeting, Sciences Po., Paris, France. Retrieved from http://www.allacademic.com/meta/p245805_index.html

Crowson H. M. (2009). Are all conservatives alike? A study of the psychological correlates of cultural and economic conservatism. *Journal of Psychology, 143*, 449–63.

De Dreu, C. K., Greer, L. L., Handgraaf, M. J., Shalvi, S., Van Kleef, G. A., Baas, M., et al. (2010) The neuropeptide oxytocin regulates parochial altruism in intergroup conflict among humans. *Science, 328*, 1408–11.

Donaldson, Z. R., & Young, L. J. (2008). Oxytocin, vasopressin, and the neurogenetics of sociality. *Science 322*, 900–904. (Correction: (2009) Science 323, 1429a).

Ebstein, R. P., Israel, S., Lerer, E., Uzefovsky, F., Shalev, I., Gritsenko, I., et al. (2009). Arginine vasopressin and oxytocin modulate human social behavior. *Annals of the New York Academy of Science, 1167*, 87–102.

Ebstein, R. P., Salomon, I., Chew, S. -H., Zhong, S., & Knafo, A. (2010). Genetics of Human Social Behavior. *Neuron, 65*, 831–844.

Eisenberger, N. I., Liberman, M. D., & Williams, K. D. (2003). Does rejection hurt? An fMRI study of social exclusion. *Science, 302*, 290–292.

Endres, T., & Fendt, M. (2009). Aversion- *vs* fear-inducing properties of 2,4,5-trimethyl-3-thiazoline, a component of fox odor, in comparison with those of butyric acid. *Journal of Experimental Biology, 212*, 2324–2327.

Fast, N. J., & Tiedens, L. Z. (2010). Blame contagion: The automatic transmission of self-serving attributions. *Journal of Experimental Social Psychology, 46*, 97–106.

Fowler, J. H., & Christakis, N. A. (2008). Dynamic spread of happiness in a large social network: Longitudinal analysis over 20 years in the Framingham Heart Study. *British Medical Journal, 337*, a2338.

Frith, U., & Frith, C. (2010). The social brain: Allowing humans to boldly go where no other species has been. *Philosophical Transactions of the Royal Society of London. B., 365*, 165–176.

Gelstein, S., Yeshurun, Y., Rozenkrantz, L., Shushan, S., Frumin, I., Roth, Y., & Sobel, N. (2011). Human Tears Contain a Chemosignal. Science ePub ahead of print. doi:10.1126/science.1198331

Giganti, F., & Esposito Ziello, M. (2009). Contagious and spontaneous yawning in autistic and typically developing children. *Current Psychology Letters, 25*, 1. Retrieved from http://cpl.revues.org/index4810.html

Grape, C., Sandgren, M., Hansson, L., Ericson, M., & Theorell, T. (2003). Does singing promote well-being?: An empirical study of professional and amateur singers during a singing lesson. *Integrative Physiological and Behavioral Science, 38*, 65–74.

Gregory, S. G., Connelly, J. J., Towers, A. J., Johnson, J., Biscocho, D., Markunas, C. A., et al. (2009). Genomic and epigenetic evidence for oxytocin receptor deficiency in autism. *BMC Medicine, 7*, 62.

Gwee, P. C., Tay, B. H., Brenner, S., & Venkatesh, B. (2009). Characterization of the neurohypophysial hormone gene loci in elephant shark and the Japanese lamprey: Origin of the vertebrate neurohypophysial hormone genes. *BMC Evolutionary Biology, 9*, 47.

Harr, A. L., Gilbert, V. R., & Phillips, K. A. (2009). Do dogs (Canis familiaris) show contagious yawning? *Animal Cognition, 12*, 833–837.

Hatfield, E., Rapson, R. L., & Le, Y. L. (2009). Primitive emotional contagion: Recent research. In J. Decety, and W. Ickes (Eds.), *The social neuroscience of empathy*. Boston, MA: MIT Press.

Hatton, G. I., & Wang, Y. F. (2008). Neural mechanisms underlying the milk ejection burst and reflex. *Progress in Brain Research, 170*, 155–166.

Israel, S., Lerer, E., Shalev, I., Uzefovsky, F., Riebold, M., Laiba, E., et al. (2009). The Oxytocin Receptor (OXTR) contributes to prosocial fund allocations in the dictator game and the social value orientations task. *PLoS ONE, 4*, e5535.

Iwata, E., Nagai Y., & Sasaki, H. (2008). Social rank modulates brain arginine vasotocin immunoreactivity in false clown anemonefish (Amphiprion ocellaris). *Fish Physiology and Biochemistry, 36*(3), 337–345.

Joly-Mascheroni, R. M., Senju, A., & Shepherd, A. J. (2008). Dogs catch human yawns. *Biology Letters, 4*, 446–448.

Keri, S. & Benedek, G., (2009). Oxytocin enhances the perception of biological motion in humans. Cognitive, *Affective & Behavioral Neuroscience 9*, 237–241.

Kime, N. M., Whitney, T. K., Ryan, M. J., Rand, A. S., & Marler, C. A. (2010). Treatment with arginine vasotocin alters mating calls and decreases call attractiveness in male túngara frogs. *General and Comparative Endocrinology, 165*, 221–228.

Knafo, A., Israel, S., Darvasi, A., Bachner-Melman, R., Uzefovsky, F., Cohen, L., et al. (2008). Individual differences in allocation of funds in the dictator game associated with length of the arginine vasopressin 1 a receptor RS3 promoter region and correlation between RS3 length and hippocampal mRNA. *Genes, Brain and Behavior, 7*, 266–275.

Large, E. W., & Snyder, J. S. (2009). Pulse and meter as neural resonance. *Annals of the New York Academy of Science, 1169*, 46–57.

Larson, E. T., O'Malley, D. M., & Melloni, R. H., Jr. (2006). Aggression and vasotocin are associated with dominant-subordinate relationships in zebrafish. *Behavioural Brain Research, 167*, 94–102.

Lee, R., Ferris, C., Van de Kar, L. D., & Coccaro, E. F. (2009) Cerebrospinal fluid oxytocin, life history of aggression, and personality disorder. *Psychoneuroendocrinology, 34*, 1567–1573.

Levin, R., Heresco-Levy, U., Bachner-Melman, R. Israel, S., Shalev, I., & Ebstein, R. P. (2009). Association between arginine vasopressin 1a receptor (AVPR1a) promoter region polymorphisms and prepulse inhibition. *Psychoneuroendocrinology, 34*, 901–908.

Levitin, D. J. (2005). Musical behavior in a neurogenetic developmental disorder: Evidence from Williams syndrome. *Annals of the New York Academy of Science, 1060*, 325–334.

Manuck S. B., Marsland A. L., Flory J. D., Gorka A., Ferrell R. E., & Hariri A. R. (2010). Salivary testosterone and a trinucleotide (CAG) length polymorphism in the androgenreceptor gene predict amygdala reactivity in men. *Psychoneuroendocrinology, 35*, 94–104.

Marazziti, D., Masala, I., Baroni, S., Polini, M., Massimetti, G., Giannaccini, G., et al. (2010). Male axillary extracts modify the affinity of the platelet serotonin transporter and impulsiveness in women. *Physiology and Behavior, 100*, 364–368.

Marlowe FW, Berbesque JC. (2008). More 'altruistic' punishment in larger societies. *Proc Biol Sci. 275*, 587–90.

McDermott, R., Christakis, N. A., & Fowler, J. H. (2009). *Breaking up is hard to do, unless everyone else is doing it too: Social network effects on divorce in a longitudinal sample followed for 32 years.* Retrieved from http://ssrn.com/abstract=1490708

Meyer-Lindenberg, A., Kolachana, B., Gold, B., Olsh, A., Nicodemus, K. K., Mattay V., et al. (2009). Genetic variants in AVPR1A linked to autism predict amygdala activation and personality traits in healthy humans. *Molecular Psychiatry, 14*, 968–75.

Ohashi, J., Naka, I., & Tsuchiya, N. (2011). The Impact of Natural Selection on an ABCC11 SNP Determining Earwax Type. *Moledular Biology and Evolution 28*, 849–857.

Palmieri, L., Papaleo, V., Porcelli, V., Scarcia, P., Gaita, L., Sacco R., et al. (2010). Altered calcium homeostasis in autism-spectrum disorders: Evidence from biochemical and genetic studies of the mitochondrial aspartate/glutamate carrier AGC1. *Molecular Psychiatry, 15*, 38–52.

Patel, A. D., Iverson, J. R., Bregman, M. R., & Schultz, I. (2009). Experimental evidence for synchronization to a musical beat in a nonhuman animal. *Current Biology, 19*, 827–830; supplemental data, Movie S1. Synchronization to Music in Experimental Trials at Three Tempi (MOV 6380 kb), retrieved from http://download.cell.com/current-biology/mmcs/journals/0960-9822/PIIS0960982209008902.mmc1.mov

Patel, et al. (2009). Experimental evidence for synchronization to a musical beat in a nonhuman animal. *Current Biology.* doi:10.1016/j.cub.2009.03.038

Patel, et al. (2008). Studying synchronization to a musical beat in nonhuman animals. *Annals of the New York Academy of Sciences.* Retrieved from http://www.birdlovers only.org/docs/Study_NYAS.pdf

Penenberg, Adam L., "Social Networking Affects Brains Like Falling in Love," Fast Company July 1, 2010 (downloaded from :http://www.fastcompany.com/magazine/147/doctor-love.html)

Perry, A., Bentin, S., Shalev, I., Israel, S., Uzefovsky, F., Bar-On, D., Ebstein, R.P. (2010). Intranasal oxytocin modulates EEG mu/alpha and beta rhythms during perception of biological motion. *Psychoneuroendocrinology 35*,1446–53.

Prehn-Kristensen, A., Wiesne, C., Bergmann, T. O., Wolff, S., Jansen, O., Mehdorn, H. M., et al. (2009). Induction of empathy by the smell of anxiety. *PLoS ONE, 4*, e5987.

Preti, G., & Leyden, J. J. (2010). Genetic influences on human body odor: From genes to the axillae. *Journal of Investigative Dermatology*, 130, 344–346.

Raafat, R. M., Chater, N., & C. Frith, (2009). Herding in humans. *Trends in Cognitive Sciences, 13*, 420–428; (Correction: *Trends in Cognitive Neurosciences, 13*, 504).

Robinson, P. H., Cahill, M. T., & Bartels, D. M. (2009, September 20). *Competing theories of blackmail: An empirical research critique of criminal law theory*. University of Pennsylvania Law School, Public Law Research Paper No. 09–27; Brooklyn Law School, Legal Studies Paper No. 171. Retrieved from http://ssrn.com/abstract=1477400

Rodrigues, S. M., Saslow, L. R., Garcia, N., John, O. P., & Keltner, D. (2009). Oxytocin receptor genetic variation relates to empathy and stress reactivity in humans. *Proceedings of the National Academy of Science,USA, 106*, 21437–21441.

Salimpoor, V. N., Benovoy, M., Longo, G., Cooperstock, J. R., Zatorre, R. J. (2009). The rewarding aspects of music listening are related to degree of emotional arousal. *PLoS ONE, 4*, e7487.

Salmina, A.B., Lopatina, O., Ekimova, M.V., Mikhutkina, S.V., & Higashida, H. (2010). CD38/Cyclic ADP-ribose System: A New Player for Oxytocin Secretion and Regulation of Social Behaviour. *Journal of Neuroendocrinology, 22*, 380–392.

Saucier, D. A., & Webster, R. J. (2010). Social vigilantism: Measuring individual differences in belief superiority and resistance to persuasion. *Personality and Social Psychology Bulletin, 36*, 19–32.

Seip, E. C., van Dijk, W. W., & Rotteveel, M. (2009). On hot heads and Dirty Harries: The primacy of anger in altruistic punishment. *Annals of the New York Academy of Science, 1167*, 190–6.

Seltzer, L. J., Ziegler, T. E., & Pollak, S. D. (2010). Social vocalizations can release oxytocin in humans. *Proceedings of the Royal Society. B. Biological Sciences*. doi: 10.1098/rspb.2010.0567

Senju, A., Kikuchi, Y., Akechi, H., Hasegawa, T., Tojo, Y., & Osanai, H. (2009). Brief report: Does eye contact induce contagious yawning in children with autism spectrum disorder? *Journal of Autism and Developmental Disorders, 39*, 1598–602.

Senju, A., Southgate, V., White, S., & Frith, U. (2009). Mindblind eyes: An absence of spontaneous Theory of Mind in Asperger syndrome. *Science, 325*, 883–885.

Shamay-Tsoory, S. G., Fischer, M., Dvash, J., Harari, H., Perach-Bloom, N., & Levkovitz, Y. (2009). Intranasal administration of oxytocin increases envy and schadenfreude (gloating). *Biological Psychiatry, 66*, 864–70.

Singer, T., & Steinbeis, N. (2009). Differential roles of fairness- and compassion-based motivations for cooperation, defection, and punishment. *Values, Empathy, and Fairness across Social Barriers: Annals of the New York Academy of Science, 1167*, 41–50.

Soley, G., & Hannon, E. E. (2010). Infants prefer the musical meter of their own culture: a cross-cultural comparison. *Developmental Psychology, 46*, 286–92.

Spitzer, M., Fischbacher, U., Herrnberger, B., Grön, G., & Fehr E. (2007). The neural signature of social norm compliance. *Neuron, 56*, 185–96.

Tamma, R., Colaianni, G., Zhu, L. L., DiBenedetto, A., Greco, G., Montemurro, G., et al. (2009). Oxytocin is an anabolic bone hormone. *Proceedings of the National Academy of Science USA*, *106*, 7149–7154.

Tobin, V. A., Hashimoto, H., Wacker, D. W., Takayanagi, Y., Langnaese, K., Caquineau, C., et al. (2010). An intrinsic vasopressin system in the olfactory bulb is involved in social recognition. *Nature*, *464*, 413–417.

Toyoda, Y., Sakurai, A., Mitani, Y., Nakashima, M., Yoshiura, K., Nakagawa, H., et al. Earwas, osmidrosis, and breast cancer: Why does one SNP (538G>A) in the human ABC transporter ABCC11 gene determine earwax type? *The FASEB Journal*, *23*, 2001–2013.

Ukkola, L. T, Onkamo, P., Raijas, P., Karma, K., & Järvelä, I. (2009). Musical aptitude is associated with AVPR1A-haplotypes. *PLoS ONE*, *4*, e5534.

Walum, H., Westberg, L., Henningsson, S., Neiderhiser, J. M., Reiss, D., Igl, W., et al. (2008). Genetic variation in the vasopressin receptor 1a gene (AVPR1A) associates with pair-bonding behavior in humans. *Proceedings of the National Academy of Science USA*, *105*, 14153–6.

Way, B. M., Taylor, S. E., & Eisenberger, N. I. (2009). Variation in the mu-opioid receptor gene (OPRM1) is associated with dispositional and neural sensitivity to social rejection. *Proceedings of the National Academy of Science USA*, *106*, 15079–84.

Wirén, A., Gunnarsson, U., Andersson, L., & Jensen, P. (2009). Domestication-related genetic effects on social behavior in chickens - effects of genotype at a major growth quantitative trait locus. *Poultry Science*, *88*, 1162–1166.

Wray, G. A. (2007). The evolutionary significance of cis-regulatory mutations. *Nature Reviews, Genetics*, *8*, 206–216.

Wray, M., Miller M., Gurvey J., Carroll J., & Kawachi I. (2008). Leaving Las Vegas: Exposure to Las Vegas and risk of suicide. *Social Science and Medicine*, *67*, 1882–1888.

Young, L. I., & Wang, Z. (2004). The neurobiology of pair bonding. *Nature Neuroscience*, *7*, 1048–1054.

Zak, P. J., Kurzban, R., Ahmadi, S., Swerdloff, R. S., Park, J., et al. (2009). Testosterone administration decreases generosity in the ultimatum game. *PLoS ONE*, *4*, e8330.

CHAPTER 28

EMPATHIC DISTRESS FATIGUE RATHER THAN COMPASSION FATIGUE? INTEGRATING FINDINGS FROM EMPATHY RESEARCH IN PSYCHOLOGY AND SOCIAL NEUROSCIENCE

Olga Klimecki[1] and Tania Singer

How selfish soever man may be supposed, there are evidently some
principles in his nature, which interest him in the fortunes
of others, and render their happiness necessary to him, though
he derives nothing from it except the pleasure of seeing it.
—Adam Smith, 1853, p. 3

KEY CONCEPTS

- Compassion fatigue is introduced as a form of pathological altruism since it is altruistically motivated and gives rise to symptoms of burnout.
- Empirical findings are discussed that dissociate different forms of vicarious responses.
- We conclude that the term *compassion fatigue* should be replaced by the term *empathic distress fatigue*.

ALTRUISM, WHICH IS usually defined as an unselfish concern for the welfare of others, was identified early on by scientists and philosophers such as David Hume, Adam Smith, and Auguste Comte as a crucial component of our social interactions (for reviews on this topic, see Batson, Fultz, & Schoenrade, 1987; Wispé, 1986). However, despite the strong positive connotation of altruism in our society, there are also downsides to altruism, which can be subsumed under the umbrella term of *pathological altruism*. Depending on how the term is defined, many different forms of pathological altruism exist, ranging from

Williams syndrome to politically motivated suicide (discussed in Chapters 9 and 15, respectively). In their chapter on codependency (Chapter 4), Michael McGrath and Barbara Oakley define pathological altruism in general as "the willingness of an individual to place the needs of others above him- or herself to the point of causing harm—whether physical, psychological, or both—to the purported altruist." In this chapter, we begin by describing compassion fatigue—a form of burnout—as an example of how an excess of altruism in caregivers may result in suffering and actually lead to decreased levels of helping. After reviewing definitions of the concepts related to empathy and compassion, we discuss how these concepts have been studied scientifically in the fields of social and developmental psychology and social neuroscience. Finally, we propose an integrative model and argue that *compassion fatigue* should instead be renamed *empathic distress fatigue*. We close the chapter by outlining suggestions for promoting prosocial behavior while circumventing pathological altruism in the form of compassion (or empathic distress) fatigue.

Compassion Fatigue as a Form of Pathological Altruism in Caregivers

Compassion asks us to go where it hurts, to enter into places of pain, to share in brokenness, fear, confusion, and anguish. Compassion challenges us to cry out with those in misery, to mourn with those who are lonely, to weep with those in tears. Compassion requires us to be weak with the weak, vulnerable with the vulnerable, and powerless with the powerless. Compassion means full immersion into the condition of being human.

—McNeill, Morrison, & Nouwen, 1982, p. 4

Baumeister and Vohs (2007) provide a cogent definition of compassion as "the emotion one experiences when feeling concern for another's suffering and desiring to enhance that individual's welfare." Typically, compassion involves two components: the affective feeling of caring for a suffering person, and the motivation to relieve the other person's suffering. In this regard, the term *compassion fatigue*, first introduced by Joinson (1992), describes a state of reduced capacity for compassion as a consequence of being exhausted from absorbing the suffering of others[2] (Figley, 2002; Sabo, 2006). We argue that compassion fatigue can be regarded as a manifestation of pathological altruism for the following reasons:

- The source of compassion fatigue is altruistic: Caregivers with compassion fatigue were initially motivated by the prosocial aim of alleviating the suffering of others by means of their empathic care.
- The consequence of this form of altruism, however, is pathological, since compassion fatigue negatively affects the caregiver's mental and physical health (see also Chapter 11).

To better understand the nature of compassion fatigue, the following section will describe the negative consequences of compassion fatigue for clinicians and give an account of its causal mechanisms.

Compassion fatigue, or burnout, has been reported to be very frequent in caregivers, with prevalence rates ranging from 40% to 80% and to have adverse effects on the people who experience it (for a recent review, see McCray,

Cronholm, Bogner, Gallo, & Neill, 2008). Shanafelt and colleagues (2002) assessed the prevalence and effects of burnout by mailing clinicians anonymous surveys, such as the Maslach Burnout Inventory (Maslach & Jackson, 1981) along with questions regarding patient care practices and depressive symptoms. This cross-sectional study showed that 76% of the responding medical residents reported symptoms of burnout in the domains of high depersonalization (e.g., "I've become more callous toward people since I took this job.") and emotional exhaustion (e.g., "I feel emotionally drained from my work."). Furthermore, Shanafelt and colleagues reported that half the residents who feel burned out suffer from depressive symptoms. The adverse effects of compassion fatigue on clinician's health were substantiated by a longitudinal study in which burnout was shown to predict mood disorders and poor general health in physicians (Hillhouse, Adler, & Walters, 2000). In addition to negative effects on the caregivers, burnout has also been associated with an increase in self-reported medical errors (West et al., 2006) and suboptimal patient care practices (Shanafelt et al., 2002). These and similar studies suggest that the consequences of compassion fatigue are wide-ranging and affect the caregivers' health and interaction with patients. In light of these alarming consequences, the question arises as to why caregivers are sometimes overwhelmed by compassion.

> More than all other factors, including the patient's disability and the time spent caregiving, it is the perceived suffering that leads to depressive symptoms in the caregiver.

Schulz and colleagues (Schulz et al., 2007) argued in their review that, more than all other factors, including the patient's disability and the time spent caregiving, it is the *perceived* suffering of the patient that leads to depressive symptoms in the caregiver. This suggests that empathy for a patient lies at the very root of compassion fatigue. Similarly, Figley (2002) described empathy as one of the main sources of compassion fatigue. This might seem counterintuitive at first glance, since compassion and empathy are said to promote prosocial behaviour. To unravel this paradox, we reexamine here the definitions that have been used to describe empathy and its consequences and review empirical findings from different fields supporting these conceptual distinctions. We show that by differentiating these concepts, a new integrative model arises that can account for mechanisms underlying compassion fatigue. This model suggests that, rather than compassion fatigue, it is empathic distress that underlies the negative consequences of caregivers who are exposed to others' suffering.

> Rather than compassion fatigue, it is empathic distress that underlies the negative consequences faced by caregivers who are exposed to others' suffering.

Definitions of Empathy and Related Concepts

Broadly speaking, empathy occurs when observing or even simply imagining another person's affective state triggers an isomorphic affective response. Importantly, the person experiencing empathy is aware that the source of his or her emotional response is the other person's affective state (for comprehensive reviews, see Batson, 2009b; de Vignemont & Singer, 2006; Eisenberg, 2000; Hoffman, 2000; Singer & Lamm, 2009; Singer & Leiberg, 2009). As outlined by Singer and Lamm (2009), empathy is a vital first step in a chain of emotional responses that lead towards feelings of compassion, empathic concern, or sympathy.[3] There is a crucial distinction between empathy as opposed to compassion, empathic concern, and sympathy. Empathy refers to "feeling with"—it involves vicariously sharing the same feeling with another person. The other forms of vicarious affective responses refer to "feeling for" and are not necessarily isomorphic to the target's affective state. Empathizing with someone else's sadness implies that we also feel sad. Having compassion, sympathy, or feelings of empathic concern for someone who is feeling sad or distressed does not necessarily mean that we are also feeling sad or distressed. Instead, it means we have feelings of concern for the other ("feeling for"), as well as a motivation to alleviate the other's suffering. Feeling compassion can also imply that we have positive feelings related to love for the suffering other. As we discuss in more detail below, a number of social and developmental psychological studies have shown that these other-oriented feelings motivate prosocial behavior (see Batson et al., 1987 and Eisenberg, 2000 for a review). However, these prosocially motivated and other-oriented feelings of compassion, sympathy, or empathic concern are not the only way of responding to others' suffering. Empathizing with others may also give rise to so-called feelings of *empathic* or *personal distress*. In this case, empathizing with the suffering of another person leads to strong feelings of distress and aversive emotions in the observer. It has been suggested (Batson, O'Quin, Fultz, et al., 1983; Eisenberg et al., 1989) that, in contrast to compassion, sympathy, and empathic concern, which are all three other-oriented emotions that promote prosocial behavior, empathic distress and personal distress are aversive and self-oriented emotions that often lead to withdrawal behavior motivated by the desire to protect oneself from negative emotions.

The different steps involved in an empathic response can be illustrated by the following example: Upon hearing that a friend of ours is sad because her grandmother is dying, our first reaction would be empathy, which means that we would share the feeling of sadness and thereby know what our friend is going through. Empathy is the first step connecting us with the affective and motivational states of the other. In the next step, we would either transform this empathic response into compassion or empathic distress depending on our disposition, personality, emotion regulation ability, and the situation. If we reacted with compassion, we would feel pity or concern for our friend and, motivated by this other-oriented feeling, act in a prosocial way by trying to alleviate our friend's suffering. However, if we reacted with empathic distress, which is a self-oriented response linked to withdrawal, we would be overwhelmed by our own sadness and try to avoid the aversive situation by leaving our friend alone with her sadness. In the following, we will discuss empirical evidence for such distinctions, first from social psychology, then from developmental psychology, and finally from social neuroscience.

Empirical Evidence from Social Psychology

To understand from a social psychological perspective how empathy and prosocial behavior are linked, Batson and his colleagues (1987) postulated and tested two core hypotheses:

1. Since the feeling of empathic concern is other-oriented, it should give rise to prosocial motivation. In other words, people who experience

empathic concern should strive to relieve the suffering of the person in need.

2. The experience of empathic distress is self-oriented. Therefore, people who experience empathic distress should primarily be motivated to reduce their own negative affect. This can be done either by avoiding the distressing situation altogether or by alleviating the other person's suffering.

Batson proposed that the relation between empathy and helping could be investigated by manipulating the ease with which the observer can escape witnessing the suffering of another person. He reasoned that people who respond to others' suffering with personal distress should primarily seek to reduce their own negative affect. So, when someone is suffering as a result of witnessing a distressing situation in which escape is easy, the primary motive of reducing one's own negative affect should result in the person leaving the situation without providing help (in the above example, one would avoid seeing the sad friend or change the subject whenever she speaks of her dying grandmother). However, if a person experiences distress in response to suffering in a situation that is not easy to escape from (for example, when hearing the distressed friend sob at night when sharing a hotel room), the distressed person should help the person in need, since the vicariously induced distress can be reduced by alleviating the other's suffering. Conversely, people who experience empathic concern for the person in need should help irrespective of whether it is easy or difficult to escape since their primary motivation is prosocial and other-oriented. Based on this theoretical framework, Batson and colleagues were able to test how empathy is related to prosocial motivation. They expected to observe low levels of helping when people experienced personal distress and when it was easy to escape witnessing the suffering of the other, since withdrawal would be an adaptive first response to protect oneself from the vicariously experienced negative affect. Conversely, people who experience personal distress but do not have the opportunity to escape the suffering stimuli easily, should provide help, since this is the most efficient way to reduce their own negative feelings. Furthermore, in this framework, the ease of escape should not matter for persons who experience empathic concern, since they would be motivated by the desire to help the needy person in all situations. So, helping rates should always be high in people who experience empathic concern.

To test their hypothesis, Batson and colleagues used a paradigm in which subjects watched another person receive electric shocks in an ostensible learning experiment. After a few trials, subjects were given the opportunity to relieve the other person's suffering by taking the remaining shocks themselves. In one experiment, the researchers manipulated the participant's emotional response to the person receiving shocks by using an emotion-specific misattribution technique (Batson, Duncan, Ackerman, Buckley, & Birch, 1981). Subjects who reported reacting with more empathic concern to the suffering person as a consequence of the experimental manipulation showed high rates of helping in both the easy and the difficult escape condition. However, subjects whose dominant response to the suffering was distress showed lower helping rates in the easy escape condition compared with subjects in the difficult escape condition or subjects with high empathic concern. In another experiment, Batson and colleagues (1983) showed that subjects who reported being more distressed from observing suffering helped significantly less in the easy escape condition than in the difficult escape condition. Furthermore, the general pattern of results supported Batson's claim: Subjects who reported more empathic concern showed comparatively high levels of helping in both the easy and the difficult escape condition. This and many more experiments (for review, see Batson, 2009a) confirm the hypothesis that empathic concern acts as a precursor of altruistic motivation, whereas personal distress leads to a self-oriented response. As will be outlined in the next paragraph, parallel research in developmental psychology has extended these findings to children.

Empirical Evidence from Developmental Psychology

> Empathic concern acts as a precursor of altruistic motivation, whereas personal distress leads to a self-oriented response.

In the domain of developmental psychology, Eisenberg and colleagues (1989) studied how children's responses to needy others differed from adult's reactions. One of their studies used a paradigm similar to that developed by Batson and colleagues; it focused on the easy escape condition, since it best differentiates between altruistic and selfish motives. In addition to measuring subjects' individual rates of helping behavior, Eisenberg and her colleagues also recorded facial expressions and heart rate while subjects watched a video clip of a hospital scene depicting a woman and her two injured children, who were suffering from the consequences of a car accident. After viewing the film, subjects reported their emotional reactions and were given the opportunity to offer help to the woman in the film by assisting her with some household tasks (in the case of adults) or to help the injured children by gathering together homework materials (in the case of children). In line with the hypothesis that sympathy promotes prosocial behavior, this experiment showed that, for adults, self-reports and facial expressions of sympathy predicted helping. Interestingly, children's verbal reports of distress and sympathy were not related to their prosocial behavior, suggesting that children's capacity to report self-experience may be underdeveloped. However, children's facial display of distress tended to be negatively related to their helping behavior: Children who showed more facial signals of distress tended to help less. Taken together, the general pattern of results supports the claim that empathic concern promotes helping, whereas personal distress is linked to a self-oriented motivation. Several other developmental psychological studies have confirmed with various measures (ranging from facial and behavioral to physiological reactions to the distress of others) that children's increased empathic concern is positively correlated with higher helping rates (for a review, see Eisenberg, 2000).

Empirical Evidence from Social Neuroscience

As pointed out in previous paragraphs, to predict prosocial motivation, it is crucial to differentiate between the different reactions that follow empathy. Social neuroscience has recently significantly advanced our understanding of the different neural substrates of empathy, particularly through functional magnetic resonance imaging (fMRI; for recent reviews, see Decety & Lamm, 2009; Singer & Lamm, 2009). In these studies, brain responses were acquired while participants were receiving painful stimulation themselves or were empathizing with others in similar situations. Guided by the assumption that empathy would be very strong for one's partner, Singer and colleagues (2004), for example, invited couples to participate in an experiment in which the woman's brain activity was measured by means of fMRI while her partner was sitting next to the scanner. During the measurement, either the female or the male partner received painful stimulation through electrodes that were attached to the back of the hands. An arrow indicated who would be stimulated next and whether the stimulation would be painful or nonpainful. Interestingly, this study revealed that certain parts of the neural "pain matrix" show increased activation in both conditions; that is, in the direct experience and in the observation of pain. More specifically, the brain areas that were activated more strongly during the experience of pain and empathy for pain were the anterior insula (AI) and the anterior cingulated cortex (ACC), which both play a crucial role in processing bodily and feeling states (see also Singer, Critchley, & Preuschoff, 2009). These findings have been replicated (Bird et al., 2010; Hein, Silani, Preuschoff, Batson, & Singer, 2010; Singer et al., 2006, 2008) and corroborated by several other empathy-for-pain studies that also found increased activation of AI and ACC when subjects merely observed pictures, photographs, or videos depicting body parts, faces, and people in painful situations (Cheng et al., 2007; Gu & Han, 2007; Jackson, Brunet, Meltzoff, & Decety, 2005; Jackson, Meltzoff, & Decety, 2006; Lamm, Batson, &Decety, 2007; Morrison, Lloyd, di Pellegrino, & Roberts, 2004; Morrison, Peelen, & Downing, 2007; Saarela et al., 2007; Singer et al., 2006). Importantly, a recent meta-analysis by Lamm and colleagues (2011) across nine independent fMRI studies on empathy for pain showed consistent involvement of a core network involving AI and ACC in self-pain and empathy for pain (Figure 28.1). The routes leading to activation of this core network, however, differ depending on the type of paradigm used. More specifically, a neural

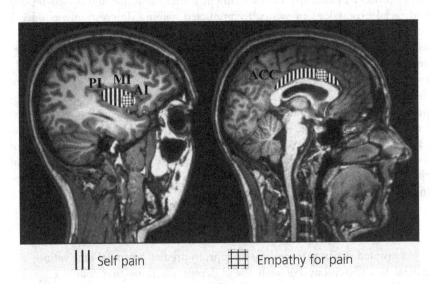

||| Self pain   ⊞ Empathy for pain

FIGURE 28.1
Schematically depicted shared networks for pain as experienced by oneself as opposed to one's empathy for the pain being experienced by another. Activation related to empathy for pain in another is depicted checkered, whereas activation related to the direct experience of pain in the subject him- or herself is shown with stripes. Overlapping activation between both conditions (also checkered) is localized in the anterior cingulate cortex (ACC) and the anterior insula (AI). MI, medial insula; PI, posterior insula

circuitry processing somatic features was involved along with the AI and ACC when pictures of body parts or faces in painful situations were shown to induce empathy. In contrast, the above-mentioned paradigms, which involved a real-life situation with the suffering person being present in the scanner environment while abstract cues indicated when and to whom pain would be inflicted, induced activation in networks involved in inferring abstract mental states of others, that is, networks involved in Theory of Mind and mentalizing.

Although neural correlates of empathy have been observed in numerous studies and across different paradigms, empathic brain responses have also been found to be modulated by multiple factors (for a recent review, see Hein & Singer, 2008). There are situations in which stimuli that usually lead to empathy fail to induce increased responses in empathy-related brain networks. For example, Singer and colleagues (2006) investigated how empathy and its neural underpinnings depend on the perceived fairness of people suffering pain. In their study, the participant who was subsequently being scanned first played an economic game with two other volunteers, who in fact were confederates, and who behaved either fairly or unfairly. This manipulation induced the participant to like the fair confederate and dislike the unfair confederate. In a second step, the subject who was scanned, and the two other participants who were seated next to the scanner received painful or non-painful stimuli. First, Singer and coworkers confirmed the existence of a shared neural representation for self-experienced pain and the observation of pain in fair players in the AI and the ACC. Interestingly, only female subjects also showed increased activation in these regions when witnessing unfair players receiving pain, suggesting that women empathized with both fair and unfair players in pain. In contrast, men showed significantly less activation in the AI when witnessing unfair players as opposed to fair players receiving pain. Notably, the reduction in the men's empathic neural response toward unfair players was accompanied by a rise in activation in the nucleus accumbens, a region that has previously been linked to reward-processing (for recent reviews, see Knutson & Cooper, 2005; Schultz, 2000). This link between activation in a reward-processing area and punishment was further supported by the observation that activation in the nucleus accumbens in men correlates positively with their self-reported desire for revenge.

The observation that the readiness to empathize crucially depends on the nature of the social relation has received additional support from a recent study in which Hein et al. (2010) report that male soccer fans show a greater empathic response in the left AI when witnessing the pain of a fan of their own favorite team (in-group) as compared to a fan of a

> Readiness to empathize crucially depends on the nature of the social relation.

rival team (out-group). Intriguingly, the intensity of activation in the insula predicted the amount of altruistic helping later on. In contrast, the intensity of nucleus accumbens activation observed when watching out-group members suffering pain was associated with a reduction of empathic brain responses in AI and correlated with reduced helping for the out-group member. In other words, when empathy-related activation in AI while seeing someone else suffering was high, neural activation in the nucleus accumbens was low, whereas nucleus accumbens activation was elevated when activation in the AI in response to another person's suffering was low. These findings corroborate the suggestion that empathy motivates prosocial behaviour, and an absence of empathy accompanied

> Empathy motivates prosocial behavior, and an absence of empathy accompanied by *schadenfreude*—reflected in elevated activation in nucleus accumbens—predicts a lack of helping.

by *schadenfreude*—reflected in elevated activation in nucleus accumbens—predicts a lack of helping.

Another study relevant to the present chapter showed that empathic brain responses can be modulated as a function of the observer's experience. Cheng and colleagues (2007) compared the neural response of volunteers who observed needles being inserted into different body parts. Some volunteers were physicians who practice acupuncture, whereas others were naïve participants with no experience in practicing acupuncture. The results showed that naïve participants showed activation in the neural network related to empathy in response to the stimuli, whereas physicians did not. One potential explanation is that the physicians were able to either not engage in any empathic response or to inhibit their empathic response toward the patient's pain at an early stage.

The question arises as to which neural networks are actually involved when people adopt a loving attitude toward others, particularly in light of the potential dissociation of empathic distress and empathic concern. Although findings in this realm are not yet as abundant as in the domain of empathy for pain, the evidence for distinct neural structures converges: Bartels and Zeki studied romantic love (2000) and maternal love (2004) by means of fMRI and found overlapping activations for both types of love in the middle insula, the dorsal part of the ACC and the striatum (comprising the putamen, globuspallidus, and caudate nucleus). Similar activation patterns were reported by Beauregard and colleagues (2009), who observed increased activations in the middle insula, the dorsal ACC, the globuspallidus, and the caudate nucleus when their participants adopted a stance of unconditional love toward pictures of individuals with intellectual disabilities compared to just looking at these pictures. Converging evidence for the involvement of the striatum in feelings of love comes from another study that shows that activation in the caudate nucleus is linked to seeing a beloved person (Aron et al., 2005). Furthermore, Vrticka et al. (2008) report increased ventral striatum activation in response to smiling faces. As reviewed by Zeki (2007), the reported areas are linked to reward processing and are awash with oxytocin and vasopressin receptors—neuropeptides that play a crucial role in attachment and bonding (see Depue & Morrone-Strupinsky, 2005, for a review). Interestingly, increases in middle insula activation were also reported to be more pronounced in expert as compared to naïve meditators who were listening to distressing sounds while they were in a compassionate state (Lutz, Brefczynski-Lewis, Johnstone, & Davidson, 2008). The finding that the middle insula is up-regulated in response to aversive stimuli during loving-kindness meditation is promising since it suggests that these meditation techniques are efficient in activating neural networks of love and positive emotions, even in light of distressing stimuli. However, much more research is necessary to substantiate which neural networks are involved in positive social emotions such as love and compassion.

An Integrative Model

Looking at the different studies presented in this chapter, it might at first seem confusing that, despite empirical evidence from psychology revealing that

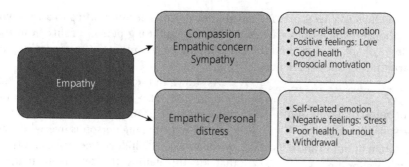

FIGURE 28.2
A schematic model depicting two different forms an empathic reaction can take.

compassion is a necessary precursor for prosocial behavior, the same behavior has been linked to compassion fatigue and burnout in caregivers. We suggest that this confusion can be resolved by taking a close look at the definition of empathy and its related concepts. As outlined above and illustrated in Figure 28.2, one should distinguish between empathy, which denotes sharing someone's feelings ("feeling with"), and the consequences of empathy, which can take at least two different paths.

As illustrated by the upper path in Figure 28.2, empathy can result in feelings of concern, compassion, or sympathy *for* another person. The other-oriented focus of the compassionate response is essential, because it prevents the empathizer from identifying with the suffering. In other words, the compassionate person responds with feelings of love and concern to the observed suffering, while at the same time being able to regulate their own negative feelings caused by an empathic response and being aware that it is *the other person* who is suffering. Empirical evidence for the importance of self–other distinction in determining which path an empathic response will follow was reported by Lamm and colleagues (2007). In their study, which combined behavioural measures with fMRI, participants viewed video clips depicting patients who reacted to a medical treatment with painful or nonpainful facial expressions. The behavioural results show that participants reported higher personal distress when they imagined themselves in the patient's situation (self-perspective), whereas participants reported more empathic concern when they cognitively differentiated between the patient and themselves (other-perspective). Likewise, Eisenberg (2000) underlines that the realization of being different from the suffering person without being indifferent toward him or her is an important prerequisite for the development of prosocial behaviour. In other words, the compassionate person has the capacity to help because he or she is not overwhelmed by distress, but instead guided by feelings of concern, love, or affection toward the other.

This view on compassion is very close to the Buddhist notion of loving kindness (a feeling of warmth and caring toward oneself and others, Salzberg, 2002), because both share the same core emotions of positive affect and feelings of love and concern. The crucial difference between these two concepts is that, whereas loving kindness is experienced towards nonsuffering beings, compassion is felt for suffering beings. As will be discussed below, initial evidence suggests that compassion (or loving kindness) can even

> The other-oriented focus of the compassionate response is essential, because it prevents the empathizer from identifying with the suffering.

have beneficial effects on the empathizing person's health, leading to a win–win situation in which both parties benefit: The suffering person profits from the help he or she receives, and the empathizing person profits from the feelings of warmth he or she experiences.

> The realization of being different from the suffering person without being indifferent toward him or her is an important prerequisite for the development of prosocial behavior.

As shown in the lower path of Figure 28.2, empathy may also give rise to aversive emotions of empathic or personal distress. In this case, the empathizing person is overwhelmed by the vicariously induced negative emotions that are threatening the self. Note that, in contrast to a compassionate response in which the observing person does not identify with the suffering, the self–other distinction becomes blurred during empathic distress as the observer is overwhelmed by the experience of negative emotions. As outlined in the section above, this distinction is supported by the behavioural results reported by Lamm and colleagues (2007). Furthermore, the fMRI data of this study show that adopting the self-perspective leads to increased activation in brain areas involved in the processing of threat or pain, such as the amygdala. This suggests that the different experiences related to whether one adopts a self-focused or other-focused perspective are accompanied by distinct neural responses. Since identifying with the suffering of others induces empathic distress, the empathizing person will most likely try to reduce these harming feelings and attempt to withdraw from the difficult emotional situation, even if that means losing the opportunity to provide help. This withdrawal response may in fact be very adaptive, given that the studies described above on burnout in caregivers show that being overwhelmed by others' distress can have detrimental consequences for the mental and physical health of the affected person.

> Adopting the self-perspective leads to increased activation in brain areas involved in the processing of threat or pain, such as the amygdala. This suggests that the different experiences related to whether one adopts a self-focused or other-focused perspective are accompanied by distinct neural responses.

With this model in mind, we propose that the term *compassion fatigue* is slightly misleading, since it suggests that caregivers are tired of feeling too much compassion, whereas the definition we use implies that the feeling of compassion should actually protect against burnout. Therefore, we argue that the term compassion fatigue should be replaced by *empathic distress fatigue*, since the nature of burnout described in caregivers closely resembles the state of empathic distress. Both, burnout in caregivers and empathic distress, are characterized by the experience of negative emotions, which lead to a self-oriented response with the desire to alleviate one's own distress and both have negative effects on health. So, instead of abstaining from empathic responses altogether, physicians and caregivers in general should aim at maintaining high levels of empathy and learn how to transform empathy into compassion and loving kindness before being trapped by empathic distress. It is important to note here that the schematic model depicted in Figure 28.2 does not make any prediction about whether feelings of empathic distress and compassion can also be developed and experienced simultaneously while being exposed to a suffering person. It is plausible to assume that we can experience a mixture of both feelings at the same time and that it is rather a question of which path is predominantly activated that will determine whether negative or positive outcomes will be observed in the long run.

The importance of a compassionate approach in physician–patient interactions is indisputable and was nicely illustrated in a study by Fogarty and colleagues (1999). The researchers showed women with breast cancer short videotapes about the treatment before the women saw the physician. One video contained an "enhanced compassion" segment in which the physician says: "You know you have a very bad disease, but we are going to take care of you." Fogarty and colleagues report that women who saw the "enhanced compassion" video were less anxious than women who saw the control video. This finding underpins how crucial a compassionate approach is for a good physician–patient interaction. Given the high prevalence and the adverse effects of burnout among caregivers, the question arises as to how one can maintain a high level of compassion, and by this, profit from the beneficial effects that a health profession can entail (for a discussion of the positive effects of caregiving, see Post, 2005). Recently, there has been growing research interest in the question of how compassion might be promoted. Although solid findings in this area are still scarce, certain streams of research on meditation suggest that mindfulness and loving-kindness training can have beneficial effects on the mental and physical health of those who practice it. Meditation training based on mindfulness, loving kindness, or both, have been shown to have beneficial effects on markers of immune function (Davidson et al., 2003), reduce negative affect and stress (see Chiesa et al., 2009 for a recent review), decrease illness symptoms, and finally, to increase positive affect (Fredrickson, Cohn, Coffey, Pek, & Finkel, 2008). Importantly, the beneficial effects of meditation also extend to caregivers. Shapiro and colleagues (2005) have found that mindfulness-based stress reduction in healthcare professionals decreases perceived stress and promotes self-compassion. A recent review by Irving and colleagues suggests that various other studies found empirical evidence showing that mindfulness-based training improves physician's mental and physical health (Irving, Dobkin, & Park, 2009).

Conclusion

In summary, despite the scarcity of studies that allow for causal inference (for a review, see Toneatto & Nguyen, 2007), accumulating evidence suggests that certain forms of meditation offer effective ways of circumventing compassion fatigue in caregivers by promoting an attitude of empathic concern and compassion that is associated with a skillful use of adaptive emotion-regulation mechanisms and a clear self–other distinction that makes one less vulnerable to the repeated experience of distress and suffering.

Acknowledgments

We would like to thank Matthieu Ricard—a long-term Buddhist practitioner whom we study regularly while he is immersed in different meditative states in the MRI scanner—for the fruitful and inspiring discussions on the nature of empathy and compassion. His first-person perspective on the nature and differences between empathic states and compassionate states have inspired the distinction between compassion fatigue and empathic distress fatigue, as he reported that compassionate states are associated with wholesome states and could never lead to burnout, whereas engaging in empathic states alone can lead to unbearable suffering. In addition, we would like to thank Regula Ott for her help with the figures.

Notes

1. Corresponding author: Olga Klimecki, Max Planck Institute for Human Cognitive and Brain Sciences, Department of Social Neuroscience, Stephanstr. 1a, 04103 Leipzig, Germany, Telephone: +493419940 2681, E-Mail: klimecki@cbs.mpg.de

2. In addition to the phrase *compassion fatigue*, terms such as *secondary traumatic stress* and *burnout* are also used to describe the negative consequences of intense emotional engagement with patients (for review, see Najjar, Davis, Beck-Coon, & Carney Doebbeling, 2009; Thomas & Wilson, 2004). For simplicity, we will use these three terms interchangeably in this chapter.

3. Although these concepts can be further differentiated, these terms are often used synonymously (Batson, 2009b). Whereas Eisenberg (2000) primarily uses the term sympathy, Batson (2009a) rather refers to empathic concern. Since it would be beyond the scope of this chapter to introduce the fine-graded differences, we will use the three terms interchangeably.

References

Aron, A., Fisher, H., Mashek, D. J., Strong, G., Li, H., & Brown, L. L. (2005). Reward, motivation, and emotion systems associated with early-stage intense romantic love. *Journal of Neurophysiology, 94*, 327–337.

Bartels, A., & Zeki, S. (2000). The neural basis of romantic love. *Neuroreport, 11*, 3829–3834.

Bartels, A., & Zeki, S.(2004). The neural correlates of maternal and romantic love. *Neuroimage, 21*, 1155–1166.

Batson, C. D. (2009a). Empathy-induced altruistic motivation. In M. Mikulincer, & P. R. Shaver (Eds.), *Prosocial motives, emotions, and behavior* (pp. 15–34). Washington, D.C.: American Psychological Association.

Batson, C. D. (2009b). These things called empathy: Eight related but distinct phenomena. In J. Decety, & W. Ickes(Eds.), *The social neuroscience of empathy* (pp. 3–15). Cambridge, MA: MIT Press.

Batson, C. D., Duncan, B. D., Ackerman, P., Buckley, T., & Birch, K. (1981). Is empathic emotion a source of altruistic motivation? *Journal of Personality and Social Psychology, 40*, 290–302.

Batson, C. D., O'Quin, K., Fultz, J., Mary, V. M., & Alice M. (1983). Influence of self-reported distress and empathy on egoistic versus altruistic motivation to help. *Journal of Personality and Social Psychology, 45*, 706–718.

Batson, C. D., Fultz, J., & Schoenrade, P. A. (1987). Distress and empathy: Two qualitatively distinct vicarious emotions with different motivational consequences. *Journal of Personality, 55*, 19.

Baumeister, R. F., & Vohs, K. D. (2007). *Encyclopedia of social psychology*. Thousand Oaks, CA: Sage Publications.

Beauregard, M., Courtemanche, J., Paquette, V., & St-Pierre, E. L. (2009). The neural basis of unconditional love. *Psychiatry Research, 172*, 93–98.

Bird, G., Silani, G., Brindley, R., White, S., Frith, U., & Singer, T. (2010). Empathic brain responses in insula are modulated by levels of alexithymia but not autism. *Brain, 133(5)*, 1515–1525.

Cheng, Y., Lin, C. P., Liu, H. L., Hsu, Y. Y., Lim, K. E., Hung, D. et al. (2007). Expertise modulates the perception of pain in others. *Current Biology, 17*, 1708–1713.

Chiesa, A., & Serretti, A. (2009). Mindfulness-based stress reduction for stress management in healthy people: A review and meta-analysis. *The Journal of Alternative and Complementary Medicine, 15*, 593–600.

Davidson, R. J., Kabat-Zinn, J., Schumacher, J., Rosenkranz, M., Muller, D., Santorelli, S. F., et al.(2003). Alterations in brain and immune function produced by mindfulness meditation. *Psychosomatic Medicine, 65*, 564–570.

de Vignemont, F., & Singer, T. (2006). The empathic brain: How, when and why? *Trends in Cognitive Sciences, 10*, 435–441.

Decety, J., & Lamm, C. (2009). Empathy versus personal distress - Recent evidence from social neuroscience. In J.Decety, & W. E.Ickes(Eds.), *The social neuroscience of empathy* (pp. 199–213). Cambridge: MIT press.

Depue, R. A., & Morrone-Strupinsky, J. V. (2005). A neurobehavioral model of affiliative bonding: implications for conceptualizing a human trait of affiliation. *Behavioral and Brain Sciences, 28*, 313–350.

Eisenberg, N. (2000). Emotion, regulation, and moral development. *Annual Review of Psychology, 51*, 665–697.

Eisenberg, N., Fabes, R. A., Miller, P. A., Fultz, J., Shell, R., Mathy, R. M.et al. (1989). Relation of sympathy and personal distress to prosocial behavior: A multimethod study. *Journal of Personality and Social Psychology, 57*, 55–66.

Figley, C. (2002). Compassion fatigue: Psychotherapists' chronic lack of self care. *Journal of Clinical Psychology, 58*, 1433–1441.

Fogarty, L. A., Curbow, B. A., Wingard, J. R., McDonnell, K., & Somerfield, M. R. (1999). Can 40 seconds of compassion reduce patient anxiety? *Journal of Clinical Oncology, 17*, 371.

Fredrickson, B. L., Cohn, M. A., Coffey, K. A., Pek, J., & Finkel, S. M. (2008). Open hearts build lives: Positive emotions, induced through loving-kindness meditation, build consequential personal resources. *Journal of Personality and Social Psychology, 95*, 1045–1062.

Gu, X., & Han, S. (2007). Attention and reality constraints on the neural processes of empathy for pain. *Neuroimage, 36*, 256–267.

Hein, G., & Singer, T. (2008). I feel how you feel but not always: The empathic brain and its modulation. *Current Opinion in Neurobiology, 18*, 153–158.

Hein, G., Silani, G., Preuschoff, K, Batson, C.D., & Singer, T. (2010). Neural responses to ingroup and outgroup members' suffering predict individual differences in costly helping. *Neuron, 68*, 149–160.

Hillhouse, J. J., Adler, C. M., & Walters, D. N. (2000). A simple model of stress, burnout and symptomatology in medical residents: A longitudinal study. *Psychology, Health & Medicine, 5*, 63–73.

Hoffman, M. L. (2000). *Empathy and moral development*. Cambridge, UK: Cambridge University Press.

Irving, J. A., Dobkin, P. L., & Park, J. (2009). Cultivating mindfulness in health care professionals: A review of empirical studies of mindfulness-based stress reduction (MBSR). *Complementary Therapies in Clinical Practice, 15*, 61–66.

Jackson, P. L., Brunet, E., Meltzoff, A. N., & Decety, J.(2006). Empathy examined through the neural mechanisms involved in imaging how I feel versus how you feel pain. *Neuropsychologia, 44*, 752–761.

Jackson, P. L., Meltzoff, A. N., & Decety, J. (2005). How do we perceive the pain of others? A window into the neural processes involved in empathy. *Neuroimage, 24*, 771–779.

Joinson, C. (1992). Coping with compassion fatigue. *Nursing, 4*, 116–121.

Knutson, B. & Cooper, J. C. (2005). Functional magnetic resonance imaging of reward prediction. *Current Opinion in Neurology, 18*, 411–417.

Lamm, C., Batson, C., & Decety, J. (2007). The neural substrate of human empathy: Effects of perspective-taking and cognitive appraisal. *Journal of Cognitive Neuroscience, 19,* 42–58.

Lamm, C., Decety, J., & Singer, T. (2011). Meta-analytic evidence for common and distinct neural networks associated with directly experienced pain and empathy for pain. *Neuroimage, 54,* 2492–2502.

Lutz, A., Brefczynski-Lewis, J., Johnstone, T., & Davidson, R. J. (2008). Regulation of the neural circuitry of emotion by compassion meditation: Effects of meditative expertise. *PLoS ONE. 26;3(3).*

Maslach, C., & Jackson, S. E. (1981). The measurement of experienced burnout. *Journal of Occupational Behaviour, 2,* 99–113.

McCray, L., Cronholm, P., Bogner, H., Gallo, J., & Neill, R. (2008). Resident physician burnout: Is there hope? *Family Medicine, 40,* 626–632.

McNeill, D., Morrison, D., & Nouwen, H. (1982). *Compassion: A reflection on the Christian life.* New York: Doubleday.

Morrison, I., Lloyd, D., diPellegrino, G., & Roberts, N.(2004). Vicarious responses to pain in anterior cingulate cortex: Is empathy a multisensory issue? *Cognitive, Affective, and Behavioral Neuroscience,4,* 270–278.

Morrison, I., Peelen, M. V., & Downing, P. E. (2007). The sight of others' pain modulates motor processing in human cingulate cortex. *Cerebral Cortex, 17,* 2214–2222.

Najjar, N., Davis, L., Beck-Coon, K., & Carney Doebbeling, C. (2009). Compassion fatigue: A review of the research to date and relevance to cancer-care providers. *Journal of Health and Psychology, 14,* 267–277.

Post, S. G. (2005). Altuism, happiness, and health: It's good to be good. *International Journal of Behavioral Medicine, 12,* 66–77.

Saarela, M. V., Hlushchuk, Y., Williams, A. C., Schurmann, M., Kalso, E., & Hari, R. (2007). The compassionate brain: Humans detect intensity of pain from another's face. *Cereb.Cortex, 17,* 230–237.

Sabo, B. M. (2006). Compassion fatigue and nursing work: Can we accurately capture the consequences of caring work? *International Journal of Nursing Practice, 12,* 136–142.

Salzberg, S. (2002). *Loving-kindness: The revolutionary art of happiness.* Boston, MA: Shambhala.

Schultz, W. (2000). Multiple reward signals in the brain. *Nature Reviews Neuroscience, 1,* 199–207.

Schulz, R., Hebert, R. S., Dew, M. A., Brown, S. L., Scheier, M. F., Beach, S. R.et al. (2007). Patient suffering and caregiver compassion: New opportunities for research, practice, and policy. *Gerontologist, 47,* 4–13.

Shanafelt, T., Bradley, K., Wipf, J., & Back, A. (2002). Burnout and self-reported patient care in an internal medicine residency program. *Annals of Internal Medicine, 136,* 358–367.

Shapiro, S. L., Astin, J. A., Bishop, S. R., & Cordova, M.(2005). Mindfulness-based stress reduction for health care professionals: Results from a randomized trial. *International Journal of Stress Management, 12,* 164–176.

Singer, T., Seymour, B., O'Doherty, J., Kaube, H., Dolan, R., & Frith, C. (2004). Empathy for pain involves the affective but not sensory components of pain. *Science, 303,* 1157–1162.

Singer, T., & Lamm, C. (2009). The social neuroscience of empathy. *The Year in Cognitive Neuroscience 2009: Annals of the New York Academy of Sciences, 1156,* 81–96.

Singer, T., & Leiberg, S. (2009). Sharing the emotions of others: The neural bases of empathy. In M.S. Gazzaniga (Ed.), *The cognitive neurosciences IV.* Cambridge, MA: The MIT Press.

Singer, T., Seymour, B., O'Doherty, J. P., Stephan, K. E., Dolan, R. J., & Frith, C. D. (2006). Empathic neural responses are modulated by the perceived fairness of others. *Nature*, *439*, 466–469.

Singer, T., Critchley, H. D., & Preuschoff, K. (2009). A common role of insula in feelings, empathy and uncertainty. *Trends in Cognitive Sciences, 13*, 334–340.

Singer, T., Snozzi, R., Bird, G., Petrovic, P., Silani, G., Heinrichs, M. et al. (2008). Effects of oxytocin and prosocial behavior on brain responses to direct and vicariously experienced pain. *Emotion, 8*, 781–791.

Smith, A. (1853). *The theory of moral sentiments.* London: Henry G. Bohn.

Thomas, R. B., & Wilson, J. (2004). Issues and controversies in the understanding and diagnosis of compassion fatigue, vicarious traumatization, and secondary traumatic stress disorder. *International Journal of Emergency Mental Health, 6*, 81–92.

Toneatto, T., & Nguyen, L. (2007). Does mindfulness meditation improve anxiety and mood symptoms? A review of the controlled research. *The Canadian Journal of Psychiatry/La Revue canadienne de psychiatrie, 52*, 260–266.

Vrticka, P., Andersson, F., Grandjean, D., Sander, D., & Vuilleumier, P. (2008). Individual attachment style modulates human amygdala and striatum activation during social appraisal. *PLoS ONE, 3*(8), *1–11*.

West, C. P., Huschka, M. M., Novotny, P. J., Sloan, J. A., Kolars, J. C., Habermann, T. M. et al. (2006). Association of perceived medical errors with resident distress and empathy: A prospective longitudinal study. *Journal of the American Medical Association, 269*, 1071–1078.

Wispé, L. (1986). The distinction between sympathy and empathy: To call forth a concept, a word is needed. *Journal of Personality and Social Psychology, 50*, 314–321.

Zeki, S. (2007). The neurobiology of love. *FEBS Letters, 581*, 2575–2579.

PART VI

SYNTHESIS OF VIEWS ON PATHOLOGICAL ALTRUISM

CHAPTER 29

HELL'S ANGELS

A Runaway Model of Pathological Altruism

Marc D. Hauser

KEY CONCEPTS

- Pathological altruism emerges as a by-product of a runaway process of selection for in-group favoritism and self-deception.
- In-group favoritism coupled with self-deception or denial of the other, leads to pathological commitment to one group's ideology, coupled with out-group antagonism that can lead to mass genocides.
- Self-sacrifice and martyrdom represent the ultimate forms of pathological altruism, at least from the perspective of the victims. From the perspective of the pathological altruist's group (e.g., religion), however, it is divine altruism, revered, and adaptive for the martyr's faith.
- When pathological altruism runs away, it can lead to mass genocides, as obstinate cooperators disregard the humanity—and human rights—of all who interfere with the ideological cause.

OUR PARENTS, AND generations before them, tried to teach us that everything is good in moderation, including sex, rock and roll, and even drugs such as alcohol and coffee. But there are at least two problems with this wisdom, and both derive from the concept of moderation: What is moderate for one is excessive for others, and once a taste of the moderate wets the appetite, it is hard to control the desire for more. A majority of the essays in this fascinating volume suggest that altruism may be similarly characterized. Altruism, in moderation, is good— smiled upon by angels. But in the absence of important control mechanisms (see Chapter 2, O'Connor et al.; Chapter 9, by Riby et al.; and Chapter 16, by Brannigan), it too can turn to excess, and create a living hell for the altruist, as well as for other members of society. Altruism is pathological when it is blind to the diversity of consequences.

Here, I would like to weave together several strands running through a number of chapters in this volume to suggest that the pathological side of altruism can, like many diseases of the mind and body, be traced to a set of capacities

> Altruism is pathological when it is blind to the diversity of consequences.

that were, in their origin, highly adaptive. The core idea is simply this: Pathological altruism emerges as a by-product of a runaway process of selection for in-group favoritism and self-deception. Thus, unlike some who wish to argue that the mere presence of a particular behavior implies that it must have a selective advantage, I suggest instead that many traits emerge as evolutionary by-products, of which the components may have been selected, but not the end product; I also suggest that even the end product can be selected for, following suggestions by Tobeña (Chapter 15), and Kanazawa (Chapter 25). Thus, pathological altruism, like many other diseases of the mind and body exposed by the logic of Darwinian medicine (Trevathan, 2007; Wiliams & Nesse, 1991), evolved from the degeneration of otherwise adaptive capacities.

The notion of a runaway process emerged from discussions of sexual selection, and in particular, Sir Ronald Fisher's (1930) insight that female choice can drive the expression of a male trait to excessive proportions. More specifically, Fisher noted that from the female's perspective — the typically choosy sex — it would be adaptive to show preferences for males—the competitive sex—that carry a trait that is favored by natural selection. As the preference for this trait increases in frequency, the attractiveness of the trait will increase or amplify the advantage of mate choice. What results, so Fisher argued, is a runaway process of coevolution between preference and trait that could cause an exaggeration of the trait beyond its naturally selected optimum. What can counteract this runaway process is low survival rates of males carrying such traits, causing a decrease in the benefits accrued to females.

As an example of a runaway process, consider the observation, consistently made in a wide variety of species, that females prefer males with bigger or longer appendages, whether they are tails or antlers (Andersson, 1994). In its origin, this preference picks out a trait that is linked to male–male competition—e.g., a male with slightly bigger antlers is slightly better at defending his territory, and thus, his resources. Once this is established, preference and trait are genetically coupled, causing both to coevolve over time leading to more and more females who prefer larger and larger antlers, or whatever trait they set their eyes or ears on. And once the runaway process is gallivanting along, survival selection may not be able to reverse the process. As such, runaway processes are potential agents of extinction. And it is here that a link to pathological altruism emerges: Once it is set in motion, it too can lead to extinctions in the form of massive genocides (see Chapter 15, by Tobeña and Chapter 16, by Brannigan).[1]

Before I turn to in-group favoritism and deception, a note about my understanding of pathological altruism. The authors of this volume interpret the concept in different ways, with some splitting it up into various forms (e.g., Widiger and Presnall's Chapter 6, Homant and Kennedy's Chapter 14, and Turvey's Chapter 13), often relying on either clinical distinctions or personality theory, whereas others step back to take a more encompassing singular definition (e.g., Oakley, Knafo, and McGrath's Chapter 1 and Perlin's Chapter 12). However, for most authors, (with interesting exceptions contained in Perlin's Chapter 12 and Traphagan's Chapter 21), what makes a person pathologically altruistic is that he or she deviates from some sense of a norm of altruism,[2] of what is common, typical, or expected. Thus, pathological altruism consists of apparently selfless acts that only concern the welfare of others, are often indiscriminate, and frequently both self- and other-injurious. But this definition quickly runs into problems. For one, if a pathological altruist's "stated aim or implied motivation" (see Oakley et al.'s Chapter 1) is to help others, whereas in fact their behavior injures either the self or other, then such actions are indistinguishable from the deceptive psychopath who states that he will help you, but in fact engages in an extortion scam (think Madoff). This would be a mistake, but also shows how critical it is to identify the underlying psychology.

A second point is that those definitions based on societal norms (see Li & Rodin's Chapter 11) are exceedingly difficult to assess because, as in all corners of morally relevant behavior, there are justifiable exceptions. For example, as Tobeña notes in Chapter 15, cases that are clearly excessive and concerned with the welfare of others, need not be pathological, as in the case of suicide bombers: Their self-sacrifice is for the benefit of the group, of the ideology and faith they follow. In the eyes of their group members, they are heroes, pathology-free; similar arguments appear in Bachner-Melman's Chapter 7, on eating disorders, and the link between starvation and gaining proximity to the divine, and Gandhi's Chapter 18 on sacrifice for a cause. And, from an evolutionary perspective, they represent a strategy that would pay off in terms of intergroup competition or what Bowles and colleagues have referred to as *parochial altruism* in the service of human warfare (Bowles, 2009; Choi & Bowles, 2007). Thus, what is pathological altruism from the standpoint of the victim is gloriously healthy altruism from the standpoint of the self-sacrificial martyr and his ideological tribe.

Although I acknowledge the merits of conceptual splitting, I will focus on the form of pathological altruism that results from excessive self-sacrifice to some other individual or group of individuals. Although this may limit the implications of what I have to say, I hope it minimally provides an illustration of how a runaway process can lead to detrimental consequences for humanity.

In-group Favoritism

Every social species, from the eusocial ants and bees to the social birds and mammals, shows intense affiliative behavior and investment toward some individuals, while engaging in violent behavior toward others. In species with parental care, such valenced interactions start with early rearing, selectively targeting kin over nonkin. Of course, there are exceptions, as when parasitic cuckoo species dump their eggs in a host's nest, duping the host into rearing a behemoth nestling from a different genera. From parental care to broader networks of kin-biased helping, and up to within-group solidarity in competition with other groups, we see extensive evidence of investment biases, of favoring one group of individuals, often at a cost to others that are either excluded, or worse, violently attacked. The point is straightforward: In-group biases are evolutionarily ancient, and the result of a long history of selection that paid off in terms of survival and reproductive success.

What makes humans different—dangerously so—are the novel ways in which we represent in-group favoritism and out-group antagonism, and the fact that in-group biases or prejudices are often implicit or unconscious (Banaji, 2001; Richerson & Boyd, 2005; Tafjel, 2004). These are psychological *accessories* that are magnets for pathological altruism. Unlike any other species, we symbolically mark members of the in-group, distinguishing them by means of appearance (e.g., clothing styles, hair cuts), associations with structures (e.g., churches, universities, corporate buildings), or expressed opinions (e.g., ideology, faith, academic arguments). But our symbolic labeling doesn't stop here. With the same swiftness that we provide identity badges for the members of our tribe, we also label those outside, often by means of representations that dehumanize.

> In-group biases are evolutionarily ancient, and the result of a long history of selection that paid off in terms of survival and reproductive success. What makes humans different—dangerously so—are the novel ways in which we represent in-group favoritism and out-group antagonism, and the fact that in-group biases or prejudices are often implicit or unconscious

Recent work by Haslam (2006) suggests that dehumanization takes two distinctive routes, with some evidence that this process is consistent across cultures (Haslam, Kashima, Loughnan, Shi, & Suitner, 2008). One route dehumanizes by means of enhancing the animal qualities, whereas the second takes away qualities of human nature by objectifying and mechanizing. The animalistic route often finds its way to organisms that are either dangerous (e.g., vipers) or dirty (e.g., vermin) and thus, in both cases, significant health hazards. The mechanistic route, in contrast, extracts core properties of human nature, such as agency, free will, and the rich social emotions, and in so doing, allows for the other to be used instrumentally (e.g., prostitutes) or to be owned as property (e.g., slaves).

Once individuals travel down these routes, both corrosive and inspiring emotions kick in, with disgust leading the charge on the animalistic side, whereas happiness and elation mediate the mechanistic side. Disgust, in its origin, evolved as a warning signal, alerting the individual to an impending health threat (Rozin, Haidt, & McCauley, 2000). The rational response to a health threat is to distance oneself from the threat, or better yet, destroy it. This original representation of disgust is rapidly transformed into a social, and more importantly, moral representation, as the threat is both deserving of the surgeon general's warning, as well as the judicial warning (Rozin, 1997). The target of disgust is both a health and moral hazard. Destroying it is not only appropriate, but obligatory for the well-being of the in-group.

The mechanistic route enables the dehumanizer to perceive the other as property, something that should not only be protected, but prized and valued. And with property comes a sense of reward, of self-worth, and value. And as with disgust, the original experience of happiness and elation are transformed into a judicial experience, including the psychology that underpins contract law and its jurisdiction over property.

This is a brief history of in-group favoritism. What it reveals is that, in its origins, it was a highly adaptive psychological process, leading to important fitness benefits, both by caring for kin, and by defending against lethal enemies. But as the history of mass genocides reveal, this capacity, especially when it is coupled with its partner in crime—self-deception or denial—can reach extremes, ultimately undermining basic human rights and leaving a trail of breathless bodies.

Self-deception

Like in-group favoritism, the capacity for deception is also evolutionarily ancient, present in viruses, bacteria, and of course, other animals. As Trivers (2001, 2010) has argued, deception is an adaptive psychological mechanism that, in cases such as self-deception, can run amuck, resulting in great tragedies.

Deception arises when some aspect of reality, either external or internal, is suppressed or manipulated—lies of omission and commission. Cases in the animal kingdom are plenty (Cheney & Seyfarth, 1990; Hauser, 1996; Trivers, 1985): insects mimicking sticks, plovers feigning injury, roosters falsely announcing food to seduce hens, and monkeys crying wolf. From an evolutionary perspective, deception is highly adaptive, as it enables individuals to gain an upper hand in competition. Truth in advertising doesn't pay in a world where defection pays more. Thus, in many situations, it will pay for individuals to appear tougher, sexier, or more caring than they are because if the foil works, they will gain more resources. More resources means better health, more babies, and a longer life— the currency of evolutionary fitness. Once deception has this adaptive edge, there is pressure for self-deception. Self-deception arises when unconscious processes have manipulated conscious processes to gain control over behavior. Thus, not only does it pay to deceive others, it pays to deceive oneself, to really believe that one is tougher, sexier, and more caring. But, as discussed by Turvey (Chapter 13), self-deception is a form of cognitive distortion that can become pathological if unchecked. And, from an evolutionary perspective, it is likely to go unchecked, or at least unnoticed, once it couples with in-group favoritism and rapidly runs away.

With this perspective on self-deception in place, we can now begin to explain how the pathological side of altruism might have evolved from an originally adaptive origin. One route would be through a costly signaling (Zahavi & Zahavi, 1997) or show-off perspective. On this view, demonstrations of extreme altruism would indicate that the altruist can bear the cost, at some level, and this might be seen as attractive, and in fact, an honest signal of fitness. As Boone (1998) has suggested, this perspective might well explain the evolution of magnanimity: Apparently wasteful displays of altruism or apparent generosity may be designed (in an evolutionary sense) to reveal the capacity to incur short-term costs for long-term gains as a high status individual. This approach has been used to account for a range of phenomena, including general aspects of cooperation, hunting among hunter-gatherer societies, language and animal communication, and religious displays (Bulbulia, 2004; Gintis, Smith, & Bowles, 2001; Smith, Bird, & Bird, 2003; Sosis, 2000). Once an advantage accrues to apparently extreme altruism, the psychological rewards may become addictive, and uncontrollable, leading to pathology. And here, self-deception would act as a spectacularly powerful facilitator, creating a positive illusion of grandiosity for the ego, and a diminution of all that is human for the other. Coming full circle, we are back to a dehumanizing process (Haslam, 2006).

> Self-deception is a form of cognitive distortion that can become pathological if unchecked. And, from an evolutionary perspective, it is likely to go unchecked, or at least unnoticed, once it couples with in-group favoritism and rapidly runs away.

Runaway Altruism

When the process of in-group favoritism couples with self-deception, a runaway process is triggered that inevitably leads to pathological altruism, including sports-based hooliganism, street gang violence, suicide bombings, and massive genocides. In each of these cases, individuals functionally lose their individual identities for the identity of their in-group, and in so doing, enter into a process of denial and moral amnesia that enables dehumanization of the other. These are dangerous liaisons. Once in play, they are difficult to break because each process rewards the other, while simultaneously fending off the capacity to engage in self-control (see Chapter 16, by Brannigan, on the relationship between inhibitory mechanisms and genocide).

Consider street gang violence. Street gangs have an identity, and often a charismatic leader with specific goals. Though explicit violence is not necessarily one of these, individuals in gangs are 20 times more likely than at-risk individuals of the same age to engage in drive-by-shootings, ten times more likely to commit homicide, eight times more likely to carry out a robbery, three times more likely to commit a public assault, more likely to carry a gun to school, and more likely to use a gun during an altercation (Huff, 1998; Wood & Alleyne, 2010). Such violence is often carried out in the name of the gang. It is pulled off by various forms of self-deception, including moral justification and dehumanization of the victim, as well as positive illusions that inflate the power of the gang while falsely minimizing other gangs and individuals.

It takes little to scale up from street gang violence to massive genocides. The underlying psychology is functionally the same. Individuals lose their connection with the complexities of reality, deny the importance of individuals in the out-group to serve an ideological or faith-based movement, work for the movement in a selfless manner, self-deceiving in the service of deception. And here, too, the Janus face of altruism surfaces, appearing heroic from the perspective of the in-group and horrific from the perspective of the dehumanized and victimized out-group. The atrocities that emerge in genocides, and the frequency with which they occur, suggest that if anything, it is a misnomer to think of such altruism as pathological, especially if pathology is conceived of as some deviation from a norm. The history of mass genocides is both too old and too rich to consider selfless altruism as deviance (Goldhagen, 2009).

> The only solution is to remain vigilant to the dangerous alliance between prejudice and self-deception, poised to take the legs out of the runaway process.

The historical record may, however, provide a way of refining how we think about pathological altruism, and in particular, the emphasis placed by some authors on its supposed indiscriminate nature. When we look at the sacrifices made by individuals and groups of individuals during recent terrorist activities, it is clear that they are anything but indiscriminate. Thus, as revealed by the analyses of Atran (2003), the modeling work of Bowles and colleagues (Bowles, 2009; Choi & Bowles, 2007), as well as the studies of Tobeña (Chapter 15), extremely costly altruism often emerges in the context of out-group antagonism or parochial altruism. And it is such acts that lead to war, including the genocidal cleansings that have resulted in Rwanda, Germany, and Yugoslavia, to name a small sample of recent atrocities. If this analysis is right, *pathology* may not be the correct diagnosis. In the same way that we are forced to reject philosophical and theological characterizations of evil as a rare stain on our species' clean slate (Kant, 1793/1998), replacing it with the view that it is common and part of our biological capacity, so too might we be forced to reclassify extreme cases of altruism as adaptive from the perspective of the in-group, though toxic from the perspective of the outgroup. The only solution is to remain vigilant to the dangerous alliance between prejudice and self-deception, poised to take the legs out of the runaway process.

Notes

1. Interestingly, Pacheco and Santos' (Chapter 23) game theoretic model predicts that pathological altruists can actually galvanize cooperation by annihilating the evolutionary advantage to defectors. My intuition here is that if this so-to-speak *messianic effect* is real, it will do so in the service of favoring the in-group and ultimately, obliterating other groups.

2. At times, the notion of norm is used in a somewhat analogous fashion to the evolutionary concept of a *norm of reaction* (Lewontin, 1983). For an interesting discussion of how the evolutionary perspective on norms can be applied to the psychological domain, and more importantly, the moral domain, see Gibbard (1990).

References

Andersson, M. (1994). *Sexual selection*. Princeton, NJ: Princeton University Press.

Atran, S. (2003). Genesis of suicide terrorism. *Science, 299*, 1534–1539.

Banaji, M. R. (2001). Implicit attitudes can be measured. In H. L. Roediger, J. S. Nairne, I. Neath, & A. Surprenant (Eds.), *The nature of remembering: Essays in honor of Robert G. Crowder*. Washington, DC: American Psychological Association.

Boone, J. L. (1998). The evolution of magnanimity: When is it better to give than to receive? *Human Nature, 9*(1), 1–21.

Bowles, S. (2009). Did warfare among ancestral hunter-gatherers affect the evolution of human social behaviors? *Science, 324*, 1293–1298.

Bulbulia, J. (2004). Religious costs as adaptations that signal altruistic intention. *Evolution and Cognition, 10*(1), 19–42.

Cheney, D. L., & Seyfarth, R. M. (1990). *How monkeys see the world*. Chicago: University of Chicago Press.

Choi, J. K., & Bowles, S. (2007). The coevolution of parochial altruism and war. *Science, 318*, 636–640.

Fisher, R. A. (1930). *The genetical theory of natural selection*. Oxford: Oxford University Press.

Gibbard, A. (1990). *Wise choices and apt feelings*. Cambridge: Harvard University Press.

Gintis, H., Smith, E. A., & Bowles, S. (2001). Costly signaling and cooperation. *Journal of Theoretical Biology, 213*, 103–119.

Goldhagen, D. (2009). *Worse than war*. New York: Public Affairs.

Haslam, N. (2006). Dehumanization: An integrative review. *Personality and Social Psychology Review, 10*(3), 252–264.

Haslam, N., Kashima, Y., Loughnan, S., Shi, J., & Suitner, C. (2008). Subhuman, inhuman, and superhuman: Contrasting humans with nonhumans in three cultures. *Social Cognition, 26*(2), 248–258.

Hauser, M. D. (1996). *The evolution of communication*. Cambridge, MA: MIT Press.

Huff, C. R. (1998). *Comparing the criminal behavior of youth gangs and at-risk youth*. . Washington, DC: US Department of Justice, Office of Justice Program, OJJDP.

Kant, I. (1998). *Religion within the boundaries of mere reason*. Cambridge, UK: Cambridge University Press. (Original work published 1793).

Lewontin, R. C. (1983). Gene, organism and environment. In D. S. Bendall (Ed.), *Evolution from molecules to men* (pp. 273–285). New York: Cambridge University Press.

Richerson, P. J., & Boyd, R. (2005). *Not by genes alone: How culture transformed human evolution*. Chicago: University of Chicago Press.

Rozin, P. (1997). Moralization. In A. Brandt, & P. Rozin (Eds.), *Morality and health*. (pp. 379–401). New York: Routledge.

Rozin, P., Haidt, J., & McCauley, C. R. (2000). Disgust. In M. Lewis, & J. M. Haviland-Jones (Eds.), *Handbook of emotions* (2nd ed., pp. 637–653). New York: Guilford Press.

Smith, E. A., Bird, R. B., & Bird, D. W. (2003). The benefits of costly signaling: Meriam turtle hunters. *Behavioral Ecology, 14*, 116–126.

Sosis, R. (2000). Costly signaling and torch fishing on Ifaluk atoll. *Evolution and Human Behavior, 21*, 223–244.

Tafjel. (2004). An integrative theory of intergroup conflict. In M. J. Hatch, & M. Schultz (Eds.), *Organizational identity* (pp. 56–65). Oxford: Oxford University Press.

Trevathan, W. R. (2007). Evolutionary medicine. *Annual Review of Anthropology, 36*, 139–154.

Trivers, R. (1985). *Social evolution*. Menlo Park: Cummins Publishing Co.

Trivers, R. (2001). Self-deception in service of deceit. In R. Trivers (Ed.), *Natural Selection and Social Theory: Selected papers* (pp. 255–293). New York: Oxford University Press.

Trivers, R. (2010). Deceit and self-deception. In P. M. Kappeler, & J. B. Silk (Eds.), *Mind the gap: Tracing the origins of human universals* (pp. 373–394). Berlin: Springer Verlag.

Wiliams, G. C., & Nesse, R. M. (1991). The dawn of Darwinian medicine. *The Quarterly Review of Biology, 66*(1), 1–22.

Wood, J., & Alleyne, E. (2010). Street gang theory and research: Where are we now and where do we go from here? *Aggression and Violent Behavior, 15*, 100–111.

Zahavi, A., & Zahavi, A. (1997). *The handicap principle*. New York: Oxford University Press.

CHAPTER 30

ALTRUISM GONE MAD

Joachim I. Krueger

Originally—so they decree—unegoistic actions were praised and called good from the perspective of those to whom they were rendered, hence for whom they were *useful*; later one *forgot* the origin of the praise and, simply because unegoistic actions were *as a matter of habit* always praised as good, one also felt them to be good—as if they were something good in themselves.
—Friedrich Nietzsche (1887/1998)

KEY CONCEPTS

- Personality-based approaches to pathological altruism are either typological or dimensional, with distinct implications for the question of how pathological altruism is propagated.
- In a mixed population of individuals with different social preferences, altruists do poorly. They may not see it that way, however, which makes their behavior pathological.
- In a Volunteer's Dilemma, altruists suffer when interacting with other altruists.
- When interpersonal dilemmas are nested within intergroup dilemmas, the meaning of altruism is contingent on perspective.
- Evolution has favored parochial morality (altruism), leaving us with the intractable problem of how to satisfy the local group and the general population at the same time.

A VOLUME ON pathological altruism is bound to provoke. By standard morality, altruism is one of the highest goods, both in intention and consequence, so how can it be pathological? The equation *altruism = good* runs deep in everyday imagination and in scholarly texts (Nietzsche dissenting). Altruists help others, and the standard assumption is that the benefit to others is greater than the cost to the self. This assumed inequality immediately raises the possibility of pathology. If I spend a dollar so that you can have a dime, my behavior is not just self-damaging, which is definitional of altruism, but the damage to me is out of proportion with the benefit to you. I may have miscalculated, which would only be a matter of cognitive error, but I also could have strange, perhaps pathological, motives.

395

The goal of this volume is to explore the conceptual, neuroscientific, and behavioral boundary conditions of (pathological) altruism. The collective conclusion is that altruism ought not to be thought of in simple "the more, the better" terms. My objective here is to contribute to this discussion by revisiting some of the conceptual and definitional issues from a social-psychological and game-theoretic point of view. I will argue that altruistic acts may turn out to be irrational, maladaptive, or destructive in a variety of circumstances that are not necessarily foreseeable or controllable. In other words, altruism may go mad, not only because of individual personality flaws but also because of irreducible complexities in the environment.

> Altruism ought not to be thought of in simple "the more, the better" terms.

Conceptual Issues

Most contributors to this volume assume that altruism exists. The counter position is that close inspection of the actor's motives or the behavior's long-term consequences will always reveal egoism (Chapter 24, by Kanazawa). According to this latter view, to which I am sympathetic, the perception of altruism is an illusion. Acceptance of this "altruism-as-illusion" perspective can reshape the framework of research. The question is no longer "Is this behavior egoistic?" Instead, it becomes "In what way is this behavior egoistic?" If there is no altruism, how can that which does not exist be pathological? But there is behavior, from time to time, that is more beneficial to the other than to the self. For convenience, and perhaps illogically, I will refer to this type of behavior as pathological altruism.

Many mammalian species, and humans in particular, are highly interdependent. Individual organisms need one another to survive and thrive. Mechanisms of inclusive fitness and reciprocal altruism ensure that individuals do not behave selfishly in the narrow sense (Hamilton, 1964). Parents care for their young, and recipients of favors tend to reciprocate (Trivers, 1971). Both these mechanisms are selective in the choice of the *alter*. Offspring will likely transmit one's genes, whereas exchanges with reciprocators are mutually beneficial. Neither of these mechanisms requires "pure" altruism. I never understood why this state of affairs should be deemed unsatisfactory. If benefitting relatives and reciprocators rewards both parties, the overall well-being is greater than it would be if only one party (alter) benefitted, while the other suffered (ego).

> The search for altruism that is pure in the sense of being uncontaminated by egoism is, in my view, an outgrowth of moralistic or muddled thinking.

The search for altruism that is pure in the sense of being uncontaminated by egoism is, in my view, an outgrowth of moralistic or muddled thinking. It is moralistic because it assumes that pure altruism is superior to impure or "blended" altruism. Would we really feel better about the human race if it could be shown that some individuals are truly altruistic? The search for saints should be left to religion, not science. If we found these true altruists, what would it say about us? Everyone else would probably feel worse. More shame, more guilt. If we accept that true altruism does not exist, no one needs to worry about invidious comparisons with saints.[1]

> Without proper reflection of costs, benefits, and probabilities, empathy opens the door to pathology.

The search for true altruism signals muddled thinking because it sets motives to benefit the self and motives to benefit the other into competition. The goal then is to find a beneficent act that cannot be attributed to egoism; in other words, the goal is to protect the motive to benefit the other from being discounted. The decades-long debate (with data) between Batson (e.g., Batson, Sager, Garst, Kang, Rubchinsky, & Dawson, 1997) and Cialdini (e.g., Maner, Luce, Neuberg, Cialdini, Brown, Sagarin, & Rice, 2002) suggests that there is always room for a credible egoism hypothesis. A proponent of the egoism hypothesis can always fall back on the claim that the motive to benefit another is a personal preference, and that personal preferences are by definition self-regarding.

The claim that *any* behavior is egoistic by definition smells like a conversation stopper, but it does not have to be. The trouble with preferences is their elasticity. A body of work on self-regulation examines intertemporal choices. The basic idea is that humans sometimes choose passionately that which they know they will regret later. In the same way that it is difficult to decline the immediate consumption of a cookie for the pleasure of having two cookies tomorrow, it is difficult to ignore one's empathic-distress response and not help reflexively. Yet, in many circumstances, emotion-based decisions to help are far less efficient than decisions based on a careful weighing of actions and consequences (Loewenstein & Small, 2007). Like Schopenhauer, many authors trace altruistic behavior to the capacity for empathy (e.g., Homant and Kennedy, in Chapter 14; McGrath and Oakley, in Chapter 4). Empathy is important in that it stimulates a person's desire to help, but it is a poor guide to figuring out how much to help and how to distribute help across needy recipients. Without cool utilitarian reflection, empathy opens the door to pathology.[2] I hasten to point out that I use the term "pathology" in a strictly consequentialist manner; that is, with sole reference to the outcomes of behavior. This conceptualization can conflict with a clinical definition of pathology. In a provocative study, Koenigs and colleagues (2007) found that patients with damage to the ventromedial prefrontal cortex made better utilitarian judgments than normal controls. They were more likely to save many lives over a single, empathy-arousing one.

> If it is irrational to yield to social influence at the expense of self-interest, the bulk of the classic social psychological compliance research amounts to a project on pathological altruism.

If failures to self-regulate can make people choose that which they do not prefer (one cookie now rather than two cookies later), so can social influence guide people away from acting in their self-interest. In a classic experiment, Regan (1971) showed how clever deployment of the norm of reciprocity can get people to return more than they received. The key is to present a small, unsolicited favor or gift, and then to ask for a larger favor in return. Compliant individuals act irrationally because the norm of reciprocity does not demand submission to escalating requests. Normatively, the burden is on the first mover to elicit reciprocity that matches the original investment.

In his wide-ranging research program on compliance, Cialdini (2001) showed how people can be subtly manipulated to do desirable things (donate blood, give to charity, pick up litter) that, if left to their own devices, they would not do. By definition, compliant people act to gratify the wishes of others, not their own. If executed well, compliance techniques obscure the violation of self-interest.

The target of social influence may experience a temporary or even lasting change of preference. If it is irrational to yield to social influence at the expense of self-interest, the bulk of the classic social psychological compliance research amounts to a project on pathological altruism.

There is, however, a *cui bono* question in some instances. In Milgram's (1974) studies of obedience, for example, most participants were influenced to go against their personal preferences (i.e., not to shock another person), but their actions were simultaneously altruistic (benefiting the experimenter and Milgram's career) and destructive (presumably harming the confederate). The presence of multiple targets of behavior is a common feature of the real world that is often neglected in scientific work. By focusing on cases involving one actor (ego) and one target (alter), the typical research design overlooks the possibility that a single behavior can be both altruistic with respect to one person, and—for lack of a better word—competitive with respect to another. Consider, for example, the common human aversion to inequity. An employer (parent) granting privileges to some employees (children) but not others can be seen as both altruistic and unfair.

Let us pursue the sensitivity to inequity a bit further. If A sees B treating C unfairly, A may punish B. In a typical experiment, the cost to A is smaller than the harm to B, yet, A's behavior is often labeled "altruistic punishment." The reasoning is that A perceives her action as educational, and the data show that third-party punishment works (Fehr & Fischbacher, 2004). The qualifier "altruistic" may be infelicitous. First, the short-term consequences are negative for both A and B, whereas the long-term consequences are only probabilistically positive. Second, A's motivational state is ambiguous. Besides altruistic motives ("I spank you for your own good!"), self-righteous motives might be at work (Chapter 5, by Brin). Person A may wish to uphold social norms or seek vengeance, even on behalf of others.[3] Indeed, some people punish cooperators, apparently for the sheer pleasure of it (Herrmann, Thöni, & Gächter, 2008). I suspect the label "altruistic punishment" was chosen because its incongruity was guaranteed to draw attention.

The punishment of defectors (or cooperators) in economic game situations is difficult to conceptualize as altruism (pathological or otherwise) because egoistic motives continue to matter. The social-psychological approach addresses this problem by isolating cases in which people's behavior conflicts with their stated self-interest. On this view, pathological altruism is a form of irrationality. The pathology deepens inasmuch as irrational behavior is repetitive (Chapter 3, by Vilardaga and Hayes). Consider from a psychophysical point of view how people can become trapped into a pattern of altruistic behavior that they do not desire. Coombs and Avrunin (1977) proposed that "good things satiate, whereas bad things escalate." Altruistic acts yield diminishing returns to the other, whereas the aversiveness of the costs to the self accelerates. At the point at which the benefits to the other outstrip the costs to the self, the person should no longer help. This cross-over point may be easily missed, however, because it is harder to estimate (and easier to overestimate) from an outside than from an inside perspective.

I am focusing on these social-psychological perspectives because the bulk of this volume is dedicated to the personality approach. Although this latter approach is important, one should bear in mind that the range of pathologically altruistic behaviors is likely to be much greater than the proportion of individuals who can be classified as pathological altruists. The personality approach to pathological altruism comes in two forms: typological and dimensional. The typological approach is more prominent in the chapters of this volume. This view asserts there are some people who are pathological altruists in their essence, and they can be categorically distinguished from everyone else. The perspective underlying the typological approach is epidemiological. You either have the disease or you don't, and the primary goal of research is to optimize classification.

Like some contributors to this volume, I suspect there are limitations to the typological approach (Baron-Cohen, in Chapter 27; Perlin, in Chapter 12). Many human behaviors can occur in excess somewhere, under the right circumstances. The constraints of the adapted mind all but guarantee it. Hence, the dimensional approach has some promise because a variety of pertinent measures of individual differences exist with known distributions of scores.

According to the dimensional approach, there is continuous variation in the strength of particular personality characteristics over individuals. This approach offers an interesting perspective on the vexing question of why (pathological) altruists have not died out. Consider a distribution of individuals along a continuum running from extreme egoism to extreme altruism, and suppose that individuals with scores in the tails of the distribution are less reproductively fit than individuals with scores near the center. In each generation, the tails of the distribution are cut off; yet, the distribution has the same shape in the next generation. The logic is simple. Each individual's manifest score can be thought of as the sum of a true score and error. The distribution of true scores has a smaller variance than the distribution of the manifest scores. What is cut off in each generation is error. If distributions were not truncated, they would become wider in each generation, which evidently is not the case.[4]

Social Dilemmas

In traditional experimental work, the role of the agent of social influence (e.g., the person seeking to induce compliance) and the role of the target of influence are neatly separated. In contrast, game theory emphasizes the interdependence among (potentially) rational actors. In a social dilemma, "two or more individuals have choices to make, preferences regarding the outcomes, and some knowledge of the choices available to each other and of each other's preferences. The outcome depends on the choices that both of them make, or all of them if there are more than two" (Schelling, 1984, p. 214). Consider the Prisoner's Dilemma. Each person chooses between cooperation and defection, which results in four possible outcomes, conventionally labeled T (unilateral defection or Temptation), R (mutual cooperation or Reward), P (mutual defection or Penalty), and S (unilateral cooperation or Sucker). The payoffs associated with these events decrease in this order.

In a Prisoner's Dilemma, cooperation is not unambiguously altruistic. A person can cooperate with the expectation that the other cooperates too. If choice of one's own strategy is correlated with expectation, cooperation is simultaneously egoistic and altruistic (Krueger & Acevedo, 2005). Besides inclusive fitness bias and reciprocity, such "evidential decision making" is the third possible way in which a social good can be realized without pure altruism. In contrast, a person who cooperates while expecting that others will not is being (pathologically) altruistic. Observers view such a person as highly moral, although not very smart (Krueger & DiDonato, 2010).

Types of Player and Psychological Value Transformations

In a social dilemma, the objective payoff ranking is T > R > P > S. One way of unpacking the ambiguities of cooperation is to examine the subjective meaning people ascribe to the payoffs. A person whose subjective ranking corresponds to the objective one may be called an individualist. Individualists defect unless they believe their own behavior is diagnostic of the behavior of others. Otherwise, whatever the other person does, defection yields a better deal (T > R and P > S). Social preference theories suggest that not everyone is an individualist (van Lange, de Cremer, van Dijk, & van Vugt, 2007). Transformation of the objective payoffs into subjective ones comes in three major forms. Whereas individualists' overriding motive is to maximize their own payoffs, prosocials want to maximize joint payoffs. They most prefer mutual cooperation, with the chain of inequalities being R > T > P > S. They cooperate if the other person cooperates, otherwise they defect (assuming they know the other person's choice). Competitors want to minimize the other person's payoff (T > P > R > S). Finally and crucially, altruists want to maximize the other person's payoff (S > R > P > T), and hence they cooperate.

What happens when the four types mix? To what extent do they get what they want, and how are their returns affected by changes in the mix of types in a group where everyone interacts with everyone else? For a quantitative demonstration, assume that the values assigned to the four possible outcomes are interval-scaled from 1 to 4, where 4 represents the most valued outcome.

Consider a group comprising an individualist, I, a prosocial person, P, a competitor, C, and an altruist, A. Table 30.1 shows each person's subjective payoff for each pairing as well as the sum of each person's payoffs. The altruist is happy ($M = 3.67$) to be suckered by the individualist and the competitor, and achieves the second highest payoff through mutual cooperation with the prosocial. The competitor is less happy ($M = 3.33$). This person suckers the altruist, but has to settle for the second best outcome of mutual defection with the other two players. The individualist and the prosocial are least happy ($M = 2.67$) because they attach little value to mutual defection, which they each encounter twice. Note that, in this analysis, I assume that players do not make second-order inferences—as for example, the competitor defecting against the altruist knowing this is what the altruist wants.[5]

If subjective happiness is a proxy for fitness, altruists should multiply faster than the other types. But there is a catch. If we add nine altruists to the group, as shown in Table 30.2, the average altruist does worse than types I and C and is tied with type P (3.17). Only when players of type I or C are added to the group, the individual altruist thrives, or is tied in first place with the person of type P type. In other words, *the altruist's success is self-limiting.* The whole group does

TABLE 30.1   SUBJECTIVE PAYOFFS FOR THE PLAYERS LISTED IN THE ROWS IN A GROUP OF FOUR TYPES OF SOCIAL PREFERENCE

Ten of type	I	P	C	A	M (individual efficiency)
Individualist (I)	—	2	2	4	2.67
Prosocial (P)	2	—	2	4	2.67
Competitor (C)	3	3	—	4	3.33
Altruist (A)	4	3	4	—	3.67

TABLE 30.2   SUBJECTIVE PAYOFFS IN A GROUP OF FOUR TYPES OF SOCIAL PREFERENCE

Ten of type	I	P	C	A	*M* (individual efficiency)
Each person of type					
I	2.17	2.17	2.33	3.67	2.59
P	2.17	3.67	1.25	3.67	2.69
C	3.08	3.83	2.33	3.83	3.27
A	3.92	3.17	3.92	3.17	3.55
M (group efficiency)	2.37	3.53	3.00	3.29	

better when altruists are added (see column means in Table 30.2), but the individual altruist does worse. Altruists need others to exploit them, which works best if there are many other types and few altruists.

I believe there is reason to doubt that subjective happiness is a critical predictor of reproductive success. The transformation of objective payoffs into personal preferences could be a psychological event with little impact on actual fitness.[6] For this reason, I reconsider the actual payoffs of the game. As shown in Table 30.3, all

TABLE 30.3   OBJECTIVE PAYOFFS IN A GROUP OF FOUR TYPES OF SOCIAL PREFERENCE

	I	P	C	A	*M*
Individualist (I)	—	2	2	4	2.67
Prosocial (P)	2	—	2	3	2.33
Competitor (C)	2	2	—	4	2.67
Altruist (A)	1	3	1	—	1.67

nonaltruist types outgun the altruist by a wide margin. Table 30.4 shows that when nine players of each type are added to the group, one type at a time, the altruist systematically suffers (row means). Only when prosocials come in does A do better than I and C because P defects against those. Although it is clear that the group does best overall (column means) when altruists predominate, the question is *how* they can dominate if the selection pressures work against them.

TABLE 30.4   OBJECTIVE PAYOFFS IN A GROUP OF FOUR TYPES OF SOCIAL PREFERENCE

Ten of type	I	P	C	A	*M* (individual efficiency)
Each person of type					
I	2.17	2.17	2.17	3.67	2.55
P	2.08	2.83	2.08	2.83	2.46
C	2.17	2.17	2.17	3.67	2.55
A	1.17	2.67	1.17	2.67	1.92
M (group efficiency)	2.08	2.78	2.08	2.83	

Nested Games, the Volunteer's Dilemma, and the Meaning of Altruism

We think we know an altruistic act when we see one. But do we? Following Malthus, Garrett Hardin (1968) regarded unfettered breeding as the greatest threat to human welfare. A person who puts more children on the planet is like the farmer who puts more cattle on the commons, thereby contributing to its destruction. To breed is the real-life equivalent of game theory's defection—the result is disaster. As Hardin (1998) put it, "The psychic gains of parenthood are offset by economic losses channeled through the whole population" (p. 682). Meanwhile, some countries (e.g., Germany, Japan) have birth rates well below the replacement rate (United Nations, 2006). These same countries have generous systems of social welfare. A person who does not have to rely on her own children to support her in old age can rationally forego offspring and vacation from Arizona to Zimbabwe. Now, *not* to breed is to defect.

In an intergroup situation, breeding can simultaneously be an act of cooperation and an act of defection (Krueger, 2007). Groups sometimes compete, not by killing members of the other group, but by adding members to their own ranks. Here, breeding is a cooperative (altruistic) act with respect to the in-group, but a selfish act with respect to the out-group. The logic of war is the same. The individual chooses between enlisting and defecting (literally). Within the group, the "Universal Soldier"[7] is an altruist, or so they tell him. "Killing for me my friend, and me for you," as Donovan put it in his classic song. Relative to the other group, the enlister is an aggressor.

Altruism tends to be parochial; that is, a person's choice is construed as cooperative or competitive depending on how it affects other members of the in-group (Bernhard, Fischbacher, & Fehr, 2006; Brannigan (pp. 225–236); Tobeña (pp. 207–224). From the bird's eye view, however, defection from local in-groups is the highest form of altruism. Humanity as a whole might benefit the most if individuals made no sacrifices for their local groups. When interpersonal dilemmas are seen in the context of intergroup relations, it becomes possible to explain the latter with reference to the former (Bowles, 2009). Note that this model is parsimonious in that it does not require any assumptions about how individuals interact with individual members of outgroups (see Choi & Bowles, 2007, or Hammond & Axelrod, 2006, for examples of less parsimonious models including both intra- and intergroup behavior). Likewise, it is not necessary to assume that a group acts as a unit to defect against another group.

The result of this analysis is that behavior intended to be cooperative or altruistic within the context of the in-group can become destructive in a larger intergroup context. Social categorization into in-groups and out-groups is nothing but a crude way of representing social distance. Members of in-groups are closer to us and more similar to us than are members of out-groups. When, in a more fine-grained approach, social distance is scaled on a continuum, it becomes evident that generosity (altruism) increases sharply when the other person is very close to the self (Jones & Rachlin, 2006).

Being kind to kin has all the advantages of boosting inclusive fitness. Yet, certain types of social dilemma can induce irrational and self-defeating behavior that fits the definition of pathological altruism. Here, distant individuals or out-group members need not even be part of the behavior's context. Consider the

Volunteer's Dilemma (Diekmann, 1985). A and B have a choice between volunteering and defecting. If both select the same strategy, they both suffer. Only if one volunteers is the defector spared. For a perfectly selfish person, the best strategy is to always defect, hoping that the other will volunteer. The most efficient strategy is to volunteer with $p = 0.5$ because it entails a 50% chance that one person will be spared and a 25% chance that it will be you. Now what happens when the social distance between A and B varies? Preliminary results show that willingness to volunteer goes up as distance declines (Krueger & Ullrich, unpublished). The hitch is that at very small distances, such as between siblings or best friends, some people volunteer with $p > 0.5$, which means they court the disaster of mutual altruism. What is more, some do this while at the same time predicting that the other person will volunteer with $p > 0.5$. In other words, two altruists accept disaster for both with eyes wide open. Isn't that pathological?

From the perspective of social dilemmas, strategic behavior cannot be understood without knowing the person's expectations of other people's actions. A robust finding is that people project their own choices onto others (Krueger, 2007). As we have seen, egocentric predictions are beneficial in the Prisoner's Dilemma and all other games in which mutual cooperation is the most efficient outcome. It follows that pathological altruism—that is, cooperation coupled with the expectation of defection—is rare in such dilemmas. In contrast, social projection can drive a person crazy in the Volunteer's Dilemma, because here rationality demands that we choose the opposite of what we think others choose. It follows that pathological altruism, or choosing to volunteer while expecting that others will also volunteer, is common in this dilemma.

Conclusion

If altruism has been a problem from a theoretical point of view, so too is pathological altruism. I have tried to supplement the many fascinating ideas and findings presented in this volume by carrying the flag for social psychology. Traditionally, social psychology has had a great interest in understanding conflicting human action tendencies, although the conventional formula has been a bit simplistic (*altruism = good, aggression = bad*). From a game-theoretic perspective (Nietzsche and most authors in this volume assenting), I have suggested that it is time to revise this formula. My hope is that the study of altruism will remain interdisciplinary and that social psychology will play a vital part.

Admittedly, I feel a little undercut in my effort to serve my field because the fifth edition of the *Handbook of Social Psychology* (Fiske, Gilbert, & Lindzey, 2010) no longer has a chapter on altruism. The word "altruism" is mentioned on only seven pages out of 1,500, three of which are in a chapter on social justice. The words "prosocial behavior" appear on eight pages, scattered over chapters on gender, evolutionary psychology, and morality. The word "helping" does not appear at all.

Why do research and write papers, when others don't? Let it be remembered that science is a "gift economy" that does not reward individual contributions.[8] The work has an element of altruism, and one hopes that it is not a pathological one.

Notes

1. If it is difficult to separate the pure altruists from the blended ones, it must be all the more difficult to distinguish pathological from nonpathological kinds within the former group.

2. Empathy with members of out-groups can *reduce* goodwill in an intergroup situation (Vorauer & Sasaki, 2009). I will return to the parochialness of altruism below.

3. I recognize that my own prior argument on discounting puts limits on the force of this criticism. Perhaps the label "altruistic" is justified even if altruism is only one of several motives at play.

4. Arguing from a typological view, Pacheco and Santos prove mathematically that altruists survive in a mixed population if their resistance to extinction is written into the code. They define altruists as individuals who "do not let themselves be influenced by anyone—they are *obstinate* . . . . Although they do not imitate anyone, their altruistic behavior can be imitated by others" (p. 303, this volume). Tautologically then, "successful behaviors will be imitated and spread in the population" (p. 302, this volume).

5. Which brings to mind the old joke of the masochist who says to the sadist "Hurt me" and the sadist says "No!" The point here, to which I will return shortly, is that objective outcomes are more important than subjective ones.

6. Let my friends in the positive psychology movement demur.

7. Find the music at http://www.youtube.com/watch?v=PT6NRc37T_8

8. I fearlessly quote from Wikipedia, itself a brilliant example of gift-economic efficiency: "Scientists produce research papers and give them away through journals and conferences. Other scientists freely refer to such papers. All scientists can therefore benefit from the increased pool of knowledge." Retrieved March 30, 2010 from [http://en.wikipedia.org/wiki/Gift_economy.

References

Batson, C. D., Sager, K., Garst, E., Kang, M., Rubchinsky, K., & Dawson, K. (1997). Is empathy-induced helping due to self-other merging? *Journal of Personality and Social Psychology, 73,* 495–509.

Bernhard, H., Fischbacher, U., & Fehr, E. (2006). Parochial altruism in humans. *Nature, 442,* 912–915.

Bowles, S. (2009). Did warfare among ancestral hunter-gatherers affect the evolution of human social behaviors? *Science, 324,* 1293–1298.

Choi, J. -K., & Bowles, S. (2007). The coevolution of parochial altruism and war. *Science, 318,* 636–640.

Cialdini, R. B. (2001). *Influence: Science and practice* (4th ed.). Boston, MA: Allyn and Bacon.

Coombs, C. H., & Avrunin, G. S. (1977). Single-peaked functions and the theory of preference. *Psychological Review, 84,* 216–230.

Diekmann, A. (1985). Volunteer's dilemma. *Journal of Conflict Resolution, 29,* 605–610.

Fehr, E., & Fischbacher, U. (2004). Third-party punishment and social norms. *Evolution and Human Behavior, 25,* 63–87.

Fiske, S. T., Gilbert, D. T., & Lindzey, G. (Eds., 2010). *Handbook of social psychology* (5th ed.). New York, NY: Wiley.

Hamilton, W. D. (1964). The genetical evolution of social behavior. *Journal of Theoretical Biology, 7,* 1–52.

Hammond, R. A., & Axelrod, R. (2006). The evolution of ethnocentrism. *Journal of Conflict Resolution, 50,* 926–936.

Hardin, G. (1968). The tragedy of the commons. *Science, 162*, 1243–1248.

Hardin, G. (1998). Extensions of "The tragedy of the commons." *Science, 280*, 682–684.

Herrmann, B., Thöni, C., & Gächter, S. (2008). Antisocial punishment across societies. *Science, 319*, 1362–1367.

Jones, B., & Rachlin, H. (2006). Social discounting. *Psychological Science, 17*, 283–286.

Koenigs, M., Young, L., Adolphs, R., Tranel, D., Cushman, F., Hauser, M., & Damasio, A. (2007). Damage to the prefrontal cortex increases utilitarian moral judgements. *Nature, 447*, 908–911.

Krueger, J. I. (2007). From social projection to social behaviour. *European Review of Social Psychology, 18*, 1–35.

Krueger, J. I., & Acevedo, M. (2005). Social projection and the psychology of choice. In M. D. Alicke, D. Dunning, & J. I. Krueger (Eds.), *The self in social perception* (pp. 17–41). New York, NY: Psychology Press.

Krueger, J. I., & DiDonato, T. E. (2010). Person perception in (non)interdependent games. *Acta Psychologica, 134*, 85–93.

Krueger, J. I., & Ullrich, J. (unpublished). *Volunteers' dilemma and social distance*. Working paper, Brown University.

Loewenstein, G., & Small, D. A. (2007). The scarecrow and the tin man: The vicissitudes of human sympathy and caring. *Review of General Psychology, 11*, 112–126.

Maner, J. K., Luce, C. L., Neuberg, S. L., Cialdini, R. B., Sagarin, B. J., & Rice, W. E. (2002). The effects of perspective taking on motivations for helping: Still no evidence for altruism. *Personality and Social Psychology Bulletin, 28*, 1601–1610.

Milgram, S. (1974). *Obedience to authority*. Princeton, NJ: Princeton University Press.

Nietzsche, F. (1998). *On the genealogy of morality: A polemic* (M. Clark, & A. J. Swenson, Trans.). Cambridge, MA: Hackett. (Original work published in 1887).

Regan, D. T. (1971). Effects of a favor and liking on compliance. *Journal of Experimental Social Psychology, 7*, 627–639.

Schelling, T. (1984). *Choice and consequence*. Cambridge, MA: Harvard University Press.

Trivers, R. L. (1971). The evolution of reciprocal altruism. *The Quarterly Review of Biology, 46*, 35–57.

United Nations, Department of Economic and Social Affairs. (2006). *Social indicators: Indicators of childbearing*. Washington, DC: Author. Retrieved from http://unstats.un.org/unsd/demographic/products/socind/childbr.htm

Van Lange, P. A. M., de Cremer, D., van Dijk, E., & van Vugt, M. (2007). Self-interest and beyond: Basic principles of social interaction. In A. W. Kruglanski, & E. T. Higgins (Eds.), *Social psychology: Handbook of basic principles* (2nd ed., pp. 540–561). New York, NY: Guilford.

Vorauer, J. D., & Sasaki, S. J. (2009). Helpful only in the abstract? Ironic effects of empathy in intergroup interaction. *Psychological Science, 20*, 191–197.

CHAPTER 31

PATHOLOGY, EVOLUTION, AND ALTRUISM

David Sloan Wilson

KEY CONCEPTS

- The concept of a pathological adaptation might seem like a contradiction of terms, but traits that count as adaptive in the evolutionary sense can be harmful to others and even to oneself over the long term.
- When altruism is defined in terms of behavioral consequences, it is inherently vulnerable to exploitation by selfishness and evolves only when altruists manage to confine their interactions with each other. Even when altruism evolves because it is more successful than selfishness, on average, some altruists still encounter selfish individuals and are harmed by their own behavior.
- Social environments are pathological when they are structured to make altruists vulnerable to exploitation. Much can be done to create social environments that favor altruism as a successful behavioral strategy.
- Altruism at one level of a multitiered hierarchy (e.g., within groups) can be used for selfish purposes at higher levels (e.g., between-group conflict). The costs and benefits of altruism are repeated at all levels.
- When altruism is defined in psychological terms, it can be regarded as a proximate mechanism for motivating altruistic behavior. Just as there are many ways to skin a cat, there are many proximate mechanisms for motivating altruistic behavior that can be expected to vary among individuals and cultures.
- The analysis of pathological altruism in this volume should be extended to other traits associated with morality and group-level functional organization.

A PATHOLOGY, BY definition, is something that we would rather be without. Evolution adapts organisms to their environments, which seems desirable. The idea that adaptations might count as pathological therefore seems like a contradiction of terms. Yet, *pathological adaptations* are an expected outcome of evolution.

Before applying the concept of pathological adaptations to the subject of altruism, consider the case of risky adolescent behaviors. Teens are especially prone to high-risk behaviors such as unprotected sex, substance abuse, and violence. The dominant paradigm for explaining these behaviors can be termed the mental health model; it assumes development takes place optimally in nurturing social environments and is compromised in harsh social environments, resulting in these pathological behaviors.

Evolutionary theory suggests another possibility (e.g., Ellis, Figueredo, Brumbach, & Schlomer, 2009; Nettle 2010). Humans have experienced the full range of social environments, from nurturing to harsh, since before they were humans. When the going gets tough, the tough don't fall apart—they behave in ways that are adaptive in harsh environments. This means adopting strategies that ensure immediate survival and reproduction,

> **PATHOLOGICAL ADAPTATION**
>
> A trait that is favored by natural selection but harms others or even the individual over the long run.

whatever the cost to others or even oneself over the long term. Adaptations to harsh environments go beyond conscious decision-making and include developmental switches that take place early in life—even before birth, as in metabolic strategies triggered by nutritional stress (Gluckman & Hanson, 2004).

Recognizing the adaptive nature of risky adolescent behaviors does not provide justification. Such behaviors still count as pathological as far as societal and long-term individual welfare are concerned. We still have every reason to do without them, but recognizing their evolutionary basis leads to solutions that were not forthcoming when they were regarded as pathological in all respects.

Behavioral Altruism

Now that we have clarified the concept of pathological adaptations, we can apply it to the concept of pathological altruism. Altruism can be defined in terms of behavioral consequences or psychological motives. Both need to be understood from an evolutionary perspective, as outlined in parts I and II of Sober and Wilson (1998). At the behavioral level, altruism is inherently vulnerable to selfish-

> When judged in terms of societal benefits, altruism is generally good and selfishness is generally pathological. Does this mean that we should counsel everyone to be altruistic? Not necessarily.

ness. The only way for altruists to survive in a Darwinian world is by interacting with other altruists and avoiding interacting with selfish individuals. Conversely, selfish individuals only succeed by gaining access to the social benefits produced by others. When selfish individuals interact with each other, they lose. It follows that the fate of altruistic and selfish social strategies in a Darwinian world depends entirely on how individuals employing the strategies are grouped. All evolutionary theories of social behavior reflect these considerations, regardless of what they are called (e.g., multilevel selection theory, inclusive fitness theory, or game theory; Wilson & Wilson, 2007).

The costs and benefits associated with altruism and selfishness can result in a number of pathologies that are reflected in the chapters of this volume. When judged in terms of societal benefits, altruism is generally good and selfishness is generally pathological. Does this mean that we should counsel everyone to be altruistic? Not necessarily. Consider a social environment in which everyone is behaving selfishly. Advising someone to behave altruistically in this situation would be harmful for that person and would not increase the frequency of altruism in the population. Getting people to behave altruistically remains an important objective, but we must be smarter about how we go about doing it.

In real human social interactions, people employing highly prosocial strategies are remarkably good at finding each other. In one ingenious study (Sheldon et al. 1999), college freshmen filled out a prosociality scale when they first arrived on campus. Four months later, they filled out the same scale and were provided copies to give to three associates of their choice. These groups—each consisting of a focal individual and their three associates—then played a game with both cooperative and selfish options. Within each group, individuals differed in their prosociality score, and the lowest scorers were indeed more likely to employ the selfish option in the game. However, the more prosocial focal individuals had managed to find associates during the first 4 months of college who are were also more prosocial. The segregation of high- and low-prosocials into different groups was only partial but compensated for the disadvantage of prosociality within groups.

In our study of human prosociality at a city-wide scale, we measured a very high correlation between the prosociality of the individual and the prosociality of their social partners—even higher than the correlation expected among full siblings in the classic kin selection model (Wilson, O'Brien, & Sesma, 2009). Those who gave also received, at least on average, but it is the nature of statistical correlations that there will always be exceptions to the rule—individuals who are highly prone to give but not fortunate enough to find like-minded social partners (Wilson & Csikszentmihalyi, 2007).

It is interesting to reflect upon what counts as pathological in this situation and what can be done about it. Imagine a person who is highly prone to be altruistic. Statistically, she is likely to become associated with other altruists and all will be well, but instead she's unlucky and becomes associated with selfish individuals who exploit her. Is her altruism pathological, and what should she do about it? A person in this situation has only four options:

1. Change partners and find more altruistic associates
2. Attempt to make her current associates more altruistic
3. Defensively turn off her altruism to protect herself
4. Remain altruistic and continue to be exploited

Option 4 might count as pathological, but option 3 is at best a short-term solution. The best options are 1 and 2, which do not change the behavior of the altruist but rather create the social environment that enables altruism to succeed as a social strategy.

> Engineering a social environment to favor altruism is possible—if that environment is cleverly designed with checks and balances.

Conversely, imagine an individual who is highly prone to be selfish and is typically avoided by altruists, but who gets lucky and manages to sink her hooks into one. She is thriving, especially compared to her victim. It is thanks to this situation that selfishness persists in the population; otherwise, it would never be advantageous and would go extinct. Nevertheless, we wouldn't counsel the selfish individual to keep it up; moreover, it seems strange to call the *altruist* pathological for being victimized.

What's pathological in both of these situations, as least from the societal perspective, is a social environment that rewards selfishness and punishes altruism as a behavioral strategy. The solution is to engineer the social environment to favor altruism as the most successful evolutionary strategy. This is less utopian than it might seem. Elinor Ostrom won the 2009 Nobel Prize in economics for showing that people are capable of avoiding the tragedy of the commons, but only if certain conditions are met (Ostrom 1990, 2005). Briefly, these conditions are well-defined groups, mechanisms to ensure those who benefit are also those who contribute, consensus decision-making, the ability to monitor transgressions, graduated sanctions to punish transgressions, and swift conflict resolution mechanisms. A burgeoning literature in experimental economics shows that altruism can succeed or fail in the laboratory by adding or removing these conditions, and that most people readily adopt altruistic strategies when the conditions are present, thus providing a practical set of guidelines for structuring our social environments to favor altruistic social strategies.

Even when altruists are as good as gold toward each other within groups, their altruism can be the source of violence and other forms of exploitation against other groups. Between-group conflict pervades both the animal and human world. It is inescapable as an empirical fact and makes perfect sense from an evolutionary perspective. Such violence is indeed pathological when judged in terms of the welfare of all groups, but it is often adaptive for the offending groups. This provides yet another example of pathological adaptation.

Multilevel selection theory shows that the costs and benefits of altruism and selfishness are repeated at every level of a multitiered hierarchy of groups (Wilson & Wilson, 2007). Groups committed to prosocial relations with other groups can succeed to the extent that they interact with like-minded groups. Rogue groups can be punished and excluded from prosocial interactions, and so on. Establishing the conditions identified by Ostrom might be more difficult at higher levels of a multitiered hierarchy, but it is encouraging to know that it is theoretically possible and to have a clear set of guidelines for what to do.

Psychological Altruism

To understand psychological in relation to behavioral definitions of altruism, it is helpful to recall the proximate–ultimate distinction in evolutionary theory. Every evolving trait requires two explanations; why it exists compared to many other traits that could exist (ultimate causation), and physical mechanisms that cause the trait to be expressed in actual organisms (proximate causation). Just as there are many ways to skin a cat, there are often many different proximate mechanisms that can cause a given trait to be expressed. The proximate explanation need not resemble the ultimate explanation in any way whatsoever, other than to cause the trait to be reliably expressed. These considerations are Evolution 101 for a biologist, but they can be novel when applied to human-related subjects.

When a behavior that counts as altruistic in behavioral terms is expressed by any given individual, it is caused by a proximate mechanism of one sort or another. It might be empathy, a sense of duty, the promise of a heavenly afterlife, the desire to enhance one's reputation, or many other possibilities. Philosophers and psychologists like to debate which of these count as altruistic or selfish, but there is a sense in which it doesn't matter. I don't care whether you pay your bills with checks or a credit card, so why should I care whether you're nice to me because of a sense of empathy or a sense of duty? As long as two proximate mechanisms reliably cause the same behavior, it's wrong-headed (from an evolutionary perspective) to make an important distinction between them. The proximate–ultimate distinction cautions us against placing much stock in psychological definitions of altruism and selfishness.

> Our analysis of beliefs and practices should be guided by a single overriding consideration: *What do they cause people to do*?

As one remarkable example, an edited volume titled *Altruism in World Religions* (Neusner & Green, 2005) begins with an essay by William Scott Green, an esteemed religious scholar, who claims that when altruism is defined so that self-sacrifice is a necessary component, it is foreign to the religious imagination. Religions inspire their believers to behave altruistically in behavioral terms, but they never think of it that way. After all, the very word "altruism" didn't exist until it was coined by Auguste Compte in the 19th century, making it a secular concept. Green challenged the other religious scholars contributing to the volume to put his claim to the test—they ended up agreeing with him. It would be hard to imagine a better example of proximate mechanisms that don't resemble the behaviors they produce.

Insofar as cultural evolution is an ongoing and open-ended process, we should find tremendous diversity in the beliefs and practices that cause people to behave altruistically and selfishly, defined in behavioral terms. Our analysis of these beliefs and practices should be guided by a single overriding consideration: *What do they cause people to do*? All other considerations, such as whether a belief is rational, is supported by factual evidence, or is conceptualized as altruistic or selfish makes sense only insofar as they are related to the primary consideration (Wilson, 2009). That is business as usual for an evolutionist, and it needs to guide the study of human altruism and selfishness. Since cultural evolution can result in outcomes that count as pathological, no less than genetic evolution, we should expect beliefs and practices framed in terms of altruism to lead to pathological outcomes some of the time. It is gratifying to see this kind of "evolutionary social constructivism" (Wilson, 2005) featured in this volume, along with more strictly biological themes that are equally important, such as genetically based differences in behavior.

So far, I have explored how altruism, defined in terms of both behavioral consequences and psychological mechanisms, can have pathological manifestations. I end by stressing the need to go beyond altruism. There is more to morality and groups functioning as adaptive units than the beliefs and practices that we associate with altruism (Joyce, 2006; Sober & Wilson, 1998). These, too, can have pathological manifestations and can benefit from the treatment provided for altruism in this volume.

References

Ellis, B. J., Figueredo, A. J., Brumbach, B. H., & Schlomer, G. L. (2009). Fundamental dimensions of environmental risk: The impact of harsh versus unpredictable environments on the evolution and development of life history strategies. *Human Nature, 20*, 204–268.

Gluckman, P., & Hanson, M. (2004). *The Fetal Matrix: Evolution, development, and disease.* Cambridge, UK: Cambridge University Press.

Joyce, R. (2006). *The evolution of morality*. Cambridge, MA: MIT Press.

Nettle, D. (2010). Dying young and living fast: Variation in life history across English neighborhoods. *Behavioural Ecology, 21*, 387–395.

Neusner, J., & Green, W. C. (2005). *Altruism in world religions*. Washington, DC: Georgetown University Press.

Ostrom, E. (1990). *Governing the commons: The Evolution of institutions for collective Action*. Cambridge, UK: Cambridge University Press.

Ostrom, E. (2005). *Understanding institutional diversity*. Princeton: Princeton University Press.

Sheldon, K. M., Sheldon, M. S., & Osbaldiston, R. (2000). Prosocial values, assortation, and group-selection in an N-person prisoner's dilemma. *Human Nature, 11*, 387–404.

Sober, E., & Wilson, D. S. (1998). *Unto Others: The evolution and psychology of unselfish behavior*. Cambridge, MA: Harvard University Press.

Wilson, D. S. (2005). Evolutionary social constructivism. In J. Gottshcall, & D. S. Wilson (Eds.), *The literary animal: Evolution and the nature of narrative* Vol. 2005 (pp. 20–37). Evanston, IL: Northwestern University Press.

Wilson, D. S. (2009). Rational and irrational beliefs from and evolutionary perspective. In D. David, S. J. Lynn, & A. Ellis (Eds.), *Rational and irrational beliefs* (in press). Oxford: Oxford University Press.

Wilson, D. S., & Csikszentmihalyi, M. (2007). Health and the ecology of altruism. In S. G. Post (Ed.), *The science of altruism and health* (pp. 314–331). Oxford: Oxford University Press.

Wilson, D. S., O'Brien, D. T., & Sesma, A. (2009). Human prosociality from an evolutionary perspective: Variation and correlations on a city-wide scale. *Evolution and Human Behavior, 30*, 190–200.

Wilson, D. S., & Wilson, E. O. (2007). Rethinking the theoretical foundation of sociobiology. *Quarterly Review of Biology, 82*, 327–348.

ABOUT THE EDITORS

Barbara Oakley is an associate professor of engineering at Oakland University in Michigan. Her work focuses on the complex relationship between neurocircuitry and social behavior. Among her varied experiences, she has worked for several years as a Russian translator on Soviet trawlers in the Bering Sea during the height of the Cold War; she met her husband while working as a radio operator at the South Pole station in Antarctica; and she has gone from private to regular Army Captain in the U.S. military. Oakley is a recent vice president of the IEEE Engineering in Medicine and Biology Society, the world's largest bioengineering society, as well as a fellow of the American Institute of Medical and Biological Engineering. Her books include *Cold-Blooded Kindness* (Prometheus Books, 2011), *Career Development in Bioengineering and Biotechnology* (coedited, Springer, 2008), *Evil Genes: Why Rome Fell, Hitler Rose, Enron Failed, and My Sister Stole My Mother's Boyfriend* (Prometheus Books, 2007), and *Hair of the Dog: Tales from Aboard a Russian Trawler* (WSU Press, 1996).

Ariel Knafo is an associate professor at the Psychology Department, The Hebrew University of Jerusalem. He is interested in all potential influences on individual differences in social behavior and values, ranging from genetics to culture, and may have been the only person belonging to the International Association for Cross-cultural Psychology and to the Behavior Genetics Association at the same time.

Eager to get exposed to a full range of human experience, he has trained in departments of psychology (The Hebrew University), education (Ben Gurion University), and Psychiatry (Institute of Psychiatry, London). His current research deals with the genetic and environmental contributions to empathy and altruism and how children's genetics affect their own behavior and the way parents react to them. In 2007, he received an Early Career Scientific Achievement Award from the Society for Research in Child Development . But he sees his three children as his greatest achievement, and tries to avoid seeing them through the eyes of a developmental psychologist.

Guruprasad Madhavan is a program officer in policy and global affairs at the National Academy of Sciences, National Academy of Engineering, Institute of Medicine, and the National Research Council—collectively known as the National Academies—in Washington, D.C. Madhavan received his doctorate in biomedical engineering and, among other awards and honors, was selected as one of the *New Faces of Engineering* of 2009 in *USA Today*. He is an elected member to the administrative council of the International Federation for Medical and Biological Engineering, and is a co-editor of *Career Development in Bioengineering and Biotechnology* (Springer, 2008). He enjoys searching for black swans.

David Sloan Wilson is a Distinguished Professor of Biology and Anthropology at Binghamton University, State University of New York. He applies evolutionary theory to all aspects of humanity. He is best known for championing the theory of multilevel selection, which has implications ranging from origin of life to the nature of religion. He is author of nearly 200 scientific articles published in biology, anthropology, psychology, and philosophy journals. His books include *The Natural Selection of Populations and Communities* (1980), *Unto Others: The Evolution and Psychology of Unselfish Behavior* (with Elliott Sober; Harvard, 1998), *Darwin's Cathedral: Evolution, Religion, and the Nature of Society* (Chicago, 2002), and *The Literary Animal: Evolution and the Nature of Narrative* (co-edited with Jonathan Gottschall; Northwestern, 2005), *Evolution for Everyone: How Darwin's Theory Can Change the Way We Think About Our Lives* (Bantam, 2007), and *The Neighborhood Project: An Evolutionist Contemplates Changing the World—One City at a Time* (Little, Brown, 2011).

ABOUT THE CONTRIBUTORS

Francisco J. Ayala is University Professor and Donald Bren Professor of Biological Sciences and Professor of Philosophy at the University of California, Irvine. Dr. Ayala is a member of the National Academy of Sciences (NAS), a recipient of the 2001 National Medal of Science, and served as Chair of the Authoring Committee of *Science, Evolution, and Creationism*, jointly published in 2008 by the NAS and the Institute of Medicine. Dr. Ayala has received numerous awards, including the 2010 Templeton Prize for exceptional contribution to affirming life's spiritual dimension, and honorary degrees from universities in nine countries. He has been President and Chairman of the Board of the American Association for the Advancement of Science and President of Sigma Xi—the Scientific Research Society of the United States. Dr. Ayala has written numerous books and articles about the intersection of science and religion, including *Darwin's Gift to Science and Religion* (Joseph Henry Press, 2007) and *Am I a Monkey?* (Johns Hopkins University Press, 2010). He teaches classes in evolution, genetics, and the philosophy of biology.

Rachel Bachner-Melman is a clinical psychologist specializing in the treatment and research of eating disorders. She coordinates the eating disorders unit in the Adult Psychiatric Ward at Hadassah University Medical Center in Jerusalem, Israel, and lectures in psychology at the Rothberg International School of the Hebrew University of Jerusalem. Her doctoral thesis was on the genetics of anorexia nervosa, and she has published over 40 articles and book chapters, mostly on eating disorders. Originally from Australia, she has lived in Israel for 25 years. She has a love for modern languages, and in addition to psychology degrees from the Hebrew University, has degrees in linguistics and Germanic languages from Australian National University, in translation from Geneva University (French, German) and Bar Ilan University (Hebrew), and in education and French from the Hebrew University. Her other loves include music, theater, dance, and, above all, her four terrific children. (Photo Courtesy: Dr. Nimrod Friedman)

Simon Baron-Cohen is professor of developmental psychopathology at the University of Cambridge and fellow at Trinity College, Cambridge. He is director of the Autism Research Centre in Cambridge. He holds degrees in human sciences from New College, Oxford, a Ph.D. in Psychology from University College London, and an M.Phil in clinical psychology at the Institute of Psychiatry. He held lectureships in both of these departments in London before moving to Cambridge in 1994.

He is author of *Mindblindness* (MIT Press, 1995), *The Essential Difference* (Penguin UK/Basic Books, 2003), and *Prenatal Testosterone in Mind* (MIT Press, 2005). He has edited a number of scholarly anthologies, including *Understanding Other Minds* (OUP, 1993, 2001), *The Maladapted Mind* (Erlbaum, 1997), and *Synaesthesia* (Blackwells, 1997). He has also written books for parents and teachers, such as *Autism and Asperger Syndrome: The Facts* (OUP, 2008), and *Teaching Children with Autism to Mind Read* (Wiley, 1998). He is author of the DVD-ROM *Mind Reading: An Interactive Guide to Emotions* (Jessica Kingsley Ltd, 2003) and *The Transporters* (www.thetransporters.com, 2007), an animation for preschool children with autism to help them learn emotion recognition. Both of these were nominated for BAFTA awards.

He has been awarded prizes from the American Psychological Association, the British Association for the Advancement of Science (BA), and the British Psychological Society (BPS) for his research into autism. For 2007, he was president of the Psychology Section of the BA, vice president of the National Autistic Society, and received the 2006 Presidents' Award for Distinguished Contributions to Psychological Knowledge from the BPS. For 2009, he is vice president of the International Society for Autism Research (INSAR). He is patron of several autism and disability charities (Autism Anglia, Red2Blue, Autism Yorkshire, and Speaking Up). He is a fellow of the BPS, the British Academy, and the Association for Psychological Science, and co-editor in chief of the new journal *Molecular Autism*. For 2010, he is chair of the NICE Guideline Development Group for adults with autism spectrum conditions. His current research is testing the "extreme male brain" theory of autism at the neural, endocrine, and genetic levels.

Bernard Berofsky went into the study of philosophy in order to solve the free will problem. He is frustrated that it has so far resisted his best efforts, but has high hopes for his new book *Nature's Challenge to Free Will* (Oxford University Press, forthcoming). Prior to that, he published *Liberation From Self*, *Freedom from Necessity*, various anthologies, and numerous articles in major philosophical journals. He is currently professor emeritus in philosophy at Columbia University and an executive editor at the *Journal of Philosophy*. The solution to this vexing philosophical problem would have come upon him sooner had he not decided to turn to sports car driving and racing as a response to his midlife crisis and to magic, because he finds it is easier to do the impossible than most things that are possible. (He performs stage magic under the name Sebastian.)

Jack W. Berry is assistant professor in the Department of Psychology at Samford University in Birmingham, Alabama, and codirector of the Emotion, Personality, and Altruism Research Group (EPARG) at the Wright Institute, Berkeley. He holds a Ph.D. in psychology from the Wright Institute and held a postdoctoral research fellowship at the UAB Injury Control Research Center, Department of Immunology-Rheumatology, University of Alabama at Birmingham. From 1997 to 2004, he was director of research of the Marriage Assessment, Treatment, and Enrichment Center in the Department of Psychology at Virginia Commonwealth University.

Dr. Berry's academic specialty areas include personality and individual differences, psychometrics, research methodology, and statistical analysis. Much of his research has focused on prosocial personality traits such as guilt, empathy, forgiveness, moral identity, and altruistic personality dispositions. He has also conducted research on the influence of personality configurations in risk of traumatic injury and in adjustment following injury. An active research consultant, he has provided statistical and measurement consultation to researchers in a wide range of scientific disciplines and has collaborated on many randomized clinical trials of cognitive-behavioral interventions in rehabilitation psychology. He is currently on the editorial board as a statistical consultant for the journal *Rehabilitation Psychology*.

Katherine D. Blizinsky is a PhD candidate in the Northwestern University Interdepartmental Neuroscience Program and a 2009 recipient of the Neuroscience Early Years Training Grant. Katherine completed her undergraduate work at Smith College and University of Washington. Her work has appeared in journals such as *Proceedings of the National Academy of Sciences* and *Molecular Psychiatry*. Her research interests lie at the intersection between stress, genetics, and mental health. When not in the lab, Katherine enjoys dancing, swimming, and making people laugh with reckless abandon.

Augustine Brannigan is professor of sociology at the University of Calgary. His first book, *The Social Basis of Scientific Discoveries* (CUP, 1981), was a landmark contribution to science studies. His more recent book, *The Rise and Fall of Social Psychology* (de Gruyter, 2004), provided a critical evaluation of the misuse of the experimental method in the classical American social psychology. Professor Brannigan's work on prostitution and pornography led to his contribution as an expert witness in several criminal trials. He has also written extensively on crime causation. Most recently, he undertook extensive fieldwork in Rwanda to study the 1994 genocide, and he is currently completing a new book on genocide. Outside of his academic career, he is an active alpinist in the Banff area. As an intrepid student of scuba diving, he has logged over 350 hours of bottom time in recreational diving throughout the Caribbean and the South Pacific.

David Brin has a triple career as scientist, public speaker, and author. His 1998 nonfiction book—*The Transparent Society: Will Technology Force Us to Choose Between Freedom and Privacy?*—won the Freedom of Speech Award of the American Library Association.

Some of Brin's novels have been *New York Times* bestsellers that have been translated into 20 languages, and have won multiple Hugo, Nebula, and other awards. His 1989 ecological thriller, *Earth*, foreshadowed global warming and other dangers, as well as near-future trends like the World Wide Web. A 1997 movie directed by Kevin Costner was loosely based on Brin's novel *The Postman*.

Although he explores many fields, heedless of credentials, Brin does have degrees from Caltech and the University of California, San Diego (Ph.D. in physics, working with Nobelist Hannes Alfven); he was also a fellow at the California Space Institute and the Jet Propulsion Lab. Brin now lives in San Diego County with his wife, three children, and a hundred very demanding trees.

Vicki Bruce is professor and head of the School of Psychology at Newcastle University, having previously held chairs at the universities of Nottingham, Stirling, and Edinburgh. She has researched the field of face perception and recognition since she began her doctoral studies in Cambridge in 1974, supervised by Alan Baddeley. She has watched with interest as her field has blossomed over the past 35 years, with social cognition now one of the hottest topics in contemporary cognitive neuroscience. Vicki has contributed over 150 publications to the field, including books, chapters, and journal articles not only about faces, but also about a wider range of topics in visual perception and cognition. Outside work, she enjoys walking up hills (rather slowly), playing bridge (rather badly), and eating (rather a lot).

Robert A. Burton graduated from Yale University and the University of California at San Francisco medical school, where he also completed his neurology residency. At age 33, he was appointed chief of the Division of Neurology at Mt. Zion-UCSF Hospital, where he subsequently became associate chief of the Department of Neurosciences. In addition to his professional writing, he has written three critically acclaimed novels and his recent *On Being Certain: Believing That You Are Right Even When You're Not.* He also throws stones at popular culture in his neuroscience and culture column at Salon.com—*Mind Reader.* His next book will be an investigation of what philosophy and neuroscience can and cannot tell us about ourselves. His working title is "A Skeptic's Guide To The Mind." He lives in the San Francisco Bay Area.

Bobby K. Cheon is a doctoral student of social psychology at Northwestern University. He received his B.A. in cognitive science from the University of Virginia.

His research interests involve exploring the role of culture on the psychological and neural processes that underlie intergroup perception and bias. He has received support from scientific agencies in Korea, Singapore, and the United States on research projects examining the interplay of neurobiological and cultural processes on racial prejudice and intergroup empathy. His work has appeared in journals such as *Nature Neuroscience* and *Behavioral and Brain Sciences.*

In his spare time, Bobby enjoys the company of friends and family, and finding personal and scientific inspiration through travel.

Joan Y. Chiao is an assistant professor of psychology at Northwestern University, and is an affiliated faculty member of the Neuroscience Institute, the Cognitive Science Program, and Asian-American Studies Program. Professor Chiao received her doctoral degree in psychology from Harvard University in 2006, and a B.S. in symbolic systems from Stanford University in 2000. Her research interests include cultural neuroscience of emotion and social interaction, social and affective neuroscience across development, social dominance and affiliation, and integrating psychology and neuroscience research with public policy and population health issues. She recently edited a Progress in Brain Research volume on *Cultural Neuroscience: Cultural Influences on Brain Function* (Elsevier Press, 2009) and is an editor for the journals *Social Cognitive and Affective Neuroscience, Frontiers in Human Neuroscience,* and *Social Neuroscience.* When not psychologizing, Professor Chiao enjoys cooking and traveling the world with her family and friends.

Arun Gandhi was born in 1934, in Durban, South Africa. He spent 1956 to 1987 in India, working as a journalist and promoting socioeconomic programs for the poor and the oppressed classes. With his wife Sunanda, he rescued about 123 abandoned newborn babies from the streets and placed them in loving homes around the world. They also began a Center for Social Change, which transformed the lives of millions in villages in the western Indian state of Maharashtra.

In 1987, Sunanda and Arun came to the United States; in 1991, they started the M. K. Gandhi Institute for Nonviolence at the Christian Brothers University in Memphis Tennessee. In 2007, the Institute was moved to the University of Rochester, New York, and in 2008, Arun resigned the Institute to change focus and start the Gandhi Worldwide Education Institute. This new institute's mission is to build Gandhian schools for the very poor and exploited children of the world. Arun's thoughts follow those of Sophocles, who once said: One word frees us from all the weight and pain of life. That word is *love*.

Marc D. Hauser's research sits at the interface between evolutionary biology and cognitive neuroscience and is aimed at understanding how the minds of human and nonhuman animals evolved. By studying nonhuman animals (monkeys, apes, dogs) in both the wild and in captivity, as well as human infants, adults, and clinical populations (e.g., psychopaths), Hauser's work has unlocked some of the mysteries of language evolution, conceptual representation, social cooperation, and morality. He is the author of more than 200 papers and five books, including *The Evolution of Communication* (1996, MIT), *Wild Minds* (2000, Holt), and *Moral Minds: How Nature Designed Our Universal Sense of Right and Wrong* (Harper Collins/Ecco). He is currently working on a book called *Evilicious: Why We Evolved a Taste for Being Bad* (Viking/Penguin) that his daughter believes will sell because it sounds like "bootylicious."

Steven C. Hayes is Nevada Foundation Professor at the Department of Psychology at the University of Nevada. An author of 32 books and more than 430 scientific articles, his popular book *Get Out of Your Mind and Into Your Life* was featured in *Time Magazine* among several other major media outlets, and for a wonderful week outsold *Harry Potter*.

Steve has four children, ages 40, 21, 18, and 4. If he survives this, he will have had minor children in the home for 55 years before the youngest goes to college. His favorite music is trance, techno, and chill—he is the oldest raver in the place when trance DJs come to town.

Robert J. Homant received a doctorate in social and clinical psychology from Michigan State University in 1972. After an eight-year career as a prison psychologist, he became a professor of criminal justice at the University of Detroit (now UD Mercy). He actualizes any sensation-seeking needs with the Detroit Men's Senior Baseball League, which accordingly named the bottom division of its oldest age bracket after him. While he may occasionally get thrown out taking a chance on the bases, he is in no danger of being accused of risky altruism.

Ali Jawaid graduated with a medical degree from Aga Khan University, Pakistan, in 2007. While in medical school, he proposed a multipronged model for the management of children with attention deficit hyperactivity disorder, with a focus on behavioral and social interventions. Subsequently, he completed a post-doctoral fellowship in Neurodegenerative Diseases at Baylor College of Medicine, Houston. He is currently an MD/PhD student at Institute of Neuropathology, Zurich. At the age of 26, he has over 35 scientific peer-reviewed articles to his credit. His other academic interest is mentoring medical and college students on research methodology and ethics. Outside of work, Ali has another passion—exploring the world as much as he can.

Satoshi Kanazawa is Reader in Management in the London School of Economics and Political Science, and Honorary Research Fellow in the Department of Psychology at Birkbeck College University of London. He has written over 80 scientific articles and chapters in psychology, sociology, political science, economics, anthropology, criminology, biology, and medicine. He shares his observations in his popular blog *The Scientific Fundamentalist* at the Psychology Today website (http://www.psychologytoday.com/blog/the-scientific-fundamentalist). He is the author of *Why Beautiful People Have More Daughters* (Penguin, 2007) and *The Intelligence Paradox: Why Intelligent People Do Unnatural Things* (Wiley, 2012). His credo in science is, "If the truth offends people, it's our job as scientists to offend them."

Daniel B. Kennedy is a forensic criminologist who received his doctorate from Wayne State University in 1971 while serving as a probation officer in Detroit. His exposure to crime victims during those years led him to develop one of the first college courses in victimology, which he taught at the University of Detroit Mercy for over 20 years. Dr. Kennedy's current efforts involve participation in litigation on behalf of crime victims around the country.

Olga Klimecki is a doctoral student with Prof. Tania Singer at the Department of Social Neuroscience at the Max Planck Institute for Human Cognitive and Brain Sciences in Leipzig, Germany. She studied psychology at the University of Mainz, Germany, for three years and then completed her Master of Neuroscience at University College London in 2007 before starting her PhD thesis with Tania Singer at the Laboratory for Social and Neural Systems Research at the University of Zurich, Switzerland. She is currently working on the neural substrates of emotional plasticity. More specifically, she is examining in how far compassion and empathic distress can be differentiated as well as how training in loving kindness and compassion can influence empathic and prosocial behavior (as assessed with behavioral measures) and empathy-related brain activity (as measured by functional magnetic resonance imaging, fMRI).

Joachim I. Krueger received his initial training in psychology in his hometown at the University of Bielefeld, Germany. His very first course was a laboratory on prosocial behavior, taught by Susan Streufert. At the University of Oregon, in beautiful Eugene, he received his Ph.D. and first taste of the *Journal of Personality and Social Psychology* in 1988. Mick Rothbart, Robyn Dawes, and Lew Goldberg shaped his thinking about social categorization, rationality, and personality, respectively. Over the last few years, Krueger has argued that research participants are not as stupid as portrayed in *JPSP*, whereas research workers are not as smart as they'd like to think. He believes that the entire pattern of under- and overestimation of self can be modeled by a simple regression equation. When not thinking deep thoughts, Krueger enjoys blogging for *Psychology Today*. Krueger could not have finished his chapter for this book without the nonpathologically selfless help from his friends Mika MacInnis and Judith Schrier.

Thomas B. Lewis is an assistant clinical professor of psychiatry at the University of California, San Francisco, School of Medicine (UCSF), and professor at the Fromm Institute at the University of San Francisco (USF). Dr. Lewis received his M.D. from UCSF, where he also trained as an intern and a resident in psychiatry. Dr. Lewis was a fellow in the Affective Disorders Program at UCSF for 3 years, and also served as the associate director of the Affective Disorders Program. Knowledgeable in psychopharmacology and psychobiology, Dr. Lewis has written and lectured extensively on a broad range of topics for audiences ranging from the American Association for the Advancement of Science to Google University. Dr. Lewis is also one of the authors of *A General Theory of Love* (Random House, 2000), a nonfiction book for the general public that elucidates the psychobiology of emotion and human relationships. Dr. Lewis' main area of professional interest is the intersection between neuroscience and human experience, in phenomena such as love, empathy, morality, and the law.

Madeline Li is an assistant professor in the Department of Psychiatry at the University of Toronto and a clinician-scientist in the Department of Psychosocial Oncology and Palliative Care and Division of Behavioral Sciences and Health Research at the Princess Margaret Hospital, University Health Network. She is a cancer psychiatrist who conducts research in the areas of psychoneuroimmunology and genetics as contributors to behavioral and psychiatric disorders in cancer patients. She divides her time between her patients, her research, her husband, children, and dog, and her love of marathon running, all the while struggling to contain her own pathological altruism in the process.

Vani A. Mathur is a graduate student in the Northwestern Psychology Program. She received her B.S. in human physiology from Boston University in 2005. She is most interested in pain processing and perception, and clinically and publicly relevant applications of pain research. Her work has appeared in journals such as *Annals of the New York Academy of Sciences*. Other than the human brain, Vani's loves include the ballet, BBQ, and her friends and family.

Michael McGrath is a board certified forensic psychiatrist, licensed in the State of New York. He is a clinical associate professor in the Department of Psychiatry, University of Rochester School of Medicine and Dentistry, Rochester, New York, and Medical Director & Chair, Department of Behavioral Health, Unity Health System, Rochester, New York. He also serves as medical director to a chemical dependency program and was a supervising physician for a sex offender program. Dr. McGrath obtained an undergraduate degree in sociology and worked as a police office for the Penn Central Railroad before returning to school and eventually traveling to Israel to study medicine.

Dr. McGrath divides his time among administrative, clinical, research, and teaching activities. His areas of expertise include forensic psychiatry and criminal profiling, as well as sex offenders and addictive disorders. He has lectured on three continents and is a founding member and past president of the Academy of Behavioral Profiling. Dr. McGrath has authored or coauthored ten articles in peer-reviewed journals and ten chapters in textbooks on subjects ranging from the diagnosis of bipolar disorder to sexual asphyxia to criminal profiling.

Jane N. Nathanson has been providing social work and rehabilitation services to individuals, families, and groups in need of guidance and support as related to crisis intervention, disability, and elder care management, and personal and career development since 1975. In 1987, she extended her private practice to offer counseling and consulting for pet owners, veterinary clinic staff, and humane services providers with regard to the dynamics of the human–animal relationship and the challenges of confronting critical illness, end-of-life caregiving, and death. In 1999, she became a member of the Hoarding of Animals Research Consortium and proceeded to design, implement and develop The Animal Hoarding Human Services Project for the Massachusetts Society for the Prevention of Cruelty to Animals. In addition to providing these services of crisis intervention, case management and coordination of community resources, Ms. Nathanson additionally receives referrals from the Animal Rescue League of Boston, out-of-state animal protection organizations, and self-referrals of animal hoarders and their family members.

Lynn E. O'Connor is professor at the Wright Institute, Berkeley, California, and director of the Emotion, Personality, and Altruism Research Group (EPARG, URL: http.www.eparg.org). Holding a Ph.D. in clinical psychology from the Wright Institute, she works as an educator, researcher, clinician, and consultant. With a specialty in chemical dependency, Dr. O'Connor worked as a researcher at the Haight Ashbury Free Medical Detoxification and Aftercare Project, and evaluator at Walden House Adolescent Program, a residential treatment program for addiction. From 1998 to 2004, Dr. O'Connor served as director of evaluation at the Wright Institute, and cofacilitated a psychotherapy research seminar, with Joseph Weiss, founder of an integrative biopsychosocial theory of psychotherapy.

Since 1990, Dr. O'Connor and Dr. Jack Berry, codirector of EPARG, have been collaborating on studies of altruism, empathy-based guilt, positive motivation, personality, and psychological problems from an evolutionary and cross-cultural perspective. Funded by private foundations and housed at the Wright Institute, EPARG includes psychologists and professionals from other institutions and disciplines. In recent years, Drs. O'Connor and Berry were joined by psychopharmacologist Dr. Thomas Lewis, collaborating on a study of psychopathology, personality, temperament, and neurotransmitter circuits. Since 2008, Professor O'Connor has also been studying Tibetan Buddhism as a method counteracting pathogenic guilt, and the role of pathogenic guilt in posttraumatic stress disorder (PTSD). Presently, students working with Dr. O'Connor are investigating the connection between empathy-based guilt and green behavior, the role of empathy-based guilt in forgiveness, the effects of stigma on mental illnesses, and the use of Internet-based social media in today's military. In addition to conducting research and teaching, Dr. O'Connor maintains a small private practice, seeing individuals in psychotherapy, and providing clinical and research consultation to psychologists and other mental health providers in the San Francisco Bay Area.

Jorge M. Pacheco is a full professor at the Department of Mathematics and Applications of the University of Minho (Portugal). He studied theoretical physics at the University of Coimbra (Portugal) and obtained his Ph.D. at the Niels Bohr Institute (Denmark, 1990). He is active in a variety of research topics, ranging from quantum many-body physics to the mathematical description of complex processes such as somatic evolution of cancer, the evolution of cooperation, the evolution of culture, and complex network science.

Gary J. Patronek graduated from the University of Pennsylvania School of Veterinary Medicine (VMD) and Purdue University (Ph.D.), where he completed a fellowship in epidemiology. While director of the Tufts Center for Animals and Public Policy at the Cummings School of Veterinary Medicine at Tufts, he founded the Hoarding of Animals Research Consortium (HARC), an interdisciplinary research group of investigators from several different institutions who worked collaboratively from 1997 to 2006 to study the problem of animal hoarding. Dr. Patronek published the first paper defining this behavior in the public health literature and continues to lecture, write, and investigate this topic. He is currently an independent consultant and an adjunct Clinical Assistant Professor at the Cummings School of Veterinary Medicine at Tufts.

Michael L. Perlin is professor of law, director of the online mental disability law program, and director of the international mental disability law reform project in the Justice Action Center at New York Law School (NYLS). Formerly a public defender in Trenton, New Jersey, and formerly director of the New Jersey Division of Mental Health Advocacy, he has taught at NYLS since 1984, and is the author of 21 books and over 200 articles on all aspects of mental disability law. Under his direction, New York Law School now offers 13 online, distance-learning courses in mental disability law (along with an online master's and advanced certificate program). He is on the board of advisors of Disability Rights International, and serves on the editorial board of multiple law-and-behavioral science journals. He is currently working on a seven-volume, third edition of his treatise, *Mental Disability Law: Civil and Criminal* (Lexis-Nexis Publishers); his most recent book, *International Human Rights and Mental Disability Law: When the Silenced are Heard*, was published in August 2011 by Oxford University Press. His recent research focuses also on the role of neuroimaging testimony in the criminal trial process, and the relationship between mental disability and the death penalty. He has also just published an article, "Oh Mercy: Blood on the Cusp," in *Montague Street: The Art of Bob Dylan*.

Professor Perlin posts his reviews of Dylan concerts regularly on the Web, and is working on an article on Dylan's jurisprudence. Besides those at Dylan concerts, his favorite days are those spent cooking, hiking, birdwatching, and attending kirtan concerts with his wife, Linda; going to baseball and basketball games with his son, Alex; and fishing for striped bass in the waters of Chatham Harbor, Cape Cod, with his daughter, Julie.

Karol M. Pessin has been a biotechnology intellectual property lawyer for over 20 years, and has held various senior positions in private practice and industry. She writes under a pseudonym about neuroscience, enjoys perusing PUBMED, and has spent quite a long time trying to figure out why people act the way they do. Ms. Pessin received her J.D. from the University of California at Berkeley, and holds a degree in botany from the University of Maryland.

Jennifer Ruth Presnall is a graduate student in the clinical psychology program at the University of Kentucky. Her research and clinical interests include diagnosis and treatment of personality disorder from a Five-Factor Model perspective. She plans to pursue a clinical career with an emphasis on personality disorder treatment. She agrees with the elusive orator Henry J. Tillman that "life is something that everyone should try at least once."

Deborah M. Riby is a lecturer in the School of Psychology at Newcastle University. She completed her Ph.D. on "Face Perception in Williams syndrome and Autism" at Stirling University in 2007. She then remained at Stirling University for an additional year as a postdoctoral researcher on an ESRC-funded project for which she was a co-grant holder. That project produced the first published eye tracking research to explore social attention in individuals with Williams syndrome and was featured in *Scientific American: Mind Matters*. Outside of work and following her relocation from Scotland, Debbie is currently enjoying exploring the North East of England with her husband and her "Angel of the North"—her 5-year old daughter.

Gary Rodin is a professor of psychiatry at the University of Toronto who holds the Harold and Shirley Lederman Chair in Psychosocial Oncology and Palliative Care at Princess Margaret Hospital in Toronto. His recent work has been focused on the psychology of advanced disease and on developing therapeutic interventions to alleviate the suffering associated with it. This chapter is an opportunity for him to reflect on the philosophical problem of balancing altruism and self-interest, on the perils and pleasures of caregiving, and on how to find balance between the passions of work and those of family and personal life.

Francisco C. Santos studied physics at the University of Lisbon (Portugal) and earned his Ph.D. in compvuter science at the Free University of Brussels (Belgium, 2007). After 3 years as associate researcher in Brussels, he is currently an associate researcher of the New University of Lisbon (Portugal). His interests span several aspects of complex adaptive systems, from the structure of social networks and the dynamics of human cooperation, to the evolution of social norms and reputation-based systems.

Tania Singer received her Ph.D. in psychology from the Freie Universität Berlin in 2000, and was awarded the prestigious Otto Hahn Medal of the Max Planck Society for best dissertation of that year. She was a Postdoctoral Fellow at the Max Planck Institute for Human Development, Berlin, until 2002, at the Wellcome Department of Imaging Neuroscience, London, from 2002 to 2005, and at the Institute of Cognitive Neuroscience, London, from 2005 to 2006. She was appointed Assistant Professor for Social Neuroscience and Neuroeconomics at the University of Zurich in 2006 and promoted to Full Professor and Inaugural Chair of Social Neuroscience and Neuroeconomics in 2008. She has been co-director of the Laboratory for Social and Neural Systems Research at the University of Zurich from 2007 until 2010. Since 2010, she has been Director of the Department of Social Neuroscience at the Max Planck Institute for Human Cognitive and Brain Sciences, Leipzig. She is Fellow of the Association for Psychological Science, Senior Fellow of the Mind and Life Institute, Associate at the Swiss Centre for Affective Sciences (Geneva), Honorary Research Fellow at the Laboratory for Social and Neural Systems Research (Zurich) and Associate Member of the Institut Jean Nicod (Paris). Her research interests include social neuroscience (empathy, fairness, social emotions); neuroeconomics (decision making, cooperation); lifespan, cognitive, and social psychology (development of social functions).

David J. Stiver is reference librarian and assists with Special Collections and coordinates digitization projects at Graduate Theological Union in Berkeley, California. He also manages data collection and the website for the Emotion, Personality and Altruism Research Group, Wright Institute, Berkeley. His online projects include digital content from GTU's Special Collections (callimachus.org/gtu), a site on the art and image of the cross (www.crosscrucifix.com), and a web biography of his father (www.stanleystiver.com).

Adolf Tobeña was born in Graus, Aragon-Spain, in 1950. He studied medicine at the University of Barcelona from 1967 to 1972, proceeding on to psychiatry training from 1973 to 1977 at the Clinic Hospital in Barcelona. Dr. Tobeña became a full professor of psychiatry at the Autonomous University of Barcelona in 1997, and has happily served as the chairman of the Department of Psychiatry and Forensic Medicine since 2000—perhaps happily, since he hasn't seen patients, as a clinician, for decades. Dr. Tobeña is the author of 14 books and 160 papers in neuroscience and psychiatry journals. He is also a visiting professor at the Institute of Psychiatry, University of London, and at the Universities of Groningen, Tel Aviv, and Venice International. He was a popular columnist in the Barcelona media on "neurosocial" and political topics and directed a widely followed radio program on "science and society" for years at the main broadcasting network in Barcelona, until his views came to be considered too unconventional and "biologically" oriented. Dr. Tobeña was a recipient of the "Avui" Award on Scientific Journalism in 1991; the City of Barcelona Award on Science in 1992; the "Serra i Moret" Award (Catalonian Regional Government) on Civic Promotion in 1994; and the European Award "Estudio General" on Scientific Popularization in 2004. His books include *Anatomia de la Agresividad Humana* (2001), *Mártires Mortíferos: Biologia del Altruismo Letal* (2004), *Cerebro y Poder* (2008), and *Values, Empathy and Fairness across Social Barriers* (coedited with S. Atran, K.Ochner, A. Navarro, and O. Vilarroya, 2009).

John W. Traphagan is associate professor of religious studies and anthropology at the University of Texas at Austin. He has written about 50 scientific articles and chapters in anthropology, medical, and religious studies journals and books and is the author of *Taming Oblivion: Aging Bodies and the Fear of Senility in Japan* (SUNY Press, 2000) and *The Practice of Concern: Ritual, Well-Being, and Aging in Rural Japan* (Carolina Academic Press, 2004). He also has co-edited several books, the most recent being *Imagined Families, Lived Families: Culture and Kinship in Modern Japan* (SUNY Press, 2008) with Akiko Hashimoto. He agrees with the comment of jazz great Miles Davis: "Don't play what's there, play what's not there."

Brent E. Turvey spent his first years in college on a pre-med track, only to change his course of study once his true interests took hold. He received a bachelor of science degree from Portland State University in psychology, with an emphasis on forensic psychology, and an additional bachelor of science degree in history. He went on to receive his master's of science in forensic science from the University of New Haven, in West Haven, Connecticut. Since graduating in 1996, Mr. Turvey has consulted as a forensic scientist and criminal profiler with many agencies, attorneys, and police departments in the United States, Australia, China, Canada, Barbados, and Korea on a range of rapes, homicides, and serial/multiple rape/death cases. He has also been court qualified as an expert in the areas of criminal profiling, forensic science, victimology, and crime reconstruction.

Brent is the author of *Criminal Profiling: An Introduction to Behavioral Evidence Analysis*, 1st, 2nd, 3rd, and 4th Editions (1999, 2002, 2008, 2011); and coauthor of *Rape Investigation Handbook*, 1st and 2nd Editions (2004, 2011), *Crime Reconstruction*, 1st and 2nd Editions (2006, 2011), *Forensic Victimology* (2008), and *Forenic Criminology* (2009)—all with Elsevier Science. He is currently a full partner, forensic scientist, criminal profiler, and instructor with Forensic Solutions, LLC, and an adjunct professor of justice studies at Oklahoma City University. He can be contacted via email at bturvey@forensic-science.com.

Carol Van Hulle graduated in 1991 from Augsburg College, Minneapolis, Minnesota, with degrees in math and psychology. She decided to trade lakes for mountains and headed to Boulder, Colorado, to attend the Institute for Behavior Genetics at the University of Colorado. When not studying, she logged many miles hiking and biking, but obstinately refused to learn to ski. After earning her Ph.D. in 2000, Carol returned to her Midwestern roots and now works at the University of Wisconsin studying the development of emotion regulation and child psychopathology. In her spare time, she hangs out with her three cats, husband, and son, and occasionally helps out with her father's reforestation project.

Roger Vilardaga is currently a doctoral student at the University of Nevada, Reno. He received his bachelor degree at the University of Barcelona in Spain, where he studied psychology and minored in epistemology and theory of science. He has authored 12 empirical and theoretical publications and has received clinical training in several varieties of behavior therapy including traditional cognitive behavior therapy, acceptance and commitment therapy, functional analytic psychotherapy and dialectical behavioral therapy. His main interest is the investigation of core psychological processes that lead to either optimal human functioning or psychopathology. He is widely known among his close family members (mostly mom and dad), and he likes fighting cultural assimilation by being called rʊ'ʒe.

Thomas A. Widiger is the T. Marshall Hahn Professor of Psychology at the University of Kentucky. He received his Ph.D. in clinical psychology from Miami University (Ohio) and completed his internship at Cornell University Medical College. He currently serves as associate editor of *Journal of Abnormal Psychology*, *Journal of Personality Disorders*, *Journal of Personality Assessment*, and the *Annual Review of Clinical Psychology*. He is the recipient of the 2010 Distinguished Scientist Award from the Society for a Science of Clinical Psychology, for which he received a very lovely lamp that he will display each Christmas.

Carolyn Zahn-Waxler is a research scientist in the Departments of Psychology and Psychiatry at the University of Wisconsin. She is also affiliated with the Center for Investigating Healthy Minds at the Waisman Center. She received her B.A. in psychology at the University of Wisconsin and her Ph.D. from the Institute of Child Development at the University of Minnesota. Before moving to Madison, she was a research psychologist at the National Institute of Mental Health in Bethesda, Maryland, where she headed the Section on Development and Psychopathology at NIMH. She served as associate editor and then editor of *Developmental Psychology*, a journal of the American Psychological Association, for nearly a decade. She also served on the APA Council of Editors; as president of the Developmental Division of the American Psychological Association; and as a member of the Governing Council for the Society for Research in Child Development. She is an APA Fellow.

Throughout her career, she has studied the origins and development of empathy and caring behaviors. These longitudinal studies have followed children from the first years of life to adolescence. They have focused on the role of genes, temperament, family life, and socialization experiences that foster or impede altruism and compassion in children. She has also conducted longitudinal studies on the role of emotions in the development of psychopathology in adolescents and on risk and protective factors in the development of conduct problems in children from preschool to adolescence. In addition to numerous scientific publications based on these and other studies, she has written about the intergenerational transmission of depression from mothers to daughters from a personal perspective. She served on the Task Force on women and depression for the lieutenant governor of Wisconsin, and works to destigmatize mental illness. She is currently interested in translational questions—i.e., how scientific advances can inform the use of practices that encourage empathy, kindness, altruism, and positive emotions in children. She enjoys laughing, family, friends, yoga, loving-kindness meditation, lay ministry, creative writing, group singing, designing and knitting afghans, and other activities that deter pathological altruism and foster authentic compassion.

INDEX

Note: Entries followed by *f*, *t*, and n correspond to figures, tables, and notes respectively.

pseudoaltruism, 182–184
psychological, 262–270, 263*f*, 312–315, 409–410
psychotic versus nonpsychotic, 168n26, 179*t*, 182
punishment as part of altruism. *see* altruism, costly; punishment
reciprocal
  cultural differences in, 279
  general explanation of, 59, 194, 194*t*, 312, 396
  in relation to cancer caregiving, 139, 144
  self-serving, ultimately seen as, 11
and Relational Frame Theory, 40*f*
as a relative concept, 293–297, 350
risky and safe, 198–204, 199*ts*
scrupulosity and religious obsession with morality, 17, 166n11
self- versus other-directed, motivation in, 139
self-sacrifice as part of, 31, 166n13, 322
selfish, 166n15
situational, 194*t*, 194–195
and social Darwinism, 166n15
societies, central role in human, 31
strategies in, to avoid being taken advantage of, 408–409
strong, 212
suicide attackers share, 207
tolerant, 214
and victimization. *see* victimization
altruism, pathological. *see also* altruism; altruist, pathological
and abusive relationships. *see* abusive relationship(s)
and agreeableness. *see* agreeableness
and "altruistic pathology," 168n33
and animal hoarding, 107–115
and anxiety. *see* anxiety
and battered women. *see* battered women
"born of suffering," 203
and caregiving, problematic, 140–147, 149, 322
and certitude, pathological. *see* certitude, pathological
in children
  connections between empathy, guilt and depression, 321–338
  in relation to fetal testosterone, 326–327
  who are highly prosocial, 6, 7*f*, 13
  who become animal hoarders, 109–111
  who go on to have eating disorders, 96–98
and codependency, 5, 49–68
and cognitive bias. *see* bias, cognitive
and cognitive dissonance. *see* dissonance, cognitive

and cognitive distortion. *see* distortion, cognitive
and compliance. *see* compliance
and concern for appropriateness, 94, 99–100
a contextual behavioral (Relational Frame Theory) approach to, 5, 31–42, 37*f*, 39*f*
costly altruism in relation to. *see also* aggression, maternal; altruism, parochial; punishment, altruistic
and developmental pathways of depression, 6, 323*f*, 324–325, 324*f*
in group dynamics, 253–254
in relation to parochial altruism, 392
suicide attacks and biological origins of, 212–214
from a cultural perspective, 161–162, 275–285, 292–293
defensive altruism in relation to, 179*t*, 182, 185–187
definition difficult because of justifiable exceptions, 389
definitions
  Chapter 1 (Oakley, Knafo & McGrath) Long definition: Any behavior or personal tendency in which either the stated aim or the implied motivation is to promote the welfare of another. but instead of overall beneficial outcomes the 'altruism' instead has irrational (from the point of view of an outside observer) and substantial negative consequences to the other or even to the self, 3, 4
  Simple definition: Well-meaning efforts that worsen the very situation they mean to help, 6
  Chapter 3 (Vilardaga & Hayes), Generally used to refer to (a) the actions of individuals with the intention of promoting the welfare of others that cause needless harm to themselves or others, (b) an excess of the 'self-sacrificing' aspect of altruism implicit in most common definitions of altruism itself, and (c) a repetitive pattern of this feature that makes the pattern of action more pervasive and problematic, 32
  Chapter 12 (Perlin), the willingness of a person to irrationally place another's perceived needs above his or her own in a way that causes self-harm. Put another way, it involves an excessive,

Printed in the USA/Agawam, MA
July 10, 2015

618657.001